GRIEVANCE GUIDE

EIGHTH EDITION

*A15045 797413

by the
BNA EDITORIAL STAFF

HD
6972.5
.G74
1992
West

The Bureau of National Affairs, Inc., Washington, D.C.

Copyright © 1959, 1964, 1968, 1972, 1978, 1982, 1987, 1992
The Bureau of National Affairs, Inc.
Washington, D.C.

Library of Congress Cataloging-in-Publication Data

Grievance guide / by the BNA editorial staff. — 8th ed.
   p. cm.
   ISBN 0-87179-751-8
   1. Grievance procedures—United States. I. Bureau of National
Affairs (Washington, D.C.)
HD6972.5.G74   1992
658.3'155—dc20   92-24178
                                                                              CIP

Authorization to photocopy items for internal or personal use, or the internal or personal use of specific clients, is granted by BNA Books for libraries and other users registered with the Copyright Clearance Center (CCC) Transactional Reporting Service, provided that $0.50 per page is paid directly to CCC, 27 Congress St., Salem, MA 01970, 0-87179-751-8/92/$0 + .50

Published by BNA Books
1250 23rd Street, N.W., Washington, D.C. 20037-1165

Printed in the United States of America
International Standard Book Number: 0-87179-751-8

PREFACE

Grievance Guide, first published in 1959, has been updated and reissued serveral times to reflect current thinking on the "common law" of employee relations as established by arbiters' rulings on grievances presented under union contracts.

Although arbiters do not set binding precedents in their awards in individual grievances, their rulings on particular issues tend to follow a similar general pattern. Based on an analysis of these awards as published by The Bureau of National Affairs, Inc. (BNA) over the years, a "common law of the shop" may be detected that provides a guide to handling employee grievances in any setting.

The practice of using arbitration by third-party neutrals to settle employee grievances had its origins during World War II, when companies and unions were forced to develop a technique for resolving their disputes peacefully. At that time, BNA introduced its *War Labor Reports* to cover these arbitration awards.

After the war, it soon became clear that the idea of arbitrating labor disputes was to become increasingly popular. Therefore, BNA introduced a reporting service, *Labor Arbitration*, as part of its *Labor Relations Reporter*, which is the "grandaddy" of all labor information services, having been launched in 1937.

During the 1950s BNA began publishing *Grievance Guide* for employers and unions on arbiters' handling of grievances. The guide has been continuously updated as part of two BNA information services—the *BNA Policy and Practice Series* for employee relations executives and the *Union Labor Report* for union officials and representatives. These looseleaf reference services are kept current by biweekly supplements, and are the source of the material for the *Grievance Guide*.

Grievance Guide presents a current compilation of BNA's guide to the common law of grievance arbitration. Citations are provided to the full text of the arbitration awards in BNA's *Labor Arbitration*. Thus, for example, a citation to an award at 98 LA 183 is to Volume 98 of *Labor Arbitration*, page 183.

The eighth edition of *Grievance Guide* was prepared by Todd L. Bunce, editor with the *BNA Policy and Practice Series* and *Union Labor Report*.

                                    Bill Manville
                                    Managing Editor
                                    BNA Policy and Practice Series
                                    and *Union Labor Report*

INTRODUCTION

Grievance Guide addresses the problems that unions and employees encounter in the day-to-day business of living under a collective bargaining agreement by using, as examples, arbitration awards handed down by impartial arbiters. The arbitration cases chosen are those which the editors thought would best illustrate general arbitration principles in many collective bargaining situations. Awards based on complex or unusual factual situations or interpreting highly unusual contract language have been omitted.

KEEP THESE POINTS IN MIND—

▶ Arbiters are not bound by precedent. Their function is to give the most appropriate judgment in interpreting collective bargaining agreements. Arbiters do, however, take note of rulings handed down by other arbiters.

▶ No two collective bargaining agreements are identical. Small differences in language may make all the difference in the outcome of a dispute.

▶ The meaning of a contract clause may be determined in large part by the past practice of the parties — i.e., how the bargaining agreement has actually been interpreted or applied in the workplace setting.

▶ The fact that employer conduct is permitted under a bargaining agreement does not make it lawful or proper, and vice versa. Therefore, problems in contract administration (particularly in discipline and discharge cases) should be researched only by checking the material in this section and other relevant sections

CONTENTS

Preface iii
Introduction v

Part 1. Discharge and Discipline: In General
Just Cause for Discipline 3–6
Disciplinary Procedures 7–12
Types of Penalties 13–18
Proving Misconduct 19–22

Part 2. Discharge and Discipline: Categories
Absenteeism 25–33
Insubordination 34
  Refusal to Obey Directives 35–43
  Abusive Behavior 44–50
  Union Activity 51–53
Misconduct 54–55
  Damaging Company Property 56–60
  Dishonesty 61–66
  Dress and Grooming 61–70
  Fights and Altercations 71–74
  Gambling 75–76
  Discourtesy 77–81
  Garnishment 82–85
  Horseplay 86–89
  Off-Duty Misconduct 90–97
  Outside Employment 98–102
  Sleeping & Loafing 103–106
  Strike-Related Activities 107–115
  Sexual Harassment 116–122
  Miscellaneous 123–125
Substance Abuse 126
  Intoxication & Alcoholism 127–134
  Drug Abuse 135–142
  Drug Testing 143–147
Unsatisfactory Performance 148–149
  Incompetence 150–153

Contents—Contd.

Carelessness	154–159
Disability	160–166

Part 3. Safety and Health
Introduction	169
Safety Rule Violations	170–171
Smoking Rules	172–174
Acquired Immune Deficiency Syndrome (AIDS)	175–178

Part 4. Seniority and Its Application
Calculating Seniority	181–186
Order of Layoff	187–193
Layoff Notice & Pay	194–197
Bumping & Transfer to Avoid Layoff	198–204
Worksharing	103–106
Recalls From Layoffs	209–216

Part 5. Leave of Absence
Paid Sick Leave	219–225
Personal Leave	226–237
Leave for Union Business	238–244
Arranging Leave	245–249
Maternity & Adoption Leave	250–256

Part 6. Promotions
Posting of Vacancies & Bidding	259–265
Bases for Promotion	266–273
How Ability Is Measured	274–280
Transfer	281–286

Part 7. Vacations
Vacation Eligibility	289–296
Vacation Scheduling	297–301
Vacation Pay	302–308

Part 8. Holidays
Eligibility for Holiday Pay	311–322
Pay for Holiday Work	323–327

Part 9. Health & Welfare Benefits
Health & Welfare Benefits	331–338

Contents—Contd.

Part 10. Management Rights
Management Rights 341–354
Compulsory Retirement 355–359
Subcontracting 360–363

Part 11. Union Rights
Union Rights 367–374

Part 12. Strikes & Lockouts
No-Strike Pledges 377–382
Strike Penalties 383–391

Part 13. Union Security
Union Security 395–401

Part 14. Checkoff
Checkoff 405–408

Part 15. Wages and Hours
Incentive-Pay Plans 411–415
Job Evaluation 416–421
Overtime Work & Pay 422–432
Premium Pay for Weekend Work 433–436
Premium Pay for Shift Work 437–439
Reporting & Call-In Pay 440–445
Hours Schedules 446–451
Wage Guarantee & SUB Plans 452–457

Part 1

Discharge and Discipline: In General

Just Cause for Discipline

IN BRIEF

A basic principle underlying most disciplinary procedures is that management must have "just cause" for imposing the discipline. This standard often is written into union contracts or read into them by arbitrators. Even in the absence of a contract, it sums up the test used by employees in judging whether management acted fairly in enforcing company rules.

While the definition of "just cause" necessarily varies from case to case, one arbitrator has listed seven tests for determining whether a company had just cause for disciplining an employee:

▶ Was the employee adequately warned of the consequences of his conduct? The warning may be given orally or in printed form. An exception may be made for certain conduct, such as insubordination, coming to work drunk, drinking on the job, or stealing company property, that is so serious that the employee is expected to know it will be punishable.

▶ Was the company's rule or order reasonably related to efficient and safe operations?

▶ Did management investigate before administering the discipline? The investigation normally should be made before the decision to discipline is made. Where immediate action is required, however, the best course is to suspend the employee pending investigation with the understanding that he will be restored to his job and paid for time lost if he is found not guilty.

▶ Was the investigation fair and objective?

▶ Did the investigation produce substantial evidence or proof of guilt? It is not required that the evidence be preponderant, conclusive, or "beyond reasonable doubt," except where the alleged misconduct is of such a criminal or reprehensible nature as to stigmatize the employee and seriously impair his chances for future employment.

▶ Were the rules, orders, and penalties applied evenhandedly and without discrimination? If enforcement has been lax in the past, management cannot suddenly reverse its course and begin to crack down without first warning employees of its intent.

▶ Was the penalty reasonably related to the seriousness of the offense and the past record? If employee A's past record is significantly better than that of employee B, the company properly may give A a lighter punishment than B for the same offense (50 LA 83).

GUIDELINES

In addition to the checklist outlined above, another arbitrator that these guidelines are "well accepted":

● The employer should enjoy reasonable discretionary powers to prescribe rules of conduct.

- The employer should publicize these rules either be direct publication or by consistent enforcement.
- The employer should apply his disciplinary policies "seriously and without discrimination."
- The employer should regard industrial discipline as corrective — not punitive.
- The employer should avoid arbitrary or hasty action when confronted with a situation.
- The employer should evaluate each situation in the light of the employee's disciplinary record.
- The employer should tailor the punishment to fit the crime. (48 LA 336)

Still, another arbitrator listed the following criteria generally applied in evaluating just cause for discipline:

Equal treatment — All employees must be judged by the same standards, and the rules must apply equally to all. This does not mean, however, that the same penalty always must be given for the same offense.

Rule of reason — Even in the absence of a specific provision, a contract protects employees against unjust discipline and permits a challenge to any company procedure that threatens to deprive employees of their rights.

Internal consistency — The pattern of enforcement must be consistent, whether a company disciplines on a case-by-case basis or uses a rule book.

Personal guilt — Even though two employees are involved in the same act of misconduct, the same penalty need not be meted out to each. Such things as prior disciplinary records may be considered. (47 LA 1104)

Just Cause for Discipline Upheld

Initially, if management has acted in good faith upon a fair investigation and fixes a penalty not inconsistent with similar cases or what would be fair and just under the circumstances, an arbitrator should not attempt to "second guess" management, an arbitrator ruled. If it can be said that the causes for discharge are just and equitable and would appeal to fair-minded individuals as warranting discharge, the grievant must suffer the consequences of his actions, the arbitrator emphasized. (Smith & Wesson-Fiocchi Inc., 60 LA 366)

In this regard, just cause for discipline has been upheld:
- Where a sales clerk failed to follow proper store procedures and displayed unbecoming conduct toward fellow employees and customers. (Goldman's Department Store, 65 LA 592)
- Where a drill press operator negligently misdrilled an aircraft part and then attempted to cover up the mistake by throwing the part into a trash bin. (Rohr Industries Inc., 65 LA 982)
- Where an employee made excessive use of the employer's telephone to transact personal business in violation of company policy. (Canned Foods Inc., 65 LA 409)
- Where an employee made telephone threats that a bomb was going to blow up the employer's plant. (Vulcan Materials Co., 64 LA 773)
- Where an employee, while on vacation, refused to accept company telephone calls and telegram advising the worker of his shift on his return to work. (Anaconda Co., 61 LA 1221)
- Where an employer discharged an employee who was observed sitting in a bar of a restaurant with a glass of beer in front of him in violation of terms of his reinstatement from a prior discharge for alcoholism requiring him, among other things, not to consume alcoholic beverages from that point on "anywhere, at any time." (Sterling Drug Inc., Local 342, 67 LA 1296)
- Where a cab company discharged an employee for purchasing gasoline on separate occasions from sources other than company garage, which was forbidden by agreement, where record of employee establishes commission of other offenses. (DeSoto Cab Co. and Teamsters, Local 265, 67 LA 643)
- Where an employer discharged a driver salesman for falsifying and tampering with cash tickets, even though contract did not contain an express pro-

vision that discharge shall be only for "cause" or "just cause," since the agreement as a whole expressed the parties' adoption of the "just cause" concept. (Dayton Pepsi Cola Bottling Co., 75 LA 154)

• Where an employer discharged a shift electrician for failing to pass a test that the electrical superintendent administered to determine his competence in correcting malfunctions of paper machines for which he was responsible, since the union did not provide impartial experts to challenge the fairness of the test and there was no evidence that the superintendent devised the questions so deliberately difficult that the worker could not be expected to answer them. (St. Regis Paper Co., 74 LA 896)

• Where an employer discharged an employee after she refused to raise her pants leg in order to reveal the nature of bulges that a plant guard had observed, since it is not customary for people to have bulges under their pants leg and it would have been a clear dereliction of duty for the guard to observe such conduct and do noting about it. (Aldens Inc., 73 LA 396)

• Where an employer imposed a 10-day suspension on an employee for drinking beer during a four-hour off-duty interval of her split shift under a plant rule prohibiting employees from consuming alcoholic beverages of any kind during a tour of duty, since management communicated the rule adequately to employees and applied it in a uniform and even-handed fashion. (General Telephone Co. of California, 77 LA 1052)

• Where an employee audio-recorded, and made no effort to stop recording, a counseling session held to end her unauthorized use of audio and video equipment in the workplace. (Prescription Health Services, 98 LA 16)

• Where a telephone company operator was suspended for three days when she rudely addressed a customer and failed to give her name when asked. (American Telephone & Telegraph, 98 LA 102)

• Where a home-delivery meal driver was discharged for failing to deliver hot meals to certain senior citizens, since he tried to falsify records and the misconduct was so egregious that it threatened the senior citizens' health. (Bay County Division on Aging, 98 LA 188)

Just Cause for Discipline Not Upheld

Arbitrators are unwilling to uphold an employer's disciplinary action where management has failed to meet certain requirements. Just cause for discipline was not found:

• Where a city employee who received gifts from a city supplier was discharged, while other city officials, guilty of the same offense, were only suspended. (City of Binghampton, 65 LA 663)

• Where an employer discharged a locomotive brakeman who accidentally shot himself in an attempt to shoot a crow alongside the employer's railroad track, since the worker's action was not related to railroading. (Erie Mining Co., 65 LA 880)

• Where an employeee was discharged for obtaining payroll information on fellow employees, from the employer's desk drawer, which was made the basis of a union grievance, since there was no company rule declaring the drawer and its contents off limits. (Meat Fair Meat Market, 65 LA 1112)

• Where an employer discharged a bench inspector for harassing the employer during a four year period by filing 16 grievances and writing notes of protest to management, since most of the worker's grievances had merit. (Caterpillar Tractor Co., 62 LA 645)

• Where an employer disciplined a registered nurse for complaining about inadequate staffing of intensive care and coronary care units to head nurse, since nurse had right under Sec. 7 of the Taft Act to discuss and complain about staffing, assuming there was no "harassment" of head nurse. (Auburn Faith Community Hospital, Inc. and California Nurses Assn., 66 LA 882)

- Where a federal agency employer issued an official reprimand to an off-duty federal protective officer for misrepresenting himself as a police officer during spot check conducted by state county police that revealed employee's possession of firearm, since the employee had a clean work record and had never been convicted of an offense against the law. (General Services Admn., Public Buildings Service and Government Employees, AFGE, Local 1733, 66 LA 639)

- Where an employer discharged an employee who pleaded guilty to smoking marijuana, which he had taken from his car in the company parking lot, at a restaurant during his noontime break, since the employer failed to promulgate a rule which clearly alerted employees that the act was forbidden and penalized by discharge. (Gamble Bros. and Carpenters, Local 3125, 68 LA 72)

- Where an employee was discharged for urinating on the floor of his delivery vehicle by choice and not by necessity, even if the worker's conduct was offensive; since there was nothing in the parties' contract subjecting an employee to immediate discharge merely because his personal behavior is offensive and vile. (Pepsi Cola Bottling Co., 76 LA 54)

- Where a retail food store discharged a bakery counter employee for offering to make a birthday cake for a family friend, thereby causing the friend to cancel an order she was placing with another bakery counter employee, since the worker's conduct was an isolated event involving the sale of a cake that cost only $10.95, and the employee did not deprive the employer of any other sales of baked products. (Patton Sparkle Market, 75 LA 1092)

- Where an assistant bookkeeper was discharged over an incident in which she allegedly spent the night with a married store manager at the home of a co-employee following a party, since an employee's off-duty conduct away from company premises was not subject to discipline or discharge, under the contract, unless it adversely affected the operation of the employer's business. (Ralph's Grocery Co., 77 LA 867)

- Where an employee was discharged for poor performance who suffered stroke and accompanying memory loss, since his illness may have contributed to his job performance. (Pepsi-Cola General Bottlers, 98 LA 112)

- Where an employee was suspended for 24 hours for insubordination — picking up his own paycheck at the employer's finance office without authorization. (Shelby Co. Government, 98 LA 126)

- A one-day suspension of a firefighter for alleged negligent response to a hillside fire was ruled excessive, even though the fire truck which he was driving had to be towed out of mud, and his driving the truck downhill resulted in property damage, for which the town had to pay. (Allingtown Fire Dist., 98 LA 263)

- Where a police officer with a 13-year good record received a 30-day suspension for hitting handcuffed prisoner in holding cell who was trying to spit in his face for a second time, since he used only enough force to counteract assault. (Redwood City, 98 LA 306)

Disciplinary Procedures

IN BRIEF

In ruling on the fairness of discipline for such offenses as insubordination, misconduct, absenteeism, and poor work, arbitrators do not concern themselves merely with whether the workers involved are guilty. They also examine the procedures followed by the company in punishing the workers and the nature of the punishment itself.

Many agreements specify procedural requirements for discharge or discipline. In many cases arbitrators have refused to uphold management's action in discharging or disciplining an employee where management failed to fulfill some procedural requirement specified by the agreement, such as a required statement of charges against the employee, or a notice or investigation requirement, or a requirement for a hearing or joint discussion prior to the assessment of punishment. (56 LA 694, 55 LA 764, 55 LA 677, 54 LA 361)

However, in numerous other cases compliance with the spirit of such procedural requirements has been held to suffice where the employee has not been adversely affected by the failure of management to accomplish total compliance with the requirements. (56 LA 973, 55 LA 1102, 55 LA 118, 53 LA 342, 52 LA 1213, 52 LA 951)

Every employer is forced at some time or other to administer discipline, but there are good ways and bad ways of doing it. A study of many successfully administered policies reveals this pattern:

▶ Company rules are carefully explained to employees. This is especially important in the case of new employees. Indoctrination courses, employee handbooks, bulletin board notices, and many other forms of bringing rules to the attention of employees, are used.

▶ Accusations against employees are carefully considered, to see if they are supported by facts. Witnesses are interviewed, their statement recorded, and careful investigation made to see that both sides of the story are available and fairly presented. Circumstantial evidence is kept to a minimum in judging the facts, personality factors and unfounded assumptions are eliminated.

▶ A regular "warning" procedure is worked out and applied. Sometimes all warnings are in writing, with a copy handed to the employee and one filed in the employee's record in the personnel office. Sometimes first warnings are orally delivered, but a written record of the warning is filed away. Warnings are given for all except the most serious offenses—those which management has made clear will call for immediate discharge.

▶ Some companies bring the union into the discipline case early in the procedure. Copies of warning notices go to the union. The union is given advance notice of other disciplinary action which management intends to take. Sometimes the action is held up until the union has time to make its own investigation.

▶ Before disciplinary action is taken, the employee's motive and reasons for the violation of rules are investigated. Then the penalty is adjusted to the facts—whether the employee's action was in good faith, partially justified, or totally unjustified.

▶ Before disciplinary action is taken, the employee's past record is taken into consideration. A good work record and long seniority are viewed as factors in the employee's favor, particularly where a minor offense is involved, or where it is a first offense. Previous offenses are not used against the employee unless he was reprimanded at the time they occurred, or warned that they would be used against him in any future disciplinary action.

▶ Companies make sure that all management agents, and particularly first-line supervisors know the company's disciplinary policies and procedures, and carefully observe them. This is particularly important in the case of verbal warnings, or informal reprimands.

▶ Discipline short of discharge is used wherever possible.

GUIDELINES

Right To Adopt Rules

It is generally agreed that management is authorized to make and to post reasonable rules of conduct that are not inconsistent with the collective bargaining agreement. (97 LA 542, 93 LA 1082, 90 LA 625, 90 LA 341, 88 LA 1164, 88 LA 931, 84 LA 856, 83 LA 1308, 82 LA 581, 81 LA 672, 74 LA 312, 74 LA 58, 73 LA 357, 73 LA 34, 72 LA 133, 71 LA 716, 71 LA 1, 63 LA 896, 63 LA 467, 60 LA 924, 60 LA 778, 60 LA 645, 59 LA 883, 11 LA 689, 7 LA 150)

Once promulgated the rules may be subject to challenge through the grievance procedure as contrary to the contract or as arbitrary, unfair, or discriminatory. (65 LA 1077, 63 LA 267, 63 LA 138, 60 LA 938, 28 LA 583, 10 LA 113)

While management's right to make reasonable rules is recognized, particular rules may be voided if they are unreasonable, vague, ineffective, or arbitrary. (97 LA 675, 96 LA 122, 95 LA 495, 85 LA 921, 75 LA 397, 74 LA 412, 73 LA 850, 73 LA 443, 27 LA 717, 27 LA 99)

The test of reasonableness of a rule is whether or not the rule is reasonably related to a legitimate objective of management. (55 LA 283) Rules must be reasonable, not only in content but also in application.

EXAMPLE: An employer improperly required male employees on the day shift to wear neckties while allowing male employees on the second shift not to wear them, and permitting female employees to wear anything they desired, an arbitrator ruled. Pointing out that enforcement of the rule discriminated against male employees based on sex, in violation of the contract, the arbitrator concluded that rule was not predicated on a reasonable standard, it appearing that the neckties were required based on the personal taste of the department head. (Union Tribune Publishing Co., 70 LA 266)

DISCIPLINARY PROCEDURES

Even reasonable rules have been held unenforceable if they (1) have not been brought to the attention of employees (18 LA 866), (2) infringe unduly upon an employee's private life (18 LA 400), or (3) are applied discriminatorily (26 LA 934).

EXAMPLE: An employer could not enforce a rule prohibiting employees from wearing beach clothes when walking to and from plant gates, in amplification of its general safety rule barring wearing of loose clothing or jewelry when employees are around moving machinery, an arbitrator ruled. The rule went substantially beyond the scope of the general rule, and constituted unreasonable interference with the personal freedom of employees to come and go from their work places, the arbitrator concluded. (Babcock & Wilcox, 73 LA 443)

EXAMPLE: An employee was improperly discharged for violating a work rule that required him to work until he heard the quitting bell, an arbitrator decided, since the reasonableness of the rule required that it be applied to all employees in a similar manner, and that the employee be able to hear the "sound of the quitting bell" when it rings. (Visador Co., 73 LA 578)

Posting of Plant Rules

The decision as to whether to post plant rules is management's and the posting of rules ordinarily is not a condition precedent to management's right to discipline employees for violations.

EXAMPLE: In rejecting a union's contention that an employer could not discipline employees in the absence of properly promulgated and communicated plant rules, an arbitrator observed that many plants operate without formal rules, relying on the rules of common sense. Employees are assumed to have a modicum of common sense the arbitrator concluded, emphasizing that employers have the right to expect that even a minimal degree of common sense is exercised by employees. (Davey Company, 60 LA 917)

Other arbitrators have held that plant rules need not be in writing (Ohio Power Co., 50 LA 501); that a company's reliance on the "grapevine" to announce a new disciplinary policy was proper (Pacific Northwest Bell Telephone Co., 48 LA 498); and that there is no one way of either establishing or publicizing a rule, which can become effective through the accumulation of experience and practice and need not be announced at a given time and place. (Eastern Airlines Inc., 44 LA 459)

However, except where the nature of the prohibited activity is such that employees should know it is improper, plant rules should be communicated to employees in some manner. Thus, in the absence of posted rules management's freedom of action may be more restricted than it would be if rules were posted.

Consistent Enforcement

Where management has winked at violations of a rule, it should announce its intention to require observance of the rule before it hands out heavy penalties. This is especially true where the rule applies to conduct that, unlike stealing or assaults on supervisors or co-workers, is not inherently objectionable. Lax enforcement of rules may lead employees reasonably to believe that the conduct in question is sanctioned by management. (94 LA 297, 93 LA 302, 66 LA 953, 63 LA 995, 20 LA 342, 21 LA 729, 28 LA 65, 42 LA 87, 46 LA 161)

This does not mean that the same discipline must be meted out to each individual in a group, even where each is equally culpable. Such things as prior disciplinary and work records may be considered. (65 LA 1151, 47 LA 1104)

While arbitrators have no jurisdiction to pass upon management's treatment of its supervisors, they may set aside penalties imposed upon rank-and-file workers if supervisors who were guilty of the same offense are let off free or given lesser penalties. Thus, when both a supervisor and a worker were cleared of the offense, the arbitrator found management guilty of double standards when it reinstated only the supervisor. (39 LA 823)

Pay for Time Spent in Disciplinary Interview

Is a worker who is being questioned or interviewed to determine possible disciplinary action entitled to pay for the time spent in this way? At least one arbitrator has ruled that workers could not be docked for the time spent in disciplinary interviews held on company time. Both management and the worker stand to profit from such interviews, he pointed out, and there is no reason why the employee should have to suffer a monetary loss. (Bethlehem Steel Co., 19 LA 261)

Similarly, a union steward's pay was improperly docked one-half hour because the worker left his job early to discuss his own disciplinary grievance with union attorneys, an arbiter ruled, it appearing that the steward left the plant with the permission of the employer. (County Sanitation District, 64 LA 521; see also 74 LA 601, 73 LA 789, 73 LA 872)

Furthermore, another arbitrator ruled that workers should be paid for time spent in a disciplinary conference held on their off time. In this instance, the workers were called in on a Saturday, so the arbitrator awarded them four hours' pay for the time spent in conference under the call-in-pay provision of the contract. (Bethlehem Steel Co., 21 LA 579)

However, an employee was not entitled to pay for time spent in a grievance meeting where a fight between the worker and a co-employee was discussed, an arbitrator decided, since the contract expressly stated that the "company will not pay for time spent at meetings." (Brockway Glass Co. Inc., 74 LA 601)

Staggered Penalty

Where management penalizes a group of workers by suspending them, can it stagger the suspensions so that the workers are not all off at the same time? Arbitrators have ruled that management has the right.

EXAMPLE: In one case where workers struck in violation of the contract, the arbiter reasoned that if management suspended everyone at once, the result would be a work stoppage, the very thing the disciplinary action was intended to penalize. (United States Steel Corp., 40 LA 598)

EXAMPLE: Another arbitrator came to a similar conclusion, adding that although management was not free to schedule the discipline "at its convenience" any time after the stoppage, it was entitled to reasonable latitude in deferring the time of the suspensions. (Bethlehem Steel Co., 39 LA 686)

Notice to Union

Where a contract calls for notice of disciplinary action to be given to the union, arbiters are likely to require strict compliance with such a provision. They operate on the theory that a worker's rights are seriously abridged if the union is not given a chance to get in on the ground floor.

Even if the disciplined employee clearly was guilty of misconduct, the penalty may be mitigated if the union was not given proper notice. Thus one arbiter ordered a discharged employee reinstated without back pay where the company failed to adhere to the contractual requirement of consultation with the union over discharges. (Hayes Mfg. Corp., 17 LA 412; see also 94 LA 7, 86 LA 503, 65 LA 690, 64 LA 425, 64 LA 67) Another arbiter ruled that a company that had failed to comply with notice requirements had to give an employee pay for time lost between the date of his discharge and the date of the first grievance meeting, even though his discharge was for just cause. (National Lead Co., 13 LA 28; see also 75 LA 1119)

Moreover, where it has been the company's custom and practice to give notice of disciplinary action to the union, even though the contract did not require it, one arbitrator ruled that the discharge of a worker without notifying the union was improper. (Coca-Cola Bottling Co., 9 LA 197)

Challenging New Rule

A union lost any right to challenge the discharge of a worker for violation of a new plant rule forbidding drinking during lunch breaks, when it did not protest when the rule was posted, an arbiter ruled. A worker was caught drinking on his lunch break and was fired. The arbiter denied the union's grievance, holding that management was justified in enforcing a new rule which it considered had full union support. (International Pipe & Ceramics Corp., 44 LA 267)

Union's Right to Disciplinary Forms and Reports

The personnel forms management develops are its own business and ordinarily need not be given to the union, one arbiter has ruled. He suggested, though, that this rule may not hold where a form is used in imposing discipline.

When an employer developed three new personnel forms to replace a single reprimand form, the union demanded that it be given a copy whenever one of the forms was used. Management was willing to supply one that was to be used solely for reprimands, but it refused to fork over one used to record attendance and changes of address or one entitled "Employee Performance & Conduct Memo."

The arbiter said the employer had the right to develop his own forms without any discussion or negotiation with the union. And if a form was to become merely part of management's records, he added, the union had no more right of access to it than management had to union records. He noted that the employer had an established practice of supplying reprimand, and he said he considered this a sound practice. So he concluded that the new reprimand form had to be given to the union whenever it was used; the Performance & Conduct Memo had to be supplied only if used as a reprimand; and the attendance and change of address form could be withheld altogether. (Harshaw Chemical Co., 32 LA 86; see also 73 LA 148)

Union Representation During Investigation

If a contract gives employees the right to union representation when disciplinary action is taken against them, do they also have the right to have a union official on hand when the employer is conducting preliminary investigations held prior to disciplinary action? Arbiters are divided on this question. Some feel that employees have the right to union representation during preliminary investigations on the theory that this is the beginning stage of a grievance. (Independent Lock Co. of Alabama, 30 LA 744; see also 66 LA 581, 60 LA 1066, 60 LA 832, 60 LA 9)

On the other hand, some take the position that union representation is not required unless the employee actually requests it (73 LA 1092), is charged with an offense, or until the beginning of the investigation. One arbiter ruled, for example, that an employer was justified in refusing to allow a union steward to participate in a scheduled mechanics' apprenticeship meeting concerning pay, since the employees must have reasonable grounds to believe that a meeting might be used to support disciplinary action against them in order to be entitled to union representation. (Clow Corp., 64 LA 668)

Union Representation Waived

Under a contract giving a disciplined employee the right to representation, what happens if the employee is not in the plant when he's discharged or other discipline is imposed? Arbiters generally hold that representation requirements are waived if the employee is absent when action is taken against him or if the penalty is imposed via mail or telegram. (Lyon Inc., 24 LA 353; E. J. Kress Box Co., 24 LA 401)

EXAMPLE: An employer did not violate a contract's provision requiring the presence of union representation at the discharge of an employee when the company sent a telegram to the employee at his home notifying him of his discharge, an arbitrator ruled. The arbiter reasoned that: (1) the contract required the presence of a union representative "if practical" and the presence of a union representative at the home of the grievant when the telegram was delivered was not practical; and (2) the contract provision contemplated that discharges would occur on company premises during regular working hours. (Rexall Drug Co., 65 LA 1101)

Types of Penalties

IN BRIEF

The type of penalty assessed for wrongdoing usually is either a temporary suspension or discharge. A temporary suspension, or "disciplinary layoff," results in loss of pay (and sometimes seniority) for the period of suspension and mars the employee's record. When an arbitrator reinstates a discharged employee without back pay, the end result is not unlike suspension.

Warnings are a lesser type of discipline. Failure to warn an employee of the consequences of violating a rule is one of the most frequent reasons given by arbitrators for setting aside disciplinary layoffs or discharges.

Management may be on shaky ground if it attempts to use types of penalties other than warnings, suspensions, and discharge. However, increasingly common forms of conditioned reinstatement are appearing in the form of last-chance agreements and disciplinary probation.

Factors relevant to an arbitrator's review or evaluation of management's penalties include:
- ▶ The nature of the offense,
- ▶ Due Process and procedural requirements,
- ▶ Pre-discharge conduct of the employee,
- ▶ Double jeopardy,
- ▶ Employee's past work record,
- ▶ Employee's length of service with the company,
- ▶ Employer's lax enforcement of company rules, and
- ▶ Discriminatory or disparate treatment of the employee.

GUIDELINES

Discipline Other Than Discharge

The fact that a contract gives the right to discharge for cause or mentions certain offenses that are grounds for discharge usually does not mean that management may not impose lesser forms of discipline. Under the principle that the greater includes the lesser, arbitrators have upheld management's right to impose degrees of penalties.

But if a contract specifies a procedure of progressive discipline, such as warnings, suspension, and discharge, arbitrators may not uphold management's right to apply other types of penalties, particularly if such measures contravene other provisions of the contract. Thus, arbitrators have held that employers had no right to apply the penalties of denial of a promotion (9 LA 47), denial of holiday pay (16 LA 317, 13 LA 126, 25 LA 332), loss of seniority (30 LA 519), denial of incentive earnings (29 LA 512), and forcing public apologies (22 LA 528).

EXAMPLE: When an employee went for his paycheck, the payroll clerk was carrying on a personal telephone conversation. The employee waited 10 minutes, then broke the connection to get the clerk's attention. She complained about his conduct, and he was told to apologize. When he refused, he was fired.

The employee was unnecessarily rude to the clerk, the arbiter figured, since he could have attracted her attention in some other way. But a short layoff would have been adequate discipline, he said, for the offense was minor and the clerk's conduct irritating. The company's attitude, the arbiter found, put the employee on the spot; he was required to say he was wrong when he felt he was not. The company's action, the arbiter held, was out of line. (Magnavox Co., 28 LA 449)

Warnings

Arbitrators in general seem to feel that some form of warning should precede a discharge (75 LA 819, 75 LA 1254, 64 LA 778, 64 LA 563), except where the employee is guilty of serious misconduct such as stealing or intoxication on the job. (64 LA 880, 17 LA 334, 3 LA 181)

A written warning is particularly important where a worker has been let off lightly for past offenses and management intends to crack down on future offenses. (77 LA 940, 65 LA 894) A discharge for a "last straw" offense might be set aside unless the worker was warned previously that he would be dealt with more severely. (74 LA 814, 65 LA 829, 64 LA 981, 23 LA 284, 29 LA 599)

Progressive Discipline

For most offenses, management is expected to use a system of progressive discipline under which the employee is warned or given disciplinary suspensions before being hit with the ultimate penalty of discharge. A common pattern is: oral warning, written warning, disciplinary layoff, and discharge. (77 LA 207, 72 LA 1285, 72 LA 350, 60 LA 656)

However, management is not bound by a progressive-discipline formula in cases of serious offenses. Some offenses, such as stealing, loan-sharking, or drunkenness on the job, are regarded as so serious that no specific warning or prior disciplinary action need precede discharge. Employees are presumed to know that such serious offenses will lead to discharge. (66 LA 286, 27 LA 768)

EXAMPLE: If progressive discipline were to apply to every case, one arbitrator noted, an employee who brutally assaulted his foreman or a fellow employee would get off with a simple warning slip if it were only his first offense. Thus, he held, the schedule of penalties spelled out in the contract was intended to apply to the offenses referred to and other violations of specific contract provisions and was not intended to apply to other offenses, including serious infractions of plant rules. (Alliance Machine Co., 48 LA 457)

EXAMPLE: As one arbitrator explained:

"The policy of progressive discipline does not mean that for any given employee each penalty must necessarily be more severe than the immediate preceding one, regardless of the offense involved .... What progressive discipline does mean is that progressively more severe penalties may be imposed on each given employee each time any given offense is repeated.

"Progressive discipline also means that after a specified number of offenses, regardless of whether the offenses are identical or not, the company may have the right to discharge the given employees.

"Both of these ... interpretations of progressive discipline avoid the inequitable meting out of discipline, and at the same time serve the dual purpose of progressive discipline, namely, the discouragement of repeated offense by employees and the protection of the right of the company to sever completely its relationship with any employee who by his total behavior shows himself to be irresponsible." (Bell Aircraft Corp., 17 LA 230)

Double Jeopardy & Delays

It is a well recognized principle that discipline should be reasonably prompt and that a penalty, once announced, should not be increased absent evidence that the offense was more serious than it looked at first.

The principle of double jeopardy has been applied by arbitrators to prohibit the imposition of two successive penalties for the same offense, such as a recorded warning and a suspension. (76 LA 758, 12 LA 129, 13 LA 551, 18 LA 86, 24 LA 356, 59 LA 414, 90 LA 435, 96 LA 657, 97 LA 8, 97 LA 60, 97 LA 121, 97 LA 393, 97 LA 774, 98 LA 102)

However, one arbitrator pointed out, that the legal "double jeopardy" rule assumes that a full hearing has been held and that disclosures at that hearing are the basis for the penalty imposed. But "normal industrial plant disciplinary procedures" do not contemplate the kind of hearing which is the basis of the legal rule, he pointed out. He upheld the discharge of employees who already had received a layoff for participating in a wildcat strike where evidence obtained after the layoff showed that they were leaders in the strike. (International Harvester Co., 13 LA 611; see also 74 LA 1012, 81 LA 564, 83 LA 833, 85 LA 302, 91 LA 544)

Court and company penalties — The fact that an employee has paid a fine or served a jail sentence for acts committed in connection with this employment does not preclude management from imposing discipline for the same acts. An arbitrator, however, may consider the legal punishment in determining the severity of the penalty imposed by management. (Westinghouse Electric Corp., 26 LA 836)

EXAMPLE: An arbitrator ruled that the Air force was justified in imposing a three-day suspension on an employee after the worker pleaded guilty and was convicted of making fraudulent claims against the U.S. Government, since the double jeopardy defense does not apply where the misconduct of the employee also amounts to a violation of the law. (Air Force, Dept. of and Government Employees, AFGE, Local 1857, 74 LA 949)

Delays — Management may delay in imposing a penalty for a reasonable time, but arbitrators sometimes find that excessive delay is almost the same as double jeopardy, since an employee then has the threat of the penalty hanging over him for months. (Ashland Oil & Refining Co., 28 LA 874)

It has been held that an employee is entitled: (1) to expect full discipline within a reasonable time, and (2) to assume that the penalty received is the complete one. (8 LA 234, 9 LA 606, 12 LA 344)

Demotion as Discipline

Many arbitrators disapprove of demotion as an ordinary tool of discipline. It permits unequal penalties for similar offenses, they reason, and may have side effects more drastic than the intended punishment, as where a demoted employee subsequently loses his job because of the change in his seniority status. (Lukens Steel Co., 42 LA 252)

Other arbiters, however, have allowed demotions for such matters as carelessness and negligence, poor work attitudes, and incompetence. (74 LA 1131, 74 LA 991, 66 LA 588, 60 LA 197, 59 LA 988)

But in such cases approval frequently is grounded on the theory that the demotion is not really a form of discipline but an adjustment required by the employee's inability to do his job. (12 LA 266, 17 LA 328, 18 LA 457)

EXAMPLE: An employee who had worked for a supermarket chain for about 14 years had served two long stretches as head of a meat department. Each time he had been demoted to cutter, first class, for unsatisfactory performance. Nevertheless, he talked the company into giving him another shot at running a department. He was told at that time, however, that he would have to maintain a satisfactory profit margin.

Although the company could not point to specific defects in the employee's subsequent handling of the department, his profit margin consistently was below the all-store average, was below his predecessor's average, and was, in fact, the worst of any of the company's 40 stores. After 14 weeks of this, the employee was warned in writing; a week later, the picture not having improved, he was demoted.

An arbitrator upheld the demotion, but he clearly did not view it as discipline. Instead, he treated the employee's 15 weeks as a department head as a trial period during which he had failed to demonstrate his ability to handle the job. (Hart's Food Stores Inc., 43 LA 934)

Discharge v. Resignation

Where the facts and circumstances are such as to lead management reasonably to conclude that intent to resign exists, the matter may be treated as a resignation (or "voluntary quit") even though the individual never actually stated his or her intent to quit. (97 LA 297, 96 LA 585, 93 LA 1047, 92 LA 930, 92 LA 259, 90 LA 1194, 90 LA 149, 86 LA 1160, 86 LA 888, 60 LA 619, 30 LA 225, 26 LA 786, 25 LA 608)

EXAMPLE: Because of an increase in workload, an employer cancelled vacations scheduled to begin in August, and informed the two employees who were affected that later dates would be assigned. The grievant, disregarding the employer's notice, did not call in for his work assignment on August 21, and, when contacted by a company representative, reported that he was going on vacation. The employee was told that, if he did so, his act would be construed as a voluntary quit. Upholding management's viewpoint, the arbiter stressed that the scheduling and taking of vacation time is a "mutual responsibility," under which the employee may select his leave dates provided they are agreeable to the company. It is clear that the grievant's chosen vacation time was not agreeable, the arbiter observed, pointing out that the other employee whose leave was cancelled was able to reach agreement with the company for a later vacation date. (B.B.D. Transportation Co. Inc., 66 LA 64)

EXAMPLE: An employee voluntarily quit and was not discharged, an arbiter held, when the worker angrily left the plant without either clocking out or reporting to his foreman following confirmation that the job he had bid on was awarded to someone else. Rejecting the union's contention that the employee at the time of his walkout was suffering from acute stomach pains that precluded his clocking out, the arbiter ruled that although it is possible that the employee's anger over not getting the job had caused him to become ill, the evidence did not establish that the worker was so incapacitated as to justify his leaving the plant without either punching out or first notifying his foreman. (Owens Manufacturing Inc., 63 LA 585)

However, the fact that an employee leaves work without permission because of dissatisfaction or upset over something that has occurred does not necessarily mean that management may be justified in treating the worker as a voluntary quit. (97 LA 297, 88 LA 1265, 88 LA 597, 86 LA 144, 82 LA 569, 75 LA 1147, 74 LA 980, 70 LA 497) Arbiters have held that the test is whether the employee intended permanently to sever his connection with the company. As one arbitrator stated:

"The overwhelming weight of authority holds that there is no voluntary quit by reason of an employee's refusal to perform work to which he is assigned. Unless some affirmation of an intent to quit the job is manifested by the employee, the employer's subsequent refusal to let the employee continue his status constitutes a discharge rather than a resignation." (Oklahoma Furniture Mfg. Co., 24 LA 522; see also 41 LA 913, 921)

Similarly, employees have been held not to have voluntary quit their jobs when they are forced by other commitments or circumstances to miss or stay away from a job.

EXAMPLE: An employee whose military training extended beyond a return-to-work date — specified in a memo granting a leave of absence — did not voluntarily quit his job, despite the fact that the memo stated that failure to report would be considered a resignation, since the employer failed to demonstrate a clear and unequivocal intent to sever the employment relationship. (Rustco Products Co., 92 LA 981; see also 96 LA 216)

By the same token, the mere fact of leaving the job or going home has been held not to constitute a voluntary quit. (66 LA 858, 42 LA 845, 41 LA 386, 41 LA 27)

Even when an employee is warned that persisting in a certain action or behavior will be construed as a quit, the employee's persistence might not be viewed as a voluntary quit. (67 LA 1061, 66 LA 19, 45 LA 97)

Furthermore, if the intent to resign is not adequately evidenced, or if a statement of intent to resign is involuntary or coerced, an alleged resignation will be treated as a discharge and subject to the usual test of "just cause."

EXAMPLE: A foreman who offered to resign from his job was constructively discharged, an arbiter ruled, where the foreman made the offer following the employer's indication of its dissatisfaction with the worker's performance as supervisor. The employer also had stated that the employee would not receive any salary increases.

Concluding that it was reasonable for the foreman to assume that the employer was really telling him that he might as well look for another job, the arbiter pointed out that the company's plant superintendent admitted that he would have terminated the foreman had the worker not resigned. (Rodman Industries Inc., 59 LA 101)

Mental State at Time of Quit

When an employee who is suffering from a mental illness or disturbance announces an intent to resign, an arbitrator may have to decide whether the worker was capable of making a rational decision at the time.

EXAMPLE: An employee suffered from a nervous condition and was unable to sleep or eat for several days. During this period, the worker approached his supervisor and for no apparent reason said: "I quit. I saw you smiling at me." The supervisor immediately called two union stewards to his office, and asked the employee to repeat the statement. The employee, however, did not reply, but instead retrieved his tools, picked up his electric oven, and left the plant. Subsequently, the employee was admitted to a mental institution for observation. Following a two-week stay there, he returned to the plant, attacked a union steward, and damaged the steward's car. At the time, the employee still was under psychiatric care and was receiving medication. A few months later, the psychiatrist told management that the employee was able to return to work. However, the employer, contending that the employee had voluntarily quit, refused to allow him to return to the job.

Agreeing with the position that the employee had suffered a nervous breakdown when he allegedly quit and was not responsible for his statements that day, the arbitrator held that the employee did not have the necessary mental capacity to make a meaningful decision to quit work. The employee should be reinstated, the arbiter decided, but only if two psychiatrists affirm that he is mentally fit to return. (Herr-Voss Corp., 70 LA 497)

EXAMPLE: For several years, an employee suffered from a mental condition that frequently caused irrational reactions to employment situations. After the employee experienced a new nervous disorder, a physician stated that the condition was "not totally disabling," and recommended that the worker be allowed to return to work on a limited basis. However, after being back at work for only a short period of time, the employee decided that it would be in his own "best interest" to quit.

After management reluctantly accepted his resignation, the employee's doctor contended that the worker was in no condition to make prudent decisions.

Finding that the employee was in a rational frame of mind when he reached the "deliberate decision" that the tensions associated with his work were more than he could handle, an arbitrator ruled that he voluntarily quit his position. Despite efforts by management and union officials to dissuade the employee from quitting, he was determined to abide by his decision, the arbitrator pointed out. (Kellogg Co., 71 LA 494; see also 74 LA 980)

Rescinded Resignations

Generally, an employee who voluntarily quits loses his status as an employee. Therefore, if he subsequently tries to rescind the resignation, the decision as to whether to accept the retraction is considered to be within the sole discretion of management. (40 LA 469, 29 LA 700)

EXAMPLE: Where an employee's resignation and subsequent request to withdraw it were an admitted attempt to defraud the company by gaining time off with pay, an arbitrator ruled that the employer's refusal to honor the withdrawal was reasonable, even though contrary to its past practice. (A.R.A. Manufacturing Co., 67 LA 1195; see also 53 LA 1103)

On the other hand, some arbiters have held that extenuating or mitigating circumstances may justify a departure from "rigid" application of the general rule.

EXAMPLE: An employee who resigned after being charged with being off company premises and using marijuana was entitled to rescind his resignation after getting an opportunity to evaluate the facts, an arbitrator ruled, where the recision caused no detriment to the employer. (Renaissance Center Partnership, 76 LA 379)

Proving Misconduct

IN BRIEF

Generally, in most disciplinary cases, and especially in discharge cases, the burden is on management to prove the guilt or wrongdoing, particularly where the contract requires "just cause" for discharge. (55 LA 435, 54 LA 1, 52 LA 1164, 48 LA 567)

The amount or degree of proof required to prove misconduct, however, is not a cut-and-dried matter. It may vary with the severity of the alleged offense, the type of evidence at hand, and the individual arbitrator.

Strict observance of legal rules of evidence usually is not necessary, unless expressly requested by the parties.

GUIDELINES

Determining the Degree of Proof

In disciplinary or discharge hearings, arbitrators frequently tend to stress burden of proof considerations. In such cases, the arbitrator is concerned with two areas of proof. The first involves proof of wrongdoing, and the second—assuming that the employee's guilt has been established—concerns the issue of the appropriate penalty.

The degree of proof required by arbitrators for proving misconduct may vary, depending on the type of offense the employee allegedly has committed. Arbitrators generally agree that a "preponderance" of the evidence, "clear and convincing" evidence, or evidence "sufficient to convince a reasonable mind of guilt" is necessary to uphold management's disciplinary action in cases involving ordinary misconduct. (77 LA 978, 77 LA 569, 77 LA 483, 77 LA 210, 75 LA 574, 74 LA 877, 74 LA 737, 73 LA 1278, 73 LA 1167, 73 LA 760, 73 LA 531, 71 LA 949, 60 LA 125, 60 LA 899, 63 LA 952, 65 LA 784)

A higher degree of proof, however, may be required where the alleged misconduct is punishable under criminal law or regarded as morally reprehensible. In such cases, the common law standard of "proof beyond a reasonable doubt" may be required. (64 LA 1099, 66 LA 619)

EXAMPLE: One arbitrator, ruled that the penalty of discharge was too severe for an employee who allegedly participated in an attempt to steal company-owned property, since the employer failed to establish the worker's guilt beyond a reasonable doubt. The "drastic nature of the sanction of discharge" requires a higher standard of proof, the arbitrator pointed out, emphasizing that not only is a discharged employee out of a job, but also (especially where the worker is discharged for dishonesty) the opportunities for reemployment are greatly reduced. (Daystrom Furniture Co. Inc., 65 LA 1157)

Similarly, an employer failed to establish beyond a reasonable doubt that an aluminum ladder and other items found in an employee's garage were company property that the worker had removed from the employer's premises, an arbitrator decided. The charge of theft, the arbitrator noted, was based on a statement by the employee's estranged wife that her ex-husband had brought the property home from work. Although the employee may have removed the property from company premises, it was equally as possible that it was not removed by him and that his disgruntled ex-wife set up the situation, the arbitrator pointed out, concluding that there was no proof that the worker stole the materials. (Standard Oil Of Ohio, 75 LA 588; see also 74 LA 1163, 73 LA 1066)

Evidence Gathering

When management discharges or disciplines an employee, it should have enough facts in hand at the time of the action of establish "just cause." Efforts to build up a good case by extensive research after a grievance is filed generally will be a waste of time, since arbitrators usually hold that management's case must stand or fall on the basis of facts it had at the time it acted. (12 LA 108, 10 LA 117, 1 LA 153)

The most important evidence in a discharge or discipline proceeding usually comes in the form of testimony from witnesses—the facts which led to the employer's disciplinary action being of great importance. (77 LA 721, 75 LA 1147, 73 LA 771, 73 LA 610, 71 LA 1109, 71 LA 949)

In weighing the credibility of evidence offered by management and the union, an arbitrator might consider the following.

● Any conflict or contraction in the evidence;

● Any inconsistency in the testimony of the accused employee and other witnesses (60 LA 703, 64 LA 107); and

● The source of the witnesses' testimony — whether it is first-hand knowledge or merely hearsay and gossip.

● The arbitrator might also observe the demeanor of witnesses while on the stand, and will credit or discredit the testimony according to his own impressions of the witnesses' veracity. (Inland Steel Container Co., 60 LA 536)

Witnesses

One arbiter devised the following criteria to be used to determine the credibility of witnesses' testimony; including, but not limited to:

● the relative strength of their recollections;

● the consistency in testimony given on the same subject at different times during hearings and in different fora;

● the showing of obvious bias or prejudice;

● showing of emotional stress or other feelings that would impair ability to respond to questions carefully and accurately;

● evasiveness;

● the quality and reasonableness of testimony; and,

● the existence of corroborating testimony. (Safeway Stores Inc., 96 LA 304)

Arbiters sometimes bring in outside experts for impartial study of the disputed matter. (6 LA 218, 18 LA 447, 21 LA 573)

Arbiters have accepted testimony of handwriting experts and have based their awards principally on such testimony.

EXAMPLE: Similarly, in a case involving the discharge of an employee for allegedly writing and posting three obscene notices slandering female employees, the arbitrator ignored the employee's refusal to take a lie detector test, holding that he was within his rights in so refusing. But he relied on the testimony of a handwriting expert in upholding the discharge. He noted that the examiner's qualifications as an expert were substantial and that his identification of the employee as the author was both positive and firm. (Seaview Industries Inc., 39 LA 125)

Polygraph Tests

Arbiters generally have been reluctant to uphold discipline based on the results of lie detector/polygraph tests. Some arbiters have held that test results can be given no weight whatsoever in determining guilt.

EXAMPLE: Granting that such tests are used extensively in government and industry, one arbitrator said, the fact remains that most courts have ruled them inadmissible as evidence in criminal and civil cases. The same rule should apply to arbitration proceedings, the arbitrator concluded. (Continental Air Transport Co., 38 LA 778; see also 75 LA 574, 75 LA 313, 71 LA 1202, 70 LA 909, 70 LA 100, 68 LA 581, 64 LA 453, 44 LA 709, 45 LA 1155)

Further, another arbiter discounted the use of polygraph-test results in a proceeding involving a discharge for theft, where state law forbade the reference to, or use of, polygraph tests in court proceedings. (Deer Lakes School District, 94 LA 334)

However, traditional arbitral skepticism about the reliability of polygraphs may be changing, according to one arbiter, who observed that arbiters have begun to adopt a "more favorable attitude" toward such testing in recent years. He cautioned, however, that "polygraph tests are more useful in verifying the truthfulness of testimony than in detecting its unreliability." (Daystrom Furniture Co. Inc., 65 LA 1157)

Similarly, another arbiter maintained that "the pace of acceptance of polygraph results has accelerated somewhat in recent years" and that the tests "can provide helpful supplemental evidence" in industrial discipline cases. (Bowman Transportation Inc., 64 LA 453; see also 88 LA 1019, 77 LA 1259)

Other arbitrators have held that test results may be considered as a "factor of evidence" but may not serve as the sole basis of proof. (39 LA 470, 39 LA 893, 43 LA 450)

Others have said that an employee's refusal to submit to a test cannot be used against him, especially where the company is fishing for a guilty party among a group of employees and hasn't yet accused anyone. (73 LA 304, 32 LA 44, 39 LA 470)

EXAMPLE: One arbitrator set forth these guidelines on the use of lie detector tests in cases involving dishonesty: The company could offer these tests to employees on a voluntary basis when there was a reason to suspect them of dishonesty and could consider the failure to take a test as an additional possible factor in determining whether to proceed with discharge action. However, where the company had nothing else to go on but an employee's unwillingness to take a test, it could not use this factor as a basis for discipline. (Lag Drug Co., 39 LA 1121)

However, one arbiter, upheld an employee's discharge for refusal to cooperate in the investigation of a theft where the missing articles were found in the employee's car and he refused to offer a satisfactory explanation or to take a test. (Allen Industries Inc., 26 LA 363)

Use of 'Bugs,' TV Surveillance

Suspension of a telephone operator for poor work performance was upheld by an arbitrator, where supervisors used a multiple listening device to monitor her performance. Discipline needn't be limited to eyewitness observation by supervisors, it was held. (Michigan Bell Telephone Co., 45 LA 689)

However, use of a TV surveillance system was knocked down by another arbitrator, but only on the ground that installation of the cameras was a substantial enough change in working conditions to require negotiation with the union. The arbitrator did not completely close the door to the use of closed circuit television as a tool of supervision. For one thing, he rejected the union's claim that this constituted an unlawful invasion of privacy or spying.

In ruling that the TV system had to go, the arbitrator relied heavily on the fact that the company failed to show any particular need for or benefit to be derived from the system. (EICO Inc., 44 LA 563)

Unnamed Accusers

Some arbitrators have refused to sustain discipline based on charges by persons whom the employer either refused to identify or to produce at the arbitration hearing. (24 LA 538, 22 LA 320, 13 LA 433)

However, where a discharge was based on the report of a professional "spotter" employed to detect irregularities, an arbitrator held the company did not have to produce the spotter at the hearing, since this would have destroyed his effectiveness. (Shenango Valley Transportation Co., 23 LA 362)

Biased Accuser

The arbitrator might examine the relationship between the employee and his accuser. Arbitrators generally recognize that the accused employee has "a strong incentive for denying guilt," in that the worker stands immediately to gain or lose in the case (48 LA 812), and that normally there is no reason to presume that a supervisor, for example, would unjustifiably select and accuse the employee of misconduct. Nevertheless, the testimony of the accuser is subject to doubt and might be carefully scrutinized if there is evidence of ulterior motives or ill will against the accused employee. (60 LA 206, 60 LA 688, 63 LA 244, 64 LA 304)

EXAMPLE: An employee was discharged for being a goof-off. Two of his fellow workers said they'd rather clock out and go home than be assigned to work with this employee because of his habit of wandering off and leaving them to shoulder the whole load.

It so happened that one of these employees was a brother-in-law of the discharged employee's foreman and the other was a neighbor of the foreman. The discharged employee on an earlier occassion had turned in the foreman for being intoxicated on the job.

The arbitrator didn't put any stock in the testimony of the foreman's allies, but relied instead on the testimony of other employees who said they'd never had any trouble working with the discharged employee. (Scientific Data Systems Inc., 53 LA 487)

Part 2

Discharge and Discipline: Categories

Absenteeism

IN BRIEF

Generally, arbitrators agree that chronic or excessive absenteeism is just cause for discharge. However, the real problem has been to determine when absenteeism is excessive. No general rules can be laid down, thus arbitrators consider a variety of factors in deciding such cases.

In determining whether an employer acted reasonably in disciplining an employee for absenteeism or tardiness, most arbitrators use a case-by-case approach, focusing on the particular facts and circumstances of the immediate situation. Several factors are examined by arbitrators, including:

▶ The length of, and time during which, the employee had a poor attendance record (64 LA 12, 74 LA 623, 94 LA 409, 95 LA 1169);

▶ The reasons for the worker's absences (64 LA 672, 74 LA 1185, 98 LA 57);

▶ The nature of the employee's job;

▶ The attendance records of other employees (64 LA 483);

▶ Whether the employer has a clear disciplinary policy relating to absenteeism, which is known to all employees and which is applied fairly and consistently (63 LA 1315, 65 LA 919, 77 LA 249); and

▶ Whether the employee was adequately warned that disciplinary action could result if the worker's attendance record failed to improve. (63 LA 148, 71 LA 129, 71 LA 744, 72 LA 347, 98 LA 105, 98 LA 203)

--- GUIDELINES ---

REASONS FOR ABSENTEEISM

Balancing the employee's right to job security against the employer's right to expect a reasonable degree of job attendance is the primary task of arbitrators dealing with a problem of excessive absenteeism. In achieving this balance, the arbitrator's decision often turns on whether the employee has provided a reasonable or justifiable excuse for being absent from work. Some of the problems in striking this balance are discussed below.

Chronic Illness

Illness is probably the most common excuse given by employees who are absent from work. Although it is reasonable for employees to be excused for occasional absences due to illness, management does have the right to guard against false claims of sickness.

In evaluating whether excessive absenteeism due to illness justifies the disciplinary penalty, arbiters often consider whether or not the employee's attendance record has fallen below an acceptable range for an unreasonable period of time. In determining this, management may consider the employee's previous attendance record, his length of service, his desire to be a faithful employee, his efforts to improve, the nature of the absences, the extent to which they exceed the norm, the effect upon efficiency and morale, and the prospects for the future. (41 LA 551)

EXAMPLE: One arbiter ruled that illness, injury, and other incapacitation by forces beyond the employee's control are mitigating circumstances, excuse reasonable periods of absence, and are important factors in determining excessive absences. However, he said, if an employee cannot maintain an "acceptable attendance record" due to chronic bad health or a being prone to injury, an employer may discharge the employee after having sought to improve the attendance through counselling and warnings. (Louisville Water Co., 77 LA 1049; see also 48 LA 615, 74 LA 507, 76 LA 509, 77 LA 1049, 78 LA 673, 79 LA 128, 79 LA 916, 80 LA 7)

EXAMPLE: An employer was held justified in discharging an employee for excessive absenteeism, where the employee's physical condition caused the worker to be absent from the job 16 to 100 percent per year over a 12-year period. (60 LA 1122)

Similarly, a company properly discharged an employee who had been absent because of illness 14 or 15 weeks out of a six-month period. In upholding the discharge, an arbiter said: "No plant can operate profitably unless it can depend on fairly regular attendance of employees. Any situation which results in or tends toward unprofitable operations is against the best interests not only of the company but of the employees themselves." (Celanese Corp. of America, 9 LA 143; see also 74 LA 205, 74 LA 362, 74 LA 531, 74 LA 623, 74 LA 681, 74 LA 858, 94 LA 41, 94 LA 409, 95 LA 1169, 97 LA 653)

Management's case for justifying a discharge will be strengthened if it has sought through counseling, warnings, and health care to rehabilitate the employee (94 LA 971). But the fact that the final absence would not by itself support discharge is immaterial, so long as the company has given adequate warning.

Even if the reasons offered for each individual absence seem proper, employees may be disciplined for excessive absenteeism, if the absences become so frequent as to render the employee's services of little or no value to the company (15 LA 593, 18 LA 86, 23 LA 663, 39 LA 187, 64 LA 672, 74 LA 1024, 96 LA 649, 98 LA 105).

It is generally felt, however, that employees should be put on notice and given an opportunity to improve before the discharge penalty is invoked. (Ambac Industries Inc., 72 LA 347; see also 64 LA 1283)

It may be relatively easy for a company to justify a discharge for excessive absenteeism where the employee has had frequently recurring illnesses for short periods over a long period of time showing symptoms of psychosomatic origin or chronic bad health. On the other hand, it may be more difficult for it to justify the termination of an employee with several genuine illnesses, each lasting a long time. (36 LA 1042; see also 75 LA 430)

Alternatively, an arbiter reinstated an employee where an employer's attendance-control policy in a collective bargaining agreement recognized the mitigating nature of an employee's illness — in this case, a chronic kidney stone — in determining proper discipline. The arbiter said that valid "no-fault" absentee plans must distinguish "malingering and honest misfortune." (Owens-Brockway Packaging Inc., 96 LA 950; see also 98 LA 112)

Also, the discharge of an employee whose off-duty back injury had caused him to be absent sporadically, was premature and possibly without just cause, despite claims that the employer had a responsibility to protect the worker and itself from the risk of further injury and that there was no indication that absenteeism would improve, where doctor's statements do not limit employee's work activities after his recovery. (92 LA 837)

Further, just cause did not exist to discharge a 28-year employee suffering from anxiety and depression, even though she had accumulated seven absenteeism-related discipline slips in 23 days and did not seek treatment until more than two weeks after discharge. A letter from a treating psychologist confirmed that she was unable to care for herself or to act rationally during period in question. (96 LA 1174)

Alcoholism

Generally alcoholism is viewed as an illness, and many companies have developed programs aimed at spotting and rehabilitating alcoholics. (95 LA 553, 73 LA 1193, 71 LA 158) But management is not obligated to retain indefinitely an employee whose alcoholism keeps him or her from delivering on a regular basis.

EXAMPLE: An employee had been warned on numerous occasions concerning his attendance. Lack of improvement resulted in a seven-day disciplinary suspension. This was followed by more counseling concerning the seriousness of his absenteeism and his drinking problem, and finally by a 30-day suspension pending discharge with the understanding that he would be given "one more chance" if he committed himself to the state alcoholic hospital and successfully underwent treatment. After temporarily getting "on the wagon," the employee subsequently fell off with the result that he lost a week from work and woke up in the state hospital again. The company finally decided to discharge him.

Refusing to set the discharge aside, an arbiter said that when a "last-chance" agreement has been reached, another chance must rest entirely within the company's discretion. If he were to rule otherwise, it might jeopardize the chance of other employees to obtain reinstatement on the same condition, he noted. (Mohawk Rubber Co., 47 LA 1029)

Similarly, an employer properly discharged an alcoholic who had received his fourth warning notice for excessive absences instead of allowing the worker to take retroactive credit against his paid vacation for his unexplained absences, an arbiter ruled. Pointing out that it is not unfair for an employer to place more stringent reporting requirements on an employee who has had warning notices about poor attendance, the arbiter concluded that management did not act precipitously. (General Electric Co., 72 LA 355)

For more arbitral standards and decisions concerning employee alcoholism, see the chapter on Intoxication & Alcoholism, in this section.

Imprisonment

Arbiters are by no means unanimous in their attitude toward absence caused by confinement in jail. Some hold that it is just cause for discharge, while some say that it is a sufficient excuse for absence. In between are those who hold that it is not necessarily one or the other and that disposition depends on the circumstances.

In determining the propriety of discipline for an absence caused by a jail sentence, a number of factors may be taken into consideration. These include the duration of the absence, the nature of the act causing the confinement and the effect the employee's reinstatement would have on plant morale, the ease or difficulty of having the absent employee's duties performed by others, the employer's past practices with respect to absenteeism generally and to arrest-caused absences specifically, the employee's length of service, his prior disciplinary record, and his record for dependability. (74 LA 860, 74 LA 1245, 75 LA 967, 86 LA 673, 87 LA 500, 87 LA 691, 87 LA 1273, 89 LA 1150, 94 LA 1206, 96 LA 216)

EXAMPLE: An employee with 37 years of service was arrested in a local movie house on a morals charge. He was held in a jail a couple of days before being released, and later was tried, convicted, and sentenced to a year and a day in prison. Upon his release, he began receiving treatment from doctors and psychiatrists toward elimination of the "sociopathic personality disturbance, sexual deviation," that had landed him in jail. The company decided to terminate him permanently.

While conceding that the employee was mentally ill and that his illness had manifested itself in a way that was repugnant and unlawful, an arbiter directed his reinstatement. The illness did not impair his ability to do his job, the arbiter noted, and the company had not shown that it could not be eliminated or substantially improved by medical treatment. Nor was it shown that the employee's absence had affected the efficiency of his department or had significantly increased the company's insurance charges. And aside from sheer speculation, there was no basis for finding that his return would result in bad feelings or tensions in his department. All of this, plus his spotless employment record of 37 years, convinced the arbiter there was not just cause for discharge. (U.S. Steel Corp., 41 LA 460)

On the other hand, after juggling his schedule in order to appear in court on a workday, an employee was convicted of a felony and incarcerated. The worker's wife reported his whereabouts to the company the following day, and, after he had missed a week of scheduled workdays, the employee was issued a suspension for an unjustified absence. Later, upon considering the worker's record of prior absenteeism and discipline, management decided to change the penalty to a discharge. The union, on behalf of the prisoner, requested that the company grant the worker either his vacation leave or a leave of absence until the employee was given a work release, which occurred four weeks later. Management contended it had no obligation to do so and stuck by the discharge.

Saying there was no reason the company should consider the employee's imprisonment to be in error or forced upon him for reasons beyond his control, the arbiter asserted that management "is not required to sit idly by and, in effect, carry an employee who is serving a jail sentence for acts committed against society." Finding that the employer had no contractual obligation to place the worker on annual leave, the arbiter concluded that the worker's confinement, in light of his prior discipline and "significant absenteeism problem," warranted discharge. (United States Steel Corp., 69 LA 225; see also 72 LA 613, 73 LA 196, 86 LA 1237, 88 LA 167, 88 LA 1092, 89 LA 804, 91 LA 1225)

Religious Beliefs

Management's right to discipline an employee for absences caused by his religious beliefs is complicated by the ban on religious discrimination in Title VII of the federal Civil Rights Act and by similar bans in many state FEP laws.

Guidelines issued by the Equal Employment Opportunity Commission call for employers to make reasonable accommodations to the religious needs of their employees when this can be done without undue hardship to the business.

Weather Conditions

On occasion, bad weather, civil disturbances, or other outside conditions make it difficult for employees to report to work. However, even when an "Act of God" is considered a reasonable excuse for absence, there still may be difficulties in determining how long the condition remains an acceptable excuse.

EXAMPLE: Under an absentee control program that assigned "points" to employees for certain types of tardiness and absence but not for "Acts of God," an employer wrongly assigned points to employees who were absent from work one day after a severe winter storm that was considered an Act of God, an arbiter ruled. Despite management's contention that strict enforcement of the absence program was necessary and that conditions did not have a "sufficient impact" on the total work force since 80 percent of the employees were able to report, the arbiter maintained that the company could have extended the Act-of-God allowance to the 20 percent who were still hindered by snow and ice the following day, without retarding or impairing the overall effectiveness of the absence program. (Environmental Elements Corp., 70 LA 912; see also 95 LA 906)

Similarly, although an employer had the right to establish a "snow day" policy excusing absence of employees due to weather conditions only when more than 50 percent of employees were absent, an arbiter decided that the application of the policy on the day a snowfall caused absence or tardiness of 36 percent of employees was improper because the employees were not notified of the policy. (Marley Cooling Tower Co., 71 LA 306)

'Personal Business'

Employees at times are reluctant to disclose their reasons — good or bad — for wanting to take time off from work. To avoid unpleasant situations, employers frequently are willing to accept personal business as a valid excuse for absences in some situations.

However, when a company decided to crack down on absenteeism because of suspected abuses, an arbiter held that it could require employees to come up with something more than "personal business" as an excuse for absences. It is appropriate in such cases, the arbiter said, for the company to inquire into the *general* nature of the business without invading the privacy of the employee's personal affairs.

Since it would be next to impossible to prescribe a set formula covering every situation, the arbiter advised, each personal absence should be diagnosed and treated separately. (Fairbanks Morse Inc., 47 LA 224)

This case-by-case approach generally is followed by arbiters.

EXAMPLE: "Personal reasons" were held an acceptable excuse where the employer ordinarily accepted that excuse, even though the disputed absence occurred on the day before a scheduled vacation (McLouth Steel Corp., 31 LA 386).

On the other hand, suspension of an employee was held justified where all he would say was that he had been "out of town" (American Steel & Wire Co., 12 LA 47).

Likewise, an employee, with a record of extensive absenteeism and failing to call in or give explanation for his absences, gave as an excuse for a one week's absence that he had been out on "personal business." Because this explanation was considered inadequate, he was asked on several occasions to come up with a more substantive explanation. When he failed to do so, he was terminated. Only then did he explain that the reason for his absence was a highly personal situation involving domestic difficulties which he found embarrassing to make public.

If the employee had not had the poor past record of unexplained absences, the company might have been in the position to have given him the benefit of the doubt, an arbiter said. But in view of his record, a request for an explanation was justified. (Mead Corp., 51 LA 1121)

NOTIFICATION OF ABSENCE

Company rules usually require both notice to the employer when the employee is going to be absent and a justifiable excuse for such an absence. Notice alone, without a good excuse, does not fulfill the employee's obligation. On the other hand, a good excuse for the absence does not necessarily justify an absence without notice.

Lack of Notice

If employees are expected to give notice of their absences, a failure to attempt to meet this requirement may justify discipline, regardless of the merits of the reason for the absence. (60 LA 680, 63 LA 1262, 81 LA 657, 98 LA 23)

EXAMPLE: An employer that imposed "last-chance" re-employment on an employee with a drinking problem was justified in discharging the employee after he absented himself from work for more than one week without complying with a condition requiring the worker to give notice of an intended absence and the circumstances involved to either of two general supervisors. (United States Steel Corp., 63 LA 274, see also 74 LA 507)

Similarly, an employer's lack of notice to an employee concerning proper work procedures has led to the disallowance of discipline for what constitutes an "excused absence" (45 LA 532; 30 LA 231), or when a doctor's excuse is required for return to work. (47 LA 441)

Failure to Notify Not Voluntary Quit

An employee's failure to notify an employer of his or her whereabouts or reasons for an absence can be considered a "voluntary quit." However, occasionally, if the employee's reasons are good enough, a discharge may be reduced to a suspension. (96 LA 216, an employee's imprisonment; and 95 LA 881, an employee's drug relapse)

Defective Notice

If an employee makes a good-faith effort to comply with the notice requirement, but is unable to do so, he is more likely to be treated leniently. But a sincere effort at compliance should be demanded.

EXAMPLE: An employee was taken ill shortly before the time he was to leave for work. Having no telephone, he asked a fellow employee to transmit the message to management. The message never arrived.

An arbiter credited the employee with an honest effort to meet the notice requirement. The employee's obligation is met, the arbiter said when "he employs a means of reporting that is, under all circumstances, reasonable and calculated, in all probability, to result in actual receipt of the notice." (Goodyear Clearwater Mills, 11 LA 419; see also 72 LA 312, 73 LA 133)

EXAMPLE: An employee who wanted to overstay his vacation mailed a letter to this effect to the employer at the end of his originally scheduled vacation period. The company's rule specified that absence without notice "for three consecutive working days" meant termination. The employee's letter was mailed within the three day period, but the employer did not receive it until later.

The employee did not meet the notice requirement, an arbiter held. The employer must actually receive notice within the three-day period, the arbiter concluded. (Lear Sieglar Inc., 48 LA 276)

OTHER ABSENTEEISM PROBLEMS

Special absenteeism problems, apart from the issues of excuse and notice, are discussed below.

Overstaying Leaves, Vacations

Vacations, layoffs, and leaves of absence often give rise to absenteeism problems when employees report back late. Arbitrators tend to judge these situations as they would any other other absenteeism case, with particular attention to the reason for the absence and the consistency of the company's enforcement of rules against leave-stretching.

EXAMPLE: An employee did not return to work until one week after the end of her scheduled two-week vacation. She claimed that she could not get transportation back from the distant place where she spent her vacation unless she waited for her husband to finish his three-week vacation.

Discharge of the employee for violating the company's rules was upheld by an arbiter. He was of the opinion that she probably had deliberately chosen not to return to work on time. In any event, she had demonstrated an irresponsible attitude toward her job. (Packaging Corp. of America, 42 LA 606)

EXAMPLE: In another case where an employee overstayed her vacation by a week, an arbiter found that her excuse was good enough to warrant reducing her discharge to a suspension without pay. Her reason for her absence was an attempt to save her marriage, which the arbiter felt out weighed the employer's need for her presence. (Vellumoid Co., 41 LA 1129; see also 74 LA 847)

Past Leniency

The fact that management has been lenient with an employee in the past does not necessary bar it from resorting to discharge if he persists in his misconduct. A decision to give an employee a break in hopes that he will straighten out will not later be held against management by an arbiter. But where management, over an extended period of time, gives only lip service to a rule of conduct, arbiters will insist that discharge be preceded by effective notice that the rule will be enforced.

EXAMPLE: In an effort to get a delinquent employee to mend his ways, management sent him a total of five "final" warnings over a three-year period. It finally decided to terminate him.

Overruling the discharge, an arbitrator noted that the "final" warnings all read exactly alike. Thus it was not suprising that the employee did not think anyone actually was concerned about his absences. If somewhere along the line management had let the employee know that it meant business, either by specific warning or disciplinary suspension, then discharge for subsequent absences probably would have been upheld. Instead, management had completely nullified the effectiveness of its warnings by repeatedly threatening discharge and then taking no disciplinary action, the arbiter concluded. (Limestone Greer Co., 40 LA 343)

Absence on Usual Day Off

When management schedules work on a Saturday, holiday, or other day that normally is not a working day, it usually runs into a higher degree of absenteeism than usual. Arbiters are agreed, however, that, as a general principle, the right to schedule work belongs to management, except to the extent that this right has been specifically limited by contract.

Even where a contract gives employees the right to decline to work on a Saturday or holiday, arbiters usually have held that once an employee accepts an assignment to work on such an overtime day, his duty to the company is the same as it would be on a regular work day. (11 LA 947, 12 LA 770, 29 LA 672)

Insubordination

The offense of absenteeism often is compounded by insubordination where employees after being denied permission to take time off, take the time anyway. Arbitrators usually find just cause for discipline in such cases. (43 LA 1070, 24 LA 593)

Failure to Report

An employer properly discharged an employee for refusing to report to a job offered under reinstatement award, where union officials urged him to accept position pending arbitral clarification of award and resolution was "equivalent" to former job, and the worker had been reinstated on probation and without back pay because of previous improper resort to self-help. (97 LA 489; see also 96 LA 740)

However, just cause did not exist to discharge an employee for "unauthorized absences" following automobile accident, even though he did not report on first date specified in medical release, where the date of his actual return was one week after the return-to-light-duty date specified by chiropractor. Further, the date of the worker's actual return was one week prior to the earliest date he would be released for regular duties, and was the date of release letter, and the employer had told the worker on similar occasions that there was no light-duty work, and the worker was entitled to a period of readjustment. (97 LA 572; see also 95 LA 784, 95 LA 881, 95 LA 1135, 96 LA 38, 98 LA 194)

TARDINESS

While not as serious an offense as an absence without excuse or notice, tardiness is properly a subject for discipline. (77 LA 947, 76 LA 1066, 76 LA 324, 74 LA 290, 74 LA 205, 72 LA 347, 71 LA 129) Since the reported cases commonly involve discipline of employees for a combination of absenteeism and tardiness, it would appear that the employee who is guilty of one is likely also to be guilty of the other.

As with absenteeism, a program of progressive discipline (e.g., counseling, warning, suspension) generally is viewed as the proper way to encourage a delinquent employee to mend his ways. (63 LA 54, 63 LA 739, 65 LA 1028, 81 LA 297, 82 LA 141, 83 LA 337, 83 LA 1281, 84 LA 1058, 86 LA 517, 86 LA 686, 86 LA 1077, 89 LA 1237, 90 LA 131, 91 LA 231, 91 LA 339, 93 LA 441, 95 LA 983, 97 LA 708) But, also as with absenteeism, excessive and consistent tardiness can reach the point of rendering an employee no longer suitable for employment.

When Does Tardiness Begin?

Can employees be counted tardy if they are not at their work stations at the time the contract says the workday starts, even though they clock in on time?

EXAMPLE: Under a contract that failed to specify whether the workday began at the time clock or at the work station, an arbiter held, management had no right to fire a worker for tardiness because he did not clock in before the beginning of his shift.

According to the contract, the "standard day shift" ran from 7:30 a.m. to 4:00 p.m. The Company construed this to mean that workers had to be at their work stations by 7:30, and it issued a notice stating that they'd be considered late if they failed to clock in before then. A worker who persisted in clocking in exactly at 7:30 was given a written warning. He appealed the matter to a union-management committee but was turned down. Eventually he was discharged on three counts, one of which was tardiness.

The arbiter, noting that the company bore the burden of proof, decided that the charge of tardiness would not stand up. Nothing in the contract, he pointed out, established whether the parties intended the workday to begin at the time clock or at the work station: therefore there was no basis for the company rule. For either the grievance committee or the arbiter to "interpret" the contract on this issue would actually be an amendment to the contract, and therefore improper, the arbiter concluded. (Pacific Air-Motive Corp., 28 LA 761, see also 85 LA 207, 92 LA 658, 95 LA 248)

On the other hand, an arbiter decided that an employer properly suspended an employee who either had another worker punch in for him so that he could go to the convenience store, where the plant manager saw him 10 minutes after the start of the shift; or punched in himself and then temporarily left the plant.

(Peerless Mfg. Co., 73 LA 915; see also 84 LA 613, 85 LA 411)

Tightening Rules on Tardiness

If it becomes necessary for a company to adopt stricter rules on tardiness, are there any limitations on the penalties it can impose?

One arbiter has taken the position that a new set of rules on tardiness must be judged not only on their merits but also by how they compare with past practice. Applying this reasoning, he refused to approve a rule that departed radically from past practice.

EXAMPLE: After trying a number of approaches to the problem of tardiness, a company finally laid down a rule stating that an employee would be discharged if he was tardy 12 times in a 12-month period.

An arbiter held that this rule was arbitrary and unreasonable. Looking at past practice, he found that none of the rules promulgated by the company in the past eight years had provided for discharge without prior warning. Moreover, the penalty of discharge had never been invoked on the basis of as few as 12 instances of tardiness in a 12-month period. It sometimes may be okay to define "chronic tardiness" in terms of a fixed number of instances of tardiness, the arbiter said, but in his view it was unreasonable to do so where the number of instances of tardiness was reduced from the number allowed in the past, where notices were not issued to the employee, and the rules made no provision for a graduated system of penalties. (The Maccabees, 27 LA 99)

Similarly, another arbiter ruled that a company had no right, after signing its first contract, to start docking workers for tardiness. Nobody had ever been docked for tardiness before the contract was signed. Further, the company had agreed that no clause in the contract would be interpreted to "imply a lowering of the working conditions heretofore existing."

The arbiter found the contract language of special significance, since it was a first contract, and said it granted the workers all rights, privileges, and benefits they previously enjoyed plus the new ones in the agreement. He concluded that to start docking for tardiness after the contract became effective was a lowering of previously existing conditions. (Hellenic Lines Lte., 39 LA 31; see also 97 LA 988)

Likewise, an employer violated a contract provision obligating parties to keep shop rules and penalties in effect without change for the duration of the bargaining agreement, an arbiter ruled, when it promulgated a new rule setting new discipline for tardiness. The employer's action was an improper modification of offenses and penalties under the contract the arbiter reasoned, concluding that the evidence established a past practice by which employees regularly had been disciplined under existing rules for tardiness and absence. (Wolverine Aluminum Corp., 74 LA 252)

However, a reasonable rule on discipline for tardiness was upheld by another arbiter as not conflicting with employee rights under a union contract. (U.S. Steel Corp., 44 LA 829)

Insubordination

IN BRIEF

One of the most firmly established principles in labor relations is management's right to direct the workforce. Insubordination, then, is a cardinal industrial offense since it violates this right. Arbitral decisions in discipline cases involving insurbordination overwhelmingly are governed by the "obey now, grieve later" rule laid down many years ago. (Ford Motor Co., 3 LA 779) In that case, the arbiter declared that "an industrial plant is not a debating society." Rather, "its object is production," the arbiter stressed, and "when a controversy arises, production cannot wait." Therefore, when objecting to an order, a worker's proper course of action is to first comply with the directive and then file a protest. The principal exception to this standard, arbiters agree, is where carrying out the order would endanger workers' health or safety. In addition to failure or refusal to comply with an order, abusive behavior-from profane language to physical violence-toward management qualifies as insubordination, since such actions impinge on the employer's ability to direct the workforce.

When considering the propriety of discipline in either type of case, arbiters will weigh the degree of insubordination involved. As one arbiter noted, an employee "may quietly say that he does not think that he should follow instructions ...; he may become 'wordly abusive'; or he may engage in open conflict with his supervisor." While "each action may, it is true, be generally classified as insubordination," the arbitrator emphasized, "there is none the less a difference." (Micro Precision Gear & Machine Corp., 31 LA 575; see also 41 LA 1176, 44 LA 254, 44 LA 289, 47 LA 175, 52 LA 61, 53 LA 274.) In addition, arbiters generally will hinge the severity of the discipline on whether the employee was given specific warning of the consequence of the insubordination (31 LA 575, 38 LA 218, 52 LA 217) or had previously engaged in such behavior (43 LA 864, 44 LA 193, 45 LA 361, 65 LA 748)

Refusal to Obey Directives

IN BRIEF

Most cases of insubordination involve a worker's refusal or failure to follow the directive of a duly designated member of management or comply with an established procedure. On reviewing the propriety of discipline in such cases, arbiters generally consider not only the magnitude of the offense and prior occurrences of such behavior but also whether:
▶ The order or procedure in question was clearly expressed;
▶ The employee was made aware of the possible consequences of the action; and
▶ The discipline was applied in a nondiscriminatory and progressive manner.

GUIDELINES

Rules, Orders, & Procedures

Violations of clearly expressed orders typically constitute insubordination and provide grounds for discipline.

EXAMPLE: An employee was properly suspended for refusing to obey an order to move her car. After the employee refused to comply with a request to move her automobile that was parked in a restricted area on the company's parking lot, she was issued a ticket by the safety manager. The ticket warned the employee that she was parked illegally in an area reserved for motorcycles. When the employee refused to accept the ticket, her supervisor ordered her to accompany him to the associate manager's office where she would be given a memo directing her to move the car. However, the employee again refused to comply, and, subsequently, was suspended for insubordination. The employer argued that the employee was "flagrantly" insubordinate in failing to move her car and report to the manager's office. The union, on the other hand, insisted that the worker should not have been required to report to the manager's office without a union representative.

It has long been established that an employee first must follow an order and then turn to the grievance procedure for further relief; the arbitrator declared, upholding the disciplinary action. Pointing out that an "air of insubordination" surrounded the employee's conduct, he concluded that the worker's "open defiance" of management's directives constituted just cause for discipline. (Federal Correctional Institution, 75 LA 295; see also 93 LA 203, 96 LA 212, 96 LA 633)

However, an employee who was charged with five separate acts of insubordination during a 20-minute period was improperly dismissed because he was not warned about his behavior, another arbiter ruled. The employee first was told to adjust the brakes on a piece of machinery. Refusing to comply, the employee used obscene language toward his supervisor. The supervisor then ordered the worker to report to a manager. When the employee refused to obey that command, the supervisor told him to punch out and leave the premises. The employee, however, insisted on staying and worked at his machine until management summoned the police to remove him from the premises. Subsequently, management discharged the worker, maintaining that he had committed five separate acts of insubordination by refusing to comply with orders to repair a machine; talk to the manager; Stop working; clock out; and leave the premises. Protesting the discharge, the employee claimed that since all the incidents took place within 20 minutes, they constituted a single infraction.

Rejecting the employee's argument that the insubordinate acts constituted a single incident, the arbiter pointed out that the employee was "instructed to perform or not to perform several distinctly different tasks or acts." Although holding that the worker was "guilty of committing several acts of insubordination," the arbiter decided to overturn the discharge because of a procedural error" made by the worker's supervisor. Noting that the supervisor had "failed to forewarn" the worker of the grave consequences of his disobedient behavior," the arbiter stressed that such a warning "might have shocked" the worker "back to his senses." (St. Regis Paper Co., 75 LA 819; see also 93 LA 773, 95 LA 302, 97 LA 592, 98 LA 131)

A refusal to take a polygraph examination, many arbiters agree, warrants special consideration and does not automatically constitute insubordination. For example, one arbiter declared that a company's demand that a worker take a lie-detector test was an invasion of the right of privacy and the constitutional protection against self-incrimination, even though the worker had signed pre-employment forms agreeing to take such tests. The employment form had not been agreed upon by the union, the arbiter found, and could not stand up as an individual contract. (Lag Drug Co., 39 LA 1121; see also 39 LA 332 and 38 LA 778.)

Similarly, another arbiter stressed that polygraph test results are "generally held to be inadmissible evidence" in arbitration proceedings. Furthermore, the arbiter continued, refusing to take such tests is "analogous to refusing to work under hazardous conditions, because it "exposes the employee to another sort of danger, that of self-incrimination." An employee who submits to a polygraph test may be forced to reveal information that "may be placed in the hands of the employer to his future detriment, whether accurate or not, and whether or not material to the investigation at hand," the arbiter pointed out. Even though management had required the test only after a series of in-house thefts, the arbiter concluded, it improperly discharged a worker for failing to take the exam. (Temtex Products Inc., 75 LA 233) However, another arbiter decided that management was within its rights to discharge a worker for a similar refusal, especially since the employee had signed a pre-hire agreement to submit to lie detector tests at the employer's request. "Employees may be required by their employer to undergo polygraph tests as a part of an investigation, and may be disciplined or discharged for refusal to submit to such a test," the arbiter asserted, especially "when the employees sign a statement at the time they are hired agreeing to submit to a polygraph test during their employment at any time the employer may request." In the present case, the arbiter observed, the employee failed to comply with the agreement he made at the time he was hired. The company was within its rights in requiring the employee to take the test and discharging him when he refused to do so, the arbiter concluded. (Grocers Supply, 75 LA 27)

Failure to comply with procedures typically leaves the worker open to discipline. The grievance process, arbiters agree, is the proper mechanism for protesting directives once the worker has complied with the order. (40 LA 562, 43 LA 46)

EXAMPLE: An employee who refused to report to his supervisor at the beginning and end of his shifts was properly discharged. The worker was clearly informed of the procedure and warned of the consequences of noncompliance, but repeatedly refused to follow the check-in procedures on the grounds that the rule was unreasonable and discriminatory since it applied only to a two-employee unit.

"The mere fact that an order is directed at two people does not per se render it discriminatory," the arbitrator asserted. Noting that management often had difficulty locating workers in the unit due to their inability to answer pages when performing certain tasks, the arbiter decided that the employer's "rule of check-in and check-out" was "reasonable." Despite his supervisor's warnings, the employee "continued to flout the rule," the arbiter stressed, upholding the worker's discharge. (Washington Hospital Center, 75 LA 32)

Similarly, an employee who refused to sign a form making him responsible for company-issued tools was properly discharged for insubordination, an arbiter decided. An employee was assigned to a job that required the use of special tools. He also was told that he would have to sign a voucher that said that a sum equivalent to the value of the tools would be deducted from the worker's paycheck in the event that the equipment was not returned. The employee refused to sign the voucher, even though his supervisor told him to do so. Subsequently, management discharged the worker for "deliberate refusals to comply with work instructions and unreasonable insubordination." Protesting the discharge, the employee argued that he had refused to sign because he believed that the form amounted to a "blank check" for the company to make unauthorized deductions from his wages. Stressing that he had "never" signed for a tool before and "was not starting now," the employee claimed that in the past supervisors commonly took responsibility for the workers' tools.

The arbiter said that "it is clear" from the worker's "own admission that he was insubordinate." The employee's attitude, "amounted to a deliberate defiance of the legitimate exercise of managerial authority in terms of the requirement that employees sign for the tools and materials they are issued." Rejecting the worker's argument that signing the voucher was equivalent to signing a "blank check," the arbiter stressed that was "no evidence that the employer had ever made improper or unauthorized deductions from employee paychecks in the past as a result of their having signed the voucher." (Budd Co., 75 LA 281)

EXAMPLE: A teacher who required his students to complete an examination during a bomb threat was properly suspended for failing to comply with established procedures. The teacher protested the discipline, arguing that false alarms were common at the school and that it was within his "judgment to allow the students to complete" the important exam. The arbiter, however, agreed with management that the teacher had endangered the pupils by requiring them to stay in the building and "deliberately and willfully" disobeying "clear and reasonable policy and legal guidelines." Since the teacher's actions were most serious" and his judgment in the situation "clearly faulty," the arbiter declared, the one-day suspension was for just cause. (Whitehall-Coplay School District, 76 LA 325)

Meanwhile, given the importance of established work procedures, some arbiters have held that an employee may not be disciplined for insisting on complying with such practices even in the face of orders to the contrary.

EXAMPLE: An employee was improperly suspended for refusing to sign a time card his supervisor had altered, an arbitrator decided. The worker, a union steward, attended a grievance meeting that started a half hour before the end of his shift. At the end of the two-hour meeting, the employee clocked out. His supervisor subsequently changed the worker's time card to reflect the time he had stopped working rather than the time he had left work. The employee refused to sign the time card, claiming that the card had been "tampered with." Following the worker's repeated refusals to initial the card, management suspended him for insubordination. The worker protested, claiming that he did not sign the card because he disagreed with its contents.

The supervisor's insistence that the worker sign the card, "in the face of his fear of signing away his claim" for pay, "served no legitimate business purpose and did not constitute a valid work order," the arbiter declared, since the employer was "free" to calculate the worker's pay in any way it thought proper, whether or not the worker signed the time card. Since the employee had not refused a valid work order, the arbiter continued, he could not be guilty of insubordination. Stressing that an "essentially trivial" incident "ought not result in serious consequences," the arbiter decided that the employer did not have "proper cause" to suspend the worker. (Kilsby Tubesupply Inc., 76 LA 921)

EXAMPLE: A worker who had followed one set of procedures for 11 years was improperly discharged for refusing to follow new operating procedures, an arbiter ruled. A messenger for an armored car service, who was entrusted with delivering and picking up bags of currency, previously had been required to pack and seal damaged bags in another container. Suspecting that currency was being "extracted" from holes or tears in the bags, management established a new policy requiring messengers to break the seal on a bag and count the currency whenever a hole was discovered. Confronted with this situation, the employee, however, refused to obey the directive, even though a supervisor ordered him to do so. When the worker continued to insist that "tampering" with the seal would be illegal, he was discharged for insubordination.

Although finding that the employee did defy a clear order that did not involve an illegal or contractually forbidden act, the arbitrator ruled that the penalty of discharge was too severe. For 11 years, the employee had been taught by "direction, custom, and practice" never to break the "sacrosanct seal," he stressed, concluding that the employer could not expect to 'turn back the clock" on such experience and training simply by issuing a new directive. (Brinks Inc., 76 LA 1120)

Safety & Working Conditions

The leading exception to the "obey now, grieve later" standard arises when an employee has reasonable cause to believe that the work ordered performed is unusually hazardous, substantially injurious to the health, or abnormally dangerous. When an employee raises the issue of safety as a reason for refusing to obey orders, some arbiters have taken the position that the worker has the burden of proving the existence of unsafe conditions. (61 LA 607, 62 LA 605, 63 LA 653, 64 LA 369) On the other hand, most arbiters have held that an employee is protected in refusing to perform work, even if in actuality conditions are safe, as long as he honestly believes that the situation is hazardous. As one arbiter put it, the employee should not be disciplined if he is "sincere in his belief of danger and so long as he makes a 'reasonable' appraisal of the potential hazards." (A.M. Castle & Co., 41 LA 666; see also 30 LA 833, 67 LA 486)

Furthermore, both the Taft and Occupational Safety and Health Acts prohibit certain disciplinary measures against workers who refuse to perform under hazardous conditions. Noting that, under the Taft Act, quitting work in good faith because of abnormally dangerous conditions is not a strike, the U.S. Supreme Court has held that employees refusing to work on the basis of this provision cannot be disciplined so long as there is objective evidence that the work is dangerous to that degree. (Gateway Coal Co. v. Mine Workers, US SupCt, 1974, 85 LRRM 2049) Likewise, the Court has upheld similar rights provided workers by OSHA. In one case, for example, the Court ruled in favor of two employees who had refused to work on a suspended screen from which a coworker previously had fallen to his death. Arguing that the workers were engaging in illegal acts of "self-help," management suspended the two for the rest of the day and issued them written reprimands for insubordination. Dismissing the employer's allegations, the Court found that the workers were protected by OSHA regulations that served to further the Act's fundamental objective of preventing occupational deaths and serious injuries. It would be a deviation from the purpose of the Act to construe it as prohibiting an employee, with no other reasonable alternative, the freedom to withdraw without fear of reprisal from a work environment that he or she reasonably believes is highly dangerous, the Court concluded. (Whirlpool Corp. v. Marshall, US SupCt, 1980, 8 OSHC 1001)

EXAMPLE: A worker was improperly suspended for insubordination after refusing to operate a vehicle he believed was in unsafe condition, an arbiter ruled. After experiencing problems over a prolonged period of time with the vehicle's brake system, the worker told his supervisor that he had no "desire" to continue operating the machine. Finally, after again being assigned to the vehicle, the employee said he'd "rather not" operate it. He was then suspended for a "clear act" of disobedience. Finding, however, that the worker's desire not to operate the vehicle was based on a legitimate concern for his personal safety, the arbiter decided that the suspension was unjust. (Georgia Pacific Corp., 76 LA 808; see also 98 LA 72)

Similarly, another arbiter ruled that a refusal to obey an order may be justified by a good-faith fear for personal safety, whether or not the danger actually exists. In that case, an outside electrician refused to throw two high voltage outside switches unless another outside electrician were present, not the inside electrician the company promised. Discharging the employee for insubordination, management insisted that a worker who relies on safety factors to justify a refusal to obey an order must demonstrate that a danger actually exists. Dismissing this argument, the arbiter stressed that the employee's fear was "real" enough, and warranted his reinstatement. (Hercules Inc., 48 LA 788)

However, in another case, an arbiter held that a group of employees erred in refusing to work under abnormal conditions, despite the protective equipment furnished by management. The employees refused to work in the presence of an acid mist, which they considered abnormally dangerous to their health, although the Company offered to provide respirators to filter out 95 percent of the mist. The employees, however, refused to wear them, contending that use of the respirators would not reduce the danger of the acid. The arbiter found the company's arguments the more convincing, and pointed out that the employees showed only that here were "abnormal conditions" in the work area, not that such conditions were "abnormally dangerous." In upholding the suspensions for the refusal to work, the arbitrator added that the employees could not assume that the respirators would have been ineffective. (Bunker Hill Co., 65 LA 182)

Even if an employee is not in danger himself, he may be justified in refusing to perform a work assignment out of consideration for the safety of others, it has been held. Thus, an arbiter found a company in error when it disciplined a worker for refusing to work with another worker who performed his job in such a way as to endanger the safety of others. (Midland Structural Steel Corp., 30 LA 38)

"*Hazardous v. uncomfortable*" is sometimes the boundary line for what constitutes a proper as opposed to improper refusal to obey a work order or assignment. In deciding whether employee claims of dangerous working conditions are valid, arbiters may have to distinguish between mere discomfort on the employee's part and a real threat to occupational health or safety.

EXAMPLE: An arbitrator found that an employer's use of portable commodes at a shipyard was not a serious threat to the safety and health of the employees, since there was no evidence that the toilets themselves were unsanitary. The employees had objected to the toilets, claiming that it was unpleasant to use such facilities without the benefit of hot and cold running water. The arbitrator concluded that the employees had not proved that any disease or ailment had been contracted by the use of the facilities and that, therefore, there was no basis for their complaint. (National Steel and Shipbuilding Co., 64 LA 466)

Where working conditions are uncomfortable, as distinguished from hazardous, it is generally agreed that the proper method of securing relief is to file a grievance or request permission to leave. An employee who walks out to protest the heat or the lack thereof normally is subject to discipline, although arbitrators may reduce discharge penalties if they find mitigating circumstances.

EXAMPLE: Seven employees who were working on overtime told their foreman they were going home on a day when the temperature in the plant approached 100 degrees. Their foreman told them they were making a mistake, but they left nevertheless.

An arbitrator reduced the discharges imposed by management to two-week disciplinary layoffs. He agreed with the company that the employees had violated the well recognized standard of conduct in industry that an employee does not leave during a shift—either regular or overtime — without permission. But mitigating circumstances were found here, particularly in the foreman's vague response, which was at best only a half warning. He probably could have forestalled the walkout if he had told the employees that they had a duty to remain and that they would be disciplined if they left without permission, the arbitrator observed. (Phelps Dodge Aluminum Products Corp., 52 LA 375)

EXAMPLE: A woman who claimed extreme nervousness moved her work area farther away from the noisy area of the plant despite her foreman's order to remain until she substantiated her complaint with a doctor's slip. Upholding her discharge, the arbiter found that the woman repeatedly disobeyed orders to stay at her regular work station, ignored a warning of discharge, and "acted with full knowledge of the consequences." (Scripto Inc., 48 LA 980)

However, a distinction may be made between working conditions that are merely uncomfortable and conditions that are so bad as to make it unreasonable for management to require employees to continue working. The latter type of situation was found by an arbiter in a steel fabricating plant where the heat was turned off for renovation during the winter and the thermometer dipped to 20 degrees. Disciplinary suspensions of workers who walked out were set aside by the arbiter. (Berger Steel Co., 46 LA 1131)

On the other side of the coin, safety rules may be established and enforced by management in order to protect the health and safety of the workforce. Absent specific contract provisions to the contrary, most arbiters agree, management has the right, as well as the obligation, to promulgate and enforce reasonable safety rules and regulations. (61 LA 824, 63 LA 574, 64 LA 894, 65 LA 360, 65 LA 751)

EXAMPLE: Observing that such rules must bear a reasonable relationship to the promotion of safety and health on the job, as well as "being reasonable" in application, an arbiter ruled that management was justified in enforcing a requirement that employees wear safety shoes. Failure to wear the shoes, the arbiter noted, was a potential health hazard to workers handling heavy objects. (Ingalls Iron Works Co., 61 LA 1154)

However, arbiters also have held that the punishment must fit the crime, i.e., that extenuating circumstances must be considered in weighing the propriety of a disciplinary penalty.

EXAMPLE: An old-time miner objected to a new rule requiring the wearing of safety glasses, complaining that the glasses, in his view, were more hazardous than helpful. After being given several warnings, he was told to wear the glasses or else, and he chose the latter.

An arbitrator conceded that management had authority to discharge, after suitable warning, for refusal to comply with the safety-glasses regulation. But because the employee's record was good and his fears apparently were genuine, the arbitrator was moved to permit him to return, but without back pay and provided he pledged to cooperate in the future. (Bunker Hill Co., 43 LA 1253)
Overtime Assignments.

In the absence of contract language specifically permitting or forbidding management to compel overtime work, arbitrators generally hold that overtime work may be required. But before discipline is imposed for a refusal to work overtime, certain conditions usually must be met:

• The overtime must be reasonable in amount.

• A notice must be given except in emergencies.

• Overtime must be distributed equitably on a departmental basis.

• It must be assigned first to qualified workers who are willing to work extra hours.

• Only if there are not enough willing workers may unwilling employees be required to work overtime. (Sunbeam Electric (P.R.) Co., 41 LA 834)

The general "rule of reason" often applied to required overtime-that it must be of reasonable duration; commensurate with employee health, safety, and endurance; and ordered under reasonable circumstances (Texas Co., 14 LA 146)—"has generally been construed to mean that an employee's refusal may be justified, and that reasonable excuses for not working overtime must be accepted." (American Body & Equipment Co., 49 LA 1172) Common types of excuses are reviewed below.

Claims of physical inability, when substantiated, may protect a worker from reprisals for refusing to work overtime. As one arbiter asserted, "that genuine illness is a proper excuse for non-performance of a work assignment—overtime or regular—goes beyond reasonable question." (United States Steel Corp., 63 LA 608)

EXAMPLE: An employee who had a "recent history of disability and severe back pain was justified in refusing to obey a supervisor's order to work overtime due to the "serious hazard" posed by such work, one arbitrator decided. (Pet Dealers Supply Co., 60 LA 814)

However, in another case, an arbiter found that management properly disciplined an employee for refusing overtime because he was "sick" from the "heat." The worker's "excuse of sickness," the arbiter decided, was "for the sole purpose of avoiding overtime work and did not represent a true account of his physical condition at the time such excuse was made." (Becton, Dickinson & Co., 60 LA 913)

Employees' religious beliefs and practices may lead to scheduling difficulties. Although employers are required to make reasonable accommodations to sincerely held beliefs an employee's religious involvement may not automatically be considered a valid reason for refusing to work overtime.

EXAMPLE: One arbitrator held that employees' refusal to work on Christmas and New Year's Eves was not punishable as insubordination in view of the "peculiar and sacred" place those holidays occupy in the culture and in view of the irretrievable loss that would result if the employees followed the "work now, grieve later" rule. (Kaiser Steel Corp., 31 LA 567)

However, in upholding the discharge of an employee who refused overtime because he had "certain duties to perform as a minister," another arbiter ruled that this very high calling does not entitle an employee to exceptional consideration." (Food Haven Inc., 62 LA 1246)

Similarly, in another case involving religious reasons, an arbiter insisted that "chaos" would follow if an employee were permitted to "determine for himself, for reasons sufficient to him, whether he will regularly not work on a workday which management has the right to schedule." Combustion Engineering Inc., 49 LA 204)

Personal inconvenience or hardship resulting from extra work requirements also is cited as an excuse for refusing overtime. Depending on the severity of the hardship, arbiters may accept the excuse as a valid reason for the refusal.

EXAMPLE: "There are circumstances of emergencies, disasters, and perils, unforeseeable and foreseeable, where all but the very most vital needs of a good faith employee must give way to working the overtime," an arbiter observed. However, he continued, in most cases there must be some give and take between employer and employee, to reach a "common sense" adjustment of overtime problems. With that reasoning, the arbitrator found a company unjustified in forcing an employee to work on the day her house was being moved to a new location. (Southwestern Bell, 61 LA 202)

However, a company had the right to reject an employee's attempt to use his car pool as a permanent exemption from overtime duty, an arbitrator ruled, even though the employer had encouraged employees to form car pools and was required by contract to excuse employees from overtime, where overtime would cause hardship or serious inconvenience. (American Can Co., 65 LA 12)

Moonlighting, generally is not recognized as a valid excuse for refusing overtime. Employees owe their first loyalty to their primary employer, and cannot use a second job as a reason for avoiding required extra work. (Shamrock Oil Co., 41 LA 1250)

However, where management has followed a policy of trying to accommodate overtime assignments to employee wishes, discharge was too severe a penalty for a moonlighting employee who refused the extra work. Reducing the termination to a disciplinary suspension, the arbiter stressed that substitute workers were available to handle the overtime and that other employees with the same work assignment had been excused. (Budd Co., 52 LA 1290)

Mitigating Circumstances

Unique conditions surrounding an alleged incidence of insubordination have lead arbiters to reduce or completely set aside discipline for the infraction.

EXAMPLE: An arbiter reversed the discharge of a union trial-board member for insubordination after he left work without permission to attend a union convention, despite the general application of the "obey-now, grieve-later" rule to insubordination cases. Because the international union ordered a trial board to reconvene at a convention, the employer was required to grant a leave of absence to any employee "designated by the union" to attend a convention "or other official union business." Further mitigating, internecine union politics made swift resolution of the member's predicament unlikely before the convention, the arbiter concluded. (Dole Refrigerating Co., 96 LA 787)

EXAMPLE: An arbiter reduced from a discharge to a suspension the penalty imposed on a 60-year-old employee who violated a plant rule prohibiting workers from sitting during their tour of duty. Although acknowledging "management rights to impose plant rules unilaterally," the arbiter stressed that "to sustain actions taken thereunder, such rules must be within the bounds of reason, considering all the circumstances surrounding their application." "The no-sit-down rule in a cement plant where operations are at least semi-automatic and therefore to an extent monotonous, temperatures at least at some spots above normal, and floors hard," the arbiter declared, "would seem to go beyond the bounds of reason." (Ideal Cement Co., 13 LA 943)

EXAMPLE: Another arbiter overturned the discharge for insubordination of a professional employee who failed to follow new policy and procedures after being told to use her own discretion about how to run a detached facility. The employee, as the sole laboratory technician at a clinic located five miles from her supervisor, had to exercise more independent judgment than might otherwise have been required, the arbiter noted, adding that the physical separation undoubtedly made effective communications difficult and contributed to a number of misunderstandings. Furthermore, the arbiter pointed out, the employee, upon challenging the policy changes, had been assured by her supervisor that she could continue to use her discretion in regards to the facility's operating procedures. (Permanente Medical Group, 52 LA 217; see also 98 LA 194)

However, another arbiter ruled that a supervisor must be the judge of when and what tasks are to be performed. In that case, the employee, a service worker, claimed that he was too busy to comply with his supervisors' instructions. Although the pressure of dealing with the public may increase the potential for friction, the arbiter emphasized, it does not warrant abandoning the standard of "obey now, grieve later." It would be destructive of proper employer-employee relations, the arbiter concluded, to allow workers to be he final judge of what instructions they would follow or honor. (National Lawyers Club Inc.,52 LA 547)

Abusive Behavior

IN BRIEF

Abusive behavior toward members of management constitutes insubordination and, therefore, grounds for discipline. Within this general category are several types of offenses of varying degrees of severity, ranging from displaying a disrespectful attitude to verbally abusing or even physically assaulting management representatives. Each class, of course, and the circumstances surrounding the specific insubordinate behavior will determine the appropriateness of a disciplinary penalty. Nevertheless, arbiters typically uphold the ultimate employee has directed threats, penalty of discharge in cases where an abusive language, or physical violence toward management. (51 LA 633, 51 LA 688, 63 LA 765, 63 LA 1130, 65 LA 631, 65 LA 1119, 66 LA 206, 67 LA 426, 92 LA 3, 94 LA 1277, 95 LA 895, 97 LA 121) "Where this type of grievous on-the-job misconduct occurs," one arbiter has stressed, an employer "is obligated in the protection of its employees to mete out stern disciplinary action promptly and consistently." (51 LA 462) Following are arbitral reviews of discipline for abusive behavior.

GUIDELINES

Physical Assault

An assault upon a supervisor is considered a very serious offense, particularly where it would have the effect of under- mining employees' respect for management's authority if it went unpunished. Most arbitrators agree that management's right to control operations in an efficient manner rests on the assumption that employees will exhibit respect for their supervisors. Assault and battery upon a supervisor, for example, was described by one arbitrator as "the antithesis of civilized conduct and the behavior code of employment." (51 LA 462) Similarly, another arbitrator maintained that threats by an employee to inflict bodily harm on a supervisor were "a potent form of intimidation no less serious than actual physical attack." (50 LA 232)

To be considered insubordination, the assault need not occur on company property or during working hours if it is work related and has its roots in the employer-employee relationship. But it would not be considered insubordination if the assault occurs off company property and outside of working hours and results from a purely personal matter. A distinction is drawn between the civil law which governs the normal relations between people and the private law of industrial relations which governs job-related relationships.

In cases where an employee is accused of physically abusing a supervisor, arbitrators generally consider:
- The type of assault committed;
- The degree of violence involved;
- Whether the employee was the aggressor in the altercation; or
- Whether the worker merely was exercising the right to self-defense.

EXAMPLE: An employer was held justified in discharging an employee who was the aggressor in a fight with his supervisor on company premises, even though the supervisor might have struck the first blow. Remarking that the employee exceeded his right to self-defense by chasing the supervisor with a piece of iron after the fight had ended, the arbitrator ruled that the use of a dangerous weapon constituted an aggravated infraction of the plant rules. (Southern Iron & Equipment Co., 65 LA 694)

Similarly, an arbitrator upheld the discharge of a delivery truck driver who assaulted his supervisor during an argument that occurred when the supervisor tried to improve the driver's efficiency. While the employee's frustration and anger at repeatedly being told that his work was not up to par might have been understandable, his frustration was no excuse for the method he used to manifest his emotions, the arbitrator decided, asserting that a contrary conclusion would invite "industrial anarchy." (United Parcel Service Inc., 67 LA 861)

EXAMPLE: An employee was properly discharged for assaulting his supervisor after an argument in which the foreman collapsed and died of a heart attack. Although the worker argued that he was not guilty of an "assault," since he hadn't physically attacked the foreman, the arbiter decided that the discipline was just. The argument, coupled with the worker's shaking a rod in front of the supervisor's face as a "weapon to threaten or intimidate the foreman," put "great stress" on the deceased. "Making verbal threats and poking the rod at the supervisor's face" were sufficient grounds for discharge, "just as pulling a knife would be enough," the arbiter reasoned, pointing out that in the latter case there would be "no question that a supervisor would not have to be stabbed before a discharge was proper." (Quality Electric Steel Castings Inc., 74 LA 558)

Likewise, an arbiter ruled that two employees were properly disciplined for "supporting" an off-duty assault on a supervisor by blocking the exit and refusing to intervene in the scuffle. Even though the employees did not "physically participate" in the assault, the arbiter noted, they did "aid and abet" the attackers. Since they prevented others from coming to the supervisor's assistance, stood by "passively," and failed to "attempt to restrain" the attackers, they were "accomplices to the assault," the arbiter ruled, and deserved the suspensions. A failure to uphold management's right to punish workers for such conduct, the arbiter concluded, "unquestionably would have an intimidating effect on a foreman's willingness to exercise discipline in his department." (Murray Machinery Inc., 75 LA 284)

However, another arbiter decided that a worker was improperly discharged for kicking a supervisor, who had bent over to pick up something he'd dropped, on the grounds that the kick was a "spontaneous kind of horseplay without malice or evil intent or any feeling of animosity or anger." While management argued that the kicking incident jeopardized the "respect, consideration, and loyalty" that the supervisor needed to function on the job, the arbiter found the contrary to be true. There was much "playing around" in the "relaxed" atmosphere of the worksite, the arbiter pointed out, declaring that a "playful kick can be a compliment among friends." (Tyrone Hydraulics Inc., 75 LA 672)

Off-duty assaults, as noted above, typically are viewed by arbiters in the same light as on-premises misconduct. While acknowledging that public authority is available to deal with those who willfully commit assault and battery, one arbiter declared that management still preserves its right to maintain discipline and protect members of supervision from retaliatory action by disgruntled employees, whether inside of or away from the plant. (U.S. Steel Corp., 35 LA 227)

EXAMPLE: An employee who followed a supervisor to his residence and punched him was properly terminated, an arbiter decided. After an argument on the job, the employee and his supervisor agreed to meet at a nearby parking lot to "box it out." The supervisor went to the parking lot, but left before the employee arrived. When the employee was unable to find the supervisor at the lot, he went to the manager's residence and threw a punch at him. The employer subsequently discharged the worker for "seriously offensive conduct." To condone "violence, intimidation, and threatened attacks on supervisory personnel, for whatever reason and wherever committed," the employer argued, would "lessen efficient production and undermine authority." Protesting the discharge, the worker contended that his conduct was "only incidentally related" to the workplace and "was not so reprehensible as to justify his discharge."

The employee's "aggressive" behavior was the "culmination of a brooding resentment" toward his supervisor, the arbiter found. Stressing that the worker had "plenty of time to reflect and back off," the arbiter decided that the employee's pursuing the supervisor to his residence warranted the discipline imposed by the company. (Texstar Automotive, 74 LA 210)

Threats of Violence

In determining the propriety of management's disciplinary action in situations where an employee allegedly has threatened to assault a supervisor, arbitrators might consider the following:
- Was the employee's language directed toward the supervisor in an insulting manner and in front of other employees?
- Did the employee intend to carry out the threat of bodily harm?
- Was the employee provoked?

EXAMPLE: In one case, an arbitrator decided that an employer was justified in discharging an employee who had reacted to an assigned task of picking up dog manure "by dumping the manure on the supervisor's desk, breaking the supervisor's office window with a steel pipe, and threatening to 'bust' the supervisor's head." Even assuming that the supervisor, by words or gestures, had provoked the employee's conduct, there was no justification for the employee's threat of physical violence, the arbitrator reasoned. Noting that the employee's assignment did not represent a threat to his health or safety, the arbiter stressed that the worker had committed three serious offenses in succession, each of which standing alone merited dismissal. (Marley Cooling Tower Co., 66 LA 325)

EXAMPLE: In another case, an arbitrator ruled that an employee who had threatened to have his foreman killed by a hired assassin was properly discharged. Emphasizing that the employee's threat against the foreman's life, which was made in front of co-workers, had "a chilling effect on the entire work force," the arbitrator pointed out that, if the employer condoned the employee's conduct, then other workers might be tempted to engage in similar misbehavior, without fear of reprisal. (Protective Treatments Inc., 61 LA 1292)

Similarly, a worker was terminated for just cause after he followed his supervisor's car one morning, swerved in front of the other vehicle, and then threatened to kill the foreman. Dismissing the worker's denials of the incident, the arbiter found that the supervisor's "positive testimony" carried more weight. Furthermore, the arbiter noted, the employee had a history of run-ins with various supervisors, as well as having recently been suspended for absenteeism. (Central Soya Co. Inc., 74 LA 1084)

Likewise, management properly discharged a worker for raising his fist against a supervisor and telling the foreman to "lay off me, boy, or I'm going to beat your ass." Protesting the discipline, the worker maintained he had been responding to racial remarks, and that he hadn't threatened the supervisor, but only told him to "get the hell out of my face before things happen that we don't want to happen." Rejecting the employee's claims, the arbiter pointed out that even if he had made the latter remarks, these words "certainly promised physical harm if the supervisor did not modify his behavior to comply" with the employee's wishes. In addition, while the supervisor might have made some derogatory racial utterances, the arbiter observed, the employee's "proper response" would have been something other than "mayhem."

ABUSIVE BEHAVIOR

(United Parcel Service Inc., 76 LA 1086; see also 92 LA 3, 94 LA 1277, 95 LA 895, 97 LA 121)

However, in another case, an arbiter decided that discharge was too severe for a 12-year employee with an otherwise spotless record who had threatened to run over a supervisor with a Mack truck. The arbiter agreed with the employer that the worker's threats were a "direct subversion of the company's right to maintain order and to direct the work force," and scored the worker's attempt to "exercise selfhelp" over the matter leading up to the altercation. Nonetheless, while the conduct "justified punishment," the arbiter ruled, termination was too severe in light of the "principles of progressive discipline." Instead, he concluded, a "substantial layoff" would be "in order." (Brockway Glass Co. Inc., 74 LA 601; see also 95 LA 302, 95 LA 519, 95 LA 543, 97 LA 473, 97 LA 750)

Abusive Language

Generally arbitrators do not require companies to put up with verbal abuse of their foremen by employees. Use of profane and obscene language by an employee does not necessarily subject him to drastic discipline, but if such language is used to embarrass, ridicule, or degrade a supervisor, it would be considered an insubordinate act, especially if other employees were present to hear it.

But when profane, obscene, or abusive language is coupled with a refusal to obey an order or other insubordinate act of the employee, arbitrators typically uphold a discharge or other severe penalty. (Hastings Mfg. Co., 26 LA 713)

Profanity toward management generally is upheld as grounds for discipline. However, except where employees have consistently used such abusive language even in the face of repeated warnings to cease, arbiters generally will not sustain discharge for profanity alone. On a few occasions, arbiters also have accepted employee claims that profanity-or "shop talk"-is a normal practice in the work place.

EXAMPLE: An employee who used obscene language and made a vulgar gesture toward a foreman should have been suspended, not terminated, an arbitrator ruled. The arbiter noted that the incident occurred during a series of mechanical breakdowns that left the shop in "turmoil." Finding that the "profane words and gestures" had a "relevant significance" to the "frustration, excitement, and confusion that prevailed," the arbiter ordered that the discharge be reduced to a three-day suspension. (Mead Packaging Co., 74 LA 881)

Similarly, another arbiter ruled that discharge was too severe a punishment for a long-term employee who went into a rage at a grievance meeting held to discuss her alleged use of foul language toward her supervisor. Insisting that it could not condone or tolerate this type of behavior, the employer discharged the worker for "gross insubordination." However, reducing the penalty, the arbiter pointed out that the worker was a well-trained, long-term employee who had held several positions within the company. Under the circumstances, the arbiter concluded, she deserved a "last chance" to correct her unacceptable behavior. (TRW Inc., 76 LA 782; see also 94 LA 610, 94 LA 767, 94 LA 1075)

However, another arbiter upheld the discharge of an employee who used profanity and in very obscene terms suggested that his foreman perform an act of indignity upon himself. The foreman told him he would be given a warning for such language and started to walk away. The employee called after him and repeated the remark with emphasis. Ten to 20 employees were in the vicinity at the time.

In upholding the employee's discharge, an arbitrator conceded that the term used was in common usage in the plant. But, he said, the way in which it was used is the important consideration. Use of the term in ordinary banter may be tolerated, but it is vastly different when such an expression is used in anger and with the intent to degrade and insult the recipient. The company must maintain the respect of both employees and supervisors; it cannot condone repeated insubordination, such as this, without losing this respect. To permit one employee to be disrespectfully insubordinate, the arbiter concluded, could undermine the morale of the entire work force. (Paragon Bridge & Steel Co., 43 LA 864)

Name-calling, according to one arbiter, may be just cause for discipline where:

- The employee, instead of executing an order, argues about it and calls the supervisor a name.
- The employee calls the supervisor a name in front of other employees.
- The employee calls the supervisor a name privately but afterward brags to other employees about telling off the boss.
- The employee calls the supervisor a name privately, is warned by the supervisor, but continues to indulge in the name-calling. (Arkansas Louisiana Chemical Corp., 35 LA 887)

In some name-calling cases, arbitrators have reduced discharge penalties in view of mitigating factors, such as the employee's good work record, common use of profanity in the shop, or reciprocal use of profanity by the supervisor. (25 LA 439, 27 LA 611, 39 LA 58, 39 LA 661, 39 LA 849, 64 LA 751, 64 LA 1065, 65 LA 25, 94 LA 1087)

However, calling a supervisor a "liar" usually is regarded as a major offense that may warrant the discharge penalty. A discharge for this offense was upheld even where the employee had an "erroneous impression" that led him to think the supervisor had told an untruth. (Pacific Mills, 3 LA 141)

Similarly, another arbiter noted that "most people would consider the accusation 'liar' to be more abusive and contemptuous than some casual vulgarism." In that case, the employee not only called his supervisor a liar in front of union and management officials, but also refused to follow work assignments and even sprayed his foreman with a high-pressure hose. Finding that the worker's conduct was "no simple act of incivility," but rather "an. egregious expression of contempt for supervisory authority," the arbiter ruled that management was within its rights to terminate the employee. (ITT Continental Baking Co., 75 LA 764)

One employee managed to maintain his job after calling his foreman a "damn liar" only because he had a good past record and because there were no other employees within hearing at the time. Furthermore, there was some evidence that the foreman had first used abusive language. (Higgins Industries Inc., 25 LA 439)

Disrespectful Attitude

Few things are likely to annoy a supervisor more than the employee who always replies with a flip or sour remark when told to do something. However, it often is difficult to draw a line between defiance or disrespect of the type that undermines discipline and harmless, so-called healthy, griping. And it is not at all rare for a supervisor to put up with questionable remarks and then finally to blow his stack.

Back talk and grumbling may be tolerated over a period of time without precluding management from deciding that an employee finally has gone too far. It may be necessary, however, to warn the employee that management's patience has run out before serious disciplinary action is taken.

EXAMPLE: An employee who had been with the company about 20 years talked virtually all the time, including times when nobody was around. He always insisted on having the last word and almost invariably would go off muttering disapproval when given an order. Twice on one day, his foreman's orders drew "I-know-my-job" retorts. This led to an exchange that culminated in discharge.

An arbitrator reduced the discharge to a 3½-month suspension. The umpire conceded that the employee, along with his extremely active tongue, apparently had a persecution complex, and his own special brand of anything-you-can-do-I-can-do-better. But all of this was nothing new to his fellow employees or supervisors. While he had engaged in misconduct on the day of his discharge, his conduct on innumerable occasions in the past might similarly be characterized as objectionable. A slight variation in his 20-year theme shouldn't precipitate anything so drastic as discharge, the umpire said. (Armour Agricultural Chemical Co., 40 LA 289)

Disparaging remarks about a supervisor or about management or the company in general are not unheard of in employee conversation. Normally, such remarks, even if overheard by a supervisor, are not considered grounds for disciplinary action.

EXAMPLE: After a company instituted a crackdown on previously tolerated practices, two employees were overheard making derogatory remarks about the company president. They were discharged for this and for failing to observe the newly instituted rules. On being terminated, one of the employees used profanity in directly addressing the president.

Finding little to support the claim of rules violations, the arbitrator also found the case based on the derogatory remarks to be extremely weak. It wasn't shown that such remarks were uncommon, that the statements were malicious in character, or that they affected morale and productivity. The only incident where the employer actually was confronted with disrespectful conduct was after he had fired these employees. As this occurred subsequent to the discharge, it could not properly be used as grounds to sustain the discharge. (Top World, 51 LA 1285)

EXAMPLE: A worker was improperly discharged for criticizing management policies at a stockholders' meeting. The employee, who worked as a stock boy, was the son of a woman who owned 49 percent of the firm's common stock. When his mother became ill, the employee represented her at a meeting of the company's board of directors. During the meeting, the worker expressed several criticisms of management policies, as well as of the company's president, attorney, and accountant. Subsequently, management discharged the employee, contending that his "attitude toward work had changed considerably" and that he had begun to act more like a manager than an employee. While the employee was vocal in his criticism of company policies and "challenged the competence" of various management officials, the arbiter noted, he was "registering complaints and criticism not as an employee but as a representative of his mother." Consequently, the arbiter ruled, the remarks were not proper grounds for discharge. (Hopwood Foods Inc., 74 LA 349)

Mitigating Circumstances

Regardless of the type of abusive behavior displayed by the employee and its severity, arbiters may reduce disciplinary penalties where the employer or management representatives have helped to create situation in which personality conflicts are more likely to flare up.

EXAMPLE: An employee who had worked for a company 33 years without an incident of insubordination became inebriated at the company Christmas party and threw the contents of a can of beer in the face of the industrial relations manager while letting loose with a stream of profanity. Management subsequently suspended the worker for 30 days for insubordination.

An arbitrator, however, overturned the penalty. The offense was not committed during working hours nor under the conditions of plant discipline, the arbiter observed, and the employee's conduct appeared to be the result of consuming too much alcohol rather than being connected with the employment relationship. Furthermore, the arbiter noted, despite prior incidents of drunken fights at the annual holiday party, the company continued to furnish free and unlimited liquor at the affairs, thereby running the risk of "predictable consequences." (Hopper Paper Co., 30 LA 763)

Similarly, another arbiter decided that an employee was improperly reprimanded for expressing anger during a meeting with his supervisor, who had precipitated the altercation. The employee requested emergency leave to attend to a family crisis. However, the employee's supervisor wanted to know more details about the family emergency before approving the leave. When the employee refused to provide any more information, a heated argument ensued between the two men. Upset over the supervisor's attempts to elicit more details about the leave request, the employee became agitated and expressed himself in angry tones. Responding in a similar fashion, the supervisor pointed his finger at the employee and threatened to charge him with insubordination. Following the altercation, 'the employee was reprimanded for disrespectful conduct.

Finding that the supervisor had engaged in a pattern of harassment against the employee, the arbitrator reversed, management's disciplinary action. The supervisor's "excited" response to the employee's remarks contributed substantially to the heated nature of the discussion, the arbitrator noted, holding that the employee's anger, although improper, was excusable. The supervisor's own "intemperate" conduct in dealing with a subordinate constituted unacceptable work place behavior. (Veterans Administration, 75 LA 733; see also 81 LA 176, 81 LA 385, 90 LA 1302, 91 LA 482, 91 LA 905, 92 LA 28, 92 LA 340, 92 LA 521, 92 LA 871)

Furthermore, an arbiter ruled that just cause did not exist to discharge three non-English-speaking employees who allegedly were involved in a shop-floor confrontation with a supervisor. The altercation had resulted in a "charged atmosphere" on the shop floor after the collapse and death of a union steward immediately following a grievance meeting. The steward's death, the language and cultural differences between management and the employees affected the clear interpretation of events, and the employer could not prove the workers' involvement in the incident, the arbiter said. (Polycast Technology Corp., 97 LA 704)

Also, an arbiter held that just cause did not exist to discharge an employee for fighting with his supervisor after being given a work assignment. Even though he concededly struck the supervisor in the face and threatened to throw him from a catwalk, this was the employee's first offense in an outstanding 20-year work record, and moreover, the arbiter said, the new, young supervisor's management style was harassing and provocative. (Ball-Incon Glass Packaging Corp., 98 LA 1)

However, an arbiter upheld the termination of a worker who slugged his foreman, even though the supervisor had provoked the argument by calling the worker a term used in the plant as a derogatory way to refer to inexperienced, unskilled employees. According to the arbiter, regardless of provocation, physical violence other than in self defense is universally condemned. At the same time, the arbiter stressed, management should be obligated to do everything possible to end the use of "trigger" words or terms in the working environment. (Pioneer Finishing Co., 52 LA 1019)

Union Activity

IN BRIEF

In cases involving alleged insubordination by union stewards or an alleged reach of plant rules, arbitrators generally look to see whether the offense was committed when the union representative was acting in official capacity or merely as a rank-and-file employee. If the steward were insubordinate as an employee, then the penalty properly is the same as for any other employee under similar circumstances, since the behavior does not constitute concerted protected activity under the Taft Act. (92 LA 3, 63 LA 765, 62 LA 432)

But where the steward is "on business," the usual requirement of "obey now, grieve later," does not apply if the order given is in conflict with the union's rights. (98 LA 131) This principle has been extended to cases where union officials refused to obey orders in the good-faith, albeit mistaken, belief that the orders violated the contract.

No consensus exists, however, on whether management has a right to discipline a union official where he or she does not act in good faith but rather in knowing disregard of the contract and management's rights. (85 LA 70) One school holds that union officials have a blanket immunity from discipline by the employer for their official actions, regardless of good or bad faith, and that management's recourse is through the grievance procedure. The contrary view holds that evidence of bad faith destroys the shield usually accorded union officials.

GUIDELINES

Grievance Investigation

If a steward, pursuant to the contract, seeks permission to leave his job to investigate a grievance, management cannot withhold permission unreasonably. It is not the supervisor's prerogative to decide whether or not the matter in dispute is a legitimate grievance and therefore subject to investigation.

EXAMPLE: A union steward asked his foreman for a pass to investigate the discharge of a probationary employee. His foreman refused and referred him to the general foreman. The general foreman argued that the discharge of a probationary employee was not a grievable issue and told the steward to go back to his job or risk discharge. The steward refused and was discharged.

An arbitrator set the discharge aside. "There is a clear distinction," the umpire said, "between the case of a supervisor telling an employee to go back to his job, and a supervisor telling the union to stop investigating a grievance." When the duly authorized representative of the company told the duly authorized representative of the union to stop investigating a grievance, the company was issuing orders to the union, and it was the steward's duty, as a representative of the union, to insist upon the union's rights. If the steward had been rough, rowdy, belligerent, or insolent in his attitude, some disciplinary action might have been warranted, but that was not the case here. (International Harvester Co., 16 LA 307)

Similarly, another union steward asked his foreman for permission to attend a meeting between two employees and a company vice-president, but he was refused. The steward left his station at break time to attend the meeting anyway, and was back at his work station by the end of the break period. Later, he was discharged for insubordination.

In reversing the discharge, the arbitrator noted that the steward had not been given reprimands for such conduct. The foreman who refused the employee permission to attend the meeting also admitted that he did not think the steward was guilty of insubordination. (General Fireproofing Co., 61 LA 389)

However, a steward correctly was suspended for refusing a repeated order to return to work station after being denied admittance to an injury-review meeting between bargaining-unit employee and management, an arbiter said, irrespective of whether the employer violated the employee's right to representation. The steward had no right to attend the meeting because no formal grievance had been filed, the arbiter concluded. (Ethyl Corp., 96 LA 255; see also 95 LA 909, 90 LA 856, 88 LA 145)

Leave for Union Business

Contract provisions for leaves of absence for union business vary greatly, and whether such leave should be granted depends not only on the particular contract clause, but also on the facts and context of each case, with particular reference to the good faith of both parties. (C & D Batteries, 32 LA 589; see also 96 LA 60, 80 LA 201, 80 LA 1055, 78 LA 969, 76 LA 648, 75 LA 66, 71 LA 349, 71 LA 696, 64 LA 709, 58 LA 252, 54 LA 1130)

The employer is entitled to enough information regarding the nature of the union business involved and the probable duration of the absence to permit it to make an intelligent choice as to granting or denying leave. Internal affairs of the union and union "secrets" need not be divulged. (78 LA 8, 69 LA 831, 64 LA 1274, 50 LA 1140, 42 LA 632, 35 LA 873, 32 LA 589, 11 LA 569)

Leave for union activity may encompass organizational activity outside of the bargaining unit at a plant affiliated with the employer (80 LA 403, 74 LA 916, 74 LA 501, 74 LA 396, 64 LA 975, 58 LA 253, 50 LA 1140, 35 LA 873), but it does not include *political activity* (76 LA 648, 64 LA 1089, 37 LA 249, 8 LA 350, 5 LA 428)

An employer may approve leave for union business on a conditional basis in certain circumstances. (41 LA 739, 37 LA 475, 37 LA 249, 36 LA 400) Past practice has influenced arbiters' decisions in granting leave for union business. (76 LA 1273, 75 LA 66, 70 LA 887, 43 LA 670, 15 LA 611, 14 LA 574, 11 LA 1074, 11 LA 569)

Debates with Supervisors

Although a steward has the right to process a grievance energetically and may dispute a supervisor's decision, he may be subject to discipline if he becomes abusive to the supervisor.

EXAMPLE: In an argument over a grievance, a foreman and steward exchanged angry words. The foreman then warned the steward that if he continued his display of ad temper "he had better punch his time card and leave." The company subsequently issued the steward a letter of warning for his conduct.

In upholding the disciplinary action, the arbitrator said: "A steward cannot be disciplined for actively pursuing grievances or presenting his arguments in a positive manner. A distinction must be drawn, however, between presenting arguments in a positive manner and being argumentative. There is a difference between attacking the logic of a decision and attacking the man who made the decision. Moreover, we cannot ignore tone of voice or attitudes. These may be just as important as the words used." (Westinghouse Electric Corp., 38 LA 1226)

UNION ACTIVITY

Similarly, another arbiter upheld the suspension of a union steward for using abusive and threatening language toward members of management.

Responding to a steward's request for permission to speak with a co-worker, a supervisor asked the steward what the two were going to discuss. According to the supervisor, the steward became angry at the question and replied with an obscenity. Later, a manager asked the steward to explain his use of the obscenities. Denying that he had used such language, the employee contended that the supervisor was a liar. The manager then noted that other supervisors had made similar complaints about the steward and stressed to the worker that such abusive language was "uncivilized." The employee then told the manager you can kiss my ass." Subsequently, the employee was suspended for three days for using abusive language toward members of management.

Acknowledging that "the right of the union steward to do his job properly must be protected," the arbiter said that "mere militancy or zealousness on his part will not justify punishment, nor can a steward be limited to the language of polite society in fulfilling his role." On the other hand, "management cannot function properly if employees who are also union stewards can with impunity verbally insult and abuse members of management." (Hobart Corp., 75 LA 907; see also 91 LA 482, 90 LA 462, 88 LA 512, 81 LA 1115, 81 LA 888, 88 LA 821)

However, where another steward was discharged for using profane language during a joint union-company meeting and "also threatened the employer's managerial control, the arbitrator disagreed with management's view of the incident and reinstated the employee. The employer conceded that the profane language alone would not have justified discharge in the context of the meeting, but added that it drew the line at the steward's threat, "I'll tell you how to run your job."

The arbitrator reasoned that although such outbursts are undesirable, they are also sometimes unavoidable: In the context of the meeting, the arbitrator concluded that there was no real threat to management's control, because despite the verbal threat, management was free to do as it pleased, subject to the grievance machinery. (Kaiser Engineers Inc., 63 LA 1051; see also 96 LA 56, 89 LA 361, 85 LA 716)

Misconduct

―――――――――――― **INTRODUCTION** ――――――――――――

The term "misconduct" applies to a multitude of industrial offenses, from displaying discourtesy to customers to engaging in picket line violence. In all cases of misconduct, however, arbitral reviews are characterized by the interplay of three factors:

▶ *The nature of the offense* — Some types of misconduct, obviously, are of a more serious nature than others and warrant more severe discipline. An arbitral maxim established early in modern U.S. industrial relations is that "extremely serious" offenses "usually justify summary discharges without the necessity of prior warnings or attempts at corrective discipline," while "less serious infractions of plant rules or of proper conduct" call "not for discharge for the first offense (and usually not even for the second or third offense) but some milder penalty aimed at correction." (Huntington Chair Corp., 24 LA 490) For example, while arbiters seldom sustain a discharge for a single instance of rudeness to clients, they are apt to uphold termination where a striking worker physically assaults a replacement employee. Additionally, within a category of misconduct, offenses may be punished differently, based on their relative seriousness. Thus, employees running an illegal numbers racket warrant more severe disciplinary measures than do those involved in an informal sports pool, although both actions may violate the same rule against workplace gambling.

▶ *The burden of proof* — The seriousness of the offense determines the degree of proof arbiters require to uphold the discipline imposed. Where the offense is relatively minor (and the discipline appropriate for misconduct of this magnitude), arbiters generally will sustain management's action based only on a showing that the "preponderance of the evidence" supports the allegations of improper behavior. On the other hand, where the misconduct is "of a kind recognized and punished by the criminal law," arbitrators typically follow the lead of another industrial relations pioneer by requiring that the worker's guilt be "clearly and convincingly" established with "proof beyond a reasonable doubt." (Kroger Co., 25 LA 906; compare other arbiters' "clearly and convincing" standard: 97 LA 30, 97 LA 564)

▶ *The circumstances surrounding the case* — Many a misconduct case has been won or lost not so much on the merits of the charges as on the presence or absence of certain key factors. In rounding out a review of the propriety of discipline, an arbiter typically will examine management's prior enforcement of the rules and its compliance with the due process and procedural requirements of the disciplinary mechanism and the employee's own knowledge of the rules, past work history, and length of service with the organization.

The ways in which arbiters balance these factors in specific types of misconduct cases are examined in the following sections.

Damaging Company Property

IN BRIEF

Indication of a deliberate intent to inflict damage is the primary factor weighed by arbiters deliberating discipline for the destruction or defacement of employer property. This consideration distinguishes vandalism or sabotage from negligence or carelessness, in which damage results not so much from a purposeful move to destroy as from a failure to follow procedures. (Discipline for property damage due to gross negligence is discussed in the chapter beginning on page 154.)

Thus, where malicious intent is proven, the actual dollar value of the damage takes on relatively little significance, with many arbiters upholding the ultimate penalty of discharge even though the damage may be slight. (94 LA 979, 92 LA 709, 77 LA 865, 73 LA 538, 72 LA 704) Conversely, absent evidence of a malicious intent and provided that the worker is not, alternatively, guilty of gross carelessness, arbiters generally will overrule discharge even though there may be considerable property damage. (74 LA 257, 73 LA 98, 68 LA 1341)

---- GUIDELINES ----

The Matter of Intent

To sustain discharge for malicious destruction of employer property, arbiters generally require proof beyond a reasonable doubt that the worker willingly and knowingly engaged in the alleged act with full awareness of its consequences. Once this is established, however, they will uphold management's right to impose discipline as it sees fit on the theory, as one arbiter explained, that management "is entitled to insist that employees respect the employer's property and to protect that property from abuse." According to the arbiter, this management prerogative derives from the fact that "every worker's job is potentially threatened when employees engage in needless acts of vandalism against their employer's tangible property."

Based on this reasoning, the arbiter sustained the discharge of a worker caught tampering with the lock box fitted over the thermostat controlling the temperature in his work area. Although this was "not the most destructive of acts," it reflected an "insensitivity to the underlying obligation of employment," the arbiter declared, concluding the employer was justified in viewing the otherwise minor incident as a "willful act of property damage" that warranted termination. (National Car Rental System, 72 LA 704)

EXAMPLE: A worker caught using a hammer to bang on a soft-drink machine was properly suspended under a work rule prohibiting "intentional destruction of any property, tools, or materials of the company," an arbiter held. The employee claimed that he had been handed the hammer "as a joke" during his unsuccessful attempts to retrieve his money from the nonfunctioning machine and that he had used the tool with never "a thought to any dam-

DAMAGING COMPANY PROPERTY

age which might occur to the machine." Dismissing the worker's contention that he should not be disciplined since the element of intent was lacking, the arbiter found that regardless of whether the employee thought the whole affair was a "joke," it was "plain that he was intentionally hitting the machine with a heavy tool." (The Flexible Co., 48 LA 1227)

Likewise, an arbiter ruled that an employee was properly discharged for hitting and breaking the glass face of a malfunctioning time clock where work rules provided for discipline for "damage to or destruction of" company property "through negligence or deliberate intent," even though the worker maintained that he had not intended to break the clock. Although granting that the worker "was frustrated and irritated, perhaps justifiably so in view of the history of malfunction of the clock," the arbiter declared that "nevertheless, there was no justification for his action." The worker "intended to strike the clock, that deliberate act damaged company property, and his discharge was for proper cause," the arbiter concluded. (National Services Industries Inc., 73 LA 538)

However, distinguishing "premeditated effort" from a "loss of restraint," another arbiter overturned the discharge of a worker who broke the glass on a malfunctioning vending machine while trying to retrieve his purchase. Finding it "commonplace for human beings to bang on or kick a machine which does not deliver the promised goods," the arbiter decided that the "provocation offered by the machine" plus the employee's otherwise clean work record militated against termination. (Goldblatt Tool Co., 74 LA 257)

Similarly, another arbiter ruled that just because a worker shook and kicked a cafeteria vending machine, this "assault" did not constitute a dischargeable offense since the machine was not damaged in the incident. Dismissing management's charge of "vandalism," the arbiter pointed out that this label required the two elements of intent and damage. Here, however, even "if there was malice, there was certainly no defacement or destruction," he stressed. Furthermore, the employee's conduct was in accordance with "applicable mores," which hold that "vending machines are most imperfect creatures, subject to being physically abused without penalty when they malfunction," the arbiter observed, In short, he concluded, the worker "committed no industrial offense, and the employer was entitled to administer no discipline." (Cosden Oil and Chemical Co. Inc., 68 LA 1341)

EXAMPLE: An employee was properly discharged for breaking a machine while making a "mockery" of following the tips a manager had given her to improve her performance, After being shown how to correctly place slats of wood on a conveyer belt, the employee exaggerated the procedures, finally pushing some sticks into the machine and breaking one of the chains. In upholding the discharge, the arbiter noted that the employee had a history of unsatisfactory work and earlier had been transferred to the conveyor line as an alternative to dismissal. (Decorative Cabinet Corp., 17 LA 138)

Vandalism

Vandalism as noted above combines the elements of intent and damage and therefore constitutes grounds for severe discipline most arbiters agree. However, especially where graffiti is alleged, arbiters may overturn a discharge for vandalism if management has been lax in enforcing rules against drawing on the walls. The prime consideration here is whether the employee was aware that the action was prohibited,

EXAMPLE: Discharge was too severe for an employee caught painting the words "peace, love, and brotherhood" on a door frame, an arbiter decided, precisely because management had never warned employees that it would not tolerate graffiti. The employer also allowed scrawls and drawings to remain on the walls for extended periods of time, the arbiter noted, pointing out that this inaction may well have contributed to the worker's lack of concern about a rule prohibiting this type of activity, Although management has the prerogative to decide what will be allowed to appear on its walls and what the penalties for infractions of the rules will be, these rights cannot be exercised arbitrarily and inconsistently, the arbiter observed, concluding that the extreme penalty of outright dismissal was far too harsh a punishment for this particular, and first-time, offense. (Russell Stanley Corp., 66 LA 953)

Alternatively, where a prohibition was well communicated, management was justified in disciplining a worker for vandalism, In that case, the employer had experienced several acts of vandalism in its restrooms, including episodes in which workers caused toilets to overflow by deliberately stopping them up with rolls of toilet paper. The vandalism resulted in water damage to the walls and floor tiles in the restrooms, After the employer determined that a certain restroom was the primary target of the vandalism, it posted security guard in an adjacent storage room for surveillance. The guards stuffed a roll of toilet paper in one of the toilets and posted a sign on it saying "do not use." Later, an employee entered the restroom, removed the sign, and used the commode, By the time the guards entered the restroom, the employee had flushed the toilet several times, causing it to overflow. Although the employee disclaimed any responsibility for the overflow, he was suspended for one week for deliberately damaging company property.

Finding that the employer's version of the incident was "consistent, cogent, and free of any significant discrepancies or incongruities," the arbitrator upheld the discipline. Pointing out that the employee did not offer to help clean up the mess when confronted by the guard, he concluded that the worker's denial of responsibility for the overflow displayed "a primary concern over culpability, fault, responsibility, and blame, rather than a primary concern over minimizing the damage." (General Electric Co., 74 LA 161)

Sabotage

Sabotage is a particularly distasteful offense, arbiters concur, in that it aims to deliberately subvert the employer's operations.

EXAMPLE: Intentionally starting a fire to dramatize an allegedly unsafe working condition was sufficient cause for discharging an employee, an arbitrator decided,

On the day when an air pollution inspector was observing working conditions in another part of the plant, a worker deliberately started a fire at his work station by throwing oil-soaked lead scraps into a vat filled with molten lead. The resultant fire shot flames 4 to 5 feet in the air. When the employee admitted starting the fire in order to get the inspector to take a look at conditions in his work area, he was discharged.

The arbiter noted there was no dispute about the employee's actions or why he took them. However, he continued, "the 'good' motive to improve unpleasant or even unhealthy conditions of work is wholly disproportionate to the seriousness of this conduct." Furthermore, the worker's self-righteous attitude about what he had done could be reasonably interpreted as a harbinger of further hazardous acts, the arbiter noted, concluding that, under these conditions, the employer was justified in discharging the worker. (F.E. Olds & Son, 64 LA 726)

Similarly, citing the "rights" of an employer "to manage its operation with care and concern for the safety of all its employees," another arbiter upheld the discharge of a worker caught setting his work glove on fire in violation of a rule that prohibited sabotaging or willfully destroying company property. Finding management's version of the incident to be more credible, the arbiter noted that "while the supervisor obviously lacks any incentive for making the charge," the worker, "who stands to lose, has every incentive for denying the charge." With the evidence it presented, the arbiter concluded, the employer "amply met its burden of persuasion." (Cavalie Corp., 77 LA 865)

EXAMPLE: An employee was properly suspended for disconnecting wires from company speaker equipment, an arbiter decided, finding that the action created a safety hazard in the plant. Displeased with the volume of music coming in over the public address system, the worker disconnected the wires in the speaker located next to his work station. Maintaining that the action threatened the effectiveness of its communication system, management suspended the worker for "willful destruction of company property." Arguing that the action amounted to tampering with, rather than destroying, company property, the worker claimed that at most he should be given a written warning.

The arbiter, however, found that pulling the wires from a speaker is more akin to destruction of property than to mere tampering. Furthermore, he noted, the employee's conduct posed the risk of serious property damage. (Mayville Metal Products Co., 64 LA 1239)

EXAMPLE: A company had been plagued by frequent breakdowns of a conveyor, caused by foreign objects thrown into the works. Within a six-month period, there had been 43 such incidents. Employees were questioned about one of the breakdowns, which was caused by a small horseshoe-shaped object. One employee reluctantly admitted he had seen another take such an object from a storage bin and put it in his pocket. Although this employee denied committing the sabotage, management fired him. Applying the test of "proof beyond a reasonable doubt," the arbitrator upheld the discharge. The credibility of the witnesses, the circumstantial evidence, and corroborating testimony indicated the guilt of the discharged employee, the arbiter decided. (Aladdin Industries Inc., 27 LA 464)

However, management erred in firing a worker for sabotage where the evidence did not conclusively establish his guilt. One night outside the employer's premises, a security guard saw a man throw what looked to be a lighted object into a trash bin. A second guard also observed someone walking along a street just 35 feet from the bin shortly after the first guard called for assistance. Based on the guard's identification, an employee subsequently was discharged for attempted arson.

The arbitrator overruled the discharge, since the employee had an alibi for his whereabouts at the time of the incident, and since the first guard's identification was highly doubtful. The guard made his observation from a distance of about 100 yards and the street was poorly lit, the arbitrator pointed out. (Greyhound Lines-West, 61 LA 44)

Conspiracy to commit sabotage also is a dischargeable offense. However, to be sustained, this allegation requires proof beyond a reasonable doubt that the employee was actively involved in the planning of the activity. Mere presumption of guilt, or superficial investigations, are insufficient for discharge.

EXAMPLE: A manufacturing plant had been plagued by several incidents of sabotage, including a fire. Two employees admitted to setting the fire, and implicated a third co-worker in the conspiracy. The co-worker was then indicted by civil authorities and discharged by the employer.

In reversing the discharge, the arbitrator ruled that the employer's action was premature, since the indictment only raised a presumption of guilt, and the employer imposed the discharge penalty on the basis of doubtful information, However, because the co-worker was with the other two employees when they discussed setting the fire and knew the nature of the act but did nothing to prevent it, the arbitrator found him negligent and withheld pay back from the reinstatement order. (Donaldson Co. Inc., 60 LA 1240)

EXAMPLE: An employer properly suspended all five workers on a crew after none would admit responsibility for sabotaging a piece of equipment, an arbitrator ruled.

After returning from their regular 20-minute lunch break, the crew reported that the machine they had been using was broken down. Investigating the problem, a supervisor discovered that an electrical hookup was missing from a control panel. The supervisor decided that sabotage had occurred because the wire had been manually removed. When all the employees denied any involvement in or knowledge of the sabotage and none would admit tampering with the control panel, management suspended the entire crew.

The missing wire "was removed by some human agent," the arbitrator agreed, and "its removal constituted sabotage to the equipment," While acknowledging that the evidence implicating the employees was "entirely circumstantial" and the company did not consider "the nature of the involvement of individual crew members," he pointed out that the wire tampering could not be "explained reasonably except by assigning the blame to one or more members" of the crew. Even if all the crew members were not directly involved, all were "guilty of conspiring to obstruct the employer's investigation of the matter," the arbiter decided. (Koppers Company, 76 LA 175)

Dishonesty

IN BRIEF

Discharge for dishonesty would seem to be an unquestioned right of management. Yet, the discharge penalty is reduced or reversed in a high majority of the arbitration cases in this area.

The reason for this is that arbitrators demand a higher standard of proof in these cases and frequently are reluctant to stigmatize an employee as "discharged for theft," with the potential this has for causing a permanent loss of employment. (Commercial Warehouse Co., 62 LA 1015) According to one arbitrator, when an employee is accused of criminal behavior, such as theft of property, the worker is likely to suffer, in addition to other sanctions, a "diminution" of reputation of the "severest sort" in the employment community. More than almost any other accusation, a theft charge greatly diminishes the accused worker's ability to become re-employed, the arbitrator pointed out, concluding that a higher degree of proof than the traditional civil standard of a "preponderance of evidence" was in order. (General Electric Co., 70 LA 1097)

The evidence required to support a discharge for dishonesty frequently is stated as "proof beyond a reasonable doubt," while a lesser degree of proof, such as "preponderance of the evidence" is accepted in cases that do not involve overtones of moral turpitude. (71 LA 1109, 65 LA 1157, 65 LA 1091, 63 LA 849, 63 LA 648, 48 LA 891, 28 LA 65, 25 LA 906)

Because of this reluctance to label an employee a "thief," both management and arbitrators have a tendency to seize upon some other violation of company rules as justification for disciplinary action when in truth the real reason is the suspected dishonesty. This often results in cases where the penalty seems excessive for the offense that is the basis for the discipline.

GUIDELINES

Falsification of Job Applications

Arbitrators generally agree that discipline is warranted where an employee is shown to have falsified work records or employment forms. However, there must have been more than an oversight or a lapse of memory; a deliberate act with intent to defraud usually must be shown.

Also, the present consensus of arbitrators seems to be that after some reasonable period of time, falsification of an employment application should not operate as an automatic cause for discharge. Indeed, many arbitrators have ruled that a lengthy period of satisfactory employment should bar a subsequent discharge for falsification provided the facts falsified are not of such a nature as to endanger the present and future employment relationship. (29 LA 192, 21 LA 560, 17 LA 230)

Arbitrators also have decided that:

● Where falsification was deliberate and material to the employment and where no mitigating factors existed, a period of limitations was not applicable. (91 LA 1261, 85 LA 834, 65 LA 1084, 60 LA 987)

● False statements on applications for employment is a dischargeable offense even if the company's rules do not specify such conduct as cause for dismissal. (55 LA 581, 43 LA 233, 42 LA 323)

• Misstatement as to the employee's medical history will justify discharge if the employee's physical condition, if known, would have disqualified him for the type of work for which he applied. (94 LA 249, 86 LA 640, 76 LA 520, 74 LA 354, 72 LA 1171, 64 LA 1260, 60 LA 1113, 55 LA 581, 39 LA 142, 36 LA 889)

• Failure to mention prior employers on an application may be cause for discharge, since such information is material for the assessment of the applicant's qualifications. (93 LA 124, 81 LA 158, 65 LA 797, 62 LA 389, 55 LA 581, 34 LA 143, 12 LA 207)

• But if failure to divulge names of former employers is used merely as an excuse, when discharge is for another reason, then the employer's disciplinary action may be overruled. (60 LA 509)

• Misstatements as to whether or not an applicant's relatives work for the company may be grounds for dismissal. (73 LA 512, 71 LA 1168)

• Willful and deliberate falsification of a job application to conceal an applicant's prior workers' compensation claims — which would affect an employer's hiring decision — may be a dischargeable offense. (91 LA 951)

On the other hand, arbitrators have allowed for minor discrepancies on the application form on the theory that it's a natural tendency for a worker to put his best foot forward in applying for a job. Some exaggerations or "puffing" are permitted.

Another consideration used by some arbitrators is whether the employee would have been hired if he had disclosed the true information at the time. In other words, they require that the true facts, if known, would have been a bar to employment.

EXAMPLE: On his employment application, a worker replied "no" to the question "Have you ever had a back injury?" Four years later, in the course of treatment of an on-the-job injury, it was discovered that the employee had had back trouble off and on for 25 years.

A discharge for falsifying the employment application was upheld. While acknowledging that the employee may have answered the way he did because he didn't regard himself as disabled, the arbitrator noted that this meant substituting the employee's judgment for that of the company as to his qualifications for employment. While the company might also have concluded that the employee wasn't disabled so as to disqualify him for employment, it was entitled to have a full and accurate disclosure of all relevant health information in order to make a judgment. (Zia Co., 52 LA 89; see also 93 LA 381, 94 LA 690)

EXAMPLE: On the employment application form, a worker checked "no" to questions asking if he had a skin disease or rash. Five months later he developed hand eczema, and the company physician referred him to a specialist. In relating his medical history, the worker told the specialist he had had the disease intermittently since he was 16 years old. The worker was subsequently discharged for lying on the application form.

In overruling the discharge, the arbitrator noted that the employee honestly believed that he no longer had the condition at the time he applied for the job. However, the arbitrator concluded that reinstatement should be probationary and terminable upon a disabling outbreak of the condition. (Springday Co., 64 LA 1129)

EXAMPLE: An employee was improperly discharged for failing to mention on his employment record that he had been hospitalized, an arbitrator ruled. Although the employer's charge against the employee was valid, it was merely an excuse to fire the employee because of his heart condition, the arbitrator decided. Finding that the heart 95:83
condition was insufficient to warrant discharge, the arbitrator ordered reinstatement, but without back pay. (Rockwell International, 60 LA 869)

Disclosing Criminal Convictions

Failure to mention a criminal conviction in answer to a question requesting it is not necessarily grounds for dismissal.

DISHONESTY

If the employee reasonably believes the conviction has been expunged from the public record, then his omission of the conviction is made in good faith, and discharge may be unjustified. (Kaiser Steel Corp. 64 LA 194)

EXAMPLE: A worker was improperly discharged for "falsifying his application form" by not listing previous illegal arrests. But, the arbiter continued, even though both arrests were thrown out of court as illegal, the past cannot be erased, and the worker must share some of the blame for his discharge since he failed to make a frank disclosure on his job application. The arbiter directed reinstatement, but without back pay. (American Airlines Inc., 47 LA 119)

Moreover, other mitigating factors often lead to reversal or modification of disciplinary action where an employee has omitted his criminal past on an application form.

EXAMPLE: An employee who had committed armed robbery as a teenager, 25 years earlier, answered "no" to a question on a job form concerning criminal convictions. In reducing his discharge to a short suspension, the arbitrator considered: (1) the employee's sincere belief that a "governor's proclamation" obliterated his conviction, (2) the worker's 25 year history as a good citizen, and (3) the employee's good work record. (American Stevedoring Corp., 65 LA 801)

EXAMPLE: In consideration of a worker's good record and trouble-free period of employment, another arbiter voided discharge for a two-year-old falsification of job application forms. The employee had falsified the reason for leaving a prior job, and had failed to list an arrest. The arbiter directed reinstatement—but without back pay and with the charges and disciplinary suspension to remain a part of his permanent record. (Ward Mfg. Co., 46 LA 233; see also 77 LA 569)

However, Where falsification is deliberate and relates to a material fact, and where the work record is poor, the employer may be justified in discharging the employee. (93 LA 738, 91 LA 1193, 74 LA 176, 71 LA 1126, 71 LA 100)

EXAMPLE: An employee was arrested on a gun possession charge which revealed a previous conviction he had omitted from his job application. The employer properly discharged the employee, an arbitrator ruled, since the worker deliberately concealed a prior felony conviction. (Houdaille Industries, Inc., 65 LA 797) (See also 81 LA 675, 81 LA 988)

Omitting "Positive" Information

Although employees may be discharged for omitting information of a damaging nature from their application, discharge was not upheld in the rare instance where an employee omitted 'positive" information.

EXAMPLE: In this case, a utility man who did not list his bachelor of arts degree, masters degree and completion of work towards a doctorate degree, was improperly discharged an arbitrator decided, despite knowledge of a company's policy of not hiring people with a college education for "blue collar" jobs. Noting that the discharge merely was a pretext for getting rid of an "undesirable" employee, the arbitrator concluded that the falsification did not result in injury to the employer since the employee demonstrated his competence as a good worker. (Hofmann Industries Inc., 61 LA 929)

Falsifying Work or Time Records

Falsifying records by claiming credit for work not done is a serious offense that clearly justifies discharge. The falsification however, must be deliberately intended to cheat the company. Where there is doubt, discharge may be set aside. (96 LA 823, 95 LA 401, 84 LA 600, 83 LA 170, 81 LA 1004, 76 LA 213, 75 LA 45, 73 LA 1278, 72 LA 391, 71 LA 142, 63 LA 837, 62 LA 1015, 62 LA 934, 62 LA 14, 61 LA 363, 48 LA 891, 47 LA 966, 38 LA 1157)

EXAMPLE: An employee who filled out his production record to reflect completion of a specified period of incentive work when in fact a portion of such period was spent training new employees was improperly discharged for dishonesty, an arbitrator ruled. Emphasizing that the employer's system for recording and distinguishing between "incentive" and "training" was confusing, the arbitrator concluded that the company charged the employee with committing a crime, but failed to prove the worker's guilt beyond a reasonable doubt. (H. R. Terryberry Co., 65 LA 1091)

EXAMPLE: Two employees punched their time cards to reflect half-hour lunches when in fact they had taken two-hour lunches. In addition, one of the workers punched the card of the other, enabling the co-worker to leave early for deer hunting. Both employees subsequently were discharged by the employer.

In reversing the discharge, but withholding back pay, the arbitrator found the unblemished work records of the employees to be mitigating factors. The employer had previously allowed employees to leave early early without punching out, the arbitrator noted, concluding that the company did not have a rule specifying discharge as the penalty for falsifying time records. (Great Atlantic & Pacific Tea Co. Inc., 63 LA 79)

EXAMPLE: An employee was wrongly discharged for punching a co-worker's time card one half-hour early, an arbitrator ruled, since the employee believed the co-worker was sick. The employee's action was devoid of any intention to cheat the company, the arbitrator reasoned, emphasizing that the employer's past practice allowed employees to punch each other's cards. (Park 'N Fly of Texas Inc., 64 LA 1009)

EXAMPLE: One arbitrator decided that a discharge for falsifying records was improper where the employer encouraged the employee's action. An auto mechanic had made a $120 repair estimate for a car which required only $9.50 in repairs at another shop, and advised auto repairs on another car that a state inspector later said were unnecessary. The employee was discharged, but the arbitrator reversed the employer's action, since the employer had pushed its mechanics to sell repair services. (Fidesta Co., 64 LA 803)

Falsifying Expense Accounts

Falsifying expense accounts to reflect costs not incurred by the employee may be grounds for discharge. In such cases, the employee is usually warned first by employer, then discharged for a subsequent violation. A satisfactory work record may not be considered a mitigating factor where the employee is a repeat offender, or where he is evasive about answering questions concerning his conduct. (81 LA 393, 75 LA 154, 75 LA 40, 64 LA 934, 64 LA 110)

Falsifying to Obtain Health Benefits

False statements to obtain medical insurance or other health benefits may also serve as grounds for discharge. In cases where employees receive double benefits illegally by withholding information about their insurance sources, obtain benefits for persons not properly covered under plans by claiming they are family members, or make false reports of medical treatment for compensation, arbitrators have upheld discharge. (96 LA 1090, 96 LA 644, 95 LA 46, 87 LA 160, 85 LA 643, 82 LA 604, 65 LA 623, 63 LA 768, 62 LA 493).

However, in this category, as in others involving conscious dishonesty or moral turpitude, the employer must meet the burden of proof beyond a reasonable doubt. (Dunlop Tire & Rubber Corp., 64 LA 1099; see also 89 LA 8, 95 LA 759)

Stealing Company Property

Arbitrators, generally, believe that no employee needs a rule to tell him that stealing company property is wrong and that it constitutes a chargeable offense. (76 LA 1216, 76 LA 939, 76 LA 592, 76 LA 373) This is true even of items of relatively little value. Companies simply don't want to retain employees who demonstrate they cannot be 95:84a fully trusted, and management is aware that small thefts can produce great losses if sufficient numbers of people are involved.

Frequently, however, the claim will be made that the employee didn't think an item was of any value to the company or thought it had been thrown away or would be. (Emge Packing Co., 61 LA 250)

DISHONESTY

For that reason, it often is wise to have a clearly stated policy concerning the disposition of scrap, the equipment that may be used or borrowed, and the "sampling" of company products by employees. Perhaps it will not be feasible to cover all possible contingencies, but an established procedure for clearing questionable items may save a lot a grief.

Arbitrators tend to modify discharge penalties where the value of the stolen goods is relatively small and the employee's seniority is relatively long. Thus, discharge was deemed too harsh for taking two cents worth of crackers (Spartan Stores Inc., 33 LA 40), theft of five beers by a long-service brewery worker (Pabst Brewing Co., 29 LA 464), stealing a pair of coveralls by a seven-year employee with a good record (Chrysler Corp., 24 LA 549), and pilfering building materials worth about $10 (Peoples Gas Light and Coke Co., 44 LA 234; see also 77 LA 648, 71 LA 989)

However, in one case, an arbitrator upheld discharge for theft of $1.10, even though the employee had been with the company 28 years and had a good record. The arbitrator said he might have imposed a lighter sentence if the employee had admitted his mistake. Instead, he had tried to get off the hook by inconsistent, evasive, and implausible statements and sometimes outright falsehood. Such conduct doesn't call for leniency, the arbitrator said. (Hawaiian Telephone Co., 43 LA 1218)

Similarly, an employee with 12 years of service was properly discharged for stealing a package of ham, an arbitrator ruled. The employee had committed other thefts during the previous year, the arbitrator pointed out, emphasizing that her behavior had become so notorious in the plant that not only her employer but her co-workers as well were concerned. (Manhattan Brand Food Products, 62 LA 405)

Likewise, stealing a can of Spam was sufficient cause for discharge, an arbitrator decided, even though the employee had five years of satisfactory service. The employee blatantly disobeyed a foreman's order to return the can of food which was the property of the employer's customer, the arbitrator concluded. (Kane Transfer Inc., 63 LA 858; see also 77 LA 133, 40 LA 533)

Circumstantial Evidence As Proof of Theft

Circumstantial evidence may be sufficient to justify discharge for pilferage.

EXAMPLE: In one case, an employee was seen secreting company products on her person by a co-worker who notified a plant guard. The guard notified a supervisor, who directed her to recover the items from the employee.

However, the employee and the guard were alone when the goods were recovered. The stolen items were returned to the processing line and so disappeared as evidence. The employee later denied the guard's testimony concerning the theft.

In upholding the discharge, the arbitrator ruled that the testimony of the co-worker, the guard, and the supervisor was sufficient circumstantial evidence to prove the employee's guilt. (Max Factor & Co., 61 LA 886)

Lie Detector Limitations

In cases where management relies on lie detector tests to prove the guilt of an employee charged with pilfering, arbitrators may either prohibit the introduction of such evidence, or admit it but require that the employer's allegations be corroborated by some other type of proof. Most arbitrators agree that lie detector tests are usually unreliable and that an employee canot be discharged simply for refusing to submit to a polygraph examination. (71 LA 1202, 70 LA 909, 70 LA 100, 68 LA 581, 64 LA 453)

EXAMPLE: One arbitrator, held that an employer improperly imposed indefinite suspensions, which were equivalent to discharges, on two employees for refusing to take a lie detector test. The employer had required its workers to submit to lie detection tests as part of a system for curbing thefts of company property. Saying that it is uncertain whether polygraph tests record lies or only psychological changes caused by stress, the arbitrator maintained that the use of such tests raised serious constitutional questions about whether the employees' privacy rights were violated.

Emphasizing that the employer had "extended" the use of lie detector tests by insisting that a refusal to submit would subject an employee to dismissal, the arbitrator concluded that the polygraph requirement was improper. (Art Carved, Inc., 70 LA 869)

Similarly, an employer improperly discharged employees who failed to pass a polygraph test to determine their involvement in theft of silver bars used by the company, an arbitrator decided, where management claimed that the employees took the test voluntarily, but the employees believed that they had to take the test. (Bunker Ramo Corp., 76 LA 857)

On the other hand, an employer properly discharged an employee for refusing to take a lie detector test that on his hire he agreed to take at any time during his employment whenever the employer requested it, an arbitrator decided, where the motor vehicle registered in the worker's name had been found by the police to contain some $5,000 worth of company property. While the guilt or innocence of the employee in respect to the merchandise was not at issue, the question of whether the employer may require the worker to honor a written promise to submit to a polygraph test was, the arbitrator concluded. (Grocers Supply Co. Inc., 75 LA 27)

Search and Seizure Procedures

Most arbitrators agree that the constitutional protections against illegal searches and the use of evidence obtained from such searches are not applicable to the workplace, particularly if the searching employer has probable cause to believe that a theft has occurred. (66 LA 307, 51 LA 469, 50 LA 65)

EXAMPLE: One arbitrator held that an employer was entitled to tighten up its security rules and begin inspecting the purses of female employees as they were leaving work. Despite the union's contention that the searches were an affront to the employees' dignity, the arbitrator concluded that management had a "paramount" right to search the purses since they might contain stolen property.

(AMF/Harley-Davidson Motor Co. Inc., 68 LA 811)

However, another arbitrator held that an employer did not have the right to search employees' lunch bags for stolen goods. The workers' privacy rights, the arbitrator declared, clearly included the right to be free from such searches. (Anchor Hocking Corp., 66 LA 480)

Arrests for Thefts

What course of action should an employer take if an employee is arrested by the police and charged with theft of company property? Management may be on dangerous ground in relying solely on actions by the police or what happens in court as a basis for discipline. Discharge or even suspension of an employee simply because he has been arrested for a crime connected with his work may be overturned by an arbitrator and is almost sure to be set aside and back pay ordered if the charges are dropped or the employee is acquitted (62 LA 901, 39 LA 1242, 39 LA 859, 35 LA 77).

EXAMPLE: An employee was suspended from his job and arrested for theft after a search of his home by police and company officials recovered company glassware. Although the case was dismissed in court because the search warrant and the search were improper, the employee was still discharged by the employer.

In reversing the discharge, the arbitrator found a lack of direct evidence that the items recovered in the employee's home had been taken by him. The only evidence, the arbitrator noted, was the testimony of three persons, two of whom were admittedly hostile toward the employee. (Imperial Glass Corp., 61 LA 1180; see also 71 LA 1113)

On the other hand, Where the company has made an inquiry into the facts and has substantial evidence of guilt, discharge has been upheld, despite the fact that criminal charges were dropped. (76 LA 133, 61 LA 663, 44 LA 711, 38 LA 93, 32 LA 44, 31 LA 674)

Dress and Grooming

IN BRIEF

What is desirable or necessary by way of grooming and dress standards will vary greatly from company to company depending especially on the nature of the business and the type of work being performed by different employees. Therefore, the approach to setting and enforcing standards may range from a single code handed down by top management for all employees to separate codes for different employee groups.

While management is concerned with an employee's appearance from the standpoint of the organization's public image, as well as from the standpoint of job safety and health factors, employees often are opposed to broad company prohibitions or requirements regarding dress and grooming, considering them an infringement on their personal rights.

When ruling on the right of employees to determine their own clothing or hair styles, arbitrators usually point out that this right may be limited by the nature of the employee's job. Arbitrators generally are aware of the effect of changing times on dress and grooming habits, and unwarranted interference by management with an employee's preference for a particular mode of dress or hair length is prohibited. On balance, however, arbitrators recognize management's legitimate business reasons for regulating the personal appearance of employees.

In dealing with discipline for violation of dress and grooming standards, arbitrators make these points:

▶ The standard must be clear, unambiguous, and consistently enforced.

▶ The standard must be reasonably related to a business need of the company, although it is recognized that "business need" includes the need to keep employees from being distracted by outlandish or overly revealing attire.

▶ The standard must be reasonably attuned to contemporary mores and attitudes toward dress and grooming. As styles change, the standard may have to change.

GUIDELINES

Reasonable Regulations

The prevailing view is that management has the right to require employees to cut their hair and change their dress when long hair or the manner of dress reasonably threatens the employee's relations with customers or other workers, or when a question of safety is involved.

However, most arbitrators hold that a reasonable relationship must be shown between the employer's image (or health and safety considerations) and the need to regulate employee appearance. (77 LA 807, 55 LA 1020, 61 LA 645, 62 LA 357, 63 LA 467, 63 LA 1203, 63 LA 345, 66 LA 439, 70 LA 28, 91 LA 24)

Whether or not any particular hair rule or dress standard meets the test of reasonableness depends on a variety of factors, including the nature of the employer's business and the degree of public exposure the employee encounters on the job. (51 LA 292, 64 LA 376, 64 LA 783, 92 LA 1161, 93 LA 855)

Moreover, most arbitrators agree that management's grooming standards must be clear, unambiguous and consistently enforced. (52 LA 1282, 62 LA 175, 63 LA 345, 64 LA 940)

In upholding the suspension of an employee who refused to cut his hair in comformance with management policy, one arbitrator offered the following questions as additional criteria for determining discipline pursuant to grooming code violations:
• Did the bargaining agreement restrict, prohibit, or qualify the employer's right to establish grooming standards?
• Was the rule adequately communicated to all employees?
• Did the affected employees have an adequate opportunity to comply with the employer's grooming requirement?
• Was there sufficient evidence to establish that the employee's violation of the grooming code created a health or safety hazard or that it was injurious to the employer's public image? (American Buslines Inc., 64 LA 471)

The Public Image

The employer's public image is a matter of concern, particularly where an organization offers services to the public or where the employee comes in contact with the company's customers. Although there is general agreement among arbitrators that the employer has a legitimate interest in the presentable appearance of employees who are visible to the public (71 LA 22, 69 LA 141, 68 LA 31, 64 LA 471, 63 LA 467), one arbitrator pointed out that some arbiters may require management to present direct evidence that long hair, sideburns, mustaches, or beards have caused a loss of business or provoked complaints from the public. Other arbitrators, however, have been willing to accept an employer's reasonable business justification, even without empirical proof. (City of East Detroit, 61 LA 485)

Following are some examples of arbitrators' rulings on "public image" issues.

EXAMPLE: An employer had a right to require employees who were in contact with the public to present a favorable personal appearance by maintaining certain weight standards, an arbitrator found, in considering the discharge of an overweight flight attendant. Dismissing the argument that maintaining weight standards is more difficult for women than men, the arbiter concluded that the employer enforced its standards in a reasonable manner and had provided the employee with an ample opportunity to correct her overweight condition. (American Airlines, 68 LA 527; see also 75 LA 1273, 74 LA 1115, 74 LA 1017)

On the other hand, an airline employer did not have the right to prohibit a male flight attendant from growing a neat beard, an arbiter decided. The employer had argued that its no-beard rule was necessary to ensure that its employees promoted a conservative image, which, it claimed, was a business asset in a competitive industry. Rejecting this contention, the arbiter held that management failed to prove that the employee's beard would damage the company's public image or its business activities. (Pacific Southwest Airlines, 73 LA 1209)

Similarly, another arbiter ruled that a store owner improperly suspended a cashier and a checker for "unkempt" and "messy" hair that failed to conform to the firm's unwritten policy regulating employees' hair length. Although knowledging that an employer may establish reasonable rules governing workers' appearance, the arbiter decided that, given the type of work done by the two employees, the length of their hair did not interfere in any way with the efficient performance of their jobs. Furthermore, the arbiter noted, the one or two customer complaints about the employees' hair length were "minor, vague, remote, and indefinite," and thus carried only "slight weight." (Big Star No. 35, 73 LA 850; see also 75 LA 798)

However, and employer's desire to present a "clean shaven, clean cut image" to its customers was upheld by another arbiter, who ruled that management had the right to prohibit all workers from wearing beards. In this case, the arbiter explained, the no-beard issue was "pared to the bone by the absence of any hygienic overtones," since the grieving worker was not employed in the "delicatessen, the bakery, or other food preparation areas in the store." Although the company, absent "specific studies," could only claim, "somewhat empirically," that its clean-shaven image was "at least part of its touchstone of success as seen in its rising position in the market," the arbiter decided, maintenance of this image formed a "reasonable" basis for the no-beard rule. (Randall Foods No. 2, 74 LA 729; see also 77 LA 953, 77 LA 705)

Safety and Health

Safety and health considerations may be valid reasons for management's restrictions on an employee's personal appearance. However, the employer must show a reasonable relationship between the application of the grooming standard and the health or safety factor. (74 LA 412, 69 LA 824, 62 LA 357, 61 LA 645)

EXAMPLE: An arbitrator ruled that a fruit-processing employer properly discharged an employee for refusing to trim his long mustache, since the employer's grooming rule was designed to protect the company's products against hair contamination, rather than to regulate employee appearance. (Tree Top, Inc., 66 LA 8)

Likewise, a meat packing company's rule prohibiting the wearing of wigs and hair pieces in the plant for reasons of sanitation was upheld by an arbitrator on the grounds that such items fall into the same category as "street clothing," barred from the plant as a possible source of contamination. (Marhoefer Packing Co., 51 LA 583)

In many cases involving *no-beard* rules, the safety issue is whether an employee should be required to shave off his beard before using a facial respirator or gas mask. (69 LA 824, 68 LA 912)

EXAMPLE: A black employee who suffered from a skin condition, "pseudofolliculitis" which is common to black males and is aggravated by shaving, was ordered by management to shave his beard before using a respirator. Claiming that he should be allowed to test whether he could get a proper seal with the respirator before being required to remove the beard, the employee charged the employer with discrimination. Insisting, however, that the beard constituted a safety hazard since it prevented the employee from obtaining a good seal with the respirator, the employer maintained that any worker who had to wear special breathing equipment on the job should not have a beard, sideburns, or a moustache that might interfere with the proper functioning of the equipment. The arbitrator, however, ruled that management improperly had refused to comply with the worker's request to conduct empirical tests of the respirator's sealing ability on bearded employees. Allowing the employer to apply its no-beard rule uniformly without conducting such tests, the arbitrator maintained, would effectively bar many black males from rightful employment because of a skin condition peculiar to their race. (Niagara Mohawk Power Corp., 74 LA 58)

Similarly, an arbitrator decided that management improperly had relied on visual observation to determine that an employee's beard would prevent him from obtaining a positive seal with a fresh air mask. The employer's visual observation was insufficient in light of clear evidence that facial hair did not automatically prevent a positive seal, the arbitrator said, concluding that the proper way to determine if the employee could wear the mask safely over his beard was to conduct a test of the device's sealing ability on the worker. (Phillips Petroleum Co., 74 LA 400)

Likewise, the disciplinary action imposed on a firefighter, whose allegedly "long and excessively bulky" hair was in violation of the department's grooming standards, was not upheld by an arbitrator, since the evidence failed to establish that the worker's hair interfered with the proper wearing of headgear or that the employee's hair style exposed him to added personal injury. (City of Los Angeles, 66 LA 694)

On the other hand, an employer properly issued a rule prohibiting facial hair in the area where a respiratory face mask was sealed and, therefore it had just cause to discharge an employee who refused to shave his beard, an arbitrator ruled. Rejecting the union's contention that the employer's policy was brought about merely by its desire that employees be clean shaven and not by the desire to provide a safer place to work, the arbitrator pointed out that the evidence established that a better seal could be achieved between the face and the mask if the face was clean shaven. Even though a good seal could be achieved if the employee with facial hair has enough time properly to adjust the mask, the arbitrator concluded that in an emergency situation time is of the essence, and additional length of time might be disastrous to the worker and fellow employees. (Hess Oil Virgin Islands Corp., 75 LA 771)

Additionally, when employees' work involves the operation of machinery, arbitrators will generally uphold safety rules restricting the wearing of loose-fitting clothing, dangling jewelry, and long, unprotected hair, which might become entangled in a machine.

Sex Bias in Appearance Rules

Besides the mass of arbitration cases arising from management attempts to regulate the wearing of beards, mustaches, sideburns, and long hair by male employees, the question has been raised whether male grooming codes constitute illegal sex discrimination.

EXAMPLE: An arbitrator ruled that a necktie requirement imposed by one department head in a company was inconsistent with a contractual ban on sex discrimination as well as the employer's new, "swinging" public image. The union had protested that male employees in other departments were not required to wear ties and that the employer's dress policy had "gradually degenerated" into letting female employees wear anything they wished, including jeans, sweaters, tank tops, and other informal apparel. Observing that, not only were female employees allowed to "go with the vogue," but the company had launched a public relations campaign in which male employees were photographed wearing ties, turtleneck shirts, sport shirts, and "all sorts of attire," the arbitrator concluded, that the necktie rule was "arbitrary, capricious, and totally inconsistent" and that it was "predicated upon the personal taste of one department head." (Union Tribune Publishing Co., 70 LA 266)

Uniform Accommodations

Where employees are required to wear uniforms, accommodations may have to be made in certain circumstances, arbitrators have found.

EXAMPLE: A public transit company, which furnished and paid for uniforms for its bus drivers, was required to either provide female employees with women's pants or to pay for those the drivers had special ordered. On discovering that they were to be provided with men's uniform pants, most of the women drivers ordered instead comparable pants designed to fit a women's body and equipped with a side, rather than front, zipper. When they were billed for the cost of the pants, the women drivers refused to pay. Saying that the women 95:89 have at least the right to expect to be provided with women's clothing, the arbitrator held that the employer's policy failed to meet the implied test of reasonableness. (Taylor Enterprises Inc., 67 LA 1285)

EXAMPLE: Another arbitrator decided that a hospital employer, which required all operating room employees to wear pants for health reasons, had to allow a technician, whose religion forbade women to wear pants, the chance to design an alternative uniform rather than be transferred from the operating room. (Hurley Hospital, 70 LA 1061; see also 75 LA 1300)

Fights and Altercations

IN BRIEF

Tensions, misunderstandings, and jealousies can strain employees' relationships in the working environment. Such emotions often cause employees to become involved in heated disputes and fights among themselves or with their supervisors. Since these disturbances obviously are not conducive to workplace harmony and efficiency, management frequently attempts to counteract individual or group antagonisms through various personnel and human relations techniques.

Such methods, however, may not always prove effective in preventing interpersonal conflicts among employees, particularly where hard feelings have erupted into a fight. In cases involving fighting or aggressive misconduct, arbitrators generally agree that, in the absence of mitigating circumstances, management has the right to invoke disciplinary penalties, including discharge, in order to minimize disruptions, which easily could have an adverse impact on plant operations and employee morale. (97 LA 356, 94 LA 773, 94 LA 767, 94 LA 610, 88 LA 418, 75 LA 1246, 74 LA 1113, 73 LA 1248, 71 LA 884, 63 LA 952, 63 LA 3)

Where fighting occurs, arbitrators have reduced discharges to less drastic penalties when it is shown that the violence was provoked. In such cases, one arbitrator said, a company reasonably could discharge the employee who provoked the assault without discharging the one who finally resorted to violence. (Goodyear Decatur Mills, 12 LA 682; see also 98 LA 1)

GUIDELINES

Considering All Factors

Fights on the job are a serious matter, one arbitrator asserted, emphasizing that, in order for a discharge to satisfy the "just cause" requirements, all relevant factors surrounding the fight must be considered. (Harshaw Chemical Co., 46 LA 248; see also 92 LA 871)

In determining the propriety of discipline meted out to employees involved in fighting, arbitrators usually consider the following:

- The length of service and the overall work record of the employee (Dorsey Trailers Inc., 60 LA 1305; see also 93 LA 1277);

- Whether the employee's misconduct consisted of a single, thoughtless blow or a series of deliberate acts (American Motors Corp., 51 LA 945);

- Whether the blow was struck with a dangerous instrument, a clenched fist, or an open hand, etc. (Polysar Inc., 91 LA 482, 81 LA 569, 66 LA 1005, 60 LA 917);

- The effect of the employee's "breach of shop-etiquette" on the morale, safety, and work habits of other employees (C-E Building Products Inc., 60 LA 506);

- The presence or absence of mitigating factors, such as provocation (Boeing Co., 51 LA 1153; see also 76 LA 1249, 76 LA 244), discrimination, or a failure by

management to take preventive action (Zinsco Electrical Products, 65 LA 487); and
• Whether the incident indicated that the employee has vicious tendencies, a serious emotional instability, or dangerous propensities toward such conduct (Pioneer Rubber Co., 53 LA 283; see also 75 LA 12).

Abusive Language / Threatening Conduct

Mere cursing or the use of abusive, obscene, or vulgar language in and of itself is not sufficient basis for discipline of an employee, arbiters generally hold. (97 LA 750, 95 LA 302, 95 LA 543, 90 LA 1302, 81 LA 1077, 81 LA 1051, 76 LA 195, 75 LA 1205, 75 LA 553, 73 LA 663)

Much depends on the manner and spirit of its use. Such language may be used to lend color to one's remarks, or it may be hurled as slurs and epithets designed to goad or jeer another into a fight.

In deciding whether cursing and using threatening language warrants discipline, a test used by many arbitrators is whether the conduct violated reasonable job decorum so as to cause apprehension or reaction in another employee which might hamper production. This test clearly is met where the conduct almost inevitably will provoke a fight. (95 LA 1021, 95 LA 895, 77 LA 1259, 75 LA 288, 75 LA 258)

However, certain employee abusive language and threats are sufficient to warrant discipline or discharge. (88 LA 512, 88 LA 418, 85 LA 1011, 81 LA 865)

EXAMPLE: An employer properly discharged an employee for threatening to blow up a plant and the home of the assistant manager after the manager chastised him for insubordination, an arbiter ruled, despite the fact that the employee's threat was made in the heat of anger. (D & D Poultry, 81 LA 553)

EXAMPLE: An arbiter ruled that there was just cause to suspend a local union president for directing obscenities, abusive language, and falsehoods at his supervisor and accusing management of lying and being "out to get" employees. Although the local president's remarks were made during a union-management meeting, where his actions would normally have been considered "protected activity" under the Taft Act, the arbiter said that his conduct was so "egregious and disrespectful" that they lost protection of the Act. (Trans-City Terminal Warehouse Inc., 94 LA 1075; see also 92 LA 3, 90 LA 585, 81 LA 821)

Assessing Aggression

Determining who was the aggressor and apportioning penalties in accordance with degrees of responsibility are other important arbitral functions in cases involving fights. (91 LA 905, 72 LA 441, 52 LA 1142)

EXAMPLE: One arbitrator ruled, that an employer improperly discharged an employee who was involved in a fight with a co-worker in the lunch room. The fight began after an argument between the workers in which both used obscenities. After an incomplete investigation, management decided to discharge both employees, on the mistaken belief that they were equally responsible for the altercation, the arbitrator observed. Emphasizing that the evidence clearly established that the co-worker was the aggressor because, after the argument ended, she "resumed the affair" and struck the first blow, the arbitrator stressed that the co-worker had no right either to strike the employee or grab her purse, which the co-worker allegedly believed contained a dangerous weapon. (Affiliated Hospitals of San Francisco, 64 LA 29)

Similarly, an employer did not have just cause to discharge an employee who pulled a knife during the course of an argument with a co-employee after the co-employee taunted the employee with racial slurs and dared him to use the knife, an arbitrator ruled. Pointing out that the co-employee provoked the fight, the arbitrator ruled that the employer had engaged in disparate treatment by not disciplining the co-employee. Noting that the employee had a good work record during his nine years with the employer, the arbitrator concluded that the employee pulled the knife because he was frightened, not because he was being aggressive. (Welch Foods Inc., 73 LA 908)

Off-Duty Fights

Ordinarily employees aren't subject to discipline for misconduct committed off company premises.

EXAMPLE: One arbitrator held that an off-duty fight between two employees during a poker game was not just cause for discipline absent any harm to the employer. "No evidence takes this case outside the general rule that off-duty indiscretions do not permit discipline," the arbitrator ruled, emphasizing that there was no proof whatsoever that the employees were unable to work together after their off-duty altercation or that any other employee refused to work with either of them. (Honeywell Inc., 68 LA 346)

However, an exception often is made to this general rule in the case of off-duty fights that are job related, particularly where the fight is between a rank-and-file employee and a supervisor. (Heaven Hill Distilleries Inc., 74 LA 42)

EXAMPLE: In upholding the discharge of an employee for a violent assault on another employee, an arbitrator cited the following circumstances as warranting action by management:

● The attack occurred very near the plant at a place where other employees were known to be present.

● It occurred during the scheduled working day.

● It stemmed from activities inside the plant that were a part of the employment relationship.

● Other employees could have been expected to become involved, and did.

● The attack had a disruptive effort upon plant operations, morale, and efficiency. (Victorian Instrument Co., 40 LA 435)

Similarly, other arbitrators have noted that the employer has an obligation to maintain order and safety on its premises, which includes more than just the plant. Therefore, discharges have been sustained for assaults on company parking lots and against employees leaving the company premises. (29 LA 820, 30 LA 948, 50 LA 407)

Mitigating Circumstances

In rare circumstances, discharge may be considered too severe a penalty for assault, particularly if the worker is "acting under substantial provocation." (92 LA 521, 92 LA 340, 92 LA 28, 87 LA 877) In one case, for example, an arbiter ruled that management lacked just cause to discharge an employee for striking a co-worker who used "abusive and provocative" racial slurs.

Further, an employees medical or psychological condition may or may not mitigate an arbiter's discipline. (90 LA 1137, 89 LA 432, 83 LA 966)

EXAMPLE: In another case, an arbitrator held that an employer was not justified in discharging an employee who struck a co-worker with a two-inch pipe. The co-worker had called the employee "bad names," the arbitrator noted, and also had threatened him with a piece of timber. The employee was faced with a real threat of danger, the arbitrator pointed out, adding that in an attempt to avoid the encounter, the employee had walked away from the co-worker twice before fighting.

"It should be obvious that an employee suffering an unprovoked attack should not be expected to calmly keep his hands by his side while being clobbered," the arbitrator asserted, maintaining that when fighting is a "reasonable self-defense" mechanism, it does not constitute just cause for discharge. Finding that the employee's conduct was provoked, but that his self-defense measures were excessive under the circumstances, the arbitrator reduced the discharge to a two-month suspension. (Central Foundry Co., 63 LA 731; see also 95 LA 519)

Moreover, mitigation also may be found in the failure of management to head off an impending conflict, such as where it knows of bad blood between employees and fails to take readily available steps to keep them apart. (Zinsco Electrical Products, 65 LA 487)

Also, an arbiter held that an employer did not have just cause to discharge their non-English speaking employees who allegedly were involved in a confrontation with a supervisor on a shop floor, where the altercation resulted from a "charged atmosphere" on the floor immediately after the collapse and death of a respected union steward. Further, the arbiter ruled that language and cultural differences between the employees and management precluded a clear interpretation of events. (Polycast Technology Corp., 97 LA 704)

Gambling

IN BRIEF

Gambling of some type occurs in most organizations, whether it be the relatively innocuous sports pool or lunch-hour poker game or the more serious organized "numbers" racket. In deciding on discipline for alleged on-premises gambling, arbiters typically consider whether:

▶ The evidence connecting the employee to the gambling is substantial and convincing and supports the charge that the worker engaged in the prohibited activity on company property and/or time. (51 LA 707, 45 LA 247, 41 LA 823, 39 LA 859, 18 LA 938, 12 LA 699)

▶ The nature of the offense justifies the penalty. For example, discharge may be appropriate where the employee previously had been disciplined for gambling but too severe in cases of first offense. (95 LA 937, 95 LA 148, 86 LA 297, 52 LA 946, 49 LA 1262, 28 LA 97, 22 LA 210, 16 LA 727, 12 LA 21) Similarly, even though it may have tolerated sports pools or holiday turkey raffles, management may be warranted in cracking down on employees involved in illegal bookmaking or numbers operations. (33 LA 175, 22 LA 210, 17 LA 150, 13 LA 253)

GUIDELINES

Rationale for Discipline

Management is within its right to promulgate and enforce rules against on-premises gambling, most arbiters concur, since, as one employer put it, "organization and morale would be seriously affected" if such activity were permitted. As phrased by the employer in that case, "the evils which run concurrently with gambling, namely ill feeling, cheating, fighting, and the lure of 'easy money,' could disintegrate a highly productive work force and reduce its efficiency beyond measure." "If the company and its employees are to reap the benefits of successful operation," that employer emphasized, "any factors which curtail industrial efficiency and production must be completely eliminated." (Brown Shoe Co., 16 LA 461)

Based on similar reasoning, arbiters have upheld discipline where the employer is able to show that the worker engaged in gambling on company premises, even though he may have been on his own time.

EXAMPLE: A worker who engages in illegal activity on company property — even during his free time — is not carrying out his responsibilities as an employee, according to one arbiter. Although management was unable to prove that the worker in this case was writing numbers on company time, the arbiter upheld the discharge, since the "numbers slips" found on the employee demonstrated that he was conducting his activities at the plant. Dismissing the worker's arguments that the discharge was unwarranted since the activity took place "off-the-clock," the arbiter declared that "during all times that an employee is *on* company property, he must be deemed to be an *employee*" and must "conduct himself properly in discharging his responsibilities as such employee." In short, the arbiter concluded, the worker, while at the plant, "may not engage in illegal activities whether he does so on his 'free time' or not and whether he *uses* company property (i.e., a company telephone) or not in order to further his illegal activities." (Jones & Laughlin Steel Corp., 29 LA 778)

Similarly, another arbiter sustained the discharge of an employee for running an illegal numbers racket on company property, despite evidence that he conducted the gambling on his own time. Since the gambling took place inside the plant, it was "inextricably bound up with his employment status," the arbiter ruled. (Bethlehem Steel Co., 45 LA 646)

However, an arbitration board overruled the dismissal of an employee who was arrested on company property with numbers slips in his possession and who subsequently pleaded guilty to a gambling charge. Dismissing management's allegations that the existence of the slips showed that the worker had engaged in the illegal activity on its premises, the board concluded that such possession did not constitute clear proof that "there had been gambling or accepting of wagers" by the worker on company property. (Jenkins Bros., 45 LA 247)

Nature of the Offense

Organized gambling generally is viewed as a serious offense by arbiters. Given that charges of criminal conduct may be involved, however, arbiters will require that management meet stringent standards of proof to sustain a discharge decision. Thus, where an employee was apprehended with hundreds of dollars in small bills and change and a sheet of lottery numbers, an arbiter upheld his discharge. (Bethlehem Steel Co., 45 LA 646) Similarly, another arbiter decided that an employee's guilty plea to charges of illegal gambling on company property was just cause for discharge, since the employee's otherwise good work record did not outweigh the fact of his misconduct. (Jenkins Bros., 45 LA 350)

However, the discharge of an employee for allegedly engaging in a numbers racket on company time and property was set aside by an arbiter because management failed to meet its burden of proof. While agreeing with the employer as to the "harmful effects of playing numbers, the arbiter declared that he did not "believe an employee, especially one with long seniority, should lose his job for engaging in the numbers racket, unless there is substantial and convincing proof that the employee did so act," and stressed that "our system of justice and the recognized principles applied under it are based on the same belief." (Chrysler Corp., 12 LA 699)

Unorganized gambling, on the other hand, meets with more leniency from arbiters.

EXAMPLE: Employees involved in a "check pool" on company time and property were improperly discharged, an arbiter decided, despite a work rule prohibiting on-premises gambling, since the rule was established to guarantee that standards of "good conduct" were followed, it was not properly applied here since the pool was not shown to be detrimental to these standards. Further, management properly should have followed its own policy of issuing warnings for violations of conduct rules instead of terminating the workers for a first offense, the arbiter said. (Black Diamond Enterprises Inc., 52 LA 945)

However, a board of arbitration upheld the discharge of three employees caught playing poker. Dismissing the workers' protests, the board pointed out that management twice before had warned them about gambling on company time and property. (Brown Shoe Co., 16 LA 461)

Discourtesy

IN BRIEF

Employees, particularly those involved in serving the public, are expected to be courteous and solicitous toward business patrons. As a general rule, arbiters will uphold discipline in situations where employees are guilty of abuse either toward co-workers or members of the public with whom they come in contact, if the following conditions are met:

▶ The evidence convincingly supports the allegations of discourtesy. (95 LA 771, 83 LA 224, 71 LA 805; 65 LA 592; 64 LA 96)

▶ Adverse consequences, such as "public embarrassment" or disruption of operations, clearly have resulted from the abusive behavior. (98 LA 102, 95 LA 771, 94 LA 983, 93 LA 24, 82 LA 1186, 72 LA 723; 70 LA 432; 69 LA 1031; 65 LA 1098)

This section examines arbitration cases involving employees' discourtesy toward customers and members of the public as well as cases involving workers' complaints of discourteous behavior from supervisors. Discourtesy exhibited by employees toward supervisors generally constitutes insubordination and is discussed in the section beginning on page 34.

GUIDELINES

Due-Process Considerations

Evidence of employee discourtesy toward an employer's business patrons is generally accepted by arbiters as a just basis for management's disciplinary decisions. However, most arbiters are careful to distinguish between "hearsay" evidence that an employee may be guilty of alleged abusive behavior and actual testimony that the misconduct took place. For example, one arbitrator approvingly cited as a "sound and good practice" the "policy of obtaining written complaints" from customers that document the employee's guilt. (Safeway Stores Inc., 64 LA 563)

EXAMPLE: Discharge was improper for a bus driver who was accused of having attempted to kiss a female passenger while on duty, an arbiter decided. While acknowledging that the employer had "a most serious obligation for the health, welfare, and safety of its passengers," the arbiter pointed out that management based its case almost entirely on the testimony of a 17-year-old woman who was "unable to give dates or the description of passengers on the vehicle." Ruling that such testimony is "hardly the highest degree of proof," the arbiter concluded that the company failed to produce evidence sufficient "to remove any reasonable doubt" as to what actually occurred. (Capital District Transportation Authority, 72 LA 1313)

An employee's past record of displays of poor conduct toward business patrons may be sufficient cause for discipline.

EXAMPLE: An arbiter ruled that an employee was justifiably discharged for repeatedly insulting customers, since on two earlier occasions the worker had narrowly escaped termination for similar behavior. Reasoning that the worker's history was "rife" with incidents involving conduct that intimidated and embarrassed customers, the arbiter decided that it was very "doubtful" that the worker would improve his conduct if given yet another chance. (Great Atlantic and Pacific Tea Co., 71 LA 805)

EXAMPLE: Discharge was proper for an employee who failed to follow store procedures and displayed unbecoming conduct toward fellow employees and customers, another arbiter ruled. Although the employee had been warned about her undesirable behavior, the prevailing evidence showed that she disregarded the employer's regulations regarding proper employee conduct. Since the worker had been adequately warned that her continued disobedience of company rules would result in dismissal, the arbiter concluded that discharge was reasonable. (Goldman's Department Store, 65 LA 592)

However, an arbiter decided that an employee was improperly discharged despite her history of rude, abusive conduct toward customers. Discharge was based on the receipt of several complaints, both oral and written, that detailed the employee's misconduct. The arbiter refused to uphold the worker's claim that such complaints were "hearsay," explaining that "written complaints are clearly admissible for the limited purpose of showing that the company was receiving complaints" about the worker's attitude from its customers. Nonetheless, the arbiter overturned the discharge because the employer failed to live up to its obligation to ensure "justice and due regard for the reasonable rights" of its workers. The employer's handling of the matter was deficient in two respects: first, the employer did not give the worker "an opportunity to explain her version of the incidents which resulted in the complaints by various customers," and second, its failure to advise the worker that complaints were being lodged against her "lulled" her into thinking that the behavior was acceptable. (Apollo Merchandisers Corporation, 70 LA 614; for other cases involving due process considerations, see 70 LA 614 and 50 LA 177)

Degree of Discipline

Adverse effects resulting from an employee's discourtesy and the existence of clearly stated rules on employee behavior are important considerations in arbitral determinations of the proper severity of discipline.

EXAMPLE: One arbiter set aside discipline in a case where the employer contended that a worker violated an "unwritten" courtesy policy. Contending that this unwritten policy called for the "protection of confidential information" concerning patrons, the employer had suspended the worker for using improper language and talking in a "loud excited voice" about a movie celebrity who was on the work premises. Declaring that management had not "defined 'confidentiality' in terms of employee behaviors" nor "given proper advance notice of the rules," the arbiter said that absent clearly promulgated policies the employer could justify the discipline only by showing that adverse "consequences" resulted from the worker's behavior. (Rochester Methodist Hospital, 72 LA 276)

Public-service employees are one group of workers whose day-to-day responsibilities involve the general public and who are expected to display courteous behavior, even though they themselves may encounter situations where members of the public are abusive. Particularly since such employees often work in an unsupervised capacity, arbiters usually uphold the right of employers to discharge workers who are consistently unable to deal with people.

EXAMPLE: "Public embarrassment" was sufficient cause to discharge a worker who cursed at a motorist after hitting his car and refused to give his name or driver's license number, an arbiter found. While it was "reasonable" for the employer, being "dependent on public goodwill and trust for its existence," to demand high standards from its drivers, the arbiter declared, the worker's record reflected a pattern of careless and irresponsible behavior that warranted discharge. (Central Blood Bank of Pittsburgh, 69 LA 1031; see also 65 LA 1098)

EXAMPLE: A bus operator who physically ejected two passengers from his bus after an argument over transit rules was properly discharged, an arbiter ruled, even though the employee contended that he had been provoked when one of the passengers hit him on the head. Finding that the worker's unsupervised job required him to interact with members of the public who might engage in "every conceivable mode of conduct," the arbiter agreed that management could not depend on the employee to demonstrate reasonable and controlled behavior in his dealings with the public. (Metropolitan Atlanta Rapid Transit Authority, 72 LA 723)

Similarly, a worker's accumulated record of rule violations, including several instances of documented discourtesy to passengers, properly prompted his discharge, another arbiter maintained. Asserting that the company's business "requires even-tempered, trustworthy drivers who consistently provide good service to their customers," the arbiter decided that the employee had proved himself unreliable with respect to the firm's operating procedures. (Jacksonville Coach Co., 70 LA 432)

However, other arbiters have set aside or reduced discipline in cases where a worker's angry outburst was provoked.

EXAMPLE: An employee who assaulted two teenage boys after they threw snowballs at his van was improperly discharged, an arbiter ruled. While the worker "unquestionably" should have "held his temper" rather than commit an "extremely poor act of judgment" that was "bound to reflect unfavorably upon the company," the arbiter asserts that the employee clearly had been "provoked" by the assault. While the fact of provocation did not excuse the employee's conduct, the arbiter maintained, it went "far to mitigate against the imposition of the most severe penalty at the company's command." The previous infractions of the worker "did not establish a record of such gravity" that the assault could be considered a "last straw," the arbiter held, reducing the discharge to a 30-day suspension. (New Jersey Bell Telephone Company, 68 LA 931; see also 57 LA 773)

Patient care is another area in which charges of discourtesy are frequent. However, employees who are responsible for the care and treatment of patients operate under slightly different circumstances from public-service workers, since their charges — those who are ill — may sometimes misinterpret actions. As a result, arbiters are careful to scrutinize the validity of charges filed by complainants, and will consult employees' past records to determine if there were previous instances of abusive or discourteous behavior.

EXAMPLE: A nurse's aide who allegedly directed obscene language at a patient while lifting her abruptly from her bed was improperly discharged following a superficial investigation of the matter, an arbiter ruled. Pointing out that the worker was tired after a "long and arduous" shift, the arbiter decided that the discipline was "overly harsh." While the worker "may have acted without the highest degree of care to which the patient was entitled," the arbiter declared, her actions were not "maliciously intended," but rather were the "result of normal human frailty." (Viewcrest Nursing Home, 72 LA 1240; see also 53 LA 350)

Similarly, a state-owned hospital was not justified in discharging an employee for allegedly striking a mental patient during a scuffle, another arbiter decided, since management had failed to establish that the employee had intentionally or maliciously abused the patient. Finding no evidence of prior sadistic behavior or improper treatment of patients by the employee, the arbiter dismissed management's charges of premeditated abuse toward the patient and reduced the dismissal to a suspension. (Faribault State Hospital, 68 LA 713)

Likewise, an arbiter set aside discipline for an employee who was accused of abusing a mental patient with curses and threats. Saying that the complaints of "mental patients must be viewed with caution," the arbiter found it "disturbing that management would elect to believe the testimony of three mental patients in preference to the testimony of its own personnel." "Even those who are 'well' sometimes misinterpret the actions of others," the arbiter maintained, ordering the written reprimand removed from the worker's record. (Veterans Administration Medical Center, 74 LA 830)

On the other hand, an arbiter upheld the right of management to discharge a nurse for refusing to medicate a patient and for extreme rudeness toward two other patients. Ultimately, the arbiter said, it is the patients' well-being that is the primary concern of the employer. Since the employer had given the worker adequate chances over a three-year period to improve her discourteous behavior, the arbiter decided, the discharge decision was justified. (Elizabeth Horton Memorial Hospital, 64 LA 96; see also 91 LA 451, 83 LA 44, 81 LA 306)

Internal Discourtesy

Dissension and fighting among the workforce can be the basis for discipline, particularly if such behavior is noticeable by business patrons or otherwise disrupts operations. (NOTE: Where arguments among employees degenerate into brawls, workers properly are subject to discipline for fighting, discussed in this section beginning on page 71).

EXAMPLE: A worker's refusal to apologize to a black co-worker for using the word "nigger" in her presence was sufficient grounds for a suspension, an arbiter ruled. Although the worker claimed that she had not meant anything "racial," the arbiter declared that her remark had a "racial bias which indeed is a form of discrimination," and the use of such a term was "socially undesirable and racially derogatory." The very fact that the black employee considered herself to be abused or insulted by the comment, the arbiter said, was reason enough to uphold the discipline. (Memorial Hospital, 71 LA 1252)

EXAMPLE: In another case, an arbiter decided that discipline was unjust for an employee who had been shot by his co-worker during an argument. The employer had allowed 11 months to pass before disciplining the worker for his part in the incident, waiting until a criminal trial had investigated the shooting incident. Finding that the delay in discipline was unreasonable, the arbiter stressed that this decision does not mean that disciplinary action must be taken within a specified period of time. On the other hand, an employer may not wait an unreasonable length of time, pending criminal action against another employee, before notifying a worker of possible discipline. (City of Flint, Mich., 69 LA 574)

Turning the tables, employees have brought to arbitration complaints of discourtesy from management.

EXAMPLE: An employer violated its contractual obligation to promote a harmonious relationship between the company and the union by refusing to discipline a manager who verbally and physically abused an employee, an arbiter decided. Although agreeing with the employer's argument that the union had no right to tell management how to discipline its supervisors, the arbiter ruled that the foreman was guilty of abusive conduct. Management, the arbiter concluded, was obligated to take steps to ensure that such conduct did not occur in the future. (San Antonio Packing Co., 68 LA 893)

Other forms of "managerial" discourtesy must fall within the realm of clearly unreasonable conduct in order to be considered violations of work-place policies.

EXAMPLE: Casual remarks between supervisors about the behavior of a subordinate did not violate a contract provision requiring management and employees to show mutual respect for each other, an arbiter decided. While emphasizing that "it goes without saying that criticism of employees is best left to private discussion," the arbiter stressed that the supervisors had meant the remarks "lightly." "To call the situation disrespectful," he noted, "would be tantamount to ruling that supervisors cannot supervise." (Veterans Administration Hospital, 71 LA 856)

EXAMPLE: In a similar case, an arbiter ruled that a manager was not disrespectful toward a worker during an interview in which he left the door to his office open and leaned back in his chair with hands behind his head. Disagreeing with the employer's contention that the "dignity and respect" policy applied only to relationships between workers and their direct supervisors, the arbiter exclaimed that the employer certainly could not be suggesting that managers "could be ill-behaved toward employees other than those" over whom they had direct supervision. However, as regards the employee's allegations, the arbiter found that she had failed to present any "objective facts" showing that the manager "intentionally" failed to conduct himself with "dignity and respect" during the session. (Veterans Administration Medical Center, 75 LA 793)

Garnishment

IN BRIEF

Garnishments, arbitrators acknowledge, create numerous clerical and administrative burdens for employers, as well as involuntarily plunging them into the midst of an employee's personal financial difficulties. Especially where a worker has incurred excessive wage levies, arbiters sympathize with an employer's "natural wish to avoid the time, inconvenience, and expense of extra bookkeeping, extra accounting procedures, the necessity to file written returns with the attaching officer, as well as the additional trust liability for the funds that he is required to hold and his statutory liability for any failure to hold and to pay according to the instructions of the attaching officer." (35 LA 139) Based on such reasoning, one arbiter found that, "into the abstract, there is nothing unreasonable about an employer rule which provides that more than one garnishment within a year will constitute grounds for employee discharge." (63 LA 912) However, another arbiter held that a rule that permits discipline for repeated garnishments is unreasonable. (97 LA 444)

In practice, this right is bounded by several considerations, including federal and state garnishment laws that dictate the propriety of discipline for wage attachments.

The standard principles generally applied by arbiters in garnishment cases mandate that a rule providing for discipline in such situations: "must be reasonably predicated on saving the company from inconvenience, cost, liability, or the imposition of other serious burdens"; "must not be unreasonable" in terms of the penalty assessed for infractions; "must be applied without discrimination"; and "must be clear, unambiguous, and well-known by employees." (48 LA 1331)

However, even when these principles are satisfied, arbiters sometimes find that extenuating circumstances warrant discipline of lesser severity than discharge. Such mitigating circumstances, according to one arbiter, may include situations where the employee lacked knowledge of the debt; had complied an otherwise unmarred work record; arranged to discharge the debt through bankruptcy or resolved an imminent wage attachment through other means; or fell into debt because of income losses caused by chronic layoffs. (63 LA 1157; see also 82 LA 1004, 57 LA 31)

GUIDELINES

Rulings and Warnings

Rules and warnings are two items that arbiters typically look for in reviewing discharge for garnishment. Arbiters are unlikely to disturb a discharge made in accordance with a garnishment rule that has been enforced consistently. Even if there is no specific rule dealing with garnishment, a discharge probably will be upheld if the worker has been warned and has failed to improve.

EXAMPLE: An arbiter ruled that an employer had just cause to discharge an employee who refused to make peace with the Internal Revenue Service, which had garnished his wages. The employee, who was unmarried, had submitted a tax form claiming 14 dependents which he did not have. Further, the employee threatened to sue the employer if it withheld any money from his paycheck. The arbiter upheld the discharge despite the employee's claims that he had made a tax protest which was protected by the First Amendment, and his contention that, under the Federal Consumer Credit Protection Act, no employer may discharge an employee because his or her earnings have been subjected to garnishment for any one indebtedness. (Las Vegas Building Materials Inc., 83 LA 998)

EXAMPLE: A company acted within its rights in discharging a worker whose wages were garnished three times in less than four years, an arbiter ruled. The employee argued that the dismissal was unlawful, interpreting a Secretary of Labor opinion letter to hold that if an interval between garnishments exceeds one year, discharge based on the second levy would constitute termination for one garnishment, an action prohibited by the Consumer Credit Protection Act. The arbiter, however, found that the Act clearly was intended to protect only a "certain class of employees—those with only one indebtedness on which garnishments have been issued." "It is impossible to read into it any protection for the employee who has multiple garnishments for multiple indebtednesses," the arbiter stressed. Pointing out that the worker had been counselled following the first garnishment, warned after the second that an additional levy would result in dismissal, and given a week in which to prove his claim that the third wage order was in error, the arbiter concluded that "there was certainly nothing precipitous about management's action in this case" and that the dismissal was entirely proper. (BBC Manufactured Buildings Inc., 77 LA 1132)

EXAMPLE: An employer was justified in invoking a rule of conduct and discharging a garnishee who also had caused numerous delinquent credit complaints to be sent to the firm, despite management's repeated counseling. While the employee protested that the termination violated the Consumer Credit Protection Act's prohibition against discharge for garnishment for one indebtedness, the arbiter found that the single garnishment was not the sole reason for the discipline. Rather, he stressed, "the cause of termination was a protracted record of financial irresponsibility which caused unreasonable demands upon the company." Under the circumstances, he concluded, the federal law could not be construed so as to make the employee "invulnerable to consequences of unacceptable patterns of behavior." (Continental Air Lines Inc., 57 LA 31; see also 77 LA 1132, 72 LA 850, 71 LA 832)

However, another arbitrator ruled that management had no right to fire a worker whose pay was garnished for three weeks in a row under one court order. Workers whose wages were attached were punished by warnings for the first two offenses and discharge for the third. In this case, the arbitrator held that three withholdings under one court order could not be considered three separate offenses. (Bagwell Steel Co., 41 LA 303; see also 78 LA 799, 71 LA 538)

EXAMPLE: Another arbiter upheld disciplinary action against a garnisheed employee, even though the employer had no rule concerning garnishments. In that case, the worker continued to receive notices of garnishment, despite counseling and verbal warnings from management. Eventually the employer issued the worker a written warning, advising that a "recurrence of two garnishments in one week will result in immediate termination." The employee subsequently was discharged for violating this provision.

Finding sufficient cause for discharge, the arbiter ruled that management had acted fairly and objectively, particularly since it had attempted to assist the employee in his financial difficulties through counseling. Since the worker continued to show irresponsibility and created administrative expense for his employer, the arbiter ruled, management was within its rights to fire him. (Lear Siegler Inc., 63 LA 1157)

However, an employee's discharge was not justified where the employer's warning to the worker about his garnishments was clouded by a conversion concerning an unrelated suspension, an arbitrator decided. In addition, the arbiter noted, management had delayed a month before communicating with the union about the employee's possible discharge. (Virginia American Waterworks, 63 LA 912)

Similarly, discharge for excessive garnishment was overruled by an arbitrator, despite 21 garnishments against the employee, since the employer admitted the rule was not usually applied in such instances, and would not have been invoked except for other complaints against the worker, including poor attendance and criminal misconduct. (Rexall Drug Company, 65 LA 1101)

EXAMPLE: Under a plant rule requiring a second garnishment within 12 months before discharge, discharge was not justified for an employee who received a first notice within 21 months following reinstatement from an earlier discharge for violation of the rule, despite an employer-union agreement to reinstate the employee on the condition that he would be subjected to immediate discharge if found guilty of one more violation. (FMC Corp.-Vitafreeze, 57 LA 314; see also 97 LA 444)

Repeated incidents of garnishment justify severe disciplinary penalties, many arbitrators have ruled.

EXAMPLE: A three-day suspension imposed on an employee for incurring eight garnishment orders in as many months "was not only reasonable but lenient as well," an arbiter agreed. The worker was a "chronic offender in the area of garnishments," the arbiter noted, pointing out that one year previously, he had been given a one-day suspension for incurring five wage attachments. Furthermore, prior to the latest suspension, the worker had been warned by management that additional orders would result "in discipline up to and including discharge." Nevertheless, the arbiter stressed, the worker "made no effort to seek outside help in the form of personal bankruptcy or a trusteeship to take care of his financial problems" until the company was faced with yet another garnishment order. In view of the considerable progress the worker had made since then "toward getting his financial affairs in order," the company "could have overlooked the last garnishment," the arbiter noted, adding, however, that "it did not, nor was it required to overlook it." "Based on the record as a whole," the arbiter concluded, the company's decision to suspend the employee "was not arbitrary, capricious, or unreasonable." (Diem and Wing Paper Co., 72 LA 850)

EXAMPLE: Over a period of four and a half years, a worker's indebtedness resulted in four separate court orders and two actual garnishments against his salary. Management counseled the employee several times about his financial problems, and finally warned him that one more garnishment order would result in his discharge. When another order was issued, the employer terminated the worker, who protested that it was "unfair for management to fire any employee for 'a financial bind.'"

Upholding the discharge, the arbitrator noted that management "made every reasonable effort to counsel" the employee about his financial troubles and also conducted "an investigation to assure the validity and source of the encumbering debts." Despite the employer's "guidance and counseling," the worker "entangled" the company "in the mesh" of his problems "throughout virtually the entire period" of his employment, the arbiter observed. Just as "employees resist employer control and discipline for off-premises, non-work related incidents," the arbitrator concluded, so "employers should have a corollary right to be free from measurable expense and involvement" in workers' personal problems. (Shawnee Plastics Inc., 71 LA 832)

EXAMPLE: An employer properly discharged an employee who violated a plant rule by causing three garnishments to be served on the company within 12 months. The rule was reasonable, according to the arbitrator, since the employer was not obligated to undertake the administrative burden of dealing with employees' financial problems outside the plant. (Federal Paper Board Co. Inc., 60 LA 924)

Extenuating circumstances sometimes lead arbitrators to reduce discharges for garnishment to less severe disciplinary penalties. In one case, for example, an arbiter nullified a worker's termination for three wage attachments because of "mitigating" circumstances that included family illness. (American Airlines Inc., 47 LA 108)

EXAMPLE: An employer improperly discharged a worker for incurring two garnishments, an arbiter ruled, despite a work rule providing that more than one garnishment may constitute just cause for discharge without warning. The termination "fell short of what was 'just,'" the arbiter found, because of four extenuating factors: the worker had a good record; the garnishments resulted from debts that the employee had merely cosigned; management failed to inform the worker of possible programs for making voluntary wage deductions or to help him in any other way, as it had done with another employee in similar circumstances, and the employee had since "demonstrated his responsibility by diligently paying off debts on a business accountable to the creditors." (Delta Concrete Products Co. Inc., 71 LA 538)

Horseplay

IN BRIEF

In determining how to handle incidents of horseplay on company property, a distinction may be made between joking that involves only a remote possibility of injury and acts that involve a high risk of serious injury. Conduct of the latter type clearly warrants a more serious penalty even if disastrous consequences luckily do not result.

Saying that "horseplay is a 'first cousin' to willful intent to damage," one arbiter listed the following criteria to set apart the more serious actions: "Premeditated; malicious; done with evil intent or with a bad motive or purpose; intent to commit a wrong through actual or implied malice; doing something with knowledge that it is likely to result in injuries or with reckless disregard of its probable consequences." (Ozark Lead Co., 69 LA 1227)

GUIDELINES

Degree of Danger

"Arbitral notice can be taken," one arbiter maintained, "that horseplay exists" in any workplace "where a group of men are gathered together." "The real question is how frequent and how serious the horseplay is," he stressed, explaining that "there is a line between simply kidding around and dangerous and vicious acts." (Erwin Mills Inc., 51 LA 225; see also 93 LA 580)

The distinction between relatively harmless horseplay and conduct that creates serious dangers is indicated in the following cases.

EXAMPLE: For some time, employees had engaged in occasional horseplay when management's back was turned. Most often this took the form of blowing an employee's hat off with an air hose or throwing pieces of hard rubber used in shipping the company's products. On one occasion when the rubber squares were flying, an employee who was struck in the head retaliated by sneaking up behind an employee and dropping a lighted cigarette in his back pocket. After about five minutes, the employee entered a spray booth where highly combustible paints, lacquers, and solvents were used. Fortunately, another employee noticed smoke coming from the victim's back pocket and helped him snuff out the coals. The prankster also dropped a lighted cigarette in the pocket of another employee who also managed to escape injury.

Refusing to set aside the prankster's discharge, an arbiter noted that his conduct showed a serious disregard for the personal safety of others. In allowing the first employee to walk into the spray booth, the prankster created a serious fire hazard. The second employee was working on a cutting machine at the time the hot-seat was administered. These incidents could not be considered in the same class with the throwing of rubber squares or the misuse of the air hose, the arbiter concluded. (Decar Plastics Corp., 44 LA 921)

EXAMPLE: A 30-day suspension was not too harsh for an employee who exploded firecrackers in the work area, an arbiter ruled. Although the discipline was much more severe than that previously imposed for the same offense, the arbiter observed that the company had posted a notice that horseplay would not be tolerated in the plant because of the safety risks, and thus, it was justified in taking stronger action when the rule was violated again. An employee who indiscriminately shoots firecrackers in the presence of other people who are trying to work is showing contempt and disregard for the safety and well-being of his fellow workers, the arbiter stressed. (Midland Ross Corp., 65 LA 1151)

EXAMPLE: Returning from a work assignment, an employee spotted a snake on the road, which he proceeded to capture and bring with him to the job. There, the worker was instructed by a foreman to find a container in which the reptile might be kept until the end of the shift. Holding the snake in front of him with two hands — a procedure which ensured, according to the worker, that co-workers could "get out of the way" if they so desired — he marched through various work areas until he finally located a can. Snake still in hand, he was preparing the container when a co-worker, who suffered from a heart condition, entered the room. Because he was "scared to death of snakes," the co-worker "left in a hurry," pushing other employees out of his way. Subsequently, the snakehandler was discharged for violating a work rule against "irresponsible behavior" on the job.

"That some people are frightened by snakes, even though the fear may be irrational, must be acknowledged and known to reasonable persons," the arbiter declared. The employee's indifference to co-workers' possible fears — as exemplified by his "showy parade" through the workplace — indicated, the arbiter decided, that he was "not willing to adhere to an appropriate standard of conduct" — which the arbiter defines as "no more than the reasonable behavior of a responsible adult." Emphasizing the "real potential for injury or harm" created by the employee's behavior, the arbiter concluded that the discharge "was for just cause and equitable under the circumstances." (J.R. Simplot Co., 67 LA 645; see also 89 LA 297, 76 LA 339, 75 LA 592, 75 LA 305, 75 LA 290, 74 LA 785, 73 LA 912)

However, if the employer fails to show malicious intent on the part of the employee or potential for serious injury or damage as a result of the horseplay, an arbiter will be reluctant to uphold the ultimate penalty of discharge. (Ozark Lead Co., 69 LA 1227; see also 75 LA 672, 54 LA 281, 48 LA 1278)

EXAMPLE: Discipline short of discharge was held warranted where an employee pulled back a supervisor's chair, causing her to fall. The employee's conduct showed a lack of judgment, the arbiter found, but it was not shown to have been a malicious act. A ten-week suspension without pay, the arbiter concluded, ought to be enough to impress upon the culprit that employees have an obligation to "conduct themselves as mature individuals rather than as lighthearted juveniles." (Fisher Electronics, Inc., 44 LA 343)

Similarly, an employer improperly discharged an employee for throwing a pie in the face of a management consultant, an arbiter decided, where the employee mistakenly received the impression that the consultant generally was willing to participate in practical jokes. Pointing out that there was an excellent working relationship among plant personnel, including management at all levels and employees and union officials, the arbiter noted that the reason for such an excellent relationship was in part due to the presence of room in the plant for a "little fun." Considering all the circumstances, the arbiter concluded that the employee should be given another opportunity to demonstrate his desire and ability as an employee. (Clay Equipment, 73 LA 817)

Mitigating Circumstances

Aside from determining the degree of danger involved in an employee's actions, arbiters will often take into consideration the worker's record of past performance and conduct, as well as management's responsibility in the situation, in determining the proper penalty for horse-play. (96 LA 828, 91 LA 1402)

EXAMPLE: Although an employer correctly maintained that it must impose severe punishment on violators of a three-times posted rule against horseplay, an arbiter found, immediate discharge was too severe for a worker who smeared red ink on a machine handle. In lessening the penalty to a suspension, the arbiter pointer out that the employee had five years' service with a good record, that he readily confessed to the transgression when asked about it, and that, although the offense was serious, it was not "sufficiently heinous to support a summary discharge." (Southeast Container Corp., 69 LA 884)

EXAMPLE: An employee who was prone to needling other employees had harassed a fellow worker all morning. In retaliation the other man came up behind the grievant and grabbed him in a bearhug, placing most of his 265 pounds on the grievant's head and shoulders. The greivant thereupon drew a pocket knife and made a slicing motion toward the other worker, for which he was later discharged. In lightening the penalty to reinstatement without back pay, the arbiter noted that the grievant's nearly perfect record of 19 years' service supports the conclusion that he is not a "chronically mean or vicious" person. (Erwin Mills Inc., 51 LA 225)

EXAMPLE: The discharge of a worker whose horseplay actually resulted in injury to a fellow employee and could have caused damage to equipment was overturned because of the worker's unblemished work and conduct record. "Adequate punishment" for the improper conduct, the arbiter decided, was a disciplinary suspension without pay. (Butler County Mushroom Farms, 41 LA 568)

EXAMPLE: An employee was improperly discharged for dangerous horseplay, which, up till then, had been overlooked by management, an arbiter ruled. The accumulation of a flammable substance on surfaces in the employee's work area prompted occasional incidents of prankish pyromania, including employees' lighting the backsides of co-workers' uniforms and igniting the hangers on a conveyor belt that passed through the area. Although no employee had been disciplined for such antics before, one worker was terminated when his horseplay resulted in fire damage in an adjacent work area. Concluding that the "use of any fire" in the area represented "a reckless disregard for the safety of persons and property," the arbiter observed that management had taken "no action to stress the seriousness of this offense." Since the company had not responded to prior misconduct, the employee had reason to expect that this latest fire would also be tolerated, the arbiter concluded, holding that discharge was too harsh, under the circumstances. (Owens-Corning Fiberglass Corp., 70 LA 916)

EXAMPLE: An employer was not justified in discharging for horseplay a worker whose actions resulted in his own injury and created a safety hazard for others, an arbiter ruled, where the employee had a mental and nervous disability that required treatment. Even though the employer had provided a three-month leave for psychiatric treatment, the arbiter concluded, the arrangement did not ensure the necessary reports and proper safeguards for the employee's return to work, as in the company's handling of similar cases. (Foster Wheeler Corp., 57 LA 1171)

Rehabilitative Effect

Discipline short of discharge may be advocated for employees guilty of mild horseplay to see if they can be taught a lesson.

EXAMPLE: A company was within its rights in disciplining a third-shift employee who was guilty of "teasing" his female co-workers by transferring him to the first shift, with attendant loss of his shift differential, an arbiter said. But for the action to have a rehabilitative value, the arbiter pointed out, the employee should be given a chance to prove that he profited from the experience. Accordingly, the company was directed to give him another try on the third shift. (Sobel Metal Products Inc., 54 LA 835)

Off-Duty Misconduct

IN BRIEF

As a general rule, arbiters hold that an employer may not discipline a worker for off-duty activities, since "to do so would constitute an invasion of the employee's personal life by the employer and would place the employer in the position of sitting in judgment on neighborhood morals, a matter which should be left to civil officers." (Menzie Dairy Co., 45 LA 283)

Nevertheless, while agreeing that the "private life of an employee is beyond the reach of his employer," other arbiters have pointed out that the effect of the conduct of a worker's job relationship may prevail over considerations of "privacy." Thus, Elkouri and Elkouri (How Arbitration Works; BNA Books, 1985) concluded that the right of management to discharge an employee for conduct away from the workplace depend on the effect of that conduct on plant operations. (41 LA 713, 28 LA 434, 28 LA 312)

One arbiter noted that management may be entitled to discipline workers for off-duty misconduct where "there is a direct and demonstrable relationship between the illicit conduct and the performance of the employee's job." "The consequences of all other conduct is to be left for correction or punishment by civil and moral authority existing for that purpose," the arbiter stressed, cautioning that even where the conduct results in "very substantial embarrassment to an employer," it "cannot be merely assumed that particular conduct—even conduct so gross as to result in a criminal conviction—is related to job performance." (Internal Revenue Service, 77 LA 19)

To support discipline for off-duty misconduct, management should be prepared to show that the worker's outside activity had a readily discernible harmful effect on company operations. Thus, arbiters will uphold discipline where the employer is able to prove that:

▶ The conduct renders the workers unable to perform the job satisfactorily and/or leads other personnel to refuse to work with the employee. (96 LA 244, 95 LA 169, 89 LA 1, 67 LA 1296, 58 LA 1293, 52 LA 1266, 39 LA 1165, 33 LA 735, 23 LA 229, 22 LA 1, 15 LA 42)

▶ The misconduct jeopardizes the employer's operations by, for example, creating publicity that harms the organization's public image. (97 LA 585, 96 LA 1208, 96 LA 454, 96 LA 181, 95 LA 358, 95 LA 169, 91 LA 6, 69 LA 508, 67 LA 1296, 65 LA 280, 60 LA 173, 53 LA 1266, 53 LA 203, 49 LA 117, 47 LA 62, 45 LA 498, 38 LA 1003)

Where management is unable to show a relationship or "nexus" between the misconduct and on-the-job performance or prove adverse effect to the business, arbiters typically will rule against the discipline imposed for off-

OFF-DUTY MISCONDUCT

duty activities. (97 LA 801, 96 LA 325, 95 LA 319, 95 LA 162, 92 LA 669, 91 LA 930, 91 LA 193, 90 LA 41, 90 LA 38, 88 LA 749, 88 LA 275, 87 LA 1261, 77 LA 19, 71 LA 1004, 71 LA 82, 68 LA 254, 66 LA 1037, 66 LA 639, 66 LA 220, 64 LA 832, 64 LA 528, 63 LA 1265, 63 LA 917, 63 LA 350, 63 LA 291, 61 LA 587, 60 LA 801, 60 LA 314)

GUIDELINES

Off-Duty Misconduct on Company Premises

Generally, off-duty employees have a obligation to observe plant rules while on company premises and may be subject to discipline for their misconduct even though the misconduct (which often will adversely impact employee morale, discipline, or other legitimate company interests) occurs while they are off duty and in a nonworking area of the plant (e.g., the company cafeteria or parking lot). (65 LA 1233, 65 LA 1236, 65 LA 1177, 65 LA 1182, 64 LA 528, 63 LA 36, 50 LA 766, 50 LA 403, 49 LA 1253, 49 LA 370, 48 LA 1099, 48 LA 695, 45 LA 817)

Adverse Impact

To sustain discipline for off-duty misconduct, arbiters generally require that management clearly demonstrate how the incident has negatively affected the employment relationship. (78 LA 806 (verbal abuse of plant manager at company picnic); 79 LA 1187; 76 LA 387 (possession/sale of cocaine); 76 LA 347 (theft); 74 LA 1293 (burglary); 74 LA 1084 (threatening foreman); 70 LA 756 (vandalizing supervisor's home); 69 LA 876 (shooting incident); 69 LA 507 (parking in "no-parking" zone near plant); 69 LA 379 (possession of heroin); 68 LA 1245 (shoplifting); 60 LA 172 (possession of stolen property); 57 LA 725, 56 LA 1221 (incest); 49 LA 117 (intoxication); 47 LA 62 (KKK Acting Grand Dragon); 46 LA 346 (fight); 39 LA 1025 (employee with "sordid" private life whose work required him to enter private homes)

EXAMPLE: An employer properly fired a store clerk after he fatally beat a 71-year-old woman who had intervened in an argument he was having with his wife on a downtown street. Although convicted of manslaughter, the worker argued that he should be allowed to continue on the job through the prison release program. The arbiter, however, agreed with management that the employee's conduct was of such a brutal nature as to severely damage relations with customers and co-workers. Finding that the widely publicized assault would tend to create anxiety among fellow employees and hesitancy among customers about entering the store, the arbiter decided that the fear of violence could be as harmful to a business as violence itself and therefore justified the discharge penalty. (Commonwealth of Pennsylvania, 65 LA 280)

EXAMPLE: Management properly issued a written warning to an employee whose parking infractions threatened the organization's "amicable relations" with area residents.

Despite the existence of free parking facilities provided by the employer, a number of workers persisted in parking their cars on residential streets adjacent to the plant, thereby inconveniencing local residents. Attempting to cooperate with city authorities, the employer incorporated into its work rules a parking ban. Nevertheless, one employee continued to violate the ban, and was issued a written warning. According to the employee, the discipline was improper since it covered a matter entirely outside the employment relationship.

The "neat question" in the case, the arbiter pointed out, was whether or not the employer had "an exaggerated notion of how much supervision or influence" it could exercise over employees away from the job. An employee's off-duty activities often can serve as the basis for "very severe discipline," the arbiter noted, if the worker's conduct makes it "difficult or impossible" for the employer to conduct its business. "The relations between a business enterprise and its neighbors" are "vital considerations" for an employer, particularly one located in a residential area, he stressed. "One of the facts of modern life," he continued, "is that shortages of parking spaces can lead to controversies which become virtual feuds." Thus, while the employee's decision to risk a parking ticket was "essentially his own business," his conduct also created a "serious problem"—the "wrath" and "antipathy" of local residents—for the employer. (Electronic Memories & Magnetics Corp., 69 LA 507)

Similarly, an arbiter upheld the termination of an employee for off-duty misbehavior where the work entailed entering customers' homes. The arbiter termed the employee a bad risk because of his association with disreputable characters capable of using to their advantage inside information on customers' residences and because of the worker's contempt for minimum standards of acceptable social behavior. (Gas Service Co., 39 LA 1025)

Likewise, another arbiter ruled that the discharge of an employee for after-hours behavior was fully warranted, since the misconduct stamped him as an individual capable for resorting to violence and, therefore, potentially dangerous to co-workers. (Central Packing Co. Inc., 24 LA 603)

EXAMPLE: An employer was justified in discharging three employees who were found guilty in court of possessing supplies that were part of another company's shipment. Finding that the employer's operations were closely linked to the theft area and that the employees previously were suspected of stealing company property, the arbiter decided that the discipline was for just cause.

The employer's business interests were substantially harmed in view of the small size and close-knit character of the community, the arbiter reasoned, emphasizing that the employees' reinstatements would have an adverse effect upon the employer-employee relationship and, thus, were not warranted under the circumstances. (Inspiration Consolidated Copper Co., 60 LA 173)

However, another arbiter ruled that an off-duty shooting in self-defense was not sufficient grounds for termination. Although convicted of second-degree manslaughter, the power lineman was allowed to serve out his sentence on probation. The employer, however, terminated the worker, contending that his continued employment would have an adverse effect on the business, since his duties required him to enter customers' homes.

Rejecting the employee's arguments, the arbiter gave more weight to the testimony of several community leaders who attested to the confidence they had in the worker and their lack of objection to his coming into their homes on company business. Such testimony, the arbiter found, was convincing evidence that the worker's continued employment would have no adverse effect on the company, whereas the failure to reinstate him might harm the organization's reputation. Since the primary reason for the discharge—adverse effect—had been disproved, the arbiter concluded, the termination was improper. (Alabama Power Co., 66 LA 220; see also 78 LA 1311 (selling marijuana); 77 LA 867 (homosexual conduct); 73 LA 1042 (vehicle damage); 71 LA 1004 (firing gun); 71 LA 82 (possession of marijuana); 68 LA 346 (fighting); 68 LA 254 ("affair" with fellow employee); 46 LA 307 (romantic liaison in hotel); 44 LA 133 (bankruptcy); 43 LA 242 (contributing to the delinquency of a minor); 41 LA 460 (morals offense); 37 LA 1040 (narcotics conviction); 35 LA 315 (invoking Fifth Amendment in congressional investigation); 29 LA 451, 28 LA 434 (intoxication); 23 LA 808; 20 LA 175, 15 LA 42)

Similarly, another arbiter found that an employer had erroneously concluded that a worker's off-duty misconduct had tarnished its public image. After quarreling with his wife, the employee grabbed a shotgun and went into the woods behind his home. A short time later, a state police trooper was called to the scene, and, upon arriving, ordered the employee to come out of the woods. As he emerged, the worker's shotgun discharged, grazing the trooper slightly. The officer arrested the employee and took him to jail. As a result of the publicity the incident received in two local newspapers, the employee was discharged. However, stressing that the publicity about the shooting was limited to two local newspapers, which did not reveal the employee's association with the company, the arbiter ruled that the discharge was improper. The employee's work did not require him to deal with the public, the arbiter found, and the employer's customers had no reason to fear the worker because of the incident or the newspaper publicity. (Valley Bell Dairy Co., 71 LA 1004)

EXAMPLE: Two male employees were improperly suspended for "mooning" a woman, an arbiter decided.

After work, the two employees went to a cocktail lounge for a few hours. Later, as they headed for their car in a parking lot, they noticed a group of women "laughing" and "carrying on" behind them. One of the women blew a "rape" whistle, which the employees considered to be a "practical joke." In response, the workers dropped their trousers and exposed their buttocks to one of the women. The woman reported the mooning to the police, and, when management learned of the incident, it issued the workers one-day suspensions for misconduct that adversely affected the "efficiency" of the employer's operation.

"There can be little doubt," the arbiter asserted, that the employees' "concerted baring of their asses" was "sophomoric and foolish" and fell "substantially short of earning them a merit badge." However, he stressed, an employer must have sensible "expectation concerning the conduct of employees on their own time," and may not "exaggerate unduly what the public may think of incidents having no bearing on their job." Under this standard, the arbiter concluded, the employer had no basis for relating the "conduct of the two employees in this single and isolated occasion with the performance of their work." (U.S. Internal Revenue Service, 77 LA 19)

Likewise, an airline company was not justified in discharging a service employee who, after completing his shift, won a $20 bet from fellow workers by "streaking" in front of the airport's terminal wearing only a ski mask, a T-shirt, and cowboy boots. Remarking that the employee's conduct apparently was not lewd and that it caused no morale problems among other employees, the arbiter concluded that the alleged adverse publicity resulting from the worker's behavior could be considered no more than minimal. (Air California, 63 LA 350)

Effect of Arrest

As preceding examples demonstrate, arbiters generally will not uphold a discharge for off-duty misconduct that is predicated solely on the employee's having been arrested for the incident. On the other hand, most will agree that management is justified in suspending an employee pending the outcome of trial on the charges. A suspension in such circumstances should not be considered disciplinary in nature, some arbiters have held, since it is unrelated to the final verdict as to the employee's guilt or innocence. Instead, the suspension should be viewed as an act of self-defense on management's part that is intended to eliminate a potential detriment to or impairment of the organization's business. (See 48 LA 391, 45 LA 498, 29 LA 442, 26 LA 570, 22 LA 851)

EXAMPLE: Management was within its rights to establish a company rule automatically subjecting employees to immediate suspension without pay upon their indictment or arrest for criminal activity, an arbiter ruled. Rejecting the union's argument that the rule was unfair and unjust in that it convicted an employee before he had a chance to show his innocence, the arbiter agreed with the employer that some of a worker's off-duty behavior could relate directly to the conduct of a business and therefore be subject to company rules. According to the arbiter, off-duty conduct that could be subject to management control included actions that would adversely affect employee morale, discipline, and other legitimate company interests. (Virginia Chemicals Inc., 65 LA 760)

EXAMPLE: A driver-salesman arrested on a variety of obscenity charges should be (1) suspended pending trial, (2) discharged if found guilty, or (3) reinstated if proven innocent or the charges were otherwise dropped but to a position not involving contact with customers, an arbiter recommended. Suspension was clearly warranted in the case, the arbiter held, because of the possible damage to the company's image and good will if it continued to employ the driver. The duties of the job necessitated a close personal relationship with customers, he noted, stressing that the seriousness of the charge increased the risk of harm to the company. (Menzie Dairy Co., 45 LA 283)

Such a suspension may be questioned, however, where a lengthy trial results in an extended loss of employment. In these types of cases, arbiters have suggested that management would do better to conduct its own investigation of the incident and decide upon the appropriate disciplinary action.

EXAMPLE: Two employees were indicted for committing criminal acts of violence against nonstrikers during a strike. When they returned to work at the end of the strike, the company temporarily suspended them. The employees emphatically denied the guilt, but several months passed without any indication of the date when they would be brought to trial.

A temporary suspension at the time they returned to work was justified, an arbiter ruled, since the employer reasonably could conclude that their return at the time would disrupt plant operations. But the suspension should not have continued beyond 60 days without the company's making its own investigation and taking appropriate disciplinary action. (Plough Inc., 54 LA 541)

Conviction Considerations

Arbiters typically uphold discipline meted out to an employee whose off-duty misconduct results in a criminal conviction, especially where work rules provide for punishment in such cases. Thus, one arbiter ruled that management was within its rights to discipline a worker convicted of possessing illegal drugs where negotiated work rules mandated discipline simply upon "conviction of a felony involving drugs." The employer did not need to investigate the case nor prove an adverse impact on its own reputation or the performance of its workforce, since the rule was a mutually negotiated provision of its contract with the union, the arbiter said. However, finding that off-duty possession and use of drugs was not as serious an offense as such misconduct on company premises, the arbiter decided that discharge was too harsh a penalty for the first-time offender and, therefore, reduced the discipline to a suspension. (Nugent Sand Co., 71 LA 585)

Arbiters also will uphold a discharge where the conviction results in harm to the organization's image. (69 LA 776, 68 LA 697, 65 LA 1203, 38 LA 891)

EXAMPLE: A gas company employee convicted of embezzlement at his part-time job was properly discharged, an arbiter ruled. The arbiter noted that the company as "understandably concerned" about the risk of bad public relations, especially since its employees held a strong position of trust with respect to customers' homes. The fact that this particular employee did not have access to customers' residences was not known to the general public, the arbiter pointed out. (New Haven Gas Co., 43 LA 900)

Where the court tempers the conviction by, for example, suspending part of the sentence or permitting a work release, arbiters generally require that, absent compelling circumstances, management show similar leniency. Thus, arbiters have warned, employers may not base a discharge upon a conviction while ignoring the fact that the employee has received a suspended sentence with probation. (60 LA 430, 37 LA 1040)

EXAMPLE: Management improperly discharged a worker who was convicted of possessing marijuana but placed on probation, an arbiter decided, dismissing the employer's contention that the disposition of the court was not relevant in light of the worker's confession of guilt to violating a company rule against use of illegal drugs. Management, the arbiter said, failed to present evidence that the worker's arrest had adversely affected its operations or the performance of coworkers, or that the reported drug activity had any impact on the worker's own performance, his record of attendance, or any other aspect of the employment relationship. (Indian Head Inc., 71 LA 82)

Effect of Acquittal

An acquittal, on the other hand, does not necessarily eliminate the possibility of discipline. Management may preserve its right to take disciplinary action against an employee who has been acquitted of the charges in a court hearing, subject to review within a mutually agreed-upon forum. As one arbiter declared, "in the absence of a contrary stipulation by the parties, determinations by other tribunals of issues arising on the facts are not binding on the arbiters." (Chrysler Corp., 53 LA 1279; see also 54 LA 541) Another arbiter explained that, regardless of acquittal in criminal trial, the finding of a disciplinary proceeding may establish that the employee did, in fact, commit the act in question. In such cases, the arbiter said, "it matters not that the rigorous protection in the criminal law has saved the individual from criminal penalties because such fact does not constitute a bar to the employer's right to protect itself or its other employees." (New York City Health & Hospital Corp., 76 LA 387)

EXAMPLE: An arbiter upheld the discharge of an employee for damaging company property, even though a jury had acquitted the employee of the criminal charge of malicious destruction of property. The arbiter held that the jury's action did not foreclose him from making his own judgment on the evidence presented to him, observing that he did not know what evidence or arguments were presented in the criminal action, what rules of law were applied, and what elements of evidence persuaded the jury to reach the verdict it did. (Chrysler Corp., 53 LA 1279)

However, where an employer has agreed to base its disciplinary decision on the outcome of a trial, it may not ignore an acquittal to which it objects. "It is essential to good labor-management relations," one arbiter stressed, "that grievance settlements not be disturbed in the absence of conclusive showing of changed conditions." (Standard Oil Co., 13 LA 799)

EXAMPLE: Following the "logic behind the reasoning," an arbiter thus ruled that city management improperly discharged a police officer for "unbecoming" conduct after it had agreed to return the officer to the payroll if he were acquitted of morals charges. Management later said that the agreement was not a binding contract since "essential elements" of the contractual process were missing and that, in any event, the settlement had been made by the former chief of police, who had retired prior to the officer's acquittal. Rejecting these arguments, the arbiter found that at the time the agreement was made, the since-retired police chief had full authority to settle grievances and impose discipline, and that the city could not now renege on that settlement. Furthermore, the arbiter pointed out, "even though given ample opportunity," city managers were unable to show "any conclusive change in the circumstances which would permit them to rescind the agreement." (City of Pontiac, Mich., 77 LA 765)

Morally Reprehensible Conduct

Management may be presented with a tough decision where an employee is convicted of criminal conduct that is regarded as immoral or repugnant by society. On the one hand, there is the threat to employee and/or customer relations that may be presented by returning the employee to the job. On the other, the argument may be made that punishment of the employee should be left to the courts and that the employee should not be placed in "double jeopardy" by loss of employment as well.

In resolving this dilemma, arbiters tend to weigh the employee's past record against the threat of a recurrence of the misconduct. Thus, an employee who pleaded guilty to a charge of taking indecent liberties with a nine-year-old girl and who spent about eight months in a state mental hospital was given a conditional reinstatement. The employee's record of 16 years' employment without prior incident was cited as some indication that he could continue as a satisfactory employee, while the fact that he had been a factory worker was seen as minimizing any adverse affect upon the morale or efficiency of other employees, as well as the public at large. Citing the worker's lack of public contact, the arbiter noted that the case might have been different if he had been a retail clerk in a toy store. (Armco Steel Corp., 43 LA 977)

Some of the considerations to be weighed in such cases were reviewed by an arbiter who ordered the reinstatement of an employee who sought to return to his job after serving a nine-month jail sentence after being arrested on a morals charge at a motion picture theater. The arbiter noted that:

- The employee had a 37-year, unblemished work record.
- The nature of the offense did not impair the employee's ability to perform his job functions.
- The underlying psychiatric problem that led to the offense did not, in itself, render the employee unfit for further employment.
- Aside from supposition, it was not shown that either supervision or fellow employees would be subjected to resentments or tensions impairing the department's operation if the employee were to be reinstated. (United States Steel Corp., 41 LA 460)

EXAMPLE: Where an airline purser was arrested once in an altercation arising from his taking pictures of nude males in a hotel room, an arbiter converted a discharge to a 90-day suspension. But when the employee subsequently pleaded guilty to criminal charges involving the photographing of a nude minor, a discharge penalty was upheld. The cumulative effect of these incidents exposed the airline employer to potential damage, the arbiter said, noting that "some people may be given pause" in riding planes "under the control of persons who are so inept at managing their own affairs." (Northwest Airlines Inc., 53 LA 203)

Social "Transgressions"

Certain cases labelled as "misconduct" involve no criminal activity, but rather represent transgressions of societal "taboos." In such cases, arbiters generally require that management conclusively demonstrate how the employee's private affairs can have a negative impact on the employment relationship.

EXAMPLE: "In this age of so-called enlightenment and permissiveness, it would be difficult to assess the impact that the private lives of fellow employees have on the work force," an arbiter declared, overturning the discharge of an employee who had an affair with a coworker.

Upon learning that the workers, both married, had become intimately involved, management gave them the option of resigning or being fired. While the man chose to resign, the woman refused to accept the ultimatum and was subsequently discharged for conduct unbecoming an office employee. Reinstating the worker, the arbiter dismissed the employer's contentions that the discharge was necessary in order to protect the organization's good name. Agreeing with the employee that her private life had no adverse effect on the organization or on her job performance and finding that the employees were "consenting adults," the arbiter concluded that the "punishment did not fit the crime." (Operating Engineers, 68 LA 254)

Similarly, an employer erred in discharging two married workers for "unbecoming conduct" after catching them in an embrace. Interpreting the phrase to mean "conduct that is so open and notorious that it affronts fellow workers or customers and is carried on while the employee is on duty," the arbiter decided that this definition did not agree with the facts of the case. The transgression "did not occur on the employer's time, did not affront any customer, and was not the subject of complaint by a fellow employee," he pointed out, concluding that the discharge was too severe. (Williams Bros. Markets, 64 LA 528)

EXAMPLE: A cashier at a supermarket was permitted to continue to work until shortly before the birth of her first illegitimate child. But when she subsequently sought maternity leave for a second pregnancy, management asked her to resign. When she refused, she was fired.

Rejecting the company's claim of damage to its customer relations, an arbiter noted that customer-employee relations in a supermarket are not as intimate as they are in a small neighborhood grocery. Moreover, the first pregnancy apparently had not injured the company. He also rejected a claim that the discharge was justified by the possibility that parents might forbid their daughters to work at the store. The worker was not charged with sexual misconduct on the premises, and there was no evidence that she was a bad influence on the other girls. In fact, the arbiter said, her case might serve to underscore the dangers inherent in an illicit sexual relationship. (Allied Supermarkets Inc., 41 LA 713)

An employer that dismisses an unwed pregnant employee also is likely to encounter legal problems. The courts have held that discharging a worker, married or not, for pregnancy is unlawful sex discrimination under Title VII of the 1964 Civil Rights Act since pregnancy is a condition unique to women. A company's claim that its action stemmed from abhorrence of premarital sexual activity was rejected by an appeals court, which found that the employee involved was terminated not because of her sexual conduct but because she was pregnant and unmarried. Making a distinction between wed and unwed pregnancy in application of employment policies, the court decided, had no rational relationship to the normal operation of the company's business. (Jacobs v. Martin Sweets Co., CA 6, 1977, 14 FEP Cases 687)

Outside Employment

IN BRIEF

Employee "moonlighting"—holding a second job during off hours—can sometimes pose problems for the employer. While employees may argue for their rights to do as they please during off hours and to use their skills and knowledge to augment their income, outside employment may interfere with management's need for full productivity during working hours and loyalty from employees. Outside employment may be a cause for disciplinary action where:

The issue of dishonesty is raised, such as when an employee fraudulently takes sick leave in order to work on the outside job. (91 LA 1261, 91 LA 647, 90 LA 16, 83 LA 48, 67 LA 606, 66 LA 177, 64 LA 856, 63 LA 941, 62 LA 732)

The outside employment adversely affects the employee's primary job through poor performance, absenteeism, or tardiness. Additionally, arbiters generally uphold discipline where the second job causes a worker either to neglect routine job duties or refuse to carry out regularly scheduled overtime. (89 LA 1062, 66 LA 1071, 66 LA 177, 62 LA 779, 41 LA 1126, 37 LA 1095)

A conflict of interest arises between the outside employment and the employee's primary job, particularly when the second employer is a competitor, and trade secrets or special skills are involved. (94 LA 841, 87 LA 1140, 86 LA 1073, 85 LA 286, 82 LA 1259, 74 LA 1066, 73 LA 164, 72 LA 855, 71 LA 762, 68 LA 13, 67 LA 985, 67 LA 632)

In all of the above situations, an important consideration in determining the kind of discipline warranted is whether or not the contract or a "reasonable" management rule or policy expressly forbids outside employment or business ventures. (91 LA 1261, 67 LA 606, 54 LA 381, 52 LA 818)

--- GUIDELINES ---

Dishonesty in Moonlighting

Just cause for discharge usually is found where an employee falsely claims sick leave in order to work on a second job. Such cases usually are treated as instances of misconduct akin to dishonesty rather than as simple absenteeism. (98 LA 122, 58 LA 827, 52 LA 314)

EXAMPLE: A worker was properly discharged after having been discovered plowing a field of corn for spring planting while on sick leave, an arbiter ruled. The employee's activities during his period of sick leave constituted a business venture for profit that was prohibited by the bargaining agreement, the arbiter ruled, noting that the employer had a clearly stated rule which did not permit leaves of absence for the "purpose of any other employment or business venture." (Farmland Foods, 67 LA 606; see also Rock Hill Printing & Finishing Co., 37 LA 254)

EXAMPLE: Another arbiter held that an employer properly discharged an employee who had admittedly lied when he denied working at another company during a period when he was on sick leave because of injuries sustained in an automobile accident. The arbiter found that the employee's continued absence, although he was able to work, caused scheduling difficulties and loss of production during a critical season. The employee's dishonesty, the arbiter declared, "showed a clear intent to deceive the company for the purpose of obtaining a personal benefit." (I. B. Goodman Mfg. Co., 62 LA 732)

However, an employee may be able to escape discipline for working elsewhere while on sick leave if no intent to cheat is involved.

EXAMPLE: Just cause for discharge was held to be lacking where an employee took a second job involving light work while recuperating from a heart attack. The employee had sought to return to his primary job, but both his doctor and the company doctor had recommended against it, and the company also turned down his request for lighter work. The employee's failure to notify the company of his other job and his denial at one point that he was working was held to constitute at most bad judgment, rather than dishonesty. (American Bakeries Co., 43 LA 1106; see also Mercoid Corp., 63 LA 941)

EXAMPLE: An arbiter set aside the discharge of an employee who rode a tiger in a novelty animal exhibition while on leave for an occupational back injury. Reasoning that the worker could have reinjured himself during the stunt, the employer contended that he should have obtained its written permission to engage in the off-duty employment. However, based on a description of the event, the arbiter found that the tiger-riding activity posed no "foreseeable risk" of injury to the employee, and concluded that it was unreasonable for the employer to consider such activity as detrimental to either itself or the employee. (Randle-Eastern Ambulance Service, 65 LA 394;

see also Rock Hill Printing and Finishing Co., 64 LA 856)

Similarly, the discharge of an employee who was found tending bar at a local tavern while on sick leave was set aside by an arbiter on the basis of testimony from the tavern owner and the employee that they were old friends, the employee was not compensated, and he often used the tavern as a "second home." (Standard Brands Inc., 52 LA 918)

Working for Competition

Arbiters generally concede that management has the right to bar employees from working for a competitor during their off hours. Such employment not only gives the competitor the benefit of experience provided by the full-time employer, it frequently does so at bargain-basement prices. At the same time, the worker may unintentionally harm the primary employer by divulging trade secrets, or such proprietary information as new designs or sales figures.

EXAMPLE: An employer has the right to establish a rule against working for a competitor, one arbiter decided. In applying such a rule, a company is not required to establish beyond doubt that the employee's moonlighting has damaged its business or led to a financial loss, the arbiter said, maintaining that management can take action against the offending employee where it "reasonably" infers that the outside employment might lead to disclosure of information or the use of special skills. (Ravens-Metal Products Inc., 39 LA 404; see also 96 LA 526, 71 LA 762)

However, arbiters insist that employers inform their workers through clearly established rules that any outside employment is forbidden. Even when the evidence is clear that a worker has broken a rule against outside employment, many arbiters require that management allow the employee a chance to relinquish the secondary job before enforcing a final decision to discharge.

EXAMPLE: After learning that two of its workers had accepted part-time employment with a competitor, the employer gave them a formal warning that further such activity would be cause for discharge. Although ruling that the employer was justified in barring the outside work, the arbiter considered the warnings in the case unjustified. While management had the right to forbid the outside employment, the arbiter said, it could not impose discipline at the same time it gave notice of its policy. (Mechanical Handling Systems Inc., 26 LA 401; see also Phillips Petroleum Co., 47 LA 372)

EXAMPLE: An employer that required all employees to disclose any moonlighting activities, improperly discharged a worker for failing to reveal his part-time job with a competitor, since the employer had terminated the worker without giving him a chance to resign from the second job. Other employees in similar situations, the arbiter noted, had been allowed an opportunity to relinquish their outside interest before any disciplinary action was invoked. (William Feather Co., 68 LA 13)

Similarly, discharge was improper where an employee was not afforded a reasonable opportunity to disengage himself from a business that his primary employer considered a conflict of interest, another arbiter ruled. Although the employer contended that the worker's part ownership in a local bar competed with its retail business, the arbiter decided that the employer had failed to prove that the bar was a competitor. If the employer's interest in the operation competed with his primary job, the arbiter noted, then the employer should have allowed the worker a chance to have given up his interest. (Albertson's Inc., 65 LA 1042; see also 96 LA 1)

Direct Competition

Arbiters agree that management has the right to discharge an employee when the worker's off-duty activity constitutes direct competition because the business is similar to that of the employer. (57 LA 1258, 55 LA 1044, 53 LA 1176)

Such activity "is not a mere case of 'moonlighting'," one arbiter stressed. Upholding an employer's action, he explained: 'I do not consider this discharge as disciplinary. (The employee's) ownership of a competing business was not, strictly speaking, an offense. But it was a condition, created by him, that made his continued employment by the company intolerable." (Firestone Retread Shop, 38 LA 600)

Workers soliciting business for personal gain while on company time also should be liable for discipline, arbiters agree. "It is an established rule of employment law," one arbiter said, "that an employee may not use for his own benefit and contrary to the interest of his employer, information obtained in the course of the employment." Ruling that an employer had "just cause" for discharging workers who were soliciting business for private gain on company time and working in competition with the employer, an arbiter stressed that "no employee needs to be told that if he is soliciting company customers on company time and property for a competing business, that he runs a great risk of losing his job." (Alaska Sales and Service Co., 73 LA 164; see also Jacksonville Shipyards Inc., 74 LA 1066)

EXAMPLE: Another arbiter converted discharge to a disciplinary layoff where the employee had been siphoning business from his employer. In this case, the employer had a specific rule forbidding employees to solicit during working hours with the intent of obtaining work ordinarily performed by the company. Nevertheless, noting such mitigating factors as the employee's good record and the absence of any evidence that the employer had actually lost money, the arbiter held that giving the worker a second chance would benefit both the company and society. (Heinrich Motors Inc., 68 LA 1224; see also Patton Sparkle Market, 75 LA 1092)

Other Conflicting Employment

Even where the second job is not with a direct competitor, management still may claim that it inherently conflicts with the employee's responsibilities and obligations to the primary employer.

EXAMPLE: An arbiter ruled that a wholesale distributor of cigarettes would be justified in discharging a salesman, if the worker did not divest himself of his interest in a private vending machine business serving the employer's retail customers. Pointing out that the employee's outside business activity created a conflict of interest, the arbiter concluded that the employer's legitimate business interests required that the company be able to discharge the employee so long as the worker refused to terminate "those outside, but closely related, business activities, which caused economic harm to the employer." (Phillips Brothers Inc. 63 LA 328)

Such an issue frequently has been raised by employers in the publishing industry. Here are some examples of how arbiters have ruled in these cases:

• An arbiter ruled that an employee violated an employer prohibition against outside activities that created "clear conflict of interest," by writing and publishing a book about the employer, based on his work as an investigative reporter covering a story of the employer's financial problems. Further, even though the employee had permission to use his story without restriction toward a book, the arbiter said, the journalist commented on the employer in a derogatory fashion, thus violating the employer rule. (United Press International Inc., 94 LA 841)

• A publisher had the right to give one of its reporters a choice between his job with the paper and an outside job as editor of a union weekly that espoused political views contrary to the newspaper's editorial policy. (Niagara Falls Gazette, 41 LA 899)

• A publisher did not show just cause for discharging two circulation managers for operating a local beer tavern. The arbiter rejected the company's contention that a bias against beer existed in a large segment of the community, noting that the sole test of community morals is that which has been crystallized by statute or ordinance into positive mandate. Since dealing in beer is a legal business, the employees were not engaged in activities of a detrimental nature to the newspaper. (Memphis Publishing Co., 48 LA 931)

• A publisher did not have the right to order one of his advertising salesmen to quit a night-time job in a local department store, notwithstanding the publisher's contention that other advertiser-stores might view it as a conflict of interest. As a remedy, the publisher was directed to make the employee whole for wages he lost by relinquishing his part-time employment. (Lowell Sun Publishing Co., 43 LA 273)

• A publisher had the right to fire its drama critic for accepting outside work as a press agent for a summer theater and allowing her name, which was also the name of her column in the newspaper, to be used in promoting the summer theater. (Tribune Publishing Co., 42 LA 504)

Other Adverse Interference

Moonlighting that does not involve working for a competitor or otherwise conflicts with the primary job usually is not regarded as just cause for discharge, in the absence of contractual prohibition on outside employment. On the other hand, a company was held to be within its rights when it adopted a rule prohibiting the holding of a second full-time job, on the ground that this would have a natural and obvious tendency to interfere with an employee's work. (Goodyear Tire & Rubber Co., 41 LA 1126). Moreover, outside employment normally will not be considered an excuse for poor performance, absenteeism, tardiness, or a refusal to work overtime.

EXAMPLE: An arbiter held that an employer properly issued a written reprimand to an auxiliary engineer who published an article in a newspaper which attributed an alleged atrocious safety record to the employer, despite the claim that the employee's action were entirely without malice. (San Diego Gas & Electric Co., 82 LA 1039)

EXAMPLE: An employer had just cause for discharging a worker who took three days off to harvest his corn crop despite a specific order to report to work, an arbiter decided. The need to harvest and the potential economic loss if he failed to so, the arbiter ruled, did not excuse the worker's failure to fulfill his obligation to the employer. Furthermore, the arbiter decided, management had the right to discipline without giving written warning, since the employee had blatantly refused to carry out its specific instructions. (Dryden Manufacturing Co., 66 LA 1071)

EXAMPLE: In the course of preparing reprimands to an employee for spoiled work, management stumbled onto the fact that he was a moonlighter. The reprimands were changed to a discharge when the employee refused to give up his second job. An arbiter set aside the discharge on the ground that management had insufficient backing for its conclusion that it was injured by the worker's other job. Although his two jobs allowed him only about five hours of sleep a day, his foreman saw no signs that the employee was suffering from lack of sleep and instead had given him rapid promotions. There also was no showing that he was less efficient or spoiled more work than non-moonlighters. (United Engineering & Foundry Co., 37 LA 1095)

Similarly, another arbiter reinstated a worker who had been discharged for excessive absenteeism on the condition that he stop working in any outside business for one year. On several occasions, the employee had failed to report to work because of arm and neck pains. When management discovered that he was working at a garage on the days he had called in sick, it terminated the worker. Although finding that the worker's outside venture had interfered with his regular job by causing him to be excessively absent, the arbiter concluded that the worker's prior satisfactory job performance and length of service warranted a second chance. (Microdot Inc., 66 LA 177)

In contrast, an arbiter held that an employer improperly discharged a flight attendant whose "bohemian" lifestyle and work as a professional artist were described in a magazine feature article that identified him as working for the employer. Even though the employee failed to get the required pre-publication review, approval, and permission from the employer, the arbiter pointed out, neither the employee's artistic endeavors nor the article constituted work "detrimental to, or in conflict with, the company's interest." (Trans World Airlines Inc., 93 LA 167)

Sleeping & Loafing

IN BRIEF

Discharge is generally acknowledged to be a proper penalty for sleeping on the job as long as there is a plant rule or established practice making discharge the penalty for such an offense. (98 LA 183, 86 LA 430, 81 LA 1263, 77 LA 1143, 74 LA 115, 72 LA 1275, 27 LA 510, 22 LA 498) Discharge also is regarded as warranted if the dozing involves any danger to the safety of employees or equipment. (81 LA 955, 76 LA 232, 76 LA 18, 73 LA 705, 26 LA 472, 21 LA 676, 20 LA 50)

Although discharge may be accepted as a just penalty for sleeping on the job, the employer has a heavy burden of proving that the employee was in fact sleeping. Not only must the employer prove that the employee was actually asleep rather than just resting with his eyes closed, but he also must show that the company's rule against sleeping was applied fairly and consistently. (95 LA 452, 91 LA 30, 90 LA 1053, 88 LA 991, 64 LA 77, 61 LA 686, 27 LA 512, 27 LA 137, 19 LA 380, 14 LA 907)

─────────── **GUIDELINES** ───────────

Penalty for Sleeping

Generally arbitrators have held that where management has strictly enforced no-sleeping rule, the discharge of a worker for violating it is fully justified in principle. In the absence of a specific rule, awards indicate that arbitrators consider the degree of responsibility of the worker's job and the circumstances under which he was found asleep in deciding what penalty is proper.

EXAMPLE: In the opinion of one arbitrator, sleeping-on-the-job cases fall into three categories: (1) the worker who is ill or tired for a good reason and who drops off involuntarily while trying to work; (2) the worker who has been out whooping it up while off duty and who yields to the need for sleep during working hours; and, (3) the worker who makes preparations, hides out, and goes to sleep as a regular practice. Employees in the last group deserve the severest discipline, the arbitrator advised.

In this case a maintenance man was found asleep on a blanket in a remote section of the plant with his shoes off and an alarm clock set to wake him just before the end of his shift. His preparations for sleeping, together with the fact he had been moonlighting, suggested to the arbitrator that sacking out on company time was a habit with him. The arbitrator concluded that his conduct put him into the third class of offenders and that the company was within its rights in firing him. (Collins Radio, Co., 30 LA 121)

On the other hand, an arbitrator decided that discharge was too severe a penalty for a worker who wasn't feeling well and was found sleeping when no work was available. The arbitrator distinguished between this instance and that of sleeping while an unattended machine was running, and thus reduced the penalty. (Nestle Co. 45 LA 524; see also 94 LA 340)

Sleeping During Break

Can a worker be disciplined for sleeping during lunch breaks or rest periods? The answer to this question may depend on whether the worker took steps to make sure that he would wake up before the break was over. In one instance where an employee took such measures and had good intentions, his discharge was overruled.

EXAMPLE: An employee usually ate at his work station, but on a day when he had a headache, he told his group leader he was going to lie down in the rest room and asked the leader to come and get him in 15 to 20 minutes. After about 15 minutes, a foreman discovered him, and he was fired for sleeping on the job with intent to deceive.

In light of all of the circumstances, an arbitrator decided the employee should be reinstated with back pay. Since he told the group leader where he was going, he obviously wasn't trying to hide anything. Moreover, he was entitled to a break and hadn't been away from the job more than the permissible length of time. Finally, his machine was not in operation when he left it so there was no risk of damage to the company's products. (Kawneer Co., 30 LA 1002)

However, where the circumstances showed that a worker might have remained asleep throughout the rest of his shift, an arbitrator upheld the disciplinary action.

EXAMPLE: Employees in the packing department at one company were allowed two break periods each shift. The breaks were taken without immediate supervision, and the company and union had agreed that employees were on the "honor system." When a foreman caught two employees lying down and asleep during a break, they were fired.

An arbitrator okayed the discharges. The employees, he pointed out, had deliberately placed themselves in a position conducive to sleep. If this sort of conduct were allowed, he commented, the entire department, in the absence of supervision, might go to sleep during a break and remain asleep indefinitely. (Phillips Chemical Co., 22 LA 498)

Proof of Sleeping on Job

Can a worker be disciplined for sleeping on the job merely on the basis of impressions someone gets by observing him from a distance? Most arbitrators agree that there must be convincing evidence that the worker was asleep. (83 LA 468, 81 LA 1009)

EXAMPLE: A worker had begun his assignment of holding the brake of an overhead crane during a grinding operation when a foreman and several other people walked up. Seeing the worker's head nodding and his eyes shut, the group concluded he was sleeping. Although the worker's foreman arrived 10 minutes after the grinding began and found the worker awake, the company dished out a two-week suspension. The worker admitted he had been drowsy, but he said his eyes were shut only because they were smarting from the oil and brake fluid in the crane cab. The union contended that from the 25- or 30-foot distance from which the worker was observed, no one could tell whether he as asleep.

The arbitrator felt that the worker could not have fallen completely asleep in the 10 minutes. Finding discipline unjustified, he said the witnesses only assumed the worker was asleep, since they were not close enough to be sure. (John Deere Ottumwa Works, 27 LA 572)

Similarly, a supervisor discovered an employee lying on a pile of plastic-covered bags on the roof of the plant, after the worker had been paged on a public address system twice without success. Although the worker explained that he was merely resting to relieve a toothache, he was nevertheless discharged for sleeping on the job.

In overturning the discharge, the arbitrator ruled that the burden of proof was not met by the company. Noting that the supervisor testified that the employee's eyes were open and he was lucid when he was found, the arbitrator concluded that, there was no evidence that the employee had actually prepared the "bed" on which he was resting, leaving in doubt the "premeditated" nature of his action. (Costal Resin Co. 61 LA 686; see also 71 LA 1041)

Mitigating Factors

In determining whether management's disciplinary penalty for sleeping on the job is warranted, arbitrators may consider mitigating factors including the employee's inadvertently or accidentally falling asleep, the employee's work record, or any medication or temporary physical discomfort which may have caused the worker to fall asleep. (95 LA 1006, 91 LA 443, 86 LA 1096, 81 LA 1200, 77 LA 1200, 76 LA 643)

EXAMPLE: An employee was discharged for sleeping on the job and for verbally abusing a supervisor who tried to awaken him. The employee thought the supervisor was a lower-level employee. However, after learning the identity of the supervisor the worker apologized for his behavior.

Finding that the employee's conduct caused no harm and that he did not realize that he was insulting a supervisor, the arbitrator ruled that the employee's work record and lack of prior disciplinary action were sufficient reasons to warrant reinstatement. (Union Carbide Corp., 66 LA 702)

Similarly, an employee who had taken codeine for a toothache was hit in the genitals by a valve arm he was polishing, and knocked to the floor. To relieve the pain, the worker laid down across some packing boxes in a corner of the shop. He was soon approached by a foreman who suspended him for sleeping on the job. The worker was later discharged.

In reversing the discharge, the arbitrator found that the employer's contention that the lights had been turned off in order for the employee to escape detection was at best doubtful, if not false all together. The sleepless night the employee spent because of a toothache, prior to the incident, was considered a mitigating factor the arbitrator ruled, concluding that the foreman summarily suspended the worker without any investigation into his reasons for falling asleep. (Crown Cork and Seal Co., 64 LA 734)

On the other hand, an employer properly discharged an employee for sleeping on the job that was caused by his various medical problems, including obesity which resulted from his bad eating habits, an arbitrator decided, despite the fact that the worker did not intentionally go to asleep to avoid working. Noting that the presence of an employee who is asleep at work is not conducive to an employer's public image, the arbitrator pointed out that a company had the right to expect the employee to present himself fit for work. Finding that the employer attempted rehabilitative measures, and progressive discipline to correct the employee's behavior, the arbitrator concluded that under the circumstances discharge was warranted. (City of Iowa City (72 LA 1006)

Last-chance agreement — An employee found sleeping on duty was properly discharged, an arbiter ruled, despite the fact that his "Weingarten rights" were violated, since he had signed a last-chance agreement stating that next incident of sleeping on the job would result in his discharge. (Maui Pineapple Co., 86 LA 907)

Penalty for Loafing

Is discharge too severe a penalty for the first offense of loafing on the job? Although management may feel that once a worker is found guilty of loafing he has lost his value as an employee, an arbitrator may reduce a discharge penalty and give the loafer another chance.

EXAMPLE: A company's charges against the employee were that he loafed on the job and as a result of his loafing, his work area was not cleaned properly, and he neglected to tend to a bin which ran over and caused loss to the company. Management stated that it had previously realized that he was deficient in his duties and had reinstructed him. When he failed again he was discharged.

The employee was ordered reinstated with back wages, less two weeks' pay for a disciplinary layoff. The arbiter found that the company had reinstructed the employee in his duties but had not specifically warned him at the time of the reinstruction, as was customary. The arbiter also found that the irregularities complained of were no greater than those of other employees who had been reprimanded or laid off but not discharged. (International Minerals & Chemical Corp., 4 LA 127)

Strike-Related Activities

IN BRIEF

Work stoppages may present a wide range of disciplinary situations, including:

▶ Illegal job actions, such as contractually prohibited slowdowns or wildcat strikes. In such circumstances, discipline is warranted by the sole fact of the walkout or slowdown, and may be applied either to all participants or only to those responsible for initiating or prolonging the action. (97 LA 1006, 96 LA 294, 93 LA 1097, 90 LA 24, 89 LA 1226, 89 LA 1257, 89 LA 880, 89 LA 227, 87 LA 188, 86 LA 622, 85 LA 1017, 85 LA 692, 84 LA 185, 83 LA 552, 82 LA 226, 81 LA 183, 81 LA 179)

▶ Offenses committed during an authorized strike. Although discipline may not be invoked for a legal work stoppage, any misconduct that occurs during the walkout — e.g., picket-line misconduct — is grounds for punishment, provided that there is concrete evidence to support the charges and absent any mitigating factors. (94 LA 929, 90 LA 969, 90 LA 502, 89 LA 126, 87 LA 394, 87 LA 188, 87 LA 103, 87 LA 99, 84 LA 919, 84 LA 367, 83 LA 608, 83 LA 501, 83 LA 487, 83 LA 327, 81 LA 1977, 81 LA 969)

▶ Misconduct following a settlement. Hostility engendered during a strike may continue after the return to work, most frequently in the form of intimidating behavior toward strike breakers. While agreeing that such misconduct justifies discipline, many arbiters hold that a lesser punishment than would be exacted for similar behavior under "normal" circumstances is most appropriate, given that "human emotions do not always respond to command."

The following discussion examines in greater detail how arbiters view these types of situations and the factors they consider in weighing discipline imposed for strike activities.

GUIDELINES

Illegal Work Stoppages & Slowdowns

In cases of work slowdowns, arbiters tend to uphold discipline even though, as one arbiter noted, the employer may not be able to present "direct evidence and proof of concerted activity." In such situations, the arbiter stressed, "the employer is required only to establish a prima facie case based on circumstantial evidence which would lead the reasonable person to conclude that the employees' action were more probably concerted." At that point, "the burden of coming forward with evidence to rebut such prima facie presumption shifts to each employee because each employee would be best able to produce substantiating or corroborating evidence to support any contrary contention."

In the case at hand, the arbiter decided that management had established a probable case for its allegations that a group of 21 employees was involved in an illegal work stoppage when none of the workers could provide any alternative explanation for failing to report in on the day in question. Accordingly, he concluded, the employer was justified in issuing disciplinary layoffs. (Longview Fibre Co., 69 LA 1182; see also 48 LA 949, 4 LA 744)

EXAMPLE: Three-day suspensions were appropriately levied against employees who engaged in a group "sickout," another arbiter held, precisely because the workers could not support their claims of illness with medical certificates. Although the employees argued that doctors' statements properly were required only in case of an extended illness, the arbiter ruled that management was within its rights to demand the documentation —and impose discipline for lack thereof—since it legitimately suspected the workers of "abusing the sick leave privilege." (Barbers Point Federal Credit Union, 76 LA 624)

EXAMPLE: A worker was properly discharged for limiting her production, an arbiter decided, finding that her work record and working conditions indicated that the decline in production was due to a "deliberate slowdown." Stressing that management had imposed the ultimate penalty of discharge only as a last step in a series of progressive disciplinary measures, the arbiter rejected the worker's claim that her 33 years of service militated against discharge. Although agreeing that usually "long service with a good record weighs heavily in favor of an embattled employee, "the arbiter concluded that, nonetheless, "no union, company, or arbiter can always and forever shield an employee from a contractual result of an act of pure folly in a context where the ultimate result was known or should have been known to the individual employee." (Martinsburg Mills Inc., 48 LA 1224)

However, long service has led other arbiters to overturn discharge for work slowdowns. For example, citing the worker's long record of satisfactory performance, one arbiter converted a dismissal for a deliberate slowdown to a four-week layoff. (Reed Roller Bit Co., 29 LA 604; see also Armour & Co. 8 LA 1)

Honoring a picket line also may be grounds for discipline where such action leads to a violation of contract provisions banning interference with work performance or operations.

EXAMPLE: Based on the no-strike clause of its collective bargaining agreement, an employer was justified in suspending workers who refused to cross another union's peaceful picket line to perform their work duties, an arbiter decided. Although the employees argued that the no-strike agreement did not apply here, the arbiter ruled that their refusal to perform their duties was, in fact, a work stoppage in violation of the contract provision, which specifically stated that there would be "no strike, work stoppage, slowdown, or any other interference with or impeding of work." By agreeing to this provision, the employees had waived their statutory rights to refuse to cross a picket line, the arbiter found, concluding that their actions warranted two-day suspensions. (Monongahela Power Co., 64 LA 1210)

Similarly, another arbiter held that management properly disciplined its inspectors for reporting late to their assignments because they had honored an informational picket line. The parties' bargaining agreement specified that employees were "responsible for not taking sides or personally becoming involved in an industrial dispute between the management and the employees of the official establishment or plant to which they are assigned." Rather, in such cases they were to report to work "as scheduled" unless "otherwise directed by their supervisor."

There was "no question" that the employees were aware of both the contract provision and their assignments, yet "voluntarily" chose to honor the picket line and thus report late, the arbiter declared, finding the employees "guilty as charged." As for the propriety of the discipline, the penalty imposed was a oneday suspension for "failure to follow instruction to report as scheduled," the arbiter noted, stressing that "had the agency so desired, the charge could have been that of engaging in an illegal activity—a strike—with the statutory penalty of discharge." When "weighed against the offense committed," the arbiter concluded, "the penalty is not too severe." (U.S. Dept. of Agriculture, 75 LA 36)

However, despite the existence of a no-strike/no-slowdown agreement, an arbiter reinstated a worker discharged for honoring a picket line set up by another union at the worksite. The controlling factor in this case was a second contract provision that barred disciplinary action against an employee who "refuses to go through or work behind any primary picket line, including primary picket lines at the company's place of business." Finding that the picket line was an extension of one set up at the company's wholly owned subsidiary and thus was properly classified as a "primary" line, the arbiter ruled that the employee's actions were protected from reprisal. (Coca Cola Bottling Co., 72 LA 73; see also 89 LA 1227, 84 LA 5, 72 LA 706, 69 LA 1024)

Wildcat strikes are grounds for severe discipline, arbiters overwhelmingly agree, absent any indication that the workers were prevented from reporting to the job through "duress, coercion, intimidation, or the like." Declaring that "willing participation in a work stoppage is among the most heinous of industrial offenses," on arbiter stressed that dismissal in such circumstances would not be "too severe" a penalty or one that would "shock the conscience of an arbiter." Accordingly, that arbiter ruled that management was justified in dismissing 132 workers who refused to end a wildcat strike in the face of union officials' instruction to return to the job. Finding no evidence that any of the employees were prevented from showing up for work, the arbiter concluded that each thus was "an employee responsible" for the unauthorized strike as defined under the contract and appropriately subject to the agreement's provision authorizing discharge for illegal work stoppages. (American Air Filter Co., 47 LA 129)

For practical purposes, however, most employers do not go to the extreme of discharging all wildcat strikers. As one arbiter explained, "a company that is the victim of an illegal strike cannot be expected to 'cut off its nose to spite its face' by firing all participants." (Charles Mundt Sons, 46 LA 982) Consequently, most arbitration cases dealing with wildcat strikes involve selective discipline, with the issue under debate the question of whether management properly could and did apply discipline to only certain of the strikers or whether in doing so it acted in an arbitrary, capricious, or discriminatory manner. Especially where the employer has selectively applied the discharge penalty, some arbiters may require clear proof that the workers thus disciplined deserved being singled out because they were either instigators of the illegal activity or at least more active in it than other employees. Absent such evidence, the dismissals may be overturned. (67 LA 1250, 61 LA 148, 28 LA 121, 27 LA 321, 24 LA 761)

Other arbiters do not set such strict parameters and will uphold the propriety of selective discipline under a wider range of circumstances. (93 LA 1097, 77 LA 505, 66 LA 626, 63 LA 677, 61 LA 896, 55 LA 1159, 53 LA 75, 53 LA 45, 52 LA 1047, 40 LA 1209, 35 LA 590) "No agreement provision and no obligation to justice compels the company to discipline in every case of employee misconduct," an arbiter declared. "Inequality of treatment in disciplinary matters does not amount to unjust discrimination if there are rational grounds for distinguishing between those to be disciplined and those not to be disciplined," the arbiter maintained, stressing that "it is only where the grounds for distinction are irrational, arbitrary, or whimsical that disciplining of some employees and not others may be looked upon as unjust and discriminatory." (Ford Motor Co., 41 LA 609)

EXAMPLE: Management properly charged all wildcat strikers with five absences each under its absence control program, regardless of the actual amount of time an individual worker spent off the job and despite the union's contention that disciplinary measures should be governed by the parties' no-strike agreement rather than the absenteeism program. Both the "literal application of the terms" of the absentee policy and a strict assessment of discipline for violating the no-strike clause "would have resulted in the termination of the majority" of its employees, management pointed out, with the result that the organization would have suffered the "same detrimental effect on production as the unauthorized work stoppage itself."

Finding it a "fundamental prerogative of management to select the form and extent of disciplinary action as long as it is not specifically restricted from doing so by the agreement, as long as cause is demonstrated, and as long as equal treatment is accorded," the arbiter agreed with the employer that it had "discretion to apply the absentee policy as it chooses in the context of a wildcat strike, whether the application be literal, something less stringent than literal application, or no application at all." (Kennecott Copper Corp., 77 LA 505)

However, in another case, management erred in discharging four of 26 wildcat strikers. Although acknowledging the employer's right of discretionary punishment in such cases, the arbiter pointed out that the discipline should be applied to a "representative group" rather than being levied in a completely arbitrary manner. If the company had conducted a thorough investigation, the arbiter noted, it would have found that other employees had greater responsibility for the walkout and were more deserving of discipline. (Homer Laughlin China Co., 67 LA 1250)

Use of Selective Discipline

Instigation of the work stoppage or slowdown, as is noted above, generally is regarded as one justification for the application of selective discipline.

EXAMPLE: Holding that the initiators of a walkout bear a heavier responsibility for the misconduct than other strikers, an arbiter sustained management's move to suspend only the first employees to leave work. The arbiter found that the selective discipline was further justified in that the company could not have given all 800 workers disciplinary layoffs without shutting down the plant. (Goodyear Atomic Corp., 27 LA 321)

EXAMPLE: Three employees were properly discharged for attempting to prevent co-workers for reporting to the job and inciting a wildcat strike to protest what they considered to be prior unjust discipline, an arbiter ruled. Rejecting the employees' contention that the stoppage was justified since management had failed to respond to their legitimate grievances, the arbiter upheld the employer's argument that the workers had flagrantly violated the contract. Stressing that one of the most serious and disruptive acts an employee can perform is to lead a wildcat strike, the arbiter concluded that in inciting the illegal activity, the workers knew they had embarked on a dangerous course of action. (National Mine Service Co., 69 LA 966; see also Warner & Swasey Co., 65 LA 709)

Similarly, another arbiter ruled that a worker was properly dismissed for causing an unauthorized work stoppage following a dispute with his supervisor. Any disagreement "with company policy or the actions of his supervisors" should have been pursued "through the grievance procedure," the arbiter ruled, declaring that an employee who "disregards the contractual dispute settlement mechanisms and engages in self-help subverts the fundamental nature of the collective bargaining relationship." Since the worker "knowingly caused a work stoppage" in violation of the contract, the arbiter concluded, the discharge was warranted. (Traverse City Iron Works, 76 LA 21)

However, an arbiter reinstated five workers who were discharged for organizing an illegal strike since the contract's no-strike clause failed to specify, and management had not warned them, that they could be dismissed for their actions. Besides failing to make clear the range of discipline possible, management officials "stood or sat idly by while employees around them argued about walking out" and some supervisors even "actively encouraged the walkout." (Superior Switchboard & Devices Division, 75 LA 1107; see also 96 LA 294)

EXAMPLE: Where the evidence did not support management's allegations that an employee had attempted to incite a walkout, an arbiter ordered the worker's reinstatement. Not only was the crewman who made the accusations an unreliable witness, the arbiter pointed out, but also there were no signs of job desertion to corroborate the story. (Payne & Keller Inc., 70 LA 114; see also 55 LA 548, 28 LA 121)

Union leadership also may be a basis for selective discipline in cases where union officials have not carried out their responsibility of promoting adherence to a contract's no-strike/no-slowdown clause. Arbiters consistently have held union leaders to a higher standard of responsibility than the rank-and-file in such cases. "A shop steward's duty in the face of an unauthorized work stoppage is well settled," an arbiter declared, explaining that "not only should he make a determined effort to prevent the stoppage before it begins, but upon its development must actively and unequivocally attempt to bring an end of the stoppage at the earliest possible moment." "Only in this way," the arbiter asserted, "can the steward comply with his responsibility to uphold the integrity of the contract and its orderly processes for dispute settlement." (United Parcel Service Inc., 47 LA 1100)

Other arbiters similarly have stressed that union officials have "an especial obligation to refrain from committing overt acts designed to encourage others to walk out or stay out." Pointing out that such officials have been "chosen to be custodians of the agreement, guardians of its rights, and monitors of its obligations within the prescribed procedures," one arbiter concluded that "hence, if they engage in overt acts which flout the agreement's most solemn obligations, they engage in a specific class of acts which set them apart from the rank and file." (Mack Trucks, 41 LA 1240; see also 14 LA 986, 4 LA 744)

EXAMPLE: Declaring that union officials "must give more than 'lip service' to their obligation" to prevent illegal work stoppages, an arbiter ruled that an employer properly imposed more severe discipline on union delegates than on rank-and-file workers for participating in a stoppage. The contract specified that "in the event of an unauthorized slowdown, boycott of overtime, or any other form of strike," union officials were to "immediately notify participating employees that the conduct is in violation of the agreement" and "instruct participating members to resume normal operations at once." Nevertheless, the arbiter found, the union delegates not only failed to honor this pledge but even went so far as to encourage the members in their "recalcitrancy" by actively taking part in the stoppage. Rejecting the delegates' contention that complying with the contract provision would have meant acting "as double agents," the arbiter pointed out that one "can't have his cake and eat it too." "Having accepted the honor of the titled delegate position and the accompanying leadership," the arbiter concluded, the officials "must accept the responsibilities of the position." (New Jersey Bell Telephone Co., 77 LA 1038; see also 68 LA 618, 49 LA 27, 43 LA 608, 41 LA 732)

However, where union officials have attempted to prevent or halt a work stoppage without success or where they are not contractually bound to take such affirmative action, arbiters have overturned discipline selectively levied against them. (64 LA 1210, 64 LA 425, 55 LA 1159, 29 LA 644, 8 LA 758, 7 LA 183)

EXAMPLE: An employer improperly suspended a union steward for demonstrating "negative leadership" by standing outside the plant gate rather than reporting for work during an illegal job action, an arbiter decided. Although the steward came to the plant on all three days of the illegal strike, he went home after being unable to get through the blocked entrance, the arbiter found. Observing that the steward had not carried a picket sign and had never before been disciplined during his eight years of employment, much less involved in an illegal strike, the arbiter concluded that the charges against him were "arbitrary and unjust." (Powermatic/Houdaille Inc., 65 LA 1245)

EXAMPLE: A union official who eventually tried to halt a wildcat strike was improperly discharged, an arbiter decided. However, in light of the official's initial participation in the illegal action, the arbiter decided, a one-year probation was in order. (Cyclops Corp., 45 LA 560; see also Quanex, 73 LA 9)

Misconduct During Legal Strikes

Even where a work stoppage is lawful, employees may be justifiably disciplined for misconduct committed in association with the strike. Recognizing that the term "misconduct" covers a multitude of offenses, from taunting strikebreakers to assaulting supervisors, several arbiters have outlined general criteria by which the propriety of discipline may be judged. In addition to deciding whether the evidence is sufficient to support the allegations, arbiters will pose such questions as:

● "What is the extent of participation? In any mob situation the degree of involvement of the individual in any action is important."

● "What was the nature of the violence? This has both quantitative and qualitative aspects. Participation in several incidents is more serious than in only one. Some actions are more reprehensible than others. Shouting insults and shoving are of a different order from striking a person."

● "Was the violence provoked? To the extent that the violence is retaliatory and defensive, it is less culpable than if undertaken as an act of aggression."

● "Was the violence premeditated or undertaken on the spur of the moment? Premeditated violence is the more inexcusable."

● "What will be the impact of the punishment? Discharge is more of a penalty for an old man than a young one; for a long service employee than a short service employee."

● "Was the disciplinary action discriminatory? A company is under some obligation to treat persons similarly situated in a comparable, although not necessarily identical, manner. Violence can hardly be said to be the real basis for discharge if other unjustifiable factors enter in." (Cudahy Packing Co., 11 LA 1138; see also Swift & Co., 12 LA 108)

Expanding on these guidelines, another arbiter has determined that reviews of strike misconduct also should be influenced by the following considerations:

● "How serious was the offense in terms of injury to persons or damage to property?"

● "Were remedies at law available and were they involved?"

● "Was the conduct destructive of good employee-employer relations?"

● "Was the conduct destructive of good community relations?"

- "Will the discipline restore good relations, or is it the result of a spirit of vindictiveness?"
- "Was the conduct such that the employee could be reabsorbed into the work force?" (J.R. Simplot Co., 64 LA 1061)

EXAMPLE: A striking employee who verbally and physically abused a supervisor at a local social club was justifiably discharged, an arbiter ruled. The employee's behavior was particularly blameworthy in that the incident occurred away from the picket line and thus was not the result of "inflamed group passions," the arbiter found. Reinstating the worker in the face of the damage to the employer-employee relationship, the arbiter concluded, would be a "visible and highly public vindication" of the abusive behavior. (General Telephone Co. of Kentucky, 69 LA 351; see also 92 LA 578)

Likewise, an employer was justified in discharging a picketing striker for "streaking," mooning," and using racial slurs against replacements, under a strike settlement agreement authorizing dismissal only for picket line misconduct "that would be considered serious under normal working conditions." The arbiter rejected the worker's arguments that, even if he were guilty of the allegations, such behavior was not so serious as to warrant discharge. Rather, finding that "any one of these three actions would constitute misconduct if engaged in within a plant operating normally," the arbiter specified that "any would create a major disturbance, interrupt production, upset plant discipline, and bring opprobrium to the company." Furthermore, while the use of racial epithets alone "might or might not be considered serious enough to warrant immediate discharge within a plant," the arbiter stressed, "occurring on a picket line such language can only be calculated to injure the company, its standing in the community, and to reflect discredit upon the public relations image of the company and union alike." (H & L Tooth Co., 66 LA 1020).

However, a striking employee was improperly discharged for tire-slashing, since management failed to "continue and complete a comprehensive investigation of the matter sufficient to establish the employee's culpability." The "circumstantial" evidence, while suggesting that the worker may have been responsible for the damage, did not meet the "burden of proof" standard for upholding the dismissal, the arbiter concluded. (Collins Foods International Inc., 77 LA 483; see also McDonnell Douglas Astronautics Co., 74 LA 726)

Mitigating factors also may lead an arbiter to reinstate a worker discharged for picket line misconduct.

EXAMPLE: Citing a "satisfactory" work history, one arbiter reduced to a six-month suspension the termination penalty levied against a worker for throwing ball bearings through the window of a guard house during a strike. Furthermore, although the company argued that the employee was a "rabble rouser" whose return to the work force could "create the possibility of discord and hostility rather than enhance a peaceful, working relationship," the arbiter found no evidence "of prior acts of hostility toward the company nor damage to company property that would tend to justify the apprehension of the company were he to be reabsorbed into the work force." Management's "stated objective for the disciplinary action"—deterrence of future such incidents—could be better accomplished "by a lengthy suspension without pay and accompanied by a stern reprimand," the arbiter concluded (Charter International Oil Co., 75 LA 929).

Similarly, finding that the misconduct was not so "grave" as to prevent the employees' being "reabsorbed into the work force," an arbiter reduced to lengthy suspensions the discharges imposed on two employees for strike offenses. The first employee, who threatened a contractor performing work at a picket site, deserved a four-month disciplinary layoff, the arbiter decided, while the second, who kicked in the side panel of a company pick-up truck, warranted a five-month suspension. (General Telephone Co. of Kentucky, 69 LA 351)

Moreover, an employer that chooses to continue to operate its plant during a strike, regardless of the fact that such action historically invites violence, may not be justified in discharging employees for picket line misconduct, according to some arbiters. In two similar cases, arbiters reduced dismissals to disciplinary layoffs, based on the theory that a company that elects to "continue operations and engage replacements" during a strike "cannot escape a share of responsibility for the militancy and aggressiveness of the strikers." Violence usually occurs only when management decides to utilize strategies of replacing striking workers and/or deploying armed guards, one arbiter noted, deciding that by taking on the historical "inevitability" of violence in pursuing such options, an employer is guilty of "contributory negligence" that militates against outright dismissal for strike misconduct. (Washington Scientific Industries Inc., 67 LA 1004, and J.R. Simplot Co., 64 LA 1061)

Post-Strike Misconduct

"Strikes are not fought," one arbiter has pointed out, "without leaving a residue of bitterness and defeat, or arrogance and pride, in their participants." Frequently these emotions take shape in acts of misconduct directed by returning workers toward those individuals who crossed the picket line during the strike—management officials, outside suppliers, and, especially, new employees taken on as replacements. Particularly where returning strikers are warned against harboring grudges, arbiters are likely to agree that hostile behavior justifies disciplinary action.

However, unless the offense is of an extremely serious nature, arbiters generally will not sustain a discharge for post-strike misconduct, deciding, rather, that a disciplinary layoff is more appropriate punishment.

EXAMPLE: "By continuing its operations during a bitter and acrimonious strike, and settling on terms extremely disadvantageous to the union, the company encouraged hostility and bitterness among its employees, and cannot complain if, in the first 10 days following defeat, some of their anger spilled over, embarrassing several who supported it." With this assertion, an arbiter reduced to a disciplinary warning the discharge penalty management had levied against a flight attendant for spilling food and beverages on and refusing to utilize the services of other employees who had worked during a strike. Although scoring the attendant's "breach of professional courtesy of self-control," the arbiter declared that the slow process of building up post-strike cooperation "is not aided by humiliation, or by a unilateral imposition of terms and conditions of employment." The "spirit" of the back-to-work agreement, which "indicated an intention to forgive strike-related actions and restrict antagonisms to the past," should be applied here, the arbiter stressed, concluding that in the "absence of prior discipline, and given the nature of the circumstances," punishment should be "minor." (Continental Airlines, 77 LA 368)

Similarly, although "some form of discipline" was warranted, discharge was too severe for a returning striker who directed abusive language toward new hires taken on as strike replacements, another arbiter ruled. Upon returning from a six-month strike, the workers repeatedly referred to the new-hires as "scabs" and made threatening remarks to them. Management "counseled" the worker for his abusive language, but took no action until the employee arrived at work one day wearing a t-shirt with a caption that made obscene reference to the strike breakers. Citing this latest incident in an intimidating "course of conduct," the employer discharged the worker. The arbiter, however, reduced the penalty on the grounds that "'counseling' does not suffice for disciplinary action intended to correct the misconduct and apprise the employee of the seriousness of his actions." Absent explicit warning that discharge would result if the employee continued to intimidate the new hires, the arbiter concluded, suspension was a more appropriate discipline. (Chromalloy American Corp., 72 LA 838)

EXAMPLE: An employer was justified in disciplining an employee for making inflammatory remarks immediately following a strike, an arbiter decided. During the month-long work stoppage, the employer's trucks were operated by drivers from another company. On the day following strike settlement, one of the drivers was having difficulty starting a truck when an employee laughed and said he hoped the truck blew up. Later, management found that the truck would not start because the gas tank has been filled with water. Although there was no evidence connecting the worker to the sabotage, management issued him a five-day suspension for making a serious threat at a time when tension was still "high." Agreeing that the statement was indeed "inflammatory and threatening," the arbiter pointed out that in making such comments on the first day back at work, the employee naturally stirred up the driver's concern and apprehension. However, while the comment was "further magnified by the fact that an act of sabotage had taken place," the arbiter continued, the worker should be disciplined only for the totality of his "actual involvement" in the post-strike misconduct. Ruling that the five-day suspension was excessive in light of the just cause standard, the arbiter ordered that the discipline be reduced to a two-day layoff. (Emery Industries Inc., 72 LA 110)

EXAMPLE: Five employees who engaged in post-strike staring tactics against replacement workers were properly suspended, an arbiter decided, since the employees had been sufficiently warned about and directed to stop the harassment. (La Crosse Telephone Corp., 65 LA 1077)

Sexual Harassment

IN BRIEF

Arbiters considering cases of discipline for sexual harassment must determine: (1) whether the employee's misconduct actually was sexual harassment, and (2) whether the discipline imposed was appropriate.

In making the first determination, many arbiters rely on the Equal Employment Opportunity Commission's *Guidelines on Sexual Harassment*, which define sexual harassment as encompassing "unwelcome sexual advances, requests for sexual favors, and other verbal or physical conduct of a sexual nature" that have the "purpose or effect of unreasonably interfering with an individual's work performance or creating an intimidating, hostile, or offensive working environment."

In addition, sexual harassment may also be found when submission to the advances or requests is "a term or condition of an individual's employment." It is not necessary, however, that the object of the harassment be a subordinate of the harasser; harassment of co-workers, including the creation of a "hostile" environment, is also sexual harassment, as is harassment of clients or customers of the employer.

If an employee's conduct were, indeed, sexual harassment, the arbiter must then decide whether the discipline was justified. To make this determination, arbiters may consider whether:

▶ the victim's testimony was credible;
▶ the incident was reported to management;
▶ the harassment interfered with the victim's job performance or adversely affected the employer's operations;
▶ the behavior created an intimidating, hostile, or offensive working environment;
▶ the victim suffered any diminution in job status because of a refusal to submit to or tolerate the sexual overtures.

Collective bargaining contracts protect employees through work rules against sexual harassment in the form of anti-discrimination clauses.

Arbitration of sexual-harassment issues generally arises from grievances challenging the discharge or discipline of an employee for misconduct based in whole or in part on alleged sexual harassment of another employee rather than complaints of alleged victims of such harassment.

SEXUAL HARASSMENT

---- GUIDELINES ----

Types of Harassment

Sexual harassment constitutes a form of sexual discrimination under Title VII of the Civil Rights Act of 1964. The EEOC and the federal courts have recognized two distinct types of sexual harassment — (1) "quid-pro-quo"; and (2) "hostile-environment" harassment. "Quid-pro-quo" occurs when an aspect of a person's job is conditioned on his or her acceptance of the sexual advances or conduct of another employee (usually a manager or supervisor). Hostile-environment harassment occurs when an employee is subjected to a pattern of unwelcome, sexually-related conduct in the workplace that creates a hostile, intimidating, or offensive work environment. Arbiters have found these actions to be sexual harassment: sexual threats, insults, or innuendo; inappropriate comments; sexual gestures; and unwelcome physical touching.

EXAMPLE: A male supervisor was properly discharged for sexual harassment, an arbiter decided, because he put his arm around the waist of one woman; told another that she was attractive while looking at her and smacking his lips; spoke of sex and virginity to another; brushed an employee's uniform in the chest area and stroked her hair; and cast penetrating looks at another worker that made her feel as though she were "undressed." Although the supervisor contended that his actions were "nothing more than the expression of the freer American lifestyle," and that sexual receptivity was not imposed as a "condition" for job retention, promotion, or more desirable working conditions, the arbiter ruled that the supervisor's conduct had produced "stress and anxiety" among the female employees, which interfered with their mental health and ability to perform their jobs, the arbiter found, so the discharge was just. (University of Missouri, 78 LA 417)

EXAMPLE: An instructor who "inappropriately" touched six female students in his training class was properly suspended for five days, another arbiter ruled. Despite the worker's denial of the accusations, the arbiter pointed out that there was a "similarity" and a "ring of truth" to the statements and no evidence that the women had "conspired to 'frame'" the instructor. Emphasizing that "sexual harassment should not be tolerated anyplace," the arbiter stressed that the employer would have been "negligent in its obligations" if it had not taken action. (United States Army Signal Center, 78 LA 120)

Seriousness of Offense/Proper Discipline

One arbiter developed five criteria for determining the seriousness of the sexual harassment:

● Did the employer have a sexual harassment policy in place when the incident occurred? Was it written? Was it specific enough to make employees understand what constitutes sexual harassment, and what the consequences of infractions of this policy would be? Was the sexual harassment policy adequately disseminated to employees?

● Does the employer have an effective vehicle for employees to bring sexual-harassment complaints to the attention of management? Is the work environment such that it discourages employees from making formal or informal complaints?

● Did management know, or should it have known, of the sexual harassment practice(s) that occurred?

● Was the sexual harassment committed by the employee's supervisor on whom the employee was dependent for employment, work assignment, promotion, performance evaluation, and/or salary increases?

● What is the personal relationship between the person accused of harassment and the person(s) considered to be the "victims"?

Relevance of Past Sexual Harassment

A unique problem that has arisen involves whether evidence of past sexual harassment offenses by the alleged harasser should be relevant in arbitration of current sexual harassment cases. One arbiter considered it relevant to the extent that it established a pattern of conduct that was consistent with the accusations of the current sexual harassment victim (86 LA 254). However, in another case, an arbiter found that the employer had improperly considered prior incidents of alleged sexual harassment in deciding whether the employee was guilty of current charges (86 LA 681).

Further, an arbiter ruled that a worker was improperly suspended for allegedly filing a false sexual harassment claim against a co-employee. The arbiter said that although the alleged victim (who previously had been raped) may have exaggerated one claim and incorrectly stated a second, she had not done so intentionally intending to deceive or defraud (92 LA 653).

When Discipline is Justified

Many arbiters, relying on the EEOC guidelines to determine whether misconduct was sexual harassment, have upheld an employer's disciplinary action against the harassing employee. For example, discharge has been sustained where:

• The employee's harassment created an intimidating, hostile, and offensive working environment. (88 LA 791, and violated EEOC guidelines on sexual harassment; 89 LA 27, by writing "obscene" comments on a magazine; 94 LA 289);

• The employee adversely impacted production with repeated obscene gestures and comments to female co-workers (93 LA 721);

• The employee's profanity impacted the employer's public image (93 LA 25);

• The employee engaged in persistent and continued sexual advances that created an offensive working environment and interfered with job performance by causing co-workers to lose work time (62 LA 1272, 82 LA 921, 84 LA 915, 97 LA 957);

• The employee knowingly violated a company policy that clearly did not tolerate sexual harassment (82 LA 640);

• The employee failed to respond to corrective discipline for obscene name-calling and gesturing (78 LA 985);

• The worker relentlessly harassed, through obscene gestures and demeaning slurs, a female peer who was twice the employee's age (78 LA 690);

• The employee's misconduct had negative emotional and physical effects that diminished the job performance of the victimized co-worker (78 LA 417, 86 LA 1253);

• The worker, whose record reflected prior incidents involving physical touching, threatened to rape a co-worker (74 LA 1281, 75 LA 592).

Similarly, arbiters have upheld the lesser penalties imposed by employers where the misconduct has involved touching a female co-worker (80 LA 133, 81 LA 459) or physical restraint (75 LA 592).

Following are details of specific cases of sexual harassment in which arbiters have upheld the employer's penalty for the misconduct.

EXAMPLE: An employee was properly discharged for threatening to rape a female co-worker, an arbiter concluded, even though the employee contended that his co-worker had invented the rape threat because of an argument between the two. It is not "realistic to suppose that accusations of that kind are lightly made," the arbiter said. "Such accusations may be taken to reflect adversely on the accuser as well as the accused, and are inevitably embarrassing," the arbiter stressed, finding that the woman's testimony "should be credited." (St. Regis Paper Co., 74 LA 1281)

EXAMPLE: Discharge was proper for an employee who admitted that on two successive days he made improper advances to female co-workers in an elevator, an arbiter said. Noting that the worker had persisted in harassing one woman even after she had told him to stop, the arbiter ruled that "such conduct cannot be tolerated and is a matter which calls for severe discipline." (CPC International Inc., 62 LA 1272)

EXAMPLE: A female employee who wrote anonymous letters to a co-worker and the co-worker's husband was properly discharged, an arbiter concluded. The letters, which accused the co-worker of sexual misconduct with her supervisor, were examined by a handwriting expert, who definitely established that the employee wrote them. The employee was "incontestably guilty" of harassment that was calculated to "bring disrepute" to the co-worker and "create domestic disharmony," as well as "a psychologically repressive work environment," the arbiter pointed out. While not "unmindful" of the employee's 32 years of service and exemplary record, the arbiter adds that it is not a mitigating factor in this case because the misconduct was not only "heinous," but "in most respects more serious than other forms of sexual harassment" prohibited by the employer. (Schlage Lock Co., 88 LA 75)

EXAMPLE: A 20-day suspension was appropriate for an employee who "bluntly solicited" a female co-worker, an arbiter ruled. The employee on several occasions, both on and off the job, told the co-worker that he wished to have oral sex with her. The co-worker did not respond to the employee's advances, would "hide" from the employee when he came to her work area, reported the incidents to her supervisor, and submitted a written statement to the employer detailing the misconduct. Management suspended the worker for "disruptive harassment" for his "unceasing efforts" to win the co-worker's submission. The arbiter concluded that the misconduct "interfered" with the co-worker's job performance, adding that the facts "established to a degree of certainty one rarely encounters" a hostile, abusive, and intimidating work environment. The employer had a legal obligation to take "immediate and appropriate corrective action," the arbiter pointed out, so the suspension was justified. (Veterans Administration Medical Center, 87 LA 405)

When Discipline is Reduced

In some cases, however, arbiters found misconduct constituting sexual harassment, but held that the penalty assessed by the employer was inappropriate because of mitigating factors or because the employer failed to investigate properly the harassment complaint, failed to give the employee adequate notice of the prohibition, or failed to give the employee a chance to defend him- or herself before the discipline was imposed.

Some of the mitigating factors calling for reduced discipline cited by arbiters include:

● seniority (80 LA 19);

● a good work record and the absence of past disciplinary problems (71 LA 54, 83 LA 571, 85 LA 11);

● evidence that the misconduct amounted to an isolated incident that is not likely to recur at any time in the future (79 LA 940);

● the harassing employee's attitude (85 LA 11);

● the harassed employee's attitude (75 LA 377, 81 LA 730, 83 LA 570, 88 LA 1292, 95 LA 1097);

● the quality of proof of the worker's guilt and the thoroughness of the employer's investigation ((82 LA 25, 86 LA 254, 86 LA 681);

● management's failure to address sexual harassment specifically in policies and procedures; to follow progressive discipline procedures; or to provide proper supervision to limit "shop talk," joking, teasing, or ridicule. (71 LA 54, 74 LA 875, 85 LA 11, 86 LA 1017, 88 LA 1292, 95 LA 510);

● the employer not having given the harassing employee adequate opportunity to defend him- or herself. (86 LA 681);

- the context in which the incident occurred. (83 LA 824); and,
- the nature and amount of horseplay, obscenity, etc. prevalent in a particular work environment (90 LA 783, 92 LA 1090, 94 LA 1217).

Specific cases in which arbiters have reduced the penalties imposed by employers include:

EXAMPLE: Discharge was reduced to a written notice of violation of an employer's policy against sexual harassment for a male employee who continued to send letters, flowers, and gifts to a female co-worker despite her protestations. The arbiter refused to apply the "reasonable woman standard" in determining whether there was just cause for discharge, holding that the arbiter's jurisdiction in limited to determining whether just cause exists under the terms of the collective bargaining agreement, unless the employer can establish that the arbitrator is also bound by public policy. Public policy does not mandate discharge for sexual harassment, the arbiter stated, it merely requires that the hostile work environment be eliminated. (KIAM, 97 LA 617)

EXAMPLE: Discharge was converted to a suspension for a male employee who made obscene gestures to a female co-worker. While agreeing that the employee's behavior constituted "distasteful conduct," the arbiter pointed out that had the co-worker reported the problem to management when it first arose, the employer could have issued a strong warning or taken other steps to put an end to the harassment. (Powermatic/Houdaille Inc., 71 LA 54)

EXAMPLE: Discharge was too severe a penalty for an employee who deliberately entered a ladies' rest room and told a female occupant that he "always wanted to know what it looked like," one arbiter concluded. Although the worker displayed "poor judgment," the arbiter said, the incident did not justify dismissal of an employee with 14 years' seniority, especially since there was "nothing immoral about the employee's conduct." (Perfection American Co., 73 LA 520)

EXAMPLE: Discharge was reduced to a seven-month suspension for an employee who allegedly pinched a female co-worker's breast while making a "kissing" sound. Although the worker denied harassing the female employee, the arbiter credited the woman's testimony, pointing out that she displayed no bias or bad feeling against the male employee. However, mitigating circumstances in the case, the arbiter said, included: the worker's 28 years of employment; his reasonably good work record with the employer; the absence of past disciplinary problems in the employee's record; and the female worker's failure to report the incident when it occurred. The arbiter warned, however, that the reduction in the penalty "should not be construed to lessen the seriousness of the conduct," nor be understood in any way to relieve the employer of its duty to protect employees from sexual harassment. (Dayton Power and Light Co., 80 LA 19)

EXAMPLE: Discharge was reduced to a three-month suspension for one employee, and a six-day suspension was reduced to three days for another, by an arbiter who found that the department involved was "a disruptive place to work largely because of poor supervision, leadership, and general discipline." Supervisors themselves participated in the teasing and ridicule which were rampant in the department, the arbiter noted, so the disciplined employees "are not alone in the problem," and "they cannot be held solely responsible." (New York Air Brake Co., 74 LA 875)

In some cases, arbiters have permitted no penalty at all.

EXAMPLE: Sexual harassment did not occur, an arbiter found, when an employee made a crude, joking remark to the only woman on his work crew. While the employer's efforts to prevent sexual harassment were "admirable," it "overreacted" in suspending the employee, the arbiter concluded. The discipline was inappropriate because: a similar remark was made to a male employee; the remark was not "hostile or intimidating;" the remark was addressed to the female employee "as a member of the crew;" and the woman took the remark as a joke. "The key here," the arbiter says, "is the intent" of the disciplined employee, and that intent was not to harass. (Louisville Gas & Electric Co., 81 LA 730, 93 LA 1204)

Employer's Burden of Proof

Some arbiters equate sexual-harassment disciplinary cases as any other disciplinary case involving misconduct, without specifically mentioning a burden of proof, appearing to require the employer to establish sexual harassment by a preponderance of the evidence. (82 LA 25, 84 LA 915, 86 LA 1253, 87 LA 405, 88 LA 1292)

However, other arbiters hold that an employer must prove that the disciplined employee engaged in sexual harassment by "clear and convincing evidence." (83 LA 824, 83 LA 828, 86 LA 1017, 86 LA 1020, 89 LA 76)

Still other arbiters require that an employer prove sexual harassment "beyond a reasonable doubt." (85 LA 11, 85 LA 15)

EXAMPLE: An arbiter justified his using the beyond-a-reasonable-doubt standard by saying that a charge of sexual harassment clearly involves an accusation of moral turpitude, carrying an enormous social stigma, and that it is not overly dramatic to say that in some cases an employee's life is on the line — a marriage, a parental relationship with children, a standing in a community, relationships with other employees, etc. And, further, once the employer has proved beyond a reasonable doubt that the employee is guilty of sexual harassment, the company must still establish that the discipline imposed is "just and sufficient." (King Soopers Inc., 86 LA 254)

Harassment of Non-Employees

Employees who harass customers or clients may be disciplined if the conduct adversely affects the employer's reputation and customer relations or damages the employee's effectiveness.

EXAMPLE: A telephone repair technician was properly discharged for making obscene and harassing telephone calls to a customer, an arbiter concluded, even though the employee was off-duty when the calls were made. Because of the nature of the company's business, and the need it has for public confidence in the integrity of its repair personnel, the arbiter concludes that the employer "would not be responsible to the public" if it permitted the employee, in light of his misconduct, "to enter upon the premises of a customer to provide telephone service." (Southern Bell Telephone & Telegraph Co., 75 LA 409)

EXAMPLE: A deliveryman was properly discharged for making "sexual propositions" to customers to whom he delivered the employer's product, an arbiter concluded. The deliveryman had been barred from making deliveries at several retail stores and had been subjected to progressive discipline. The misconduct harmed the company's reputation and interfered with its business, the arbiter pointed out, and had consequences for other employees. Because the deliveryman was barred from some stores, delivery route rotation was disrupted; other drivers complained of coolness from customers with whom they had always had good relations; and one driver was threatened by an outraged husband with a gun. "A delivery man is the company's representative," the arbiter pointed out, and "has a special duty to be courteous and honorable in his dealings with customers." (Nabisco Foods Co., 82 LA 1186)

Conflicting Testimony

Sexual harassment cases often require an arbiter to resolve conflicts in the testimony given by the alleged victim and the accused, and even within different statements made by the victim.

EXAMPLE: An arbiter upheld the suspension of a male worker accused of improperly touching a female employee, despite inconsistencies between the woman's oral and written accounts of the incident. Noting that the woman might have been so traumatized by the experience that her recollection of it was clouded, the arbiter ruled that the inconsistencies in her versions of what happened did not undermine the basic truthfulness of her charges. (Fisher Foods Inc., 80 LA 133)

EXAMPLE: An employee was properly discharged for embracing and kissing a co-worker, an arbiter concluded, even though there were no witnesses and the two employees told completely different stories. The arbiter found the disciplined employee "to be a thoroughly unbelievable witness," and thus accepted the victim's version of the incident. "Employees have the right to be safe from abusive actions and it is the duty and responsibility of the company to give them this protection and further, to discipline and even discharge those employees whose misconduct justifies such a penalty," the arbiter concluded. (Care Inns Inc., 81 LA 687)

Miscellaneous

IN BRIEF

Frequently, arbitrators are called upon to resolve disputes concerning minor forms of employee misconduct such as smoking on the job, or possessing firearms on company property, in violation of plant rules. Guidelines applied by arbitrators in deciding such cases are discussed below.

GUIDELINES

Violation of No-Smoking Rule

Arbitrators agree that a company has every right to set up a rule prohibiting smoking in order to protect its property and employees' lives against fire hazard and to comply with legal requirements. (Litton Industries, 75 LA 308) (See also "Safety and Health; Smoking Rules.")

EXAMPLE: A paint manufacturer properly discharged a batchmaker for smoking in a no-smoking area where numerous large containers of flammable solvents were stored, an arbitrator ruled. Pointing out that the employee was a member of the plant safety committee charged with the responsibility of preventing the action he had taken, and he admitted knowing that the area was a "no-smoking" zone and considered to be the most dangerous area in the plant, the arbitrator concluded that the worker was lawfully terminated with good cause for violating reasonable, posted company safety regulations. (USM Corp., 71 LA 954)

However where management has permitted violations of a no-smoking rule to go unpunished over a long period of time, most arbitrators hold that the sudden firing of a worker for smoking is not justified. These arbitrators feel that if a company decides to enforce the rule strictly it must make it clear to all hands. Until such announcement is made, workers may not be summarily discharged for breaking the rule, especially if the company knows that it was being broken for some time. (69 LA 930, 68 LA 687, 51 LA 97, 8 LA 782, 1 LA 350)

Additionally, arbitrators may not uphold discharge for no-smoking violations where there is insufficient proof of the employee's alleged misconduct. (Celanese Fibers Co., 70 LA 270)

Violation of No-Firearms Rule

Arbitrators generally agree that management has the right to forbid employees from possessing firearms on company property. (69 LA 1237, 63 LA 121, 63 LA 69, 56 LA 517, 53 LA 1028)

However, arbitrators may be unwilling to uphold an employer's disciplinary action against the employee who brings a gun into the plant where the company has not promulgated or posted rules prohibiting such conduct (69 LA 613, 64 LA 291); where a no-firearms rule has not been consistently enforced in the past (77 LA 845); or where there is insufficient evidence that the employee possessed a firearm. (77 LA 1018)

EXAMPLE: A truck driver, involved in an accident, was found to be carrying a loaded gun and subsequently was discharged. The arbitrator decided that discharge was not for just cause, as the company rule against gun-toting was never made clear to the workers or enforced. (American Synthetic Rubber Corp., 46 LA 1161; see also 43 LA 568)

Loan Sharking

Arbitrators, generally agree that the practice of loan-sharking is so undesirable that the offender can be fired without warning.

EXAMPLE: An employee with many years' service with a company decided to run a loan business on the side, netting a 10-15 percent profit per week. The employer discharged the worker for violating a rule against "shameful and indecent conduct." The union argued that the employee had not been properly warned.

The arbiter ruled that the employer discharge was justified regardless of whether the company rule actually applied to such a situation. Moreover, he decided that it was unnecessary to give a warning in such a case, stating that the evils of loan-sharking are too well known, and its adverse effect on employees too obvious to require that the usual disciplinary procedures be followed. (Glenn L. Martin Co., 27 LA 768)

Similarly, an employer properly discharged employees for making loans to co-workers and making collections on company time, in violation of a rule barring solicitation of funds or property during working hours, or on plant premises, without permission of the employer, an arbitrator ruled. The arbitrator rejected the employees' contentions that making loans was not cause for immediate discharge and that progressive discipline was not used, since the workers' activity was so conducive to disharmony and disruptions in plant operations. (Mobil Oil Co., 76 LA 585)

Political Activity on Company Property

In the absence of a definite written rule against it, can a worker be fired for carrying on political activity on company property? At least one arbiter has held that discharge was too severe for this kind of offense where most employees did not know that such activity was prohibited. (Four Wheel Drive Auto Co., 4 LA 170)

Similarly, an arbiter ruled that an employer improperly suspended an employee for off-duty campaigning for candidates for a board of trustees, where the employer's rule restricting employee participation in trustee elections to voting was not reasonably related to the board's objectives, had not been uniformly enforced, and had been applied disparately. However, in the same case, the arbiter held that the employer's discipline of the workers for off-duty campaigning did not violate the Taft Act, since the union had not instigated the employees' involvement in the campaign, and the activity — trying to effect change in management — was unprotected under the Taft Act. (Joe Wheeler Electric Membership Cooperative, 89 LA 51; see also 89 LA 1054)

Failure To Report Accident

A trucking company was justified in firing a driver for failing to report an accident involving the truck he was driving, an arbiter ruled. Under causes for immediate discharge, the contract listed "failure to report an accident which the employee would normally be aware of." The evidence established beyond a reasonable doubt that this condition was fulfilled. (Maislin Bros. Transport, Ltd., 46 LA 527)

SUBVERSIVE ACTIVITY

Distributing Communist Literature

Can a worker be discharged for distributing Communist literature on company property?

If a lesser penalty ordinarily is imposed for literature distribution without permission, an arbitrator may hold that discharge is improper. (Spokane-Idaho Mining Co., 9 LA 749)

Discharge for KKK Activities

Threats of violence, boycott, and a wildcat strike justified the discharge of a publicly avowed Ku Klux Klan leader in order to avoid turning the employer's buses into "a battleground in the civil rights movement," an arbitrator decided. He reasoned that the worker's conduct went beyond mere belief when he began preaching racial hatred and religious intolerance, and that this breached the worker's duty to foster friendly relations with the public. (Baltimore Transit Co., 47 LA 62)

Substance Abuse

INTRODUCTION

While drug and alcohol abuse were once simply considered personal problems, they have gained attention in recent years as important workplace concerns. Both employers and unions now realize that substance abuse can drive business operating costs up — substance abuse can cost employers hundreds of billions of dollars each year — and worker productivity down. By increasing absenteeism, tardiness, and accident rates, substance abuse can create strained relations between management and labor and among coworkers.

With management and labor increasingly concerned over substance-abuse problems, arbitrators frequently are called on to review policy and disciplinary decisions related to such abuse. Arbiters may be asked to decide whether employees actually have abused alcohol or drugs, whether the employer's response was appropriate, and whether mitigating circumstances existed that would justify more lenient treatment.

The following chapters outline some of the common problems and viewpoints found in substance-abuse arbitration cases, including:

▶ *Intoxication and alcoholism* — While management might consider an isolated incident of on-the-job intoxication and a pattern of missed workdays caused by alcoholism as equally serious offenses, arbiters may insist that such infractions call for different employer responses. The standards arbiters use in judging discipline levied against employees who possess or drink alcohol, or are intoxicated on the job, and the circumstances warranting a chance at rehabilitation rather than an immediate dismissal, are among the issues reviewed in this chapter.

▶ *Drug abuse* — While illegal drug use might be considered a less prevalent or costly workplace problem, many employers are concerned that it poses as serious a threat to safety and health as alcohol abuse. This chapter focuses on decisions involving such topics as drug-abuse policies, evidence of drug use, off-duty drug use, and arrest and conviction on drug charges.

▶ *Drug testing* — As businesses increasingly introduce or consider drug-testing programs, the disputes increase while the controversy continues to grow over management's right to test workers for possible drug abuse. This chapter examines arbitral reasoning on such issues as the conditions entitling management to test job applicants or employees and the proper standards for, and use of, drug tests.

Intoxication & Alcoholism

IN BRIEF

Arbiters generally accept the idea that intoxication on the job may indicate that an employee has a drinking problem. However, if the worker is an alcoholic, many arbiters will view the employee's alcohol dependency as an illness rather than as simple misconduct. In such cases, some arbiters may agree with an employer's view that progressive discipline, with increasingly harsher penalties, is the best way to correct the employee's behavior. However, a growing number of arbiters believe that rehabilitation, through counseling and other alcohol treatment programs, is the key to getting the worker back on track. In such cases, if it appears that the worker is making a good-faith effort at rehabilitation, reinstatement may be ordered or the penalty may be reduced.

The following discussion of grievances that arise over intoxication and alcoholism covers:
▶ Arbiters' standards in assessing such cases;
▶ Employers' need for a policy concerning alcohol use and intoxication;
▶ Safety considerations implicated by workplace intoxication;
▶ Proper evidence of alcohol possession and intoxication;
▶ Rehabilitation and discipline of alcoholic employees;
▶ Employees' refusal to undergo rehabilitation; and
▶ Off-duty drinking and drinking during holiday seasons.

GUIDELINES

Arbiters' Standards

Three arbitration models are used most often to decide arbitration cases involving intoxication/alcoholism, according to *Alcohol and Other Drugs* (Dennenberg & Dennenberg, BNA Books, 1991):
● The straightforward application of the traditional corrective-discipline model;
● A rejection of the corrective-discipline model in favor of a therapeutic model (drug therapy, psychotherapy, behavior therapy, and eclectic therapy); and,
● A modification of the corrective-discipline model.

In cases involving the use and possession of intoxicants, arbiters have developed the approach that discharge for drinking or drunkenness generally is sustained in these situations:
● Frequent absenteeism as a result of drinking;
● Drinking on the job combined with other misconduct such as serious improper behavior or material falsification of employment records;
● Drinking on the job that results in an inability to perform the work;
● Drunkenness or drinking that has a definite destructive effect on the employer's business and/or the morale of other employees; and

- Chronic alcoholism with no sign of efforts at rehabilitation.

When such factors are not present, and where drinking on the job is a first offense, the penalty of discharge often is reduced to some lesser degree of discipline. (49 LA 190, 52 LA 989, 55 LA 1274) Moreover, long, continued service usually is recognized as a factor in an employee's favor when determining the appropriate penalty for intoxication. (21 LA 80, 23 LA 245, 24 LA 720, 55 LA 1274)

Need for Company Rules

Not every incident of intoxication on company property demands that the employee involved be treated as "sick" rather than disciplined for misconduct. Several arbiters point out that rules against consumption or possession of alcohol while on company property or company time make good sense, as do rules against employees reporting to work while intoxicated. Unless there is other evidence that the on-premises intoxication or drinking is part of a pattern suggesting alcoholism, management is free to treat the matter as a simple violation of company rules. (90 LA 960, 89 LA 838, 81 LA 630, 81 LA 449, 81 LA 318, 77 LA 1064, 75 LA 899, 75 LA 699, 75 LA 90, 70 LA 946, 67 LA 1296, 64 LA 988, 63 LA 355, 58 LA 9, 52 LA 945, 51 LA 120, 50 LA 173, 47 LA 1029, 46 LA 549, 44 LA 772, 44 LA 267, 32 LA 293, 30 LA 94, 30 LA 847, 29 LA 362, 24 LA 810, 12 LA 350, 3 LA 146)

EXAMPLE: Under a plant rule forbidding employees to possess or drink alcoholic beverages on company premises, an employee was justifiably discharged for consuming a can of beer and for possessing unopened beer cans in his automobile, an arbiter ruled. The employer's method of communicating the ban on alcohol was adequate, the arbiter found, noting that the the employee was aware of the rule. The arbiter concluded that the first-offense discharge was not excessively harsh since management had been consistent in applying the penalty of discharge to other employees who committed similar offenses. (AMF Lawn and Garden Division, 64 LA 998; see also 96 LA 1185, 77 LA 1052)

Safety Considerations

Generally, arbiters uphold an employee's discharge for intoxication where the worker's behavior endangers other employees or damages equipment. (90 LA 960, 82 LA 861, 73 LA 228, 73 LA 191, 71 LA 329)

EXAMPLE: One arbiter ruled that an employer was justified in discharging an alcoholic worker who vandalized a supervisor's home, car, and travel trailer. Although acknowledging that alcoholism is a disease, the arbiter emphasized that the "interests and welfare of the employee must be balanced with the interests and welfare of other employees and the company." A reinstatement of the employee, the arbiter said, would be perceived by other supervisory personnel as "tolerating, if not condoning, destruction of a supervisor's property by employees, thereby inhibiting supervisors in the performance of their duties." Although noting that the employee subsequently had sought treatment for his illness and apparently was progressing satisfactorily, the arbiter concluded that the "extreme vandalism"and the "associated trauma" experienced by the supervisor and his family weighed against reinstating the employee. (NCR and United Paperworkers, 70 LA 756)

EXAMPLE: An employer properly discharged an alcoholic who worked in an underground mine where even brief omissions of basic mine safety practices could lead to serious injury or death, an arbiter decided. Finding that the risks involved in the employee's occupation made his return to work inappropriate, the arbiter rejected the suggestion that if the worker was put back in his job, he would continue to seek rehabilitation. (Asarco Inc., 76 LA 163)

EXAMPLE: A heavy equipment operator was properly discharged for intoxication when he drove his road grader off the road and into a creek, injuring himself and damaging the grader. Although the employee claimed that he had a drinking problem and expressed a willingness to undergo rehabilitation, the arbiter pointed out that whether or not the employee's intoxicated condition was the result of alcoholism, he "should have recognized his condition and the danger it presented." Instead, the employee "went ahead to operate dangerous equipment," thereby "deliberately jeopardizing the safety of the grievant, his fellow employees and of the equipment with which he was charged," the arbiter noted. "Under these extreme circumstances, the company has an unchallengeable right to punish such conduct severely as a deterrent to ensure that it will never happen again," the arbiter concluded. (Freeman United Coal, 82 LA 861)

However, another arbiter ruled that an employee who was drunk while on duty and fell over the edge of the barge on which he was working was improperly discharged despite management's claims that the accident "severely jeopardized" the employee's life and the safety of others. Noting that the employee admitted he had an alcohol problem, joined Alcoholics Anonymous and became an active participant, stopped drinking, and had no prior disciplinary or poor performance record, the arbiter reduced the discharge to a 60-day suspension. (Ohio River Co., 83 LA 211)

Evidence of Intoxication

Where an employee is disciplined for alleged intoxication, a dispute often arises as to the sufficiency of the evidence regarding his state of sobriety. Arbiters have set forth these principles:

• Mere opinion evidence is not sufficient proof of a drunken condition. The evidence must be specific in describing various details of appearance and conduct so that it is clear that the person accused was under the influence of alcohol. (85 LA 1127, 85 LA 251, 83 LA 1323, 65 LA 783, 65 LA 193, 64 LA 742, 63 LA 1102, 60 LA 1030, 54 LA 145)

• Supervisors who have no medical training nevertheless are capable of recognizing when an employee is intoxicated or under the influence of alcohol if they objectively compare an employee's normal demeanor and work habits with those at the time his sobriety is questioned. (Dayton Walther Co., 77 LA 1064)

• Results of breath/blood-alcohol/urinalysis tests may be accepted as conclusive proof of intoxication. Arbiters differ over whether management is required to give a blood test in order to prove intoxication, since requiring such tests might cause undue delays and disruption of production. (Charleston Naval Shipyard, 54 LA 145; see also 90 LA 286)

EXAMPLE: An arbiter reinstated an allegedly intoxicated employee after ruling that his employer mishandled his blood test — a medical group's laboratory failed to follow procedures in a letter of understanding for illegal alcohol an drug induced intoxication, the arbiter found, reducing the discharge to a 90-day suspension, and made the employee sign a last-chance agreement requiring that the worker attend and successfully complete an alcoholic rehabilitation program and provide written proof that he was attending "Alcoholics Anonymous" meetings. Failure to do all of the above, the arbiter cautioned would again result in the worker's discharge. (Pacific Motor Trucking, 86 LA 497; see also 87 LA 972)

EXAMPLE: An arbiter reinstated a delivery driver who was discharged for refusing to submit to a blood test. A supervisor smelled alcohol on the driver's breath, and when the driver admitted to drinking a beer at lunch — after having two traffic accidents that day — the supervisor requested that the employee submit to a blood test. The driver refused to take the test and was discharged for insubordination. Overturning the dismissal, the arbiter pointed out that the employer could not fire the employee for insubordination since he was not warned that his refusal to undergo the test would be an admission of intoxication or that it would result in his dismissal. (Signal Delivery Service, 86 LA 75)

EXAMPLE: Another arbiter overturned the discharge of an employee who was not given a blood test even though management judged him to be intoxicated after observing his unusual "walking and talking patterns." Noting that "a person is not intoxicated until or unless a certain quantity of alcohol or other substance is found in one's blood," the arbiter noted that in this case, a blood test "quite clearly" was in order. "To discharge a person for suspected but unconfirmed intoxication is to discharge unjustly," the arbiter observed, concluding that, "no one knows if the grievant reported to work under the influence as he was not tested." (Durion Co., 85 LA 1127)

EXAMPLE: A print shop employee was unjustly discharged for intoxication without the results of a blood test to prove his drunkenness, said an arbiter. The employee admitted to his supervisor that he drank two beers before reporting to his shift after his supervisor smelled alcohol on his breath. The employee was discharged even though he would not take a blood test, as the employer requested. The arbiter reversed the discharge since there was "insufficient evidence" to prove that the employee was intoxicated. However, the arbiter refused to award the employee back pay, deciding that in not taking the blood test, the employee was "forestalling an independent evaluation of his condition, which was reasonably suspect." (Foote and Davis Inc., 88 LA 125)

EXAMPLE: An arbiter upheld the suspension of a worker for intoxication in the workplace based on a supervisor's observations. However, even though the employer's substance-abuse policy recommended discharge for intoxication, because the worker's blood-alcohol level was below the level set by the state motor-vehicle law for intoxication, the employer lessened the sentence to suspension. (Vivi Color Inc., 97 LA 850)

However, another arbiter upheld the discharge of an employee who was discharged for drinking but did not take a sobriety test. The discharge was upheld on the basis of witness testimony without reliance on the sobriety test, when the arbiter found that the testimony clearly showed that the employee was intoxicated on the day of his dismissal. In fact, the arbiter noted, refusal to take a sobriety tests has been held to constitute an implied admission of guilt. (Cal Custom/Hawk, 65 LA 723; see also 77 LA 1180, 76 LA 1005, 76 LA 144)

Evidence of Alcohol Possession

When plant rules clearly forbid the possession of alcoholic beverages on company property, management may use the discovery of an open container of some alcoholic drink to support the discipline of an employee. However, an observed open container does not necessarily prove that the employee is in possession of alcohol, arbiters have held. (81 LA 917)

EXAMPLE: An arbiter reduced the penalty against a truck driver who brought an open can of beer into a compulsory company meeting. Finding the employee's suspension too harsh, the arbiter noted that the employer had a "demonstrated practice" providing beer for employees, and that the worker did not flagrantly defy management authority. (Keebler Co., 88 LA 183)

EXAMPLE: A lack of evidence caused the reinstatement of an employee who was fired after the company security guard discovered him squatting behind a car in the company parking lot. The guard also found a Styrofoam cup hidden behind the rear tire of the car and after examining the contents of the cup, concluded that it was filled with some kind of alcoholic beverage. Although no bottle was found on or near the employee, and no analysis was ever made to determine the true contents of the cup, the company fired the worker. The arbiter found that the employee was fired without just cause, since the company failed to show that the worker committed any wrongdoing, even though the circumstances created some suspicion that the employee may have been drinking. (Kast Metals Corp., 65 LA 783)

However, a delivery worker was justly discharged for possession of intoxicating beverages, ruled an arbiter, calling it "more than suspicious circumstantial evidence" that two open and partially consumed cans of beer were found in the cab of the employee's truck. (Farm Stores, 81 LA 344)

Alcoholism as Mitigator

While some arbiters have been reluctant to mitigate the discipline of alcoholics (Armstrong Furnace Co., 63 LA 688; see also 75 LA 901), other arbiters are willing to give the alcoholic employee the benefit of the doubt, and are inclined to reinstate the alcoholic whenever there seems to be a possibility of recovery. (Charleston Navel Shipyard, 54 LA 145; see also 56 LA 527, 56 LA 789)

Rehabilitation vs. Discharge

The application of progressive discipline may not correct alcohol-related performance problems; it may, however, be instrumental in warning employees that they have a serious problem that can be cured only by seeking help through counseling or rehabilitation. If an employee voluntarily seeks treatment for alcoholism, an arbiter may consider such a move as a mitigating factor when evaluating the worker's job performance or attendance record. (87 LA 972, 87 LA 1039, 83 LA 211, 73 LA 1193)

However, the burden generally is on the worker to show that he has taken meaningful, affirmative action to deal with a drinking problem. Where there is convincing evidence that a discharged employee has taken positive steps to obtain care, an arbiter may reinstate the worker. Such reinstatements often are conditioned on the employee's successful completion of an alcoholism rehabilitation or counseling program, and on whether the employer knew of the employee's alcohol dependency at the time of the dismissal.

One arbiter ruled that an employer had no responsibility to "force" an employee with an alcohol-abuse problem into a rehabilitation program, after the employee had refused to enter alcohol rehabilitation voluntarily. (Pennwalt Corp., 86 LA 686)

EXAMPLE: One arbiter reinstated an alcoholic worker even though his employer had "sufficient just cause" to fire him for "excessive absenteeism and tardiness." The arbiter noted that: the employer knew that the worker's poor attendance record was the result of his alcohol-abuse problems; other alcohol-dependent employees were given second chances to improve their records; the employee had a "lengthy and more-or-less satisfactory" job performance record; "alcohol dependency is a special problem in industry which requires special treatment;" and the employee "now recognizes that he has an alcohol dependency problem and he has taken self-help measures to control it." (Youngstown Hospital Assoc., 82 LA 31)

EXAMPLE: An arbiter ruled that an employer improperly discharged a worker for "unsatisfactory attendance" when the employee was absent for an extended period because of his admission to a hospital alcoholism-treatment program. Before admitting himself to the hospital, the employee had participated in two alcoholism programs that had failed to cure his addiction. The employee's "bootstrap decision" to deal with his problem directly by seeking treatment at the hospital was an acceptable reason for being absent from the job, the arbiter ruled, pointing out that the employee had acted in a "positive manner" in response to the employer's warnings that he must "overcome his personal problem." (Warner and Swasey Co., 71 LA 158)

However, in another case, an arbiter ruled that a company was not required to reinstate an excessively absent employee when he successfully completed an alcohol rehabilitation program, since he had not disclosed his alcoholism until after he was discharged. Finding that because there was nothing in the labor agreement "exculpating an employee from his actions due to the fact that it is subsequently learned that they were due to chronic alcoholism," the arbiter rules that while the employee "is on the way to fully resolving his alcohol abuse problems," he has "no right to require this company to reinstate or rehire him." (Bemis Co., 81 LA 733; see also 90 LA 399, 86 LA 430, 82 LA 420, 80 LA 851)

Refusal to Undergo Rehabilitation

Despite the increasing recognition that alcoholism is an illness and must be treated as such, arbiters have held that management has the right to discipline an employee for drinking on the job, if the worker refuses to attempt rehabilitation.

EXAMPLE: One arbiter decided that an employer had just cause to discharge an alcoholic worker who refused to continue to participate in an institutional treatment program. Rejecting the worker's argument that he had agreed merely to enroll in the hospital's program, not to complete it, the arbiter said that it would be "absurd" to expect any beneficial results from treatment that was started but not finished. The arbiter also noted that while in the program, the employee resisted and refused to cooperate, to the point that he had been asked to leave the institution. Deciding that management had taken all "reasonable" measures to help the worker deal with his "acute and chronic" alcoholism, the arbiter ruled that the dismissal was warranted. (National Gypsum Co., 73 LA 228)

EXAMPLE: Another arbiter emphasized that while alcoholism is an illness, it is an illness which only the patient can "cure." The discharge of an alcoholic was upheld where the employee had been given repeated opportunities to bring his drinking problem under control and had failed too often for the arbiter to conclude that all would be well if only he were given another chance. (Caterpillar Tractor Co., 44 LA 87)

Conditional Reinstatement & 'Last-Chance' Agreements

Arbiters, as a solution in giving an employee a second chance, commonly are reducing an employee's discharge to a conditional reinstatement. The extent to which arbiters may properly set the terms of the reinstatement is subject to debate — in terms of both the therapeutic process and the arbitration process. Some arbiters have gone so far as to recommend the medication the employee should take. Other arbiters find this to exceed an arbiter's authority, and that they are making or interpreting clinical decisions — whether an employee is an alcoholic, the length of his or her treatment, etc. — a task, the arbiter recommends should be left up to clinicians.

Often employers and employees, as part of a substance-abuse policy, will reach a "bargain" or "quid pro quo," wherein the substance abuser will be reinstated with the proviso that the employee undergo rehabilitation and remain drug-free for the duration of his or her employment, with the knowledge that violation of which will result in immediate termination.

EXAMPLE: An arbiter upheld an employee's discharge after he had been reinstated under a last-chance agreement for misconduct stemming from alcohol abuse. The agreement stipulated that any violation of company rules would be considered violation of his one-year probation, and that any such violation could not be grieved under a collective bargaining agreement. The employee was discharged for violating a safety work rule, even though he had completed a rehabilitation program required by the last-chance agreement. (Gaylord Container Corp., 97 LA 382; see also 87 LA 973, 65 LA 803, 56 LA 319)

The arbiter posed five criteria for determining the validity of a last-chance agreement:
- Was a union representative present when the employee signed the agreement?
- Are it requirements reasonable?
- Did the employee sign it of his or her own free will?
- Did the employee understand its provisions?
- Was the probationary period of reasonable duration?

However, in one case, an arbiter reduced to a suspension the discharge of an employee who completed an alcohol-rehabilitation program, signed an agreement to remain alcohol-free for two years or face dismissal, and was discharged six months later after being arrested for driving under the influence. (Mead Products, 96 LA 240)

Employee Assistance Programs (EAPs)

Although some observers have seen the emergence of a concept that every employer has the duty to aid alcoholics and drug addicts, the primary instrument for dealing with these problems has been the voluntarily created Employee Assistance Program (EAP), run by an employer, a union, or jointly. In arbitration, the most salient question posed by the EAP movement is whether the employer who has or recognizes an EAP, or even promulgates a policy on alcohol rehabilitation, incurs an obligation to try rehabilitation before imposing discipline. That is, is the employer expected to detect incipient alcoholism in an employee and to offer assistance before the employee's poor performance leads to discharge? (For decisions involving EAPs, see: 92 LA 793, 92 LA 781, 92 LA 91, 91 LA 431, 89 LA 99, 88 LA 457, 86 LA 430, 84 LA 1030, 79 LA 182, 78 LA 302, 77 LA 1064, 77 LA 854, 75 LA 968, 75 LA 896, 73 LA 228, 72 LA 355, 67 LA 1145, 63 LA 274, 52 LA 195, 42 LA 1251)

Off-Duty Drinking

Under normal conditions, the consumption of alcohol after working hours doesn't have a direct impact upon the employer-employee relationship and therefore is not subject to discipline. (97 LA 801)

However, off-duty drinking is cause for discipline when it results in an employee's reporting for work "under the influence." (Stop and Shop Inc., 41 LA 333)

EXAMPLE: One arbiter upheld the discharge of an employee for violating a new amendment to a no-drinking rule that had been extended to meal-time drinking off company property. The arbiter pointed out that the union had led the company to believe that it saw an evil in lunch-hour drinking and would support the company in an effort to do something about it. (International Pipe and Ceramics Corp., 44 LA 267)

Off-duty drinking also may be cause for discipline where it indicates backsliding by an employee who has promised to try to bring an alcoholism problem under control. (90 LA 399)

EXAMPLE: An employee who had been with a company for 25 years and had an obvious drinking problem was justly dismissed for off-duty drinking. After issuing several written warnings about his use of alcoholic beverages, the company finally discharged him for being drunk on company property. Subsequently, the company agreed to take him back if he promised to stay off alcohol, attend AA meetings regularly, and see his doctor and follow his orders. Nearly a year later, the employee was observed by company officials drinking beer in a tavern during off-duty hours. As a result, he was discharged. The employment history demonstrated that the employee's consumption of alcohol, whether on company time or not, had a direct impact on the employment relationship, the arbiter said, finding that the employee's attitude indicated that he did not intend to improve his conduct in regard to the use of alcoholic beverages. (Emge Packing Co., 52 LA 195)

Holiday Drinking

During the holiday season, some arbiters take a more liberal view of no-drinking rules and make allowances for employees who are caught drinking alcoholic beverages on the job.

EXAMPLE: An arbiter decided that an employer properly suspended a truck driver for drinking alcoholic beverages during a warehouse party on the last working day before Christmas, and for breaking a lock on a plant gate while attempting to retrieve his vehicle. The arbiter held, however, that management was not justified in completely barring the employee from ever driving a company truck again. The "core" question, the arbiter stressed, was whether the employer's disciplinary action fit "the entire picture." Although conceding that the worker "slipped and slipped rather badly" by acting irresponsibly at the Christmas party, the arbiter noted that, in a "candid moment," most people would admit that they had engaged in similar conduct. "If we were all angels at all times," the arbiter concluded, "we would sprout wings and fly up to Heaven." (Ashland Oil Inc., 59 LA 292)

EXAMPLE: Another arbiter similarly decided that an employer was not justified in discharging an employee who was caught drinking whiskey at work on the last day before a Christmas shutdown. A supervisor had observed the employee, amidst co-workers, drinking from a pint-size bottle filled with a whiskey-colored liquid. Although condemning the conduct of the employee, the arbiter maintained that "justice tempered with mercy" should be the standard for reviewing discipline in such cases. Stressing that the employee had a long, "unblemished" work record and that drinking on the last day before the Christmas holidays was "customary" on the job, the arbiter concluded that the discharge should be converted to a suspension. (Wagner Electric Corp., 57 LA 10)

Mitigating Circumstances

An employee's work record and/or length of service may mitigate an employer's discipline for intoxication or alcohol possession. (96 LA 75, 87 LA 1039)

Drug Abuse

IN BRIEF

Arbiters generally support management's view that employees' possession or use of drugs, especially on company time and premises, is a serious offense. Increasingly, however, arbiters require management to show that that a worker's involvement with drugs has had a harmful affect on some aspect of the employment relationship.

In determining the proper penalty for drug-related offenses, arbiters will focus on issues that include whether:

▶ A drug-abuse policy has been established and clearly communicated to employees;

▶ Employees' use or possession of drugs had, or was likely to have, a negative affect on workplace safety;

▶ The drug involved was a controlled substance or a prescription drug properly used by the employee;

▶ Discipline is based on sufficient evidence of drug use, especially when management uses witnesses and polygraphs to support its case;

▶ Discipline meted out for drug involvement was on a par with that given to employees involved in alcohol-related offenses;

▶ Involvement with drugs was off-duty; and

▶ The employee was arrested or convicted on drug charges, and whether the media attention given the drug arrest or conviction has an adverse impact on the employer business or reputation.

--- GUIDELINES ---

Enforcing a Drug-Abuse Policy

As with other types of offenses, arbiters will generally uphold discipline for drug use where management has formulated a rule prohibiting it, communicated the rule to employees, and consistently applied discipline in a nondiscriminatory manner.

EXAMPLE: An employer was justified in discharging two workers who admitted to smoking marijuana on the job under a plant rule prohibiting the sale, use, or possession of alcohol and drugs on company premises, an arbiter held. The arbiter pointed out that the employees had acknowledged that they were aware of the rule, which, he added, "had been consistently administered." Finding no "mitigating or extenuating circumstances," the arbiter declared that nothing here" would warrant the conclusion "that the discharges were not completely justified." (Pepsi-Cola Bottlers, 68 LA 792)

EXAMPLE: Citing management's failure to ensure that employees understood its prohibitions against using or being under the influence of intoxicants on its premises, an arbiter overturned the discharge of an employee who had brought marijuana into the plant. "To be a basis for proper disciplinary action against an employee," the arbiter pointed out, "a rule must be reasonable in nature, clearly published, and it must be known to the employee." However, although employees were given copies of the rules, the arbiter noted, there was no follow up to ensure that they had read them. "It is a risky assumption," the arbiter pointed out, "for a firm to give rules to workers in a written form and expect them to read and understand them without some type of follow-up to confirm reading and clarity of understanding." (Ethyl Corp., 74 LA 953)

EXAMPLE: An employer that previously had been lax in enforcing its rules against reporting to work under the influence of drugs improperly terminated 25 workers for smoking marijuana during their lunch break, an arbiter found. After the employer had asked local police to help it end workplace drug use, the police raided the company parking lot, arresting or citing 50 workers. Management then discharged 25 of them for violating its drug policy. Overturning the discharges, the arbiter pointed out that the workers had been "readily observed smoking marijuana at the same time and place" day after day. The employer's inaction with respect to enforcing its rules against drug use, the arbiter concluded, had resulted in the employees' viewing the lots "as sanctuaries for this relaxation." (Lockheed Corp., 75 LA 1081)

'Last-Chance' Agreements

Often employers and employees, as part of a substance-abuse policy, will reach a "bargain" wherein the substance abuser will be reinstated with the proviso that the employee undergo rehabilitation and remain drug-free for the duration of his or her employment, with the knowledge that violation of which will result in immediate termination.

EXAMPLE: In one case, an employer agreed to finance, under an employee assistance program, the rehabilitation of an admitted substance abuser, who, in turn, committed to finishing the rehabilitation program, staying drug-free while participating in the program, and forfeiting his job if he violated either provision. An arbiter found the agreement to be "fair" and "reasonable," and that they had been fully explained to employees as part of the employer's substance-abuse policy, and upheld the employee's discharge for testing positive for cocaine after having missed several rehab meetings. (Diesel Recon Co., 96 LA 1123)

Further, an arbiter ruled that a last-chance agreement violated the due process rights guaranteed an employee under a collective bargaining agreement. The employee had failed to provide a urine sample after he had signed an agreement authorizing an employer to require unannounced drug and alcohol tests at its discretion, and the employer had rejected a union request to arbitrate the termination, citing a section of the agreement providing that "no grievances, claims, arbitration, or lawsuit will be filed" if the employee were discharged. The arbiter called the termination "arbitrary," agreeing with a union claim that the last-chance agreement ran counter to the labor contract which forbade the waiver of procedural due process protections. (Monterey Coal Co., 96 LA 457)

However, another arbiter ruled that an employee was properly discharged under a last-chance agreement even though his agreement authorized termination "without recourse to the grievance procedure." The employee was required to test for drugs during work hours based on an admitted drug dependency, and had tested positive for a substance such as valium, and had failed to inform his employer of valium prescription from a physician who was not a regular doctor. (Kaydon Corp., 89 LA 377)

Safety Considerations

Generally, arbiters are stricter in upholding discipline levied against employees who are using drugs at work or whose use of drugs outside the worksite impairs their job performance if the impaired employee would endanger other employees or the public.

EXAMPLE: A city bus driver who had been involved in an accident while on her route was justly dismissed after a blood test and urinalysis revealed the presence of habit-forming drugs in her system, an arbiter concluded. Although lacking "absolute proof" of the employee's drug use, "to allow an employee who has taken drugs to continue to drive a bus would pose a danger to the public," said the arbiter and "it is unthinkable" that such an employee "should be allowed to continue driving a bus." (Washington Metropolitan Area Transit Authority, 82 LA 150)

EXAMPLE: A police dispatcher who admitted to using cocaine off the job was properly dismissed, said an arbiter who declared that "it is incompatible with the functions of a police communications dispatcher to have a person employed in the role admittedly taking cocaine or other controlled substances." Moreover, because a person in that job "receives telephone calls from the public regarding possible life-threatening situations which must be rapidly analyzed," the arbiter said, the job requires "full concentration of the dispatcher's faculties while in the performance of their duties and the use of controlled substances such as cocaine impairs that function." (San Francisco Police Department, 87 LA 791)

However, a chemical plant employee whose job was not "in a sensitive area" was unjustifiably discharged for smoking marijuana on the premises, an arbiter held. Arguing that its business required alert employees, management insisted that an employee under the influence of drugs could "cause an erroneous mixture of chemicals" that might result in "explosions or fires." The arbiter, however, pointed out that the employee worked "in the boiler house, unloading and shoveling coal," rather than in a sensitive area where there would be the "possibility of dangerous mistakes." (Hooker Chemical, 74 LA 1032)

Nature of Abused Drug

Even when an employee's work performance is adversely affected by a prescription drug provided by a physician, arbiters still are likely to enforce management's disciplinary action.

EXAMPLE: An employee who arrived at work impaired by prescription drugs was justly discharged, an arbiter found. Both observations of the employee's behavior and medical analyses showed that the employee "was impaired and unfit for active duty when he showed up" for work, the arbiter said. "Even if all of the drugs detected in the urine and blood screens were 'prescription,' the taking of these simultaneously constitutes abuse" and defies common sense, he concluded. (Citgo Petroleum, 88 LA 521)

EXAMPLE: An employee was properly given a three-day disciplinary layoff when management determined that he reported to work under the influence of drugs, decided an arbiter. However, the employee objected to the discipline, claiming that the drug was Valium and that it had been prescribed for him by his physician. Upholding the layoff, the arbiter ruled that whether the employee's behavior was adversely influenced by his "taking medicine as prescribed or using drugs without benefit of prescription is not relevant to the fact that the employee was under the influence and therefore a risk in the workplace." (FMC Corp., 80 LA 1173)

Witnesses to Drug Involvement

When employers have disciplined workers for drug involvement, based on the testimony of witnesses to the workers' drug use or possession, arbiters look for corroborative evidence of drug involvement before enforcing disciplinary measures. Generally two types of witnesses are available to management: undercover agents, or supervisory employees and co-workers.

● *Undercover agents* — When employers who have mounted anti-drug campaigns in their workplaces hire undercover agents to detect drug use and possession, arbiters usually weigh the testimony of the undercover witness in light of his expertise and the other evidence presented, including contrasting testimony from the accused employee.

EXAMPLE: An arbiter overturned the discharge of an employee that was based on the unsupported testimony of an undercover agent. Noting that "the accused must always be given the benefit of substantial doubts," the arbiter asserted that "dismissal for alleged criminal conduct may not be upheld when the sole evidence supporting the charge is the uncorroborated testimony of an undercover informant." Corroboration could include samples of the drugs allegedly used by the employees, laboratory analyses, photographs, or tape recordings, the arbiter pointed out. (Pacific Bell, 87 LA 313, see also 97 LA 271, 95 LA 813, 83 LA 580)

EXAMPLE: Two employees were unjustly discharged for alleged drug use, an arbiter concluded, noting that management's only evidence consisted of reports from an undercover agent that "were filtered down to the company management by and through the agent's supervisor." In the arbiter's opinion, without "some type of corroboration," of the agent's reports, which might have been either "direct or circumstantial," the employee's testimony must be "superior." "To allow a job to be damaged or tarnished or taken away by uncorroborated and unsubstantiated evidence," the arbiter maintained, "would be to allow an employer to act arbitrarily and capriciously and unreasonably in many instances." (Pettibone Ohio Corp., 72 LA 1144)

However, another arbiter ruled that an employer, relying on evidence of an undercover detective, properly discharged four employees for possession and use of marijuana on company premises. The testimony of the detective was "firsthand information where the incidents testified to were backed up by reports written daily," declared the arbiter. Moreover, the undercover detective's "demeanor, the impression that his testimony was truthful, his memory, his perception," and his prior experience as a police officer shows that his testimony was "accurate and credible," concludes the arbiter, ruling that the discharges were for just cause. (Consumer Plastics Corp., 88 LA 208)

● *Supervisors or co-workers* — Management personnel or co-workers also may testify regarding an employees' drug use or possession. In such cases, arbiters will consider the strength of the testimony based on what the witness claims to have seen — or smelled.

EXAMPLE: An arbiter upheld the discharge of four employees who were witnessed by four supervisors smoking a marijuana cigarette among them. Concluding that the "chain of circumstances pointing to the guilt of the grievants goes far beyond conjecture and suspicion," the arbiter observed that the four witnesses, in sum, testified that, in addition to smelling the "pervasive and unmistakable odor of marijuana," they observed the employees: taking deep inhalations of a cigarette they passed back and forth, holding the cigarette in a "cupped fashion common to marijuana consumption," and looking "suspiciously from side to side before lighting or inhaling from the cigarette." (Cascade Steel Rolling Mills Inc., 78 LA 753)

EXAMPLE: An employer had just cause to dismiss a worker after two supervisors discovered her smoking what they thought was a marijuana cigarette in the women's locker room, an arbiter said. The supervisors testified that they found part of a marijuana cigarette on the floor of the locker room, which smelled of marijuana smoke. (Dobbs Houses Inc., 78 LA 749; see also 88 LA 633, 75 LA 642, 75 LA 597)

However, an arbiter overturned the discharge of an employee whom a supervisor discovered in the company's exercise room, which smelled of "smoking marijuana." Management must show "good and sufficient evidence to support the charges of drug use," the arbiter said, but in this case, the supervisor "was not able to say irrefutably that the odor he smelled came from the employee's smoking in the exercise room. Since "significant doubt" remained as to the employee's guilt, the arbiter ruled, to uphold the company's position would be tantamount to shifting the burden of proof to the employee, making him guilty until proven innocent. (Owens-Corning Fiberglas Corp., 86 LA 1026)

Polygraphs Evidencing Drug Abuse

Just as arbiters may find reason to suspect the reliability of management witnesses who attest to employee's drug involvement, so too may they doubt the evidence of lie-detector tests introduced to substantiate drug charges. When presented with the results of polygraphs, arbiters often require corroborative evidence before upholding discipline for drug use or possession.

EXAMPLE: An arbiter reinstated an employee who was fired after a polygraph examiner told the company that he believed the worker had been "deceptive" about his drug use. Arbiters and courts have consistently held a "jaundiced view" of both the polygraph process and the "admissibility of the results" of a polygraph exam, the arbiter asserted. Employers that want to make use of polygraph results have been advised to make sure that the test is administered by a qualified examiner, closely follows the incident in question, and is taken voluntarily, the arbiter said. At the time of this polygraph, the arbiter noted, the employee was taking prescribed medication that, according to his doctor, could have affected the results of the exam. The employer failed to "take the total circumstances under enough consideration," nor did the polygraph evidence alone support a conclusion that warranted termination, the arbiter held. (Houston Lighting & Power, 87 LA 478)

However, an arbiter upheld the terminations of several employees who had been discharged for on-the-job drug and alcohol use based on the uncorroborated testimony of an undercover agent who "passed" a polygraph test. The arbiter accorded "significant weight" to the fact that the agent's testimony was supported by the polygraph results, while all the accused employees refused to submit to the test. (Georgia Pacific, 85 LA 542)

Equal Treatment for Abusers

Arbiters sometimes will compare the discipline given to drug abusers with the discipline the employer has levied against alcohol-abusing workers, often overturning or softening discipline given drug abusers if they have been treated more harshly.

EXAMPLE: In the case of three employees discharged on their first offense of smoking marijuana on company premises, the arbiter found that the employees were indeed guilty of violating the employer's drug and alcohol policy. However, the arbiter noted that the employer regularly applied progressive discipline — not automatic dismissals — for employees' first offense in using alcohol on company property. The arbiter held that "alcoholism in industry, and as a social problem, is far more debilitating, costly, and destructive than marijuana. There is no rational or reasonable basis for treating them as distinct. Therefore to treat alcohol abuse with progressive discipline and treat drug abuse with immediate discharge is improper." (Mallinckrodt Inc., 80 LA 1261)

However, two bus company employees who smoked marijuana on the roof of their office during work hours were properly discharged rather than offered counseling through the employee assistance program, as an alcoholic bus driver had been offered, an arbiter ruled. Even though the EAP had been designed to treat both alcohol and drug-abuse problems, the arbiter declared that the company had not treated the two cases disparately, since the bus driver was an admitted alcoholic, while the dismissed drug users "denied they had a drug problem and maintained that they were recreational users." (Central Ohio Transit Authority, 88 LA 633)

Off-Duty Drug Use

In cases that involve discipline meted out for employees' off-duty behavior, arbiters will consider the relationship between the off-duty behavior and the employee's job. (For more information, see "Off-Duty Misconduct.")

One arbiter held that "discharge for misconduct away from the place of work has no basis unless the behavior harms the company's reputation or product; or the behavior renders the employee unable to perform his duties or appear at work; or the behavior leads to the refusal of other employees to work with the employee." (General Telephone Co. of Calif., 87 LA 443; see also 88 LA 425)

EXAMPLE: One arbiter upheld the discharge of an employee whose use of illegal narcotics outside of work interfered with his job performance. The arbiter ruled that the worker's "drug-induced" condition "rendered him unfit to perform his work," and therefore, the employee violated "the contractual prohibition against the use of illegal narcotics." Even though there was no evidence to show that the employee used the drugs while on duty, the arbiter concluded that "the company acted within its contractual right when it discharged" the employee "without opportunity to rectify or change his offending behavior." (Lick Fish and Poultry, 87 LA 1062)

EXAMPLE: An employee was justly discharged when he reported to work under the influence of drugs he took while off-duty, decided an arbiter. Management noticed the employee arrived at work "walking like he was somewhat in pain" and appearing "droopy-looking." After a urinalysis revealed the presence of drugs in his system, the employee admitted to using marijuana over the previous weekend, and was subsequently discharged. The arbiter reasoned that since the company's policy prohibited employees from reporting to work while "under the influence of drugs," the employee was justly disciplined although his use of marijuana had occurred while he was off-duty. (Houston Power and Light, 87 LA 478)

However, an employer improperly had discharged a worker for smoking marijuana off the premises during his lunch break, another arbiter held. The arbiter noted that "an employee's lunch period is generally considered his own time and the company's control and responsibility is even further weakened because the grievant was six blocks away from the plant." Given these circumstances, the arbiter concluded, "it is difficult to believe that any harm or danger specifically accrued to the plant or other employees" through the worker's actions. (Gamble Brothers, 68 LA 72)

Arrest on Drug Charges

Because arrest does not prove that an employee actually has committed any crime or engaged in behavior that endangers the reputation of his employer or the safety of his co-workers, arbiters are reluctant to uphold discipline against employees arrested on — but not convicted of — drug charges.

EXAMPLE: An employer unjustly suspended a worker without pay after his arrest in connection with local drug trafficking, said an arbiter. "We have not regressed to the point where the presumption of innocence until proven guilty is abandoned," insisted the arbiter. The company was "precipitous" in suspending the employee, said the arbiter, stressing that no charges had been levied against the employee and a "real investigation" had not been conducted by the employer. (Times Mirror Cable Television, 87 LA 543)

However, another arbiter ruled that the dismissal of an employee arrested on charges of cocaine possession was proper, even though the charges were dismissed. An employee who managed a community center was fired after his arrest for possession of cocaine. Pointing out that police arrest "is not a basis for determining guilt," the arbiter acknowledged that "arrest and nothing more establishing misconduct cannot sustain a discharge." Upholding the employee's dismissal nonetheless, the arbiter found that the employee's position required "great contact with the community, where success is based on trust and leadership," and that the community center "would suffer and that its programs would be undermined if a facility manager who had had drug involvement were reinstated." (Wayne State University, 87 LA 953)

Conviction on Drug Charges

Adverse effects on operations, other employees, and the employer's position in the community may provide management with sound arguments, when supported by strong evidence, for upholding a discharge in cases involving an employee who has been convicted on drug charges. (69 LA 776, 65 LA 1203) However, when a court tempers the sentence by, for example, suspending part of it or permitting a work release, arbiters generally require that management show similar leniency.

EXAMPLE: An arbiter ordered the reinstatement of a worker convicted of possession of marijuana because the court placed the employee on probation. Stressing that the "conviction and probation order must be taken as a whole," the arbiter ruled that management erred in relying only on the conviction to terminate the worker. As long as the probation order remained in force, the worker had the right to "continue in service and work with seniority rights unimpaired." (Port Terminal Railroad Assoc., 60 LA 430)

EXAMPLE: An employee whose sentence for unlawful delivery of marijuana was suspended was entitled to conditional reinstatement by his employer, absent "specific and compelling evidence" that his conviction was "harmful to the interests of the company or other employees," ruled an arbiter. Although management argued that the worker "could be a destructive influence on other employees," that his "continued employment would be damaging to the employer's reputation," and that the reinstatement might "cause other problems, such as absenteeism and tardiness," the arbiter dismissed these objections as "either hypothetical or speculative." (Intalco Aluminum Corp., 68 LA 66)

Also, an arbiter reinstated an employee convicted of drug possession, citing no indication of recidivism. (97 LA 1057)

However, an arbiter upheld the discharge of an employee convicted of three off-premises drug-dealing felonies and sentenced to a four-year prison term and who generated extensive publicity about the case and was identified as a company employee. The arbiter chided that common sense alone is enough to tell the employee that a drug conviction could result in discharge, even though the employer had no formal rule prohibiting illicit off-premises drug activity. Also emphasizing the severe, adverse impact that the publicity of the event had on the employer, the arbiter added that her continued employment and presence in the workplace would have further negative impact on the employer. (Haskell of Pittsburgh, 96 LA 1208)

Also, an arbiter ruled that the indirect harm caused by customer reading of an employee's drug arrest was sufficient to warrant his discharge even without direct evidence that the employer's reputation was damaged. (Delta Beverage Group, 96 LA 454) However, a discharge was reduced to a suspension where news accounts of an employee's drug arrest did not identify his employer and co-workers expressed no reluctance to work with him. (Mobil Oil Corp., 95 LA 162)

Further, an arbiter upheld the dismissal of a worker who was fired after his employer learned of his conviction for selling cocaine. The arbiter rejected the employee's argument that he was unjustly discharged, since the sale took place neither on company premises nor on company time. Rather, the arbiter ruled that just cause existed for the discharge "because of the impact of the arrest on the employer's product, its reputation, employee safety, plant security, and production and discipline." Specifically, the arbiter said, in light of the employee's conviction for selling marijuana two years earlier, the employer further has just cause that the employee "may continue using drugs" and "may attempt to sell drugs to other employees." (Martin-Marietta Aerospace, 81 LA 695; see also 76 LA 387, 68 LA 697)

Drug Testing

IN BRIEF

As drug testing becomes an increasingly popular method of discovering or confirming that employees are using drugs, the number of issues that arbiters must address in drug-testing grievances also increases.

Among the drug-testing issues that concern arbiters are whether:

▶ Management may impose a drug-testing policy;

▶ Management may demand that an employee be tested at random or for just cause;

▶ The results of a drug test prove that an employee's work performance is impaired;

▶ Testing procedures unjustly invade an employee's privacy; and,

▶ Samples have been carefully tested and protected against tampering and adulteration.

A 1991 American Management Association survey of 1,200 companies showed that drug testing in the workplace is more widespread than ever among U.S. employers. Three-quarters of large and mid-size U.S. companies now have drug-testing policies. The survey further found that drug testing is rarely conducted as a stand-alone policy, with only 6.5 percent of respondents saying that they test employees for drugs, but offer no other drug-preventive programs — e.g., employee assistance programs (EAPS), education/awareness initiatives, supervisory training, etc. — to address drug use.

GUIDELINES

Imposing Drug-Testing Unilaterally

Employers that unilaterally impose a drug-testing policy on their unionized workforce often encounter objections that since neither employees nor their representatives were given a role in establishing the policy, the policy is unreasonable in light of existing contract provisions. Arbiters, however, are divided over whether management may impose a testing policy without employee input.

EXAMPLE: Unilaterally promulgating a drug-testing program was within management's traditional rights, an arbiter ruled. When a truck driver continually refused to sign a form acknowledging his receipt and awareness of his employer's drug-testing policy, the company discharged him. Objecting to the discharge, the union argued that the implementation of a drug and alcohol testing policy was a subject for bargaining, and that because the policy was instituted unilaterally, the driver was right not to comply. Upholding the discharge, the arbiter ruled that "there is no question but that the company had the right to implement this drug and alcohol test policy. It is clearly an exercise of management's right and was an integral part of the company's responsibility to maintain safety, efficiency and discipline in the work place." (Concrete Pipe Products, 87 LA 601)

EXAMPLE: Another arbiter held that a testing policy, imposed without union input, was unfair. After an employer implemented a substance abuse policy, the union objected, arguing that the policy constituted new work rules, and therefore, as set out in the contract, required union-management negotiation. Calling the employers' policy "improper," the arbiter held that while "there is no doubt that there is more drug abuse in our present day society," the employer "cannot overlook a contractual clause which demands negotiations concerning rule making." (Hobart Corp., 87 LA 905)

EXAMPLE: One arbiter declared that a drug-testing policy implemented unilaterally was unreasonable because it failed to treat employees "fairly and equitably" as the contract required. The testing policy was objectionable, said the arbiter, because it mandated testing for employees whose work had no bearing on safety and who did not work with the public; provided that uncooperative employees could be charged with insubordination; dictated the testing method to be used despite the availability of many methods; did not allow employees to test a portion of their sample by a lab of their choosing; and did not mandate that the employer verify positive test results with a confirmatory test. (Bay Area Rapid Transit, 88 LA 1; see also 95 LA 729, 94 LA 393)

Management's Right to Test

Typically, testing policies call for testing employees either randomly — i.e., without suspicion of drug use — or for just cause, where management claims that it has sufficient reason to require an employee whom it suspects of drug use to undergo a drug test.

Random testing — In a minority of cases, arbiters will sanction management's use of random testing. Reasons for upholding such policies include public interest and safety, and employees' history of drug use.

EXAMPLE: An employee subject to a last-chance, conditional, return-to-duty agreement in which he agreed to submit to random, comprehensive drug screening was properly discharged when he tested positive for cocaine and PCP after he reported to work in an excited condition, threatening to kill his wife. The arbiter ruled that since being under the influence of drugs on plant property is a dischargeable offense and the worker did not offer evidence to support allegations of inadequate testing procedures or sample tampering. (Koppers Co., 94 LA 363)

EXAMPLE: A drug-testing policy implemented at a nuclear power plant was reasonable, declared an arbiter. The policy called for the periodic and random testing of all personnel who were granted unescorted access inside the plant's security fence. Opposing the policy, the union argued that the test's "random administration without probable cause offends all concepts of reasonableness and fairness." While "random testing without probable cause is abhorrent to any fair-minded person," the arbiter replied, "the disasters at Three Mile Island and Chernobyl give eloquent testimony to the disastrous effects of human error" that could occur at this power plant. Although "there is something inherently offensive about this type of testing," the arbiter concluded, "the balancing of public interest favors the imposition of the rule." (Arkansas Power and Light, 88 LA 1065)

EXAMPLE: In the case of a hospital nurse who admitted to former drug use, an arbiter ruled that her employer had just cause to request the nurse's consent to random drug testing, since she had a history of regular drug use and a proven lack of persistence in pursuing rehabilitation. Pointing out that there is "no 'certain' cure for addiction to mood-altering chemicals," the arbiter upheld the testing order, noting that the risks and probabilities of the nurse's resuming drug use "must be evaluated in the context of the job responsibilities," which could involve life-threatening situations for her patients. (Deaconess Medical Center, 88 LA 44; see also 96 LA 596, 95 LA 7, 94 LA 399, 91 LA 1385, 91 LA 1186, 91 LA 363)

For-Cause Testing — When management can furnish arguments that there was a sufficient reason to test an employee, arbiters more willingly uphold discipline that results from a positive drug test. Factors arbiters consider in these just cause determinations include:

• Safety — Although claims that drug testing is an integral part of maintaining employee and public safety in a potentially hazardous industry can help an employer justify its policy (e.g., in public transportation, see 82 LA 150), safety claims may not always override other labor relations concerns. In one case, an explosives manufacturer, arguing that working while "impaired due to drugs is extremely dangerous" in a munitions plant, instituted a drug-testing program that called for random testing of employees. Under its testing policy, the company discharged an employee for a positive urinalysis, but the employee argued that the random testing policy was unjust. Overturning the discharge, the arbiter held that, despite the employer's safety concerns, "the taking of a person's urine without any suspicion that she may have been under the influence of drugs is highly invasive of personal privacy." (Day and Zimmerman Inc., 88 LA 1001; see also 91 LA 213)

• Suspicion of employee drug use — In light of observations by management that an employee was "unsteady, staggering, swaying, and disoriented; that her eyes were glassy and her speech slurred," an arbiter maintained that the employee was properly discharged for refusing to take a drug test, since the purpose of a drug test is "to confirm whether or not an employee is under the influence" of drugs as suspected. (American Standard, 77 LA 1085; see also 97 LA 850, 97 LA 343)

• Possession of drugs on company premises — In another case, an employer forbade employees from bringing alcohol or drugs on company property. After marijuana was discovered in an off-duty employee's car parked on company premises, they requested that he take a drug test. Finding that the employee was not obligated to submit to the test, the arbiter declared that the grievant was not driving his car as an employee. Therefore, the arbiter said, "the company representatives were not entitled to instruct him to submit to testing for any purpose." (Texas Utilities Generating Co., 82 LA 6)

Contractual Obligations

An employer's decision to discharge an employee for refusing to submit to a drug test may be successfully challenged if the employer has failed to follow its contractual obligations.

EXAMPLE: An employer improperly discharged an employee who refused to take a blood test after being accused of smoking marijuana, an arbiter ruled. The employee was seen by a company manager smoking what appeared to be a marijuana cigarette. After the worker refused the manager's request to submit to a drug test, the employee was fired. While the company had reasonable grounds to order the drug test and to discipline the employee for his refusal, the arbiter pointed out, under the collective bargaining agreement two written warning notices are required before an employee may be discharged or even suspended. Accordingly, the arbiter ordered the worker reinstated. (Warehouse Distribution Centers, 90 LA 979)

Proof of Impairment

An employee may argue that basing discipline on a positive drug test is unjust since the test does not sufficiently prove that the employee was impaired by drug use. Generally, arbiters agree that drug testing alone does not provide scientific proof of impairment.

EXAMPLE: An employee argued that he was unjustly dismissed as a result of a positive drug test, since his job performance was unimpaired. However, the arbiter ruled that the company acted in a "fair, reasonable and contractually permissible manner," by discharging the employee. The employer's policy permitted it to dismiss employees who were found using drugs, the arbiter noted, and finding the positive test result to be sufficient proof of drug use, ruled that the employee was justly dismissed. (Indianapolis Power and Light Co., 87 LA 826)

EXAMPLE: While a positive drug test was "not conclusive" evidence that an employee was under the influence of marijuana, along with the positive finding, an employer had enough other evidence to justify the employee's dismissal, an arbiter decided. Moreover, the employee also "admitted use of marijuana," the arbiter added, which "violated a known safety rule," and thereby endangered his co-workers; and "was absent without notifying management." (Georgia Power, 87 LA 800)

However, another employer unjustly discharged an employee after a supervisor observed the employee's erratic behavior and after a blood test showed the presence of cocaine in the employee's system, an arbiter found. The arbiter noted that while the company had proven the employee's use of drugs, without "proof of either the inadequacy of work performance, intoxication, or the creation of a risk of harm, the proof that an employee used cocaine is insufficient to constitute just cause" for discharge. (Kroger Co., 88 LA 463; see also 88 LA 91)

Employee Privacy

Depending on the particular circumstances involved in a case, when an employee is asked to undergo a drug test, an arbiters may decide that certain drug-testing procedures overstep the privacy to which employees should be entitled.

EXAMPLE: An employee who refused to submit to urinalysis in the presence of a nurse was unjustly discharged, an arbiter held. Because the employee would have had to undress fully to provide the specimen and was refused a request for a robe, she refused to undergo the urinalysis. Consequently, she was fired. Because the employee would have had to undress completely, the arbiter maintained that the presence of the witness was "more than usually embarrassing," and the refusal to provide the employee with a robe "made the conditions of the test unreasonably onerous." (Union Plaza Hotel, 88 LA 528)

EXAMPLE: A drug-testing program that permitted observation of urination and required employees to report all prescription medicines they were taking was unreasonable, an arbiter decided. The policy was implemented over objections of the union which called the procedures an invasion of policy. Finding that the plan's prescription-reporting requirement was "vague and unreasonable," the arbiter said if it is possible for an employee to alter a urine specimen, then the "circumstances or location should be changed rather than requiring observation of urination." The arbiter ordered the parties to negotiate the testing procedures into a "reasonable form." (Sharples Coal Corp., 91 LA 1065; see also 95 LA 393)

**Chain of Custody/
Laboratory Issues**

Challenges to drug testing are sometimes based on employees' claims that the testing procedure was unsound or careless and therefore that the test results are unreliable. Where such arguments have been made, arbiters note whether the employers have guarded the sample well and tested it thoroughly.

EXAMPLE: An arbiter rejected an employee's claims that his suspension based on a positive drug test was unjust because the company could not prove that it maintained a careful "chain of possession" regarding his sample. The company exercised "due care" in securing the sample and properly identifying it as the employee's, the arbiter noted, adding that greater requirements for proper identification of the sample "might well result" in a program that would be impossible to carry out. (Union Oil Co. of Calif., 87 LA 297)

EXAMPLE: Overturning the discharge of an employee whom management thought was under the influence of alcohol while at work, an arbiter noted that the employer did not follow the sample-handling procedures established between it and the union. The procedures required that a company and union representative together mail an employee's blood sample to the laboratory for testing. In this case, however, the nurse gave the sample to the company representative, who took the sample home and kept it overnight in his refrigerator, and then mailed it to the lab the next morning without ever notifying the union. (Holliston Mills, 60 LA 1030)

EXAMPLE: Another arbiter pointed out that one crucial evidentiary test for workplace substance abuse is the analysis of medical tests. In upholding the discharge of an employee, the arbiter commended the "very careful and thorough" testing procedure implemented by the company, which included requiring the employee to undergo both blood and urine tests, and submitting the samples to two separate, professional and independent labs, each of which corroborated the positive findings of the other. (Citgo Petroleum Corp., 88 LA 521)

Unsatisfactory Performance

INTRODUCTION

Unsatisfactory work performance, arbiters agree, justifies corrective action. However, they also concur that before taking action, management should consider the nature of the problem. Unsatisfactory performance can result from very different causes, not all of which may be considered an employee's "fault." They include:

▶ Carelessness (negligence, inattention to, or simply wanton disregard of established procedures and work methods);

▶ Incompetence (inability to do the job, resulting from either a lack of aptitude or a deficiency in knowledge); and

▶ Disability (physical incapacity to perform essential aspects of a job).

Only in the first instance — carelessness — is an employee truly "to blame" for the unsatisfactory work and therefore, deserving of punishment *per se,* arbiters have held. Where unsatisfactory performance is due to incompetence or disability, arbiters generally require that, if possible, management first attempt to remedy the problem through such means as retraining or transfer. Nevertheless, employers are not obligated to carry indefinitely a worker who continues to be nonproductive and may resort to "nonculpable termination." As one arbiter commented, "the principle must be recognized that wrongdoing is not the sole basis for a just cause employment termination." "If an employee is given every fair and reasonable opportunity to perform satisfactorily and obviously is incapable of doing so," the arbiter stressed, "there is no basis for requiring an employer to continue that employee on its rolls." (Northern Telecom Inc., 65 LA 405; see also 74 LA 705, 71 LA 1099)

In reviewing terminations for unsatisfactory performance, arbiters frequently are called upon to decide between differing explanations regarding the exact cause of the employee's problem. In one case, for example, a worker claimed that "mental and emotional pressures" made it impossible for him to perform adequately. However, pointing out that the employee failed to offer any proof that his mental state constituted a "disability" rendering him incapable of doing satisfactory work, the arbiter ruled that management had properly discharged the worker for consistently failing to meet production standards. (General Electric Co., 74 LA 578)

Similarly, another arbiter sustained discharge for unsatisfactory performance, even though the union claimed that the worker was not competent to handle the job and should properly have been demoted to a less demanding position. According to the arbiter, the employer correctly considered the claim of incompetence as just an excuse to hide "negligence and disregard of warnings." (Admiral Paint Co., 60 LA 418)

The following sections discuss in detail how arbiters distinguish among the three causes of unsatisfactory performance and their decisions as to the propriety of action taken in these situations.

Incompetence

IN BRIEF

Incompetence, unlike carelessness, generally should not be treated as a disciplinary problem, since the usual remedies of warnings and suspensions clearly are inappropriate and nonproductive when the employee is, in truth, incompetent in the job. As one arbiter explained, in this type of situation, "an employee is not guilty of fault or wrongdoing," and, consequently, does not warrant "discipline" as such. However, the arbiter continued, there is a "class of nonculpable reasons which will ultimately support discharge, not because the employee is necessarily guilty of fault or wrongdoing, but, rather, because the essence of the employment relationship is so impaired that is not reasonable to require an employer to continue that relationship." Specifically, this class includes "inability to perform the work with reasonable efficiency," since, "if permitted to go on, this would impair the company's ability to make a profit, to grant wage increases in future negotiations to good productive employees, and, indeed, a company's very ability to provide jobs."

Whenever a nonculpable cause of termination arises, however, management must first warn the employee of possible consequences and work with him "to try to correct or remove the thing that is destructive to the employment relationship," the arbiter stressed. If it becomes clear "that the cause that impairs the employment relationship is chronic or of long-standing" character and that "there is no reasonable prognosis that the cause can be removed within a reasonable period of time," then "nondisciplinary termination" would be warranted. Accordingly, the arbiter upheld the discharge of an incentive rate worker who consistently failed to produce enough pieces to earn minimum wages. Pointing out that management had counseled and warned the employee for over a year regarding her inefficiency, the arbiter declared that the employer should no longer be "forced to supplement her wage beyond the work given in exchange therefor." (Florsheim Shoe Co., 74 LA 705; see also 91 LA 293)

Other arbiters similarly have upheld terminations for incompetence where management repeatedly had counselled the employee about the problem. (97 LA 378, 96 LA 556, 91 1347, 91 LA 1014, 91 LA 593, 76 LA 254, 74 LA 806, 64 LA 248, 64 LA 916, 63 LA 610) This emphasis on counselling also underlies arbitral decisions to sustain "nonculpable" discipline short of discharge where the reprimand or suspension is designed to function as a warning to the employee. (74 LA 274, 73 LA 385)

On the other hand, discipline is likely to be overturned where management: cannot substantiate the allegations of incompetence; has neglected to provide the employee with proper training or supervision necessary for learning how to do the job correctly; or has failed to give the employee adequate warning and an opportunity to improve poor performance. (97 LA 1196, 97 LA 1145, 97 LA 1045, 97 LA 931, 97 LA 549, 97 LA 12, 96 LA 957, 92 LA 850, 80 LA 176, 80 LA 13, 72 LA 988, 71 LA 396, 55 LA 231, 51 LA 642) Even where the worker is clearly incompetent, management may be able to serve its own best interests in terms of hiring expenses and workforce morale by reassigning the employee, where possible, to another job that is within his or her capabilities.

GUIDELINES

Failure to Meet Production Standards

"The employer," one arbiter has pointed out, "has regularly been held to be entitled to set production standards and discharge an employee for failure to meet them provided the standards are fair and reasonable." (Allied Employers Inc., 65 LA 270; see also 95 LA 182, 92 LA 862, 74 LA 578, 66 LA 705, 65 LA 405, 64 LA 885, 43 LA 1155, 40 LA 891, 39 LA 719, 37 LA 558, 36 LA 1442, 33 LA 913, 35 LA 794, 32 LA 485, 23 LA 217, 22 LA 101)

EXAMPLE: Stressing that "maintenance of high efficiency is important to the profitability of the company and the continued jobs of the employees," an arbitrator declared that "continued low production" on the part of any one worker "cannot be condoned." The employee had been warned several times about his "low production," but continued to work at a pace that was vastly "inferior" to that of even temporary employees, the arbiter noted. In view of these circumstances, the employer's decision to suspend the worker for three days was "neither arbitrary nor capricious," the arbiter declared, but rather "could be viewed as lenient." Cautioning the employee that management was using "progressive discipline" in an effort to drive home the lesson, the arbiter emphasized that unless he "immediately" improved his "deportment," he could "expect to be discharged without any hope of reinstatement." (Lash Distributors Inc., 74 LA 274)

EXAMPLE: A worker was properly discharged for "substandard" performance, after he botched four separate work assignments in a row, an arbiter decided. Several supervisors testified that the employee was "consistently the worst performer in the entire workforce," and even co-workers admitted that they had had to help rectify the employee's mistakes, the arbiter pointed out, ruling that the termination was "reasonable and for just cause." (Pet Inc., 76 LA 292)

When an employer resorts to the remedy of discharge for failure to meet production standards, an arbitrator judging the reasonableness of the action may consider the adequacy of the employee's training, supervision, and equipment provided to do the job, and the weight of production records, work sheets, or work samples submitted by the employer to establish the worker's incompetence.

Arbiters also agree in theory that an employer has the right to tighten work standards and require better performance, even if this is a break from past laxness. But to bring about such a reversal of past practice, management may have to do more than merely exhort employees to do better. Discipline of employees who continue to produce at the old standards may not be upheld if the new standards have not been clearly defined and communicated to the employees. (12 LA 527, 8 LA 282)

Moreover, the production standard that is set must be reasonable. One arbiter upheld termination of a substandard worker in large part because output norms were based on a "thoroughly standardized" work measurement system that had been "applied in a thoroughly professional way by a licensed and authorized practitioner." With this "valid measurement" demonstrating that the employee's output level was less than half normal capacity, management had the right to discharge her, the arbiter concluded, notwithstanding the fact that it had continued to employ the worker beyond the probationary period. (Northern Telecom Inc., 65 LA 405)

Furthermore, as another arbiter noted, "the probation clause within regard to discharge simply means that after the probationary period, the company shall be *responsible* for any discharge." In other words, management is not prohibited from terminating an employee, as long as it defends "its actions on the basis of other parts of the contract." (Sager Lock Works, 12 LA 495)

EXAMPLE: An employee who had passed his probationary period in a higher-level job was justifiably discharged for improper work performance, an arbiter ruled. Dismissing the union's allegations that the employee should never have been promoted to the position because he lacked the necessary "ability and education," the arbiter found that the worker had performed competently throughout his probationary period. Fitness for the job, the arbiter pointed out, was not confined to "technical or practical qualifications only," but included 'responsibility and reliability" as well. Agreeing with management that the employee's problem was "not a matter of competence but of negligence and disregard of warnings," the arbiter concluded that the worker had "disqualified himself for continuation in the company's employ." (Admiral Paint Co., 60 LA 418)

Inadequate Training or Equipment

Generally, management has an obligation to provide an employee with adequate training and proper equipment before disciplining the worker for incompetence. (International Register Co., 8 LA 285) However, arbitrators have held that employers are not required to maintain an indefinite training program for workers, or absolve them of all responsibility for equipment.

EXAMPLE: An employer properly removed a worker from a training program when, after seven weeks of instruction, she had been unable to "master even the most rudimentary facets" of the job, an arbiter decided. The arbiter dismissed the worker's arguments that the training program was "too short" and that management was obligated to keep her in the program for "whatever length" of time was necessary to make her "sufficiently competent" in the job. Rather, the arbiter held, in today's "industrial era of highly educated and compensated workers," companies cannot afford to "allow an employee an almost indefinite time in which to become sufficiently qualified to properly and safely handle a specific job." In any case, he declared, the worker's "lack of mechanical aptitude was the primary factor in her failure in the training program, not the make-up of the training schedule." (Allied Chemical Corp., 75 LA 1101)

Similarly, an arbiter upheld written reprimands issued to a group of workers for restricted output, notwithstanding the employees' contention that they had done "the best they could" with "faulty equipment." Even granting that there had been equipment problems, the arbiter stressed, the employees were culpable, since they had neglected their "duty" to advise their supervisor of the faulty machinery and thereby wasted the opportunity to get it repaired without "significant loss of production." (Wallace-Murray Corp., 73 LA 385)

Likewise, an employer properly discharged a chemical operator for failing to check a vacuum breaker while pumping hydrochloric acid from one tank into another storage tank, resulting in the collapse of the tank and loss of 400 gallons of acid, an arbitrator decided.

Arguing that he did not receive proper operating instructions on the pumping process and that a frozen valve was the cause of the incident, the employee insisted that he had not been negligent.

Finding, however, that the employee was trained by another operator to check the breaker, the arbitrator ruled that the worker committed a serious operating error which resulted in the tank collapsing. Pointing out that the employee's poor work record indicated that he previously had been warned on at least two occasions that his operating errors would subject him to discharge, the arbitrator concluded that the worker was "seriously remiss" in his pumping duties. (Neville Chemical Co., 74 LA 814; see also 72 LA 81)

Proof of Incompetence: Sales Records

Arbiters may be hesitant in approving discharges for inefficiency based on sales records. Unlike the output of most production workers, the work records of salespeople are subject to several factors beyond their control. These include different areas and customers, competition, product changes, and prevailing business climate. Umpires agree that these other factors must be considered before using a poor sales record to justify a discharge. Where a company failed to show that a decline in ice cream sales was the driver/salesman's own fault, for instance, an umpire overruled his discharge. (Russell Creamery Co., 21 LA 293; see also 98 LA 112, 96 LA 274)

However, another arbiter ruled that an employer was justified in discharging a department chief because of his low sales record. Although the worker argued that the drop in sales was the result of economic conditions, the arbiter decided that the true cause of the decline was the worker's "lack of application or lack of sales ability," as evidenced by the fact that his sales record "averaged only about two thirds that of his assistant's" and "ranged as low as approximately one third." Absent evidence that the assistant was a "real super salesman," the arbiter declared, the discrepancy could only be explained by the employee's unsuitability to the job. (Allied Employers Inc., 65 LA 270)

Carelessness

IN BRIEF

Undue carelessness, negligence, or wanton disregard for the employer's property or operations can provide just cause for discipline, arbitrators agree. (97 LA 1029, 97 LA 542, 95 LA 1016, 92 LA 1143, 91 LA 1284, 91 LA 1162, 91 LA 286, 76 LA 324, 75 LA 1158, 74 LA 1278, 73 LA 857, 72 LA 1051, 65 LA 829, 63 LA 753, 54 LA 1174, 52 LA 145, 51 LA 792, 51 LA 696)

While management probably should not have a flat rule of "one serious error and you're out," it does not have to wait until the building is blown up or all materials are ruined before resorting to discharge of a careless worker. The decision in each case should be based on a careful consideration of the act and related factors. One arbitrator suggested that these points should be considered:

▶ The possibility of the act's recurrence;
▶ The attitude of the erring employee, in particular the desire and ability to learn from the mistake (98 LA 188, 97 LA 162, 92 LA 1214);
▶ The actual and potential injury involved;
▶ The influence of the discipline on other employees;
▶ The effect of the mistake on the parties with whom the company deals, such as customers or the government; and,
▶ The employee's length of service. (37 LA 953; see also 95 LA 435, 93 LA 1236, 50 LA 571)

GUIDELINES

Gross Negligence

To sustain a discharge for one-time carelessness or a first offense, management usually must be prepared to prove that the employee was guilty of gross negligence — that is, an almost willful disregard of what is being done and an almost complete inattentiveness to the job with the opportunity to foresee the likely consequences. (97 LA 1029, 97 LA 542, 94 LA 21, 91 LA 1284, 91 LA 1162, 46 LA 1161)

EXAMPLE: An employer properly discharged a worker for gross negligence after she "panicked" in an emergency situation, despite eight weeks of training in emergency procedures. Instead of simply shutting off the valve that fed gas to a heater where the flame had gone out, the worker ran for help. Meanwhile, the gas continued to build up, causing an explosion that resulted in considerable damage to the heater. The arbiter dismissed the worker's arguments that the discipline was too severe because she had had only one week's experience in the job she was assigned to at the time. The company had a right, following its "thorough training" in safety procedures, to assume that all employees were "well versed and familiar with the proper safety procedures," the arbiter declared. Moreover, the employer was justified in insisting "upon competent and careful adherence to its procedures," the arbiter noted, especially where the correct response to the emergency entailed "simply shutting off a valve." Stressing that the employee's "failure to adhere to the simple safety procedures in this case resulted in extensive damage to the charge heater and perhaps more important, potential harm to fellow employees," the arbiter concluded that the termination was for just cause. (Hess Oil Virgin Islands, Corp., 72 LA 81)

Similarly, a worker who failed to follow established procedures while pumping out a tank, thereby causing the tank to collapse and 400 gallons of hydrochloric acid to be lost, was properly terminated, another arbiter ruled. Despite earlier warnings after incidents of carelessness that another operating error would subject him to discharge, the arbiter stressed, the worker showed "little, if any, positive response" to the company's efforts to "mold him into an acceptable employee." Given the magnitude of the latest incident, the arbiter decided, management was justified in the discharge. (Neville Chemical Co., 74 LA 814)

EXAMPLE: An employer properly discharged a payroll clerk for careless errors that resulted in overpayments exceeding $1,200 in a single month. Considering that the employee had received special training following an earlier discovery of errors, and that it was apparent then that she knew how to perform her job properly, the arbitrator found just cause for her discharge. (Greyhound Lines Inc., 67 LA 483)

EXAMPLE: A drill press operator negligently mis-drilled a number of holes in an aircraft part he was working on, and then attempted to cover up the mistake by discarding the part, worth about $800. When the part was later discovered, the worker was discharged for his poor work and for failure to report the mistake to his foreman. Upholding the discharge, the arbitrator pointed out that the employee was well aware of the company's stringent rule on reporting mistakes, designed to guard against the danger of defective parts in the finished passenger airplanes. He not only neglected to report his mistake, the arbiter found, but apparently went so far as to conspire with his supervisor to deceive management in order to keep his job. (Rohr Industries Inc., 65 LA 982)

However, an arbitrator overturned the discharge of a machinist who had made a costly error because of the employee's four-year blemish-free work record. Although management argued that the mistake amounted to gross negligence and warranted immediate dismissal, the arbiter ruled otherwise, since the error did not involve willfulness or recklessness or a wanton disregard for life, health, or property. Rather, he said, it amounted to a good-faith oversight on a simple step in a complicated process, and could have happened to anyone. While serious, this type of first offense does not warrant discharge, the arbiter decided, especially considering the employee's past record, his honesty in reporting the mistake, his tenure, and his responsibility. Instead, the arbiter concluded, a two-week suspension was more appropriate. (Ingalls Shipbuilding Corp., 37 LA 953; see also 97 LA 386, 96 LA 585)

Similarly, an employee was improperly discharged for negligence after the company car he momentarily had left unattended was stolen, another arbiter decided. While the employer based the discharge decision on a work rule against leaving a running vehicle unattended, the arbiter found that management did not address this issue "on a regular basis." Consequently, he said, "the company was as much at fault" in the situation as the employee. In light of the worker's past record of failing to follow established procedures, however, the arbiter concluded that a lengthy suspension was in order. (Servair Inc., 76 LA 1134)

EXAMPLE: Management improperly disciplined two workers in a case of "group responsibility," an arbiter decided. Because an operation that normally was performed by one of two workers was not carried out, the employer incurred several thousands of dollars in damages. It then disciplined both of the workers. Overturning the penalties, the arbiter came out strongly against holding an entire crew responsible for performing a task that management had not specifically assigned to any one individual. Such a practice would carry discipline to the extreme by permitting punishment of a group whenever individual responsibility could not be pinpointed, the arbiter declared, pointing out that responsibility for assigning duties rests with the supervisor. (International Nickel Co. Inc., 44 LA 376)

Neglect of Duty or Responsibility

Neglect of duty (inattention to responsibilities or ordinary negligence) may be distinguished from gross negligence in that the inattention is less intentional and, for the most part, results in less severe repercussions or involves minimal expenses. Although arbiters are unlikely to sustain terminations for isolated incidents of this type, they generally will uphold less drastic penalties, provided that these are imposed in accordance with established policies and that there is "clear and convincing evidence" to support the charge. (97 LA 66, 97 LA 60, 95 LA 873, 93 LA 302)

EXAMPLE: In one case, an arbiter ruled that management had "failed to meet its burden of proof." The arbiter thus overturned a suspension imposed on a worker who allegedly was sleeping while on emergency duty of monitoring communications channels. Although the worker, by his own admission, had been lying down, the arbiter noted, management acknowledged that he could have been watching television in this position, albeit somewhat awkwardly. The arbiter also dismissed allegations that the employee and his co-workers were neglecting their duties by watching television, since the employees were specifically instructed only "to monitor the radio and telephone and to respond to emergency situations." Although management declared that viewing television while on duty is "a transgression of common sense rules of the workplace," and "detrimental to the departmental morale and discipline," the arbiter found that the issue at hand had "nothing to do with either the inherent evils of television or the shaping of departmental discipline." Rather, he said, the question to be resolved was whether the workers "were neglecting the specific duties which their superior had assigned to them." Since the employer was unable to demonstrate that the workers had missed any "emergencies, telephone calls, or radio communications," he concluded, the suspensions were improper. (City of Cleveland, 71 LA 1041)

EXAMPLE: An employee was properly disciplined for neglect of duty after he failed to monitor several government contracts, which resulted in overpayments by the employer. Failing to find one "scintilla" of evidence supporting the employee's claim of extenuating circumstances, the arbiter ruled that management was justified in deciding to discipline the worker. However, the penalty of suspension was too severe a punishment, the arbiter decided, since management's policies prescribed an official reprimand as the appropriate discipline in such cases. (General Services Administration, 75 LA 1158)

EXAMPLE: An airline mechanic, whose negligence while performing a routine inspection risked damage to an aircraft's engine, was properly issued a written reprimand. After examining the air intake section of an airplane's engine, a mechanic conducted a "test run" of the engines. Hearing a "funny sound," he immediately cut the engines off, and then observed bits and pieces of shredded material floating in the air. These were later discovered to be that parts of the mechanic's wallet and papers, which he had left inside the engine. The employer then issued the worker a written reprimand for failing to "maintain his given responsibility." Protesting the reprimand, the employee claimed that he would not purposefully leave something in the aircraft engine intake and pointed out that no damage to the engine had occurred.

Since it is clear that the employee "did, in fact, leave his wallet in the air intake," the arbiter said, "it must be recognized that he demonstrated a lack of care for the work in question." The fact that "no actual damage occurred to the engine" is irrelevant, the arbiter stressed, since the "same inattention" which caused the employee to leave his wallet in the engine's air intake could result in his leaving behind an object that would cause damage. While accepting the employee's argument that he did not purposely leave his wallet "to be destroyed," the arbiter concluded that the employer's discipline was warranted. (Air Force Department, 76 LA 315)

Habitual Carelessness

Arbiters generally uphold management's right to discharge employees with records of chronic carelessness over a period of time, regardless of whether the culminating incident, standing alone, is sufficient to justify termination or of the causes for the carelessness. (96 LA 609, 94 LA 1080, 74 LA 1008, 73 LA 771, 32 LA 485, 23 LA 217)

EXAMPLE: An employee who persisted in her poor work habits was properly discharged, an arbiter decided. The worker's responsibilities included answering telephone calls from customers and performing routine clerical duties. However, she consistently carried on personal conversations rather than taking business calls, was frequently absent from her work station, and took inordinate lengths of time—up to nine months in one case—to process invoices, thereby losing for her employer substantial discounts for timely payments. Finding that the employee made no attempt to improve her performance despite verbal and written warnings from her supervisor, the arbiter ruled that management was under no obligation to keep on a worker who "did not diligently apply herself." to her job. (General Electric Co., 74 LA 1278)

Similarly, another arbiter upheld the discharge of an employee for "gross and habitual" carelessness. Although the employee argued that he had not had time to correct his behavior before being terminated, the arbiter found that management had properly applied a "series of progressive disciplinary measures." The worker had received a total of nine warnings and five disciplinary letters for carelessness and poor performance within a five-week period, the arbiter pointed out, stressing that the employee "knew he was getting close to discharge." (S & T Industries, Inc., 73 LA 857)

Likewise, an arbiter sustained the termination of a worker who did not perform efficiently and had a record of discipline for excessive tardiness. Although management could have terminated the worker for a previous incident, it had suspended her instead, the arbiter noted. Since this "leniency was not improving the employee's work habits," she concluded, management was justified in discharging the worker. (Trojan Luggage Co., 76 LA 324)

EXAMPLE: An employer was justified in discharging a mill worker who negligently caused the dumping of thousands of pounds of industrial paint, considering the worker's "repeated and admitted violations of safety rules either by deliberate action or by gross negligence." The arbitrator, pointing out that lesser discipline had failed to change the worker's conduct, concluded that "he was not a safe employee for other employees to work with." (W. C. Richards Co., 64 LA 382)

Accidents & the Accident-Prone

Management has the right to discharge an employee who is "accident-prone," an arbitrator has said, if it can show that the worker meets the definition of one who has "a greater number of accidents than would be expected of the average individual under the same conditions" or who has "personality traits that predispose to accident." This determination can be made, however, only after the employer explores the possibility of whether this predisposition can be corrected, the arbiter cautioned.

In the case at hand, management based its allegations on the fact that the worker filed inordinate numbers of insurance claims for on-the-job injuries. Reviewing the nature of the claims, the arbiter found that the evidence suggested that the employee "had only a propensity to file claims in instances where most employees would have been satisfied with receiving merely first-aid treatment." If this were true, he noted, "a conclusion of accident proneness would be unjustified, although a reason for warning" would exist. The arbiter suggested that management suspend the worker for a "significant period" and, upon her return to work, warn her that "while she should report all accidents, she should not exaggerate them." This technique "would shed light on whether her propensities might be remedied," he explained, whereas "without such experience, it is not clear that she was sufficiently 'accident prone' to warrant discharge as too burdensome an employee." (George-Pacific Corp., 52 LA 325)

On the other hand, another arbiter has argued, industrial discipline, particularly the supreme penalty of discharge, should not be based on the notion that an employee is "accident prone." Workers may unluckily be involved in series of accidents for which they are completely blameless, the arbiter observed, while others, who act recklessly, somehow escape accidents. According to the arbiter, it's not the former group that deserves discipline, but the latter. Under this reasoning, the test for discipline is not whether the employee was involved in accidents, but whether he is so careless and inefficient as to justify the conclusion that he is not a safe and competent employee. (Interstate Bakeries Corp., 38 LA 1109)

Driving accidents are special cases—the dangers implicit in careless operation of a vehicle typically weigh heavily in an arbitrator's decision on the propriety of discipline imposed on an employee vehicle operator whose driving judgment is in question. "Arbitrators are ordinarily reluctant to disturb disciplinary discharges," one arbiter noted, "if it means the return to the highway of an employee who may be dangerous to himself, to others, and where the legal and financial interests of the company are potentially at stake." Thus, the arbiter pointed out, discharges have been upheld where: the employee-driver had been involved in numerous accidents and/or had a poor past record; the operation involved the transportation of dangerous materials; or the worker was guilty of gross negligence or willful and wanton conduct. (48 LA 947, 30 LA 213, 24 LA 48, 8 LA 897, 5 LA 430, 3 LA 786) On the other hand, the arbiter continued, discharge has been overturned where: the alleged negligence was not conclusively proven; the employee's error presented no danger to the public; the negligence was ordinary, rather than gross, in nature; or special conditions, such as bad weather, made the accident not entirely the worker's fault. (46 LA 1161, 36 LA 537, 30 LA 830, 21 LA 457, 9 LA 775, 6 LA 913, 5 LA 3)

In the case at hand, the arbiter ruled that discharge was too severe a penalty for a worker who was involved in an accident on the worksite, even though he previously had received a three-day suspension for damage to company property arising out of a driving accident. Taking into account the weather conditions and the terrain, the worker's actions were "not so clearly negligent and so clearly in disregard of legitimate company production or performance expectations so as to warrant discharge," the arbiter found. Furthermore, the worker's record of "one prior minor accident in no way is comparable to the pattern of cases where discharge has been sustained because of a great number of accidents which were negligently caused." Finally, "in making his ill-fated attempt," the arbiter concluded, the worker "did not so substantially misjudge the danger so as to make his continued employment a grave hazard to the company." (Kaiser Sand & Gravel Co., 50 LA 571)

EXAMPLE: A truck driver was properly issued a warning for running his tractor-trailer into the rear of another company vehicle, an arbiter ruled. The worker argued that slippery road conditions had caused him to plow into the other vehicle when it suddenly stopped, and that, in any event, he should "simply have been advised in writing that an accident had occurred and that he should drive carefully in the future." The arbiter, however, found that the employee was "an experienced, veteran truck driver" who should have known "the degree of care he was required to use in the operation of his vehicle." Deciding that it was the worker's carelessness, not the road conditions, that had caused the accident, the arbiter agreed with management that the employee was guilty of "hazardous and negligent" driving that warranted a written reprimand. (Hoerner Waldorf Champion International Corp., 75 LA 416)

Similarly, a forklift operator was properly discharged for causing an accident that injured a co-worker, an arbitrator ruled.

The employee was driving a fork lift truck when he collided with another truck driven by a co-worker. In the accident, the co-worker suffered a deep gash to his forehead that required several stitches. After conducting an investigation, the employer concluded that the employee had been speeding and had failed to yield the right of way to the co-worker's vehicle. Consequently, the employee was discharged for gross negligence and disregard for safety. The arbiter decided that the evidence proved that the worker was driving carelessly, without due regard for his own safety or that of his fellow workers. Furthermore, the employee had been warned about his unsafe driving in the past, the arbitrator observed, concluding that in light of the circumstances, the penalty was not too severe. (Economics Laboratory Inc., 77 LA 73)

Disability

IN BRIEF

In most cases involving physical disability, management's right to terminate, transfer, or lay off depends on whether it has good reason to believe that the employee cannot perform satisfactorily or without undue hazard to him- or herself or co-workers. This determination, in turn, depends on an evaluation of medical evidence, job requirements, and the work environment. The mere fact of disability, taken alone, generally is not sufficient to support a personnel action, especially if the disability has been of long standing. For example, in one case an arbitrator reinstated a worker who was discharged because he was "industrially blind," it appearing that the employee has made an amazing adjustment to his disability and had worked for years without mishap. (United Gas Improvement Co., 40 LA 799; see also 94 LA 513, 67 LA 706; 62 LA 1157; 61 LA 1144)

On the other hand, when management can support its allegations with clear and convincing evidence, arbiters typically uphold the action. (96 LA 1003, 76 LA 1233, 75 LA 122, 74 LA 1205, 72 LA 1006, 64 LA 544, 61 LA 1202, 60 LA 605) Nonetheless, at least one arbiter has held that where there is little danger to others, it is up to the employee to decide whether to continue working with a bad heart. (Interwoven Stocking Co., 39 LA 918)

Discrimination against the handicapped is forbidden by the American With Disabilities Act of 1990, the Rehabilitation Act of 1973, and by state fair-employment-practice laws. Additionally, some cases of handicap discrimination have been decided on in light of constitutional guarantees, such as the right to due process.

GUIDELINES

Medical Evidence

The issue in disability cases frequently centers on conflicting medical views as to the employee's condition and ability to do the job. The general view seems to be that a company is entitled to rely on the opinions of its own doctors, as long as it gives the employees an opportunity to overcome those views before a final decision is reached. (Ideal Cement Co., 20 LA 480)

Where there are differences between a company doctor's conclusion and those of an employee's doctor, an effort should be made to reconcile the difference by, for example, having the two doctors discuss the matter. (International Harvester Co., 22 LA 138)

Where conflict persists, however, greater consideration is given to the physician who has done the most extensive examination or who is more qualified in the treatment of the injury in question. (Whitaker Cable Corp., 50 LA 1152)

Additional factors considered by arbitrators when resolving conflicting medical evidence include the following:

- The employer's decision must be based upon bona fide nondiscriminatory expert opinions and advice;
- The personal testimony of a medical witness who is subject to cross-examination is generally entitled to more weight than mere written reports where there is no difference in the degree of expertise possessed by the medical witnesses testifying; and
- In the absence of contract provisions, management is allowed to make its decision on advice from its own medical consultants as long as the advice is fair and impartial—it need not submit such advice to outside experts for their consideration. (Hospital Service Plan of New Jersey, 61 LA 947)

Raised Physical Requirements

Can an employer stiffen the physical requirements for various jobs and then discharge employees who fail to meet them? Unless there is a definite change in the nature or conditions of a job, workers may not be discharged for failing to meet physical requirements which are higher than those they met when they were hired for the job, according to most arbiters.

EXAMPLE: One company, suspecting that poor eyesight on the part of some employees was causing a lot of defective work, set up a new vision-testing program. In some cases, the visual requirements for jobs were raised. Several workers could not pass the new tests for their jobs and were discharged. The arbitrator decided that the discharges were not for good cause under the contract. He ruled that the workers could retain their jobs as long as they continued to meet the standards in effect at the time they were hired. He noted that in no case were the job requirements changed so as to make higher standards necessary. The arbitrator suggested, however, that there was nothing to prevent the company from applying higher visual standards to future placements. (Connecticut Telephone & Electric Corp., 22 LA 632; see also 97 LA 175)

Workers' Compensation Claims

In some instances, employers have tried to justify personnel actions on the grounds that the employees' medical histories indicate they are likely to become disabled, thereby making the company liable for future workers' compensation claims. At least one arbiter has held that an employer may rightfully refuse to hire on this basis. In that case, the applicants were rejected because they refused to sign WC waiver forms relieving management of liability. Noting that other applicants all had previously filed workers' compensation claims, the arbiter found that the company had reason to believe that they were "at least partially disabled." The employer was legitimately concerned that the workers would "aggravate their medical problems while performing their jobs," the arbiter pointed out. By requiring the waiver, management was "essentially informing" the trio that it had "no desire to assume any of the risk of such further aggravation,' and that they would be working 'at their own risk,' the arbiter explained, concluding that it "legitimately refused to hire" the applicants when they choose not to sign the release. (Rust Engineering Co., 76 LA 263)

Where workers have been on the payroll for some time, however, arbiters generally agree that management may not use workers' compensation claim worries to justify discharge.

EXAMPLE: A truck driver with five years' seniority received treatment under a contractual health and welfare plan for back pains, which, it turned out, were caused by congenital malformation of the lower spine. Following treatment, the worker applied for reinstatement. Management refused, claiming it had no obligation to risk the possibility of future absenteeism and claims for workers' compensation. The arbiter, however, held that the risk to the company was outweighed by the workers' interest in his job, which he had performed competently over a period of years. There was no certainty, he pointed out, that the worker would have further trouble with his back. Even if he did, his condition would not pose an immediate hazard either to himself or to other employees, the arbiter commented. Finally, he noted, the worker's doctor had stated that he could safely return to truck driving. (Bethlehem Steel Co., 29 LA 476)

EXAMPLE: A worker who had sustained 20 injuries during the last 4 years of his 18 years of employment was called into his supervisor's office and told that because he had received workers' compensation payment totaling 100 percent disability, he was considered totally disabled by the company. The worker then was discharged.

The arbitrator, however, failed to find any medical evidence that employee could not perform his job or that he was a safety hazard to himself or others. Nothing that the employee was allowed to return to work without any restrictions following two major injuries, the arbitrator reinstated the worker. (Quality Electric Steel Castings Inc., 62 LA 1157)

Similarly, discharge was overturned where an employee had already collected workers' compensation for a back injury deemed 16 percent permanent partial disability. In that case, the worker had returned to his job, which called for heavy lifting, following back surgery. After the employee was on the job for eight weeks, the company was informed of the employee's medical status, and thereafter decided to discharge him to prevent the possibility of further injury.

Despite the company's apparent good faith, the arbitrator found a lack of clear, thorough medical evidence, complicated by the employee's eight week return to the job with satisfactory results. Since there was no guarantee that the employee's reinstatement would not create a risk to himself or others, the arbitrator awarded a suspension, pending further medical evidence. (Newkirk Sales Co., 61 LA 1144)

Insurance Costs

In some instances, a company's insurance company may object to the continued employment of a disabled employee or may threaten to raise its premiums substantially if the employee is retained. One arbitrator has indicated that management is not obligated to pay substantially more for insurance to accommodate a handicapped employee. (Hiller Chevrolet-Cadillac Inc., 37 LA 629) According to another arbitrator, however, the insurance carrier should not be permitted to dictate which employees should be fired and for what reasons. This would make the negotiated restrictions on discipline virtually meaningless, he said. (Expert Dairy Service Inc., 45 LA 217)

EXAMPLE: Insurability at normal rates was an implied condition of continued employment for a truck driver, an arbitrator decided. According to the arbiter, the employer had the right to expect that it would not be exposed to unreasonable risk or expense in the employment relationship. Nonetheless, the arbiter continued, in the present case, management was under a continuing obligation to provide the disabled employee with any available work that did not involve an insurance problem. (J.A. McMahon Co. Inc., 44 LA 1274)

However, another arbiter ruled that a company could not discharge an obese employee with high blood pressure, even though it previously had had to pay a $33,000 damage award to the family of another worker who suffered a heart attack on the job. Although the company doctor had recommended the discharge, the arbiter found that the employee was not a serious industrial risk. (Great Atlantic & Pacific Tea Co., 41 LA 278)

Obesity & Hypertension

Where marked obesity is accompanied by high blood pressure or other attendant physical conditions that affect an employee's fitness for work, arbitrators have upheld management's denial of that work.

EXAMPLE: An employee whose various obesity-related problems caused him to fall asleep on the job was discharged for just cause, an arbiter decided. The employee had been hospitalized after he repeatedly fell asleep on the job. When he returned to work, management warned him about the necessity of conforming to a special diet in order to improve his condition. However, slipping back into his "errant behavior" of staying up late and consuming an "excessive" amount of junk food, the worker again started falling asleep on the job. When management's counseling and minor discipline failed to stop the problem, the employee was discharged on the grounds that he was "unfit for work."

The employer "not only gave the grievant assistance with his problem when it first learned of it," the arbiter noted, but also "took him back to work, counseled him, and followed a consistent program of progressive discipline which should have had the effect of being both rehabilitative in nature and a deterrent" to his bad habits. Despite management's reasonable and accommodative efforts," the worker himself "did little to mitigate his medical problem." The employer had "a right to expect" the employee to present himself "fit for work," the arbiter decided, concluding that the worker's repeated failures to take advantage of the opportunities given him militated against his reinstatement. (City of Iowa City, 72 LA 1006)

However, where the overweight condition has not interfered with an employee's work in the past, an employer may not say "you're too fat for me." Thus, an employee with 2 years of service was ordered reinstated, despite her obesity and high blood pressure, where her condition had not affected her job performance. (Magnavox Co., 46 LA 719)

EXAMPLE: Another arbitrator held that a company improperly denied reinstatement to two women on the ground that their obesity was deleterious to their health. The company's concern for their health should not be converted into "an essentially paternalistic attempt to regulate an employee's personal life," he said. A like disqualification, he noted, could be levied against cigarette smokers on the theory that smoking may result in short windedness that could impair employee efficiency.

But the arbitrator upheld the company in refusing to reinstate one of the workers who suffered from nervousness, hypertension, and dizzy spells, as well as obesity. (Mutual Plastics Mold Corp. 48 LA 2)

Similarly, an employee suffering from "hypertension" was properly discharged after requesting his second extended medical leave within one year, an arbitrator ruled. In this case the employee had already taken a six month leave and had been warned by the company that a reoccurrence could result in discharge. Nevertheless, the employee filed for a second leave. In the absence of a "just cause" clause, the arbitrator concluded that the "reasonable discharge" was sufficiently backed by the circumstances. (American Broadcasting Companies Inc., 63 LA 278)

Mental Illness

Although recognizing a company's natural hesitancy about reemploying a person who has a mental illness that may be of a recurrent nature, arbitrators have refused to uphold discharges where there was medical evidence that the employee had recovered to the extent that his return to work would not involve and undue risk to himself or to others. Management may not assume that such a risk exists from the bare fact that an employee has been treated for mental illness. (61 LA 121, 28 LA 333, 26 LA 295)

In cases involving immoral or socially reprehensible conduct resulting from mental illness, arbitrators may direct reinstatement on evidence that the illness has been cured. But these awards have been based in part on the assurances that the employee's fellow workers have no objection to his reinstatement. (24 LA 229, 22 LA 1, 15 LA 42)

On the other hand, arbiters generally will uphold discharges where there is evidence that the worker's continued employment presents a substantial risk to co-workers.

EXAMPLE: An employee suffering from schizophrenia was properly discharged for grabbing, shoving, and screaming at a co-worker, an arbiter agreed. The worker had been hospitalized and diagnosed as a paranoid schizophrenic shortly after being hired. When he returned to the job, management tried to place him only in low-stress situations. Nevertheless, the employee was hospitalized two more times, but again returned to work after being released. Several years later, the employee began exhibiting hostile and aggressive behavior on the job and claimed he was being picked on by co-workers. After shoving and choking a general foreman, the employee was suspended, but later was allowed to return to work when he obtained a written clearance from his physician. Thereafter, one night when employees were lined up to clock out, he grabbed a co-worker, pushed him against the wall, and shouted "Don't you ever say that about me again." Management then decided to discharge the employee, stressing that although it did not wish to discipline the worker for behavior beyond his control, it had to keep order in the plant.

The arbiter noted that the psychologist had found that the employee was suffering from a "schizophrenic illness" that caused him to "manifest paranoid thought processes focused primarily on the work situation." The medical evidence also indicated that returning the employee to work would likely trigger repeat behavior, the arbiter observed, upholding the dismissal. (Wilcox Co., 75 LA 122; see also 92 LA 1291)

Epilepsy

In several cases involving the employment of epileptics, arbitrators have ruled against discharge merely because of the existence of the disability if there was no clear evidence of a safety hazard. (12 LA 9, 15, LA 903, 20 LA 266, 38 LA 829)

EXAMPLE: An arbiter reinstated an employee with epilepsy who was discharged after seven accident-free years with a company, which acted after an Occupational Safety and Health Administration staffer commented that epilepsy "constituted a dangerous condition." During his employ, the worker had suffered two seizures on the job, neither of which resulted in injury to the employee himself, his co-workers, or company operations. According to the worker, his seizures always were preceded by at least five minutes with an "aura," primarily twitching of the face muscles. Alerted by this indicator, the employee would lie down and insert into his mouth a tool he always carried to prevent himself from biting his tongue. In addition, the employee consistently refused to operate fork-lifts or climb ladders, and regularly took medicine that helped to control the frequency of seizures.

Citing medical testimony that the employee could work safely in the plant, especially since he had advance warning of seizures, the arbiter pointed out that the worker had adjusted to this physical condition remarkably well, even to the point of enlisting the aid of his co-workers in making adjustments to his work situation. Although sympathizing with the company's "fear" of OSHA, the arbiter gave more weight to the worker's accident-free record. The discharge represented the "elevation of safety to a sacred cow," the arbiter declared, maintaining that to terminate a seven-year employee because of the possibility of future accident would convert concern with safety to "callousness." The time to decide whether or not the worker's continued employment constituted a hazard, the arbiter concluded, would be when and if an injury resulted from his condition. (Samuel Bingham Co., 67 LA 706)

However, a discharge was upheld where the employee had several seizures at work which resulted in self-injury, and the employee himself conceded that medication was not successful in his case in controlling the seizures. (Stauffer Chemical Co., 40 LA 18)

Likewise, discharge was upheld in the case of a crane operator who passed out and fell during his seizures. Hazards to himself and others existed in his continued employment, the arbitrator noted, pointing out that impartial medical experts had advised the company against retaining the worker. Not only were there no other jobs at the plant for the worker to perform safely, but he also lacked a long and satisfactory record, the arbitrator observed. (Acme Galvanizing Inc., 61 LA 1115)

Similarly, a company was justified in refusing to let an employee who had suffered epileptic seizures return to his former job, even though medical evidence indicated his condition was under control.

The employee had been a lineman for a utility company when he began having seizures. After lengthy treatment, he was cleared by his physician to return to his former job. The company doctor, however, believed he would still be a "hazard," so he was kept in the lower rated job. While conceding that medical evidence showed the employee was physically able to perform lineman's work, the arbiter upheld the company's decision not to put the employee back on a job that involved unusual hazards. (Gulf State Utilities Co., 45 LA 1252)

Discharge may be upheld even if the employee has not been examined by a physician.

EXAMPLE: Where an employee had two seizures while at work, his employer acted reasonably in discharging him out of fear of possible injury to himself and others, an arbitrator ruled. Medical testimony, given by a private doctor who had not examined the employee, failed to show that the seizures could be fully controlled in the future, and there was no other job at the plant to which the employee could be transferred, the arbitrator concluded. (Weber Manufacturing Co. Inc., 63 LA 56)

Job Reassignments

When presented with clear evidence that an employee's disability interferes with job performance or poses safety hazards, arbiters will sustain a reassignment to another position where the disability can be better accommodated, especially if this action is an alternative to discharge.

EXAMPLE: "Removing an obviously disabled man from a place of unusually hazardous exposure for him" is "the 'right' thing" to do, an arbiter explained, adding, however, that the outright firing of a disabled employee is doing the "right thing in the wrong way." Rather, management should reassign the worker to a more accommodating position, the arbiter stressed. Since in the present case, no such position was currently available, the arbiter decided, the worker properly should be placed in layoff status. (Vulcan Mold & Iron Co., 40 LA 1266; see also 92 LA 1228)

EXAMPLE: An employer properly reassigned a crane operator to another job when, following an accident, it discovered that the employee had "zero depth perception," an arbiter decided. Dismissing the employee's argument that the accident was due to the poor condition of the crane, the arbiter stressed that regardless of whether this allegation were true, "the requirement of good depth perception for anyone operating the crane is a reasonable requirement," but "particularly if the crane is in poor condition." (Foster Wheeler Corp., 54 LA 871)

Similarly, management was within its rights to demote an employee whose heart condition prevented him from competently performing his job duties, another arbiter ruled. Following his return to work from a heart operation, the employee was allowed two trial periods to work back up to normal output levels. Evaluations showed, however, that he was not performing satisfactorily, and the worker was demoted to a lower position. While the worker charged that he had not been given a fair opportunity, the arbiter agreed with management that he had had ample time to demonstrate his abilities and that the evaluation process had been fairly conducted. With supervisory and production reports showing that other employees were outperforming the worker by as much as two to one, the arbiter stressed, the demotion was justified. (Haven-Busch Co., 74 LA 1205)

Likewise, an employee whose right leg had been amputated was properly restricted to driving an automatic transmission truck, even though, as the worker claimed, there was "no evidence that his physical handicap presented a safety hazard" warranting the ban. Although the worker's safety record was "commendable," the arbiter agreed, this record was compiled primarily with automatic transmission trucks. The employer's conclusion that the worker was not qualified to use a manual clutch, the arbiter observed, was based solely on safety concerns. Management need only show a "minimal increase in risk" to establish a logical basis for its action, the arbiter stressed, concluding that the employer was justified in restricting the worker's assignments. (Des Moines Asphalt and Paving Co., 76 LA 1233)

Moreover, as one arbiter noted, while an employer "certainly" may be able to redesign a particular job to conform to a worker's medical limitations, it is not required, absent specific contract provisions, to create a "special job" for a disabled worker. (Data Transportation Co., 75 LA 1154)

EXAMPLE: Supervisors were not required to "make work" for an employee to do when medical restrictions prevented him from performing his normal duties, an arbiter stressed. The worker's obesity placed great strains on his back muscles, making it difficult for him to bend, stoop, or lift objects over 10 pounds. Although management attempted to assign work that fell within these limitation, the arbiter noted, the employee "was frequently not cooperative," and "largely determined" on his own, applying "pretty stringent" interpretations, how the restrictions applied to a particular assignment. Thus, while at one time the worker "was willing to hose down an area," on another occasion he insisted that he could not perform this type of work. As a result, the supervisors "were beginning to run out of things" for the employee to do, the arbiter pointed out. Declaring that a company is not obligated to keep on the payroll a worker who is unable "to perform enough useful productive work to warrant his continued employment," the arbiter ruled that management would be justified in discharging the employee if he failed to take advantage of a last chance opportunity to reduce his weight to optimum levels and reassume his job without restrictions. (Reynolds Metals Co., 71 LA 1099)

Part 3

Safety and Health

Safety and Health

INTRODUCTION

In general, arbiters have held or recognized that management has the right to promulgate and enforce reasonable rules and regulations to ensure the safety and health of its employees. In fact, the Occupational Safety and Health Act of 1970 requires employers to comply with specific safety and health standards. Under its "general duty" provisions, the act requires employers to furnish a workplace free of hazards likely to cause death or serious physical harm to employees.

In the three areas addressed by this chapter, the standard of "reasonableness" is the test most often used by arbiters. The questions considered include:

▶ Are safety rules promulgated by management reasonable both in application and in content?

▶ Under what circumstances may management unilaterally restrict employee smoking?

▶ Is fear of contracting Acquired Immune Deficiency Syndrome (AIDS) a reason for employees to refuse to work with persons they suspect of having the disease?

Safety Rule Violations

IN BRIEF

Arbiters generally acknowledge that management has the right to issue and enforce safety rules, but caution that such rules must be reasonably related to the purpose of ensuring a safe and healthful workplace.

Discharge for the infraction of a safety rule may be justified where an employee has persistently disobeyed safety regulations in spite of progressive discipline. Serious infractions, particularly those which endanger other workers, may subject the employee to immediate discharge, with no requirement for progressive discipline.

Safety rules must be uniformly enforced. When there has been a past practice of not enforcing a safety rule, arbiters have overturned discipline, calling it inequitable. In some cases, management's failure to comply with safety rules or regulations has been regarded as a contractual violation.

GUIDELINES

"Reasonableness" of Rules

Safety rules must be "reasonable," arbiters have held — i.e., they must have a relationship to the employee's safety in the workplace. Arbiters have rejected management's unilateral promulgation of rules that are only peripherally related to workplace safety.

EXAMPLE: A company's rule forbidding employees to wear certain types of clothing while walking between the plant gates and the shop area was unreasonable, an arbiter concluded. The walkway between the gates and the shop was a "supposedly safe pedestrian walkway," noted the arbiter. The rule thus appeared, the arbiter said, "to be an unreasonable interference with the personal freedom of the employees to come and go from and to their work places without unreasonable regimentation." Other parts of the company's rule, relating to wearing beads and finger rings, the arbiter decided, should be referred to the labor-management committee for further consideration, following which the company "may impose a reasonable rule as to beads and finger rings realistically limited to such times and occasions as when the employee is, in fact, involved in or near moving machinery." (Babcock & Wilcox, 73 LA 443; see also 94 LA 1047)

Reasonable Application of Rules

However reasonable a safety rule may be, it may be overruled by an arbiter if it is applied in an unreasonable fashion.

EXAMPLE: A blanket company rule against the wearing of beards, which derived from the incompatibility of wearing a beard and wearing a full-face respirator safely, was pronounced "arbitrary and unreasonable" by an arbiter. "The company certainly has the right and obligation to promulgate reasonable safety rules and to enforce them," acknowledged the arbiter. However, "established need for respirator use or a reasonable probability of emergency use are the underpinnings which give the beard prohibition validity," the arbiter noted, ordering the company "to rescind the overly broad beard policy and return to a previous policy, under which any beard prohibition draws its essence from the need to wear a respirator." (Allied Chemical Corporation, 74 LA 412; see also 92 LA 492, 92 LA 1214, 91 LA 987)

Progressive Discipline

Safety rules may be enforced through progressive discipline, just as any other reasonable workplace regulations, arbiters have concluded.

EXAMPLE: After sustaining a number of injuries as the result of failing to wear proper safety equipment and failing to observe proper safety precautions, a worker was progressively disciplined and finally discharged. An arbiter upheld the discharge, observing that the company's system of rules provided "for progressive disciplinary actions for successive violations of the rules and regulations, which include safety regulations." The arbiter concluded, "clearly, the safety rules requiring the use of protective equipment are reasonable," and added "since they are reasonable, and since the agreement between the company and the union specifically permits the establishment of rules and regulations, it is the duty of all employees" to abide by these rules. (Vulcan-Hart Corp., 78 LA 59; see also 98 LA 357, 96 LA 609, 96 LA 931, 94 LA 152, 94 LA 178, 94 LA 777)

Past Practice

If management fails to enforce a safety rule, especially over a period of time, the rule may be considered dormant and enforcement not permitted unless the firm notifies employees of its intent to enforce the rule.

EXAMPLE: An arbiter overturned the discipline of an employee, who had failed to use a safety belt as prescribed by a seat belt regulation that management had allowed to lie dormant for at least 20 years. "In fairness, and desire to promote favorable employee relations," maintained the arbiter, "the employer should have given notice of its intent to enforce seat belt usage and the nature of discipline to be administered for noncompliance." In the absence of "such previous warning," the arbiter concluded that "the employer's action lacked equitability." (U.S. Army Corps of Engineers, 86 LA 939)

Uniform Enforcement of Rules

Safety rules must be uniformly applied to all employees exposed to the same risks — supervisors as well as line workers — arbiters have concluded.

EXAMPLE: An arbiter reprimanded an employer for not requiring its supervisory employees to wear the same protective equipment as the workers were required to wear during periods when they were exposed to the same risks. The arbiter noted that the bargaining agreement specifically stated that "all levels of supervision of the company, the employees, and the union will cooperate fully to promote safe practices, health conditions, and the enforcement of safety rules and procedures." When supervisors "are exposed to the same risks but do not observe the same safety rules that line employees are required to observe," the arbiter said, the supervisors "are clearly violating" the agreement. "Such a violation by a foreman may not only endanger the foreman himself," observed the arbiter, but "it may also endanger employees with whom he is working." (Noranda Aluminum Inc., 78 LA 1331)

However, an arbiter reduced a written warning and a 90-day suspension from driving company trucks to a written warning for an employee who drove a tractor-trailer erratically and unsafely, in violation of a reasonable safety rule that authorized both warnings and disqualifications as penalties, since two previous rule violators were not disqualified. (Seaway Food Town, 94 LA 389)

Smoking Rules

IN BRIEF

Generally, arbiters will uphold an employer's right to impose "reasonable" smoking controls — restricting smoking to specific areas in the workplace or banning smoking entirely in the interest of safeguarding both life and property — and they sustain discipline for violations. However, mitigating factors have been taken into consideration in reversing discipline in some smoking-related cases.

Arbiters tend to reverse discipline if management has permitted violations to go unpunished in the past. (68 LA 687) Additionally, arbiters may overturn discharge for no-smoking violations where there is insufficient proof of the employee's alleged misconduct. (70 LA 270)

Employee smoking rules may be considered part of the "terms and conditions" of employment and, as such, would be a subject for mandatory bargaining. Employers that try to impose smoking controls unilaterally, in violation of their collective bargaining obligations, may face unfair-labor-practice charges.

GUIDELINES

Smoking in a Restricted Area

Fire or other hazards posed by smoking have been considered by arbiters to be adequate justification for no-smoking rules and for discipline meted out to those who disobey the rules.

EXAMPLE: An airline employee who, after being ordered to extinguish her cigarette in a no-smoking area, lit another a short time later was properly discharged, an arbiter concluded. While observing that smoking in prohibited areas was not "expressly provided as a cause for discharge," the arbiter pointed out that there are certain "critical areas," such as the aircraft fueling site, where smoking is perilous and "constitutes legal malice." The arbitrator stressed that an earlier infraction of the rule "does not create any right to smoke." (Gladieux Food Services Inc., 70 LA 544)

Mitigating Factors

Management has a duty to consider mitigating factors in smoking cases. As with other types of disciplinary actions, a too-hasty response from management to an employee's infraction may cause an arbiter to overturn the discipline.

EXAMPLE: Returning from a break, an employee entered a room clearly marked as a no-smoking area and "inadvertently" lit a cigarette, then, realizing his mistake, tried to extinguish it. A supervisor who saw the employee extinguishing the flame and exhaling "a cloud of smoke" discharged the employee on the spot, but an arbiter overturned the discharge. While acknowledging that management "forcefully and convincingly" demonstrated "the hazard of an open flame" in the no-smoking area, the arbiter observed that "consideration must be given to mitigating circumstances." The employee had an "exemplary" record, the arbiter pointed out. He added that the employee was "horrified" by his unconscious act of lighting the cigarette and thus did not have the "guilty mind" required to intentionally commit the offense of smoking in the restricted area. (Converters Ink, 68 LA 593)

Justified No-Smoking Rules

Arbiters have upheld the unilateral imposition of a no-smoking rule in cases where the rule is deemed reasonable and justified by safety, health, and business requirements.

EXAMPLE: After a discarded cigarette caused a fire, a company unilaterally decided to limit smoking to lunch and break times only, and to two designated areas. An arbiter upheld the rule, finding that banning smoking at work stations for safety reasons was "not unreasonable." The employer "established the possibility of a fire being caused" in work areas, the arbiter noted, and presented "valid safety concerns" to justify smoking prohibitions. Similarly, restricting smoking to break times was not unreasonable, given management's concern about the "impact on production" of a policy that would permit employees to leave their work stations whenever they desired to smoke. (Morelite Equipment Co., 88 LA 777)

EXAMPLE: An employer unilaterally promulgated a new plant rule that restricted smoking to the lunch room during rest and lunch periods. Upholding the employer, the arbiter maintained that revision of the plant's smoking rule was a reasonable exercise of management's reserved rights. In this case, the arbiter said, management was "not guilty of bad faith or intent on being unreasonable" because it had a "legitimate business interest and purpose in restricting the smoking privilege to the lunch room." Adding that "smoking is not a practice or working condition that the employees are dependent upon," the arbiter concluded that the rule change was "within the permissible scope of management's prerogative." (Sherwood Medical Industries, 72 LA 258)

EXAMPLE: A hospital's no-smoking policy is reasonable since the issue was not addressed in its labor agreements and most of the employees favored implementation, an arbiter decided. After 14 years of restricted smoking, the hospital imposed a no-smoking policy with the support of 78 percent of its employees and on the recommendation of a labor-management task force. At the same time, a state law banning smoking in hospitals passed for the following year. The arbiter pointed out that the labor agreements are silent on the topic of a smoking policy. Moreover, he cited management rights clauses in two relevant labor agreements permitting management to set "reasonable rules and regulations" and the fact that the unions had ample opportunity for redress through grievance and arbitration but did not act on time. (Methodist Hospital, 91 LA 969)

EXAMPLE: A company may impose a workplace ban on smoking without engaging in bargaining, an arbiter ruled. During the term of a labor agreement, the company implemented a no-smoking policy which banned smoking in work areas. The union charged that the employer had unilaterally altered "the conditions of employment," and thus was required to bargain over the change. Refusing to impose a duty to bargain, the arbiter said the employer has a "legal obligation to maintain a safe working environment." Pointing out that the Surgeon General's report states that "ambient tobacco smoke in the workplace" constitutes a health hazard, the arbiter said employers are lawfully obligated to eliminate "toxic agents" from the workplace; therefore, a total ban on smoking during working hours is "appropriate," he concluded. (Central Telephone Co. of Nevada, 92 LA 390; see also 96 LA 1179, 96 LA 499, 95 LA 1011, 95 LA 840, 95 LA 419, 94 LA 888, 92 LA 457, 92 LA 390, 92 LA 181, 92 LA 68, 91 LA 969, 91 LA 375,

91 LA 201, 90 LA 1186, 90 LA 777, 89 LA 1069, 89 LA 1065, 89 LA 937, 88 LA 1311, 88 LA 777, 87 LA 1081, 87 LA 785)

Unreasonable Smoking Bans

However, if the smoking rules are found to be unreasonable and not justified by safety, health, or business needs, arbiters may overturn the rules.

EXAMPLE: An employer's ban on smoking only in its administration building was unreasonable, an arbiter decided, noting that no one had objected to smoking in that building and that in another, adjacent building, management allowed workers "to make their own arrangements." The arbiter also rejected management's contention that it was obliged to protect members of the public from the hazards of smoke in the administration building. No such protection was provided for visitors to other buildings, therefore the no-smoking restriction was "not reasonable," the arbiter said. (Union Sanitary District, 79 LA 193)

EXAMPLE: An employer's decision to prohibit smoking by employees in nearly all areas of the workplace was not justified by either health or business needs, an arbiter ruled. While agreeing that the "relationship between health and cigarette smoking is direct and proximate," the arbitrator concluded that the rule did not clearly benefit nonsmokers, because the work area was well-ventilated, whereas the smoking restriction tended to produce heavier amounts of smoke during breaks. Furthermore, the arbitrator reasoned, there was no proof that cutting down the consumption of cigarettes during working hours directly benefited workers' health, thereby reducing absenteeism or increasing the "longevity of good employees." (Schien Body & Equipment Co. Inc., 69 LA 930)

EXAMPLE: An employer's total ban on smoking "on company premises" was unreasonable and invalid since it included "adjacent areas" such as grounds and parking lots, an arbiter ruled. Tobacco smoke outdoors quickly dissipates, the arbiter said, and employees smoking in their cars have little discernible effect on the health and safety of others. (VME Americas Inc., 97 LA 137; see also 96 LA 506, 96 LA 403, 96 LA 122, 95 LA 1163, 94 LA 894, 93 LA 1255, 93 LA 1070, 88 LA 329, 83 LA 529)

Acquired Immune Deficiency Syndrome (AIDS)

IN BRIEF

Acquired Immune Deficiency Syndrome (AIDS), a life-threatening bloodborne viral disease, has sparked widespread medical and legal concerns and raised numerous questions regarding the workplace treatment of employees or applicants with AIDS. As a relatively new issue, few arbiters to date have considered AIDS-related workplace problems. Generally, the problems that have arisen have been one of two forms: either an employee has AIDS or one or more employees refuses to work with persons who have AIDS.

Under the Taft Act, employees may refuse to work if they can present an ascertainable, factual reason that their safety or health is endangered. However, Taft Act protections probably do not extend to a refusal to work with a person who has AIDS when the overwhelming body of medical evidence indicates that fears of contracting AIDS through normal workplace contact are unreasonable. If an employee who has AIDS is covered by a collective bargaining agreement, the contract's provisions generally determine matters of sick leave, health benefits, or any disciplinary action that is to be taken.

The Americans With Disabilities Act of 1990 has adopted the definitions of the Rehabilitation Act. AIDS, therefore, is a protected disability under ADA. Moreover, the statute makes special provisions for food handlers, providing that only those persons with contagious diseases that can be transmitted through food, as listed by the Secretary of Health and Human Services, may be transferred to other jobs or denied positions as food handlers if no other reasonable accommodations can be provided. AIDS cannot be transmitted through the handling of food.

Guidelines for dealing with employees who have AIDS or may be at risk for the disease were issued in late 1985 by the Centers for Disease Control of the U.S. Department of Health and Human Services. The guidelines recommend against the imposition of employment restrictions and routine medical screening of food service, personal service, and most health care workers who have or may be at risk for AIDS.

The Occupational Safety and Health Administration standard for occupational exposure to bloodborne pathogens is designed to protect all employees, who, in the course of their work, could reasonably be expected to come into contact with human blood, or other potentially infectious material. Under the rule, employers are required to use a combination of engineering and work-practice controls and to provide personal protective clothing and equipment to shield employees from occupational exposure to bloodborne diseases or potentially infectious body fluids. In addition, employers are required to provide hazard warnings, conduct information and training programs, make hepatitis B (the human immunodeficiency virus which causes AIDS) vaccinations available, and keep medical and training records.

The federal Rehabilitation Act of 1973 may prohibit discrimination against persons with AIDS, according to a number of labor law attorneys. The Department of Justice has taken the position that people infected with the AIDS-causing virus are protected handicapped individuals under Section 504 of the 1973 Rehabilitation Act, even if they do not manifest symptoms of the disease. The Office of Federal Contract Compliance Programs, in Appendix 6D to Chapter 6 of its Compliance Manual, has taken the position that all conditions related to AIDS are covered handicaps under Section 503 of the Rehabilitation Act. These determinations are based in part on the available scientific evidence indicating that AIDS cannot be transmitted through the kind of casual contact that occurs on the job.

A majority of state and local FEP agencies have determined that AIDS is a protected handicap under their current handicap laws, and several jurisdictions have adopted laws specifically prohibiting AIDS discrimination. Testing workers involuntarily for the AIDS virus is prohibited in some jurisdictions, and strict confidentiality of the results of voluntary tests is required.

―――――――――――――― GUIDELINES ――――――――――――――

CDC Guidelines Superseded

Individuals should not be barred from work or prohibited from using telephones, office equipment, toilets or showers, eating facilities, or water fountains simply because they have AIDS, according to CDC guidelines. However, a state law requiring nursing homes to establish a written policy "for the control of communicable diseases" superseded the guidelines, an arbitrator decided.

EXAMPLE: The laws prohibiting discrimination against persons with AIDS may, at times, conflict with other laws, such as those protecting public health.

EXAMPLE: A nursing home discharged a health care worker who tested positive for antibodies to the AIDS virus. The employer argued that it was following a state law requiring nursing homes and certain other facilities to establish a written policy "for the control of communicable disease." The employer's policy specifically stated that any employee with a communicable disease would be "suspended until a negative report is received." The employee questioned whether the state law covered AIDS, and also maintained that the nursing home should have followed the CDC guidelines, both to reduce the risk of spreading the AIDS virus and to determine what steps to take when a worker tested positive for AIDS antibodies. AIDS was a communicable disease covered by the state law, an arbitrator decided, adding that "given the severity of the risk" of contracting AIDS, the employer was correct in following "the explicit requirements of state law." The CDC guidelines, the arbitrator said, "are not adequate or appropriate." Moreover, "even with the guidelines in place, the possibility of transmission exists," the arbiter maintained. Discharge, however, was improper, the arbitrator said. The appropriate step, as required by the employer's own policy, would have been to "continue the worker on medical leave, and then to suspend him until he no longer had a communicable disease." While declining to award back pay, because the employee was not eligible to return to work, the arbitrator did direct the employer to pay certain medical bills and to allow the worker to continue health care coverage. (Nursing Home, 88 LA 681)

Refusal To Work With AIDS Carrier

An employer may not discharge a worker for refusing to work with persons suspected of carrying the AIDS virus, an arbiter ruled, because the employer contributed to the worker's fears.

EXAMPLE: A prison guard who refused to conduct pat searches because he feared he would contract AIDS from inmates who presented symptoms of the AIDS virus was discharged. An arbiter ordered the discharge reduced to a lesser penalty, even though a refusal to perform assigned job duties would ordinarily merit termination. However, in this case discharge was too severe because the employer was "at least partly responsible" for the worker's "exaggerated fear of contracting the disease." A mitigating factor, the arbiter said, was an "inaccurate" memorandum from the employer that warned against the sharing of personal items, thus implying that AIDS could be transmitted through casual contact. That memorandum, the arbiter stressed, "reinforced" the worker's fears and contributed to his reluctance to believe correct medical information about the way AIDS is transmitted. The arbiter ordered reinstatement, without loss of seniority, but declined to award back pay. (Minnesota Department of Corrections, 85 LA 1185)

Medical Record Disclosure Duties

Most states have privacy laws and restrictions protecting the confidentiality of medical information. However, some unions contracts require the disclosure of medical information to their members for their protection.

EXAMPLE: Where a contract called for prison guards and their union, to be informed of inmates who had or were "medically suspected" of having a communicable disease, the employer was obligated to notify the union and the guards of inmates who tested positive for AIDS. The problem arose when an inmate died of AIDS, and some 20 other inmates requested confidential AIDS tests because they had engaged in homosexual relations with the deceased inmate. Several inmates tested positive but the union was not given their names because of the confidentiality promised them. The arbiter, while noting that the positive test results indicate only exposure, not the presence of the disease, nevertheless concluded that "a realistic and meaningful interpretation" of the contract requires the employer to release the names of the inmates testing positive. "The obvious purpose" of the contract section, the arbiter observed, "is to alert the bargaining unit employees (guards) to the need for special caution in dealing with inmates who can subject them to the risk of contracting diseases such as AIDS." (Delaware Department of Corrections, 86 LA 849.)

Environmental Differential Pay / 'Safe and Healthful Workplace'

Employees were not entitled to environmental differential pay, an arbiter ruled, because the work was not performed in "with or in close proximity to micro-organisms."

EXAMPLE: An arbiter ruled that night maintenance employees who cleaned a federal medical-center room in which the AIDS-causing human immunodeficiency virus was kept and HIV research was conducted were not entitled to environmental differential pay allowed by federal regulations for duties involving either "high degree hazard" (8 percent differential), or "low degree hazard" (4 percent). The work was not performed "with or in close proximity to micro-organisms" so as to involve "potential personal injury," or "potential for personal injury."

Moreover, according to the arbiter, the federal medical center did not violate its duty to provide a "safe and healthful workplace free from recognized hazards" and to comply with applicable laws and regulations when it permitted the maintenance workers to clean the room in which the HIV virus was kept. There was no evidence of any violation in procedures, and the federal inspectors' "notice of unsafe or unhealthful working conditions" resulted from an investigation which occurred several weeks after the completion of the HIV research. (Veterans Admin. Medical Center, 94 LA 169)

Part 4

Seniority and Its Applications

Calculating Seniority

IN BRIEF

Generally, seniority is based upon length of service, although a collective bargaining agreement may provide for exceptions such as superseniority for union officers and stewards, denial of seniority for probationary employees, and loss of seniority in whole or part under specified circumstances. Since seniority, length of service, and their concomitant rights are created by the contract, it is necessary for arbitrators to look first to the contract's language in determining the seniority status of employees. In the absence of a definition of seniority in the contract, the term is "commonly understood to mean the length of service with the employer or in some division of the enterprise." (Curtiss-Wright Corp., 11 LA 139)

An employee's relative seniority status in the company usually depends on three basic considerations — when seniority begins to accumulate, the effect of changes in work assignments on seniority, and the effect of interruptions in employment on seniority.

GUIDELINES

SENIORITY STARTING DATE

In the absence of language to the contrary, arbitrators generally hold that seniority begins to accumulate from date of hiring rather than from the later date the contract went into effect. Problems may arise, however, where formerly separate operations are merged or new businesses are acquired.

Original Hiring Date

Seniority normally is regarded as beginning with the date of hire, not the date on which seniority rights were won.

EXAMPLE: A part-time employee promoted to full-time status is entitled to seniority from the date of hire, not the date of promotion, an arbiter ruled. The contract, while excluding part-time employees from some benefits, was amended to establish a part-time seniority list, and also specifically defined seniority as arising from the date of hire. Thus, the arbiter concluded, the employer's past practice of counting seniority only from the date of full-time employment is overridden by the agreement. (Columbus Retail Merchants Delivery, 65 LA 825; see also 97 LA 1011, 94 LA 11, 93 LA 1297)

On the other hand, an arbitrator held that an employer improperly laid off several employees with greater unit seniority and retained long-service workers who had come into the unit from non-unit jobs, even though the company contended that flexibility in its operations demanded use of date of employment as basis for seniority, rather than the date of the employees' entry into the unit. Reversing the employer's action, the arbitrator ruled that seniority rights under the contract were based on date of entry into the unit. (Elmar Electronics Inc., 64 LA 912)

Change of Ownership

The extent to which seniority rights survive a change in ownership depends on the circumstances. If a new owner simply takes over from the former owner, the employees usually will retain their seniority rights based on their original dates of hire. But a more difficult situation is created where the change in ownership is accompanied by a merger of the newly acquired company with an existing unit of employees.

Some arbitrators feel that it would be unfair to the new owner's other employees if those in the newly acquired operation carried their seniority rights intact during a merger of operations. Other arbitrators are equally insistent that it would be unfair to strip the workers at the newly acquired facility of seniority rights they have earned. Some arbitrators have tried to dovetail seniority rights in the interest of fair play for both groups of workers.

EXAMPLE: Going by the letter of the sales contract, under which he agreed to assume the labor obligations of the seller, the buyer honored all accrued seniority rights of the seller's work force. But the union that represented the buyer's own work force argued that equity dictated an arrangement decreasing the newly-acquired workers' seniority.

On employee benefits, the arbitrator decided, the buyer had to honor full seniority. But on competitive status, he added, a full-seniority transfer would work an unfair advantage on the buyer's own workers. To balance these considerations the arbitrator fashioned this formula:

• The seller's workers retain full benefit seniority.

• Those who transfer with two or more years' seniority retain one-half their competitive-status seniority.

• Those who transfer with less seniority go to the bottom of the merged competitive status seniority list. (Country Belle Cooperative Farmers, 48 LA 600; see also 66 LA 1029)

Seniority in Plant Merger

When a company merges two plants having separate seniority lists, a single new list must be created, by considering length of service, relative positions on the separate lists, or both.

EXAMPLE: One arbitrator weighed these factors equally. The arbitrator reasoned that going by length of service alone would be unfair to workers in the plant where length of service was relatively low. By the same token, dovetailing the two lists according to workers' relative positions on the separate lists would be unfair to those in the plant where length of service was relatively high. The arbitrator, therefore, set up two numerical lists — one based on length of service, the other on position on the separate seniority lists. Then he figured what each worker's average position was on the two lists, and this determined the worker's position on the combined seniority list. (Moore Business Forms Inc., 24 LA 793)

EXAMPLE: Another arbitrator decided that the most equitable method for determining seniority was to make a pool of the combined jobs resulting from a merger, with each group getting a proportionate share of it. In the case at hand, the transferred work accounted for 41.3 percent of the surviving jobs, or 70 percent of what the transferred workers had contributed before the merger. Thus, the arbiter credited the transferred workers with seven-tenths of their seniority at the midpoint date of the transfers. (Sonotone Corp., 42 LA 359)

EXAMPLE: Under a multi-employer agreement that confined seniority rights to the worker's "plant," an arbitrator gave seniority preference to workers in relation to the types of operations they formerly performed at two merged plants. Those whose work was similar at both plants should be assigned from both seniority lists in the proportion that such workers at each plant bore to the total number of workers at both plants, the arbitrator directed. (Superior Products Co., 42 LA 517; see also 90 LA 1252, 72 LA 458, 71 LA 476)

CALCULATING SENIORITY

Employees Hired the Same Day

Most arbitrators give equal seniority to employees hired on the same day.

EXAMPLE: When a union urged that seniority for workers hired the same day should be computed according to the order of their physical examination, an arbitrator ruled that seniority should not be measured in units of less than one day. (Standard Oil Co. of Ind., 3 LA 758)

EXAMPLE: Another arbiter concluded that tossing a coin was the only way to resolve a dispute involving two workers with equal seniority. The contract fixed seniority "from the date of issuance of the union card." Two women were transferred into the unit on the same day and were issued union cards on the same day. Since both women enjoyed the same seniority rights, the arbiter arrived at the coin toss as the most equitable method for deciding which one would be laid off. (McCall Corp., 49 LA 183)

EXAMPLE: However, another arbiter solved the same-day hire problem by considering the shifts they worked. Thus, the first-shift worker was senior to the second-shift employee. (Robertshaw-Fulton Controls Co., 22 LA 273)

Delayed Challenges to Seniority

Arbitrators differ as to how long an employee retains the right to challenge his standing on the seniority list, unless the contract limits this period. If there is no such restriction, though, one arbitrator has said that an employee has a right to complain about the continuation of an error in the list at any time.

EXAMPLE: A company gave a man credit for too much seniority in his department, and the error went unchallenged for nine years. Then another employee filed a grievance asking that the error be corrected, thus moving him up a notch on the seniority list. The company rejected his request on the basis of a contract provision stating that grievances must be filed within 30 days of the occurence of the events involved. The time limit did not apply in this situation, the arbiter said, because if it was a contract violation to give a man extra seniority credit in the past, it was a violation to continue giving him the extra credit. The arbiter ruled, however, that the preference given to the other employee in the matters of promotion, demotion, and layoffs was beyond challenge. (Bethlehem Steel Co., 23 LA 538)

EXAMPLE: Another arbitrator, however, held that if a posted seniority has gone unquestioned for a long period of time, errors cannot be corrected even though there is no "statute of limitations" in the contract. (Creamery Package Mfg. Co., 31 LA 917)

Challenging Seniority of Others

An employee may challenge another's seniority date, one arbitrator has ruled, an arbiter ruled, where employees have the right to file grievances over the interpretation and application of the contract and the contract describes the method of computing seniority. In these circumstances, the arbiter said, the incorrect listing of a seniority date is a contract violation which any employee can protest. (Republic Steel Corp., 18 LA 907)

Responsibility for Seniority Error

Responsibility for an error on a seniority list rests with the party who prepared it.

EXAMPLE: A company prepared a seniority list, considered final and binding when a copy was given to the union. The list was in error, but, according to the arbitrator, the union was not jointly responsible for the mistake. The rule that the list was final and binding applied only to a correct list, he ruled. Since the company had the sole responsibility for preparing the list, it also had the sole responsibility for any errors. (Bethlehem Fabricators Inc., 41 LA 6; 85 LA 774)

UNITS FOR SENIORITY

Seniority units are defined by the collective bargaining agreement, either specifically or by interpretation. A seniority unit may be company-wide, multi-company, or departmental. Or it may be used upon the bargaining unit, or upon an occupational group or classification, or upon a combination of these groups.

Moreover, seniority rights may be acquired in one unit and exercised in another. For example, seniority may be based on service in the company, but its exercise may be limited to the employee's particular department. Similarly, seniority rights may be used upon different units for different aspects of the employment relations. For instance, departmental seniority may prevail for layoff and recalls, while company-wide seniority determines vacation and pension rights. (97 LA 470, 97 LA 132, 96 LA 1211, 96 LA 670, 93 LA 1192, 91 LA 763, 91 LA 605, 85 LA 489, 74 LA 2, 70 LA 786, 69 LA 1051, 66 LA 668, 63 LA 777, 62 LA 1027)

Further, the accrual of seniority may vary for different classifications of employees. For example, an arbiter held that employer's two-track seniority system for regular and temporary employees was bona fide. (Hazelwood Farm Bakeries, 92 LA 1026)

Where Unit Is Not Specified

If the seniority unit is not clearly specified, arbitrators are inclined to assume that company-wide seniority was intended, particularly if this accords with operational efficiency.

EXAMPLE: A contract specified that "accepted rules of seniority" shall apply to layoff and that acquisition of seniority would begin on the first day of employment, regardless of classification. Company-wide seniority was held to govern. If, as urged by the union, classification seniority were to apply, the employer would lose the flexibility afforded by the contract, due to the seasonal nature of the work and the varied skills of the employees, the arbitrator decided. (Great Lakes Homes Inc., 44 LA 737)

WORK ASSIGNMENT CHANGES

Where seniority is not on a company-wide or bargaining-unit basis, provision must be made for employees who transfer from one seniority unit to another. Under the most restrictive approach, the employee loses his seniority in his old job, and starts from scratch in his new one. More often, however, the employee retains or even accumulates seniority in his old job — at least for a long enough period to afford protection in case he does not work out in the new job. A third approach permits the employee to carry seniority previously acquired over the the new job.

Some contracts may be very specific regarding the seniority rights of employees promoted to supervisory positions and later returned to the unit. In cases where the contract specifically excludes the period as supervisor from the seniority calculation, the company's only defense in granting seniority may be a denial of the employee's supervisory status. (Chrysler Corp., 65 LA 544; see also 75 LA 1077, 70 LA 1217)

In the absence of contract clauses specifying the seniority rights of employees who are promoted to supervisory positions, arbitrators are divided on the seniority status of such employees when they later are demoted and returned to the bargaining unit. Some arbitrators have held that supervisors continue to accumulate seniority after promotion unless the contract specifically state otherwise. (70 LA 1246, 62 LA 1013, 43 LA 228, 34 LA 285, 31 LA 137, 25 LA 595) Other arbitrators, however, have ruled that seniority is strictly a contractual right and may not be accumulated after promotion. (32 LA 892, 31 LA 859, 31 LA 200) Still others have held that an employee forfeits all his seniority when promoted because he in effect has voluntarily resigned from the unit. (27 LA 30, 26 LA 898, 40 LA 388)

There is more apparent agreement among arbitrators that supervisors who have never been in the unit are entitled to no seniority credit on demotion. (41 LA 583, 33 LA 150, 32 LA 274, 29 LA 828)

CALCULATING SENIORITY

EMPLOYMENT INTERRUPTION

Layoffs & Leaves — Seniority generally is retained or accumulated, at least to some extent, where absence is due to illness, layoff, or other leave of absence. However in one case, an employee was properly denied seniority for the eight months of his layoff, one arbitrator decided, where the relevant contract language read: "Seniority is continuous service with the employer, compiled by time actually spent on the payroll, plus properly approved absences." The contract also listed exclusive reasons for seniority to be "broken." In upholding the employer's denial, the arbitrator ruled that the layoff was a period spent off the payroll, and not an approved absence. Furthermore, the phrase "broken seniority" was taken to mean a complete loss of seniority, the arbitrator concluded, rather than a gap in its calculation. (Firestone Tire and Rubber Co., 61 LA 136; see also 75 LA 297, 72 LA 609, 72 LA 240)

Does an employee retain his seniority when he takes a job with another employer? One arbitrator ruled that other employment during a leave of absence does not terminate seniority in the absence of a clause forbidding the taking of outside work. (Goodyear Tire & Rubber Co., 5 LA 234; see also 72 LA 663, 63 LA 941) Another arbitrator ruled, however, that an employee may not accumulate seniority simultaneously with two employers and that an employee forfeited his employee status during a layoff by working for another company. (Fairchild Engine & Airplane Corp., 3 LA 873)

Military leave — Seniority generally accumulates during leave for military service, since this is required by the law governing reemployment rights of veterans. (75 LA 696, 63 LA 750)

Effect of Unauthorized Absence

If an employee has a good reason for being absent, most arbitrators will protect his accumulated seniority even though his absence is unauthorized — unless, of course, the contract specifically provides for forfeiture.

EXAMPLE: An employee was absent for one week without permission at Christmas time. On his return the company claimed it was rehiring the employee so that his seniority would date from the day of rehire. The arbitrator agreed with the company that granting or denial of leave was a management prerogative which could not be questioned unless company action was unreasonable or discriminatory. However, in this case, the arbitrator ruled that since the absence was for good cause there should be no break in the employee's seniority. (Pittsburgh Metallurgical Co. Inc., 12 LA 95)

Refusal of Recall from Layoff

An employee who refused an offer of recall from layoff was improperly deprived of seniority, an arbitrator ruled. The employee had refused reinstatement on the night shift because employment during that shift would conflict with his religious obligations, and the employer denied seniority to the worker, arguing that the contract clearly provided for seniority denial in such cases. Overturning the employer's action, an arbitrator ruled that the company had violated EEOC guidelines which require an employer to accommodate the religious needs of employees where no undue hardship to the company will result. (American Forest Products Corp., 65 LA 650)

Loss of Superseniority

When union officials leave office, at least one arbitrator has held that their superseniority and the rights it obtained end. There was no reason, the arbiter held, why benefits and privileges that union officials acquire by virtue of superseniority should continue after they are out of office. (Rockwell Spring & Axle Co., 25 LA 174; see also 97 LA 792, 75 LA 263)

PROBATIONARY EMPLOYEES

Termination of Probationary Status

Where an employee is serving a probationary period and that period is defined as a certain number of working days, one arbiter has said, he achieves status as a regular employee the moment he clocks out on the last day of his trial period.

EXAMPLE: Under the provisions of one company's contract, all new employees had to serve a 30-day probationary period before they could become regular employees and begin to accrue seniority. During that period the company could fire an employee without being subject to the contract's "just cause" restriction. One employee clocked out on his thirtieth day of work and received a telegram that evening notifying him that he was discharged for being unsuited for the job. The arbiter concluded that the employee had become a regular employee at the time he left work and was covered by the "just cause" provision of the contract, noting that since seniority began to accrue at the conclusion of the probationary period, full status as an employee was also achieved at that time. (Lyon Inc., 24 LA 353)

Computing Probationary Period

Many questions arise in determining when a new employee completes probation and acquires seniority status. Small variations in contract language may make the difference in answering this question.

EXAMPLE: Under a contract providing probation "for the first month" of employment, an arbitrator held that an employee who worked less than a month, was discharged, was rehired 17 days later, and worked another three weeks, had completed her probationary period. Since the periods of employment were separated by only 17 days, the arbitrator decided that the company had an ample opportunity to judge the employee's suitability — the purpose of probation. (Kreisler Industrial, 27 LA 134)

EXAMPLE: A contract that defined the probationary period in terms of "continuous employment," led an arbitrator to decide that the company could require a rehired probationer to serve a completely new probationary period. (Armstrong Cork Co., 23 LA 366)

EXAMPLE: An agreement indicating an employee would be on probation until he "performed work" on 30 days within any three-month period led an arbitrator to hold that days on which an employee had been sent home because of bad weather could be discounted in figuring his probationary period. It might have been different, the arbitrator noted, if the agreement had stated the probationary period in terms of time employed. (Bethlehem Steel Co., 27 LA 300)

EXAMPLE: In an agreement defining the probationary period as "forty five working days of actual service with the company," an arbitrator decided that the employer could not exclude overtime or weekend work from the calculation of seniority, even though the employer and the union had reached an informal, verbal agreement providing that only straight time would be included. (Hoover Ball & Bearing Co., 64 LA 63)

Order of Layoff

IN BRIEF

Broadly speaking, layoff procedures fall into three categories — (1) layoffs are based solely on seniority; (2) seniority determines the order of layoff, assuming the senior employees can do the available work; and (3) seniority governs only if ability or other factors are equal. Applying procedures in the first category usually poses no serious problem; but procedures in the other two categories are fruitful sources of grievances.

Among other problems discussed in this section are those relating to the exceptions made to seniority rules and those presented by layoffs for brief periods of time.

GUIDELINES

SENIORITY V. ABILITY

Contract Requiring Equal Ability

If a contract states that seniority shall govern in layoff where ability is "equal" an arbiter is likely to hold that this means "relatively or substantially equal," not "exactly equal." Ability, arbiters reason, cannot be measured precisely.

EXAMPLE: In one case an arbiter ruled that an employer violated the contract by retaining a junior mechanic and laying off a senior one on the ground that he was not equal in skill and ability because he had never worked on certain machines that the junior man had. The arbiter stated that, as a general rule, employees within the same classification should be deemed to have relatively equal ability and skill for layoff purposes, especially when their duties are the same. In view of this, he ruled, the senior employee should have been the one retained. (Poloron Products of Pa., 23 LA 789; see also 73 LA 128)

Management's Right to Determine Ability

Arbiters have frequently held that, where a contract makes "fitness and ability" a factor to be considered along with seniority under one of the modified seniority clauses, but is silent as to how and by whom the determination of qualifications is to be made, management is entitled to make the initial determination, subject to challenge by the union on the basis that the decision was unreasonable based on the facts, or capricious, arbitrary, or discriminatory. (96 LA 1069, 92 LA 926, 85 LA 1069, 79 LA 106, 77 LA 313, 76 LA 142, 75 LA 910, 74 LA 148, 73 LA 937, 73 LA 933, 72 LA 1272, 72 LA 941, 72 LA 524, 61 LA 872, 56 LA 40, 56 LA 390, 46 LA 860, 46 LA 203, 44 LA 283, 42 LA 1093, 37 LA 801, 34 LA 271, 29 LA 394, 10 LA 284, 9 LA 515, 6 LA 838)

However, some arbiters have placed the burden of proof on the employer. They have held that management must give definite evidence that a junior employee clearly and demonstrably has greater ability in order to retain him in preference to a more senior worker. (Flexonics Corp., 24 LA 869)

EXAMPLE: Where an employer properly laid off a part-time journeyman meatcutter rather than a head meatcutter, even though the journeyman had greater seniority, an arbiter, in deciding whether the company or the union must show that the senior employee was not qualified, stated that the appropriate rule to be followed is the one generally followed when employers attempt to avoid the strict workings of the seniority system. That is — the employer must explain why it has not followed the seniority rules. In the absence of evidence presented by the employer, the contract's seniority provisions will be given full effect. If the employer presents evidence to show disqualification, then the union must go forward to rebut such proof, the arbiter concluded. (Shop Rite Foods Inc., 63 LA 60)

Factors in Measuring Qualifications

When contracts make seniority controlling in layoffs what factors should be taken into account in determining employees' qualification? Arbitrators' awards suggest these guides:

● Where a contract said seniority would govern if "ability to perform the work" was relatively equal, the only thing that should be measured was the ability to perform the particular job at stake. (Bethlehem Steel Co., 24 LA 820)

● Where a contract said seniority would govern provided ability and skill were relatively equal, a junior worker could be retained on a job in preference to a senior worker who required a much greater amount of supervision in performing the job. (Copco Steel & Engineering Co., 12 LA 6)

● Where the contract specified that seniority was to govern when management decided the abilities of two employees were "substantially equal," an arbitrator ruled against management's retaining a junior employee instead of a senior worker on the grounds that the employer's criteria for measuring qualifications were too narrow. The arbiter found that the company made its decision on the basis of only one of many functions the workers performed; that there was nothing in the contract to allow the company to judge an employee on the basis of that one function; and that the employer had never made performance of that one function a condition of continued employment. (National Broadcasting Co., 61 LA 872)

● Where senior men were demoted to "outside gang" work before junior women, an arbiter upheld the employer's action based on the implied contract criterion of "qualifications" to do the work. The work was heavy physical labor of which the two women were incapable, the arbiter ruled, adding that a general distinction between men and women would be invalid, while the use of objective standards in assessing candidates was permissible. (Morton-Norwich Products Inc., 62 LA 1241)

● Where a contract provision clearly required senior employees to have "ability to do work" if moving into an open job at the company's other plant, an employer properly laid off senior employees at one of its plants who failed to pass a test that would have qualified them for jobs, at another plant, that were being held by junior employees. (Metalfab Inc., 65 LA 1191)

● Where a contract stated that in the event of a lay-off, employees would be laid off in order of seniority, provided "remaining employees are able to perform the available work," an employer properly determined that workers who would replace a senior inspector were not able to do the job. Noting that the employer was under considerable pressure from a client that provided it with a major part of its business to improve its quality control, the arbiter concluded that the quality control manager's limitation of replacements to employees who previously had worked under him as inspectors, because they would be familiar with his methods, was a credible requirement in light of the critical nature of the work. (R.J. Tower Corp., 73 LA 933)

Use of Merit-Rating Plan

Merit-rating plans (or performance reviews) involve essentially a documentation, usually periodically made, of supervisory opinion concerning various aspects of the "fitness and ability" of an employee. A merit-rating plan may include: quantity and quality of work, knowledge of the job, ability to learn, initiative, acceptance of responsibility, ability to direct others, safety habits and accident record, attitude toward co-workers and management, attendance, and personal characteristics such as moral character, physical condition, and appearance. Other factors may include the degree of pertinent experience and training, special conditions of the job, and honors such as incentive awards or other special achievement. (U.S. Dept. of the Interior, 53 LA 657; see also 74 LA 486)

EXAMPLE: An arbiter upheld an employer's basing ability measurements on a unilateral merit-rating plan, ruling that the plan could be used because it included factors properly related to measurement of ability and skill and there was no evidence that the factors were rated incorrectly. (Merrill-Stevens Dry Dock & Repair Co., 17 LA 516)

On the other hand, where a merit-rating plan used such factors as cooperation, safety habits, personal habits, and attitude toward superiors, another arbiter ruled that the company could not use it to determine workers relative ability for purposes of layoff. Since these factors were not the same as ability to perform a job, he reasoned, the plan was an unfair measure of ability. (Western Automatic Machine Screw Co., 9 LA 606)

Similarly, a company decided to lay off a senior man with a low efficiency rating, based on a report which compared the relative efficiency of workers in a department. Because this was the first instance of the use of tests, the arbitrator held that they were improper. They could be used in the future, however, provided: (1) the ratings conform with rules that are the norm for such procedures and, (2) the workers are told about management's intentions. (McEvoy Co., 42 LA 41)

EXCEPTIONS TO SENIORITY IN LAYOFFS

Exceptions often are made to the strict application of seniority in layoffs. The most common exceptions are:

▶ Superseniority granted to union stewards and other representatives to ensure that workers remaining on the job during a layoff will continue to have union representation.

▶ Superseniority rights accorded to management to permit it to select key employees for retention during a layoff without regard to the usual seniority rules. Management-designated employees — sometimes equal in number to union representatives with superseniority — may be exempted from the operation of seniority. Employees with special skills who cannot be spared without impairing efficiency also may be exempted.

▶ The lack of any seniority rights for probationary employees, permitting management to designate individual probationers for layoff without regard to their hiring dates.

Superseniority for Union Representatives

Although arbiters have liberally construed contracts' superseniority clauses in order to ensure the fullest possible union representation, arbiters also have balanced this with the view that superseniority benefits are limited to those rights and privileges expressly stated in a collective bargaining agreement. In addition, substantial limitations on superseniority for union representatives have emerged under the Taft Act.

NLRB has ruled that superseniority clauses, which are not, on their face limited to layoff and recall, are presumptively unlawful. (Dairylea Cooperative Inc., 219 NLRB 656, 1975, 89 LRRM 1737) Further, the Board has continued to invalidate superseniority clauses applied to union officers who do not have "steward-like" grievance-handling repsonsibilities

— e.g., union negotiating committees and union executive-board members. (Gulton Eletro-Voice Inc., 266 NLRB 466, 1983, 112 LRRM 1361) This *Gulton* standard has been both accepted and rejected by arbiters. (See Ex-Cell-O Corp., 85 LA 1190 and Hunter Engineering Co., 82 LA 483, respectively)

Where the major purpose of the superseniority clause is to allow for efficient administration of the contract, arbiters have permitted layoff of union stewards when, for example, a work group was reclassified (Textron Inc., 83 LA 931), or when a temporary layoff did not impede a union's ability to administer a contract (Almet/Lawnlite Inc., 87 LA 624)

Under a union contract giving top seniority on a plant-wide basis to the bargaining-unit chair, must management retain the steward when there is no work available for him or her, and the company has retained only a few bargaining-unit employees?

Many arbiters say that under such an all-inclusive clause the union representative must be kept on the job as long as even one bargaining-unit employee is still working.

EXAMPLE: In one case arising under such a clause, the arbiter held that a shop chairman clearly had top seniority rights in the entire shop under all circumstances. He said that the superseniority given union representatives under collective agreement is not related to their functions as productive workers but stems from their special status in administering the agreement. (Freed Radio Corp., 9 LA 55)

EXAMPLE: In another case, an employer violated a contract's provision recognizing union officers' right to top seniority, an arbiter held, when it refused to recall employees who were elected to union offices during their layoff due to lack of work. While superseniority has the effect of pushing all employees to a lower position on the seniority list, it does so whether the employees are union members or nonunion members the arbiter pointed out adding that the benefits of having union officers and grievance committeemen who are not subject to as much turnover serve as a protection for nonunion members as well as union members. (Keller Industries Inc., 63 LA 1230; see also 90 LA 257, 89 LA 221, 81 LA 1242, 74 LA 987, 73 LA 13, 67 LA 741, 64 LA 1080, 39 LA 587, 36 LA 808)

However, express contractual restrictions against the transfer of union representatives, during a reduction in force, from a department or shift that they had been representing, have been upheld by arbiters. (73 LA 13, 64 LA 1080)

Further, where a bargaining agreement's superseniority clause was ambiguous and the employer had never interpreted it as granting superseniority, an arbiter ruled that an employer properly laid off a union steward during a business slowdown, where the employer was laying off employees strictly on the basis of seniority. (Curtis Sand & Gravel Co., 96 LA 972)

Moreover, an employer was allowed to reduce the workweek of union officers who held superseniority. The arbiter found that the employer merely was staggering his work schedule to spread available jobs among the work force, which did not constitute a layoff despite the reduced hours. (Wilcox Crittenden Co., 43 LA 1046; see also 74 LA 719, 72 LA 96, 70 LA 49, 66 LA 1289)

When Representatives Are Unable to Do the Work

Under the contract that gives top departmental seniority to shop stewards and also, in another article, provides that seniority applies in layoffs if employees are able to do required work, do shop stewards have the right to be retained even if they cannot do the work? Most arbiters have held that union representatives must be kept on regardless of their ability so long as other employees are still working in their departments. The purpose of a superseniority clause, they have noted, is to protect union representation during reductions in force. If stewards were laid off before other employees, the clause would be nullified and the purpose would be defeated, these arbiters have observed. (Luders Marine Construction Co., 2 LA 622; see also 97 LA 792)

Similarly, an arbiter ruled, in a case where superseniority rights conflicted with recall subject to ability to perform the work, that an employer's assessment of relative ability is irrelevant and outweighed by a superseniority provision where the retained steward can perform the work at an acceptable level. (U.S. Steel Corp., 85 LA 1113)

On the other hand, other arbiters have decided that all sections of a contract article must be read together to determine the intent of the parties. So where a contract within the same article provides for superseniority for shop stewards and then limits the application of seniority by the ability factor, it is all right to lay-off shop stewards who cannot perform required work. (Roberts-Gordon Appliance Corp., 8 LA 1030; see also United States Time Corp., 23 LA 379)

EXAMPLE: Where a contract provided for recall based on a "company's operational requirements as well as seniority and ability," and a union steward had no experience in a particular, relevant job classification, an arbiter ruled that an employer did not violate contractual superseniority provisions when it failed to recall the steward to a classification which he had never held. (Siemens Energy & Automation Inc., 91 LA 598)

Rights of Alternate Union Officers

According to one arbiter, superseniority for union stewards does not extend to their alternates. The arbiter decided one company had a right to lay off an alternate union committeeman on the ground that the benefits attached to the position rather than the worker, and alternates were not covered by the superseniority clause. There was nothing wrong with the company's extending the benefits to alternates if it wished, he said, but the union did not have the right to insist upon such extension. (Kidde Manufacturing Co., 40 LA 328)

Superseniority No Guarantee of Particular Job

Under a contract giving stewards top seniority in the area in which they serve, is a steward entitled to retain his particular job during a force reduction?

Some arbiters have held that a clause of this type simply gives a steward preferred seniority in the area which he serves — a division, a department or the plant. It does not give him the right to remain in his own job. (18 LA 780, 13 LA 628, 17 LA 291)

Of course, unless otherwise specified in a contract, superseniority ends when the union official vacates the protection and privileges of his or her office.

EXAMPLE: An arbiter ordered an employer to transfer a former union president, when he vacated his job as union president, from a job that he had during a layoff because of superseniority to a classification for which his experience and regular seniority qualified him. The contract implied that the superseniority entitlement to the position ceased when the employee vacated the protected union office; and, further, the senior employee on layoff was qualified for the job in question, the arbiter found. (Lockheed Aeronautical Systems Inc., 94 LA 137)

Superseniority for Employee with No Regular Seniority

Under a contract that permitted an employer to grant superseniority to a certain number of employees of its own choosing, one arbiter ruled that an employee who had no regular seniority was not disqualified for such superseniority.

EXAMPLE: One contract provided that an employee acquired seniority after he had worked 30 days. It also allowed the company to retain on its "working force" a certain number of employees "without regard to their seniority." When management laid off one man with seniority while keeping another who had not yet worked 30 days, the union protested; superseniority, it argued, could not be given to a worker who had no seniority at all.

The arbiter, though, sided with the company. The employee, he pointed out, was a member of the work force even though he had not worked 30 days. In the arbiter's opinion the phrase, "without regard to their seniority" meant that seniority was not a factor at all. (Bethlehem Steel Co., 28 LA 808)

Worker with Security Clearance

Can seniority rules be deviated from in order to retain a junior worker with security clearance where government-contract work requires such clearance? One arbiter held that a company could not do this in a case where it was responsible for the fact that only the junior worker had been cleared.

The company had full knowledge of its contractual obligations, he said, and could have avoided the problem if it had obtained clearance for the senior worker instead of the junior one. The only way the company could have got around its "self-imposed predicament," the arbitrator suggested, would have been to lay off somebody who had not yet achieved seniority status. Then it could have assigned the senior worker to that job, at his regular wage rate, until his security clearance came through. (Webcor Inc., 32 LA 490)

Layoff of Probationary Employees

Under most contracts, probationers must be laid off before employees with seniority are dropped.

However, one arbiter ruled that an employer properly retained probational employees who were qualified to perform the duties of their electrical tester jobs, instead of permitting their displacement by more senior employees, since the senior employees lacked the qualifications to perform the work. (Eaton Corp., 65 LA 671)

Similarly, an employer had the right to retain a probational employee who had experience in operating certain machines, instead of recalling laid-off senior employees who did not have the ability to run the machines, an arbiter held, since under the contract the employer was entitled to keep the employee on the job if he was qualified. (Bellows International, 65 LA 1280; see also 68 LA 1032)

Arbitrators usually have said that probationers do not have to be laid off in any specific order. In cases where unions have questioned management's procedure in laying off such employees, the arbitrators have held that it need not have been according to length of service because the new employees had acquired no seniority. (6 LA 760, 14 LA 963)

Layoff of Probationary Apprentices

Under a special apprenticeship agreement, one arbiter has taken the position that an apprentice is immune to ordinary reductions in force even if he is still on probation. He reasoned that it would frustrate the purpose of apprenticeship to make any apprentice subject to layoff by seniority in the absence of such a requirement in the agreement. (California Metal Trades Assn., 27 LA 105)

Layoff of Handicapped Employee

Under a contract giving handicapped employees transfer rights regardless of seniority, do they have any special protection against layoff? One arbiter ruled that once a handicapped worker had exercised his special privilege of transferring without regard to seniority, he had no further special protection. Unless the contract specifically provides otherwise, the arbiter said, handicapped employees must be treated just like other employees during a layoff. (John Deere & Co., 22 LA 383)

TEMPORARY v. INDEFINITE LAYOFFS

For temporary of emergency layoffs, management often is allowed more leeway in selecting employees than in the case of indefinite layoffs.

In the absence of contract clauses making layoff rules inapplicable to temporary layoffs, some arbiters have held that ordinary layoff procedures must be followed even where the lack of work lasted only a few hours (21 LA 400, 30 LA 441) or one or two days. (64 LA 256, 59 LA 984, 7 LA 308, 5 LA 24) The more common view, however, is that the frequently cumbersome seniority rules need not be followed in the case of a brief temporary layoff. (61 LA 506, 43 LA 1092, 41 LA 970, 12 LA 763, 4 LA 533)

In the case of layoffs caused by emergency breakdowns or other conditions beyond the control of the employer, arbiters generally have upheld disregard of seniority rules applicable in the case of ordinary layoffs. Examples include: (1) a three-day layoff due to an acute gas shortage (Atlantic Foundry Co., 8 LA 807); (2) a temporary shutdown caused by a breakdown in equipment (United Engineering and Foundry Co., 31 LA 93); and (3) an eight-day layoff due to heavy snowfall. (Riverton Lime & Stone Co. Inc., 8 LA 506)

But where it was not shown that application of seniority rules would cause a hardship, an arbiter ruled that seniority should have been followed during an emergency layoff. He found nothing in the contract to authorize the company's unilaterally established rule that layoffs did not include periods of less than three days. (Yale and Towne Mfg., Co., 40 LA 1115; see also 74 LA 844)

Temporary Layoffs for Taking Inventory

Does layoff for the purpose of taking inventory have to follow seniority provisions? Arbitrators have ruled both ways on this question. Some have said that seniority must be applied to any period of slack work, no matter what the reason.

EXAMPLE: A company closed down its plant for two days to take inventory. Certain production employees were called in to assist but the selections were not all made in accordance with seniority. The contract was silent on the exact point but did provide that seniority would govern in case of layoffs.

The question here was whether the shutdown constituted a layoff subject to seniority. The arbiter ruled that the shutdown actually "constituted a slack work period resulting in layoffs of employees within the meaning of the agreement." Therefore seniority had to be considered, and the company erred in laying off men with more seniority than some of the employees put to work to take inventory. (Warren City Mfg. Co., 7 LA 202; see also 65 LA 471)

On the other hand, in another case an arbiter held that a shutdown for inventory purposes was only a temporary cessation of operations and not really a layoff. Therefore, he said, management could select any people it wanted to help take inventory, and the remainder of the working force could be laid off without regard to seniority. (Caterpillar Tractor Co., 7 LA 555; see also 74 LA 89)

Layoff Notice & Pay

IN BRIEF

Various problems may arise when a company agrees to give either advance notice of layoff or pay in lieu of notice, but most center around two main issues. These are: (1) whether management is excused from both notice and pay under particular circumstances, and (2) the form of the notice and to whom it should be given. Beyond collective-bargaining provisions, layoff-notice arbitration decisions may be affected by state plant-closing statutes, and by the federal Worker Adjustment and Retraining Notification Act (WARN).

Some collective bargaining agreements provide for payment of a separation allowance to employees who are laid off or who lose their jobs for other reasons. Problems in this area also are taken up in this chapter.

GUIDELINES

If a contract requires advance notice of layoffs, arbiters generally hold that a layoff notice must be clear and specific and directed to the individual attention of the employees affected. Thus, one arbiter ruled that a notice requirement was not met by an employer's repeatedly telling a union at their regular joint meetings that there was a possibility of a layoff. (Phillip's Waste Oil Pick-Up & Road Oiling Service Inc., 24 LA 136; see also 61 LA 494)

Similarly, a general notice to the union of an impending layoff without identifying those to be laid off does not satisfy a requirement of written notice in advance of a layoff. The purpose of an advance notice requirement is to give employees a chance to look for other work, so the employer is required to list those employees to be affected. (Donaldson Co., 21 LA 254) Even where the layoff is as short as five days, an arbiter ruled that a general notice to the department that some men will be laid off was insufficient. If layoffs are to occur, the arbiter emphasized that, the individuals must be specifically told in advance that they are to be laid off. (Anaconda Aluminum Co., 65 LA 498)

Exceptions for emergencies — Many contracts require notice in advance of layoff except in emergencies. What is considered an emergency? Such occurrences as machine breakdowns, fire, and inclement weather generally are recognized as circumstances beyond management's control. Other situations which have been looked upon by arbiters as emergencies outside of management's control and therefore excusing the failure to provide advance notice include: (1) a strike affecting supplies, (2) an unforeseen materials shortage, (3) snowstorms, (4) unexpected business or financial crisis, and (5) gas shortages requiring plant shutdowns. (73 LA 1127, 67 LA 699, 66 LA 909, 62 LA 962, 50 LA 290, 49 LA 1140, 12 LA 726, 5 LA 295)

If a contract does not provide for exceptions to a layoff notice requirement, is management still bound to give notice or pay except in emergencies? Arbitrators have ruled both ways on this. Some have held that in the absence of a written exception in the contract, employers must meet notice requirements even in emergencies. (29 LA 706, 18 LA 227) But other arbitrators have taken the view that a clause requiring notice applies only to situations where management reasonably can give notice — and management is not obligated for pay in lieu of notice when an emergency prevents it from giving notice. (International Harvester Co., 14 LA 134)

Receipt of Notice Required

Under a contract stating that an employee "shall receive" advance notice of a layoff, one arbiter has ruled that merely "sending" a notice was not enough to relieve the employer of reporting-pay liability.

EXAMPLE: A company sent telegrams to employees who were being laid off. One employee did not get the word, although he was at home at the time it should have been delivered. He reported for work as usual the next day. The company denied his claim for reporting pay, saying that its obligation was met by sending a correctly addressed telegram.

The word "receive," the arbiter pointed means that more than the sending of a message is necessary. The contract, he said, recognized this, for it used "shall be notified" instead of "shall receive notice" in another provision. Although the employee had a telephone, no attempt was made to reach him by this means. So, the arbiter figured all reasonable efforts were not made, and the employee was entitled to pay. (Douglas & Lomason Co., 28 LA 406; see also 88 LA 594)

Penalties for Notice Violations

When an employer fails to give employees proper or timely notice of layoffs, as provided in a bargaining agreement or under state or federal law, and if the employer also fails to give an adequate written explanation for its lack of notice, it may be held liable, for example, for pay in lieu of notice.

EXAMPLE: An employer that notified a union and employees of layoffs on the morning that the layoffs were implemented was found liable to affected employees for two days' pay in lieu of notice. The arbiter ruled that the contract clearly required two days' advance notice of layoff to union or immediate written explanation for the lack of notice. Since the employer did not furnish a written explanation until the union requested it three weeks later, he said, there was no emergency. (York International Corp., 93 LA 1107; see also 86 LA 866)

However, where employees, who had 15 minutes' notice of "termination of employment" due to a plant closure and sale, are not entitled to payment in lieu of a three-day notice or to continued insurance coverage required in case of layoff, an arbiter ruled, since the employees were discharged, not laid off. The mere existence of a contract does not guarantee a continuation of employment or of employment-related benefits, and, further, the issue of a procedure for the continuation of benefits in the event of closure of sale was never discussed by either party. (Hausman Steel Corp., 93 LA 813)

Similarly, an arbiter ruled that an employer, which failed to comply with a two-week notice of termination requirement when it sent a letter of termination to employees that provided only one-week notice, need not pay a compensatory remedy since the losses were minimal. (Independent School District No. 721, 82 LA 1323)

Also, an arbiter held that an employer was not required to give laid-off employees two-weeks' notice, where a strike settlement specifically waived all "work guarantee." (Safeway Stores Inc., 85 LA 51)

And, an arbiter said that 46-days was adequate notice of an intent permanently to close a plant, where a letter agreement required 90-days' notice "if circumstances permit." The union had all the information that it needed for effects bargaining four months before the formal notice, and that there was no evidence either that the requirement guaranteed 90 days of employment or that a waiver of the time limit could only occur under "circumstances" outside the employer's control. (Commonwealth Aluminum Corp., 89 LA 1097)

Computing Notice Period

When a contract requires advance notice a certain length of time prior to the layoff, can nonworking days be counted as days of notice? At least one arbiter has ruled that they cannot. He noted that one purpose of advance layoff notice is to allow the union time to try to find other employment for the laid-off workers. This purpose, he said, would be defeated if nonworking days could be counted in the notice period. (Hoke Inc., 3 LA 750)

Similarly, an arbiter ruled that an employer had to pay eight hours wages to employees laid off without the required one day's notice, despite the employer's contention that he could not give notice because employees were not in the plant due to a vacation shutdown. The arbiter said that a vacation shutdown was like a weekend, and if employees were to be laid off they should have been notified at or before the start of work on the last day before the weekend. (Magnavox Co., 64 LA 686)

However, another arbiter ruled differently, where 24 hour notice was required before layoffs, and an employer told workers at 3:30 p.m. on Friday that they would be laid off effective 6:00 p.m. Saturday. Since Saturday was not a scheduled working day, the union maintained that the workers should have been given a full working day as notice period. Rejecting the union's position, the arbitrator found that the "24 hours notice" merely meant 24 hours following posting of layoff notice; and that there was no clear past practice governing Friday layoff notices. (White Metal Rolling and Stamping Corp., 65 LA 771)

Layoff Shorter Than Notice Period

Some contracts provide for notice a specified length of time in advance of layoff or pay for the same period in lieu of notice. Are workers entitled to pay for the full notice period when they're laid off, without notice, for a shorter period of time? A state arbitration board held that employees laid off without advance notice were entitled to pay for the full period, even though they were laid off a shorter time.

EXAMPLE: A contract said that workers would not be laid off without a week's notice or a week's pay in lieu of notice. The workers were given no advance notice when they were laid off for two days. The union claimed the company owed them a week's pay. But the company claimed it had not been possible to give advance notice.

The arbitration board conceded that application of the contract provision seemed harsh since the layoff lasted only two days, but it pointed out that it would not have seemed so if the layoff had lasted longer. The company's obligation under the contract was clear and unqualified, the board ruled; therefore one week's pay was due each of the workers. (General Baking Co., 28 LA 621)

On the other hand, the fact that a contract provides for two weeks' notice of layoff or pay in lieu thereof does not necessarily mean that employees not given two weeks' notice must be granted a full two weeks' pay, according to one arbiter.

EXAMPLE: A contract provided for two weeks' notice of layoff or pay in lieu of notice for employees with six months' service. The company made a general layoff with only a few days' prior notice. Some employees lost less than two weeks' work, but the union claimed the full two weeks' pay in lieu of notice in addition to their regular earnings for any work done within the period.

An arbiter ruled that the most reasonable interpretation of the provision was that employees were entitled to "pay in lieu thereof" only for layoffs from work which fell within the two weeks after notice was given. In other words, he said, they could expect to receive only their regular pay for the two weeks following the layoff notice. This included pay for both time worked and layoff time. (Phillip's Waste Oil Pick-Up & Road Oiling Service Inc., et. al., 24 LA 136)

Notice for Temporary Layoff

An employer attempted to avoid a contract requirement providing for two week notice in event of layoff by claiming the provision only applied in cases of permanent layoff, and that his three day notice was sufficient since the layoff was only temporary.

However, in overturning the employer's action, the arbiter read no such distinction in the contract language. A layoff is a layoff whether it is permanent or temporary, the arbiter said, and if a distinction were to be made between the two, it should have been made explicit in the contract. (International Paper Co., 60 LA 447; see also 73 LA 573)

Where Notice Is 'Impossible'

A company that had agreed to give three days' advance notice of layoffs, "except where such notice is impossible," violated the contract when employees were laid off without any advance notice due to lack of work. The arbiter ruled since the word "impossible" was not explained, it should be given its ordinary definition and only an emergency of major proportions would release the company from its obligation of giving notice. Decline or even cessation of orders does not qualify as such an emergency, the arbiter concluded. (Mobil Chemical Co., 50 LA 80)

Notice of Layoff Caused by Wildcat Strike or Slowdown

When a layoff is made necessary by an authorized and unexpected work stoppage by employees in other departments of the plant, most arbiters excuse employers from giving layoff notice or pay. One ruled that to require it under these circumstances would be completely unreasonable. (International Harvester Co., 9 LA 784)

Similarly, a slowdown has been held to be a situation that relieved an employer of the notice requirements. Under a contract that required advance notice of a layoff except in emergencies, one arbitrator held that there was an emergency within the meaning of the contract when a company had to lay off several workers on short notice because of a slowdown in one department. The arbiter said the employer was justified and did not have to give the workers layoff pay since the layoff was neither planned nor desired by the company. (Lone Star Steel Co., 28 LA 465)

Likewise, under similar contract terms, another employer was upheld for laying off workers due to a local union strike against his suppliers, since he was not given prior notice. (Burgermeister Brewing Corp., 44 LA 1028)

Bumping & Transfer to Avoid Layoff

IN BRIEF

Seniority rights lose much of their meaning if senior workers do not have a right when faced with layoff to claim jobs held by their juniors. At the same time, employers often oppose bumping on the ground that it impairs efficiency. Accordingly, bumping questions give rise to many grievances.

Even where the right to bump is expressly spelled out in a collective bargaining agreement, problems may arise. For example, may a worker bump only in his or her own department, or anywhere in the plant? May he or she displace a worker with less seniority, or only the least senior worker? May an employee claim a higher-rated job if the employee is qualified for it? Does an employee have the right to a trial period to prove that he or she can do the work?

In general, arbiters have held that bumping rights are implied by a contract providing for the application of seniority when the work force is being reduced. They have further ruled that, in the absence of express contract language to the contrary, a worker may displace any worker down the ladder who has less seniority, not merely the least senior employee. (91 LA 710, 87 LA 1107, 84 LA 1001, 76 LA 1017, 76 LA 773, 75 LA 1163, 74 LA 584)

Further, where a contract contains a provision giving senior employees the right to bump junior employees in a layoff situation, but specifies that ability and experience, in conjunction with seniority, will be determining factors in making layoff decisions, arbiters have ruled that the employer may properly allow those senior employees without training to bump junior workers with training. (98 LA 333, 98 LA 209, 86 LA 54, 85 LA 24, 84 LA 1001, 84 LA 952, 84 LA 604, 83 LA 205, 82 LA 313, 82 LA 1205)

GUIDELINES

Plant-Wide Seniority Implies Bumping

If a contract provides for a plant-wide seniority system to be applied in layoffs, most arbiters agree that bumping rights are implicit, even though they are not specifically mentioned. Such an interpretation, they say, means that a worker whose job is discontinued may displace a junior worker in an equal or lower classification provided he can perform the junior worker's job. (76 LA 899, 14 LA 938, 13 LA 843, 8 LA 816)

However, not all arbiters will conclude that bumping rights exist when not mentioned in the contract. At least one has ruled that no such rights exist unless stated in clear and unambiguous terms in the agreement. (Norwalk Co., 3 LA 535)

Bumping Rights Under Plant-Wide & Departmental Seniority

When a contract provides for both plant-wide and departmental seniority, is an employee facing layoff permitted to bump to any job in the plant held by a junior worker? Under such a provision, whether bumping rights are expressed or implied, many arbiters have ruled that departmental seniority should be applied first so that the senior worker would bump to a lower job in his or her own department. Plant-wide seniority, they say, should apply only when there are no jobs remaining within the employee's department. (38 LA 939, 30 LA 472, 3 LA 205)

Similarly, an arbiter found that under a system establishing seniority by both plant and department, the bumping rights of senior employees was limited to low-classification jobs or positions within the department over which the employee maintained posted job rights. The bumping and layoff procedure had not been reduced to a detailed written agreement, so the company argued that it was valid on the basis of past practice. The arbiter concluded that the union failed to show the existence of a contradictory practice. (United States Steel Corp., 65 LA 283)

Likewise, a dispute arose as to whether an employee with company-wide seniority could displace a junior employee, who had job-site seniority. The employer would not allow the bump, claiming the contract called for job-site seniority in cases of bumping.

Although agreeing with the employer, the arbiter nonetheless found that the contract language was inconsistent on whether job or company seniority should govern. He therefore based his decision on a combination of factors, including past practice and the union's concession that it would not have taken the same position had the grievant never worked at the same job-site. (American Building Maintenance Co., 62 LA 1027)

Bumping Limited to Choice of Classification

Under a contract permitting an employee, during a layoff, to bump a man with less seniority in any department if he had the ability to do the work, one arbiter ruled that the senior worker's choice was limited to picking a classification. Management had the right to decide which job within the classification he could fill, the arbiter ruled. (Fulton-Sylphon Co., 2 LA 116; see also 84 LA 952)

However, under a similar provision, another arbiter held that a worker could choose the job he liked best within a classification because of nonwage factors.

EXAMPLE: Under one contract, an employee slated for layoff could displace a man with less seniority in any department, provided the employee had the ability to do the job. An employee whose shift was discontinued bumped to a work crew on another shift. He requested one job on the crew but was given another. Both positions were within the same job classification and paid the same wage rate, and the company argued it had a right to decide which one the employee should have.

An arbiter, however, found that the employer was wrong. The fact that the two jobs carried the same rate did not mean there was nothing to choose between them, he said; nonwage factors made one seem more desirable to the employee. Moreover, the arbiter pointed out that past practice had been to post particular jobs on the crew for bidding. Thus, he concluded that the employee should be given the job he wanted. (Dayton Steel Foundry Co., 29 LA 191, see also 76 LA 399)

Bumping Limited to Particular Job

Under a contract providing that an employee subject to layoff was entitled to bump the employee with the least seniority in the employee's occupational group, one arbiter held that a worker was limited to bumping into only one job — that held by the least senior worker in the same job grouping. Since she was not able to do that particular job, the company was justified in laying her off, the arbiter ruled, even though workers with less seniority were kept working. He said that the contract clearly would not permit her to bump into just any job held by a worker with less seniority. (Ford Motor Co., 1 LA 462)

Further, a laid-off worker was not entitled to select the particular job on which to exercise her bumping rights where the contract referred to ability to do "required" work and willingness to accept the "work proffered." The arbiter said that the element of choice was in the hands of the company rather than the worker. (United Screw & Bolt Corp., 42 LA 669)

However, under a contract simply making seniority the governing factor in layoff, but not mentioning bumping rights, another arbiter decided that a worker facing layoff could bump any junior employee in an equal or lower classification. The employee was not limited to bumping only the most junior worker, the arbiter said. If that were the intent of the parties, they should have said so in the contract, he reasoned. (Warren Petroleum Corp., 26 LA 532)

Ability as a Factor

Where a contract allows bumping if the senior employee is capable of performing the job of a junior employee, who is to decide on the ability of the senior employee? Most arbiters hold that management has the right to determine ability. The union can challenge management's decision through the grievance procedure, but has the burden of proving that management's judgment was either wrong, arbitrary, or capricious. (75 LA 1001, 41 LA 148, 22 LA 53, 6 LA 786)

EXAMPLE: An arbiter ruled as unreasonable, arbitrary, and capricious, and an unconscionable bargain by the employer, a collective bargaining agreement's bumping clause which required employees to have 30-days' experience in the new positions and to demonstrate that employer records show such experience. (84 LA 571)

Similarly, it was the employer's past practice which dictated that senior employees were permitted to exercise bumping rights only if they could perform posted jobs without training. The arbiter honored management's practice despite the union's contention that the junior worker whom the employee wished to bump was performing "menial" tasks, since both the employee and the chief steward admitted that the junior worker could have been performing more complex tasks in that job. (Morton-Norwich Products Inc., 61 LA 494)

Need for Trial/Break-In Periods

Several arbiters have ruled that senior employees are entitled to a reasonable *trial period* in order to demonstrate their current ability. (96 LA 1069, 93 LA 1028, 82 LA 655, 82 LA 213, 88 LA 1112, 85 LA 1069, 85 LA 24, 83 LA 977, 82 LA 751, 82 LA 213, 81 LA 1248)

However, other arbiters have ruled that senior employees whose qualifications are questionable are not entitled to a trial period in a layoff situation, but, instead, are entitled to a reasonable *break-in period.* (82 LA 751, 82 LA 721, 81 LA 1100)

Another arbiter stressed that a *"trial period"* is not to be equated with a *"training period."* A trial period, the arbiter said, emphasizes a successful bidders's ability at the beginning of a period, provides criteria for determining a bidder's ability to perform in a new position, and is followed by an automatic progression in classification on satisfactory performance; whereas, a training period emphasizes prerequisite ability on the completion of a program. (93 LA 1028; see also 82 LA 655)

Still another arbiter has held that an employer may require testing to determine a senior employee's qualifications for a position to which the employee wishes to bump. (91 LA 710)

To qualify for retention during layoff, other arbiters have held that senior employees must be able to perform the necessary jobs after a reasonable break-in period, and are not entitled to any instruction or training. (96 LA 105, 61 LA 72, 23 LA 584, 11 LA 667, 7 LA 526)

Some arbiters go even further and hold that the senior employee, in order to exercise his bumping rights, must possess the ability to perform the job in question without benefit of any training or trial period. (67 LA 282, 65 LA 901, 44 LA 694, 44 LA 24)

Efficiency as a Factor

Under a contract requiring a senior worker to be able to do another worker's job efficiently in order to bump the employee, can it be assumed that the senior employee is not qualified just because he has never done the job at that company? One arbiter has ruled that such an assumption is not justified. He suggested that an employer, in judging an employee's ability to do the work efficiently, is obligated to take into consideration the employee's entire work record, including jobs the employee had at other firms.

EXAMPLE: During a force reduction at one company, a milling machine operator was not permitted to bump a junior employee who operated an engine lathe. The contract said employees would be given preference in layoff in accordance with their length of service, "subject to their ability to perform the work in question, it being understood that efficiency is a necessary requisite." Since the employee had never operated the lathe, the company argued, he could not do the job efficiently. The union, though, pointed out that the employee had had 12 years' experience at his trade and had operated engine lathes at other employers.

An arbiter sided with the union. Under the contract, he said, the company could not deny the employee the job unless it could prove he could not do it efficiently. This it had failed to do, the arbiter noted, even though checking on the employee's performance at the other firms where he claimed he had run a lathe would have been a simple matter. (Cobak Tool & Mfg. Co., 30 LA 279; see also 96 LA 681, 96 LA 189, 96 LA 117)

However, in another case, where the contract said the employee doing the bumping could do so only if "seniority to be exercised is greater than the seniority in that classification of the employee to be displaced," a truck driver who had sought to bump a less senior garage serviceman, was refused the move by the company. In upholding the company's refusal, the arbiter noted the grievant's lack of experience as a garage serviceman. (Jenkin-Guerin Inc., 64 LA 703; see also 94 LA 1190)

Upward Bumping

Can an employee about to be laid off bump a junior worker in a higher-rated job classification? Arbitrators have ruled both ways on the issue of upward bumping. Where arbiters have denied the right of a senior employee to bump into a higher-rated classification, one or more of the following reasons were used:

● The collective bargaining agreement does not expressly prohibit upward bumping. (91 LA 221, 62 LA 192, 34 LA 294, 30 LA 886, 29 LA 629, 29 LA 439, 21 LA 214, 20 LA 394, 16 LA 478, 15 LA 891)

● The layoff provisions of the agreement are broad. (44 LA 694, 30 LA 886, 20 LA 394, 14 LA 502)

● Upward bumping does not conflict with the agreement's promotion provisions. (29 LA 439, 12 LA 738)

● Past practice of the parties either supports or does not prohibit upward bumping. (62 LA 192, 44 LA 694, 21 LA 214)

EXAMPLE: One arbiter decided that where the contract stated that both ability and seniority were determining factors in bumping, "present rather than potential" ability was called for. Where the senior worker had the required ability, junior workers — including those in higher-rated jobs — had to be laid off first during a reduction in the work force. (Greater Louisville Industries, 44 LA 694)

EXAMPLE: Another arbiter denied an upward bump, although he admitted there was nothing in the contract to prohibit it, because he was not convinced the employee seeking the move could perform the higher rated work. The arbiter found that the employee could perform only about 20 percent of the job he sought, and that the contract did not provide for the training he would need to successfully carry out the duties which were being performed by a less senior worker. Because the employee failed to meet the burden of proof that he could perform the job at the time he sought it, the grievance was denied. (United Telephone Co. of Ohio, 60 LA 805)

Other arbiters have decided that bumping upward amounts to promotion. When a contract neither permits nor prohibits upward bumping but makes the promotion clause separate from the layoff provision, layoff is no occasion for promoting employees to higher-paying jobs, these arbiters have ruled. (71 LA 295, 25 LA 417, 23 LA 789, 15 LA 891)

Similarly, where a contract provided that all promotions to higher classifications should be given to the most senior qualified employee who bids for "the vacancy," an arbiter denied an upward bump. The employee, a senior mechanic, who had received a layoff notice tried unsuccessfully to bump into a higher rated classification of station mechanic. The desired job was held by another worker who had less seniority than the employee.

In upholding management's refusal to grant the upward bump, the arbiter stated that, there was not a single reported arbitral decision extending permission, approval, or even toleration of upward bumping as a means of achieving a promotion in violation and defeat of the specifically agreed promotion requirements of a collective bargaining agreement. (K.L.M. Royal Dutch Airlines, 60 LA 1053)

Likewise, ambiguity in the bumping procedures or contrary past practice also can limit the right of senior workers to bump. When a worker sought to bump into the top mill crew job, the company refused to promote him. Historically, it contended, workers had never been permitted to bump into top jobs that they actually had not performed. According to the arbiter, established past practice and failure of the contract to provide a training period for bumping supported the company's right to turn down workers whom it determines are unqualified. (Empire-Reeves Steel Corp., 44 LA 653)

However, other arbiters have denied the right of a senior employee to bump into a higher-rated classification. (85 LA 47, 84 LA 1069) One or more of the following reasons were used:

• A layoff may not be used as a means of achieving a promotion. The rationale here seems to be that a promotion can be sought only when a vacancy exists; promotions must be governed by the promotion clause a collective bargaining agreement; and, since upward bumping would result in a promotion in violation of the promotion requirements of the contract, it cannot be permitted. (76 LA 899, 72 LA 719, 71 LA 295, 38 LA 430, 26 LA 532, 24 LA 261, 23 LA 789, 22 LA 736, 15 LA 891, 14 LA 938, 3 LA 863)

• Evidence indicated that past practice prohibits upward bumping, or there is an indication that past practice allows it. (44 LA 653, 30 LA 815, 30 LA 1, 23 LA 220)

• The bargaining history indicates an intent to preclude upward bumping. (24 LA 261)

• While the collective bargaining agreement would permit upward bumping, it does not require that it be permitted. Therefore, without a showing of practice by the parties, the arbiter cannot sustain a claim to upward bumping. (38 LA 128, 30 LA 815)

Right to Second Bump

If an employee fails to qualify on the first job the employee bumps into, does the employee have the right to try out on another job held by a junior employee? Arbitrators are generally agreed that no second bump need be allowed when the contract is silent on the matter.

EXAMPLE: An employee slated for layoff was given the choice of bumping into a job held by a junior employee, as required under the contract. She chose a job she had never before performed; after a week's trial she was informed that she lacked the ability to do the job satisfactorily and was then laid off. The union protested, saying that she had not been given time enough to become familiar with the new job and that, even if her disqualification was proper, she should have been offered an opportunity to bump into another job rather than being laid off.

Ruling that the layoff was proper, the arbiter found that the employee had been given a reasonable opportunity to demonstrate her ability in the job and that she was not entitled to bump into another job, since the contract did not provide for repeated bumping. The arbiter decided that the employee herself was largely responsible for her poor selection of a job to bump into, since she had purposely passed up a job she knew she was capable of doing. (22 LA 53, 12 LA 391)

Right to Bump at Will

Can employees use their accumulated seniority to bump whenever they wish into jobs occupied by employees with less seniority? Most arbiters hold they cannot. They limit bumping rights to a situation where an employee is moved out of his job as in a layoff.

EXAMPLE: An employee bid on the creeler job and was awarded it on the basis of his seniority and qualifications. A year later because of advancing age he attempted to exercise his seniority to bump or "roll" into an oiling job. The company allowed this and the employee was discharged when he was unable to handle any of the available jobs offered him.

The employee protested the discharge, claiming that the bumping right did not apply to such a situation. The contract provided that in layoffs the last one in would be the first out.

The arbiter agreed that "This necessarily implies that a senior employee can 'roll' a junior employee when the former's job is abolished." But the arbiter limited that right solely to such a situation. He ruled that advancing age was not reason enough to permit an employee on his own initiative to pick out a job held by a junior employee and bump him. The arbiter pointed out that "the company could not operate efficiently if an employee were free to 'roll' a junior employee at any time he or she desires to do so." (Anchor Rome Mills Inc., 9 LA 595)

However, under a contract stating that employees with seniority could bump into more desirable jobs, another arbiter ruled that they could do so any time they desired. He said if the parties had meant to limit bumping rights only to situations when vacancies occurred, they should have said so in the contract. (Continental Oil Co., 8 LA 171)

Responsibility for Initiating Bumping

Who is responsible for seeing to it that the bumping provisions of a contract are carried out — the employer, or the employee and the union? Does the company have to start the bumping machinery in a layoff or should the senior worker put in a claim for the job to which he is entitled? When the contract did not specifically spell out the procedure, some arbiters held that it was up to employees to claim their rights.

EXAMPLE: One employee, a crane follower, was laid off for five months, when he was recalled as a punch helper. A week later, he bid for and was awarded a job as a rivet heater being held by a junior employee. He also put in a claim for back pay to the time of his layoff, claiming he should have replaced the junior rivet heater at that time.

The arbiter agreed with the employer that the employee had some obligation to be diligent in asserting his rights, either by himself or through his steward. If he did not do so, he should not be permitted to collect back pay from the company, for that would mean that the company was paying twice for the work — once to the man laid off, and once to the man who kept the job. (General American Transportation Corp., 15 LA 672)

However, in another case, an opposite decision was reached where an employee was bumped from his job by a senior employee, and did not realize that he had a right to another job that he had previously bid for but turned down. Three weeks later the employee was informed of his right to the other job, and so he filed a grievance when the employer refused to bump him into it.

The arbiter rejected the company's argument that the employee had waited too long after being bumped before filing the grievance. Remarking that the employee could not have known of his right despite reasonable diligence, and so could not have filed the grievance before the company informed him of it, the arbiter decided that the grievance was timely filed and proper, since it was filed one day after the employer refused to bump the worker into the desired job. (Dayton-Walther Corp., 64 LA 645)

Right to Refuse Downgrading

When a contract is silent on the matter, can an employee elect to be laid off rather than downgraded during a reduction in force, or can the employer discharge him if he refuses to accept a lower-rated job? According to one arbiter, in the absence of contract language requiring employees to take available work or be discharged, they have the right to choose layoff.

EXAMPLE: Two employees' jobs were eliminated during a reduction in force, and they were offered lower-rated jobs on the basis of their seniority. They refused to take the jobs and were discharged. The company said the discharges were for just cause since the men had refused the only work available to them.

The arbiter, however, decided that the right of senior employees to bump into or to take lower jobs was not the same as a requirement that they take such jobs. In the absence of clear contract language requiring them to take available work or be discharged, the arbiter concluded that they were free to request layoffs and subsequent rehire in line with their seniority. He ordered the company to change the separation status of the employees from discharge to layoff. (Caterpillar Tractor Co., 23 LA 313).

Moreover, employees may continue to elect layoff rather than demotion, despite the introduction of a supplemental unemployment benefit plan, an arbiter held, where this right of election had existed in the past. (United Engineering & Foundry Co., 47 LA 164)

Worksharing

IN BRIEF

During a period when work is in short supply, a reduction in the workweek may seem like a good idea to an employer. However, a union may see things differently. Particularly in situations where a collective bargaining agreement provides supplemental unemployment benefits, a union is likely to favor layoff for the few, normal working hours for the many.

There seems to be a general agreement among arbiters that if a contract (1) says nothing about worksharing and (2) requires that seniority be followed in cutting the work force, an employer may not shorten the workweek in lieu of making layoffs. If management could telescope the workweek on a whim, they reason, seniority rights would not mean much.

GUIDELINES

Management's Right to Shorten Workweek

If the contract contains no specific provisions relating to worksharing, is the employer free to cut the workweek in order to spread available work among the largest number of employees? The answer to this question depends on the interpretations placed on other types of contract clauses. If the agreement states that seniority must be followed in cutting the work force, an arbiter is likely to hold that management may not shorten the workweek in preference to making layoffs, and if the change is not arbitrary, capricious, or discriminatory.

EXAMPLE: One employer, relying on a clause recognizing its right to "curtail production," chopped a day off of the regular workweek for all employees. An arbiter decided the workweek reduction was a contract violation. The agreement, he noted, stated that force reductions were to be made in order of seniority. If management could cut the workweek to four days, it could make further reductions, he pointed out, and seniority would not mean much. (32 LA 244; see also 95 LA 482, 92 LA 1094, 90 LA 922, 90 LA 301, 86 LA 992, 83 LA 314, 82 LA 676, 82 LA 221, 81 LA 1150, 81 LA 519, 74 LA 1254, 40 LA 456, 24 LA 311)

Similarly, another employer also reduced the workweek to four days when business was bad. The contract with the union dictated that "either the hours per day or the days per week could be reduced by mutual agreement" with the union. Although the union rejected the employer's worksharing proposal, management shortened the workweek anyway. Arguing that it had the right to reduce the workweek, the employer maintained that union approval was needed only for the form of the reduction—i.e., either hours per day or days per week. The arbiter rejected this argument and ruled that the employer's action violated the employees' seniority rights. The worksharing had to be by mutual consent, the arbiter reasoned. Since there was no consent by the union, the employer's alternative was layoffs by seniority the arbiter concluded. (Aro Corp., 55 LA 859; see also 73 LA 810)

Likewise, an arbiter ruled that an employer could not institute one-and two-day plant-wide layoffs, because such "share the work" programs were in violation of a clear seniority layoff clause governing reductions in the work force. The arbiter rejected management's contention that a separate clause granting permission to lay off all employees due to "changes in customer requirements" was applicable, since the clause concerned only "unforeseen, unpredictable, unplanned and unanticipated conditions," which the present situation — a slow business period — was not. (Tecumseh Products Co., 65 LA 471)

On the other hand, clauses stating that the regular workweek shall consist of so many hours and so many days generally have been held not to prevent management from cutting the workweek instead of laying employees off.

EXAMPLE: One employer reduced the normal workweek from 40 to 35 hours by scheduling five seven-hour days when business slowed down. The union argued that this was a violation of a contract provision stating that the regular workday would be eight hours and the regular workweek five days. The arbiter disagreed, saying that this provision did not establish a guaranteed eight-hour day, five day week but was merely a statement of the normal operating schedule for purposes of figuring overtime. Nothing in the contract prohibited the employer from shortening the regular workweek, the arbiter concluded. (22 LA 473; see also 96 LA 445, 96 LA 117, 89 LA 1313, 81 LA 502, 66 LA 119, 12 LA 1163)

EXAMPLE: An employer had the right to maintain its two-shift system during an economic downturn, an arbiter decided even though the system resulted in frequent scheduling of less than eight hour workdays, where the contract clearly stated that the employer "shall have no responsibility or obligation to furnish any minimum number of hours of work per week or per day to its employees." (Dixie Container Co., 65 LA 1089)

EXAMPLE: An employer had the right to reduce the workweek to 35 hours, an arbiter ruled, where the contract gave management the unlimited right to schedule production. The reduction was reasonable during a temporary business slowdown, the arbiter concluded, rejecting the union's argument that a reduction to a 32-hour workweek was the only exception to the "regular 40-hour week." (Rex Chainbelt Inc., 52 LA 852)

EXAMPLE: In another case, although the union argued that junior employees should have been laid off so that senior employees could work a full 40-hour week the arbiter ruled that the contract clearly gave the employer the right to divide work equally in the event of insufficient demand. (Industrial Garment Mfg., 65 LA 875)

Layoff Before Worksharing

Many arbiters believe that it is only fair that regular employees or those with seniority should be kept on a regular workweek as long as possible. Therefore, they agree that probationary or short-service employees should be laid off before the workweek is reduced. (Western Automatic Machine Screw Co., 12 LA 38; see also 88 LA 594, 68 LA 838)

The point at which layoffs should stop and cutting hours should begin may be found in the specific language of the contract. One agreement stated that when it became necessary to make layoffs involving employees with two or more years of service, operations would be reduced to a single shift or to a 32-hour week before further layoffs were made. An arbiter held that this clearly required the employer to lay off all workers with less than two years' service before reducing the workweek to 32 hours. (Aetna Ball & Roller Bearing Co., 22 LA 453)

However, where the contract did not provide the answer, one arbiter said that employees should be laid off until the work group was reduced to a "reasonable minimum." When it reached the point where a further reduction in the work force would have impaired the standard of quality set for the group, then the employer could reduce the workweek, he said. (Bloom-Ease Inc., 12 LA 941)

Worksharing Before Layoff

A contract may call for a reduction in working hours before any layoffs can be made.

EXAMPLE: One agreement required a reduction in the workweek to 32 hours before employees were laid off. The employer claimed it could make layoffs to eliminate the night shift instead of reducing hours as long as the volume of work did not drop enough to justify instituting a 32-hour week. An arbiter ruled that the employer could not lay off workers as long as there was enough work to keep everybody working for 32 hours or more per week (Babcock Printing Press Corp., 10 LA 397)

Similarly, another employer could not discharge permanent employees for lack of work, but had to reduce hours of individual employees in order to comply with the contract which stated that "all work of any classification in any shop shall be equally distributed among the employees of that classification without discrimination." The arbiter reasoned that the provision was intended to apply to decreases in available work, as overtime distribution was dealt within a separate provision. The entire structural thrust of the contract, he concluded, was toward the work-sharing principal, and it would take explicit contract language to justify other conclusions. (Wilshire Mfg. Jewelers, 49 LA 1079)

On the other hand, where the contract permitted employee layoffs according to seniority after the workweek was reduced during four weeks in the year due to lack of work; and the employer laid off maintenance employees for two days on the basis of their seniority after it had reduced the workweek in their department to four days a week for four weeks, an arbiter upheld the employer's actions, despite the union's contention that the contract's "hours" provision guaranteed a 40-hour week. Such a construction would prohibit layoffs and render the contract language meaningless, the arbiter ruled, rejecting the union's argument that layoffs could not cover portions of weeks, but only full weeks. (Arcata Graphics, 65 LA 785)

In another case, an employer had the right to reduce hours of all employees, including union officers, in a department for lack of work. The contract granted union officers superseniority in layoffs, but also stated that a "reduction in hours of work or a staggering of work schedules of employees is not a layoff requiring the application of" seniority. Although the slips given employees when their hours were reduced stated that employees were being "laid off", the slips also contained the dates upon which employees were scheduled to return to work. Since the other facts indicated that the employer's action constituted staggering of work schedules, with sharing of available work among all employees, according to the arbiter, this was not a "layoff" as defined in the contract. (Wilcox Crittenden Co., 43 LA 1046)

Worksharing Instead of Layoff

A special agreement gave one employer the right to reduce the workweek for up to six weeks, instead of the original two weeks provided for in the contract. The union had sought the agreement to avoid layoffs, and this purpose was spelled out in the document and agreed to by management. However, when business slacked off, the employer still laid off workers, charging that no company would agree not to resort to layoffs regardless of a decline in business. An arbiter, however, disagreed with the employer, citing the clear, unambiguous language of the bargaining agreement calling for worksharing in lieu of layoffs. (Allen Group Inc., 64 LA 1085)

Group Affected by Worksharing

Can hours be cut for one group of workers while other groups are still operating on a full schedule? Where a contract with a provision for worksharing specifies that the shorter workweek shall apply to a single classification or department, or to the whole plant, an arbitrator will undoubtedly require strict adherence to the contract language.

EXAMPLE: One contract stated that when work slowed down in any department, hours should be reduced to 32 a week for 30 days before any layoffs were made. The employer reduced the workweek for one class of employees within a department, but not for others. The arbiter said this action was a violation of the contract because all classes of employees within the department should have been put on a shorter week. Employees whose hours were cut were awarded pay for the time they lost. (Mueller Brass Co., 3 LA 271)

Similarly, another employer "transferred" three employees out of their department and into lower-rated jobs while others in the original department continued to work overtime, although the labor agreement prohibited layoffs of regular employees until hours were reduced to 40 per week. The arbiter overturned the transfers, finding them to be outside the scope of management rights. The moves were actually layoffs from the department, the arbiter concluded, and the employees should not have been moved while others were on overtime. (Bartelt Engineering Co., 51 LA 582)

However, an employer had the right to schedule a four-day workweek for employees in its manufacturing department during a time period that a regular workweek was scheduled for employees in its parts depot and export departments, an arbiter decided, where the contract gave the employer the right to schedule four-day workweeks upon compliance with certain requirements. Pointing out that the manufacturing employees on the four-day workweek were not on layoff but on a contractually permissible shortened workweek, the arbiter concluded that the fact that the depot and export workers were not placed on four-day workweek did not convert the scheduling change into a reduction in force that required application of layoff procedures. (Hyster Co., 66 LA 523)

Recalls From Layoffs

IN BRIEF

Since nearly all collective bargaining agreements provide that recalls from layoffs be done in the reverse order of layoff, many recall problems are automatically eliminated when the order of layoff is determined. However, disputes frequently arise over such questions as an employer's right to give physical examinations on recall, whether a worker can continue on layoff rather than accept an undesirable job, and an employer's obligations with respect to recall notices.

Arbiters usually have held that management does have the right to require workers to take physical exams on returning from extended layoff. They also have said, though, that an employer may not set higher physical standards for returning employees than for those already working.

GUIDELINES

Seniority v. Ability in Recall

Under a contract which contained a seniority clause but was silent on applying seniority to recall, one arbiter ruled that a senior employee should be recalled if able to perform the required work. Management should not bypass a senior worker able to handle the work just because a junior worker could do a better job, even though the contract did not outline the recall procedure, the arbiter ruled. (Laher Battery Production Corp., 11 LA 41)

Similarly, in a case where recall was to be made by seniority and ability, but qualifications were not explicitly mentioned in the recall clause, an arbiter decided that ability to do the work was an implied factor in the contract. Additionally, the arbiter ruled that a training period for senior employees to gain full familiarity with certain equipment, which junior employees were already capable of handling, was also implied. Thus, when work for laid off employees became available, the arbiter concluded that the employer was obligated to recall senior employees who required some training, over junior employees who had in fact trained on the complex machines prior to layoff. (Thiokol Corp., 65 LA 1265; see also 95 LA 467, 94 LA 158, 82 LA 1007, 76 LA 932, 76 LA 699, 76 LA 575, 76 LA 540)

However, an arbiter ruled that, despite the fact that a senior employee was not recalled, an employer had the right to recall a junior employee to do shop work in addition to repair work on a railroad crane that he was recalled from layoff to do. The junior employee had done most of the original work on the crane when it was custom built for a customer and the customer had specifically requested the employee to do the repair work, the arbiter reasoned. (T. Bruce Sales, 81 LA 481; see also 93 LA 553)

Also, an arbiter held that an employer, determining the order of recall for two employees with identical departmental seniority, was required to recall the employee who had been laid off twice over a one-week period, rather than the other worker, who had been laid off once and recalled. (Jacksonville Shipyard Inc., 82 LA 90)

Ability, Skill & Efficiency as Factors in Recall

Under contracts making seniority governing in recall, where ability, skill, and efficiency were equal, arbiters have ruled that senior workers did not have to be given a break-in period to become proficient on jobs where junior workers had already proved themselves the most efficient through past performance. The arbitrators upheld the recall of the junior workers in preference to the seniors.

EXAMPLE: A contract provided that in recall after layoff, seniority would govern if ability, skill, and efficiency were equal. When two junior employees were recalled to their jobs, the union protested that there still were five employees on layoff who had more seniority and were qualified to do the work; two of these five should have been recalled, the union argued.

An arbiter upheld the company. While the five senior employees might have done the work proficiently after a break-in period, he found that *at the time of recall*, the junior employees were the most efficient on the jobs in question. Since the contract made seniority controlling only where efficiency already was equal and made no provision for a training period, the arbiter concluded that recall of the junior employees was proper (Curtis Companies Inc., 29 LA 50)

Similarly, another contract provided for the recall of a laid-off employee on the basis of seniority "so long as he can do the job in a reasonably efficient manner." A dispute arose when a junior employee who was operating a new machine, and who was the only qualified one to do so, went to work on a less advanced machine while the new one was being repaired. A laid off senior employee of the same classification argued that he should have been recalled from layoff status to work the older machine, which he was capable of working.

The arbiter disagreed, however. Although the junior employee was not operating the new machine during the period in question, the arbiter found that operating the new machine was an important part of the employee's duties since he was to continue working on it once repairs were completed. Furthermore the arbiter concluded there was no past practice which supported the senior employee's arguments. (Eagle-Picher Industries Inc., 65 LA 1108)

Physical Exams on Rehiring

Can laid-off employees be required to take a physical examination upon return to work? Arbitrators generally agree that, in the absence of a specific contract ban on the practice, management may require employees returning to work from extended layoffs, strikes or leaves of absence to have new physical examinations. (22 LA 632, 11 LA 364, 8 LA 1015)

However, management should follow a consistent practice in the use of medical exams. When a company bypassed a senior worker because of his past medical record, an arbiter said it was acting improperly. It should have based his recall on present medical information, as it did with other workers, the arbiter concluded. (National Lead Co., 42 LA 176)

Physical Standards on Rehiring

Most arbiters have ruled that an employer may not set higher physical standards for workers returning from layoff than are applied to workers still on the job.

EXAMPLE: An employee about to be recalled from layoff was found by the company doctor to have blood pressure higher than that permissible for new employees, although within the range allowed for persons already employed by the company. Accordingly, the employee was denied recall.

An arbiter ruled that the employee was entitled to recall, pointing out that the contract contained no provision for denial of recall rights to a laid-off employee whose physical condition would have been acceptable if he were still working for the company. (Allegheny Ludlum Steel Corp., 25 LA 214)

Likewise, an employer had no right to deny recall to a dump-truck driver who had lost his left hand and forearm in an accident while on layoff, an arbitrator ruled. The employee had been fitted with a prosthetic device that enabled him to pass driving tests and drive a tractor, the arbiter found, and so he should be given the same opportunity of recall as others. More rigorous standards could not be used by the employer the arbiter maintained. But if the doubts about the employee's safety and fitness for the job which prompted the recall denial were to materialize later, then the employee's employment could be affected just as any other worker, the arbiter concluded. (Murphy Construction Co., 61 LA 503)

Further, an employer had no right to refuse to reinstate a laid-off electrician on the basis of a doctor's report, according to another arbiter. Although the company admitted that it gave recalled workers "more tolerant treatment" in medical exams than new hires, the arbiter found that this worker was given the same examination as that given new employees. Further, the refusal to reinstate the worker was based on the possibility of future recurrence of back trouble, not on his present condition. Therefore, the employer was ordered to rehire the worker. (Weatherhead Co., 42 LA 513)

However, in one situation, even though a worker's physical condition was the same at the time of recall as it was upon layoff, an arbiter held that the employer could refuse to put him back to work to protect his health.

EXAMPLE: A 300-pound man with a heart murmur was denied recall because the company medic said it would endanger his health to work. An arbiter upheld the company's action. The fact that the man worked until he was laid off was no sign he was not endangering his health all that time, the arbiter said; it merely indicated the company did not know about his condition. When it found out, it had every right to refuse to recall him in order to protect his health, the arbiter concluded. (Potter Press, 26 LA 514)

Worker with Superseniority

An arbiter ruled that union stewards who had superseniority over employees/assemblers, whom they represented, were not entitled to be recalled ahead of the assemblers (recalled to work in a certain department), since the stewards' jurisdiction did not extend to the particular department. (Textron Inc., 83 LA 931)

Furthermore, if a worker is elected to union office while on layoff and thus acquires superseniority, is he entitled to immediate recall? One arbiter has held that management need not recall the worker in such a case until there is a job opening he can qualify for. The purpose of superseniority, he remarked, is to insure continuity in the administration of the contract, not to make jobs for union representatives. (Queen City Industries, 33 LA 794; see also 75 LA 263, 75 LA 261)

Recall of Job Steward

When workers are recalled to a job, must their job steward be recalled as well? An arbiter ruled yes in when the question arose in a construction case.

EXAMPLE: Two carpenters were assigned to a construction project, and the union properly assigned a third worker as the project's job steward. After the carpenters' work was suspended to allow plumbers and electricians to work at the site, one of the original carpenters and another later returned, but the job steward was denied recall.

The employer defended its action by arguing that it was a specialty contractor required only to have a "shop steward" who served as steward for all jobs with less than three men, and that the union's insistence on a shop steward implied its waiver of a job steward.

However, the arbiter disagreed, finding no provision in the contract to require the shop steward to perform all the functions of a job steward and nothing to substantiate the employer's claim of the union's implied waiver. (Master Builders Assn. of Western Pennsylvania Inc., 63 LA 664; see also 74 LA 987)

Refusal to Accept Lower-Rated or Different Job

Can employees refuse to accept a recall notice to a lower-rated job without jeopardizing their seniority rights? If there is nothing in the contract to the contrary, most arbiters hold that employees can refuse notices to lower-rated jobs without loss of seniority. (Service Conveyor Co., 9 LA 134)

Similarly, it has been held that employees do not have to accept recall to perform a job different from that held prior to layoff under a contract allowing workers to choose between layoff and transfer.

EXAMPLE: An employee was laid off when his department closed for vacations and maintenance. During his layoff he refused an offer of a job in another department, saying he preferred to wait for recall to his own department. When his department reopened, however, employees with shorter service were recalled ahead of him. The company said that he had waived his right to recall by refusing the other job.

The arbiter decided that, since the contract permitted employees to take a layoff instead of a transfer to another department, an employee could refuse an offer of a job in a different department without losing his right to be recalled to his own department in line with his seniority. (International Harvester Co., 22 LA 773)

Refusal to Accept Recall to Part-Time Work

A laid-off employee did not lose seniority when he rejected a recall for two-days' work per week, an arbiter ruled, since full-time employees were guaranteed a 40-hour week, and the employer's practice was to interpret guarantee to mean that employees were entitled to 40 hours' work for any week in which they worked. (S & S Meat Co., 97 LA 873)

Recall to Lower-Rated Job

When a laid-off worker does accept recall to a lower-rated job, at what rate should he be paid? One arbiter ruled that recall to a lower-rated job is the same as a transfer, and accordingly is governed by contract provisions relating to transferred employees.

EXAMPLE: A employer's contract provided that an employee transferred to a lower-rated job would continue to receive his former rate for 15 consecutive working days. A worker recalled from layoff to a lower-rated job received his old rate for only five days, whereupon he claimed that he was entitled to the old rate for 10 additional days.

The union, pointing to a contract provision that a recalled employee must accept the job offered or lose seniority, argued that since the worker did not have the option of refusing the lower-rated job he had in effect been transferred by the company. The company based its case on a past practice of not treating recalls to lower paying jobs as transfers.

The arbiter ruled in favor of the union. The word "transfer" as used in labor agreements, he pointed out, means a shift or change from one job to another; no one claimed that such a move would not have constituted a transfer if the worker had not been laid off, the arbiter noted. In his opinion the layoff did not change the picture. (National Can Corp., 25 LA 177)

However, another arbiter, while upholding the right of employees to refuse recall to a lower-rated job, did not agree that acceptance of a lower-rated job when recalled is the same as a transfer. (Service Conveyor Co., 9 LA 134)

EXAMPLE: In another case, the arbiter did not dispute the employer's right to put the employees in lower rated jobs when work in their former classification was not available at the time of recall, but he did insist that they be paid at their former, higher, rate. The arbiter based his decision on a contract clause requiring the "regular rate of pay" for employees working at lower rated jobs for the company's "convenience," and on the employer's past practice. (Allen Group Inc., 65 LA 114)

On the other hand, an arbiter decided that a laid-off bakery sales clerk was not entitled to retain her wage rate following her placement in an apprentice position that initially carried a lower wage rate. Despite the union's claim of a past practice consisting of one prior instance in which a clerk who was placed in the same type of position retained his bakery clerk rate of pay, the arbiter ruled that that single instance, under the circumstances, was insufficient to show an established past practice. (Ralph's Grocery Co., 71 LA 692)

Recall After Strike

When a contract provides for observance of seniority in layoff and recall, do recalls after a strike have to be made according to seniority? According to some arbiters, layoff and recall provisions in a labor agreement do not apply to recall after a strike.

EXAMPLE: A plant's production and maintenance employees went out on strike for 12 days. As soon as the employees agreed to come back to work the employer drew up a schedule for resuming operations and notified employees when to report.

The union claimed that the recalls were not made strictly according to seniority as provided for in the contract. The employer argued that the contract was not applicable to this situation. It pointed out that operations had to be started up bit by bit and that not all employees could be rehired together.

The arbiter ruled that the contract "was obviously not drafted to deal with a situation like this one. This situation did not involve any layoffs and hence did not involve rehiring after layoff." Therefore the arbiter ruled for the company that production could be resumed bit by bit and that employees could be called without regard to strict seniority rules. (Swift & Co., 8 LA 295)

EXAMPLE: Another arbiter likewise allowed an employer to recall junior strikers before senior strikers. The arbiter found that the workers were not in "layoff status," so the contract provision which called for seniority to govern in the case of recall from layoff did not apply. (Yoder Brothers Inc., 62 LA 476)

Similarly, another employer retained a new hire instead of recalling a senior striker, and also failed to recall a worker with 29 years seniority until after Thanksgiving holidays. The arbiter supported the employer's actions, since in the first case it was not clear that the employer was under any obligation at the end of the strike to follow seniority during the two or three weeks delay in starting of regular work, secondly there was no evidence that the employer was obligated to recall workers out of their classification and the employee was recalled as soon as work was available in his classification. (Borg-Warner Corp., 61 LA 234)

However, where a company's employees went on strike and the employer hired replacements an arbiter reinstated senior strikers, after the employer refused to do so. The arbiter ruled that the contract which had continued in force during the strike did not restrict its seniority clause to employees who were working, nor did it exclude employees not at work. However, although the arbitrator ordered back pay for employees who were refused work while junior replacements were employed, he recognized the right of the employer to determine the number of available jobs for the returning workers. (Tarcon Inc., 64 LA 955)

Likewise, an arbiter ruled that an employer was obligated to apply a contract's seniority provision in its recall of strikers, subject only to special agreements by the parties first to recall employees in certain key departments. The arbiter reasoned that recall was an "increase of working force" which the contract stated was subject to seniority, and found no agreement by the parties to ignore seniority in the recalls. (Orscheln Brake Lever Mfg. Co., 63 LA 736; see also 75 LA 113)

Refusal to Recall Senior Employee with Poor Record

Can a laid-off senior employee be refused recall as a form of disciplinary action for such an offense as poor attendance? If a contract requires that employees be recalled to work in line with their seniority, one arbiter has ruled, such other factors as a poor attendance record do not justify a denial of the employee's right to be recalled.

EXAMPLE: While the high-seniority employee at one company was on layoff, a temporary job came up and was filled with a man holding lower seniority. Management supported its action on the ground that, among other things, the employee had a record of several unexcused absences.

In rejecting the company's justification of its refusal to recall that employee, the arbiter decided that the employee's absenteeism was an extraneous issue. The employer should not have considered the employee's attendance record in considering his recall, said the arbiter, because this was something that should have been disposed of at the time the absences occurred. Such an offense, he said, should not be made the basis for denial of job opportunities for the indefinite future. (Cleveland-Cliffs Iron Co., 24 LA 599)

Recall For Overtime

Is an employer required to recall a laid-off employee to perform overtime work in the department? At least one arbiter has ruled no.

EXAMPLE: An employee who had been laid off during a cutback in the work force discovered that people in other classifications were performing overtime work that he had performed prior to the cutback. He filed a grievance charging that he should have been the one to perform the overtime.

In upholding the employer's position, the arbiter found that the employee's seniority rights extended only if a recall or hiring added to the number of employees in his former classification. Emphasizing that a basic right of management is the right to determine the size of the work force, the arbiter concluded that it would violate this right to order the employer to rehire the employee. (Avco Corp., 63 LA 288)

Failure to Send Proper Recall Notice

What constitutes proper notice of recall from layoff? If the contract specifically requires that laid-off workers be notified of recall by a certain means, most arbiters say that method must be used without exception. If the employer does not give the proper notice, these arbiters say, it may not take away the workers seniority and re-employment rights.

EXAMPLE: An arbiter held that an employer's telephone call to a laid-off employee did not trigger recall, stressing that, under the collective bargaining agreement, the employer was required to notify laid-off employees by certified mail. (Manville Forest Products Corp., 92 LA 681)

EXAMPLE: One employer's contract required that laid-off employees be recalled by registered letter and that they report within five days after receiving notice. Instead of sending registered letters, however, the firm sent the union steward a request that he tell employees to come to the plant for rehiring. One employee who was not notified by the steward and who did not report within the five-day period was permanently laid off.

The arbiter decided that the employee had not been notified of recall in the manner prescribed by the contract, that is, by registered letter; neither had she been contacted in any other way by the company. Accordingly, the arbiter ordered her reinstated with full seniority and back pay starting with the fifth day after she should have been notified. (Ohmer Corp., 13 LA 364)

Failure to Receive Recall Notice

When is an employee's failure to receive notice a valid excuse for not reporting? Some arbiters have held that a worker is entitled to back pay and full seniority when the employee's failure to receive recall notice was not his or her fault, even though the employer had met its notice requirements.

EXAMPLE: One employer complied with the contractual requirement that employees be notified of recall either by letter or telegram by mailing a notice to the apartment house where an employee lived. Through some slip of the post office, the notice was sent to the wrong apartment and the employee failed to report on time. The employee lost his seniority for failing to report on time after the recall. The arbiter found that while the company had met its obligation, the employee failed to receive the notice through no fault of his own. Under these circumstances, the arbiter decided, the employee had not been properly notified of recall and was, therefore, entitled to back pay and full seniority. (Levinson Steel Co., 23 LA 135)

EXAMPLE: In another case, the contract required the employee to respond to a recall notice within 72 hours, except on weekends and holidays, or lose rights to recall. After one telegram was allegedly ignored by the employee, a second telegram was dispatched, notifying the worker to report back to work the next day. Because the employee was out of town, however, he did not find the telegrams until later. When he did report for work he learned that he was discharged for failure to respond within 72 hours of the first notice. In overturning the discharge, the arbiter found it reasonable for the employee to have expected the second telegram to grant him a second 72 hours, which expired on the afternoon of the day he reported for work. Even though the employee could have avoided the discharge by requesting leave, checking his mail, or calling the dispatcher, the arbiter conceded, the critical issue was the status of the second telegram. (Ameron Inc., 64 LA 517)

However, if it appears that a worker has intentionally avoided receiving a recall notice or ignored it and its requirements, arbiters are likely to uphold a company refusal to rehire him. (Blackmer Pump Co., 20 LA 238)

Similarly, if an employee fails to give a contractually required notice to the employer of his desire to return to work from layoff, an employer may be justified in not rehiring the worker, if the employer does not act in a discriminatory manner when sending the recall notice. (Challenge-Cook Bros. Inc., 65 LA 533)

Likewise, an employer was not obligated to compensate employees for time that they lost when their recall was delayed because the recall letter that the company mailed was not received by them, an arbiter ruled, notwithstanding the union's contention that the employer should have used certified mail in the recalls. Pointing out that the recall procedure provided for in the contract did not specify the type of mail that had to be used by the employer in administering the recall process, the arbiter concluded that management's obligation to use reasonable means in notifying employees of their return to work was satisfied with the employer's practice of using a two-step procedure of telephone and regular mail, followed if necessary, a week later by certified mail. (Warren Molded Plastics Inc., 76 LA 740)

And, an arbiter ruled that an employee's failure to respond to an employer's recall notice within 24 hours, per the collective bargaining agreement, constituted a voluntary quit. The arbiter dismissed the union's contention that the employee was unfamiliar with the contract's notice/voluntary-quit provision. The arbiter held that it was the employee's responsibility to know the terms and conditions of the bargaining agreement, and pointed out that the employee had been laid off and recalled many times. (Stroh Brewery Co., 92 LA 930)

Rehiring Employee Who Has Lost Seniority

When a contract gives preference in hiring to former employees, one arbiter has said, the same employment standards can not be used in judging them as are used for other job applicants. He held that former workers should be given the inside track when their qualifications are as good or better than those of other applicants.

EXAMPLE: One agreement stated that "preference will be given in employment to those former employees who lost their seniority as a result of layoff and who apply for employment." When one women in this category applied for employment, she was rejected on the ground that she did not meet the employer's employment standards. The employer later gave two reasons for the rejection: (1) the employee's personnel record had been marked "do not rehire" at the time she lost her seniority and (2) a check with her former supervisor at the time she applied for employment showed he still did not want her back.

An arbiter said the firm did not give the employee preference in accordance with the contract. Instead, she was disqualified on the basis of absolute standards. The preference clause, the arbiter explained, did not give ex-employees an absolute right to available jobs, but it did give them the inside track where they were as good or better than other candidates. Here the employer did not attempt to compare the employee with other people applying for jobs at the same time. Management, the arbiter decided, had to give the worker proper consideration the next time a job opening occurred. (Libby, McNeill & Libby, 30 LA 309)

Part 5

Leave of Absence

Paid Sick Leave

IN BRIEF

Most employees are covered by collective bargaining agreements that provide some protection against wage loss due to sickness. This may take the form of sickness and accident insurance or paid sick leave. Some contracts provide for both, such as where paid sick leave covers the waiting period before sickness and accident insurance takes effect.

Most companies also permit unpaid sick leave for workers who are not covered by paid sick leave or by insurance plans or who have exhausted their paid leave or insurance benefits.

Sick-leave provisions may either be negotiated into a bargaining agreement, or a sick-leave plan or policy may be implemented unilaterally by an employer. Arbiters recognize an employer's legitimate concern in preventing the abuse of sick-leave claims, and will uphold reasonable rules regarding the documentation of illnesses, employee healthcare claim forms, and systems for policing sick-benefit plans, provided they are not arbitrary, capricious, or discriminatory. Whether an employee's absence from work constitutes sick leave is of critical importance in most cases.

GUIDELINES

Eligibility Rights

Arbitrators generally view sick leave as an earned right. This means that an employer cannot establish conditions for eligibility other than those prescribed by the contract or past practice. Thus, it has been held that—

• A company could not withhold sick leave pay until employees returned to work. (Malester Operating Corp., 20 LA 534)

• An employer could not require an employee who had been absent for six weeks to submit to a physical exam where the contract specifically stated that examinations would be required of employees absent for 90 days or more. (Buckeye Forging Co., 42 LA 1151)

• A company could not deny sick pay to an employee just because he did not file a claim for it until five months after his illness. (Republic Oil Refining Co., 16 LA 607)

• A supervisor in one department could not require that employees provide the names of their doctors to qualify for sick leave for "lengthy periods" since the rule was never communicated to workers, it was vague, and only was enforced in one department. (Milwaukee Area Dist. Bd. of Educ., 65 LA 383)

• An employer could not deny pay to employees with chronic illnesses despite the company's claim that the illnesses barred them from offering a fair return for their salaries. (United States Steel Corp., 63 LA 549)

On the other hand, arbiters have held that—

• An employer had the right to ask the nature of illness or injury of employees before granting sick leave under a contract enumerating the type of conditions that qualify for sick leave with pay and containing a method for submitting sick leave forms. (Willoughby-Eastlake City School District, Bd. of Education and Teachers, 75 LA 21)

• An employer properly denied sick pay to employees who refused to authorize access to medical records prepared by their personal physicians. (Noland, Lloyd, Foundation Inc., 74 LA 1236)

• An employee was entitled to be paid accumulated sick leave on severing his employment. (American Legion Club, 81 LA 1036)

Effect of Used Sick Leave on Credits Under New Plan

Can sick leave already taken be counted against the credits workers have coming to them under a new sick leave plan? If there is no restriction in a new plan, it is usually considered prospective in nature, without any retroactive effect, and arbiters will hold that employees start with a clean slate.

EXAMPLE: A company adopted a plan which provided for paid disability leave for a specified number of days during any 12-month period. Under this plan, the company said, benefits paid to employees in the 12-month period preceding the effective date could be deducted from the total for which they qualified under the new plan. The firm maintained that the 12-month period referred to in the contract did not necessarily mean the period starting with the effective date of the new plan, since the plan merely continued and modified a plan already in existence.

The arbiter, however, ruled that in the absence of any definition of "12-month period," the usual interpretation that a newly adopted plan is prospective must apply. The new plan, he said, could not work retroactively by charging previously paid benefits against workers' credits. Timken-Detroit Axle Co., 21 LA 196)

However, usually service acquired with an employer before a sick leave plan goes into effect can be counted toward eligibility. One arbiter noted that it is general practice to base sick leave eligibility on total service, not just on service acquired after a plan becomes effective. (Holga Metal Production Co., 19 LA 501)

Sick Pay During Layoff

Under a contract basing sick-leave rights on length of service, what happens to a worker's credits already built up if he or she is laid off? Generally, if the contract provides for retention of seniority during layoff, it is held that sick-leave rights also are retained. But in at least one situation where an arbiter found no clause that preserved continuity of service during lay-off, he decided that workers had no right to sick-leave credits acquired before being laid off. (O'Brien-Suburban Press Inc., 18 LA 721; see also 23 LA 459)

Similarly, another arbiter denied sick leave to an employee who sustained an on-the-job injury during a temporary recall from layoff. The arbiter based his decision on the contract language which specified that sick pay would be given only if the employee were unable to perform his or her scheduled work because of illness or injury. In this case, the employee returned to layoff status and had no scheduled work to be unable to perform, the arbiter found. Furthermore, there was no contract provision requiring sick pay during layoff, and no evidence of a clear past practice requiring sick pay under such circumstances. (American Bakeries Co., 64 LA 450)

Sick Pay During Strike

When strikes or other unusual circumstances occur, questions may arise as to the continued eligibility of employees already on sick leave when work interruptions take place.

EXAMPLE: One arbiter vetoed a company's denial of sick pay to an employee who was on leave when her union called a strike. The company, he said, had gone too far in assuming that the employee would have refused to work if she had been well. (Outboard Marine & Mfg. Co., 11 LA 467)

On the other hand, another arbiter ruled that an employee was not entitled to sick pay when, most employees were off duty because of a strike by another union. The arbiter reasoned that the purpose of a sick-pay provision is to pay a worker not because he's sick but because his illness prevents him from working. If no work is available, he's not entitled to sick pay. (Trans World Airlines, 41 LA 312)

In another case, an arbiter granted sick leave only in the case of employees who were excused prior to the strike and whose excuse had been extended into the strike period. Other employees were denied sick leave during the strike, regardless of whether they were actually ill. (County of Santa Clara, 65 LA 992; see also 72 LA 776, 73 LA 981)

Sick Pay During Temporary Shutdown

When a company closed down because of a hurricane, it refused to grant sick or injury pay to those workers who had been out on such leave at that time. It asserted that they had no right to benefits on a day on which they would not have been able to work even if they were well. The arbiter, however, held that they were entitled to the pay since the primary cause of their unemployment continued to be their illness or injury. Neither injury nor sick benefits were geared to work done by able-bodied workers; if this were the case, he reasoned, then those on leave could claim extra pay if able-bodied employees worked overtime. (Eastern Air Lines Inc., 41 LA 801)

Disability v. Sick Leave Pay

Receipt of workers' compensation may pose some problems under sick-pay provisions. If the clause does not specifically call for the deduction of workers' compensation from sick pay, an arbiter may award full or supplemental sick pay to an employee who also is receiving workers' compensation. (Republic Oil Refining Co., 16 LA 607; see also 27 LA 90)

EXAMPLE: One arbiter held that a company had no right to deduct disability payments from sick leave pay when past practice had been to grant the full amount of both benefits. He found nothing wrong with a worker's receiving benefits in excess of his regular wages. Sick leave pay was a negotiated benefit to which the worker had a right, the arbiter said, and he paid his share for the disability benefits. (Mohawk Airlines Inc., 39 LA 45)

Similarly, an arbiter ruled that an employer had no right to deprive an employee of sick-pay benefits by discharging him, despite the finding by three doctors that the worker had a severe disability and could receive disability benefits from Social Security. The contract provided for sick-leave payments for up to 52 weeks, and the employee contended that he was entitled to the payments. Finding no specific evidence that the employee, despite his disability, could not return to his job at the end of 52 weeks, the arbiter awarded full sick leave benefits. (61 LA 1188)

However, another arbiter, rejected an employee's claim to sick pay in addition to workers' compensation on the ground that nothing in the contract indicated the parties intended to have any sort of supplemental arrangement. To order the company to make such payments would have the effect of amending the contract, he said. (Babcock & Wilcox Co., 22 LA 456; see also 71 LA 1118)

Can management demand that an employee waive his right to workers' compensation as a condition of reinstatement after sick leave? Arbitrators have expressed opposite views on this subject.

EXAMPLE: One arbiter, in ordering the reinstatement of an employee who had a hernia, decided that the employer could require him to sign a waiver of all compensation claims that might stem from his condition. (Consolidated Vultee

Aircraft Corp., 10 LA 1950; see also 25 LA 216)

Another view is that waivers cannot be required if such a requirement is in effect a contract modification. (Royal McBee Corp., 23 LA 591)

Falsifying Sick Leave Claims

Where there is evidence that a worker falsified his claim of illness, an arbiter would probably uphold discipline of him unless the sick-leave policy or plan itself specifies how abuses are to be handled.

EXAMPLE: An arbiter upheld a two and one-half week suspension of an employee who reported in sick and was discovered the next day operating a tractor on his farm. Although the employee had been ill the day before and was still suffering from his ailment, the arbiter found he was not too sick to work, since operation of the tractor was considerably more strenuous than his duties as a television engineer. (Station KMTV, 39 LA 324)

However, discipline was overturned by an arbiter in another case where an employee admitted that he had performed outside "remunerative work" while drawing benefits under a sickness and accident plan. The plan itself specified that the penalty for engaging in such work, where not detrimental to a speedy recovery, was forfeiture of benefits, not discharge, the arbiter noted. (Corn Products Co., 44 LA 127)

Similarly, an arbiter held that an employer was not justified in discharging an employee who falsified his time card to claim sick leave improperly. The contract's sick leave provisions said the employer could reduce or eliminate sick leave privileges if abuses were found, the arbiter noted. Thus, management should have invoked these remedies instead of resorting to discharge. (Central Illinois Public Service Co., 44 LA 133)

Sick Pay for Overtime

Where a contract defined a "normal work day" as eight hours, one arbiter held that a worker regularly scheduled for a longer than normal work day could not collect sick pay for the overtime he was used to working.

The clause involved called for one day of sick leave after a year's service, two days after two years, and so on. The parties split over whether a "day" under the clause was the usual work day or the normal day as defined by the contract. The arbiter reasoned that the parties had some definite notion of the price tag when they negotiated the sick-leave clause. So he thought it likely that they were thinking in terms of a normal day. Thus, he held, the worker was entitled to sick pay for just the regular eight hours, not for the overtime. (Bell Aircraft Corp., 26 LA 558; see also 76 LA 1261, 72 LA 1201)

Sick Pay During Vacations

When a worker became ill just before his scheduled vacation, the employer charged his absence to extended vacation pay. The arbiter said that this was not proper. He held that problems arising from absenteeism because of illness occur whether or not employees are scheduled for vacations, so that circumstance should not affect the employer's responsibility to pay for sick leave. (U.S. Steel Corp., 44 LA 615)

On the other hand, payment of both disability and vacation benefits was not required by an arbiter, despite the company's history of having done so. The contract "precluded payment of disability benefits if wages were received." The arbiter said that a past practice could not modify the application of clear contract language. (Westinghouse Electric Corp., 45 LA 131)

Sick Pay During Leave of Absence

One arbiter has ruled that employees on leaves of absence are entitled to sick pay. In that case, the employee continued to accrue seniority and earn holiday pay while on leave. Thus, the arbiter decided he was still on the "active payroll" despite the employer's contention that sick pay was only provided for workers actually laboring on a day-to-day basis. Since the contract specified sick pay for all employees on the active payroll the arbiter awarded the sick pay. (Freightliner Corp., 63 LA 834)

However, another arbiter ruled that an employee on sabbatical leave was not entitled to use her accumulated sick leave because sick leave was not a "fringe benefit" under the collective bargaining agreement, which said that professional employees should receive one-half of their regular salary, plus "all fringe benefits" included in their contract. (Allegheny Intermediate Unit, 82 LA 187)

Job Rights After Absence for Illness

Can a worker returning from sick leave bump a man hired to replace him? Under contracts with seniority provisions, most arbiters uphold the right of an employee returning from sick leave to exercise his seniority to get his former job back.

EXAMPLE: When a senior worker returned from approved sick leave, an arbiter ruled that the company had to take him back even though it had hired a replacement on his job. The arbiter reasoned that the returning worker's job had not been eliminated, so he was entitled to the same protection as he would have received had he not been on leave. Therefore, he was entitled to displace the junior worker and get his job back, the arbiter concluded. (Everett Dyers & Cleaners, 11 LA 546; see also 17 LA 548)

Moreover, even under a contract that had no provision for sick leave but did have a seniority clause, an arbitration board decided that a worker who had been absent because of illness was entitled to his job under the contract. The company refused to take him back but the board found no evidence that he had quit or had been discharged. On this basis, the board said that he should still be considered an employee, even though the company had hired a replacement. The board reasoned that when the absent worker returned to work, the company had one too many employees. Therefore, the arbiters ruled, the layoff provisions of the contract should apply and whichever of these two workers had the most seniority should get the job. (Don Lee Broadcasting System, 1 LA 571)

However, under a contract stating that a worker on sick leave would be returned, if qualified, to his or her old job or one like it, an arbiter ruled that an employee who was unable to do his old job was not entitled to just any job he could do. The employee was a lineman for an electric company and was recovering from tuberculosis. His own doctor said he could work in any job that did not involve climbing or heavy lifting. The employer decided this ruled out lineman work and similar jobs and so refused to rehire him. The arbiter upheld the company, stating that the contract did not require the employer to give the man any job he could perform. He also noted that reinstatement under this contract depended on the worker's being qualified. (Southern California Edison Co., 26 LA 827)

Effect of Sick Leave on Eligibility for Automatic Increase

Should time spent on sick leave be counted in fixing the date on which an employee becomes eligible for an automatic increase? In the absence of a contract provision on the matter, some arbiters have ruled that workers do not have to be given credit for time spent on sick leave in determining their eligibility for length-of-service raises. They have observed that automatic wage increases are designed to reward workers for increased proficiency that comes from continued experience on the job. Job proficiency cannot be gained on sick leave, they noted. (Bell Aircraft Corp., 17 LA 230; see also 18 LA 847)

Sick Leave for Illness In Family

When most employees claim sick leave, it's because they're sick. But is an employer required to grant sick leave, rather than personal leave, for an employee when his children are sick? One arbiter ruled yes.

EXAMPLE: An air traffic controller for the Federal Aviation Administration was absent due to the illness of his two children. The employee had been up for most of the preceding night and was preoccupied and worried about his children. The employer, however, refused the request for sick leave, and charged the employee's day off against his personal leave. Overturning the employer's decision the arbiter found that the employer's job required alertness, perception and concentration, and the employee was incapable of working at his full ability due to his childrens' illness. The contract had a clause granting sick leave to an employee who was "incapacitated" and the arbiter concluded that the employee was indeed incapacitated by his worries and lack of sleep. (Fort Worth Air Traffic Control Center, 64 LA 45)

Doctors' Opinions

While management may have the right to require a doctor's statement as proof of illness, arbiters disagree as to whether such certificates may be required in all instances. (74 LA 189, 71 LA 1064)

EXAMPLE: One arbiter held that it was unreasonable for a company to require a doctor's certificate in all cases of sick leave since such a rule imposed a hardship on many in order to punish a few who abused their sick-leave privileges. (General Baking Co., 40 LA 387; see also 90 LA 262)

However, another arbiter held just the opposite, deciding that a rule requiring a doctor's certificate for each day of sick leave taken was reasonable. (Federal Services Inc., 41 LA 1063)

Still another arbiter decided that an employee's refusal to submit a doctor's certificate, even though his illness was genuine, relieved the company of its obligation to pay him for his leave. (Philips Petroleum Co., 45 LA 857)

Type of Certificate Required

The type of medical certificate to be accepted by management has also been an issue before arbitration. One company for example, refused to grant sick leave when a notice from the employee's doctor read simply "Treated for bronchitis. Return to work 4-22-74." Although the company claimed the notice did not provide specific language that the employee was incapable of working, the arbiter ruled that in ordering the employee not to return to work until a certain date, the doctor implied that the employee was incapable of working before that date. (United States Steel Corp. 64 LA 540; see also 75 LA 97).

Requiring Physical Exams on Return

Whether a company can require an employee returning from sick leave to get a medical clearance is another issue on which arbiters are divided.

EXAMPLE: One arbiter, held that an employee returning from a long illness did not have to obtain a medical release from his doctor since the contract said nothing about such a release. (Inspiration Consolidated Copper Co., 7 LA 86; see also 28 LA 554)

However, another arbiter concluded that a company could require employees absent for more than three days to submit to examinations by the company doctor. (Reserve Mining Co., 29 LA 367)

Still another arbiter balked at requiring an employee to consent to a company examination where she had complied with the contractual requirement that she obtain certification for work from her own doctor, and where the contract did not provide for a company doctor's evaluation. (MGM Grand Hotel, 65 LA 261)

Conflicting Doctors' Opinions

When the company's physician is of the opinion that a worker is unsuited for his or her former job but other doctors hold a contrary view, can a company refuse to reinstate the worker? In one case, finding a preponderance of the medical evidence in the worker's favor, the arbiter ordered the worker's reinstatement.

EXAMPLE: When a railroad conductor sought to return to work after a six-month absence caused by a heart condition, the company barred him on the basis of an examination by the plant physician. Though his personal doctor reported that he had fully recovered, a third physician noted that a job requiring less strain would be better. The worker then was examined by the state hospital's work evaluation unit, whose findings were favorable. Still he was unable to get his old job back.

The arbiter said the case for reinstatement was supported by the largely positive evidence, especially the findings of the work-evaluation unit. But, since he believed the company was motivated by concern for the employee's welfare, he denied back pay for the period prior to the work unit's findings. (U.S. Steel Corp., 38 LA 395; see also 73 LA 1060)

Similarly, another arbiter did award back pay to an employee at half the wage, where the company and union doctors could not agree on whether the employee who was recovering from drug addiction was capable of returning to work. Although the contract provided that in case of stalemate the two sides mutually were to appoint a third doctor to decide the issue, they did not take any steps to do so. The arbiter found that the employee became "reemployable" sometime during the course of the disagreement, but since the exact date was uncertain and both parties were at fault, only half-pay was awarded. (Air Carrier Engine Service Inc., 65 LA 66)

However, in another case where the union and company doctor disagreed, and where the union delayed in invoking the procedures for obtaining a third opinion, the arbiter ruled an employee was not entitled to disability payments at all. Here, the arbiter based his decision on the unfair advantage the employee would have had due to the lateness of the appeal had the third doctor ruled for the company. (Allegheny Ludlum Industries Inc., 64 LA 694)

Personal Leave

IN BRIEF

The vast majority of employers have a policy of granting employees leaves of absence without pay where it is necessary for personal reasons. At least, in the case of leave for illness, many employers feel that they have nothing to lose by such a policy—if the employee is a good worker and will have to be absent anyway, it is better to make some provision for getting the employee back on the payroll in regular fashion than take the chance of losing a valuable employee forever.

Usually, however, management wants to reserve the right to decide each case of personal leave on its own merits. For this reason it will phrase its leave policy in very general terms: "Leave will be granted for good cause," or "Management will approve a reasonable request for leave." The theory here, is that management holds the reins and can grant or deny a leave request at will.

However, this is not always the case. Employees have long memories, and if leave is granted in one case and denied in another, a feeling that management is being unfair may spring up and spread to other employees. In other words, if a company grants a certain type of leave—maternity leave, for example—in a few cases, it has, in effect, established a policy of granting this type of leave and, except for unusual circumstances, will have to continue to do so for morale purposes.

Except as restricted by the collective bargaining agreement, an employer has the right to grant or deny leaves of absence for personal reasons at its discretion. Unless management acts in an arbitrary or unreasonable manner in passing on a request for leave, an arbiter is unlikely to disturb its decision.

Most contracts specifically make provisions for unpaid leaves of absence for sickness, and most companies probably would grant such leave for a limited period of time even if not required to do so by contract. Leave rights based solely on past practice will also be enforced by arbiters, in most case.

Issues relating to maternity leave, funeral leave and leave for jury duty also are discussed in this chapter.

GUIDELINES

What Is Good Cause for Leave?

Although admitting that management has the right to grant or deny leaves of absence under most contracts, arbiters insist that companies apply this right reasonably and without discrimination. Sometimes they upset a company's judgment as to whether the reason for leave was good cause.

EXAMPLE: In one case a contract specified that leaves of absence "shall be granted for reasons acceptable to company and union." It also stated that seniority could be broken for three days' absence without good cause. A worker requested leave during the Christmas holidays for the purpose of securing a home for his mother. When the company disapproved his leave, he took off anyway. Upon his return to work he was considered a new employee by the company and thus lost his seniority rights.

The arbiter recognized the company's right to grant or deny leaves of absence. However, he believed that here management had been unreasonable. Since the worker had asked for leave for a good cause, the arbiter ruled, he was entitled to reinstatement with full seniority. (Pittsburgh Metallurgical Co. Inc., 12 LA 95; see also 76 LA 673, 75 LA 953, 75 LA 131, 74 LA 1284,)

On the other hand, where a union failed to show the company had discriminated against a worker in denying her leave to attend a religious function, an arbitration board held that the company's judgment could not be questioned. (Union Oil Co., 3 LA 108; see also 73 LA 1146, 71 LA 937)

Furthermore, an employer does have the right to inquire into the general nature of a worker's absence for "personal reasons." When one worker was absent in order to see another man's wife, his two-day suspension was upheld despite the claim of absence for "personal reasons." (Fairbanks Morse Co., 47 LA 224)

Falsifying Reasons for Leave

Where there is evidence that a worker falsified his reasons for wanting leave, an arbiter probably will uphold the company's right to discipline him.

EXAMPLE: An employee requesting leave presented to his foreman a telegram stating that his mother was seriously ill in another city. His foreman told him to see the general foreman at the end of the shift. The employee worked out his shift without protesting the delay and received permission to take a leave of absence. Furthermore, he told the foreman that he definitely would be back to work on a certain date. The foreman became suspicious of the employee's nonchalance about the delay and his willingness to set a date for his return, so the company hired an investigator, who discovered that the employee's mother was not seriously ill and that the employee actually was taking time off to attend a convention which was being held in the city where his mother lived. The employee was discharged upon his return.

At the arbitration hearing, the employee admitted that he knew his mother was not seriously ill but simply old and worried about her son. Although he did attend the convention from time to time, he insisted the primary purpose of the trip was to see his mother. The arbiter decided the employee had, in any event, misrepresented the reason for the leave. The employee should have explained that his mother simply wanted to see him instead of saying she was ill. The discharge was upheld. (International Harvester Co., 14 LA 980)

Regulating Leave Through Workforce Requirement

Where an employer has both a contract and past practice which outline procedures for granting leave, can it add the requirement that the workforce be maintained at a certain minimum level? One arbiter has ruled no.

EXAMPLE: An employer had a clause in the labor contract providing for leave to enable employees to cover "emergencies" arising outside of scheduled vacation time. However, the employer unilaterally set the maintenance of certain levels of the work force as a condition for granting personal leave.

The employer justified this unilateral condition as being a corollary of its reserved right to determine of size of manpower on various shifts. However, the arbiter disagreed, ruling that the new requirement was improper. Past practice had allowed employees to determine what constituted "emergencies"—which was undefined in the contract—and the employer had always acquiesced, the arbiter noted. Furthermore the arbiter reasoned that enforcing the size-of-workforce requirement would result in a "chilling effect on exercise of the employees' rights under the contract." (City of River Rouge, 65 LA 1105) Seniority Protection During Indefinite Leave

If a company grants a worker a leave of absence and then reinstates him without loss of seniority, can the union object that this is unfair to other workers and require management to reinstate the man as a new employee?

In one case, where the contract contained no leave clause, but did contain a seniority clause, an arbiter held that the union could prevent management from giving an employee seniority credit while on leave.

EXAMPLE: An employee desired to work his farm and requested an indefinite leave of absence. The company granted his request. Over a period of a year the employee returned to work only for a few scattered days. At the end of the year the company put man back on full time when he requested it. The union complained that the employee should be treated as a new employee within the meaning of the contract. The company answered that the employee had been on an indefinite leave of absence and was merely returning from his leave. While there was no leave provision in the contract, the seniority clause provided for the accumulation of seniority while on sick leave or layoff.

The award held that the employee should be rehired as a new employee.

The arbiter reasoned that if there was no limit placed on the length of leaves, a company could defeat the seniority clause by granting leaves up to two or three years in duration. He stated that the seniority clause had to be given a reasonable interpretation in order to carry out its meaning. He concluded that the clause governing seniority could not be read so as to protect the employee's seniority. (National Gypsum Co., 2 LA 566)

Promotion Rights During Leave

If a contract bases promotion on seniority, is a senior worker who is on leave when a vacancy comes up entitled to a chance at the promotion after he returns? Some arbiters feel that, unless the contract specifically waives seniority rights during leave, management is required to reopen the bids after the return of a senior worker.

EXAMPLE: An employee was on a leave of absence when a higher-paid job for which she was qualified was given to another employee who was her junior in point of security. The employee contended that her seniority had accumulated during her absence and that she was entitled to the promotion when she returned. The company based its refusal on the wording of the layoff clause reading: "In case of a layoff, if the employee next in line for return to work is not available, he then forfeits his right to the job."

When the case went to arbitration, the employee who had been absent was ordered promoted to the higher job. The arbiter stated that since there had been no question raised as to the employee's ability or physical fitness, he could not hold otherwise. He refused to apply the "layoff" clause to a situation where the employee was on an authorized leave instead of being laid off.

The "leave" clause provided for the retention and accumulation of seniority during leave, and the "seniority" clause stated that seniority was the controlling factor in promotions the arbiter emphasized, concluding that since the employee had seniority, she should be promoted. (Curtiss-Wright Corp., 9 LA 77)

Accrual of Leave Rights

When a worker voluntarily quits the company, is he entitled to compensation for leave he has accrued during the year, or may leave rights only be granted at the end of a year, like a bonus? One arbiter has said that personal leave is a form of additional compensation that employees earn upon putting in each day's work, and to which they are entitled upon quitting.

EXAMPLE: When some employees voluntarily quit, the company withheld the personal leave pay they had "accrued" during the year. Management contended that the leave time was being earned for use in the following year and, therefore, was not an earned right until then. For support, the company showed, and the union agreed, that new employees—during their first year of employment—get no leave, but draw on that year for leave during the second year. Further, the company argued that leave was a working benefit and that when the employees quit, they release and give up the rights they can only use incidental to continued work.

However, the arbiter disagreed with the company's contentions. Citing contract language providing that "any employee who leaves employment with the employer prior to the end of the calendar year shall be paid for all personal or sick leave time accrued at his regular rate at the time he leaves employment," the arbiter concluded that leave is an additional "fringe benefit" that is earned every day, and to which employees are entitled upon quitting. (Gunther-Nash Mining Construction Co., 65 LA 767)

MATERNITY LEAVE

Maternity Leave and EEOC

It should be noted that some of the decisions reported in this chapter that upon a denial of maternity leave benefits were handed down prior to the rulings by the Equal Employment Opportunity Commission on maternity leave.

Interpreting the ban on sex discrimination in Title VII of the Civil Rights Act, EEOC has ruled that a "leave of absence should be granted for pregnancy whether or not it is granted for illness." (EEOC Decision YAU-9-026, July 10, 1968, 2 FEP Cases 294)

On October 31, 1978, a pregnancy disability amendment to Title VII of the 1964 Civil Rights Act was signed into law. The impetus for amending Title VII to prohibit discrimination because of pregnancy was a 1976 U.S. Supreme Court ruling (General Electric Co. v. Gilbert, 13 FEP Cases 1657) permitting the exclusion of pregnancy from an employer's disability plan. The amendment adopted by Congress, however, has the broader effect of banning disparate treatment of pregnant women for all employment-related purposes.

The amendment provides the following:

● Prohibits terminating or refusing to hire or promote a woman solely because she is pregnant.

● Bars mandatory leaves for pregnant women arbitrarily set at a certain time in their pregnancy and not based on their inability to work.

● Protects the reinstatement rights of women on leave for pregnancy-related reasons, including credit for previous service and accrued retirement benefits, and accumulated seniority.

● Requires employers to treat pregnancy and childbirth the same as other causes of disability under fringe benefit plans.

The amendment provides the same employment protections to women who choose to terminate their pregnancies, with the exception that the employer is not required to pay for the abortion procedure itself. (see Section 17, Equal Employment Opportunity, Sex Discrimination for additional information on maternity benefits and leave)

Considering the Law

Generally, maternity leave will not be allowed unless authorized by a state statute or by a collective bargaining agreement. (89 LA 105) Arbiters are reluctant to look past the contract to complicated bodies of law. Nevertheless, at least in cases involving maternity leave, most arbiters, after some soul-searching have referred to anti-discrimination law. This is true even where the contract instructs the arbiter to make decisions based solely on the contract. As one arbiter insisted, "applicable provisions of state and federal law impress themselves upon the labor contract and not only may, but must, be given consideration in any arbitration proceeding which arises thereunder." (Wausau District Public Schools, 64 LA 187)

State laws requiring employers to provide maternity benefits still apply, even when the federal law and the Supreme Court do not go as far, arbiters have ruled. Prior to the Title VII amendment, employers in Pennsylvania and Wisconsin were required to provide sick leave for maternity disability, in accordance with state fair employment laws. (Apollo-Ridge School District, 68 LA 1235; West Allis-West Milwaukee Joint City School District. 1, 68 LA 644)

Maternity Leave Under General-Leave Clause

Do employees have a right to maternity leave under a contract providing merely for leaves of absence? One arbiter recognized that a contract clause of this kind left to the company the right to grant or deny leaves. He concluded that there was nothing in the agreement qualifying that right. Noting that there is a distinction between sickness and pregnancy, the arbiter held that this company could grant sick leave without being compelled to grant maternity leave. (American Stove Co. 8 LA 779)

On the other hand, where a company had granted maternity leave on several occasions in the past, another arbiter held that it had to continue to do so. This situation, too, was covered by a general leave of absence clause. The arbiter said, however, that management must administer the clause fairly and justly in the interests of all the employees and of the company. (Gen. Electric Mfg. Co. Inc., 11 LA 684)

Maternity Leave or Paid Sick Leave

Most contracts have a clause granting paid sick leave to employees, but seldom is the term "sick" clearly defined. Thus the arbiter must undertake to define what the sick leave provision really means with regard to pregnancy. Often arbiters are guided by other contract clauses or by the decisions of courts and government agencies. Occasionally, however, they find that no other contract provision is relevant and that the case law is either hopelessly divided or beyond the scope of proper inquiry. In these cases arbiters are on their own, and the outcome is unpredictable.

EXAMPLE: A school committee denied paid sick leave to teachers who desired it during their pregnancies. The contract provided for unpaid maternity leave "for those who desire leave," and the committee ruled that this was the only leave available for pregnancies, despite union arguments that the teachers should have a choice, and should be able to select sick leave when they did not "desire" maternity leave.

Upholding the school committee's ruling, that arbiter decided that the union improperly assumed that pregnancy was covered by the sick leave clause. Pregnancy is not a "sickness" and therefore the maternity leave clause was negotiated to protect the jobs of pregnant employees, the arbiter continued. If pregnancy were covered by the sick leave clause, the maternity leave clause would be meaningless, the arbiter concluded. (Millinocket School Committee, 65 LA 805; see also 71 LA 1178)

Similarly, another employee was denied paid leave when she took maternity leave and argued that she should be covered by the contract's sick pay provision. Finding that the employee could not be covered by a clause granting pay for "illness" or "accident," since she was neither ill nor injured the arbiter pointed out that the union, prior to the filing of the grievance, had likewise understood the clause to exclude pregnancies. (Miller

Brewing Co., 64 LA 389; see also 97 LA 383)

However, an arbiter awarded maternity pay where the contract had been changed in negotiations to include employees who "become pregnant" among employees entitled to "sick leave of absence." The arbiter ruled that the union had in fact successfully negotiated transfer of pregnancy to the paid sick leave clause from the unpaid maternity leave clause. (Scottscraft Inc., 64 LA 279)

Similarly, another arbiter granted paid pregnancy leave because "the physical disability incurred through childbirth must be deemed to be a physical indisposition covered by the meaning of sickness for employment purposes." (Milwaukee Area Technical College, 60 LA 302; see also 74 LA 1288, 71 LA 1102, 71 LA 509)

Maternity leave to long-term disability leave — an arbiter ruled that an employer improperly refused to extend an employee's maternity leave and threatened her with dismissal if she failed to report as scheduled, after she had submitted a physician's letter stating that she would be unable to return to work for two months due to complications from breast-feeding, on the ground that the employer's long-term disability plant did not "pay for breast-feeding." The doctor's letter was presumptively valid, and the employee's condition made it impossible to perform her regular case-worker duties, the arbiter said, holding the employer liable for the employee's long-term disability benefits for the period of the extended maternity leave. (County of Monroe (Michigan), 94 LA 845)

Effect of Past Practice and Nondiscrimination Clause

Usually, arbiters can look to one or more contract clauses or to past practice under the contract in order to interpret the sick leave clause. A prevalent clause is one that provides maternity leave without pay. Employers argue that the presence of such a clause indicates that absence due to pregnancy is to be treated differently from absence due to sickness. By and large, however, arbiters reject this reasoning, ruling that the general sick leave provision of the contract covers absences due to pregnancy-related disabilities, while the maternity leave provision covers other pregnancy-related absences. (60 LA 549, 64 LA 245)

The past practice of not granting paid maternity leave also is frequently cited by employers as evidence that the parties view the contract as not providing such leave. Reaction to this argument has been mixed. Some arbiters find past practice "fairly conclusive" (Walled Lake Consolidated Schools, 64 LA 239), while others find it a "unilateral pronouncement by management" and hence "not controlling." (Kaiser-Permanente Medical Core Program, 64 LA 245)

More and more contracts contain "no discrimination" clauses. Many arbiters find this clause useful in discerning whether a contract provides paid maternity leave. The effect of the provision is to refer the arbiter to definitions of discrimination formulated by EEOC and the courts. Since these definitions seldom favor the employer, the result is usually a decision in favor of the pregnant employee. (62 LA 409, 64 LA 245)

Union's Right To Be Consulted on Abandoning Practice

Even though a contract was silent on granting maternity leave, one arbiter upheld the union's right to be consulted by the company before such a leave policy was dropped. The company had started granting maternity leave unilaterally, but it had become a long-established, important, and known practice and, the arbiter said, a condition of employment. For this reason, he ruled that the union must be consulted concerning the elimination of the policy. (Northland Greyhound Lines Inc., 23 LA 277)

On the other hand, a company was justified in refusing maternity leave to a woman by virtue of its past practice of never having done so. For 15 years this policy had gone unchallenged by the union, a no complaint had been registered. When a protest finally was lodged, the arbiter ruled that it came too late. (Chattanooga Box & Lumber Co., 44 LA 373)

Maternity Leave for Unmarried Employees

Can an unmarried woman employee demand rights under a company's maternity leave policy? When this situation arose in one plant, management dismissed the worker instead of granting her leave. However, an arbitration board ordered the company to reinstate her and grant, her leave. There was no association between her conduct and her job, the board held. (Crane Co., 12 LA 592; see also 41 LA 713)

The courts likewise have held that an unmarried employee may not be fired for pregnancy. For purposes of applying Title VII, the courts have said, there is no distinction between wed and unwed pregnancy.

Maternity Leave for Adoption

If an employer has a maternity leave policy, must it offer this benefit to employees who become parents through adoption? Emphasizing that "our society places great value on adopting children," one arbiter held that a maternity leave policy should not be interpreted to preclude situations "where the family unit is increased by adoption rather than natural birth."

EXAMPLE: Under an employer's policy, employees could be granted up to six months of leave for "maternity reasons." In requesting this leave, workers were allowed to choose any combination of available sick or annual leave or leave without pay to cover the required time off. In accordance with this policy, an employee sought a three-month leave without pay to care for her newly adopted daughter. The adoption agency, the employee explained, had requested that both she and her husband take time off from work to adjust to the child, who had medical and emotional problems. Management, however, told her that she would be allowed the time off, but only after she had used up all her accumulated annual leave, since its maternity leave policy was intended to cover only situations of "pregnancy, birth, or physical incapacitation of a wife before and after pregnancy."

The arbiter decided, however, that the "maternity reasons" acceptable for leave under the policy should include the "care of an adopted child during the initial period of adjustment when the adopted child becomes a member of the new household or family." Previously, the arbiter pointed out, the employer's maternity leave grants had been "solely confined to the actual delivery period," but had made "allowances for the mother to be with her new child" following the baby's arrival at home. Noting that maternity leave is designed to help employees deal with the "problems of a mother," the arbiter stressed that "a mother with an adopted child has just as many compelling reasons for absenting herself from the job with her new child—if not more—than a mother who has been pregnant." (Office and Professional Employees, 71 LA 93)

PAID FUNERAL LEAVE

Arbitration cases involving funeral-leave provisions have turned on the precise wording of the funeral-leave or "bereavement" pay clause. Arbiters, in general, appear to lean toward the strict interpretation of such clauses.

Therefore, where a collective bargaining agreement explicitly stated that a certain number of days of paid leave would be allowed to attend the funeral of a member of the employees's immediate family, arbiters have held that such a leave provision includes attendance at the funeral and necessary travel time, but excludes absences to aid bereaved relatives or to attend to the estate. (80 LA 1305, 73 LA 115, 73 LA 96, 70 LA 830, 67 LA 536, 61 LA 510, 57 LA 951, 53 LA 1108, 53 LA 974, 48 LA 351, 47 LA 438, 45

LA 494, 42 LA 59, 40 LA 223, 36 LA 1077, 34 LA 300)

Moreover, where the contract language used is "pay for lost time" or "paid leave of absence" while attending the funeral of a family member, arbiters generally have denied such pay when the employee was already on vacation or otherwise not scheduled to work. (79 LA 82, 75 LA 1076, 75 LA 845, 70 LA 950, 68 LA 165, 62 LA 771, 61 LA 382, 58 LA 706, 57 LA 421, 55 LA 437, 51 LA 517, 46 LA 849, 46 LA 11, 45 LA 644, 45 LA 291, 44 LA 937, 36 LA 1330, 33 LA 629, 27 LA 362) But, where contract language is ambiguous or less specific, or where a conflicting practice is a factor, arbiters sometimes have ruled differently. (75 LA 845, 58 LA 852, 49 LA 768, 37 LA 1034, 37 LA 151)

However, in some cases, an arbiter may favor a *broad* interpretation on that portion of a funeral-leave clause which specifies the family members or relatives for whose funeral the leave provisions apply — e.g., consanguinity or close affinity.

EXAMPLE: Where a contract listed "brother" among other members of the family, an arbiter, emphasizing the close relationship between an employee and his step-brother, ruled that the step-brother constituted the employee's brother under the contract. (Foremost Dairies, 43 LA 616)

Similarly, an arbiter ruled that half-brothers were included in the word "brother," for purposes of a contract's funeral-leave clause, despite an employer's claim that the employee's half-brother was not represented in the community as part of the employee's family unit. Several dictionaries and the state legislature defined brother to include half-brothers, the arbiter pointed out, and, moreover, the "family-unit" test should not be applied when there is a blood relationship or where a contract lists relatives covered. (Hartman Electrical Manufacturing, 92 LA 253; see also 95 LA 455, 76 LA 1107, 71 LA 874, 71 LA 473, 63 LA 163, 62 LA 447, 61 LA 1224, 54 LA 56, 49 LA 595, 43 LA 467, 40 LA 1230, 38 LA 1029, 31 LA 603)

Contrastingly, other arbiters have leaned toward a *strict* interpretation of funeral-leave relationship clauses. (96 LA 115, 89 LA 1285, 87 LA 1042, 86 LA 1132, 83 LA 1153, 77 LA 1127, 76 LA 1107, 73 LA 1144, 71 LA 1071, 71 LA 874, 71 LA 473, 69 LA 1080, 63 LA 1036, 61 LA 1224, 61 LA 79, 57 LA 959, 51 LA 289)

Past practice, of course, may be relevant to an arbiter's decision. An arbiter held, in a case where a contract contained no funeral-leave clause but did provide for maintenance of working conditions, that an employer was required to continue an established practice of granting up to three days of funeral leave. (Commercial Motor Freight, 34 LA 592; see also 53 LA 1215)

Similarly, another arbiter ruled that an existing funeral-leave policy, recognized by both parties, of not including payment of such benefits during any period of paid absence from work (such as vacations), had carried over into a new contract provision covering paid funeral leave. (Food Employers Council, 45 LA 291)

Length of Funeral Leave

The usual provision is for "up to three days" funeral leave. Arbitrators generally agree that funeral leave is not intended solely for allowing travel time to attend out-of-town funerals, but that it also can serve the additional purpose of enabling the employee to assist with funeral arrangements. Under this view, arbiters are inclined to permit employees to have the choice of which three days to take off. Those who are attending out-of-town funerals probably will take the day before, the day of, and the day after the funeral. Those who do not need the travel time might take the three days ending with the funeral. (94 LA 317)

EXAMPLE: An arbiter found that an employee who requested Thursday, Friday, and Monday as bereavement leave, was not entitled to be paid for Monday under a contract that granted three "consecutive days" of bereavement leave, since "consecutive" means following one after the other, not "consecutive regular work days." (Gulf Printing Co., 92 LA 893; see also 96 LA 1029, 96 LA 574, 94 LA 519, 94 LA 33, 92 LA 893, 89 LA 385, 89 LA 179, 84 LA 137)

EXAMPLE: At least one arbiter who subscribed to this school of thought on funeral leave, nevertheless, thought that the employee should not have the option of taking the funeral day and the two days after the funeral, since this would not agree with either of the purposes of the three-day funeral leave. (Champaign-Urbana Courier, 53 LA 490)

EXAMPLE: An employee took off Monday, Tuesday, and Wednesday to attend the Wednesday funeral of a relative, who had died the previous Friday. The employer only granted leave for Monday, however, claiming that the contract language granting "up to three days funeral leave" meant up to three days following the death. The arbiter disagreed — finding no provision in the contract to support the employer's claim that leave centered around the death rather than the funeral, the arbiter decided that since the leave is "funeral leave" rather than "death leave," the word "days" must center on the event of the funeral. (W.G. Bush & Co., 65 LA 608)

EXAMPLE: Some arbiters have emphasized that the "up to three days" language should not be construed as a guarantee of three days' funeral leave. Thus, one arbiter refused to allow paid leave for the day after the funeral, which was spent in assisting relatives in their travel plans. This did not qualify as time spent either in attending or arranging for the funeral, the arbiter held. (Trane Co., 53 LA 1108; see also 73 LA 115)

EXAMPLE: Another arbiter also sided with the company and restricted funeral pay. The contract provided leave pay for up to three "consecutive days," provided that "pay shall be allowed only for time absent from regularly scheduled working hours on Monday through Friday." Two grievances arose under this clause. In one, an employee took off from Tuesday through Friday to attend a Sunday funeral, and the arbiter limited pay to Friday. In the second instance, the employee who took off Wednesday through Friday for a Saturday funeral and the arbiter awarded pay only for Thursday and Friday.

The arbiter reasoned that the clear, unambiguous language calling for pay only for three consecutive workdays prior to the funeral outweighed the union's argument of contrary past practice granting more liberal pay. (FMC Corp. 64 LA 1300)

Similarly, another arbiter indicated that as a general rule the company should not have to pay for time after the funeral. (Warner & Swasey Co., 47 LA 438)

However, one arbiter granted four days of funeral leave despite a contractual limitation of three days, where, the employee's sister and brother-in-law had both died, and the contract provided three days off for the funeral of the former, and one day off for the latter. The company argued that there was no provision allowing "pyramiding of leave" for multiple funerals. However, the arbiter found that the parties had negotiated the clause to enable employees to deal with the immediate problems connected with funerals, and in this case the employee spent the four days driving to and from the funerals, which was a substantial distance away. (Federal Glass Co., 65 LA 787; see also 72 LA 337)

Scope of Funeral Leave

Is a worker whose vacation is interrupted by a funeral entitled to be paid for funeral leave? Several arbiters have held that this is a subject that should be decided by negotiation rather than by arbitration.

EXAMPLE: One worker took his two-week vacation to honeymoon. His mother died after the wedding, so he canceled his plans and attended to the details of the funeral and mourning services that followed. The company granted a two-day unpaid extension of his vacation, but denied funeral-leave pay. The language of the funeral-leave clause tied benefits to loss of working time, the arbiter said, and since the worker suffered no such loss, he was not entitled to funeral-leave pay. (Maui Pineapple Co., Ltd., 46 LA 849)

EXAMPLE: Night-shift workers were entitled to the same funeral leave provisions as day-shift workers. The contract did not make any distinction between different types of workers, the arbiter held, so the company could not arbitrarily introduce different treatment of night- and day-shift workers (Lehigh Portland Cement Co., 47 LA 840)

Proof of Attendance

An employer need not extend funeral-leave pay until proof of attendance has been submitted. When a company discovered that a worker had not been to a funeral as claimed, it refused to grant him any pay. The arbiter disallowed the union's claim of "automatic" payment for funeral leave, and said that the company had the right to establish a procedure for determining whether workers met the contract requirement of funeral attendance. (Borg-Warner Corp., 47 LA 691)

Funeral Leave During Strike or Shutdown

Is an employer obligated to pay funeral leave to employees who are on strike, or who attend a funeral during that strike? At least one arbiter has ruled yes. The arbiter found that work was available, and that the employees could have worked had they reported to the employer. Therefore, since funeral pay is compensation for time not worked due to attendance at a funeral, and since the employees did in fact attend the funeral, the arbiter concluded that the presence of the strike was inconsequential. (U.S. Pipe & Foundry Co., 65 LA 111)

Similarly, an arbiter ruled that two employees were entitled to funeral leave pay even though they were attending the funeral at a time when the employer's plant was closed due to severe weather and other employees were laid off. The employer argued that to grant the employees funeral leave pay would put them in a more advantageous income position than had they been available for work during the period when the plant was closed. The arbiter found, however, that once the maximum three days of paid funeral leave provided by the contract had been granted, any subsequent work stoppage occurring because of conditions beyond the employees' control could not empower the company to diminish the funeral leave pay. (Hillerich & Bradsby Co., 70 LA 950)

JURY-DUTY PAY

The vast majority of reported arbitration decisions deal not with an employee's right to a leave of absence for jury duty, but with the resultant pay problems under pertinent contract language on jury-duty pay differential. In the absence of such a provision, arbiters have held that the employer is not required to pay jury-duty benefits to its employees. (69 LA 1102, 38 LA 113)

Further, the Jury System Improvements Act of 1978 prohibits employer from discharging, threatening to discharge, coercing, or intimidating permanent employees because they are serving or are scheduled to serve on a federal jury. Also, NLRB held that jury-duty pay is a mandatory subject of bargaining under the Taft Act. (NLRB v. Merrill & Ring Inc., CA 9, 1984, 116 LRRM 2221)

Because jury-duty contract provisions are designed to "provide competent jurors through the removal of the monetary loss that would otherwise accompany jury service" (32 LA 1, see also 76 LA 170, 74 LA 865, 49 LA 901, 40 LA 1195, 32 LA 1), arbiters have ruled that employees who are called for jury duty while on vacation (51 LA 1288) or in layoff status (76 LA 170, 65 LA 264, 50 LA 852, 39 LA 50) are not entitled to jury duty.

Computing Jury Duty Pay

What is the basis for figuring jury duty pay? One arbiter has held that such pay should be computed on the basis of the hours a worker would have worked rather than on the contractual minimum work-day.

EXAMPLE: A contract required the company to pay the difference between a "full day's pay" and the amount a worker received for each day he served on a jury. When a worker was paid the difference between his jury-duty rate and the six-hour daily contractual guarantee, he complained that he ordinarily worked more than six hours a day and so should be paid more.

Both the contract language and its interpretation in the past led the arbiter to decide that the parties' intent was to prevent workers from losing pay while serving on juries. He therefore computed the pay on the basis of the hours the employee's replacement worked, minus the time the replacement spent on other jobs, plus overtime pay for the overtime hours of work the jurist actually would have performed, less the $6 daily jury-duty rate. (American Bakeries Co., 40 LA 1195; see also 98 LA 343, 76 LA 170, 74 LA 865, 74 LA 10, 73 LA 448, 72 LA 1057)

Jury Pay for Shift Workers

Under a contract providing pay for working time lost because of jury duty, is management required to pay workers on late shifts who cannot work because of daytime jury duty? One arbiter has ruled that a late-shift worker is entitled to pay for time lost.

EXAMPLE: A contract called for payment of the difference between regular earnings and jury pay when it was necessary for an employee to be away from this work because of jury duty. An employee on the night shift demanded pay when he took off from work for three days because he had to be in court by 9:00 a.m. and his shift did not end until 8:00. The company maintained it did not have to pay the employee for time lost because the jury duty occurred outside his regular workday.

An arbiter decided, however, that the employee was entitled to pay under the contract. He lived 11 miles from the plant, and the court was 35 miles from his home. Under the circumstances, the arbiter concluded that it was necessary for the employee to be away from his work if he was to arrive at court on time and in proper condition to fulfill his obligation as a juror. (Ozark Smelting & Mining Co., 27 LA 189)

Similarly, in another case, employees on an 8 a.m. to 4 p.m. shift did not have to report to the courthouse until 1 p.m. Thus, the employer refused to compensate them for morning hours, arguing, that the employees could have worked. However, the arbiter disagreed with the employer, noting that the purpose of jury duty benefit is to permit employees to have whatever time is necessary to serve on jury duty without any financial, physical, or emotional hardship. (Leve Brothers Co., 65 LA 867)

Moreover, an employee was held entitled to jury-duty pay under one contract even though he could have worked his regular shift while on jury duty.

The company had agreed to pay the difference between an employee's wage loss and the amount he received for jury duty. It turned down one employee's claim because he was on the second shift—from 4 p.m. to 12:30 a.m. It figured he could have worked while serving on the jury if he'd wanted to and it also pointed out that the employee had not proved he'd done more than report to the courthouse each morning.

The arbiter reasoned that the purpose of jury pay is to assure employees' willing acceptance of jury service by doing away with the money loss they would otherwise sustain. Requiring a man to work his regular shift after doing his civic duty, said the arbiter, would defeat that purpose. (Greenleaf Mfg. Co., 32 LA 1)

Computing Overtime Pay & Jury Duty

Arbiters are split on whether jury duty should be counted as "time worked" in computing overtime in a week in which an employee spends one or more days on jury duty and other days on the job for a combined total of more than 40 hours. Several arbiters have held that jury duty does not count as time worked and that therefore employees are not entitled to overtime premiums when their combined hours on the job and on jury duty exceed 40 per week. (63 LA 899, 52 LA 575, 52 LA 357)

But others hold that this in effect penalizes the employee for serving on the jury and that a more equitable policy would be to count jury duty as time worked in computing overtime. (55 LA 510)

Jury Pay During Suspended Operations

Is an employer required to pay jury leave when operations at his plant are suspended? The issue arose in one case where a snowstorm shut down the plant, and the employer refused to grant jury pay to employees serving on jury duty at the time. The arbiter found management's decision proper, since jury pay was based on the availability of work the employee could perform had he not served on the jury. In this instance, since there was no available work due to the snowstorm, there was no obligation to provide jury pay, the arbiter concluded. (FMC Corp., 65 LA 264)

Leave for Union Business

IN BRIEF

Contract provisions for leaves of absence for union business vary greatly, and whether such leave should be granted depends not only on the particular contract clause, but also on the facts and circumstances involved in each case, with particular reference to the good faith of both parties. (32 LA 589)

While internal affairs of the union and union "secrets" need not be divulged, the employer is entitled to enough information regarding the nature of the union business involved and the probable duration of the absence to permit an intelligent choice as to granting or denying leave. (50 LA 1140, 42 LA 632, 35 LA 873)

One arbiter, stressing that the term "union activities" is not unlimited, held that arbiters must determine whether "the nature of a particular activity is an appropriate basis for absence" based on the twin ideas of "reasonableness and undue burden." (91 LA 1317)

Under some collective bargaining agreements, arbiters have approved the action of management in granting leave on a conditional basis. (37 LA 249, 36 LA 400, 41 LA 739) In some cases, past practice of the parties and industry practice have influenced or determined the arbiter's decision. (75 LA 66, 43 LA 670)

Questions that may arise when leave for union business is considered include:

▶ Should there be a limit on the number of employees allowed to be on leave for this purpose at any one time? (74 LA 501, 69 LA 364)

▶ What should be the maximum duration of the leave—hours, days, months or longer? (91 LA 713, 76 LA 569, 69 LA 800, 66 LA 197)

▶ Is the leave permitted for any union business? One arbiter defined normal union business as activities falling within two broad areas: (1) those performed by the union as bargaining representative of the employees; and, (2) those performed on behalf of the union as an entity (88 LA 1148, 84 LA 1042) — e.g., organizing (42 LA 632); political activity (91 LA 525 (electioneering), 84 LA 1042, 70 LA 645); and, bargaining in another plant (58 LA 523). Another arbiter raised a third category: peripheral "activity on behalf of bargaining-unit employees not arising out of the bargaining relationship." (91 LA 1317)

▶ Does management have the right to require the union to explain the purpose of the leave before it is granted? (68 LA 143)

▶ What procedures should be followed when employees return from union leave?

▶ Does management have the right to deny union leave for certain reasons, such as a compelling business need? (94 LA 283)
▶ Do company benefits accrue while an employee is on union leave? (90 LA 1071, 68 LA 1028, 68 LA 101)
▶ Should a distinction be made between business for a local union and business for an international?

―――――――――――――― **GUIDELINES** ――――――――――――――

Frequent Short Absences Not Allowed

Under a contract permitting leave of absence for union business most arbiters agree that union officials do not have the right to leave their job at frequent intervals to attend to union affairs. These arbiters uphold management's right to insist that union officials tend to their jobs regularly or demand that they take extended leave if their frequent absences interfere with production. Some arbiters hold that a company can discipline union officials for leaving their jobs too often.

EXAMPLE: When one union representative left his work place to post union notices after the company had refused him permission, he was suspended. The union claimed that the company could not discipline him because he was on leave for union business. The arbiter upheld the company's action on the ground that the union leave clause did not allow a union representative to leave his job for frequent short periods of time to transact union business in the shop. He said the clause was clearly intended to permit absences for more extended periods outside the plant. Thus, he ruled the worker was properly disciplined. (Ampco Metal Inc., 3 LA 374)

However, under similar circumstances one arbitration board, while agreeing that a company could take some disciplinary action when a union representative frequently left his job, held that the penalty could not be too severe. He said that discharge was too drastic. (Brown & Sharpe Mfg. Co., 1 LA 423)

Unlimited Union Leave Permitted

When a contract placed no limit on the length of leave for holding union office, an arbiter held that the company had no right to terminate such leave.

EXAMPLE: A worker received a leave of absence to take the position of full-time staff representative with the international union. After two years, the company notified him that it was cancelling his leave and expected him to report back to work. When he did not, he was fired. Management claimed that it was unreasonable to expect it to grant union leave for eternity, when seniority and pension rights were accruing all the time.

Whether this was equitable or not was beside the point, the arbiter said. The contract stated that union leaves "shall be available" in reasonable number. The parties' failure to place any time limitation on union leave clearly indicated to the arbiter that no such limitation was intended. (Blaw-Knox Co., 41 LA 739)

On the other hand, a local official should not be allowed to devote too much company time to union business, an arbiter ruled. Although the contract granted the worker paid time off for union business, it was not "carte blanche permission to spend as much company time as he pleased on union business," the arbiter held. He further said that having full-time union officials on the company payroll could smack of unlawful domination of the union by management. (Pratt & Letchworth, 48 LA 1345)

Area of Union Business

Can "union business" be interpreted as applying only to local union affairs? Under a contract providing for leave to be granted for union business, arbiters are likely to rule that a company may not limit this privilege to business involving just the local union. One arbitration board reasoned that there are many cases where a worker would be called upon to perform work for an international of which the local union was a member. It said that the union business may in no way involve the local union. Thus, the board ruled, the meaning of "union" in the leave provision could not be restricted to the local union. (Robertshaw-Fulton Controls Co., 11 LA 1074)

Content of Union Business

Few contracts specifically cover all instances that may be considered "union business" in the leave provisions. Distinguishing between what is and what is not "union business" is further complicated by the varied nature of union activities.

EXAMPLE: At least one arbiter ruled that serving on a political action committee was not "union business" under a contract which permitted leave for the purpose of transacting union business or representing the national union. He said that the company rightly denied a worker's request for leave to serve on a union political action committee. He decided that the contract was intended to provide leave for the purpose of taking care of business for the union in its role of bargaining agent and to represent the national union in the traditional ways. (Anchor Duck Mill, 5 LA 428)

Similarly, another arbiter agreed with an employer who refused to permit an employee to take leave to negotiate a contract between the union and another employer. The employee was a union president, and he had requested time off under a clause stating that "the business representative of the union or his agent designated in writing is to be considered a member of the shop committee and may sit in on any and all meetings." The arbiter found, however, that the contract did not contemplate time off for union representatives to negotiate a contract with third-party employers. (Leonetti Furniture Mfg. Co., 64 LA 975)

On the other hand, an employer improperly refused to give the members of a negotiating committee a second day off to complete a review of a newly negotiated contract, an arbiter ruled. Notwithstanding the employer's contentions that the contract did not provide time off for committee members and that management was only required to consider request for time off in a fair and reasonable manner, the arbiter decided that two days to review the agreement was not unreasonable if a careful job was to be done. (Hyde Park Foundry & Machine Co., 71 LA 349)

Similarly, where a contract's part-time leave provisions allowed reasonable time for elected union representatives to attend conventions or conferences of the union, an arbiter held that a man should be granted leave to attend to legislative affairs. The arbiter said that conferences might well include a meeting between union representatives and members of the state legislature. (Le Roi Mfg. Co., 8 LA 350; see also 74 LA 501)

Personal Leave for Union Business

Some contracts do not have specific clauses granting leave for union business and instead include—either implicitly or explicitly—union business as a reason for taking personal leave. Employees may sometimes experience difficulty in justifying leave for union business under these circumstances, however.

EXAMPLE: A teacher sought a paid half-day emergency leave to attend union-sponsored meeting. The employer, however, contended that meeting did not meet the criteria of "personal and compelling" reasons specified by the contract as justification for "emergency leave."

However, the arbiter sided with the employee. Noting that past practice had established a very liberal application of the personal leave clause, which was the precursor of the present clause, the arbiter pointed out that when the former clause was "dove-tailed" into the new clause, the negotiators understood that the prior leave practices would not be affected. (Lake Holcombe Joint School Dist., 63 LA 1096)

Organizational Work

Can a worker claim union business leave to engage in organizational work for the union at another company? Under a contract granting leave to a union officer "to perform his duties as an executive officer of the union," an arbiter ruled that an officer was entitled to time off for proper union activities which the officer was required and authorized to do. Applying this test, the arbiter held that organizational work authorized by union members was a proper occasion for leave. The fact that the company disapproved of the organizing was irrelevant in the arbiter's view. (Telex, Inc., 35 LA 873)

Picketing as Union Business

One arbiter has ruled that a union business leave clause does not give a large number of employees in a plant the right to leave in order to picket at the place of business of another company. He reasoned that if the union could, by merely submitting a written request, create mass absenteeism it would hamper the general operation of the plant and thus defeat the right of management to direct its affairs and working forces. He further stated that the "leave" clause had not been intended to apply to late reporting or temporarily absent employees but had been intended to refer to those on extended periods of absence. (Chrysler Corp., 11 LA 732)

Similarly, an arbiter ruled that a school board was acting within its rights when it denied teachers leave to picket another school. Their contract permitted up to 25 days off during the school year for attending "official sessions" of their union. The teachers claimed that besides picketing, they were surveying the strike scene to evaluate strategy and public relations factors in the strike. The arbiter, in denying the teachers' grievance for back pay, reasoned that the clause was designed to permit employees to participate in the internal union affairs, and not to support external business affecting an outside party. (Jackson Public Schools, 64 LA 1089; see also 76 LA 648)

When Union Refuses To State Nature of Union Business

Is a union obligated to give a reason for a request for leave for union business? Where a contract specified that leave would be granted to permit workers to engage in labor activities, one arbiter ruled that the company had the right to ask the union the purpose of any leave it requested. In order for the company to determine whether the leave was for bona fide labor activity, it would have to know the nature of the union business, he reasoned. If the union refused to give the reason, then the company was not obligated to grant the leave, the arbiter decided. (Carter Carburetor Corp., 11 LA 569)

However, another arbiter held that an employer may not inquire into the nature or location or the business to be performed. Doing so, he reasoned, would amount to prying into the internal affairs of the union.

The arbiter listed three questions which management reasonably may ask a worker requesting leave—(1) whether the worker holds a union office that entitles him to leave, (2) whether the leave is to be used for official duty, and (3) how much time off is required. (Telex Inc., 35 LA 873)

Leave for Rival Union Business

Leave to work for a union other than the contracting union is not permitted under a "union activity" clause, one arbiter ruled, although it may be permissible to grant such leave requested under some other clause in the contract.

EXAMPLE: A clause in the contract provided for leave of absence to local union representatives "chosen by the union" and to employees "elected to a full-time position with the union." Another clause provided for leave of absence for "good and sufficient reasons." An employee was granted leave to attend to his duties as an officer of a rival union. Upon his return to duty, the contracting union claimed that the employee had lost his seniority rights as his leave was unauthorized under the contract terms. The company contended that the employee was on authorized leave under both the "leave for union activity" clause and the "leave for good and sufficient reasons" clause.

In his decision the arbiter was critical of the company's action in permitting leave to work for a rival union. The arbiter felt that the company's action had violated the spirit of the contract as to what were "good and sufficient reasons." However, because it had not violated the letter of the contract, he upheld the company's granting of the leave.

In its attempted application of the "leave for union activity" clause, the company was held in error. The arbiter stated: 'Beyond any conceivable doubt, these two sections were included in the contract solely for the benefit of members of the contracting union ... when acting for the union." (Swift & Co., 6 LA 422)

Discipline for Taking Unauthorized Leave

One arbiter has ruled that where a worker in good faith requests leave and, in the face of a rejection by management, takes lave anyway, he is not subject to discipline. Union business leave, the arbiter reasoned, is for the benefit of the union and not of the individual worker. To say that a worker is personally liable if he mistakenly goes on leave, he added, would be like saying that a supervisor is personally liable if he mistakenly discharges or suspends a worker. The company's recourse in such cases, according to the arbiter, is to file a grievance against the union to test whether a good-faith absence comes within the scope of the union-business-leave clause. If it is found not, a worker taking leave under similar circumstances thereafter would be subject to discipline, the arbiter said.

On the other hand, the arbiter held, if a worker acts dishonestly or in bad faith in claiming the leave privilege, he is subject to discipline. (Telex Inc., 35 LA 873) Effect of Long Leave on Pensions Benefits

Where an employee takes a long-term union leave and then returns to active employment for a couple of years before his retirement, is he entitled to count the years of his union leave in computing his pension benefits? One arbiter has ruled yes.

EXAMPLE: An employee was actively employed by a company for 23 years, and then took a 22-year union leave. He returned to active employment with his company for two years before electing to retire. A dispute arose when his employer refused to consider the leave as "credited continuous service" under the pension plan. The employer argued that the leave should be excluded because during that time the employee was not really an employee under the contract definition of "employee" as any person who was "working" under the collective bargaining agreement. This individual, the employer continued, was a full-time officer of the union and received his compensation from it for his services.

However, the arbiter decided to credit the leave period under the pension plan. He based his award on the contractual intent of parties to include those individuals on approved leave as "employees." Also, the parties carefully delineated conditions which would disqualify employees from participating in the pension plan, the arbiter noted, but did not include approved leave. Thus, the arbiter reasoned that they did not intend for approved leave to be a cause for disqualification. (Western Textile Products Co., 64 LA 709; see also 68 LA 101)

Effect of Leave on Automatic Increase

Is a worker who takes time off to accept a full-time union job entitled to automatic increases he would have received if he had not taken leave? One arbiter held that a worker was entitled to such increases where the contract provided for reinstatement without loss of seniority following union leave. (Spartan Aircraft Co., 28 LA 859)

Time Spent Handling Grievances

While an employer may challenge, in specific cases, the amount of time claimed by union officials for grievance activity, he may not unilaterally set a limit on such time.

EXAMPLE: When the number of hours spent on grievance settlement increased greatly, the employer limited the amount of time allowed, excusing his failure to negotiate the matter on a ground that it was a reasonable measure designed merely to return to a previous practice. The arbiter dismissed this as contrary to the contractual obligation to pay for all time reasonably and actually required for handling matters under the contract. (Goss Co., 44 LA 824)

Leave to Attend Arbitration Proceeding

Is an arbitration hearing part of the paid grievance time allowed union officials? It depends on the time and circumstances of the hearing and the individual contract.

EXAMPLE: An arbiter ordered an employer that required employee/witnesses to request vacation or holiday time for time off to prepare for out-of-town arbitration hearing to continue its past practice of excusing a reasonable number of employees to prepare for arbitration, subject to last-minute personnel needs in work-related emergencies. (Texas Utilities Mining Co., 87 LA 815)

EXAMPLE: The contract required the company to pay "for all time spent during working hours investigating and adjusting grievances and complaints." A number of stewards attended arbitration hearings and gave testimony regarding various grievances. Their requests for pay for time spent at the proceedings were turned down by the company. The company said that the stewards were necessary participants in grievance adjustment, but not in arbitration hearings. The argument was upheld, and the stewards were not paid, as the time did not qualify for payment under the terms of the contract. (Consolidated Industries Inc., 43 LA 331).

EXAMPLE: For years, the chief steward walked through the plant at the start of each work day to permit the workers to make known any grievance they might have. Although it had not objected before, the company began refusing to pay for these visits unless the chief steward first requested and received permission to do so. The contract gave the steward the right to reasonable time off to investigate grievances "upon notice and approval" by management.

According to the arbiter, the practice followed by the steward for years without objection from the company was the same as notice to and approval by the company and was not subject to unilateral change by the company. (American Saint Gobain Corp., 46 LA 920)

EXAMPLE: Handling grievances need not even involve the negotiated grievance procedures, according to one arbiter. In that case, employees who gave depositions during working hours in a suit arising under Title VII of the Civil Rights Act were denied compensation for the time they took from work to file the depositions. The employer, who was alleged to have violated the Act, required the employees to take the time off without pay, contending that they were not "processing their grievances," under the contract clause which provides pay for "processing grievances," however, the arbiter awarded back pay. Emphasizing that the employees had a right to elect to take their grievance to court rather than to use grievance procedures negotiated in the contract, the arbiter concluded that they were "processing their grievances" through the court, and were entitled to back pay. (Wallace Silversmiths Inc., 64 LA 1110)

However, an arbiter held that an employer did not violate a contract requiring it to grant leaves of absence for "good and sufficient cause," when it refused to grant leave to an employee to participate in an arbitration hearing. (Youngstown Vindicator Printing Co., 88 LA 17)

EXAMPLE: One steward took time from the job to discuss his own grievance with the union attorney. The employer docked the steward for the time he left work early, but the arbiter ordered back pay for that time. The arbiter reasoned that the contract included the steward's own grievance in the phrase "formal grievances" which stewards could take company time to process. It also appeared that he had prior approval from the employer to do so, the arbiter concluded. (County Sanitation District, Los Angeles, 64 LA 521)

EXAMPLE: Arbitration is merely the last step of the grievance procedure and, as such, is governed by the grievance language of the contract, one arbiter said. Thus, the contract clause granting time off for grievance investigations entitled the local union president to accompany an industrial engineer on a union-quested time study, the arbiter decided, despite management's objection. (Hupp Corp., 48 LA 524)

EXAMPLE: In one case, an employer issued two-day suspensions to employees who took time off to testify at arbitration hearings at the union's direction, instead of obeying company orders to report for work. The company argued that the union had failed to provide adequate notice for the leaves as required by the contract, and therefore they were not valid. Although the arbiter agreed in part with the company, he reasoned that the employees were innocently caught in a tug-of-war battle between the union and the employer, and so he reduced the suspensions to only one day. (United Enginering Co., 64 LA 1274)

Arranging Leave

IN BRIEF

In setting its policy on leave of absence, management really has two separate and distinct problems: (1) short-term absences, usually due to illness, or other unavoidable failures to report for work; and (2) longer absences, for which employees can plan in advance, and which may be granted for any one of a dozen different reasons.

For short-term leaves, most employers merely require that the employee notify the employer that he or she is going to be absent. This notice must come in within a specified time, usually the first day or the first morning of the absence. Disciplinary penalties are specified for failure to make proper notification. (This subject is discussed in more detail in the section on Discipline for Absenteeism.)

For long absences, or short-term leaves which are not unavoidable, employers usually require advance notice and approval from the proper management official before the leave is taken. (94 LA 761, 74 LA 1185, 72 LA 1258, 72 LA 544, 72 LA 541, 72 LA 133)

If a company has followed a lax policy in arranging and granting leaves, an arbiter is not likely to be too sympathetic if management suddenly decides that an employee should be discharged because he or she was a bit too informal about leave-taking.

GUIDELINES

Oral or Written Grant for Leave of Absence

Employers often require that authorization for leave of absence be put in writing. Despite this requirement, management sometimes grants oral leaves of absence. In such instances the question arises as to whether the employee was on an authorized leave.

An arbiter is likely to decide that management has given up the right to discipline an employee by giving oral permission to be absent.

EXAMPLE: An employee was absent on an extended leave after obtaining oral permission from management for a leave of absence. The employee, upon returning to work, was notified by the company that he had lost his seniority rights, because the leave authorization had not been put in writing. A contract provision stated: "Management agrees that leave shall be in writing and a copy thereof sent to the union." The arbiter held that the leave was authorized and that the employee did not lose his seniority rights, finding that the provision concerning a written leave was for the protection of the company. The company, in this case, had given up its privilege to require a written leave when it granted oral permission to the employee. The company, therefore, could not use its own action, in not putting the leave in writing as an excuse to deny the employee his seniority rights. (Gem Electric Mfg. Co. Inc., 11 LA 684)

Moreover, the fact that a contract provides that employees who request leaves of absence for a period of more than six days must make application in writing does not preclude finding that an employee who orally requested time off for one day was on "leave of absence."

EXAMPLE: An employee, the fourteenth member of a work crew, requested time off to visit a friend. Under the contract, the company agreed to guarantee 13 men on the crew and to replace the fourteenth if the employee were on leave. The union, on the other hand, agreed to absorb the work of the fourteenth member if his or her absence were due to sickness, accident, or absenteeism. Both parties agreed the absence was excused, but the company referred to it as an excused "absence," and the union as "leave."

The arbiter, in holding for the union, ruled that the contract implied that a leave of absence for a period of less than six days would not be reduced to writing. There is a clear difference, he said, between "absenteeism" and being off duty with prior permission. (Emge Packing Co., 15 LA 603)

Oral Discussion with Management

If management wants to make sure that leaves will be granted only after formal authorization, it should make this requirement fairly specific in its contract or personnel policy. Otherwise, an employee may claim that he was "granted" leave of absence when the company intended no such thing.

EXAMPLE: An employee contracted tuberculosis and was told by his doctor to take a long rest. The personnel director told him not to worry and that everything would turn out okay. The employee considered the statement a grant of a leave of absence and was gone for over a year. When he returned, he discovered he had been discharged. The arbiter ordered payment of half the wages the employee would have earned from the date he applied for reinstatement until the date of the award. He reasoned that the company's interest in the health of its employees, and its liberal policy in respect to leaves of absence for illness, strongly suggested that the employee had been granted a leave of absence. The words of the personnel director, he said, when considered in the light of all circumstances, must he construed as an oral grant of leave "or a sufficient equivalent." (Morey Machinery Co. Inc., 9 LA 570)

"Reasonable Notice" for Leave of Absence

Several questions may arise when the term "reasonable notice" is used in a contract provision on leaves. Who determines what is "reasonable" and what is not "reasonable"? What length of time can be considered "reasonable"?

Unless the agreement says otherwise, the union probably can demand an equal voice in answering such questions.

EXAMPLE: A contract provided that "reasonable notice" should be given to the proper company official before an employee could leave his job. The company, without consulting the union, posted a rule stating: "reasonable notice is deemed to be 48 hours." An employee requested permission for immediate absence for a few hours and left his place of employment when the request was denied. When the company disciplined the employee, the union contended that he was on legitimate leave and should not have been disciplined. The arbiter, in discussing the "reasonable notice" issue, found that the employer had no right to set a specific period of time without first obtaining the union's consent. When the "reasonable notice" clause was inserted in the contract, he said, it became a proper subject for bargaining and management could not unilaterally fix its meaning by posting a company rule. (Ampco Metal Inc., 3 LA 374; see also 71 LA 70)

Notice to Employer to Return to Work

Contract clauses covering leave sometimes provide for notice to the company when an employee intends to return to duty. Unless the contract terms are very specific, confusion may arise as to the proper timing of the notice.

EXAMPLE: In such an instance one arbiter held that an employee had a "reasonable" time to submit his request for rehire. A union official was absent for several years on an authorized leave of absence for union business. Upon discharge from his union duties he waited 12 days before submitting a request for rehire to the company. The employer refused on the ground that he had not given the contractually required notice — i.e., immediately after his release from union duties. The company also argued that the "Increasing forces after layoff provisions in the contract required an employee to report for work within five days after he was recalled from a layoff. The union argued that the "leave-for-union-activity" clause merely required the employee to notify the company one week before he was ready to go back to work.

The employee was ordered reinstated with seniority and back pay. The arbiter held that the "Increasing forces after layoff clause had no application in fixing the period of time required for giving notice at five days. He stated that a careful examination of the leave clause failed to reveal any requirement as to a fixed period of time for giving the rehire notice and, therefore, that a "reasonable" period should be allowed. The arbiter concluded that 12 days was not too long a period of time in this instance. (Armour & Co., 10 LA 140)

Reinstatement after Leave of Absence

If any employee requests reinstatement after an extended authorized leave of absence, how much time has management to reinstate the employee?

In the absence of specific policy to cover the situation, an arbiter held in one instance that the company had a "reasonable" time. Two weeks, however, was "unreasonable."

EXAMPLE: An employee who was absent for six months on authorized leave requested that he be reinstated. Management delayed two weeks before he was put back to work. In answer to the employee's claim for two weeks' salary, the company stated that it was entitled to at least several weeks' notice before placing the employee, since the nature of its operations required that much time to plan work and set up schedules.

It seemed to the arbiter that it would be unfair to require the company to put the employee back to work on the same day he decided to return to work. Since the employee had been absent for six months, the company should have been allowed a reasonable opportunity to find out where he could best be used. Because of the nature of the operation, the arbiter concluded that the company should have found out in one week where best to place the employee. (Crawford Clothes Inc., 12 LA 1104)

EXAMPLE: Another employer was also unjustified in delaying by one week the reinstatement of an employee on leave who returned a day late from an overseas trip when he missed a connecting plane flight, an arbiter ruled. The employee did in fact fail to notify his employer of the delay — an unapproved extension of leave — but this was insufficient to justify placing him on an alternate work schedule which commenced one week later, the arbiter decided. The employer's action amounts to a suspension prohibited by a just-cause provision the arbiter maintained, since there was no evidence that the employee was not back from the trip or that he was not able and willing to resume his work. (Potlatch Corp. 63 LA 816)

EXAMPLE: An employee who had been injured on-the-job was held by an arbiter to be entitled to her former position even though she had been out for more than a year, since she had obtained a medical certificate approving her return. She had been told by the employer that she could return to her job when such a condition was fulfilled. The arbiter ruled that the contract provision permitting leave of absence for one year only was not applicable, since it was not intended to apply to forced absence for on-the-job injury. The employee had neither requested nor received formal leave of absence, and the employer, in describing conditions for the reinstatement, had not mentioned time limits. The employee was capable of performing her work since she had obtained two medical releases for work without restriction. (Texlite Inc., 48 LA 509)

However, another arbiter upheld an employer's delay in reinstating an employee on sick leave when the company physician erroneously reported that the employee had a hernia. The employer waited until another physician reported that the employee was in fact fit to return to work, before he was reinstated. The arbiter found the employer's action reasonable in light of the company physician's diagnosis, and rejected the union's argument that the company doctor might have resented the employee's earlier criticism of him, and, therefore, deliberately altered his report. (Philco-Ford Corp., 62 LA 351)

Extension of Leave

If a company requires employees on leave to renew the leave at definite periods, can it discharge an employee who does not get a leave request in before the expiration of the leave period?

When an employee is late with a request for renewal, management would seem to be within its rights in considering the worker no longer an employee of the company.

EXAMPLE: An employee requested an extension of his leave of absence two days after his original leave had expired. The contract required that such leave be renewed each six months. Another provision of the contract stated that an employee was deemed to have quit, with subsequent loss of seniority if the employee failed to report for work for three consecutive working days and had not been granted a leave of absence. The union argued that the seniority-protection clause applied in this case, as the employee had been absent only two days beyond the termination of his leave. The company took the position that the renewal had not been requested within the six-month time-limit; and, therefore, the employee had not complied with the contract.

The arbiter held that the only logical construction that could be placed upon the six-month renewal qualification was that the request for renewal of leave must be made before the expiration of the original period. He also stated that the three-day seniority-protection clause, for actively-employed workers absent without leave, had no application to absentees overdue from leaves of absence. (Campbell, Wyant, & Cannon Foundry Co., 1 LA 254)

Cancelling Leave

If management has the sole right to grant or deny leaves of absence, can it also cancel leaves which have been authorized?

Undoubtedly, the right to deny leave extends also to the cancellation of leave already granted. However, this probably should be handled by notifying employees and giving them a chance to return to work, not by changing their status from "on leave" to "quit."

EXAMPLE: An employee on the day shift was told the company was moving her to the night shift in order to avoid laying her off. For personal reasons she could not work nights. She orally requested a leave of absence, which was granted. While she was on leave, the company marked her record "quit." The employee entered a claim for vacation pay and the company answered that she was a "quit" and was not entitled to payment. A majority of an arbitration board decided that the company had the right to deny the employee the leave. The board said, however, that the denial should have been made at the time the request was made. The majority pointed out that it was entirely possible that the employee, given the choice of her job or the night shift, might have changed her decision. The board held that the company's action in changing from approval to disapproval without notifying the employee was unfair. (Anchor Rome Mills Inc. 9 LA 497)

Maternity & Adoption Leave

IN BRIEF

Many unions have negotiated maternity or pregnancy disability leaves for their members. However, interpretation of these contract clauses often involves reference to other leave provisions, such as general leave, parental leave (available to female and male employees in some form currently in 11 states, covers the birth, adoption, or serious illness of a child), family leave, or sick leave, or consideration of the employer's past practices. In addition, a number of laws, both federal and state, affect maternity-leave policies. (The disability period for a normal pregnancy usually is six to eight weeks.)

Paternity leave, a form of parental leave available to men, although usually unpaid, may consist of the right to use sick, personal, or vacation days on the birth or adoption of a child.

Although arbiters are generally reluctant to look past a labor contract to complicated bodies of law, many refer to anti-discrimination law when considering maternity leave cases. As one arbiter has pointed out, "applicable provisions of state and federal law impress themselves upon the labor contract and not only may, but must, be given consideration in any arbitration proceeding which arises thereunder." (Wausau District Public Schools, 64 LA 187)

The Pregnancy Disability Amendment to Title VII of the 1964 Civil Rights Act makes disparate treatment of pregnant women for employment purposes illegal. Therefore, employers must treat pregnancy and childbirth in the same way as they treat other disabilities. Also, government contractors must provide time off for childbearing purposes in certain circumstances under Executive Order 11246. More exacting than Title VII, E.O. 11246 requires reinstatement to the same or an equivalent position (Title VII mandates only equal treatment and would not require reinstatement in those circumstances).

Additionally, state pregnancy leave laws may have even more stringent requirements, including provisions for a minimum length of leave and for reinstatement to the same or an equivalent job. A majority of states (see below) make some provision for employees to take leave for disability resulting from the birth of a child with reinstatement to the same or similar job on return to work. Maternity leave generally is without pay once regular sick leave and vacation leave have expired. (95 LA 1042) Generally, maternity leave will not be allowed unless authorized by a state statute or by a collective bargaining agreement. (89 LA 105)

GUIDELINES

Arbitral Considerations

Collective bargaining agreements vary widely in the types and amounts of leave provided covered employees. Because of this variation, arbitral interpretations of maternity leave clauses have been affected by the presence or absence of other leave clauses, and even by the exact wording of contract provisions.

In addition to contract language, arbiters frequently consider the following factors:
- the employer's past practice;
- whether the pregnancy created a disability;
- whether the employee was laid off prior to or during the disability;
- what accommodations, if any, were appropriate for a pregnant employee;
- discrimination against or in favor of pregnant employees;
- whether maternity leave is appropriate for adoption; and
- should insurance coverage continue during an unpaid leave.

General Leave Clauses

Many contracts allow employees to apply for leaves of absence — usually unpaid — for various purposes. Whether general leave may be used for maternity purposes depends on several factors.

EXAMPLE: The presence of a general leave clause gives the company the right to grant or deny maternity leaves, according to one arbiter. In reviewing an employer's agreement, the arbiter found nothing that would qualify such a right, and, noting a distinction between sickness and pregnancy, concluded that the company could grant sick leave without being compelled to also grant maternity leave. (American Stove Co., 8 LA 779)

EXAMPLE: Another arbiter, however, held that an employer that had granted maternity leave in the past under a general leave clause had to continue to do so. The arbiter added that management must administer the general leave clause fairly and justly in the interests of all employees and the company. (General Electric Manufacturing Co. Inc., 11 LA 684)

Paid Sick Leave Clauses

Although most contracts have a clause granting paid sick leave to employees, the term "sick" is rarely defined. The result is a number of contradictory decisions, each dependent upon the specific contract language and facts of the case.

EXAMPLE: Where a contract provides for unpaid maternity leave and for paid sick leave, an employee may not take paid sick leave for maternity purposes, an arbiter ruled. Arbiters may not "go behind the contract language to probe for an intent other than the one disclosed by a simple reading of the provision as supported by practice," the arbiter points out, and since the contract differentiates between sick and maternity leave, the arbiter should as well. (Millinocket School Committee, 65 LA 805; see also 97 LA 383)

However, an administrative regulation that required employees to choose either unpaid child-rearing leave, or paid sick leave, but not both, was illegal, an arbiter concluded. The provision in the contract for unpaid leave for child-rearing does not preclude an employee from using paid sick leave for the period of time that she is physically disabled because of pregnancy, the arbiter held. (Sweet Home Central School District, 71 LA 1102)

EXAMPLE: A contract provided that pregnant employees were entitled to prenatal and/or infant care leave, to be granted on request and used in conjunction with sick leave. The contract also provided sick leave for a period of disability due to pregnancy, and contained, in the prenatal/infant care section, the provision that the "sum of such leaves will not exceed four months." From these provisions, an arbiter concluded that an employee was entitled to four months of prenatal or infant care leave, in addition to sick leave for the period of her disability, despite the employer's contention that "sum of all leaves" included the sick leave. (West Side Credit Union, 77 LA 622)

EXAMPLE: A female employee was not entitled to use a "sick leave bank" to cover the post-delivery care of her child, an arbiter ruled, explaining that the contract allowed workers to use the sick bank only if they were incapacitated by a "severe" sickness or injury. The employee claimed that breastfeeding her child after delivery constituted "sickness," but, as the arbiter pointed out, breastfeeding is not a sickness and, even assuming that it is, it clearly was not among those examples of "extraordinary physical problems" that the contract addressed for purposes of using the sick bank. (Cheektowaga Central School Board of Education, 80 LA 225)

"No Discrimination" Clauses

Many contracts include clauses prohibiting discrimination on various grounds. These clauses may be useful to arbiters in discerning whether a contract requires paid maternity leave. The effect of such a provision is to refer an arbiter to definitions of discrimination formulated by the EEOC and the courts.

EXAMPLE: Under a contract that provided unpaid maternity leave and paid sick leave for "personal illness," an employer may not deny sick leave pay to an employee because of a pregnancy-related disability, an arbiter ruled, despite the employer's past practice of never granting sick leave to employees taking maternity leave. A contractual nondiscrimination clause prohibiting discrimination "with respect to any term or condition of employment," and a state law prohibiting sex discrimination, are deciding factors, the arbiter notes. (Muskego-Norway School District, 71 LA 509)

Contract Language Changes

Even a relatively minor change to a collective bargaining agreement's language can have the effect of binding an employer to provide benefits, arbiters have concluded.

EXAMPLE: When an employer agreed to a new contract which moved a provision for a "pregnancy leave of absence" into the clause covering "sick leave of absence," it committed itself to providing paid sick leave rather than unpaid pregnancy leave, an arbiter ruled. The employer's intentions during contract negotiations are irrelevant, the arbiter said. (Scottscraft Inc., 64 LA 279)

EXAMPLE: Although an exclusion of maternity was removed from the benefits clause of a contract, the employer is not required to pay benefits for maternity-related leave, an arbiter decided. "The omission from the collective bargaining agreements of the earlier exclusion of 'maternity' and the silence of the agreements with respect to an obligation to pay such benefits are hardly the stuff from which a binding contractual obligation can be erected," the arbiter said. (Chromalloy Division, 71 LA 1178)

Employer's Past Practice

A number of decisions have hinged on the employer's past practice of either granting or not granting paid maternity leave, especially where the contract is silent or ambiguous. Not all arbiters, however, accept this argument. Some find past practice "fairly conclusive" (Walled Lake Consolidated Schools, 64 LA 239), while others find it a "unilateral pronouncement by management" and, hence, "not controlling." (Kaiser-Permanente Medical Care Program, 64 LA 245)

EXAMPLE: Under a contract providing unpaid "parental leave" for up to one year after the birth of a child, an employer could not unilaterally limit the leave to half a year, an arbiter found. The employer had agreed to the clause in several different agreements, and had, over a period of years, denied only one other request for a full year's leave. In that case, the leave requested did not coincide with the school year, but spread over parts of two different school years. The present situation, however, involved a request for leave for one school year, the arbiter noted, and was refused because of "the general dissatisfaction" of the school board with long leaves. Whether or not this "dissatisfaction" was justified, the arbiter said, the board could not reject the teacher's leave request without showing the request to be "inappropriate." (Ankeny Community School District, 77 LA 860)

Disability and Layoff Issues

A pregnant employee's right to disability benefits and the effect of a layoff on a pregnant worker are two other issues that may be presented to an arbiter.

EXAMPLE: Under an insurance plan agreement that provided accident and sickness benefits for disabled employees in a doctor's care, a pregnant employee certified as disabled by her physician is entitled to benefits, an arbiter concluded. The employee had previously suffered two miscarriages, and her physician recommended that she not do any work involving lifting, pulling, pushing, or straining of any kind. The employer initially paid disability benefits to the employee, but then decided that the payments were made incorrectly. The employee was placed on unpaid personal leave from February until June, when benefits were reinstated to cover the period of hospitalization, delivery, and recovery. The arbiter concluded that, because the insurance plan's description of disability did not specifically exclude pregnancy-related conditions from coverage, the employee should have been paid benefits in the same fashion as any other employee suffering from a temporary disability. (Caterpillar Tractor Co., 79 LA 1070

EXAMPLE: An employee who was partially disabled because of pregnancy, but able to do light work, at the time of a layoff, and who later became completely temporarily disabled, was not entitled to disability benefits, an arbiter decided, based on the contract's exact terms and the company's past practice. Had the employee been disabled at the time of the layoff, she would have been eligible for benefits, the arbiter pointed out. However, the employee's absence "was not because of her partial disability, but because no work was available, i.e., she was on layoff," the arbiter said. (Hormel Fine Frozen Foods, 75 LA 1129)

EXAMPLE: An employee who was placed on layoff while she was on a maternity leave, and replaced by a less senior employee, had to be reinstated with backpay to her former position, an arbiter concluded. By refusing to reinstate the employee when she expressed her desire to return from maternity leave, the employer "constructively discharged" the worker "without any semblance of just cause," the arbiter noted. (Pipe Fitters Union Local 636, 75 LA 449)

Accommodation Concerns

An employer may lawfully require a pregnant employee to take leave when her pregnancy adversely affects her ability to work, but it first must accord to that employee the same opportunities that other temporarily disabled workers are given to perform modified or alternative tasks.

EXAMPLE: A pregnant employee who was unable to perform the various physical tasks required by her job and who was denied a transfer to a light-duty position was the victim of sex discrimination, an arbiter decided. The worker had requested a transfer to another department, and then asked to be assigned to a light-duty position in her own department. When these requests were refused, the employee requested, and was granted, sick leave. She was without income during her pregnancy after she had exhausted both her sick leave and vacation benefits. Noting that a male employee was assigned to light duty following an operation, the arbiter asserted that the pregnant employee "faced an employment situation where she was not accorded fair and equal treatment." The arbiter concluded that the "weight of the evidence clearly supports" the employee's contention that "for whatever reason, intentionally or unintentionally," the worker had been a victim of sexual discrimination. (Cities Service Co., 87 LA 1209)

Discrimination In Favor of Pregnant Employee

At least one arbiter has concluded that the Pregnancy Disability Act prohibits discrimination in favor of, as well as against, pregnant workers.

EXAMPLE: An employer who involuntarily reassigned a female employee, rather than either of two pregnant employees ahead of the reassigned worker on the involuntary assignment schedule, violated the Pregnancy Disability Act, an arbiter concluded. Under the law, "a difference in sex is not necessary for pregnancy discrimination to occur," the arbiter notes, adding, "all that need occur is for a woman affected by pregnancy to be treated differently than 'other persons.'" The arbiter stresses that one of the pregnant women was scheduled to return from maternity leave before the date of the assignment, that the other would have been in her fifth or sixth month of pregnancy, and that neither of the pregnant workers was disabled and unable to perform the assignment. (National Weather Service, 83 LA 689)

Demotion and Discharge Decisions

An employer may demote or discharge a pregnant employee if it has a legitimate nondiscriminatory reason for the action, according to several arbiters.

EXAMPLE: Upholding an employer's right to determine if its workers are qualified for their jobs, an arbiter ruled that an employee was properly terminated when, following treatment for a difficult pregnancy and other physical disabilities, she demonstrated that she was unable to perform all her duties. While medical reports from a number of doctors who treated the employee seemed to "lean in favor" of the worker, they in fact only "add confusion and make one wonder if the later 'clean bill of health' is justified," the arbiter maintained, adding that, in any case, employers must not be "handcuffed" by doctors' statements in trying to determine if an employee is qualified for a job. (National Standard Co., 85 LA 401)

Discipline or discharge under other circumstances may not be upheld, as the following case shows.

EXAMPLE: An employer improperly terminated an employee for failing to return to work upon expiration of maternity disability leave, an arbiter decided. The worker initially had requested and been granted a leave of absence without specifying an exact return date, but later, at management's request, she submitted a new leave form on which she specified both the beginning and end dates of her pregnancy disability leave. First, it would be "most unfair," the arbiter said, "to hold an employee to exactness about [a] date when there is no exactness possible in predicting either the birth date or the date of recovery." Second, if the employer was "misled" about the employee's return date, "it was the employer's own fault." Management relied on information that was "the result of the employer's insistence on the completion of an ambiguous form under confusing circumstances" and "failed on numerous occasions to protect its interest by making reasonable and logical inquiry." (Cooperative Optical Services, 86 LA 447)

Reinstatement to Position

Reinstatement of a pregnant worker to her job or a comparable position following maternity leave is not required by Title VII, unless that is the policy for all employees on disability leave, but states are not prohibited from enacting laws that go beyond the federal statute to require reinstatement. Also, some unions have negotiated contracts requiring reinstatement priority for employees returning from maternity leave.

EXAMPLE: A teacher who had been on maternity leave for one school year notified the school district that she intended to return to work. She bid on seven open positions for which she was qualified. The contract provides that employees returning from maternity leave will "enjoy an unequivocal preference over employees requesting transfers, most teachers being reemployed by the School District, and newly hired persons," the arbiter notes, yet this teacher was not interviewed for any of the seven positions, and was, instead, reassigned to her previous job. Meanwhile, five of the seven vacancies were filled by employees lower on the priority list. Noting that the school district "undeniably failed" to give the returning teacher the priority to which she was entitled, the arbiter points out that "she should have been considered for most, if not all, of the seven vacant positions she sought." Thus, the school district must assign her to one of those positions. (Decatur School District, 86 LA 841)

Maternity Leave for Adoption

Employers who have a maternity leave policy may be required to extend the leave to employees who become parents through adoption.

EXAMPLE: Emphasizing that "our society places great value on adopting children," one arbiter has held that a maternity leave policy should not be interpreted to preclude situations "where the family unit is increased by adoption rather than natural birth." The employer's policy allowed up to six months of sick, annual, or unpaid leave, or a combination of the three, for "maternity reasons." When an employee sought a three-month leave without pay to care for her newly adopted daughter, management told her that she would have to first use all her annual leave. The arbiter decided, however, that the "maternity reasons" acceptable for leave under the policy should include the "care of an adopted child during the initial period of adjustment when the adopted child becomes a member of the new household or family." Previous maternity leave grants had not been "solely confined to the actual delivery period," but had made "allowances for the mother to be with her new child" following the baby's arrival at home. (Office and Professional Employees, 71 LA 93)

EXAMPLE: Employees who adopt children are eligible for maternity leave under a contract that granted up to one year of "maternity" leave at the request of the employee, according to another arbiter. The case arose when an employer granted personal, rather than maternity, leave to an employee who adopted a baby. The arbiter noted that the length of the leave "establishes the fact" that the parties' object was to provide substantial time for child-rearing. An adopted child requires the same amount of care as an infant raised by its natural mother, the arbiter reasoned, so an employee who adopts a child is in no less need of a maternity leave than one who gives birth. Had the contract provided time off for "childbearing," the employer might have been permitted to restrict the leave to pregnant employees, but leave provided for maternity purposes should be granted to any employee who needs to perform the "duties" of "motherhood," the arbiter determined. (Ambridge Borough, 81 LA 915)

Other Maternity-Leave Issues

Other issues that arbiters may be required to decide include:

• *Unmarried employees' rights* — When an unmarried employee sought maternity leave benefits in one plant, management dismissed the worker instead of granting her leave. An arbitration board then ordered the company to reinstate her and grant her leave, reasoning that there was no association between her conduct and her job. (Crane Co., 12 LA 592) (See also Allied Supermarkets Inc., 41 LA 713.)

- *Insurance coverage during unpaid leave* — An employee on an unpaid maternity leave was entitled to have her insurance premiums paid by the employer under a contract clause that provided insurance for "employees," an arbiter ruled. The contract between the union and the employer provided for unpaid leave after employees had exhausted their sick leave; in the past, the employer had continued insurance coverage even after the worker had begun the unpaid leave. Because the contract clause is ambiguous, in that it does not define "employee," the arbiter concluded that past practice requires insurance coverage continuation. (Greensburg Salem School District, 76 LA 241)

- *State-law effects* — In at least two cases that arose prior to enactment of the Title VII amendment, employers were ordered to pay sick leave benefits for maternity-related medical disabilities in accordance with state law, which prohibited any discriminatory practice. (Apollo-Ridge School District, 68 LA 1235; West Allis-West Milwaukee Joint City School District 1, 68 LA 644)

Currently, the following states and territories have laws providing for some form of maternity leave: California, Louisiana, Maryland, Massachusetts, Montana, Nevada, New Hampshire, Oregon, Pennsylvania, Puerto Rico, Tennessee, and Washington.

Part 6

Promotions

Posting of Vacancies & Bidding

IN BRIEF

Arbiters generally recognize that in the absence of a contract provision limiting an employer's rights in regard to filling vacancies, the employer has the right to determine whether a vacancy exists and whether and when it shall be filled. (98 LA 222, 97 LA 1197, 96 LA 1007, 96 LA 553, 95 LA 1139, 95 LA 841, 95 LA 384, 94 LA 1183, 92 LA 306, 91 LA 1213, 90 LA 1018, 90 LA 577, 87 LA 914, 86 LA 1102, 86 LA 173, 84 LA 390, 84 LA 36, 83 LA 1083, 83 LA 801, 83 LA 445, 82 LA 708, 71 LA 498, 54 LA 896, 52 LA 894, 44 LA 580, 44 LA 161) However, where duties associated with a job vacancy are reassigned and continue to be performed by employees in other jobs, arbiters will examine whether an employer has intentionally avoided contractually-required procedures for filling jobs. (97 LA 196, 88 LA 614, 85 LA 449, 85 LA 290, 84 LA 390)

Moreover, contractual provisions dealing with the posting of vacancies, but not specifically requiring management to fill vacancies have been narrowly construed by arbiters. In one case, for example, a contractual provision for posting of "permanent vacancies" was held to apply only if the employer decided that a vacancy existed. In this instance the employer had decided that there was no need to replace a promoted employee, so no vacancy existed, the arbiter concluded. (49 LA 74; see also, 46 LA 1027, 44 LA 161)

Even where a job has been posted for bid, this does not necessarily guarantee that a vacancy exists and will be filled. For example, in one case an employer was upheld in permitting a successful bidder to withdraw his bid and return to his original job, even though the latter had, in turn, been posted for bid. (52 LA 894, 43 LA 951)

It is well established that management has the right, unless clearly restricted by the agreement, to decide whether or not to fill temporary vacancies occasioned by absences due to illness, vacations, and the like. (96 LA 1007, 90 LA 577, 85 LA 1190. 85 LA 290, 55 LA 19, 43 LA 395, 41 LA 492) Contract provisions stating that temporary vacancies "will" or "shall" be filled by a stated procedure have been construed merely to specify the procedure to be used if management decides to fill a vacancy. (28 LA 538, 25 LA 885)

GUIDELINES

JOB POSTINGS

Violation of Contractual Posting Requirements

Arbiters commonly examine whether an employer intentionally reassigned job duties associated with a vacancy in order to avoid posting requirements under a contract.

EXAMPLE: An arbiter interpreted a contract clause requiring the posting of a vacancy where there was an increase in the normal complement of a classification as applying only where an employer had determined a vacancy in fact existed. Infrequent transfer of employees to assist in the department did not prove that a vacancy existed, the arbiter held. (Homestake Mining Co., 88 LA 614)

EXAMPLE: An arbiter ruled that an employer violated a wage agreement by failing to post 12 jobs after it changed shift hours from 10 a.m.–6 p.m. to 7 a.m.–3 p.m. The employer had on three occasions posted jobs subject to less substantial shift-time changes, the arbiter pointed out, and posting the jobs would give senior employees an opportunity for assignment to a more desirable shift. (U.S. Steel Mining Co., 97 LA 196)

Posting New Jobs

Generally, when a contract provides that job vacancies shall be posted, the company is required to post all vacancies, including newly created jobs.

EXAMPLE: An arbiter held that an employer violated a contract when it transferred an employee to a job that it had failed to post. Regardless of the employer's claim that it had to create the position to accommodate an employee's request for transfer, the contract required that "new" and "open" jobs be posted, the arbiter found. (Rogers-Wayne Metal Products Co., 92 LA 882)

Similarly, management filled a newly created job with someone from the outside. The union protested on the basis of a contract clause stating that "job vacancy in each department shall be posted for a minimum of 48 hours." The company replied that this was not a job vacancy, but a new job. The arbiter, however, ruled that any job opening is a "vacancy" at the instant the company decides there is a need for the job to be manned. Any other holding, he said, would undermine the posting and job-filling sections of the contract. (Borden Co., 34 LA 658)

On the other hand, an employer did not create new jobs in a manner that required the jobs to be posted or placed for bidding, an arbiter ruled, when during a process of reorganization the company created a new work group and changed the proportion of duties assigned to employees in the group. Pointing out that the changes in duties, benefits, and working conditions, were not of such a magnitude to constitute a new job classification, the arbiter concluded that the employer's "traditional prerogative" to change work within a given job classification was reaffirmed by the comprehensive management rights clause in the contract. (United Telephone Co. of the Carolinas, 71 LA 244)

Temporary Vacancies

Some arbiters have held that temporary vacancies do not have to be posted or filled in accordance with seniority. They reason that to apply this requirement to every brief vacancy would be a handicap and a detriment to the efficient management of the business. (88 LA 614, 84 LA 36, 70 LA 1275, 29 LA 589, 5 LA 695)

Relying on past practice, another arbiter decided that an employer had the right to hire college students during the summer for unskilled work, even though the union claimed that the jobs should have been treated as temporary vacancies available to all employees. Noting that there was no past practice of having the work performed only by helpers, apprentices and journeymen, the arbiter pointed out that there was no evidence that the temporary students did any work that they were prohibited from performing. (Central Illinois Public Service Co., 72 LA 874)

However, at least one arbiter believes that there is a limit to what can be considered a temporary vacancy. He said that a vacancy expected to last one year during a leave of absence should be posted and filled by the senior qualified bidder. (McLouth Steel Corp., 11 LA 805)

Similarly, an arbiter rejected management's claim that its management rights clause permitted it to fill temporary vacancies without posting. The agency had filled a team leader position with an acting team leader appointment for an unknown duration. In light of a specific clause requiring job postings, the "ceiling problems" of the agency were irrelevant, the arbiter reasoned. Had the agency awarded the job to the grieving employee, its personnel would not have increased, the arbiter concluded. (Office of Economic Opportunity, 63 LA 692; see also 96 LA 1007, 90 LA 577, 85 LA 1190, 85 LA 290)

Job Originally Filled "Temporarily"

When it becomes apparent that the person who left a job temporarily will not return, does the worker who replaced him temporarily have to be removed and the job posted for bidding as a "permanent" vacancy? At least one arbiter has said that if an employee promoted temporarily remains in the new job for a considerable period of time, his promotion becomes permanent, and the company is no longer obligated to post the job. (Bethlehem Steel Co., 16 LA 478)

Similarly, one arbiter approved management's failure to post a temporary vacancy, and its subsequent appointment of the acting replacement to permanent replacement. The employee was originally appointed to replace a worker on a short-term sick leave, and since the contract specifically exempted vacancies of 60 days or less from the posting requirement, the employer acted within the agreement, the arbiter found. Later, when it became apparent that the vacancy would become permanent, the employer posted the job, but could not find a qualified candidate, the arbiter noted. Since the worker in the acting position had demonstrated his competency in the job, his appointment as permanent replacement was proper, the arbiter concluded. (Wm. Powell Co., 63 LA 341)

On the other hand, in a situation when it became clear that a temporary summer job would turn into a permanent one, an arbiter held, a company had to post the job for bidding in line with seniority. He said that the company violated the agreement by awarding the job on a permanent basis to the worker who had been filling it temporarily.

The parties had worked out a system whereby temporary jobs were created to permit all workers to take their vacations during the summer. These jobs lasted only a couple of months or so, and they were posted and filled in accordance with seniority by workers in lower classifications. At the end of the vacation season these workers returned to their regular jobs. (Phillips Petroleum Co., 29 LA 833)

Job Posting v. Transfer

Under a contract with requirements for posting vacancies, one arbitration board ruled that an employer could not transfer a worker facing layoff to fill a vacancy instead of posting the job for bidding.

EXAMPLE: An employee at one company was scheduled to be laid off within two days when an opening occurred in another department. Instead of posting the job and allowing employees to bid on the vacancy, the firm filled it with the employee facing layoff. When an employee with higher seniority complained that he had not been allowed a crack at the job, the company justified its action by saying that the contract was broad enough in intent and language to allow it to anticipate layoffs and retain employees. The company argued that it had an obligation to maintain the workforce and to give employees the highest-paid available jobs.

A board of arbitration ruled, however, that the company could not suspend its obligation to follow the posting clause. The company's personnel situation at the time did not make any difference, the board decided. Interested employees had to be allowed to apply for the job on the basis of their seniority and ability; and besides, said the board, there was a time lag before the actual layoff was due which should have been used as a posting period. The company was ordered to reopen the job to competitive bidding. (Shell Oil Co., 24 LA 748)

Similarly, an employer violated the requirement to post a job vacancy when it promoted a junior employee over a senior employee to fill that vacancy, an arbiter ruled. The employer maintained bid lists from which it selected candidates for promotions as jobs became available. When a group leader's job became vacant, the employer examined its bid list, and found no qualified candidates. It therefore allowed the supervisor to select the most qualified candidate.

The union charged, however, that when no qualified candidates were to be found on the bid list, the employer should have posted the vacancy.

Agreeing with the union, the arbiter ruled there was a contractual requirement to post jobs when bid lists have been exhausted. As a remedy, the arbiter ordered the job to be posted, but denied the union's requested remedy of promotion of a particular senior employee to the job. The arbiter denied the remedy because it was not clear that the employee would have bid for the job. (Whirlpool Corp., 63 LA 1122)

However, in another case, an arbiter upheld management's temporary transfer of a retiring employee's duties to other employees. The duties were transferred to two other employees during a computerization process, and the arbiter found that management had the right to make such temporary transfers to the employees who were in lower classifications. However, the arbiter, to insure that the transfers were only temporary, ordered the employer to return the lost position to the unit within 90 days following bidding procedures as required by the contract. (Ohio Brass Co., 62 LA 913)

Similarly, an employer did not violate a contract provision requiring posting of new or permanently vacated jobs when it did not post job of checker after checkers who transferred or were laid off because of discontinuance of crop processing were called back to work due to resumption of the processing, an arbiter decided since: (1) the checker job was not permanently vacated, and (2) contrary to the union's contention, the checker job was not a new job. (Stokely-Van Camp Inc., 69 LA 705) Job Posting v. Assignment to Supervisor

When a bargaining unit employee retires, can the company decide not to replace him, and instead assign his duties to his supervisor? An employer who attempted to do this lost the arbitration proceeding to the union. The arbiter based his decision on the union recognition and seniority clauses, which led him to conclude that the duties of the retiring employee should remain in the bargaining unit. Since the retirement created a permanent vacancy, the job should have been posted, the arbiter decided. (Stanray Corp., 63 LA 332; see also 73 LA 1250, 70 LA 182)

Previously-Posted Jobs

What is the employer's obligation to post another job vacancy notice after it has already done so, but without successfully recruiting from its employees? According to one arbiter, the employer still has a responsibility to post the job even though it will probably do no good.

EXAMPLE: An employer posted a notice of a job opening for an experienced crane operator. The company already had one employee working the crane, but wished to train another. However, after reviewing the bids from its employees, the employer found no qualified candidates. A few months later, the crane operator left the company and a new man with proper experience was hired. The union complained that the job opening should have been posted again. The arbiter agreed. The contract language explicitly required job openings to be posted, the arbiter said. However, since the company's earlier attempt to recruit a crane operator had been unsuccessful, it was clear that no one was actually disadvantaged or hurt by the contract violation; the arbiter concluded. (Consolidated Diesel Electric Co., 65 LA 1074)

POSTING REQUIREMENTS

Information Required on Job Notice

When a contract requires notices to be posted for all vacancies, the notice need contain only reasonable identification of the vacant job, according to one arbiter. He ruled that the posting does not have to give details, such as the degree of skill required, that may be determined upon inquiry. (John Deere Tractor Co., 3 LA 742)

However, under a similar provision where the practice had been to name specific jobs in posting vacancies, one arbiter decided that the company could not suddenly change to listing merely classifications of vacancies. He said the practice of posting specific job openings by name had to be continued. (Lion Oil Co., 25 LA 549)

Similarly, an arbiter held that, under a contract, an employer's steel division must identify the specific machine by number, rather than merely stating the category of a machine, when posting vacancies in a particular occupation. The contract required an indication of "specific equipment involved," the arbiter pointed out, and substantial differences existed among machines within some categories, and the employer's job postings had included machine numbers for 26 years. (Riblets Products Corp., RPI Div., 93 LA 1049)

Notices Should Be Posted Uniformly Throughout Plant

Even though a contract did not require posting of vacancies, a company whose practice was to post jobs in some departments had to post them in all departments, an arbiter ruled. Failure to post job openings in certain departments, he said, unfairly prevented workers there from exercising their seniority rights. (National Malleable & Steel Castings Co., 4 LA 175; see also 67 LA 354)

Notice to Union

When a contract requires management to notify the union of its compliance with posting requirements, how much notification is necessary? One arbiter ruled that management properly discharged its duty when it informally notified the union through its local chairman about its decision to reject employee applicants as unqualified prior to its hiring of an outsider. Although the union argued that the employer improperly waited until after the hiring to meet with the union committee, the arbiter decided that such a meeting was not required by a strict reading of the contract. (Semling Menke Co., 62 LA 1184; see also 73 LA 516)

BIDDING

Bidding Procedure/Sufficiency of Bid

Arbiters must also rule on whether an employer has followed a bidding procedure outlined in a contract, and whether an employee's bid meets the requirements for a particular job. (91 LA 605)

EXAMPLE: An arbiter held that an employer violated a contract by awarding a second-shift die-setting position to a senior qualified bidder, instead of another employer. The senior bidder had been awarded the same position on the third shift 83 days earlier, the arbiter pointed out, and the contract expressly restricts an employee from bidding on another job for at least 90 days after the employee has begun work in a position into which he or she previously had bid, and, further, it does not make seniority a sole controlling factor in job-vacancy awards. (PSW Industries Inc., 97 LA 155)

Bidding in Same Classification

Under the promotion provisions of a contract, can a worker bid for a job in the same classification as his own? Arbitrators have generally held that, in the absence of a specific definition in the contract, "promotion" means a movement to a higher classification, not a lateral movement to a job which the employee thinks is more desirable. (21 LA 707, 23 LA 159, 24 LA 723, 30 LA 550)

However, at least one arbiter has held that promotion should be construed to include improvement in working conditions as well as increases in pay. He found nothing in a contract that restricted the term "promotion" to advancement in classification. He said such an interpretation did not interfere with management's rights or with efficiency. (Medart Co., 18 LA 701)

Bidding Downward

Can a worker bid for a job in a classification lower than his own? Under a contract providing for vacancies to be filled by promotion within a department or if not filled in that manner, to be posted for plant-wide bidding, an arbiter held that an employee could not bid down into a lower classification. He said that taking a lower-rated job was a demotion even if it provided better chances for advancement or steadier work. The bidding provision, he ruled, allowed employees to bid only for jobs at higher pay. (Superior Paper Products, 26 LA 849)

Similarly, when a senior worker requested to fill a temporary vacancy in a job rated below his own, the company had the right to refuse him, an arbiter ruled. The arbiter said that the worker could not assert seniority rights to downward transfer unless a local practice to that effect existed, which he found was not the case. (Bethlehem Steel Co., 44 LA 457)

Likewise, an arbiter held that a contract contained no language permitting downward bidding. Therefore he disallowed a worker's use of seniority to get a lower job. (Pittsburgh Plate Glass Co., 44 LA 7)

Additionally, another arbiter upheld management's refusal to permit a downward bid. The arbiter reasoned that the employer's right to "arrange" its employees had not been expressly restricted by the contract with respect to downbids, and that therefore management could reject a down-bid request when it adversely affected operations. (Longview Fibre Co., 63 LA 529; see also 83 LA 685)

On the other hand, other arbiters have come to the conclusion that senior qualified bidders have a right to a job, even though it is in a lower classification. In one case, even though the bidding clause made some reference to promotions, the arbiter decided it did not restrict movement to promotions alone. (69 LA 822, 41 LA 329, 26 LA 789, 34 LA 856, 40 LA 1305)

Similarly, in another case, under a contract stating "seniority shall govern" in transfers and promotions, the arbiter ruled that an employer could not reject a bidder solely because he wanted a downward transfer. According to the arbiter, the test of whether an employer improperly denied downward transfer was whether the denial was arbitrary or discriminatory. (Max Factor & Co., 45 LA 918)

Supervisor Bidding Rights

Can a supervisor bid for a job that opens up in a bargaining unit? Where a contract permitted an employee to continue to accumulate seniority for a year after transfer out of the bargaining unit, an arbiter ruled that a supervisor who was once in the unit could bid for a job in the unit. Since the supervisor still had seniority, the arbiter held that he had the same bidding rights as other employees. (Owens-Corning Fiberglas Corp., 29 LA 578)

However, in a case where a supervisor was not, and never had been, a member of the bargaining unit, an arbiter said he had no right to bid on a posted job. Although the bidding clause referred to "employees," the arbiter decided it clearly referred to members of the bargaining unit. Since supervisors were not members of the unit, they could not accumulate seniority under the contract, and thus had no right to bid. (Boardman Co., 41 LA 215)

Trainee Bidding Rights

Can a trainee bid for a job other than the one for which he is being trained? Under certain circumstances, one arbiter ruled yes.

EXAMPLE: Three industrial trainees bid for jobs out of the job categories for which they were being trained. The employer refused to consider the bids, claiming that they were abusing the job-bidding system. However, an arbiter found that the job-bidding clause in no way limited the rights of the employees to bid provided they had "potential capabilities for the job." In the case of two of the employees, the arbiter found evidence that they were in fact qualified for the jobs, and therefore held that management's decision was in violation of the contract.

However, the third trainee had held his job for less than two months. The arbiter said he would not overrule management's action in his case because of the brief period of employment, despite the argument that the employee lacked interest in his job. (Black Clawson Co., 64 LA 175)

Right to Trial Period

Are employees who bid on new jobs entitled to a trial or training period in which to learn the job? Some arbiters have ruled that employees must be given a reasonable opportunity, under adequate supervision, to learn how to perform the work; while others have held that an employee should be removed from the position if he or she cannot "grasp" the mechanics of the job.

EXAMPLE: A senior applicant for a higher-rated job was entitled to a trial period on the job, an arbiter ruled, where the contract stated that a senior bidder for a job shall be given an opportunity to demonstrate with "normal supervisory instructions" his qualifications to perform the job. While the employee may not have been entitled to a training period under the contract, the arbiter concluded that "normal supervisory instructions" could not be interpreted to require that the senior applicant be able, ready and willing to take over, without training or indoctrination, and fulfill all his job duties with the usual and normal supervision required by employees who have long since adjusted to a routine performance. (John Deere Chemical Co., 42 LA 443; see also 73 LA 1218, 72 LA 1238, 71 LA 1171, 71 LA 733)

On the other hand, a trial period was properly denied in a case where the employer hired an outsider for a particular job, after rejecting all in-house candidates. The union argued that candidates should have been given a 30-day trial period before being rejected, but the arbiter noted that the contractual requirement of a trial period extended only to those actually hired or promoted to new positions, and not to candidates for those positions. (Semling-Menke Co., 62 LA 1184; see also 73 LA 937, 73 LA 935, 73 LA 20, 71 LA 479)

Bases for Promotion

IN BRIEF

The right of management to promote employees is frequently qualified by seniority provisions in a labor contract. While unions tend to overemphasize seniority and forget merit and ability as the basis for promotion, management oftentimes emphasizes a supervisor's personal judgment of merit and ability and places less emphasis on a worker's seniority.

Arbiters have frequently held that, where the agreement makes "fitness and ability" a factor to be considered along with seniority, but is silent as to how and by whom the determination of qualifications is to be made, management is entitled to make the initial determination, subject to challenge by the union on the ground that management's decision was unreasonable under the facts, or capricious, arbitrary, or discriminatory. (98 LA 26, 97 LA 86, 97 LA 41, 96 LA 338, 96 LA 100, 95 LA 206, 94 LA 905, 94 LA 435, 93 LA 660, 93 LA 589, 91 LA 48, 90 LA 509, 85 LA 721, 85 LA 365, 84 LA 463, 84 LA 423, 83 LA 960, 82 LA 717, 56 LA 40, 56 LA 6, 52 LA 889, 52 LA 247) This right to determine ability may be held by management either as a residual management right or as a necessary adjunct to the right to manage the plant and direct the working force. (52 LA 889, 40 LA 697, 38 LA 132)

POINTERS —

▶ Arbiters usually let management's judgment stand in the selection of workers for promotion, unless it can be shown that the company ignored the terms of the contract or acted in an arbitrary manner.

▶ In making promotions to supervisory positions, the company normally has a free hand.

▶ If no present employee is qualified to perform a vacant job, the company ordinarily has the right to hire on the outside.

GUIDELINES

Determining Qualifications

Management, arbiters have held, has the right to judge, weigh, and determine the necessary qualifications of the respective applicants so long as the methods used are fair and nondiscriminatory. (Lockheed Aircraft Corp., 25 LA 748; see also 75 LA 2, 75 LA 494, 74 LA 1023, 74 LA 811, 73 LA 632) The qualifications compared must relate directly to the requirements of the job in question. (Pittsburgh Steel Co., 21 LA 565).

FACTORS FOR PROMOTION

Seniority as Crucial Factor

Where primary emphasis is put on seniority in determining promotion rights, arbiters have held that a better-qualified employee may not be given precedence over a senior employee capable of doing the work. To pass over a senior employee,

BASES FOR PROMOTION

an employer must be able to show that the employee is not capable of doing the job. If seniority is controlling, the company cannot ignore seniority and promote the "most-qualified" or "best-qualified" (97 LA 968, 96 LA 976, 96 LA 670, 90 LA 1020, 90 LA 243, 85 LA 885, 82 LA 426, 74 LA 788, 64 LA 146, 72 LA 693, 41 LA 353, 25 LA 631, 30 LA 460).

EXAMPLE: An employer was not allowed to promote a Grade C electrician to a Grade B vacancy for which a Senior Grade B man was available, despite the employer's contention that the senior man took an unreasonably long time to perform some of his tasks and sometimes wasted his time.

The arbiter said that the senior employee was reasonably capable of performing the higher-rated work, even though he was deficient in some of the qualifications that would make him an employee of the highest caliber. (American Monorail Co., 21 LA 589)

However, where contracts require promotion by seniority if "merit and ability are approximately equal," arbiters will consider those other relevant factors (also, see below under specific categories). (96 LA 338, 94 LA 562, 94 LA 266, 90 LA 562, 89 LA 1288, 89 LA 1035, 88 LA 420, 86 LA 111, 85 LA 393)

Burden of Proof

Where seniority is a determining factor only when ability is relatively equal, arbiters have held that management has the burden of proving, when challenged, that it determined ability correctly, not merely that it did not act in an arbitrary, capricious, or discriminatory fashion. It must be shown that the selection was "reasonable," as well as free from arbitrariness, favoritism or bias. (44 LA 283, 42 LA 1093)

EXAMPLE: One arbiter ruled that the employer's burden of proof extended to showing that: (1) the standards for comparison of job bidders' qualifications were established in good faith, (2) the standards were not patently inadequate, (3) the standards were applied fairly and impartially, and (4) a decision favoring a junior employee was not clearly unreasonable. (Atlas Powder Co., 30 LA 674)

Experience as a Factor

Experience has a definite place in determining comparative fitness, ability, and qualifications. And the experience factor need not be limited to prior experience of the job in question. Arbitrators have upheld giving preference to a junior employee where the experience of the junior employee is more closely related to the work involved than the experience of the senior employee. (93 LA 233, 84 LA 23, 83 LA 960, 83 LA 317, 82 LA 1247, 82 LA 366, 82 LA 235, 81 LA 575, 50 LA 283, 30 LA 237, 21 LA 565)

EXAMPLE: Under a contract providing that seniority would govern provided qualifications were equal, an employer was justified in promoting a junior employee with two years experience in the particular field over a senior employee with only 10 days experience, an arbiter ruled. The union did not attempt to argue that the senior employee was as qualified as the junior one, but relied on a clause providing that seniority would govern if the senior employee could perform the job. However, even under this clause, the arbiter concluded that it was doubtful that the senior employee could have qualified for the job within 10 days, since this was only as long as the traditional trial period for new jobs at the plant. (Greif Brothers Corp., 64 LA 1219)

EXAMPLE: Under a contract making seniority controlling in promotion where ability to perform the work and physical fitness are relatively equal, one arbiter said that proved ability, not potential ability, was the test for selection. Even if potential ability is about the same between two bidders, he held, management can promote the junior man if he alone can step in and take over the job immediately.

In this case, two jobs had opened up in a plant and the company posted notices of the vacancies in accordance with its general policy. The company made promotions on the basis of (a) ability to perform work, (b) physical fitness, and (c) seniority where the first two factors were equal. The company assigned two junior employees to fill the vacancy of weighman, truck sales, bypassing several applicants having greater seniority.

The arbiter ruled for the company. He pointed out that under the ability clause the company had the right to select the junior employee with demonstrated ability, as proved by experience on the job, rather than one who had never actually performed the job and had never demonstrated the particular skills which the job called for. (Pittsburgh Limestone Corp., 6 LA 648; see also 50 LA 445)

However, under a contract requiring that a vacancy be filled by the employee with most seniority where skill and ability are equal, the employer was not justified in promoting an employee with less seniority, even though he had experience in the other departments. The arbiter reasoned that this experience was fully balanced by the senior bidder's higher educational accomplishments. (Lockheed-Georgia Co., 49 LA 603; see also 72 LA 1167)

Similarly, where the contract called for promotions to be awarded to "qualified senior employees," an employer improperly failed to promote the most senior employee, an arbiter ruled. Management argued that the senior employee did not meet her supervisor's requirements. However, the arbiter noted that the evidence showed that the supervisor had told all four promotion candidates that they would "do quite well," and that he "wished he could employ all four," but had only one vacancy. (Clinch Valley Clinic Hospital, 64 LA 542; see also 75 LA 1024, 74 LA 266)

Aptitude as a Factor

Under a contract making seniority and aptitude factors in promotion, an arbiter held that a company could not refuse a senior employee a promotion on the ground that he was not able to perform the job at the time. Choosing a junior man for the promotion was not justified even if he was the only one able to perform the job, the arbiter said. There was no reason to think the senior men could not have learned it. "Aptitude," the arbiter said, means the potential to learn a job, and the bidder with the highest seniority should have been given a trial period to determine whether he had the aptitude. (Vulcan Mold & Iron CO., 29 LA 743)

Education as a Factor

Arbiters generally agree that employers may consider an employee's education when deciding whether or not to promote the worker. (96 LA 201, 94 LA 463, 88 LA 1035, 86 LA 943, 82 LA 851, 81 LA 594, 75 LA 1298, 75 LA 420, 74 LA 1248, 72 LA 1167, 72 LA 941, 72 LA 666)

EXAMPLE: An arbiter held that under a contract that provided that where skill, work record, and ability of bidders are equal in the judgment of the employer, seniority shall prevail, an employer properly awarded a posted job of plant engineer to a junior employee who had performed the duties of the job for eight months to one year prior to the job posting and had B.A. and M.A. degrees, instead of awarding the job to a senior employee who had never performed the job duties. (South Central Rural Telephone Cooperative Corp., 81 LA 594)

Determining "Ability"

Arbitrators differ on the problem of what factors can be taken into consideration in determining "ability" to do a job. Thus, one arbiter has expressed the view that management must confine its determination to whether the worker is capable of handling the job at hand; how he gets along with other people, his attendance record, and other considerations do not count. (McQuay-Norris Mfg. Co., 1 LA 305)

Some arbiters, though, are inclined to give management more latitude.

EXAMPLE: One arbiter upheld the company's rejection of a union steward for promotion. The contract gave man-

BASES FOR PROMOTION

agement a free hand in judging the ability and qualifications of workers; as long as it honestly believed another man could do the job better, the arbiter rule, its judgment could not be upset. Taking note of quarrels between the steward and management representatives, the arbiter saw no evidence of anti-union discrimination since the quarrels had no direct connection with union business. (Norwich Pharmacal Co. 30 LA 740; see also 98 LA 134, 98 LA 117, 85 LA 721, 73 LA 1215, 72 LA 752)

If a contract requires that both seniority and individual ability be taken into account in making promotions, arbiters usually will not substitute their own judgment of employees' ability for management's. Most of them seem to try to strike a balance between management's right to judge ability and workers' seniority rights. Generally they uphold the company's judgment unless it is found to be discriminatory, arbitrary or erroneous. They rule that it is the union's responsibility to prove that management's judgment was faulty.

EXAMPLE: One arbiter upheld the company's choosing of a junior applicant due to his superior overall job experience. The contract did not indicate the order of importance of the three factors — seniority, ability, and previous experience — in job assignment, thus he overruled the union's contention that these criteria are in descending order of importance. (Reliance Universal Inc., 50 LA 397)

Similarly, another contract required the employer to recognize seniority as a determining factor in promotion only if "consistent with the ability to perform the required work." In this case, the employer first promoted, but then terminated the trial periods of senior employees who, it argued, were clearly not qualified. The employees took nine days to complete a four-day electrical wiring job, then caused the flooding of a basement floor through negligence and finally connected a ground wire to a live circuit, the employer maintained.

Despite the union's argument that the employer improperly assigned the employees to work with other trainees instead of with experienced electricians, the arbiter upheld management's decision. The union's proposal was self-defeating since the contract required that job applicants have a minimum of one year's experience in the field, the arbiter reasoned, agreeing with management that the trial period clearly demonstrated the employees' incompetence. (ICI United States Inc., 65 LA 869; see also 74 LA 962)

However, where it is shown that two workers have relatively equal ability to handle a job, the senior man should not be passed over merely because a supervisor has an impression that the junior worker is better qualified, according to one arbitration panel. (Shell Oil Co., 4 LA 13)

Probationer v. Senior Worker

Even where seniority was only a secondary factor, one arbiter ruled that management could not promote a probationer who had better qualifications. The contract stated that in selecting workers for promotion, three factors would be considered — seniority, ability, and physical fitness: Where the last two factors were relatively equal, seniority would govern.

The company had no authority to promote the probationary worker, the arbiter said, even though he was the best qualified of the bidding employees. The reason was that he had no seniority, and in the arbiter's opinion the agreement required that a man possess all three promotion elements in some degree to be considered for promotion. As long as workers with seniority had bid for the job, the arbiter concluded, the probationer was not eligible. (Borden Chemical Co., 32 LA 697)

Selection for Training Leading to Promotion

If a contract provides that promotion will be based on seniority where ability is equal, can management choose a junior employee for special training leading to a promotion? One arbiter ruled that without a clear understanding with the union beforehand a company had to follow seniority in selecting workers for training that would lead to promotion.

EXAMPLE: A company decided to give special training in inspection procedures. Although it admitted that the ability of two candidates for the training was equal, the junior employee of the two was picked. After completing the course, she was assigned to a newly created higher-rated job. When the senior employee protested, the company consulted with the union and agreed to give the senior employee the special training. However, after finishing the course she was denied the disputed job on the ground that its requirements had changed in the interim.

The arbiter maintained that in this case the company was under an obligation to show the union at the outset that it genuinely needed flexibility in developing the new job and was not trying to bypass seniority rules. Since management failed to do this and let the matter drift, the arbiter ordered the company to pay the senior employee the earnings she lost by not being selected initially for the special training. (Purolator Products Inc., 25 LA 60)

EXAMPLE: In another case, an arbiter held that requiring a high school education or its equivalent was a reasonable requirement for promotional training, but that a 30-year age cutoff for bidders was too low. The educational requirement was sustained because it related to the need for mathematical ability on the job. Because the contract referred to age 65 as requirement age, the arbiter said that workers completing the training course could have enough years of useful work left to repay the employer's investment, even if the workers were older than 30. (Ball Bros. Co., 46 LA 1153)

Promotion of Union Official

Can an otherwise qualified union representative be denied promotion on the ground that the time he spends on union affairs during working hours limits his ability to do the job? Unless past practice has been to restrict the promotion of union officials engaged in their duties during the working day, a company cannot deny promotion to an employee who is otherwise qualified on the basis of his seniority and ability, one arbitration board said.

EXAMPLE: Two employees at a company were promoted to leadman jobs ahead of a union steward who had more seniority and more than enough ability to do the work. The company justified its action in bypassing the steward by saying that although he was qualified for the job in every respect, he spent too much time on union business to be able to do the leadman's job satisfactorily.

A board of arbitration decided that only the presence of an established past practice limiting the promotion of union representatives could justify the bypassing of the union steward. They found no such practice at the company and accordingly decided that the steward should have received the promotion. (Douglas Aricraft Co. Inc., 23 LA 786)

Similarly, when a worker who had shown her ability to perform a job was denied the position because she could not devote full time to it due to her union duties, an arbiter said the company had unfairly discriminated against the union. He further said that if workers "find that their union positions are handicaps in obtaining preferred job assignments, it will become practically impossible for the union to attract the leadership it needs to carry on its work." (American Lava Corp., 42 LA 117; see also 72 LA 1151)

Compulsory Promotion

Must an employee accept a promotion to a vacancy for which he is eligible against his own wishes? Under one contract stating that a promotion shall be given to the senior eligible employee in the department, an arbiter held that all this required was that the company offer the vacant job to the senior employee. He was not obligated to accept it, and if he turned it down, the arbiter ruled, it should have been offered to the next senior qualified worker. (Electro Metallurgical Co., 20 LA 281)

However, another arbiter decided that if the right to waive a promotion is not spelled out in the contract, management normally has the right to make promotions regardless of employee desires. This is true, he noted, provided the employees' job security and seniority are not jeopardized. (Gisholt Machine Co., 23 LA 105)

PROMOTION TO SUPERVISORY POSITION

Management's Right to Select Supervisors

Most arbiters agree that management has the exclusive right to select its supervisors without union interference. They limit the application of contract clauses dealing with promotion to those jobs covered by the union contract or that fall within the bargaining unit. And they specifically point out that since supervisory positions are not within the bargaining unit management has the sole and exclusive right to fill them as it sees fit. (52 LA 1183, 52 LA 463, 40 LA 321, 6 LA 16)

Moreover, when management ignores seniority to promote a highly qualified employee to a supervisory position over a more senior, but unqualified employee, it can expect the arbiter to rule in its favor, absent any explicit contract language which would give the union valid grounds for complaint. (SCM Corp., 58 LA 688)

However, when the contract does contain explicit language governing promotion to supervisory positons, management is more open to challenge from the union.

EXAMPLE: One such contract provided that the employer "will normally promote its own men in accordance with seniority and qualifications to supervisory positions." When the employer selected for promotion the most junior employee out of 45 applicants, while passing over two long-term employees with supervisory experience, the union protested, and the arbiter ruled against the employer.

The arbiter rejected management's argument that the junior employee's "ambition" was so great a qualification that it compensated for his extremely short length of service. Furthermore, the arbiter found little evidence to support management's claim that the employee had sufficient "drive" for the job and that more senior employees lacked this "drive." (British Overseas Airways Corp., 52 LA 165)

Retention of Duties After Promotion to Supervisor

Is an employer permitted to have a worker who is made a supervisor perform the same work he did while in the bargaining unit? One arbiter ruled that since a worker's duties while in the unit were largely supervisory in nature, an employer could assign him the same work after he became a supervisor. Because his duties were largely supervisory, the arbiter found no merit in the union's argument that work was being taken from the bargaining unit. He said that the union should have objected earlier when the worker was assigned the duties while still in the bargaining unit, not when he became a supervisor. (Chrysler Corp. 23 LA 247)

Similarly, an arbiter approved management's transfer of some of an employee's old duties from the bargaining unit to his new job as a supervisor. The arbiter found that the duties the employee carried with him to his new job were supervisory in nature, and that those functions not supervisory in nature had in fact been transferred to other employees remaining in the bargaining unit. (Crown Zellerbach Corp., 52 LA 1183)

PROMOTION VS. NEW HIRE

Passing Over Qualified Bidder

Unless the contract shows an intent to give employees preference over outsiders, one arbiter has held that management is not required to promote from within.

EXAMPLE: One union filed a protest when management hired an outsider to fill a designing job. A draftsman already working for the company wanted the job, and the union claimed he had the necessary ability. Since the contract stated that promotions were to be based on seniority and ability, the union argued, the inside man was entitled to be promoted.

There was some disagreement as to the adequacy of the draftsman's qualifications, but the arbiter said this aspect of the case was irrelevant in any event. The important thing, he held, was that the contract placed no restriction on outside hiring. All it did was outlined the procedure to be followed if the company decided to fill a job through promotion. If the parties had intended to give present employees preference over outsiders, the arbiter concluded, they should have said so in the agreement. (Chrysler Corp., 32 LA 988; see also 85 LA 190, 85 LA 73, 84 LA 956, 84 LA 952, 72 LA 719)

However, where a contract required consideration of unit employees on the basis of seniority and qualifications, an employer could not hire outside where several unit bidders were qualified to fill a vacancy. The arbiter reasoned that the posting provision would be meaningless if the employer could hire from the outside or promote from within as it pleased, rejecting qualified unit applicants. (The Burdick Corp., 49 LA 69)

Likewise, a city violated its recognition clause, an arbiter ruled, when its department of public works hired new employees instead of promoting from within to fill new street-sweeper machine-operator positions. The arbiter reasoned that when the city hired the new employees, they became part of the bargaining unit, and hence subject to past practice. In this case, the past practice that had developed in the department's promotional training program dictated that new sweeper operator's jobs should go to certified operators with the greatest seniority. Thus, although the actual hirings may have been proper, the placement of new hires in the operator's jobs was not, the arbiter concluded. (City of Milwaukee, 65 LA 833; see also 75 LA 511, 73 LA 1218)

Hiring from Outside When Bidders Lack Ability

If a contract requires the company to fill vacancies on the basis of seniority, assuming capacity to perform the work, can a worker be hired from the outside to fill a job? Most arbiters rule that under such a provision an employer can hire from the outside to fill a vacancy when no present employee is capable of performing the job.

EXAMPLE: To fill a vacancy on a maintenance job a company posted notice of the vacancy for bids. Of the twelve employees that bid, eleven agreed that they lacked the qualifications for the job; the twelfth was noncommittal and failed to press his claim. Under these conditions the company hired a new employee to fill the vacancy. The union opposed this action arguing that one of the bidders should have been given a trial period on the job.

The company replied that it had always been its policy to bring in men from the bottom and train them and then upgrade them to top skills rather than bring new men in at the top. But in this case, the company pointed out, there was no one available to upgrade who would be able to handle the job and in such an exceptional case it was necessary to resort to outside hiring.

The arbitration board ruled that "the circumstances warranted the company, in this case, from all the evidence, in departing from its usual and commendable procedure of upgrading and giving full opportunity to men within its own plant." The board found that since the bidders were not qualified for the job the company was justified in filling the job by new hire. (Atlantic Foundry Co., 8 LA 807; see also 96 LA 1105, 82 LA 1273, 40 LA 403, 31 LA 267)

Similarly, an arbiter upheld an employer's outside hiring when none of the four in-house bidders for a millwright's position could attest to their qualifications when asked to do so. The union argued that senior employees were to be given preference for all job openings provided they could learn to perform work within a reasonable period of time. However, the employer had proved his need for a millwright who could immediately perform complex duties, the arbiter noted, pointing out that none of the in-house bidders would have been proficient even after several months. (Kerns Desoto Inc., 64 LA 1125)

Moreover, when an employer's determination that in-house candidates are unqualified to fill a vacancy is made in good faith, he may not even be required to interview them for the position, an arbiter has ruled. (Walker Mfg. Co., 62 LA 1283)

Hiring Outside Applicant With More Training

Under a contract requiring that promotions be based on length of service, training, and efficiency, one arbiter ruled that previous training could not be a requirement for promotion to an apprentice job. He said that a company could not hire a new man in preference to a senior employee merely because the senior worker had not graduated from a vocational school.

EXAMPLE: One company selected an outside applicant for an apprenticeship instead of promoting an employee to it. After deciding that the apprenticeship itself was a training program, an arbitrator awarded the vacancy to the untrained employee instead of to the outsider who had completed a vocational training program. To deny an employee the opportunity to enter the apprenticeship program, the arbiter said, would nullify the purpose of the program. According to the arbiter, the selection of an apprentice should be made on the basis of length of service and efficiency, without regard to the training factor. The company, he said, could not have both an apprenticeship program and a requirement that applicants have prior training. (Hershey Estates, 23 LA 101)

How Ability Is Measured

IN BRIEF

In the absence of a contract provision for the method to be used or the factors to be considered in determining ability, management has been permitted or required to use a variety of methods and to consider a number of factors, including, in proper circumstances: use of written, oral, performance or aptitude tests; trial period on the job; reliance upon a merit rating plan or on the opinion of a supervisor; consideration of production records, disciplinary record or absenteeism, education, experience, physical fitness, age, potentiality for further advancement, etc. Arbiters have held that management is entitled to use any method to determine ability, as long as the method used is fair and nondiscriminatory. (93 LA 874, 93 LA 961, 90 LA 1103, 87 LA 758, 53 LA 746, 49 LA 589, 45 LA 267)

Any test used to screen applicants for a job should be designed to measure qualities that have been shown to be related to performance on that job. For example, a test designed to measure mathematical aptitude should not be used on applicants for a clerk-typist job that requires little or no work with figures. The use of tests that are not validated for job-relatedness not only is wasteful; it may be regarded as a violation of the fair employment practice laws if the result is to screen out minority-group members who lack the education or background needed to pass the tests.

GUIDELINES

Written Test as a Measure of Ability

Whether or not an arbiter approves the use of a written test to determine workers' ability in making promotions seems to depend largely on the weight the contract gives to seniority in filling vacancies.

If a contract makes seniority the governing factor when fitness and ability are equal, many arbiters allow the company to require employee candidates to take written tests. Under this kind of clause the company has to measure the relative or comparative ability of candidates for a job, and an objective written test is a fair way to do this, these arbiters hold. (M. A. Hanna Co., 25 LA 480; see also 97 LA 244, 97 LA 86, 96 LA 17, 93 LA 874, 93 LA 660, 93 LA 223, 75 LA 655, 72 LA 1307, 72 LA 434, 71 LA 116)

A frequently expressed view is that an employer may use tests to assist in deciding whether an applicant meets the job requirements but that the test results may not be relied on to the exclusion of other considerations. (29 LA 262, 29 LA 29)

EXAMPLE: An employer could use two aptitude tests in judging an employee's qualification for a job, even though the tests were never used in the past and the contract did not expressly permit them. The employer promised that the tests would not be used to pass or fail an applicant, but only as additional criteria in judging an employee's qualification; and despite the employer's decision re-

HOW ABILITY IS MEASURED

garding the applicant, he would have the right to redress under the grievance procedure. (Union Carbon Co., 49 LA 465; see also 47 LA 552)

EXAMPLE: One arbiter said an employer could use such a test, if it were fairly applied and management did not use minute differences in scores to deny promotion to senior workers. (Stauffer Chemical Co. Inc., 8 LA 278; see also 41 LA 902, 49 LA 589)

On the other hand, if a contract states that all vacancies shall be filled by the senior applicant provided he has the ability and physical fitness to perform the job, an arbiter may rule against the use of a test.

EXAMPLE: One arbiter held that this kind of clause did not permit the company to promote a worker because he was better qualified for the job than workers with more seniority. He said that since the senior worker had to be given the job if he could do the work satisfactorily, the company could not base promotion on the results of a written test. (Marquette Cement Mfg. Co., 25 LA 127; see also 41 LA 856)

Arbiters generally uphold management's right to use tests that have been specifically designed to determine an employee's ability to perform a certain job. However, they also hold that aptitude tests, not directly related to the work in question properly should be used by management only in the selection of new employees, in counseling employees, or in other general uses. But such general tests should not be used as a standard for denying a senior employee a promotion. (52 LA 633, 43 LA 1184, 34 LA 46, 41 LA 1025, 31 LA 1002)

EXAMPLE: In a ruling against the use of a general aptitude test for promotions, one arbiter said that "men were denied promotions not for lack of ability to perform the work but for lack of ability to pass written tests having little or no relationship to the jobs sought." It is quite conceivable, he said, that the company's best bricklayer could not pass a written test on bricklaying. He gave these ground rules:

• If a job does not require the ability to read and write, no written test whatsoever may be given.

• If a job requires ability to read and to copy words and figures, a written test must be limited to testing ability to read and copy words and figures.

• If it requires simple arithmetic, the test must be only of simple arithmetic. (34 LA 37)

Further, an arbiter held that an employer improperly imposed testing requirements on two candidates for reclassification to master mechanic, where they had spent the required time in lower classifications and stated that they met other agreed-upon qualifications, and, moreover, neither had been disciplined on a matter of competency, and the employer's past practice had been to presume the competency of otherwise-qualified candidates absent such discipline. (Palm Iron & Bridge Works, 97 LA 681)

Number of Required Tests

How many tests should an employee be required to take while being considered for a promotion?

After a senior employee obtained a low qualifying score on a state-sponsored aptitude test, the employer gave him the company's exam as well. The union charged that the employer was not determining qualifications in a "uniform manner," and that since specific pass and fail grades were not released by the state, the employee should have been awarded the job as the senior man.

However, the arbiter upheld management's second test for the employee. Since the state test was deficient as a selection criterion, and since the company test was directly related to the requirements of the job, it was proper for management to act as it did, the arbitrator ruled. (International Steel Co., 64 LA 1093)

Refusal to Administer Test

When a written test is properly used to screen job bidders, may an employer refuse to administer the test to employees who have failed it in the past? One arbitrator has ruled no.

EXAMPLE: An employer refused to administer a test to a job bidder for a newly created position because the applicant had failed the test when it was given as a requirement for other promotions. Management argued that allowing the employee to re-take the identical test whenever new job postings were made would enable the employee to pass the test because of his familiarity with the questions rather than because of increased knowledge gained through experience or education.

However, the arbiter reasoned that the tests were not given to ascertain an applicant's knowledge of the subjects upon which he is being tested, but rather to determine his aptitude to learn. Therefore, the arbiter concluded, all employees who bid on jobs which require them to pass tests should have the opportunity to take the required tests after they have signed bids and before the jobs are awarded. (Dayton-Walther Corp., 65 LA 529)

Testing and EEOC

While arbiters may be more inclined to permit the use of general aptitude tests for new hires, EEOC looks with equal disfavor on the use of such tests for hiring and for promotions. In either case, EEOC has said (with Supreme Court approval) use of the test may be justified only if it can be shown that success on the test is correlated, statistically with success on the job.

Oral Exam to Determine Qualifications

In a situation where the contract does not specify any method to be used to determine employees' qualifications for promotion, one arbiter has said that a company has the right to use any method it sees fit, including oral examinations. But the test should be related to the skill and knowledge required for the job and otherwise not be unfair or unreasonable.

EXAMPLE: A contract required the company to consider for promotion only those employees "who are deemed qualified to do the work." When a job opening occurred in the top classification in one department, one employee in the department was given an oral test by the foreman to determine whether he was qualified for the job. He failed to pass the exam and was denied the job. The union took the matter up as a grievance, arguing that the test was unfair because there was no prescribed standard exam and no written job description on which the test could be based.

The arbiter upheld the company's action. Since the contract did not specify a particular method for determining whether a worker was qualified for promotion, he said that it was okay to use an oral exam. Furthermore, he found that the test was a fair one, partly because all workers then in the job had previously passed the same test. (Hammarlund Mfg. Co. Inc., 19 LA 653)

Physical Test to Determine Ability

Because arbiters are more likely to uphold the use of the tests which are clearly reflective of the work to be performed than tests which have little relation to the job, physical tests may be easier to defend as a basis for determining ability in manual jobs.

EXAMPLE: An employer denied a black female employee a promotion after she failed the physical exam for the job. The union argued that the company violated the contract which called for promotions to be based on "ability, physical fitness and continuous service."

However, the arbiter upheld management's action. The employee was properly denied the promotion, the arbitrator said, because she failed to meet the requirements of the job — i.e., passing the physical exam. Since there was no evidence that the exam reflected racial or sexual discrimination on the employer's

HOW ABILITY IS MEASURED

part, the grievance was dismissed (United States Steel Corp., 65 LA 626; see also 96 LA 1033, 76 LA 432, 75 LA 148)

Merit Rating & Efficiency Rating as Measures of Ability

Some arbiters have upheld management's right to use the results of a formal merit rating plan in selecting employees for promotion.

EXAMPLE: Under a contract requiring the promotion of the senior worker where ability was relatively equal, one arbiter said that one company's merit-rating plan was an acceptable method of measuring relative ability. (Acme Steel Co., 9 LA 432)

Aptitude Test as Prerequisite to Trial Period

Is a company justified in requiring bidders for better jobs to pass aptitude tests before being given a tryout on the job? Where training workers for better jobs is an expensive process, arbiters are likely to uphold the use of tests to screen out applicants who cannot show the aptitude that would warrant the expense of a tryout, even though as senior employees, they would have first bid for the jobs. But the tests should be objective and should measure, as far as possible, the aptitude for the jobs involved. (United Rayon Mills, 14 LA 241; see also 90 LA 1282)

On the other hand, where a contract specifically provided for a trial period, an arbiter ruled that the company had no right to turn down the senior bidder for a job simply because she had failed a mathematical test. (National Seal Co., 29 LA 29)

Similarly, an employer was overruled when he sought to administer a mechanical-aptitude test to the senior employee before granting him a promotion under a contract clause awarding promotions on the basis of seniority. The employer unsuccessfully argued that the test was proper in light of the employee's lack of experience at the new job. The arbiter voided the test requirement and awarded the job to the employee subject to his successful completion of a reasonable trial period. (Monarch Tool Co., 65 LA 150)

Likewise, an employer was held to have violated the contract when it promoted a junior employee to a new position of electrical trainee on the ground that he was the only applicant who passed a written test showing extent of electrical knowledge. The arbiter ruled that the test used was not a fair measure of ability to perform the job since the position was created to give employees a chance to develop electrical skills. (Vulcan Materials Co., 49 LA 577; see also 49 LA 1160)

However, another arbiter approved management's use of a test to select candidates for an electrical training program. The arbiter found the test a valid reflector of probable success in the training program, and noted that the contract left management free to determine qualifications for the program. The selected worker was junior to a passed-over applicant, but since the contract did not specifically make seniority a factor, this was irrelevant, the arbiter added. (International Steel Co., 64 LA 1093)

Likewise, an employer did not violate a contract when it administered an aptitude test to applicants for a training program, another arbiter ruled, emphasizing that the test would screen out those who had little likelihood of learning the complex skills taught in the program. The arbiter concluded that the test was fair and reasonable, administered without discrimination, and validated to meet government requirements. (Celanese Piping Systems Inc., 64 LA 462)

Trial Period To Test Ability

When is a senior worker entitled to a chance to prove himself on a job for which he is bidding? Arbitrator's awards suggest that a trial period may be in order, in appropriate circumstances, under two common types of promotion clauses.

The first is a provision that makes seniority determining in promotions if the senior bidder is able to perform the work.

EXAMPLE: Under one contract providing that seniority should govern in promotions if the senior worker "has the competency for the job," an arbiter held that a senior worker should have been given a breaking-in period to prove he was able to do the job. The company had passed over the senior man and promoted a more competent junior worker who was able to do the job without a breaking-in period because of his past experience. This was immaterial, the arbiter said. He pointed out that the contract required the company to promote the most senior applicant who was competent, not the most competent applicant. Thus, the senior worker should be given a trial period to prove whether he could perform the job, the arbiter ruled. (Beaunit Mills Inc., 16 LA 667)

The second type of promotion clause is one which makes seniority controlling where ability is relatively equal. When a company has no objective measure of relative ability under such a provision, some arbiters say that a trial period is the best way to clear up any doubts about the ability of the senior bidder.

EXAMPLE: In one case, when a hoist-operation job opened up, the supervisor gave it to a worker in preference to an older man with more seniority. His reason was that he felt the latter worker was too old to handle the job. An arbiter pointed out that this worker was strong and rugged and his supervisor's doubt as to his ability did not justify bypassing him for promotion. Since the supervisor's decision was based on such a weak assumption the arbiter said the worker should be given a chance to prove his ability on the job. He concluded that although a trial was not necessary in all cases it should not be denied where there was a reasonable doubt of ability and where it would cause no serious inconvenience. (Ford Motor Co., 2 LA 374)

Trial Period v. Training Period

If a contract provides a trial period for promoted workers and makes seniority a factor in promotion, must management give the senior applicant for a job a trial period even though he is not qualified for the job?

According to one arbiter, there is a big difference between a *trial* period and a *training* period. A trial period must be granted only after a worker has been selected for promotion, he said, and this rules out those who do not have the necessary qualifications.

EXAMPLE: Besides granting a 12-day trial period to employees who were promoted to higher-rated jobs, one contract said that seniority would be the determining factor in promotion, "all circumstances being reasonably equal." When the company bypassed the senior bidder for a job requiring some special preparation and experience, the union lodged a complaint. It conceded the junior man was qualified and that the senior man was not, but it argued that the latter should have been given an opportunity to prove he could handle the job.

The arbiter disagreed. The contract did not entitle the senior bidder to a period of on-the-job training, he said. Management was essentially correct in arguing that the trial period became available only after an employee had been selected for promotion. However, the arbiter warned, management must be prepared to justify the denial of a trial period to a senior bidder. (Colonial Baking Co., 34 LA 356; see also 39 LA 336, 74 LA 962, 73 LA 937)

Length of Trial Period

How long a period of training should an employee be allowed to show that he can perform a higher-rated job? To a large extent, the answer to this question depends on the job to which the employee is being promoted.

EXAMPLE: In one case, an arbiter held that five weeks was not long enough to provide an adequate measure of an employee's ability as a crane operator and awarded him an additional two weeks. (Lukens Steel Co., 18 LA 41; see also 71 LA 1171)

On the other hand, an arbiter ruled that three months was a reasonable period in which to determine whether an admittedly qualified employee had the proper temperament for the higher-rated job of floor inspector. (Seeger Refrigerator Co., 16 LA 525; see also 75 LA 1101, 73 LA 935)

Moreover, it has been held that if a trial period for promoted employees is established, it should be well defined and applied equally to all employees. (Consolidated Water Co., 23 LA 427)

Past Performance as Measure of Ability

Arbitrators' decisions suggest that a worker's record of on-the-job performance should be regarded as a key indicator of ability.

EXAMPLE: Under one contract providing for job transfers based on seniority where knowledge, training, and ability were substantially equal, an arbiter held that a supervisor's preference could not overrule evidence of a senior worker's on-the-job ability. When two workers bid for a maintenance mechanic job, the junior man was promoted on the basis of the supervisor's judgment of knowledge, training, and ability. The arbiter found that the senior worker had performed the job satisfactorily in the past and this was more objective evidence of ability than the supervisor's opinion. On the ground that their work experience showed that the two men were relatively equal in skill, knowledge, and ability, the arbiter concluded that the senior man should be promoted. (Plymouth Cordage Co., 27 LA 816)

By the same token, failure to make the grade during a previous trial on a job is enough evidence that a worker is not capable of handling the job, according to one arbiter. In such an event, he said, a worker is not entitled to a second trial period. (Republic Steel Corp., 3 LA 761)

Lack of Interest as Measure of Ability

Can a senior worker be bypassed for promotion because he shows lack of interest in his work? Arbitrators have ruled that "lack of interest" cannot be considered in measuring ability, particularly where it seems to be temporary and not consistent with the employee's usual attitude.

EXAMPLE: A contract required that the senior employee be given preference in promotions where abilities were equal. In filling the job of "Job Foreman," the company bypassed a senior employee on the ground that he showed a "lack of interest" in his work. The union filed a grievance arguing that since the abilities of the two men were equal the senior employee should have gotten the job.

The arbiter agreed with the union contention. He ruled "that interest in work or lack of interest in work is a matter of incentive to exercise ability or capacity and is not one of the norms for measuring ability." The arbiter then went on to point out that this lack of interest in the present case was a temporary condition apparently contrary to the worker's customary attitude so far as could be determined from his total job history. Therefore, since abilities were equal, the arbiter held that the senior employee should have been given the promotion. (Ford Motor Co., 7 LA 324)

However, another arbiter upheld management's decision to pass over for promotion a senior worker whose performance in his present job was only marginal, who had been demoted from four other positions, and who had declined to take a job-related test to demonstrate his ability. The arbiter reasoned that since management had a responsibility to determine whether the employee was qualified for the promotion, the union's argument urging him to ignore the employee's past record could not be upheld. (United States Steel Corp., 64 LA 639)

Sex Discrimination in Weighing Ability

Arbitrators generally acknowledge that a female employee has the right to bid on a job traditionally held by male workers. Yet, many arbiters, in determining whether an employee's job classification has been adversely affected because of sex discrimination, have refused to encroach upon management's recognized rights to judge employment qualifications and to determine job content. (67 LA 833, 67 LA 23, 66 LA 180, 66 LA 1276, 62 LA 1294)

EXAMPLE: In one case, an arbitrator ruled that an employer did not discriminate against a senior female clerk-stenographer when it failed to promote her to senior accounting clerk. The job, instead, was awarded to a male applicant in the accounting department who had five years of experience in the accounting field. Finding that the employer properly determined that the qualifications of the two applicants were not "reasonably equal" and that the female employee did not have "sufficient" ability to fill the job, the arbiter held that no discrimination occurred. (Missouri Utilities Co., 68 LA 379)

However, another arbiter held that an employer violated a contractual antidiscrimination clause when it disqualified a female employee because she could not perform the job's required duties. Noting that the employer had engaged in a pattern of sex discrimination that made it impossible for the employee to receive a fair training period, the arbitrator observed that the dispute displayed "classic socio-psychological motives" in terms of male resentment of the "real competition" represented by the female employee. (Braniff Airways Inc., 66 LA 421)

Transfer

IN BRIEF

Collective bargaining agreements seldom provide special procedures applicable to the general subject of permanent transfer. However, sometimes special transfer rights are accorded to handicapped or aged workers.

Temporary transfers present a different situation. In the absence of specific contract language, arbiters usually have upheld the right of management to assign workers to new and different tasks on a temporary basis, provided such transfers do not violate seniority or other contractual rights. An important consideration in such cases often is whether the agreement contains a management clause recognizing the employer's right to direct the work force.

A transfer may take various forms, including requirements by employers that employees rotate among jobs within their classification, move from one shift to another, move from one job to another in a different classification at the same level, or move to a new machine or a new location on the same job.

While some agreements make the right to transfer employees subject to other conditions in order to protect employees' seniority or other contractual rights, arbiters generally require that any restrictions placed upon the right to transfer be clearly stated in the agreement. Several arbiters have held that management's right to transfer employees is not contingent on the employees' willingness to be transferred. (73 LA 372, 44 LA 1196, 68 LA 386, 39 LA 1074, 35 LA 162, 28 LA 437, 24 LA 399)

Various justifications have been accepted by arbiters in upholding transfers required by management, including:

▶ Business needs — e.g., reduction in work, technological changes. (94 LA 632, 76 LA 516, 67 LA 702, 66 LA 671, 62 LA 1200)

▶ The employee's presence in a given job creates some undue hazard for him- or herself or other workers. (92 LA 833, 64 LA 24)

▶ A breakdown in machinery makes it necessary to transfer an employee to another job or another machine. (Eagle-Picher Industries Inc., 65 LA 1108)

▶ Incompetence. (62 LA 798, 45 LA 229) or,

▶ Personality clash. (79 LA 203, 69 LA 1138, 67 LA 509, 67 LA 271).

GUIDELINES

PERMANENT TRANSFER

Permanent transfers may be made at the employer's insistence (Small Business Association, 66 LA 1017), the employee's request (67 LA 509, 64 LA 316), or upon the advice of a supervisor. Whether a permanent transfer stems from management's decision or from an employee's request, the procedures involved with respect to measuring the worker's ability to perform the job and to apply seniority rules are similar to those used in cases involving promotions.

Transfer to Another Plant or Locality

EXAMPLE: An arbiter found that an employer violated a contract when it moved a junior employee into another employee's millwright job on a rollerplant "A" crew and transferred the other employee to a vacant leader-shift position on bearing-plant "D" crew without his consent. The contract required that out-of-occupation transfers — i.e., from millwright occupation to leader-shift occupation — be made by reassignment of the most junior employee when such transfers are not needed to fill vacancies not filled by bidding or voluntary transfer. (Timken Co., 97 LA 146; see also 91 LA 1377, 91 LA 181, 90 LA 1252, 89 LA 1101, 89 LA 201, 81 LA 382)

EXAMPLE: An auto manufacturer was not bound to transfer workers from plants where certain models were discontinued to plants which still assembled those models. Because the same type of work was done at both plants, the arbiter said, the "operations" had been transferred. Thus, the employer was not obligated by the contract to transfer the workers, he concluded. (Chrysler Corp., 43 LA 349)

Similarly, an arbiter ruled that the permanent closure of a warehouse did not require the absorption of displaced workers by the parent employer. The arbiter found that since the contract did not include the warehouse workers as part of the "company," the contract's seniority clause, for job-transfer purposes, excluded the warehouse workers. (March Wall Products, 45 LA 551)

Transfer Into and out of Bargaining Unit

EXAMPLE: An arbiter ruled that an employer did not violate a bargaining agreement when it temporarily transferred a bargaining-unit employee to perform non-bargaining-unit work on voluntary basis, since the work in question was not bargaining-unit work. (Delfield Co., 96 LA 448; see also 97 LA 1035, 97 LA 48, 91 LA 181, 90 LA 228, 85 LA 511, 83 LA 458)

Unit Attrition by Transfer

Seniority need not prevent the transfer of a worker whose job performance is not satisfactory while retaining more able junior workers in the same classification, an arbiter ruled. This was done as part of a general movement to streamline a telephone company's desk unit. Because the general policy was aimed at upgrading the unit's performance level, the arbiter felt the employer was justified in considering ability as well as seniority. (Southwestern Bell, 45 LA 229)

Transfer to Job Employee Cannot Handle

Assuming management has an unrestricted right to transfer employees within occupational groups, can an employee complain if he or she is transferred to a job which the employee cannot perform, and then discharged for lack of qualifications?

Arbiters generally agree that where management is given the right to transfer personnel, it must be exercised reasonably. One arbiter, for example, felt that transferring an employee to a job at which she had no prior experience and which she lacked the physical ability to do was unreasonable. The employee, he said, should not have been fired for failure to qualify for the job after a short trial period. (Curtiss-Wright Corp., 11 LA 139)

Transfer for Health Reasons

Can employees be transferred against their wishes for the purpose of protecting their health? In the absence of a specific contract restriction on transfers of this nature, it is likely that an arbiter would uphold management's right to make such transfers where it is apparent that they are made in good faith, are not for discriminatory purposes, and are supported by reasonable medical findings.

EXAMPLE: A company transferred to a lighter (and lower-paying) job an employee who had undergone two operations. It did so on the advice of its plant physician, who said the employee could not safely handle his regularly heavy work. The employee wanted his regular job, however, and produced a note from his own physician saying he could return to work.

The arbiter held the transfer was proper. He declared that "management had an obligation to avoid exposing employees to undue hazards to their health or safety and that this obligation created a right, under a management-rights clause, to transfer an employee if his presence in a given occupation created an undue hazard for himself or others."

The arbiter considered it important that no discriminatory purpose was apparent in this case, that there was no question of bad faith, and finally, that the recommendation of transfer was made by the plant physician, who was more familiar with the types of work involved than the employee's personal doctor. (International Shoe Co., 14 LA 253)

EXAMPLE: A machine operator, who was involved in an accident while operating a ground-controlled crane, was properly removed from the job, an arbiter decided. A test revealed that the employee had zero depth perception, the arbiter observed, pointing out that there was no provision in the contract that barred the employer from requiring relevant physical examinations. Moreover, it was the employer's practice to remove employees from jobs because of medical considerations, the arbiter concluded. (Foster Wheeler Corp., 54 LA 871)

On the other hand, an employee who developed a skin rash, that she claimed had been caused by certain cleaning compounds used in her work, was not entitled to be transferred to other work where she would not come in contact with the compound, an arbiter ruled. Rejecting the contention that the employee was not attempting to exercise special privilege, but was merely attempting to provide the employer with a honest day's work for an honest day's pay in a nonhazardous situation, the arbiter pointed out that there was no contract provision allowing employees to shift around to fit their physical needs. While such shifting may be good business, that is not the same thing as a requirement under the contract, the arbiter concluded. (Eaton Corp., 73 LA 729)

Worker Bumped by Returning Veteran

What are the job rights of a worker who is transferred after the veteran whom he or she replaced returns to work? In the absence of a specific contract provision on the subject, one arbiter decided that an employee transferred to make room for a returning veteran has the same rights as an employee on layoff.

EXAMPLE: When a veteran returned to his old job, the man who had been hired to replace him was transferred to a lower-paying job in another department. Another employee was given the first vacancy that occurred in the veteran's department on the basis of his plant-wide seniority. The union filed a grievance, arguing that the transferred employee had first crack at the job in his old department because of his greater departmental seniority.

The arbiter noted that the contract was silent on the subject of veterans' reemployment rights. Under a draft law, however, an employer simply is required to reinstate a returning veteran, the arbiter pointed out; it can do as it pleases about his replacement. In the arbiter's view, the employer had the option of either continuing operations with a larger-than-normal work force or laying off the replacement. If it took the second alternative, the layoff would be no different from another, the arbiter said. Since the contract in this case specified that departmental seniority would govern layoff and recall, the arbiter concluded that the veteran's replacement was entitled to the job in his old department, just as he would have been had he been laid off. (Mead Corp., 22 LA 292)

Transfer When Union Business Interrupts Work

If a union official is frequently called from the job to tend to union business, can the official be transferred to a job where his or her absences would not interfere with production? One arbiter has said that such a transfer is not discriminatory in itself.

EXAMPLE: A union officer employed as a dispatch clerk was needed on her job regularly because she determined work schedules for other workers. When union business required her to keep interrupting her production work, the employer ordered her to trade jobs with another woman, where ultimately her pay and working conditions were the same as in the clerk's job. The union protested that the transfer violated a contract clause prohibiting discrimination against union members. The employer did not violate the contract's non-discrimination clause, since the transferred officer's new pay and working conditions were the same as before, and, moreover, the new job permitted her to carry out her union business. (Oliver Corp., 15 LA 65)

Limitation on Transfer of Union Officials

Is a provision that shop stewards may not be transferred without their consent limited only to transfers outside of a bargaining unit? One arbiter said that such a provision could not be given such a narrow interpretation.

EXAMPLE: When the chief shop steward at one company was transferred first to the second shift and later to the third, the union protested that the company violated the clause prohibiting transfers of stewards without their consent. The company claimed that the clause referred only to transfers outside the bargaining unit. Upholding the union, the arbiter found that a movement from one shift to another was a transfer within the general meaning of the word. (Midland Rubber Corp., 18 LA 590)

On the other hand, an arbiter ruled that an employer was not required to transfer a worker from the second shift to the first shift just because he was elected chief steward. Although the contract implied that the chief steward should be on the first shift, the arbiter said, it did not say that he must work the first shift or that the company must transfer his work from one shift to another. The company allowed the chief steward to have unlimited access to the plant, the arbiter held, which was all that was required of it. (Chrysler Corp., 42 LA 1018)

As for shifting departments, a worker's right to serve a shop steward in his or her "home" department was not limited by the employer's right to transfer him elsewhere. Thus, a company was forced to recognize a welder as steward for his home department despite the fact that he had been transferred to another department. Since the company's power to assign could have eliminated a desirable union candidate, this right should not be construed to narrow the privilege of selection. Likewise, the right of selection does not bind the company to transfer a worker back to his home department, for the purpose of representation, without prior negotiation. (New York Shipbuilding Corp., 44 LA 924)

Union officials holding superseniority may not be transferred from the units they represent. Superseniority is designed to provide continuity of representation for the units in which the officials are elected, to allow the officials to police the contract in their departments, and to make them readily available to unit members and supervision. (New York Shipbuilding Corp., 43 LA 741)

Shift Transfers

If a contract is silent on the matter, do workers have a right to chose their shifts on the basis of their seniority? Most arbiters feel that, in the absence of a specific contract provision permitting it, workers may not exercise their seniority to transfer to a shift of their choice. One union claimed that senior workers could bump juniors on more desirable shifts. It argued that seniority should be applied to shift transfers as well as governing layoffs, recalls, and demotions under the contract. The arbiter, however, decided nothing in the contract gave senior workers the right to displace juniors on other shifts. (Kuhlman Electric Co., 19 LA 199)

On the other hand, an arbiter decided that an employer violated its contract when it transferred an unwilling, senior paintmaker-helper who worked on the first shift to a position on a newly created second shift. The union had argued that junior employees who previously held the paintmaker-helper classification should have been transferred, instead of the senior employee. Although the employer contended that management had the right to assign employees to shifts and that no employee was guaranteed a daytime job when he was hired, the arbiter, nevertheless, ruled that the company's right to transfer employees from one shift to another was based on the contract's seniority provisions. Since there were other qualified employees who had less seniority than the transferred senior employee, the arbiter concluded that the employer was obligated to transfer the junior employees first. (59 LA 574)

In another case, an arbiter ruled that an employer improperly transferred junior employees during a reduction in the work force, to yard crews that worked the Monday through Friday shift, instead of transferring senior operators and material handlers whose transfer to the yard crews could have enabled them to work their normal schedule days in addition to working and receiving premium pay. (Koppers Company Inc., 67 LA 752)

Lateral Transfers

Seniority entitled a qualified worker to a lateral transfer, regardless of relative ability. So long as the man had the basic ability to perform the job, he was entitled to it over a newly hired man. The fact that he was "efficient" or "badly needed" on his present job should not stand in the way of his transfer.

EXAMPLE: A turret-lathe operator requested a transfer to a new tape-controlled tracer lathe, where the operator's job carried the same rating but offered greater opportunity for promotion. In rejecting the transfer request, the company said the worker was "one of our most efficient operators on assignments that require the full capabilities of trained operators." Under the contract, seniority, skill, and ability were made the determining factors in passing on transfer request.

The contract did not mention "efficiency" as one of the factors to be considered, the arbiter noted. An able employee should not be penalized for his ability by denying his seniority rights. (Steel Products Engineering Co., 47 LA 952)

Further, lateral transfers should not be denied simply because the job does not pay more than the previous one. If it offers a better chance for advancement, it should be considered a "promotion" and follow normal contractual procedures for promotion and lateral transfers. (Picker X-Ray Corp., 42 LA 179)

TEMPORARY TRANSFERS

Temporary v. Permanent Transfer

Since management usually retains an unrestricted right to make temporary transfers to fill short-term gaps in the work force, arbiters frequently are asked to pass on the distinction between "temporary" or "permanent" transfer where the contract contains no definitions. The dividing line often is set at a week or two. (36 LA 767, 23 LA 581)

Where contracts specify the time limit on temporary transfers, a common ceiling is 30 days.

Worker's Right to Refuse Transfer

When a contract does not spell it out, do workers have a right to refuse temporary transfers to other jobs? Where the assignment was to lower-rated work, an arbiter ordered a worker reinstated, holding that management went too far in terminating his employment for refusal to accept a transfer. (Great Atlantic & Pacific Tea Co., 1 LA 63; see also 7 LA 459)

However, another arbiter ruled that an employee must accept a temporary transfer unless the contract specifically spells out his right to refuse it. (Phillips Oil Co., 18 LA 798; see also 73 LA 497)

In a related group of cases, arbiters have upheld employee refusals to accept transfers regarded as "unreasonable." For example, an employer was held to have acted unreasonably in asking glaziers to do temporary work as painters. (3 LA 782)

Temporary Transfer to Higher-Rated Job

Is a worker transferred temporarily to a higher-rated job entitled to the regular pay for that job? If the pay practices for temporary transfers are spelled out in the contract, there is no problem. But at least one arbiter has held that, even when the contract is silent on the matter, management is obligated to pay the rate for a higher job to a man who temporarily fills the job. He reasoned that it is inherent in a classification system that an employee should receive the higher rate if he performs a job in a higher classification. (Tide Water Oil Co., 17 LA 829; see also 63 LA 487)

In-Grade Transfer to Temporary Job

In the absence of contract provisions and any established past practice, can a temporary job be assigned to a worker from another classification rather than to one in the same grade? Reasoning that a case has to be decided on the basis of logic and equity where no other guides are available, one arbitration board ruled that a man in a helper classification has more right to a temporary helper's job than an employee from another classification. They said that fairness dictated that the company give the helper the job since losing it meant a loss of pay. As long as the company failed to show that there was an unreasonable administrative burden involved, the arbiters ruled, the job should have gone to the helper. (National Carbon Co., 23 LA 263)

Voluntary Transfer to Lower-Paying Job

At what wage rate must a worker be paid who is given a choice of taking work on a lower-paying job to avoid layoff or for some other reason? Most companies make clear that where an employee is required (for company convenience) to take a lower-paying job, the employee receives a regular rate for the period; but where an employee voluntarily accepts a lower-paying job, as in a force reduction, the employee receives the rate of that job. Most arbiters have upheld this practice, even where no clear distinction was made between voluntary and required transfers. (76 LA 1017, 76 LA 854, 76 LA 516, 75 LA 682, 66 LA 709, 64 LA 24, 2 LA 119, 1 LA 546)

Part 7

Vacations

Vacation Eligibility

IN BRIEF

There is no inherent right to a vacation, arbiters have ruled. Any vacation rights that an employee may have, arise out of a collective bargaining agreement (66 LA 160, 65 LA 745, 59 LA 1245, 48 LA 965, 44 LA 1045), or evolve out of a well-established employer practice. Arbiters have recognized the twofold nature of the vacation benefit: time off from work and pay. (87 LA 932)

Even though a vacation policy is spelled out in detail in the contract, numerous questions may arise when it comes to determining the rights of individual workers. The most common disputes relate to workers who are not actively at work during the vacation season — e.g., employees on layoff — and those whose employment is terminated prior to their vacation.

Furthermore, employee absences affect vacation eligibility. The types of absences that may be held to break vacation eligibility include:

▶ Layoffs for slack work.
▶ Time lost during a strike.
▶ Time lost after a strike, before return to work.
▶ Time lost because of illness.
▶ Time lost because of occupational injury.
▶ Leaves of absence for union business.
▶ Leaves of absence for personal reasons.
▶ Leaves of absence for "civic" or military reasons.
▶ Chronic absenteeism.

GUIDELINES

Effect of Layoff

If an employee has met all the regular requirements for a vacation, there is little doubt that he is entitled to vacation pay if he is laid off before the vacation season rolls around. The usual practice is to treat vacation rights, once earned, as a vested benefit.

EXAMPLE: Where a contract stated that an employee would be entitled to a paid vacation provided he had a specified amount of service and was "in the employ" of the company on April 15, an arbitrator ruled that the employer was wrong in denying vacation pay to employees who were laid off before April 15 after meeting all the other requirements for a paid vacation. (Botony Mills Inc., 27 LA 1)

Similarly, employees who were laid off because of plant closings late in the year assumed the status of employees on indefinite layoff who would be eligible for vacation pay for vacation earned in the year of layoff, an arbiter decided. Despite a contractual provision that stated that an employee must have been actively employed at some time during the calendar year to be eligible for vacation benefits during "that calendar year," the arbiter ruled that the applicable provision was a clause that entitled employees to vacation if they were laid off for an indefinite time. (Continental Can Co., 76 LA 1212)

However, it may be different story, if the contract says employees must be "on the payroll" as of a certain date. Some, though not all, arbiters have held that when an employee is laid off he ceases to be on the payroll for vacation purposes. (23 LA 298 and 15 LA 13, but see 14 LA 1017 and 13 LA 880)

While a laid-off employee generally is entitled to previously earned vacation-pay rights, it does not follow that the time he spends on layoff will be credited towards meeting the service or work requirements for future vacations. The general rule is that vacation pay "is associated with work and does not accrue during periods of unemployment or layoff unless ... the agreement so provides expressly or by necessary implication." (67 LA 997, 64 LA 791, 64 LA 641, 64 LA 103, 34 LA 170)

Eligibility Based on "Service" & "Employment"

Many contracts base vacation eligibility on a certain amount of "service." Management's reasoning often is that "service" means actual work, and that therefore, layoff time should not be counted in figuring vacation eligibility. On the other hand, workers will argue that their "service" has not been broken while on layoff because "service" is synonymous with "seniority." This latter view has been upheld in arbitration.

EXAMPLE: Under a contract requiring a certain number of "years' service" for vacation eligibility, the company maintained that "service" meant being on the job. Therefore, it argued that a three-week layoff period should be deducted in calculating "service," with the effect that a laid-off worker would not be eligible for a vacation until a year and three weeks had passed. The union's position was that "years of service" was the same as seniority.

The arbiter noted that the contract made seniority dependent on "length of continuous service," and that in this connection "service" never was considered broken by layoffs. Therefore, the union's position was upheld as "the one ordinarily adopted," since the agreement failed to set forth specific work requirements for vacation eligibility. (St. Louis Smelting & Refining Co., 28 LA 219)

Likewise, when a contract bases vacation eligibility on "employment," some arbiters hold, this too is the same as seniority. If a laid-off worker has a right to recall on a seniority basis, then his employment is not generally thought to be ended by layoff, one arbiter noted. Thus, he reasoned, laid-off workers who fulfilled the conditions that qualified them for recall were entitled to have their layoff periods counted as employment in determining vacation credits. (Hanchett Mfg. Co., 28 LA 235)

However, one arbiter ruled that laid-off employees who continued to accumulate seniority were not entitled to vacation benefits under a contract provision entitling employees to vacation as a reward for "satisfactory service," or under a provision granting employees "earned vacation." Emphasizing that the vacation provisions laid down an actual work requirement before an employee became eligible for vacation benefits, the arbiter concluded that the provision pertaining to "earned vacation" negated any automatic accrual of employment benefits during a layoff. (Frye Copysystems Inc., 65 LA 1249)

Similarly, an employee who had several years of service with an employer was not entitled to include her 10 month layoff as part of "length of service" for vacation purposes, an arbiter decided, since there was a long-standing practice of not including layoff as part of length of service. (National Cash Register Co., 64 LA 103)

Effect of Strike

In the absence of contract language requiring a different result, arbiters are unlikely to permit employees to benefit in the accrual of vacation credits during time spent on strike, since vacation bene-

VACATION ELIGIBILITY

fits as deferred wages are part of the pay received for working for an employer. (79 LA 1294, 70 LA 636, 66 LA 745, 53 LA 784, 49 LA 55, 45 LA 512, 42 LA 102)

The effect of strikes on vacation credits rarely is treated in a contract (53 LA 170) and is seldom directly covered in the strike settlement agreement.

Many arbitration cases turn on the question of whether the strike is an "excused absence" depriving or not depriving, depending on the particular contract, employees of vacation credits. (74 LA 1061, 49 LA 113, 49 LA 55, 48 LA 213, 47 LA 319, 42 LA 929, 40 LA 689, 33 LA 638, 27 LA 251)

Other cases have involved contracts basing vacation pay on some qualifying phrase such as "hours worked" or "time worked" (68 LA 447, 38 LA 1236); "years of service" (66 LA 745, 43 LA 1); "continuous service" (63 LA 1235, 53 LA 170, 34 LA 428); "employment" by the company (49 LA 1180, 27 LA 251); being in "the employ" of the company (33 LA 837); or "scheduled working days" (62 LA 415, 47 LA 319, 33 LA 638). Arbiters have interpreted these phrases as the requiring the actual rendering of services for vacation eligibility, and as excluding time spent on strike. Therefore, they distinguish between the bare retention of employment status and the actual performance of services which fulfill the eligibility requirements. (33 LA 837, 22 LA 466, 27 LA 251)

A strike may raise several questions regarding vacation eligibility —

• Are employees who fail to return to work at the end of the strike still entitled to claim vacation benefits?

Since vacation benefits usually are considered an earned right, those who quit during a strike generally are entitled to claim their vacation pay if they have otherwise met the eligibility requirements. Vacation benefits may be denied, however, if strikers who terminate fail to meet notice requirements for resignation.

• Does time spent out on strike count the same as working time in determining service requirements for vacation eligibility?

Where vacation eligibility is tied to "continuous service," arbiters generally rule that time spent on strike should not be counted in computing continuous service. (42 LA 929, 48 LA 213, 47 LA 319, 47 LA 1164)

EXAMPLE: One arbiter ruled that an employer had the right to deduct the time that workers spent on strike against the employer in determining the employees' vacation eligibility date under a side letter incorporated in the contract, stating that credit for vacation eligibility would not be earned during time spent on strike. According to the arbiter, there was evidence that during negotiations on the side letter the parties decided that strike time would be treated as layoff time, and the union had agreed that layoff, except for certain months of a grade period, would affect vacation eligibility dates. (George Banta Co. Inc. 74 LA 388)

Similarly, in another case, an arbiter ruled that an employer properly reduced its employees' vacation benefits to reflect the work time that was lost as the result of a strike. The contract entitled employees to receive vacation benefits based on their continuous service with the employer during specified dates, the arbiter reasoned, pointing out that by linking the words "continuous" and "service," management clearly intended that employees must comply with such a requirement in order to get vacation benefits. (Ohio Power Co., 63 LA 1235)

Likewise, teachers who continued a two-week-old strike through the first three days of their scheduled one-week vacation were not entitled to vacation pay for the three-day period, an arbiter decided. The striking teachers failed to meet the school's requirement that they be in a paid status for at least one of the five working days immediately preceding a vacation in order to be eligible for the pay, the arbiter maintained, concluding that the regulation was consistent with the contract. (Hawaii Dept. of Education, 62 LA 415)

However, one arbiter ruled that taking part in a strike, even though it was in violation of the contract, was not in itself cause to deprive employees of vacation credits. In the arbiter's view, the strikers would have forfeited vacation credits if management: (1) had fired them before the vacation credits accrued or (2) had notified them that their return to work would be conditioned on a waiver of vacation credits. (Marathon Rubber Products, 6 LA 238)

Strike v. Lockout

Where a contract provided vacations for workers in "continuous service" for a specified period of time, the arbiter held that the time employees spent on strike could not be counted in computing "continuous service" but the time they were locked out could be counted. He reasoned that the lockout was voluntary on the part of the company and prevented workers from accruing the "continuous service" required for vacation eligibility. The strike, however, did not come within the exceptions to the vacations provisions, so it must be considered as a break in service. (Denver Upholstered Furniture Mfrs., 42 LA 929)

Strike as "Excused Absence"

One arbiter held that time spent by the employees on strike did not constitute "excused absence" within the meaning of a contract provision. The strike was "legal" in that it violated no law, but the arbiter doubted that it was "excused" by the employer, and further, such an interpretation would require the employer to "subsidize the strike." (Motor Car Dealers Assn. of Kansas City, Mo., 49 LA 55)

Effect Of Absences

Some contracts deal with the effect of absences on vacation eligibility by fixing a cut-off point of a designated number of absences after which the right to vacation benefits is affected. For example, it might be specified that "an employee's vacation pay will be prorated, if during the vacation-eligibility year, he was absent for more than 60 days regardless of the reasons for the absences.

In the absence of such a provision, arbitrators tend to adopt a cut-off rule of their own under which they may ignore absences of relatively brief duration but may disallow or prorate vacation pay where lengthy absences are involved.

Absence for Military Service

Special rules apply where an absence is caused by an employee's entering the military service or meeting military training obligations. Such absences generally must be counted as time worked.

EXAMPLE: An arbiter ruled that an employee who worked as a part-time ovenman for 10 and one-half months prior to entering military service was entitled to include the time that he spent in the military as "continuous employment" to be counted in determining the length of vacation that he earned under a contract entitling employees to an annual vacation after having one or more years of employment. (Vie De France Corp. and Bakers, Local 118, 74 LA 449)

Absences for Illness or Injury

Do employees who are absent because of illness or other disability lose their right to vacation pay?

In the absence of specific language in the contract, an employer may or may not have the right to deny an employee vacation pay while he is out sick or because of an injury. In deciding such cases an arbiter may look to the general contract language on vacation pay rights or to the employer's past practice.

EXAMPLE: In one case an arbiter ruled that an employee who sustained an injury in an automobile accident was entitled to receive contractual sickness and accident benefits in addition to vacation pay, notwithstanding the employer's contention that the simultaneous payment constituted "double compensation," which was not intended by the contract. Since the agreement neither expressly or implicitly denied an eligible employee the right to receive both sick and vacation benefits simultaneously, the arbiter upheld the double payment. (Airco Inc., 62 LA 1056; see also 91 LA 1083, 71 LA 460)

EXAMPLE: Even where a worker's absenteeism was partly his own fault because of excessive drinking, an arbiter held that he was entitled to vacation pay since there was proof that he also could not work because of an injury. (Chicago & Harrisburg Coal Co., 2 LA 57)

However, where a contract provided that "time lost for illness" would not affect vacation pay, an arbiter ruled that an "injury," even though occurring on-the-job, was not "illness" for purposes of computing these benefits. (Modecraft Co., 44 LA 1045; see also 85 LA 967, 74 LA 1061)

Leaves of Absence

Generally, where there is no controlling contract provision, arbiters uphold the company's right to deny vacation benefits to workers who have been on leave of fairly long duration.

Absence for Union Business

Does time spent on union business count as time worked for purposes of vacation eligibility? In some cases, arbitrators have ruled that it does not.

EXAMPLE: Under a contract, eligibility for vacation benefits hinged on a work requirement of 1,400 hours in a vacation year. The local's president was 64 hours shy of the requirement. The union pointed out that up to 340 hours of leave could be credited toward satisfying the vacation work requirement; and absence for union activity was leave time under the contract. Since the officer had spent more than 64 hours on union affairs, it added, he had a right to vacation benefits. The company replied that elsewhere in the agreement a distinction was made between "excused union activity" and "authorized leave of absence." Hence it denied the president had been on leave. The arbiter upheld the company's position, saying that if union activity had been meant to be a leave of absence there would have been no reason for making the distinction cited. (American Air Filter Co. Inc., 39 LA 942)

Similarly, where a contract's vacation clause required employees to have been "continuously in the service of the company" as of the eligibility date, an arbiter upheld the company's refusal to grant vacation to a worker who had been on union business leave for six months. The arbiter reasoned that "continuously in the service" meant "continuously available to the employer," which the man on leave was not. (Chamberlain Co. of America, 8 LA 755)

Maternity Leave

How does maternity leave affect a worker's vacation rights? At one plant where the vacation clause called for a year's "continuous employment," those who took an enforced six-month pregnancy leave forfeited their eligibility for that year, an arbiter ruled. Workers on maternity leave were not "continuously employed in the company's plant" during the year, and in this sense were "laid off." The union had argued that pregnancy was not an "illness" or a "layoff" which would interrupt a worker's continuous service for vacation purposes. The sense of the vacation provision, he found, is that benefits are a reward for actual continuous employment. (Clean Coverall Supply Co., 47 LA 272)

Effect Of Termination

The tendency to treat vacation pay as an earned right generally means that an employee who has met all of the eligibility requirements for a paid vacation is entitled to claim his vacation pay if he is terminated prior to taking his vacation.

But what if he has met all of the eligibility requirements except a requirement that he be on the payroll as of a certain date? After an extensive review of prior court and arbitration decisions, an arbiter concluded that the principle was well settled in industry, generally, that employment on the specified date is not a condition of eligibility for vacation pay and therefore that termination prior to that date does not disqualify the individual for the vacation pay that he is otherwise entitled to. (49 LA 837; see also 71 LA 781)

This principle is followed fairly closely in cases where the termination is involuntary, such as in the case of a shutdown or disability retirement.

Exceptions may be made, however, where the termination is voluntary such as a quit or a voluntary retirement. In such cases, the employer's past practice may be decisive.

EXAMPLE: A contract's clause provided that "employees after having completed six (6) months' service shall be allowed ten (10) working days' vacation with current pay during the following six (6) months," and that "employees having completed one (1) year shall be allowed fifteen (15) working days' vacation during the following twelve (12) months with current pay." When an employee quit one month after her anniversary date with the company, the employer claimed she was only entitled to a vacation balance of two days and two and three quarters hours, because the other 15 days she demanded were credited on the first anniversary and not "earned" until completion of two years service.

However, the arbiter awarded the other 15 days of vacation to the employee after finding that the history of the contract's language and the bookkeeping methods used by the employer for the past 20 years were controlling. (Columbia Typographical Union, 63 LA 507)

However, a union was out of line, an arbiter ruled, when it attempted to win for quitting employees the entire vacation benefit that they would have been entitled to had they worked a full year since their last vacation. The employer was correct in awarding the vacations on a pro rata basis, the arbiter decided, rejecting the union's argument that vacations were fully vested from the start of the vacation year. The right to accrue vacation benefits during the year was recognized by the contract and confirmed by past practice, the arbiter concluded. (Wire Sales Co., 62 LA 185)

Effect of Discharge

In the absence of specific language of disqualification, arbiters generally hold that an employee who otherwise meets the requirements for vacation pay is not disqualified by virtue of his being discharged before he takes his vacation.

EXAMPLE: An employee discharged for chronic absenteeism was ruled eligible for vacation pay where the contract did not cover the situation. The arbiter decided that to permit the disqualification would amount to an amendment of the contract. (Weaver Mfg. Co., 19 LA 325)

Similarly, discharge for cause was held by another arbiter not to disqualify a worker under a contract that did not specifically bar payments under such a condition. (General Foods Corp., 18 LA 910)

Likewise, an employee discharged for negligence was not held disqualified for terminal vacation pay under a contract that specified only that resignations or discharges for rule infractions would relieve the company of its obligation to make vacation payments, an arbiter decided. (Byerlite Corp., 12 LA 641)

Moreover, at least one state court has ruled that employees discharged for striking in violation of a no-strike clause were entitled to vacation pay earned prior to the strike. (Pattenge v. Wagner Iron Works, Wis CircCt, MilwaukeeCy, 1956, 38 LRRM 2615)

Effect of Permanent Shutdown

Are employees entitled to vacation pay when they are terminated because of plant shutdown?

Arbitrators have generally held that previously acquired vacation credits are earned, or additional wages, payable even if a permanent plant closing takes place before the vacation actually becomes due. (76 LA 1212, 12 LA 860, 13 LA 804)

Similarly, some arbiters have held that workers idled because of a shutdown were entitled to vacation pay, even though the agreement expired before the eligibility date.

EXAMPLE: In one case an arbiter noted that the employees had been laid off when the plant was closed and the contract stated that a man was not terminated until he had been on layoff for two years. Thus, he said, the workers were still in the company's employ and their earned rights survived the contract's expiration. (Botany Mills Inc., 27 LA 1)

Similarly, in another case an arbiter held that workers who lost their jobs in a plant shutdown had pro rata vacation pay coming to them because they were terminated through no fault of their own. The fact that the contract had expired before the vacation eligibility date was immaterial, he said. (Brookford Mills, 28 LA 838)

Death of Worker before Vacation or Eligibility Date

When a worker dies before receiving the vacation that is due him, are his survivors entitled to the vacation pay? Where no set rule has been developed on this problem, arbiters seem to consider what other circumstances do or do not break a worker's vacation eligibility.

EXAMPLE: Even where a contract disqualified employees who quit, retired, or were discharged from receiving vacation pay, an arbiter held that "death" was not an implied exemption as maintained by the company. In awarding accrued vacation benefits to the survivors, the arbiter stated that to hold "death" as a disqualification would be to alter the contract. (Pittsburgh Steel Co., 43 LA 860)

EXAMPLE: Where the contract required an employee to work at least 1,000 hours in one year in order to be eligible for a vacation the next year, and also provided that "if an employee shall have earned a vacation but dies before such vacation has been taken, the vacation pay shall be paid to his widow," an arbiter ruled that the widow was entitled to that pay, even though the worker died in December of the year before he was to take the vacation. The arbiter rejected the company's argument that no pay was due the widow because vacation pay went only to those still on the payroll as of January 1. Nothing in the contract specified that, he said, and the employee had worked his 1,000 hours. (Clinton Corn Processing Co., 41 LA 513)

Similarly, another company was required to pay pro-rated vacation pay to the estates of two employees who died in March and April of a vacation-eligibility year that ended on June 30. (Burnham Corp., 46 LA 1129)

Likewise, a company was required to pay vacation pay to the widows of two employees who had performed no work in the year in which their vacations would have been taken. The contracts, he noted, destroy vacation eligibility only upon quit, discharge or retirement. He held that it would be improper to modify the contract to add "death." (Pittsburgh Steel Co., 43 LA 860)

On the other hand, where a contract provided for vacation rights to be forfeited if employment was terminated prior to January 1 of the vacation year, the arbiter upheld the company which had consistently denied benefits to survivors of workers who died before January 1. The arbiter maintained that giving the language its normal meaning, death must obviously be held to terminate the employment relationship. (Bethlehem Steel Corp., 47 LA 258)

Vacation Rights of Retirees

Whether vacation pay is due employees who retire voluntarily prior to the vacation season often depends upon past practice and the wording of the contract, and particularly upon whether the contract fixes a specified date for determining vacation eligibility.

EXAMPLE: A contract's vacation pay eligibility requirements were: (1) being on the payroll on January 1, (2) having at least one year continuous service as of January 1, and (3) having worked for the company in 26 of the 52 weeks immediately preceding January 1. An employee who met requirements (2) and (3) but who retired prior to January 1 sought vacation pay.

In upholding the company's denial of vacation pay, the arbiter said the company was entitled to enforce the requirement of being on the payroll as of January 1 in this case, even though it might not be entitled to do so in cases of involuntary terminations, such as those due to shutdowns or disability retirements. (Rex Chainbelt Inc., 49 LA 646)

However, in a case where the contract did not have a vacation eligibility date an arbiter directed the payment of vacation pay in one year to an employee who had retired the prior year. The employee prior to his retirement had met the dual contract requirements of having worked at least 800 hours in the current vacation year and of having at least six months service as of the prior calendar years. (B & T Metals Co., 50 LA 205)

Similarly, an arbiter awarded a retiree vacation pay earned through the time of his retirement, despite a contractual requirement that he establish his participation in the pension plan to be eligible to receive other pension benefits. The arbiter reasoned that since the parties' contract granting unpaid vacation pay to "any employee who retires" was without limitation or qualification, the company's denial of the pay was a violation of the contract. (Rexall Drug Co., 63 LA 965)

On the other hand, another employee who scheduled his two-week vacation before the start of his retirement, but who instead went on sick leave through the retirement date, was not entitled to vacation pay, an arbiter ruled, since the contract required vacation pay or holiday pay to be used before sick leave. (Kentucky Utilities Co., 64 LA 737)

Successorship and Vacations

Is a successor company required to consider time employed by the original employer when calculating employees' vacation time? If the successor employer assumes the labor-management relationship of its predecessor, the answer probably will be yes.

EXAMPLE: One arbiter found a successor company so liable, and listed the following reasons for his decision:

● The successor company hired all of the predecessor's employees in the bargaining unit.

● The employer operates in the same manner and at same location as the predecessor.

● The change of ownership did not create a hiatus in business operations.

● The successor employer's contract contains substantially the same provisions as the old contract. (A.B.A. Diesel Parts & Service Co., 62 LA 662)

Similarly, a successor employer obligated itself to pay vacation pay to its predecessor's employees, an arbiter ruled, when it wrote a letter telling employees of their continued employment and that they would be permitted to take one or two weeks of "vacation" depending on their seniority. (Zenetron Inc. and Radionic Workers, Local 5, 74 LA 861)

Vacation Scheduling

IN BRIEF

Vacation scheduling involves a balancing of the employer's interest in scheduling vacations at such time as best meets the needs of the business with the employee's interest in taking a vacation at the most desirable time. (Houdaille Industries Inc., 61 LA 958) One arbiter elaborated some general guidelines that may be followed in striking this balance:

"Absent specific contract language, it is generally understood in industrial relations that a vacation is an earned equity and is generally to be taken in terms of the employee's preference, subject to the exigencies of the company's production and maintenance requirements. Where the contract is silent on the specific policy or procedure to be followed, it must be assumed that the employee will request his vacation at a time suitable to his own preferences and that his preference will be honored to the degree that company requirements will permit. However, where the contract is silent, it must also be assumed that managerial discretion is greater than in those cases where contract language puts the burden on management to show need for the employee to take his vacation at a particular time." (Hubinger Co., 29 LA 459)

According to another arbiter, in the absence of a contrary provision in the contract, an employer has an unrestricted right to schedule vacations and, in fact, to refuse to grant any vacations at all. Vacation rights are "creatures of contract," he explained, stressing that the scheduling of vacations involves considering both the requirements of the employer and the wishes of the individual employee whenever practical. (Berkeley-Davis Inc., 65 LA 742)

GUIDELINES

Arbiter's Vacation Formula

Faced with the problem of how workers' desire to choose the time for their own vacations can be reconciled with management's need to maintain efficient operations, one arbiter came up with a formula. It was based on a contract providing that vacations would be granted at times most convenient to workers with consideration given to maintaining production —

(1) Management establishes a quota system indicating the weeks available for vacations and the number of employees needed to work those weeks. By December 1 it must publish a vacation schedule for the following calendar year based on this quota system.

(2) Employees must indicate four vacation choices by December 10. They may split their vacations, but the minimum period is one week.

(3) Since vacation priority is based on seniority, a list is set up by assigning varying numbers of points to the various seniority groups. The company must post the list by December 15. If an employee has to settle for his second or third vaca-

tion choice, his priority points are doubled or tripled the next year.

(4) The company must publish a vacation replacement list showing whether it plans to hire replacements or will rely on overtime by present employees to maintain production.

(5) A vacation grievance committee is set up to resolve employees' complaints on schedules and replacements. (Mansfield Tire & Rubber Co., 32 LA 762)

Vacation During Sick Leave

If an employee is out on paid sick leave when his regular vacation period arrives, is he entitled to another vacation period at a later date? Sick leave and vacation leave are entirely different privileges, according to an arbitration board, so the employer should re-schedule the vacation period of an employee who is on sick leave during his regularly scheduled vacation. (Derby Gas & Electric Co., 21 LA 745; see also 25 LA 94)

Similarly, where an employee was on sick leave when his scheduled vacation came up and his vacation could not be rescheduled, an arbiter held that he was entitled to vacation pay in addition to sick pay. (Tenneco Oil Co., 54 LA 862)

Vacations During Shutdown

Many companies have a practice of scheduling vacations each year during an annual plant shutdown. In the absence of such a practice, however, management may run into trouble if it tries to require employees to take their vacations during periods of layoff due to lack of work, particularly where the layoff is for an indefinite period. An arbiter pointed out that some correlation between vacations and what otherwise would be layoffs is not only permissible, but desirable (3 LA 829, see below)

EXAMPLE: One arbiter held that management could not require employees to take their vacations during a period of indefinite layoff where to do so would destroy the substantive features of a vacation. He explained:

"A vacation is a period of rest between periods of work. A layoff is a period of anxiety and hardship between periods of work. The tremendous difference lies in the assurance of the vacationer that he will return to work at the end of his vacation and the equal assurance of the employee on layoff that he does not know when he will return to work." (Ford Motor Co., 3 LA 829)

Likewise, even where a shutdown for lack of work is for a definite period, arbiters have overruled attempts to require employees to take their vacations during that period. Usually such decisions arise in cases where management previously promised to give some consideration to employee preferences in scheduling their vacations. The reasoning is that those workers who do not choose to take their vacations during the shutdown are deprived of their opportunity to state their preferences by the unilateral scheduling of vacations during the shutdown. (97 LA 578, 96 LA 445, 93 LA 107, 81 LA 254, 31 LA 462, 32 LA 776, 48 LA 1018)

EXAMPLE: A contract said each employee must schedule his vacation in advance at a time acceptable to the company.

When the company had to shut down for two months due to a lack of orders, it claimed authority to require all workers to take their vacations at that time. However, the arbiter overruled the company's action, reasoning that those workers who did not choose to take their vacations during the shutdown were deprived of their opportunity to specify what times they wanted. Moreover, the right given the company to allot vacation periods in order to insure "orderly operation of the plant" may allow management to spread out vacations to avoid too many replacements at one time, but "orderly" is not synonymous with "economical" or "efficient," the arbiter said. (Koppers Company Inc., 42 LA 1321)

Similarly, one arbiter found that a company was not free to join the trend toward plant shutdowns for vacation, as the contract bound the employer to "endeavor to comply" with vacation requests. While acknowledging the gradual changes in factory conditions, such as increased vacation tenure and a larger work force, the arbiter still maintained that in planning a shutdown, the employer was "in fact endeavoring not to comply with requests." (Welch Grape Juice Co., 48 LA 1018)

On the other hand, an employer had the right to schedule one vacation shutdown during the summer months, an arbiter ruled, under an oral agreement giving the employer the right to schedule not more than one summer vacation shutdown per year per department. Rejecting the union's contention that the employer failed to secure contract language recognizing management's right to schedule vacation shutdowns, the arbiter concluded it was not necessary to obtain such contract language in light of the employer's longstanding past practice of scheduling vacation shutdown for legitimate business reasons, the oral agreement, and the absence of limiting language in the previous agreement. (Lynchburg Foundry Co., 76 LA 554)

Moreover, in the absence of contract language or binding past practice, management has the inherent right to fix employee's vacation time, an arbiter ruled. The company decided it no longer could afford the disruptions that accompany individual vacation scheduling, and it unilaterally designated the week of July 4th for a plant-wide vacation shutdown. The arbiter overruled union objections based on past practice, finding that the union had never participated in past disagreements over vacation schedules. (Vogt Mfg. Corp., 44 LA 488; see also 30 LA 225)

Caution: A company that unilaterally changes its past practices on vacation scheduling runs the risk of being charged under the Taft Act with violating its duty to bargain with the union over changes in working conditions.

Workers' Desires vs. Efficient Operations

Under a contract that allows workers to choose the vacation periods they want subject to requirements of the business, the company must have real and valid reasons for denying them the period they ask for. (94 LA 309, 77 LA 633, 67 LA 709, 59 LA 268)

EXAMPLE: When one company turned down a worker's request for a specific vacation period because it overlapped with that requested by another worker, an arbiter ruled against this action. Although the contract provided that the "needs of the business must be considered in scheduling vacations," the arbiter found that both workers' being gone at the same time would not necessarily conflict with efficient operations. To turn down a request for a given vacation time, the arbiter said, management should show that a vacation at that time would adversely affect production, safety, or general employee relations. (Tin Processing Corp., 15 LA 568)

Similarly, another arbiter ruled that management could not make a blanket denial of all vacation requests for a certain week, even though the contract made workers' requests for vacations subject to operational requirements. The company had announced in advance that no vacations would be given during Christmas week. In the arbiter's view, the company violated the vacation clause requiring it to make every effort to meet the desires of employees in scheduling vacations. Also, it had failed to show that absolutely no one could be spared, the arbiter noted. (Bethlehem Steel Co., 30 LA 899)

However, in other cases arbiters have upheld management's right to reshuffle vacation schedules in order to meet the needs of its business.

EXAMPLE: In one case, establishment of a "one-man, one-week" vacation rule, under which only one employee in a department could be on leave at any given time, was upheld by an arbiter as a proper exercise of management's right to ensure the orderly operation of its plants. (U.S. Steel Corp., 46 LA 887)

EXAMPLE: Where a contract gave the employer the right to schedule vacations throughout the year, an arbiter upheld management's right to allot vacations to eligible employees over the full year on an equal basis, thereby eliminating the "summer bulge" of vacations. (Laclede Steel Co., 54 LA 506)

EXAMPLE: Another arbiter ruled that management could refuse to schedule vacations during months when peak business was expected, even though that business did not materialize. The contract said management would fix vacations according to the workers' wishes "in so far as practical" and "in accordance with the needs of the business." In the arbiter's view, this gave the company the sole right to limit vacation-time selection, as long as heavy business forecasts were reasonable. (Westinghouse Electric Corp., 40 LA 972)

EXAMPLE: In a case where it had been a practice for two years to commence vacations on a Monday, an arbiter held that the company could continue this practice. The contract gave the employer the right to schedule vacations in the interest of plant efficiency. The union wanted each worker's vacation to start after his regular days off. But the arbiter said that, by starting vacations on Monday, the company was justifiably exercising its right to increase efficiency and avoid costly premium payments. (Sinclair Refining Co., 12 LA 193)

EXAMPLE: Another arbiter decided that a utility employer properly postponed and rescheduled the vacation of one member of a three-man maintenance crew, since the second member was out of town at the time and the third member would have been left alone to perform work normally done by all three. (United Telephone Co., 64 LA 906; see also 73 LA 813, 73 LA 687, 73 LA 48)

Vacation — Workers v. Foremen

Where a contract gave workers their choice of vacation dates in seniority order, the company was obligated to give workers vacation preference over foremen where the two conflicted, as long as there was no operational problem, the arbiter stated. Since nothing indicated that management assigned the vacation weeks to foremen on the basis of anticipated production needs, he concluded that foremen had to take second choice. (Air Reduction Chemical & Carbide Co., 42 LA 1192)

Likewise, adoption of an extended vacation plan did not give a company the right to abandon a past practice of allowing workers and foremen to work out the schedule, one arbiter decided. Although the company may set the total number of workers who may be on vacation at one time, it may not determine when particular workers shall be off. Rather, it is bound by past practice and must permit foremen and workers to work this out among themselves, subject only to the limits of plant manpower needs. (Reynolds Metals Co., 43 LA 1150)

Extended Vacations

In a grievance against a company's refusal to grant a worker his preferred vacation period, an arbiter provided several observations and principles for the scheduling of extended vacations in the steel industry.

Observations: Subject to the company's right "to ensure orderly operation of the plants," extended vacations should be granted "at times most desired by employees." To implement this plan, a procedural agreement was adopted permitting the company to establish plant and unit quotas and allowing workers to select vacation periods within these quotas in order of seniority.

Principles: (1) The employer is not bound to continue quotas used in a prior year. (2) He is bound to honor vacation selections on the basis of seniority within separate lines of progression. (3) He may continue to schedule vacations by calendar quarter, since this had permitted most workers to receive time off during preferred summer quarters. (4) Exceptions should be made in special cases of hardship, where granting of worker's request would not interfere with production. (Armco Steel Corp., 45 LA 120)

Additionally, another arbiter asserted that the company may not give workers entitled to regular vacations priority over extended vacationers. The company may require a worker to take his vacation during a period other than the one he requested, only when its decision is related to the need to maintain orderly plant operation. (Pittsburgh Steel Co., 42 LA 1002)

Work During Vacation

Under a contract allowing management to *request* employees to work during their vacations, at least one arbiter has held that this gives the employer the right to *compel* employees to skip their vacation.

EXAMPLE: At the end of the first week after a return to work from a strike the company issued vacation checks to all employees instead of scheduling free time. The contract specified that: "Under unusual circumstances, the management may request certain or all of the employees to work during their vacation, but in such event the employees will be paid their regular pay in addition to their regular earnings." The union contended that under this clause, management might only request, not compel, employees to work during their vacations. It argued that "request" would require the employee's *approval*.

The arbiter ruled otherwise, stating that the obvious intent of the contract was to give management the right to require work under unusual circumstances. Furthermore, it was held that the definition of "unusual circumstances" must be left largely up to the employer. The arbiter found no abuse of that discretion. (Maxwell Bros. Inc., 5 LA 449)

Vacation Pay

IN BRIEF

Frequently, arbiters are called upon to settle disputes over vacation pay, even though the contract usually specifies the method for computing the benefit. Some of the issues an arbiter may have to resolve include the following:

▶ What happens when an employee works at more than one rate?
▶ Do incentive workers get their base rate or full incentive earnings?
▶ Are overtime, shift, holiday and other premium rates and bonuses included or excluded?
▶ What is the effect of a retroactive wage increase?
▶ If employees work a different workweek from the plant's schedule workweek, which one is used as a base?
▶ Is the *date* on which vacation pay is computed clear? Is it the employee's anniversary date, the eligibility date, or the date the vacation is actually taken?

GUIDELINES

Inclusion of Incentive Pay

Should workers' incentive payments be included in vacation allowances paid them?

Incentive bonuses usually are considered by workers as a part of their earnings. Thus, if vacation payments are based on "current hourly earnings" arbiters most likely would hold that incentive pay must be included.

EXAMPLE: A company agreed that: "The rate of vacation pay per week shall be the same as the current hourly earnings for a full scheduled workweek as worked the previous two months prior to June 1st."

In spite of this language, which had appeared in various contracts, the company contended that vacations were payable on the basis of "base rate." It argued that the "base rate" had been used in the past, and that the wage-incentive payments at the plant never entered into calculations or discussions regarding vacations.

The arbiter ruled against the company, using this line of reasoning: The terms, "base rate" and "current hourly earnings" have well established and quite different meanings. The first refers to a minimum rate, the second to actual earnings of an employee. There was no reason here for ruling that the two terms were identical. Therefore, vacation pay should "be calculated on the basis of 'hourly earnings' to include incentive bonuses over and above base rate and on the basis of the workweek 'as worked' by the several employees entitled to vacation pay." (Schneider Metal Mfg. Co., 4 LA 100)

EXAMPLE: Under a contract basing employees' vacation pay on "gross earnings" of the preceding year, a lump sum paid to employees to "buy out" an old incentive plan in favor of a new one must be included in computing employees' vacation pay. The arbiter ruled that the written contract must prevail and that the ordinary meaning of "gross earnings" encompasses payment. (Johnson & Johnson, 49 LA 841)

Inclusion of Overtime Earnings

Under a contract which excludes overtime earnings from vacation pay, does this mean all earnings during overtime hours or merely the premium rate for the overtime?

One arbiter held that it was clear that a company was not obligated to base vacation pay on any earnings over 40 hours. (Webster Tobacco Co. Inc., 5 LA 164)

Even where a contract is silent on whether overtime premiums should be included in figuring vacation pay, chances are that an arbiter will not require the company to include them.

EXAMPLE: Under one such agreement that based vacation pay on average hourly earnings, defining such earnings to include regular day rates, incentive rates, and shift premiums, an arbiter ruled that overtime pay did not have to be included since it was not specifically mentioned in the definition. (Kensington Steel Co., 17 LA 662)

Inclusion of Shift Premiums

Should shift differentials be included in vacation pay which is based on "regular rate"?

At least one arbitration board gave an affirmative answer to this where the employees worked regularly on second or third shifts. (Hans Rees' Sons Inc., 10 LA 705)

On the other hand, it has been held that where shift premiums have not been included for a period of years, this past practice should prevail. (Bell Aircraft Corp., 9 LA 65)

Inclusion of Holiday Pay

Under a contract that bases vacation pay on "straight-time earnings," should holiday pay be considered part of earnings?

While management may feel that employees can hardly have "earnings" while they are off work because of a holiday, at least one arbiter has required holiday pay included, under such a vacation clause.

He held that the parties agreed in effect to treat employees eligible for holiday pay as though they had come in and worked on the holiday. He declared that:

"... Holiday pay cannot fairly be said to be similar to a shift bonus, overtime bonus, or a Christmas bonus. On the contrary, holiday pay more closely resembles vacation pay since both are paid at straight time rates rather than bonus rates."

It was concluded that holiday pay should be included in figuring "earnings." (Master Weavers Institute, 11 LA 745)

Inclusion of Vacation Pay

Under a contract providing vacation pay equal to a specified percentage of earnings for "hours worked" during the preceding year, must vacation allowances paid in that year be included in figuring total earnings?

According to one arbiter, such allowances need not be included in computing earnings unless it can be affirmatively shown that the parties intended them to be. Standing alone, he said, the words "hours worked" can refer only to hours actually worked during the year. (John Deere Spreader Works of Deere & Co., 20 LA 670)

However, another arbiter ruled that the company violated the contract which stated that "employee's gross earnings for the 52 weeks prior to January 1 of the vacation year shall be the basis for computing vacation pay" by excluding the prior year's vacation pay. Even though the employer has been computing vacation pay in the same way for ten years, the method was incorrect and constituted a continuing violation of the contract. (Huffman Mfg. Co., 49 LA 357)

Similarly, vacation pay that an employee received in 1974 was part of his "gross annual earnings" for that year for purposes of computing his vacation pay for 1975, an arbiter ruled, where the contract entitled the employee with specified length of service to vacation and vacation pay at the rate of a certain percentage of his "gross annual earnings." Despite the employer's contention that the phrase "gross annual earnings" was ambiguous and that past practice should be considered in resolving the ambiguity, the arbiter concluded that the contract language established the parties intent to consider the total "earned" amount, which included employees' vacations and holidays. (Canada-Ferro Company, Ltd., 66 LA 572)

Inclusion of Other Pay

Most other forms of pay for authorized leave time usually are included by arbitrators in vacation pay computations.

EXAMPLE: One arbiter held that vacation, holiday, bereavement, and jury duty pay must be included in computing an employee's average straight time earnings for the previous year for the purpose of computing vacation pay.

After an extensive review of prior decisions, the arbiter concluded:

"The almost consistent trend of arbitral authority is that all monetary benefits paid to an employee pursuant to the provisions of a collective bargaining agreement and incidental to his employment relationship are to be treated as earnings and included in the employee's earnings for the purpose of vacation pay. Any exceptions from the generally accepted meaning of the phrase 'straight time earnings' should be expressly set forth by specific contract language." (Ridge Machine Co., 53 LA 394)

Where Employee Works at Two Rates

If a contract bases vacation pay on the employee's "regular rate," what is his regular rate if he has worked on two or more jobs paying different rates throughout the year? Arbitrators have interpreted such provisions in different ways.

EXAMPLE: Where a man had been permanently transferred to a lower-rated job, an arbiter held that he was properly given vacation pay at that lower rate under a clause which based vacation pay on the rate of the worker's regular job. The contract defined "regular job" to mean that to which an employee is regularly assigned or the job he is working on immediately prior to his vacation, whichever is higher. The arbiter said that the lower-rated job was his regular job since he had been permanently assigned to it a week before his vacation. (Olin-Mathieson Chemical Corp., 24 LA 116)

However: Where a man was working at a job only temporarily, or where his work required him to shift frequently from one job to another, some arbiters have held that he should be paid vacation benefits at the rate he received the majority of his time during the preceding year. (Hiram Walker & Sons Inc., 5 LA 186)

Effect of General Wage Increase

When a new contract is negotiated which increases pay rates, should the old or new and higher rates be used in figuring vacation pay?

Unions may insist that rates *in effect at the time the vacation is taken* should be the basis for computing vacation pay, while management will argue that the vacation has been *earned* at the old rate.

Here again, where the contract is unclear, arbiters tend to be guided by the employer's past practice.

EXAMPLE: After reviewing prior awards, one arbiter concluded:

"Thus, in all cases that have come to the attention of the arbiter here, the unanimous view has been that where contract language is not clear, the long established past practice must be followed." (Sweden Freezer Inc., 43 LA 471)

Where there is no past practice, an arbiter may conclude that the parties must have intended that the rate prevailing at the time of vacation is the one that should be used.

EXAMPLE: A company and union negotiated a new contract during May. This new agreement granted substantial wage increases, effective June 15. The company distributed vacation pay on June 27, using old rates although it recognized the new vacation benefits as to length of service, overtime, etc. Its position was that pay rates in effect when the vacations were earned were the ones to be applied.

An arbiter disagreed. He declared that when the parties drew up their new contract it was far more likely that they were thinking of the vacations just ahead of them than of the next year's vacations. Furthermore, the new rates were to be effective for two years, and if the parties had meant to use a different rate for vacation purposes, they would have said so, according to the arbiter. It was concluded that the rate prevailing at the time of the vacations should be used. (Lynch Corp., 9 LA 115)

On the other hand, where a contract based employees' vacation pay on their hourly rate on May 1 of current year, an employer was not required to include in its employees' vacation pay a cost-of-living adjustment that became effective in the pay period beginning on May 13, 1974, an arbiter decided, despite the union's contention that the wage increase was delayed by management because of clerical problems. While the union may have intended to have the May 1 date include the cost-of-living allowance for May in the vacation pay calculations, the arbiter found that it did not communicate that position to the employer during contract negotiations, nor did it make any other communications or actions supporting that intention. (Milwaukee Press & Machine Co., 65 LA 549)

A compromise system of pay may also be worked out by an arbiter faced with the question of whether old or new rates should govern.

EXAMPLE: A company and union signed a new contract in April retroactive to March 31, which provided for a wage increase and a completely new vacation plan. Many employees would have received less vacation under the new plan, so the parties agreed that the year's vacations would be figured under the old contract. There was no discussion, however, as to rates of pay for vacation time, so the question was submitted to arbitration: Should the old or new rate be applied in figuring vacation pay.

An arbitration board held that it was the responsibility of both parties to bring up the matter of applicable pay rates and to secure an agreement on the matter. Since neither party met this responsibility, it was concluded that it would be fair "for the parties to ... share equally the benefits and penalties of their failure to fixing the rates at a point half way between those originally sought by the union and those sought by the company." (Crosley Motors Inc., 8 LA 1024)

Effect of Retroactive Increase

When a wage increase is agreed to after vacations have been taken, and the increase is made retroactive to a date preceding the vacation, should the extra pay be included in the vacation pay? At least one arbiter has said it should.

EXAMPLE: "As a general rule, when a wage increase is made retroactive," the arbiter held, "it applies to all hours for which employees have been paid during the retroactive period. That rule is applicable whether such hours are those of holidays, vacations or hours of work." (Pioneer Alloy Products Co. Inc., 5 LA 458)

Effect of Annual Improvement Increase

Must an annual-improvement factor be added to a worker's vacation pay if the increase goes into effect while he is on vacation?

In the absence of any contract provision on the subject, one arbiter ruled that such an increase must be incorporated in pay for any part of a vacation which falls after the effective date of the increase. (Ford Motor Co., 17 LA 512)

Effect of Strike

Can time spent on a strike be excluded in computing vacation pay?

The answer usually turns on the past practice of the parties or upon the wording of the contract.

EXAMPLE: Where a contract based vacation pay on "time worked," an arbiter held that management had a right to deduct strike time. (Modecraft Co., 33 LA 1236)

Similarly, an arbiter ruled that economic strikers were not entitled to vacation-benefit accrual, despite a claim that the employer had not reduced the accrual for leaves of absence and that NLRB stated in an unfair-labor-practice decision that a "leave of absence is, under the plan, the same as a strike." NLRB, the arbiter found, did not state that strike time was to be treated as a leave of absence and made no determination that vacation benefits accrued during the strike. Further, he said, the employer had pro-rated vacation accruals for leaves of absence, and vacation pay is a form of compensation that is not earned while on strike. Also, the arbiter said, the retroactive application of the contract applied to vacation-benefit accrual, despite the claim that the retroactive application was solely for the purpose of health-insurance-premium payment, since the contract did not specifically restrict the application of the effective date to select provisions. (Murphy Oil USA Inc., 92 LA 1148)

Also, an employer had the right to reduce the vacation benefits of employees to reflect their absence from work due to a strike, an arbiter decided, where the contract granted employees vacation with pay following completion of a specified period of service, since the parties intended "service" to mean "service rendered" or "worked." (Reichhold Chemicals Inc., 66 LA 745; see also 63 LA 1235)

However, under a contract providing that the anniversary date of each employee shall be his most recent date of hire by the employer and that his eligibility for vacation pay shall be computed from such date, an arbiter held that an employer did not have the right to deduct time lost due to leave of absence, layoff and strikes from the total years of service for purposes of computing employees' entitlement to vacation pay. (Blue Box Co., 61 LA 754)

Moreover, where the contract was *silent,* an arbiter was persuaded by a past practice of allowing full vacation pay in strike situations. (Mobil Oil Co., 42 LA 102)

On the other hand, past practice worked to managements' favor in a case where the company, in figuring out weekly vacation pay, followed the practice of dividing the employees' earnings in the past year by 52 weeks. In view of this practice, the arbiter saw nothing wrong in using the 52-week divisor in a year when the employees had lost six weeks' earnings due to a strike. (Blaw-Knox Co., 47 LA 1164)

Effect of WC Payments

Arbiters' views vary on whether an employee is entitled to both vacation pay and workers' compensation benefits.

EXAMPLE: An employee who received 15 weeks' pay for working and 30 weeks' pay from workers' compensation during one year was not entitled to vacation pay for that year, according to one arbiter. The contract provided that employees had a right to vacation pay if they had worked for the employer for one year, and received 40 "paychecks" within the year. Considering the union's unsuccessful attempt to include reference to WC checks, the arbiter maintained that "paycheck" meant a check for work done. (Ohse Meat Products Inc., 48 LA 978)

Similarly, employees were not entitled to have included in computation of their vacation pay time they were absent from work because of injuries received on the job, for which they were compensated under state workers' compensation law. (Modecraft Co., 44 LA 1045; see also 83 LA 969)

However: Employees who failed, due to an industrial accident, to accumulate contractually specified straight-time hours of work, were entitled to vacation pay on the basis of actual hours worked, an arbiter ruled, despite receipt of workers' compensation during the vacation period. (Solar Chemical Corp., 56 LA 99)

Similarly, an employee who was awarded 100% total disability under workers' compensation was entitled to vacation benefits for 400 weeks during which he was to receive the WC benefits, an arbiter ruled. Pointing out that the employee who continued to receive benefits from the employer was considered as being on the company "payroll," notwithstanding the fact that he was not on the "active payroll," the arbiter concluded that there was nothing in the contract to support the employer's claim that its vacation obligation was restricted to the year the worker sustained the injury. (Thomas Industries Inc., 61 LA 627)

Quit or Retirement Before Eligibility Date

Where a contract stated that employees must have a certain period of service and must have worked a certain number of days "prior to August 1 of the vacation year," to be eligible for vacation pay, the arbiter ruled that those who fulfilled the requirements but left the job before August 1, were entitled to vacation pay. It is a generally recognized principle in industry that under this type of vacation clause employment on a specific date is not a condition of eligibility for vacation pay (Telescope Folding Furniture Co., 49 LA 837; see also 83 LA 1092)

On the other hand, an employee whose last day of work was December 30, 1975 and who was placed on retirement on January 1, 1976 was not entitled to vacation pay for 1976, an arbiter ruled, under contract provisions granting vacation pay to employees who were on the payroll on the beginning of the vacation year and who have worked during the vacation year. The contract defined the vacation year as constituting the period from January 1 to December 31. Despite the union's contention that the employee was on the payroll for the period ending January 4 and therefore was "on the payroll on the beginning of the vacation year," the arbiter concluded that the employee did not work during 1976 and thus failed to meet the requirement that an employee must have worked during the vacation year to be eligible for vacation benefits. (Westvaco, 67 LA 128)

Similarly, employees who elected to retire before the period set for taking vacations were not entitled to vacation pay, an arbiter decided, under a contract stating that an employee who quits or is discharged for cause shall not be eligible for vacation or vacation pay. (York Wall Paper Co., 69 LA 431;see also 91 LA 795, 84 LA 863)

Effect of Plant Shutdown

Employees who were terminated as a result of an employer's voluntary shutdown of the plant are entitled to pro-rata vacation pay for the time worked prior to the shutdown, an arbiter ruled, even though the contract required a minimum number of hours worked as eligibility. He reasoned that vacations are additional wages and no longer considered merely period of rest. Therefore, vacation benefits already earned under the unexpired contract cannot be completely annulled by the shutdown. (National Plumbing Fixture Corp., 49 LA 421; see also 87 LA 1109, 85 LA 979, 51 LA 400)

However, an arbiter held that an employee on his layoff was not entitled to request a deferment of lump-sum payment for vacation or sick leave benefits until the expiration of his three-year recall rights or upon request for payment of benefits, under a contract which provided for the deferral of benefits to month selected in the next calendar year by an employee who retires. (Sacramento, Calif., 82 LA 996; see also 82 LA 686, 82 LA 193, 81 LA 1268, 81 LA 556)

Actual vs. Normal Workweek

Some contracts spell out what a "normal" workweek is, and then in the vacation clause they base vacation pay on the "workweek." If, under such a contract, a plant has actually been operating on a schedule longer or shorter than the normal workweek, which period should be used in computing vacation pay — the actual or the normal week? Decisions have gone both ways in solving this problem.

EXAMPLE: It has been held that the workweek as defined in the contract is the one to be used, even when management has been basing vacation pay on the actual workweek in the past. (Dunkirk Radiator Corp., 1 LA 249)

On the other hand, at least one arbiter has held that the number of hours actually being worked by employees was the proper base for vacation pay. The contract in this case based vacation pay on the "scheduled workweek in the previous calendar year" and also defined the "normal" workweek as 40 hours long. Reasoning that "scheduled" refers to a time established in advance and consistently adhered to, the arbiter decided that vacation pay should be based on the six-day week actually worked since the employees usually expected to work on Saturdays unless otherwise notified. He found that 65 percent of the time they did not receive such notice. For this reason he ruled that the six-day week was the "scheduled" workweek. (Cemenstone Co., 9 LA 41)

Individual vs. Plant Workweek

Where different employees work a different number of hours per week, another common problem in computing vacation pay arises — whether the workweek of each employee or the standard workweek for the whole plant should be used. Arbiters have held that the plant's workweek is the one to be used to avoid confusion.

EXAMPLE: Under a contract basing vacation pay on the "weekly hours worked by the company in a majority of the workweeks of the vacation year," the union contended that the weekly average of actual hours worked by all employees should be used in computing vacation pay. An arbiter upheld the company's view that the number of hours scheduled for the whole plant should be the base. He reasoned that the word "company" in the clause refers to a whole and not isolated parts of the operation. The union's position, he said, would cause much confusion and destroy the meaning of established work schedules. (G. C. Hussey & Co., 5 LA 446)

Similarly, in another case an arbitration board decided that the exclusion of overtime payments from vacation pay pointed "to a definite workweek in the plant as a whole." (International Harvester Co., 9 LA 35)

Effect of Changes in Workweek

Where the length of the workweek has varied from time to time during the vacation year, which period should be used in figuring vacation pay?

One arbiter has held that the workweek in effect at the time the vacation is taken is the proper one. (General Controls Co., 12 LA 852)

However: Under a contract that specified 48 hours as the base for figuring vacation pay, an arbiter held that the company could not reduce vacation benefits to 40 hours' pay just because the workweek had been reduced to 40 hours. (Kempsmith Machine Co., 5 LA 520)

Part 8

Holidays

Eligibility for Holiday Pay

IN BRIEF

Holiday pay does not exist as a matter of law (53 LA 1165), as one arbiter said; or as another held, "There is no inherent right to holiday pay, and none exists except as set forth in the labor agreement" (46 LA 102). Therefore, although holiday pay is recognized as an earned benefit, pay for holidays not worked is usually conditioned upon an employee's compliance with certain, contractually stated work requirements. Most collective bargaining agreements, for example, require both a stipulated minimum period of service, and work on designated days surrounding the holiday, before an employee is entitled to holiday pay.

It is generally agreed that the purpose of "surrounding-days" work requirements is to prevent employees from "stretching" holidays (53 LA 1206, 49 LA 468, 48 LA 1101) and to ensure a full working force on the day before and the day after a holiday (46 LA 102, 40 LA 673). (For arbitration cases involving surrounding-day issues, see: 98 LA 319, 98 LA 258, 97 LA 484, 95 LA 1100, 93 LA 598, 93 LA 473, 91 LA 816, 88 LA 972, 88 LA 769, 85 LA 640, 82 LA 448, 81 LA 943, 81 LA 494, 81 LA 196)

Thus, a significant consequence of the work requirements clauses, according to one arbiter, is that the "failure of an employee to comply with them as a condition precedent to holiday pay operates to disqualify him from receiving such benefit." (Motch & Merryweather Machinery Co., 51 LA 723)

Arbiters have upheld management decisions not to award holiday pay to workers who fail to meet such work requirements, despite employees' claims that they were absent through no fault of their own. (91 LA 345, 69 LA 604, 69 LA 189)

In cases where employees claim that an illness prevented them from meeting the holiday work requirement, eligibility for holiday pay may depend on whether the workers are able to provide a valid medical excuse for their absences. (93 LA 537, 92 LA 571, 92 LA 228, 91 LA 1174, 81 LA 943, 81 LA 330, 73 LA 414, 70 LA 1273, 70 LA 1046, 70 LA 935, 67 LA 638, 67 LA 97, 64 LA 625, 63 LA 982)

If a contract grants holiday pay without restriction, chances are that a laid-off worker is entitled to it — particularly if the layoff is brief. In deciding whether to award holiday pay to laid-off employees, an arbiter may examine the specific language of the contract, the timing and length of the layoff period, or the employers' reasons for instituting the layoffs. (96 LA 1218, 82 LA 1170, 71 LA 611)

GUIDELINES

WORK REQUIREMENTS

Incomplete Day's Work

If workers must work both the day before and the day following a holiday in order to qualify for holiday pay, do they have to put in *full days?* What if workers are absent *part* of one of the qualifying days? It is generally recognized that the real purpose of such a provision is to prevent stretching of holidays. Going on this assumption, most arbiters hold that workers who take time off for good reason on the day before or after the holiday have fulfilled their requirements under this kind of holiday clause.

EXAMPLE: One arbiter made the distinction between "stretching" a holiday and "arranging the necessary adjustments to make the holiday available." Thus, he said that a worker who left work a half hour early the day before a holiday so he could catch a train was eligible for holiday pay. (John Deere Tractor Co., 9 LA 21)

EXAMPLE: Where an employee was 36 minutes late to work on the day before a holiday, he was held to be qualified for holiday pay because he had worked on the scheduled working day as required by the contract. (Lake City Malleable Inc., 25 LA 753)

EXAMPLE: An employee who received permission from her foreman to visit her doctor during pre-holiday shift was entitled to holiday pay for Dec. 30 and 31, an arbiter decided, since she returned to finish her shift as requested by the foreman. (ITT-Phillips Drill Division, 69 LA 437)

On the other hand, it has been held that partial absences are to be considered as depriving an employee of holiday eligibility under a before-and-after-work requirement.

EXAMPLE: One arbiter held that workers who received permission to leave early on the day before or after Christmas Day were not entitled to holiday pay under a strict interpretation of the requirement. He based his decision on the fact that the parties had discussed the clause at great length and agreed upon it in order to avoid disputes over excused absences. (American Bemberg & North American Rayon Corp., 10 LA 384)

Definition of "Working Day"

Is a "working day" the day which actually precedes or follows a holiday, regardless of whether an employee was scheduled to work on that day, or is it the first day preceding or following a holiday on which an employee is told to come in and work? An arbiter would probably hold that "working day" was the first day on which management expected work from an employee.

EXAMPLE: A contract obligated any employee "to work his full shift on both the working day before and the working day after the holiday."

A holiday fell on Thursday. An employee worked the preceding Wednesday, and was told not to work on the day following the holiday, Friday. She was scheduled to work on Monday, but did not report.

The employee contended that Friday should be considered the "working day after the holiday." Management argued that "working day" meant a day on which an employee was actually scheduled to work, and that Monday should be considered the "working day."

The arbiter agreed with management. He held that ordinarily "working day" referred to a day on which an employee was expected to work. He noted also that minor variation from schedules were the rule. In other words, there was no evidence that the instructions to some employees not to work on the Friday following the Thursday holiday were connected with the occurrence of the holiday. (American Thread Co., 10 LA 250).

ELIGIBILITY FOR HOLIDAY PAY

Eligibility Days Not in Holiday Week

Under a holiday clause requiring work on the day before and day after the holiday, do these eligibility days have to be in the same week as the holiday? In many instances arbiters have held that they do not.

EXAMPLE: A company promised to pay holiday pay "provided such holiday falls or is celebrated within the regularly scheduled workweek, and provided further that such employee works the workday previous to and the workday following such holiday."

A holiday fell on a Thursday and the plant was closed for the rest of that week. An employee was denied pay for the holiday because he was absent the next Monday.

An arbitration board majority upheld the company's position that the days preceding and following a holiday on which work was required did not have to fall in the same workweek as the holiday. The opinion stated that:

"It is likely that the union will discover upon investigation, that in nearly all cases where a clause such as this is in a contract, it is applied so that the "workday" before or after the holiday may be in a workweek other than that in which the holiday occurs." (Veeder-Root Inc., 11 LA 33; see also 12 LA 886, 41 LA 776)

Saturday as a "Work" Day

If Saturday is a scheduled work day, can workers who fail to report for overtime on Saturday be denied pay for a Monday holiday which follows? In answering this question, arbiters look at the exact wording of the agreement.

EXAMPLE: Under a contract that required employees to work the regularly scheduled work day before and after the holiday to be eligible for holiday pay, workers were held entitled to pay, for a Monday holiday, even though they failed to report for work scheduled for the preceding Saturday. The arbiter found that the contract defined a regular week's work as consisting of 40 hours, Monday through Friday, inclusive. In view of this, he said, Saturday could not be considered a regularly scheduled work day. (Hinde & Dauch Paper Co., 22 LA 505)

EXAMPLE: At another plant workers failing to report for Saturday work were held ineligible for holiday pay for the following Monday because the contract did not limit the hours employees could be required to work. The arbiter decided that they had not met the contract's requirement of working on the last scheduled work day, even though it was overtime. (Great Lakes Spring Corp., 12 LA 779)

EXAMPLE: In order to count Saturday as a scheduled work day, when it is overtime work that is involved, an arbiter ruled that the company must have the right to force such overtime work. In this case, where the contract spoke of normal Monday-through-Friday workweek and of "requests" to work on Saturday or Sunday, Saturday was not allowed to be counted as the last "scheduled" work day before a Monday holiday. (Amron Corp., 47 LA 582)

EXAMPLE: Where an employer had the right to require Saturday overtime work, an arbiter held that employees who failed to report for such work prior to a Monday holiday thereby failed to meet the requirement that they work the last scheduled work day prior to the holiday. (Sargent-Welch Scientific Co., 54 LA 923; see also 73 LA 777)

Failure to Work Scheduled Holiday

Many contracts state that holiday pay is not required for workers who fail to report on holidays when work is scheduled. In spite of such apparently clear contract language, many problems have come up when workers have claimed their holiday pay, even though they did not work. In such cases, arbiters give considerable weight to the method used in informing employees that work had been scheduled, as well as to past practice.

EXAMPLE: In one instance an arbiter ruled that it was enough for a company to post notices a week beforehand that work was scheduled for the following Monday, a holiday. Since many workers on vacation called in to find out if work was scheduled for the holiday, the arbiter decided that others on vacation had no valid claim to holiday pay on the ground that they had not received sufficient notice. (Bethlehem Steel Co., 22 LA 781)

EXAMPLE: At another plant it was held that workers who failed to show up for scheduled work on Christmas day were properly denied holiday pay. The fact that the foremen asked them whether they planned to work on the holiday did not mean that they had a choice of working or not, the arbiter said. (Bethlehem Steel Co., 25 LA 680)

Similarly, workers who refused to report for holiday work, after an emergency call-in, lost their right to holiday pay, under a provision making ineligible those who were requested or scheduled to work and failed to do so. An arbiter held that this did not require advance requests or scheduling for holiday work as contended by the union. (Firestone Tire & Rubber Co., 29 LA 469)

However, although one arbiter recognized a company's right to make changes in the work schedule, he ruled that one day's notice to report for work on a holiday was not enough. Thus, in spite of the contract provision denying holiday pay to those failing to report for work on a holiday when scheduled, the arbiter concluded that the absent workers were entitled to holiday pay. (Bethlehem Steel Co., 23 LA 271)

Holiday Pay After Termination

When terminated workers receive accumulated vacation pay, they also may be entitled to pay for holidays falling within the period covered by the vacation allowances, according to one arbiter.

EXAMPLE: Some employees who were terminated in May and June received from one to three weeks' accumulated vacation pay. The union contended that certain of them should have received additional pay for Memorial Day and the Fourth of July since these holidays fell during the weeks covered by their vacation pay. In rejecting this claim, the company relied on two contract provisions — one stating that an employee had to work his scheduled work days before and after a holiday to qualify for pay and another saying that a laid-off employee would get holiday pay only if the layoff occurred in the holiday week.

An arbiter found neither clause controlling. He reasoned that the purpose of the work requirements was to prevent holiday stretching; and that, although the layoffs did not take place during the holiday weeks, the company by granting vacation pay deferred the effective dates of the layoffs beyond the holiday weeks. Hence he concluded that the applicable clause was one granting holiday pay in addition to vacation pay for a holiday falling during an employee's vacation. (Continental-Emsco Co., 31 LA 449)

EFFECT OF SHUTDOWN

Permanent Shutdown

Are employees eligible for holidays which come after a plant closes down permanently? Although arbiters have ruled both ways on the problem, their decisions seem to turn on whether individual workers are otherwise eligible for the holiday pay rather than the facts surrounding the shutdown itself.

EXAMPLE: Where one plant shut down on New Year's Eve, an arbiter held that employees were not eligible for pay for New Year's Day because they had not worked the following day as required by the contract. (Calif. Metal Trades Assn., 11 LA 788)

Temporary Shutdown

Most arbiters have ruled that workers fulfill their work requirements for pay for a holiday falling during a temporary shutdown if they work the last scheduled working day before it and the first scheduled working day after it. Such a ruling is usually based on the assumption that a plant's closing down is something which workers cannot control.

EXAMPLE: In one case an arbiter pointed out to the company that the contract required work on the working days before and after a holiday rather than the day before and after the holiday. Since the workers had worked December 30 and had been told not to report again until January 5 the arbiter held that these were the working days. So, he concluded, the workers were entitled to pay for New Year's Day. (Aerolite Electronic Hardware Corp., 10 LA 215)

EXAMPLE: Employees who worked the day before the Christmas Day holiday which fell on Thursday and who did not work on the succeeding Friday because the employer temporarily had shut down operations were entitled to holiday pay for Christmas Day, an arbiter decided, even though they failed to work the following Monday. The employees, the arbiter stated, were qualified for the holiday pay since they worked the day before the Christmas holiday and were excused from working on the day after the holiday. (Reilly Tar and Chemical Corp., 66 LA 835; see also 75 LA 651)

However, in another case, employees who did not work the last shift on the workday before the start of a two-week vacation shutdown were not entitled to holiday pay for the fourth of July holiday that fell during the shutdown period, an arbiter held, since there was a past practice requiring employees, when a holiday falls during a shutdown, to work the day before and the day after the shutdown to be eligible for holiday pay. (Regal Ware Inc., 65 LA 795)

Additionally, it has been held that a month-long shutdown does deprive workers of holiday pay under a before-and-after work requirement, whereas a brief shutdown of only three days does not have this effect. (Vulcan Detinning Co., 4 LA 483). Also workers were properly denied pay for a holiday falling during a shutdown where the contract specified that holidays must fall within a scheduled workweek. An arbiter ruled that no scheduled workweek was in effect. (Sefton Fibre Can Co., 12 LA 101)

Involuntary Shutdown

When a company was shutdown because of a strike by another union, an arbiter decided that the workers were not entitled to pay for the holiday that fell during the shutdown. Certain of the assumptions underlying a labor contract precluded the holiday-pay claim, he said, and primary among these was that the company must be operating and able to provide employment opportunities. Since the company had to suspend publication involuntarily through no fault of its own, the arbiter concluded that a liberal reading of the contract would raise an obligation never expected or intended by the parties. (Publishers' Assn. of New York City, 40 LA 140)

EFFECT OF LAYOFF

In Absense of Eligibility Requirements

When a contract contains no specific eligibility requirements, are employees on layoff entitled to holiday pay? A common argument for awarding them pay is that companies might lay off their employees for the express purpose of avoiding holiday payments if laid-off workers were held ineligible. Some arbiters have held that those on just a temporary layoff do not lose their rights to holiday pay.

EXAMPLE: One arbiter ruled that the equities of a situation required that workers laid off because of a machine breakdown should be paid holiday pay since the breakdown was not their fault. (Thompson Mahogany Co., 5 LA 397)

EXAMPLE: Another arbiter found that, in a somewhat seasonal industry where layoffs were fairly regular, workers would suffer a serious inequity if they lost holiday pay just because of a layoff when they had worked throughout most of the contract year. (Otto Guggenheim & Co. Inc., 11 LA 1130; see also 10 LA 887)

EXAMPLE: In keeping with the strict language of the contract, an arbiter required that an employer abandon a past practice of 14 years. The only requirement for holiday pay was that the "employee actually works during the payroll week in which the holiday falls." A separate clause said that a worker would lose his standing as an "employee" if he was laid off for 12 consecutive months. When seven workers, who had been laid off for a little over nine months were recalled the day after Labor Day, they qualified for holiday pay under the terms of the contract. The employer's practice of not granting holiday pay if the return followed the holiday was ruled improper. (Anaconda Aluminum Co., 48 LA 219)

On the other hand, it has been held that if the layoff is bona fide, workers should be denied holiday pay. One arbiter noted that, if holiday pay were granted, laid-off workers who had secured jobs somewhere else would get holiday pay from two companies. (Tenney Engineering Co., 10 LA 307)

Before & After Holiday Work Requirement

Are laid-off employees considered as having met a requirement for working on the days preceding and following the holiday? (96 LA 1218)

EXAMPLE: One arbiter ruled that the parties must have intended that workers on layoff should receive holiday pay even though they did not work on the days before and after the holiday. His reasoning was that there would have been no reason to write a contract clause requiring employees to have earned some wages within the 30 days before the holiday if the parties had meant to exclude laid-off employees from holiday-pay eligibility. (Thomas L. Leedom Co., 21 LA 740; see also 75 LA 729)

EXAMPLE: Another arbiter decided that employees who were laid off indefinitely between 1 and 3:30 p.m. on the day before a Thanksgiving holiday, which was their last scheduled workday prior to the holiday, and who otherwise met the employer's work requirements, were entitled to a full holiday's pay for the holiday. The arbiter concluded, however, that the employees were not entitled to holiday pay for other holidays that fell during the layoff period which lasted from five to seven months. (Premiere Corp., 67 LA 376)

However, it has also been held that laid-off workers are not exempt from work requirements.

EXAMPLE: One arbiter reasoned that if he ruled otherwise, workers laid off for a whole year could claim pay for all six holidays provided by the contract. This, he said, would conflict with the fundamental purpose of the work requirement, that is, to cut down the monetary cost to the company. (Chrome-Rite Co., 12 LA 691; see also 82 LA 1170, 72 LA 528, 71 LA 609)

Employees on the Payroll

If the holiday-pay clause of a contract applies only to those workers on the payroll, are laid-off employees considered on the payroll? Generally arbiters hold that laid-off workers are not technically on the payroll, and thus are not entitled to the benefits of that status.

EXAMPLE: In trying to define "on the payroll" one arbiter found help in another section of a contract. The sick-leave clause specified that workers were on the active payroll if not laid off. So he reasoned that persons who were laid off were not on the payroll and, therefore not entitled to holiday pay. (Armour & Co., 9 LA 338)

Similarly, under another holiday clause with an on-the-payroll requirement an arbiter ruled that laid-off workers did not go on the payroll until they went back to work. (The Flintkote Co., 26 LA 526)

Recalled After Holiday

Are employees who are recalled from layoff after a holiday entitled to holiday pay? One arbiter has ruled yes.

ELIGIBILITY FOR HOLIDAY PAY

EXAMPLE: Employees were recalled from layoff within two to three weeks after the Memorial Day holiday. The arbiter ruled that the workers were entitled to pay for the holiday, since the contract entitled an employee who has been absent as a result of a short-term layoff to holiday pay if he has worked "within" 30 calendar days of the holiday. (Consolidated Aluminum Corp., 66 LA 938; see also 72 LA 840)

Workers on Disciplinary Layoff

Can workers who fail to meet the work requirements because of disciplinary layoff be denied holiday pay? In most cases arbiters hold this practice to be justifiable.

EXAMPLE: In one situation an arbiter concluded that if the parties had meant to provide holiday-pay eligibility for workers on disciplinary layoff, the contract would have said so. He based his decision on the fact that other sections of the contract specifically mentioned "disciplinary layoff" as being covered. (McInerney Spring & Wire Co., 11 LA 1195; see also 11 LA 1181)

However, at least one arbiter has held that the company was wrong in denying holiday pay to an employee who was on a two-day disciplinary layoff on the days immediately preceding and following the holiday. The arbiter pointed out that the purpose of requiring an employee to work the days before and after a holiday is to discourage him from stretching the holiday on his own volition. But in this case the employee was not absent by his own choice. Since he had been ordered not to report for work, the arbiter said he could not be held responsible for missing the days which the contract required for eligibility. Accordingly, the company was ordered to pay him for the holiday. (Inland Steel Co., 20 LA 323)

EFFECT OF STRIKE

Workday Before or After Holiday

Even where employees failed to work the full workday before a holiday due to a breach-of-contract walkout, arbiters have held the employees entitled to holiday pay, absent a showing that the strike was a result of a premeditated plan and that the part-day's work was intended only as token compliance with the holiday-pay eligibility requirements. (20 LA 349, 16 LA 317)

On the other hand, Other arbiters have held that employees who, because of a work stoppage, do not work the complete day before or after a holiday do not qualify for holiday pay. (93 LA 473, 85 LA 51, 62 LA 681, 68 LA 835, 35 LA 117, 11 LA 462, 40 LA 673)

Absence of Agreement

Holiday pay normally does not accrue during a strike if there is no collective bargaining agreement in effect when the strike occurs. This principle has been applied to strikes that take place after the expiration of a contract, to lawful strikes under a wage reopener, and to unauthorized strikes during the contract term. (74 LA 1058, 24 LA 561, 30 LA 671, 33 LA 681, 36 LA 1276, 37 LA 3, 43 LA 539)

As one arbiter explained:

"When an employee has chosen to detach himself temporarily from the contract effects by a strike or stoppage running through a holiday, he has surrendered the holiday benefit just as surely as he surrenders pay on any other day of such a stoppage. The surrender is certainly not lessened by the fact that the stoppage is an unauthorized one during the life of the agreement and barred by its terms." (Hellenic Lines, Ltd., 38 LA 339)

However, one arbiter allowed holiday pay for New Year's Eve Day where a legal strike beginning on the day after a contract expired made it impossible to work the "next scheduled workday." (A. O. Smith Corp., 51 LA 1309)

Retroactive Agreements

A special problem arises when a strike-settlement agreement is made retroactive to the starting date of the strike. Does this mean that the strikers should be paid for holidays occurring during the strike?

EXAMPLE: In one case, a claim for holiday pay was denied on the grounds that: (1) the new contract required work on scheduled work days before and after the holiday, (2) the plant was operating during the strike and work was available on the pre- and post-holiday work days, and (3) the strikers had failed to meet the eligibility requirement by working on those days. (Alside Inc., 42 LA 75)

Similarly, strikers were not entitled to holiday pay for the Labor Day holiday which fell during the strike period, an arbiter ruled, even though the parties entered into a strike settlement agreement which retroactively reinstated expired contract provisions that were not modified in the new contract, includ ing the holiday pay provision. Noting that the strike prevented the employees from complying with the employer's holiday work requirements, the arbiter pointed out that the parties did not make a special provision for requiring payment of holiday pay for Labor Day. (Packaging Corp. of America, 62 LA 1214)

No Work Requirement

If employees are out on strike at the time a holiday comes up, does that make them ineligible for holiday pay? Sometimes, if there was no work requirement for holiday-pay eligibility, it has been held that workers on strike were entitled to pay for holidays falling during the strike. (Royle & Pilkington Co. Inc., 18 LA 451)

Refusal to Cross Picket Lines

Can workers who are absent because they refuse to cross picket lines be denied holiday pay on the ground that they do not meet work requirements? Generally arbiters have held that holiday pay does not have to be paid in such cases even if the contract gives workers the right to respect picket lines.

EXAMPLE: One arbiter with this view said that it is one thing for an employer to agree that employees may respect picket lines, but it is something else again to approve their absence when they do. (Schlage Lock Co., 30 LA 105; see also 25 LA 687, 54 LA 754).

Likewise, an arbiter ruled that an employer was not obligated to pay holiday pay or birthday pay to employees for July 4 holiday and birthdays of some of the employees that fell during the time when they were honoring picket lines of another union. In absence of a contract provision requiring such payments, the arbiter concluded that the union should bear economic loses falling within the period of its economic and adversary struggle with the employer. (Pearl Brewing Co., 68 LA 221)

EFFECT OF VACATIONS

When Vacation Includes Holiday

When a scheduled vacation period includes a holiday, are workers still entitled to pay for the holiday? Several arbiters have held that eligible workers have the right to pay for a holiday even though it does fall within a vacation period.

EXAMPLE: In one situation where a plant shutdown for vacations beginning July 3, an arbiter ruled that the employees were justified in their claim for pay for the Fourth. The company argued that, even though the contract said July 4 was a holiday, it should not have to give employees vacation pay and holiday pay for the same day. But the arbiter said that, once the workers had qualified for paid vacation and paid holidays, the right to these earnings could not be cut off by the company's timing of the vacation period. (Koler Cigar Co., 8 LA 143)

EXAMPLE: In a similar instance an arbiter held that workers should be paid for holidays falling within their vacations even if they chose the time of their vacations themselves. He said this was not shifting any loss to the company, but only requiring it to pay the worker as much if he chose a vacation in which there is a holiday as he would have received if he chose one without a holiday. (Tioga Mills Inc., 10 LA 371)

However, an employee was not entitled to pay for a holiday that fell during a scheduled vacation, an arbiter decided, where the holiday also fell during a wage re-opener strike. The worker, the arbiter held, was not excused from working on the last regularly scheduled workday before and the first workday after his vacation in order to be eligible for holiday pay. (Union Carbide Corp., 65 LA 189; see also 65 LA 795)

Late Return from Vacation Including Holiday

When a worker returned from vacation a day late, was he entitled to pay for a holiday that fell during the vacation period? One arbiter held that he was, since eligibility tests for vacations and holidays were separate.

EXAMPLE: The contract provided for an extra day's pay when a holiday fell during a vacation period, and also stated that workers must work the day before and after a holiday to be eligible for holiday pay. The company argued that the worker did not meet the work test for holiday-pay eligibility since he did not show up the day after his vacation.

The worker did qualify, the arbiter decided, since the holiday-during-vacation clause had to be entirely separate from the work-test clause. Otherwise, he reasoned, the contract could be interpreted to require workers to show up for work on the days "immediately" preceding and following a holiday, even though they were on vacation. (Streitmann Supreme Bakery of Cincinnati, 41 LA 628)

EFFECTS OF ABSENCE

Absence for Illness

Are workers who are out sick entitled to holiday pay? Arbiters' reasoning leads to different conclusions on this question.

(93 LA 537, 92 LA 571, 92 LA 228, 91 LA 1174, 81 LA 943, 81 LA 330, 73 LA 777, 73 LA 414, 72 LA 607, 71 LA 1067)

EXAMPLE: One contract stated that workers would not lose straight-time pay because of holidays. So an arbiter denied pay for New Year's Day to a worker who was absent for illness from December 29 to January 5. He reasoned that the sick employee did not lose pay because of the holiday since he would not have worked if the day had not been a holiday. (General Mills Inc., 10 LA 53)

EXAMPLE: An employer was not required to pay holiday pay to an employee who was sick and missed a workday following Thanksgiving holidays, an arbiter ruled, where a doctor's statement confirming the employee's sickness was insufficient to constitute a grant of "sick leave" for purposes of establishing holiday pay eligibility. (Rheem Mfg. and Steelworkers, 62 LA 837)

EXAMPLE: An employee who failed to obtain a doctor's certificate certifying to his illness on the day after Christmas holiday was not entitled to holiday pay for the Christmas holiday, an arbiter decided, despite the employee's contention that he was too sick to consult his physician. (Weil-McLain Co., Inc. and Sheet Metal Workers, 64 LA 625)

EXAMPLE: An employee who sustained an injury to his finger but who was certified as capable of returning to work on a workday that fell on a legal holiday was not entitled to holiday pay, an arbiter held, where the contract limited holiday pay only to employees who worked the last full scheduled workday prior to and the first full scheduled workday after a holiday. (Belknap Inc., 69 LA 599)

EXAMPLE: Where a contract provided for both paid sick leave and paid holidays, an arbiter held that a worker who was receiving sick pay for Christmas and New Year's Day could not get holiday pay for those days, too. The arbiter reasoned that if the parties had meant to duplicate sick pay and holiday pay for the same days, they would have clearly stated it in the agreement. He noted further that this had never been done in the past. (Standard Oil Co. (Indiana), 26 LA 206)

On the other hand, an employee who was absent on his last scheduled workday prior to a holiday was entitled to holiday pay an arbiter decided, despite his failure to obtain a physician's statement as required by his employer. The worker was unaware that when he became sick the day in question was his last scheduled work day prior to the holiday because the work schedule had not been posted, the arbiter reasoned. (United States Steel Corp., 67 LA 97)

Similarly, an employee who claimed to be sick on the day after a holiday was entitled to pay for that holiday, an arbiter ruled, notwithstanding the employer's contention that the employee failed to provide a legitimate doctor's excuse for his absence. Noting that the contract did not provide for substantiation of excuse for holiday pay in order to render a qualified employee eligible for such pay, the arbiter concluded that the employee's post holiday sickness constituted a legitimate excuse, absent any challenge to the truthfulness of his claim of illness. (Hubbell Metals Inc., 67 LA 638)

Likewise, where a contract clearly waived a day-before-and-after work requirement for holiday pay in the case of sickness, an arbiter said, it meant that workers out sick were entitled to holiday pay, no matter when their illness began. (Bakers' Negotiating Committee, 24 LA 694)

Absence Due To On-the-Job Injury

Are employees who are absence because of an on-the-job injury entitled to holiday pay? Some arbiters have ruled yes.

EXAMPLE: Employees were entitled to holiday pay for holidays falling while they were receiving workmen's compensation as a result of on-the-job injuries, an arbiter decided notwithstanding the employer's contention that the employees were on "leave of absence" and, thus, disqualified from receiving the pay under the contract. Pointing out that the leave of absence provision in the contract related to unpaid leaves for reasons of "sickness, personal injuries or further educational study," the arbiter observed that the fact holidays were paid days, as opposed to days off with pay, suggested that the holiday pay was part of the employee's regular wage. (Walworth County, 71 LA 1118)

EXAMPLE: Another arbiter decided that in accordance with established past practice, as well as the contract, an employee who was ill and who suffered an occupational injury, certified by a doctor, was entitled to pay for only the first holiday occurring during the period in which more than one holiday occurred. (Chardon Rubber Co., 71 LA 1039)

Absence for Union Business

If workers do not meet holiday eligibility requirements because they are absent on union business, are they entitled to holiday pay? In one case an arbiter answered "Yes" to this question. The holiday clause required employees to work on the day preceding and following a holiday in order to be eligible for holiday pay. The arbiter based his decision on a contract provision stating that time lost in conducting union business would be counted in figuring service and attendance records. (International Harvester Co., 11 LA 1166)

Involuntary Absences

Is a worker entitled to holiday pay if his failure to meet work requirements was due to circumstances beyond his control? Some arbiters have ruled in favor of the employees in such cases.

EXAMPLE: This problem came up under one contract which required employees to work the scheduled days before and after a holiday to be eligible for holiday pay, except in the case of "justified absence." On the last scheduled workday before the Fourth of July, some employees could not get to work because of a bus strike.

Arguing that their absence was not justified, the company denied them holiday pay. But an arbiter held they were entitled to it. Noting that the purpose of a work requirement in a holiday clause is to prevent holiday stretching, he concluded that these workers were absent because of the bus strike and not because of a desire to lengthen their holiday. (Bemis Bros. Bag Co., 25 LA 429; see also 28 LA 390)

Similarly, an employee who was three minutes late in reporting for work after New Year's holiday because of an ice storm was entitled to holiday pay, an arbiter ruled, despite a contract provision requiring the employee to work the last full scheduled work day prior to and after a holiday in order to be eligible for unworked holiday pay. (Vertex Systems, Inc., 68 LA 1099)

On the other hand, one arbiter ruled that a company was justified in sticking to the letter of its contract which contained before-and-after work requirements with exceptions for illness or layoff only. Consequently, he decided that workers who were absent the day before a holiday because of a bad snowstorm could not draw holiday pay. (Steinway & Sons, 7 LA 289)

Similarly, an employer properly refused to approve the absence of an employee on a workday after Thanksgiving holidays due to adverse weather conditions, an arbiter decided. Therefore, the arbiter concluded that the employee also was properly denied holiday pay. (Tennessee Dickel Distilling Co., 69 LA 189)

Likewise, an employee who did not report for work on the workday after New Years Day holiday, despite the lifting of a road blockade that had been imposed several hours earlier in the day because of bad weather conditions, was not excused from submitting a reasonable excuse for his absence for purposes of establishing holiday pay eligibility, an arbiter ruled. (Electrical Repair Service Co., 69 LA 604)

Effect of Disability or Retirement

Are employees who are out on a disability leave of absence or who retire from the company on the day before a holiday entitled to holiday pay. Arbitrators have expressed varying views on this issue.

EXAMPLE: One arbiter ruled that an employee who went on disability retirement immediately after his disability leave of absence had expired was entitled to be paid for eight holidays occuring during his leave of absence. Despite the employer's contention that the employee had lost all of his holiday benefits because of his failure to return to work for one day after his extended absence, the arbiter finds that management's interpretation of the contract's holiday provision did not bear a reasonable relationship to its purpose of preventing an employee from improperly extending his holiday absence. The alleged past practice of the employer of not paying holiday pay in similar situations was not binding, the arbiter concluded, in view of the evidence that the employer followed this practice without the knowledge of the union. (Ideal Basic Industries Inc., 68 LA 928)

However, another arbiter ruled that an employee whose last day of work was Dec. 30, 1975, and who was placed on retirement status on January 1, 1976, was not entitled to holiday pay for New Year's Day holiday, notwithstanding the contention that since the employee did not work the regularly scheduled working day after New Year's Eve and New Year's Day holidays but nevertheless was given holiday pay for New Year's Eve holiday he should be paid for the New Year's Day holiday as well. Finding that the employer's decision to allow payment for the first holiday was in the nature of a gift for the employee who was about to retire, the arbiter concluded that employee's entire stance changed on January 1, when he no longer was considered an employee. (Westavco, 67 LA 128)

HOLIDAYS FALLING ON NON-WORK DAYS

Saturday Holidays

Holiday clauses which simply designate certain days as paid holidays invite the question: When those listed holidays fall on Saturday what happens to workers' eligibility? Are they still entitled to pay for the holidays, or have they lost their rights?

In finding an answer to this as well as other eligibility problems, many arbiters construe a provision for paid holidays as a negotiated wage increase. Pay for a certain number of holidays is often considered to be part of the employee's annual compensation. Thus in the absence of clear contract language prohibiting it, it is frequently held that, no matter what day a holiday falls on, workers should be paid for it.

EXAMPLE: In one case where the holiday clause was ambiguous, an arbiter reasoned that if he denied employees pay for holidays falling on Saturday, he would be adding to a proviso to the contract which was not intended. (Carson Electric Co., 24 LA 667)

Furthermore, where a contract stated that Saturday was a regular four-hour working day, one arbiter held that employees were entitled to a full eight-hour's holiday pay when a holiday fell on Saturday. (Safeway Stores Inc., 7 LA 599)

On the other hand, many arbiters back up management's viewpoint that the purpose of a paid holiday clause is to protect workers from loss of pay caused by a holiday falling during the regular workweek. They reason, then, that if workers are not ordinarily scheduled to work on a day when a holiday occurs, they can not draw holiday pay under an unrestricted holiday clause. Thus it has been held that a Saturday holiday should not be paid for when a contract merely lists paid unworked holidays without going into the matter of the days the holidays fall on. (Standard Grocery Co., 7 LA 745)

Likewise, where it had been the past practice not to grant pay for Saturday holidays, arbiters have ruled that employers did not have to begin to do so all of a sudden under an ambiguous holiday clause. (M. E. Stern & Co. Inc., 1 LA 635; See also 8 LA 335)

Saturday as Scheduled Work Day

If a contract limits holiday pay to those holidays which fall on a scheduled work day, and a holiday falls on Saturday, do employees rate the pay for it if they have been working overtime on Saturdays? In several instances arbiters have denied pay for Saturday holidays under this kind of requirement.

EXAMPLE: Under a contract granting pay for a holiday "falling on the employee's scheduled work day," a union demanded pay for New Year's Day, which fell on Saturday. Until November, the plant had been on continuous operations, with employees working a five-day week and sometimes overtime. From November on, however, business fell off, and employees worked no more than five days a week, Monday through Friday. The union contended that since management had scheduled work for some employees on some Saturdays during eleven-twelfths of the year, it should pay all employees for the Saturday New Year's holiday.

Ruling against the union, the arbiter stressed the contractual requirement that the holiday must fall on "the employee's scheduled work day," and concluded that "New Year's Day not having been a scheduled work day for any of the employees, none of them under the provisions of the agreement are entitled to pay for that day." (Minnesota Mining & Mfg. Co., 12 LA 165)

Pay for Holiday Work

IN BRIEF

Nearly all contracts that take up the subject of holidays specify premium pay for holiday work. The premium pay may be expressed as holiday pay plus pay for hours worked, or simply as pay at a given rate for hours worked.

It is the latter type of clause that gives rise to most of the disputes over pay for holiday work. The question is whether a worker is entitled to the premium rate only, or to the premium rate plus what he would have received had he not worked. The answer to this question must be based on careful reading of the contract.

After reviewing prior rulings, one arbiter held that a holiday provision that calls for (a) straight-time pay for holidays, and (b) double-time for work on a holiday has been interpreted to call for triple-time only where:

▶ It is provided that the premium time for work on a holiday shall be given "over and above straight holiday pay" (26 LA 573); or,

▶ There has been an established practice of awarding holiday pay in addition to the premium pay provided for actual holiday work (16 LA 1951); or,

▶ The provision for holiday pay fails to contain the limiting words "when not worked" (26 LA 491).

On the other hand, this arbiter continued, where a contract is silent on the question of whether holiday pay as such should be awarded in addition to premium pay for working on a holiday, two reasons prevail for denying it:

1. If triple pay is contemplated, it should be expressly provided for in the contract inasmuch as it is not usual in industry practice. (22 LA 564)

2. An award of holiday pay in addition to premium pay for the work performed on a holiday would permit two provisos of the contract to apply to the same hours. (25 LA 432, 39 LA 1262)

From this review of prior awards, the arbiter concluded that triple-time for holiday work was not required under the contract before him. (Southern Standard Bag Corp., 47 LA 27)

GUIDELINES

Failure to Meet Work Requirements

Even though workers at one plant failed to meet the work requirements for pay for an unworked holiday, an arbiter ruled that they were entitled to premium pay for work on a holiday as provided by the contract.

EXAMPLE: One provision of a contract said that a worker would receive pay for certain holidays not worked, provided he worked his full schedule on the day before and after the holiday.

Another provision stated that a worker who was required to work on a holiday would be paid double-time for all hours worked. Two workers who did not work on the days preceding and following a holiday but who did work on the holiday were paid only straight time for their holiday work. The company claimed that this was proper, since they had not met the requirements applying to unworked holidays.

The arbiter disagreed. He said that the two provisions, while appearing in the same section of the contract, were independent of each other and had different purposes; one was intended to penalize the company for scheduling holiday work, the other to discourage the practice of stretching holidays.

So, he concluded, a worker was entitled to double-time for holiday work even if he did not meet the eligibility requirements for pay for an unworked holiday. (Alpha Cellulose Corp., 27 LA 798)

EXAMPLE: Employees were entitled to premium pay for working scheduled work on Thanksgiving Day holiday, an arbiter ruled, under a contract provision entitling employees to eight hour's pay at two times the regular rate for required work on specified holidays. The employer had contended that the employees did not report for scheduled work on the day after the holiday and thus were not entitled to premium pay under a separate contract provision barring employees from receiving holiday pay unless they work the last scheduled work shift prior to and the next scheduled work shift after the holiday.

Rejecting the employer's argument, the arbiter noted that the contract provisions were inconsistent and susceptible to two different constructions. Emphasizing that he did not accept the employer's construction which would cause a forfeiture of premium pay, the arbiter said that while the parties may have intended that no employee was to receive holiday pay for days not worked unless he complied with the work requirement, employees were nevertheless entitled to premium pay for holidays actually worked regardless of attendance on day before or day after holiday. (Rangaire Inc., 66 LA 775)

However, employees who worked their schedule shift on the Thursday before Good Friday holiday and the holiday itself but who did not work their scheduled sixth day of work on Saturday did not meet the employer's post-holiday work requirement, an arbiter decided, and thus were entitled to only time and one-half for their Friday work. (Tenco Tea Co., 68 LA 214)

Work on Holiday, Which Also Is Premium-Pay Day

When an employee works on a holiday, which also happens to be a premium pay day (such as the sixth or seventh day of work), complicated questions are likely to arise. The principle problem seems to be whether pyramiding (paying overtime rates on overtime rates) should be required. Arbiters have held that employees are entitled to two overtime rates.

EXAMPLE: Certain employees worked on a Saturday holiday, after having worked the regular workweek of Monday through Friday. They were paid time and one-half for the Saturday holiday worked, and claimed they should have received triple-time. They contended they were entitled to time and one-half for having worked more than 40 hours a week plus time and one-half for having worked on a holiday.

The contract provided that (1) time and one-half would be paid for work after eight hours a day or 40 hours a week; (2) "no overtime shall be paid on overtime"; and (3) when certain holidays, including the one involved here, were worked, "time and one-half additional shall be paid."

An arbitration board ruled that the provision prohibiting pyramiding of overtime was applicable only to daily and weekly overtime work, and that the word "additional," in the holiday pay clause meant "additional to such other pay as would be received on the day involved." Therefore, it was concluded that employees were entitled to triple-time — time and one-half for hours worked over 40 in the week and time and one-half for holiday work. (L. A. Jewish Community Council 11 LA 869)

EXAMPLE: Another arbiter decided that employees were entitled to contractual triple-time pay for work that they performed on a Friday holiday after they rejected the offer of the employer to trade the Friday holiday for Saturday and to waive triple-time pay for work on Friday, in favor of time and one-half pay for Friday as if it were Saturday work, in order to accommodate employer's production needs.

Pointing out that the contract provided that holidays that fall on Saturdays will be celebrated on preceding Friday and that the employer will pay triple time pay for work performed on holidays, the arbiter held that absent the employees' agreement to the proposal, they were contractually entitled to Friday holiday in celebration of New Year's Eve and to triple-time pay should they be required to work on Friday. However, employees who agreed to trade the Friday holiday for the Saturday holiday and to waive triple-time pay for work on Friday are estopped from claiming that they were paid improperly, the arbiter concluded. (General Tire & Rubber Co., 71 LA 813)

Also, an arbiter ruled that employees were entitled to be paid at two and one-half times their regular wage rate for working on their sixth consecutive working day, which fell on Memorial-Day holiday. The employer's past practice, for at least five years, had been to pay employees who worked on holidays, which were their sixth day of a payroll week, two and one-half times their regular rate for that holiday. (Epicurean Inc., 85 LA 1109)

On the other hand, Arbiters have ruled against pyramiding of premium pay for weekly overtime on top of premium pay for a worked holiday.

EXAMPLE: A contract provided time and one-half pay for Saturday work, straight-time pay for certain unworked holidays, and double-time for work done on holidays. The parties also had agreed that a holiday falling on a Saturday would not be paid for if it were not worked. The union requested triple-time pay for any Saturday holiday on which work was performed. It argued that work on a Saturday holiday should be paid for at the premium rates for both the Saturday (an overtime day) and the holiday.

The arbiter ruled that:

"The parties have agreed on double time as the appropriate premium for holiday work. But there is no necessity that this means double the overtime rate when the periods coincide. The purposes of overtime and holiday pay are separate. For work on Saturday the parties have agreed on a rate of time and one-half.

"If the Saturday should coincide with a holiday the higher premium for holiday work will prevail. The arbiter is not convinced that the premium should be pyramided. It is a reasonable provision that holiday work shall be paid for at double-time, but that this be uniformly applied as double the straight-time rate." (Heating & Air Conditioning Contractors, 11 LA 816; see also 74 LA 345)

Daily Overtime on Holiday

What rate should be paid an employee for overtime hours on a holiday? Under a contract providing double-time for holiday work and time and a half for more than eight hours work in one day, one arbiter allowed employees to collect pay at triple-time since the contract did not expressly prohibit pyramiding of premiums.

On the basis of the same reasoning, the arbiter also held that time and one-half the double-time rate was in order for work on a sixth day (after 40 hours' work) when the sixth day also was a holiday. (Phelps Dodge Refining Corp., 9 LA 474)

Similarly, Under a contract providing that all hours worked on a specified holiday shall be paid for at a rate of two times employee's regular hourly rate plus regular holiday pay, an arbiter decided that an employer improperly denied employees triple-time rate for work performed on a Labor Day holiday. (Theodore Mayer & Brothers, 62 LA 540)

Likewise, an arbiter decided that the forty hours beyond which overtime was payable to employees should include the hours that employees worked on a holiday and daily hours worked in excess of eight, even though the employer paid overtime rates for hours worked in excess of eight in any one day and already had paid premium rate for work performed on the holiday. (Northwest Protective Service Inc. 65 LA 930)

Holiday Rate for Incentive Workers

Under a contract providing double time for hours worked on a holiday, incentive workers were entitled to twice their full earnings, according to one arbiter. The company thought that it only had to pay workers their full straight-time earnings plus a premium of eight times the base rate. It argued that this had been the practice for eight years without protest from the union. But the arbiter said that past practice is immaterial where it is clearly in conflict with the plain language of the contract. The agreement said that workers would "receive double-time for hours worked on any of the designated legal holidays." Clearly, the arbiter ruled, this meant the incentive base rate plus incentive earnings plus shift premium, all multiplied by two. (Ford Motor Co., 27 LA 142)

When Does Holiday Begin?

Premium pay was meant to apply to all time worked during the "calendar day" definition of Thanksgiving, according to one arbiter.

EXAMPLE: The night shift did not end until 1 a.m. Thanksgiving morning, but the company refused to pay double time as the workers demanded. It argued that since the contract was silent as to whether holiday premium pay was based on the work day or calendar day, its past practice of paying straight time only when a regular shift overlapped a calendar holiday was controlling. According to the arbiter, Thanksgiving Day is not a technical term with special meaning in labor-relations parlance; therefore, its normal meaning of midnight to midnight was binding, and the workers were entitled to double pay for the hour worked on the holiday. In addition, the "past practice" had not been used often enough to render it binding. (Grand Rapids Die Casting Co., 44 LA 954)

Birthday/ Holiday Pay

An employee was entitled to holiday pay for his birthday that fell on a Sunday, an arbiter ruled, under a contract provision requiring the employer to recognize employee's birthday as holiday but "where individual's birthday falls on his regularly scheduled day off, he shall receive holiday pay for that day treating it as a birthday holiday." The decision was made notwithstanding the employer's contention that the employee was required to observe his birthday on following Monday pursuant to separate contract provision stating that any holiday falling on Sunday be celebrated on the following Monday. The arbiter reasoned that the provision relating to birthday holidays is specific and thereby controlling, and that the specific provision equalizes long-run holiday alllowances to employees. (American Smelting & Refining Co., 65 LA 1217)

Similarly, an employer was obligated to pay double-time pay to an employee for work that he was scheduled for on his birthday, which was paid for at double time pay under the contract, an arbiter ruled, notwithstanding the employer's contention that scheduling the employee on his birthday was an error. Since the contract clearly gives the employer the right to direct its working forces; having made the choice to schedule the employee on his birthday, the employer was bound by that choice, the arbiter concluded. (Thomas Truck & Caster Co. and Machinists, Local 566, 74 LA 1276)

Furthermore, an employer did not have the right to discontinue a past practice of allowing employees to work on their birthday-holiday, an arbiter ruled, since: (1) the management rights' provision of contract did not give the employer the right unilaterally to eliminate the practice, and (2) absent an effort by management during contract negotiations to get the union to agree to discontinuance of the practice, the union had the right to believe that the practice was part of the agreement covering holidays by custom and usage. (United Salt Corp. and Chemical Workers, 72 LA 534)

Gift Giving

In deciding whether management can unilaterally alter or discontinue a gift-giving policy, arbiters usually consider whether the gifts constituted a past practice that had become a part of the collective bargaining relationship. (69 LA 1250, 67 LA 979, 67 LA 769, 64 LA 571, 62 LA 879, 62 LA 209)

EXAMPLE: One arbiter held that an employer improperly discontinued a practice of giving employees gift certificates that were redeemable for $10 worth of food. Emphasizing that the certificates had gained the status of an employee benefit and a mutually recognized past practice, the arbiter ruled that the employer was bound to continue the practice unless it could be altered or eliminated through negotiations with the union. (Advance Die Casting Co., 65 LA 810)

On the other hand, an arbiter decided that an employer properly discontinued its practice of giving Christmas turkeys to employees following a decrease in demand for the company's products. Finding no express language in the contract that required the employer to distribute food on an annual basis, the arbiter held that the turkeys were, at most, voluntary gifts. Reasoning that the employer's voluntary gift policy was predicated upon the attainment of favorable economic results, the arbiter concluded that the turkey distribution could be discontinued as a result of an "adverse, unprofitable earnings period." (Proform Inc., 67 LA 493)

Part 9

Health and Welfare Benefits

Health & Welfare Benefits

IN BRIEF

Disputes rarely arise between management and the union over the amount of benefits due workers under a health and welfare plan. This is spelled out in careful detail in the policies issued by the insurer and, therefore, is out of the parties' hands. In some instances, however, where the collective bargaining agreement was more liberal than the insurance policy purchased by the employer, arbiters have held that the bargaining agreement was controlling.

In the absence of specific contract language, the eligibility for coverage of employees who are absent from work because of layoff or for other reasons may be a source of disagreement. The employees' seniority status under the basic contract and the employer's past practice often are the determining factors in such cases.

GUIDELINES

Arbitrability of Insurance Disputes

Disputes under an insurance plan are generally not proper subjects for arbitration when the insurance is separate from the contract. Settlements of disputes of that nature are generally held to be topics for negotiation. (Mobil Oil Co., 43 LA 1287)

However, where the insurance plan has been mentioned in the collective agreement and figured in the parties' contract settlement, arbitration becomes the method for settlement of grievances. (Torrington Mfg. Co., 45 LA 1176)

EXAMPLE: Where a contract stated that any difference arising between parties concerning working conditions or interpretations of contract which could not be adjusted amicably by parties shall be settled and determined pursuant to arbitration procedure, an arbiter ruled that a grievance seeking insurance benefits for an employee who suffered a heart attack was arbitrable, despite an employer's contention that the dispute was between the employee and the insurance carrier. Doubts regarding the proper contractual interpretation should be resolved in favor of arbitrability, the arbiter concluded. (Louisville Cooperage Co., 63 LA 165; see also 91 LA 62)

Who Is Covered

In determining which employees qualify for coverage under an employer's insurance plan, an arbiter may focus on the parties definition of who is a "regular" employee. In addition, the arbiter may take into consideration any past custom or practice regarding employees' eligibility.

EXAMPLE: According to one arbiter, an employer's 20 year practice established a longer-than-normal waiting period for purposes of life insurance coverage. While employees were considered "regular" for most purposes after the expiration of their probationary period, the arbiter pointed out that it had been the custom to wait six months before issuing life insurance to workers. Noting that the workers were aware of this practice, the arbiter disallowed a claim for a worker who had died after working only four months. (Clinton Paper Co., 48 LA 702)

However, in another case where an employer tried to treat workers who worked less than 30 hours a week as "not regular employees" for purposes of welfare-fund coverage, an arbiter said that this was improper. Any employee whose hours systematically were scheduled in advance was a regular employee, the arbiter concluded. (Veterans Linen Supply Co., 46 LA 741)

Likewise, a contract providing that welfare benefits shall be applicable only to regular and full time employees did not preclude a sick employee from receiving sickness benefits, an arbiter decided, despite an employer's contention that the employee no longer was a regular employee when he was discharged for being physically unfit to perform his job. The contract, the arbiter reasoned, was designed to exclude only part-time and temporary employees but does not exclude sick workers who may be able to return to work within a specified time. (Witco Chemical Co., 61 LA 1188)

On a related matter, an employer was not required to place salaried employees in a common pool with hourly-paid employees for the purpose of computing employee premiums for a long-term disability insurance plan, an arbiter decided, even though placing employees in separate groups resulted in a premium increase for hourly-paid workers and a decrease in benefits for salaried workers. Notwithstanding a contract provision that stated that unit employees will be "extended the same general benefits under the same terms and conditions as other company hourly employees," the arbiter concluded that conditions of employment, including insurance benefits, that the employer established for its non-union salaried employees was not subject to union review. (Charter International Oil Co., 71 LA 1073)

Coverage of Dependents

Frequently, arbiters are called upon to resolve disputes that focus on whether an employee's dependents are entitled to benefits under a company's insurance plan. In determining whether there are any restrictions or limitations on dependent coverage an arbiter may review the labor agreement, the language of the insurer's policy, the intentions of the parties, as well as any conventional and recognized practice of insurance companies that may have a bearing on the issue. (92 LA 263)

EXAMPLE: Employees' claims that were submitted for surgical fees for their dependents were subject to a "customary and reasonable" limitation under the major medical portion of an insurance agreement, an arbiter decided. The union contended that it obtained an agreement from the employer that the disputed limitation had been eliminated from the plan entirely. Arguing, however, that this was not the parties' intention, the employer claimed that the elimination of the limitation applied to surgical charges only and not to the major medical portion of coverage.

In order to reach a decision, the arbiter said it was necessary to rely upon what would be considered as a generally understood and accepted practice. Therefore, to aid in determining what was generally the conventional and recognized practice for applying the "customary and reasonable" limitation, the arbiter conferred with various insurance companies, insurance consultants, members of the medical profession, and executives of a county medical society. Finding that none of the sources contacted indicated that they knew of any agreements that did not leave some limitation on surgical charges such as the "customary and reasonable" constraint, the arbiter ruled that the limitation had not been eliminated under the major medical portion of the insurance agreement. Noting that the union itself realized that there must be some limitation, the arbiter concluded that no employer can be expected to open itself up to uncontrolled medical charges. (CWC Textron, 73 LA 15)

EXAMPLE: A company had a hospitalization plan for office workers with somewhat smaller benefits than the plan covering the bargaining unit. Company policy stated that employees who were also dependents of employees could not have double coverage.

While one bargaining-unit worker's wife was employed in the office, she became pregnant. Five months later she quit. When she delivered her child, the company paid her hospitalization benefits under the office plan. Her husband claimed the higher benefits for her as his dependent under the bargaining-unit plan. But the company argued that, because she was an employee at the time she became pregnant, she could not be insured as a dependent. Even if she could, it claimed, maternity coverage required a nine-month waiting period in either case, and it had not been that long since she quit and became covered as a dependent.

The arbiter said the nine months should be figured starting with the date the husband's insurance became effective, not the date the dependent became covered. In addition, the arbiter threw out the company's argument that the woman was an employee when her pregnancy began. Her status as her husband's dependent when she went to the hospital was what counted, the arbiter concluded. (Minnesota Mining & Mfg. Co., 32 LA 843)

EXAMPLE: An employer was not permitted to deduct Medicare benefits received by dependents from the minimum benefits specified in a collective bargaining contract, an arbiter held, even though a rider to the insurance company's master policy provided for such deductions. The rider, which went into effect when Medicare became effective, was issued after the effective date of the prior agreement, the arbiter noted, and the union objected strenuously to it at the time. There was no intention that the subject was discussed in negotiation of the current contract or that the union agreed to the deductions. (Indiana General Corp., 52 LA 45)

EXAMPLE: An employer did not violate its contractual obligation to provide major medical and life insurance benefits when its insurance carrier rejected an employee's application for dependent coverage for his wife under group health insurance on the ground that the spouse was not insurable based on her past medical record, an arbiter ruled. Even if the carrier erred in its determination that the employee's wife was not insurable, the employer provided benefits through the carrier's plan, the arbiter pointed out. Thus, the grievant's dispute was with the carrier and not employer, the arbiter concluded. (TSC Industries Inc., 71 LA 787)

Coordination of Benefits

Insurance companies in their agreements with employers often insert a "coordination of benefits" clause which has the effect of prohibiting family's recovery of double benefits in cases where husband and wife work for separate employers who provided separate hospitalization coverage for each. Arbitrators are split over the effect of such clauses on the employer's obligations under the union contract. (62 LA 493, 58 LA 984)

One school of thought is that the possibility of double coverage is one of the benefits under the union contract and that it therefore may not be terminated unilaterally by the employer without the union's consent. (52 LA 557, 54 LA 583)

Other arbiters, however, take the position that the intent of the parties in negotiating for insurance benefits was not to permit an employee to make a profit out of the group insurance plan. They therefore find no objection to coordination of benefits. (47 LA 1142, 49 LA 833, 54 LA 335)

Coverage of Absent Employees

Generally, in determining whether an employee who has been absent from work because of layoff, sickness, or a leave of absence is entitled to health and welfare benefits, arbiters must analyze and interpret the specific provision of the contract relating to those benefits. (65

LA 611, 64 LA 993, 64 LA 709, 62 LA 677, 61 LA 1188, 60 LA 411, 60 LA 162)

However, where the contract's language is ambiguous, arbiters must look to any established custom or past practice to interpret its application. (59 LA 635, 57 LA 674, 57 LA 335)

EXAMPLE: One arbiter ruled that an employee, who was recalled from a layoff but prevented from reporting back to work because of illness, was entitled to disability benefits since there was no past practice of denying sickness benefits in such cases. Although the employer conclusively proved that sickness benefits were never paid to laid-off employees who had not returned to the active payroll, the arbiter concluded that the employer's denial of the benefits to a "recalled" employee who failed to report to work due to illness did not have the "support of an established and accepted practice." (McCabe Powers Body Co., 64 LA 958)

EXAMPLE: In another situation where a contract required the company to pay 75 percent of the cost of hospitalization and surgical insurance for all employees, an arbiter ruled that the company had to keep up its share of the premiums for workers on indefinite layoff. He noted that the contract provided for the retention of seniority rights for two years after layoff. So these workers were still employees, he decided. For this reason he held that the company had to make insurance payments for the laid-off workers for at least two years afterward. (National Lead Co., 30 LA 333)

EXAMPLE: In a similar manner, one arbiter held that management could not terminate the insurance coverage of a worker on a two-year disability leave. Noting that since the worker had retained her seniority and that her name was on the latest seniority roster, he decided that she was still an employee within the meaning of the contract, so the company had to pay the premiums. (Dayton Economy Drug Co., 40 LA 1182)

EXAMPLE: Another arbiter ordered a company in a similar situation to keep up insurance payments for sick and injured workers for the duration of its contract. He based his decision on the company's practice under the previous contributory plan, which was to go on paying its share of the premiums for workers on extended absence as long as they paid their part. (Dayton Steel Foundry Co., 28 LA 595)

However, in some cases companies have not been required to make premium payments to health and welfare plans for absent workers. One arbiter, for example, allowed a company to continue to make payments into a group insurance fund only for persons on the payroll at the time the payments became due because it had done this for eight years without protest from the union. (Crown Upholstering Co., 20 LA 422; see also 94 LA 924, 94 LA 770)

In cases where an employee is prevented by illness from being at work at the time life insurance benefits are negotiated and thereafter dies without returning to the job, arbiters might examine various sources, other than the contract, to determine if the workers's beneficiaries are entitled to any compensation. (64 LA 676, 53 LA 304)

EXAMPLE: In deciding whether to deny payment to the beneficiaries of an employee who died while on sick leave, one arbiter emphasized that the group policy issued by the insurance carrier to the employer, as well as the explanatory handbook prepared by the insurance company for distribution to employees covered by the plan, had to be considered. (60 LA 69, 39 LA 198)

Coverage of Pregnant Employees

In determining an employer's obligations to pay pregnant employees or pregnant dependents healthcare benefits, arbiters generally examine and interpret the specific language of the insurance plan and the bargaining agreement.

EXAMPLE: An employee who took maternity leave was not entitled to sick pay under a contract obligating an employer to provide sickness and accident benefits for employees who were absent due to "illness" or "accident" an arbiter ruled, where the employee did not suffer medical complications during the prenatal period and otherwise experienced a "normal delivery." The employee was not "ill" within the meaning of the contract the arbiter reasoned. (Miller Brewing Co., 64 LA 389)

EXAMPLE: A single female employee who had a miscarriage was entitled to maternity benefits under a contract providing group insurance benefits to eligible employees including "usual reasonable customary-maternity benefit," an arbiter held, notwithstanding an employer's contention that the employee was ineligible on the ground that "usual reasonable customary" benefit applied only to employees who were under "family coverage" and not to the employee because she had "individual coverage." The arbiter found that maternity benefits were available to single employees with individual coverage in absence of clear contract language to the contrary. (Lear Siegler Inc., 63 LA 593; see also 95 LA 942)

Coverage of Strikers

Are employees who are out on strike, or who have not been recalled after a strike, eligible for health and welfare benefits? At least one arbiter and a state court have come to the conclusion that a striker is still an "employee" and therefore eligible for benefits.

EXAMPLE: During contract negotiations, the union at one company went out on strike. As part of the settlement of the dispute, the company agreed to reinstate all the strikers as they were needed. One of the strikers died before he was recalled for work, and the company refused to pay death benefits under the life insurance policy in effect "for all employees covered by this agreement," because the employee had not been working at the time of his death.

The arbiter said the company had to pay the benefits because it would have treated the employee as a continuing, rather than new, employee if he had returned to work before his death, which he had been willing and waiting to do. (Sidney Blumenthal & Co. Inc., 12 LA 715)

EXAMPLE: About three months after a union went on strike, one of the strikers was injured as the result of an accident that had no connection with the strike. Because of this injury, the employee was hospitalized and did not fully recover until a month after the rest of the strikers had returned to work. The company turned down his claim for disability benefits under the insurance plan in effect for it employees on the ground that he was not an "active" employee at the time of the injury.

A state court ruled that the claimant had not lost his status as an employee by going out on strike, so he was entitled to benefits since the employer had not notified employees that their insurance coverage would be cut off during the strike. The court found that the company had discontinued premium payments for employees on strike, so it ruled the employer, rather than the insurance carrier, liable for the benefits payments. (Tedesco v. Turner & Seymour Mfg. Co., Conn CtComPls, Litchfield Cty, 1954, 35 LRRM 2691)

EXAMPLE: When employees went on strike, the employer cancelled the hospitalization program without notifying the union or its members of his action. He contended that the strike had terminated the contract and that the cancellation of the insurance was a legitimate counter tactic. The arbiter held that the union's exercise of its right to strike did not destroy the contract relationship, so the employer had no right to cancel the insurance. Therefore, the employer was held liable for the claims of two men who were hospitalized during the strike. (National Seating Co., 45 LA 476)

However, in another case, cancellation of sickness and accident insurance during a strike was in keeping with the terms of the contract. Several workers suffered disabilities before the parties reached a settlement which again extended the coverage. These workers claimed benefits, but were not awarded them by the arbiter. He said that to do so would be to backdate the coverage to the period of the strike, which would be contrary to the terms of the contract. (E.J. Lavino & Co., 43 LA 213)

Retroactive Coverage

Suppose some employees are out sick when a new health insurance plan goes into effect. Can they claim benefits under the plan? At least one arbiter had decided that although persons out sick may be employees as far as other benefits are concerned, they are not covered employees for health insurance purposes until they return to work.

EXAMPLE: Several employees who were out on sick leave when a health insurance plan went into effect put in claims for health benefits, saying that under NLRB rulings they were "employees," and that the plan covered "employees in the bargaining unit." The arbiter rejected their claims on two counts. First, he said that since the plan limited the coverage with respect to laid-off employees, it was logical to make a similar distinction for those on sick leave. Second, he pointed out that insurance is by its nature prospective and designed to protect employees against future contingencies. He ruled, therefore, that employees could not be covered until they returned to active status in the company. (Schlitz Brewing Co., 23 LA 126)

Discrepancy Between Contract & Insurance Policy

When an employer-union contract conflicts with the terms of the insurance policy covering the employees, which one takes precedence? Arbitrators generally have held that an employer must live up to the agreement made with the union. In the case of a discrepancy, therefore, the company usually is held liable for benefits which the insurance carrier will not pay but which employees are entitled to under the union agreement.

EXAMPLE: An employee at one company was laid off because of illness and drew sick benefits for a period of 13 weeks. He did not return to work, and died more than a year after his absence started. His family claimed benefits provided by the contract and the insurance policy at the time of the employee's sickness layoff. However, the insurance policy for the employee had expired. The family, backed by the employee's union, maintained that the employee had been on a layoff status for the entire period of his illness and therefore had been covered by the union contract and its insurance clause for the same period. The company insisted that the employee's layoff had ended when his 13 week's sick benefits ended and that liability under the insurance clause had stopped there.

However, an arbitration board went along with the employee's family and the union and ruled that the employee was in the same position as a laid-off employee. Hence the company had to pay the claim, even though the carrier was no longer liable. The Board pointed out that the contract provided for seniority accumulation during a continuous layoff period of up to two years. Furthermore, they said that the contract provided insurance for "the employees and their dependents," but did not mention the status of employees on layoff or leave of absence. Since there was no distinction in the contract between active and laid-off employees with respect to benefits, the Board ruled that the company should have kept up the insurance and, since it did not do this, must pay the insurance benefit. (Jenkins Brothers, 22 LA 364)

EXAMPLE: An employee at one company lost four weeks' work because of illness. When she applied for the $10-a-week sick benefit specified by the union contract, the insurance carrier rejected her claim on the ground that she had been treated by a chiropractor rather than by a physician or osteopath as required by the insurance policy. An arbiter ordered the company to pay the sick benefits. The employee clearly was entitled to them, he pointed out, since the contract granted them after three months' service and did not call for a doctor's certificate or other proof of illness. (Crown Cotton Mills, 32 LA 3)

On the other hand, where the union agreement was ambiguous, an arbiter used insurance-plan standards as a guide to whether or not the employer was liable for benefit payments.

EXAMPLE: The contract with the union said simply that employees would be paid $2 for calls at a doctor's office and $3 for calls at home or a hospital. Since there were no other restrictions written into the agreement, the union said that payments to employees under the medical plan had to be made for all doctors' visits, while the company argued that benefits were payable only when employees were totally disabled and absent from work.

The arbiter upheld the employer's point of view. Since the contract did not describe eligibility rules, he said, it did not settle the matter. Therefore, he decided the union was bound by the standard eligibility provisions of comparable insurance plans, and they paid benefits only if employees were unable to work. Also, the background of negotiations showed that the union had suggested a plan at a cost of 40 cents a month per employee. At this figure, the arbiter noted, it was not possible to provide the comprehensive coverage which the union claimed was required by the contract. (Weaver Mfg. Co., 15 LA 471)

Who Pays for Insurance Rate Increase?

If the insurance carrier raises its rates on a contributory health and welfare plan, who is responsible for paying the increase — the employer or the employees? There is no problem, of course, if the agreement states that both the company and the employees pay a specified percentage of the cost. Then the parties would share equally the burden of any increase.

But, where a contract said that employees would pay a certain dollars-and-cents amount, with the employer paying the difference, one arbiter required the company to pay the increase. He ruled that by agreeing to pay the difference, the company had assumed the risk of a possible change in rates. (Goodman Mfg. Co., 15 LA 489)

Similarly, in a case where the company paid a flat dollar amount and workers picked up the balance plus any increase, one arbiter held that management had to pick up any increase for retirees. The contract stated that the "above mentioned" plan applied to retired people, but did not fix any limit on the company's contribution for them. Since the contract required management to provide medical coverage for retirees, and in fact the company already was paying more than the contract specified for their insurance, the arbiter said management had to pick up the increases, too. (National Lead Co., 38 LA 772; see also 54 LA 472, 71 LA 699)

Furthermore, even though workers were supposed to pay the full cost of the premium for dependents, management could not pass on an increase to them, another arbiter held. Dependents' coverage was a negotiated benefit offered to the workers at a monthly price of $1.95. Since the contract bound the company to maintain existing benefits "for the duration of the agreement," it had to pay the premium boost, the arbiter concluded, emphasizing that; any change in the amount of the workers' contribution would have to be negotiated. (Goshen Rubber Co., 38 LA 1231)

Who Gets Insurance Dividends?

If a negotiated insurance plan says that costs are to be split equally between the company and its employees, dividends from the insurance company should be divided 50-50, one arbiter has held.

EXAMPLE: One union negotiated a package deal that included increased hospital and medical benefits. The cost of these benefits was to be shared equally by the company and the workers. After the plan had been in effect for a while, the company received some dividends from the insurance carrier. It pocketed half of these and applied the other half against future employee contributions. The union protested, arguing that the dividends represented deferred wages and therefore belonged entirely to the workers.

The arbiter, though, said the company did right. The insurance agreement, he pointed out, did not provide for a fixed contribution by the company; it stated that costs were to be shared equally. Insurance dividends are an element of these costs, so it is fitting to divide them equally, the arbiter concluded. (Philip Carey Mfg. Co., 27 LA 651)

However, where the company paid a flat cents-per-hour per employee toward the cost of insurance, another arbiter said the workers were entitled to the full amount of an insurance rebate. The company's contribution of 5½ cents was payable whether the rates went up or down, the arbiter emphasized. Since the company had not made any overpayments, the arbiter held, the entire rebate should go to the workers. (Perkins Machine & Gear Co., 41 LA 435)

Part 10

Management Rights

Management Rights

IN BRIEF

Many arbiters recognize that, in the absence of a bargaining provision to the contrary, an employer retains all managerial rights not expressly forbidden by law. In many cases, arbiters have ruled that a specific contractual clause, containing either an express or implied limitation, is necessary in order to restrict management rights.

In other cases, some arbiters, at least with respect to certain issues, have taken the view that limitations upon management rights are not necessarily confined to those rights listed in a specific provision of the labor agreement. However, the restrictions may exist as "implied obligations" or "implied limitations" under a general provision of the contract, such as a recognition, seniority, or wage clause.

Additionally, arbiters may effectually modify management rights by imposing a standard of reasonableness as an implied term of the contract. Moreover, many arbiters are reluctant to uphold arbitrary or bad faith managerial actions that adversely affect employees, even where the contract expressly permits management complete discretion in the disputed matter.

Management rights continue to be limited by federal legislation designed to protect employee rights. Recent examples are: the Worker Adjustment Retraining Notification Act, requiring employers to give their employees 60-days' advance notice of covered plant closings and mass layoffs; the Drug Free Workplace Act, requiring covered employers to establish drug awareness programs; and the Employee Polygraph Protection Act, which limits employers' use of polygraph examinations on applicants and employees.

GUIDELINES

Rights Retained When Not Limited by Contract

Most arbiters agree that management retains all its rights that are not given up in the contract. This is so even if the agreement does not list all the rights that have been retained by management or has no management-rights clause at all.

EXAMPLE: An employer had the right to suspend employees for infraction of plant rules, an arbiter ruled, notwithstanding the union's contention that the contract permitted discharge for just cause but was silent on suspensions. Pointing out that the right to dismiss employees necessarily includes the right to impose lesser penalties, the arbiter observed that the omission of a management rights clause does not divest the employer of its inherent right to take disciplinary action less than dismissal for just cause. Noting that the employer's failure to suspend employees for the last several years did not defeat that right, the arbiter concluded that a related contract provision recognizing the right of the employer to take "disciplinary action including discharge" was an express acknowledgment that management had the right to suspend employees. (Sequoia Rock Co., 76 LA 114; see also 96 LA 1033, 91 LA 1251, 74 LA 1139, 71 LA 632, 41 LA 506, 15 LA 274)

On the other hand, the fact that a company retains all rights not given up through specific contract provisions does not mean it has a free hand to take any action it wants in the name of management rights. It is well established that a company's decisions made under a management-rights clause are subject to arbitration just like any other disputes over the interpretation or application of the agreement. (McInerey Spring & Wire Co., 9 LA 91)

EXAMPLE: An employer was required to apply "cause" or "just cause" as the standard for determining the propriety of an employee's discharge, an arbiter ruled, notwithstanding the employer's contention that the contract did not contain an express limitation of its right to discharge the employee, and therefore it retained discretion to terminate employees at will. Noting that the agreement did state that certain acts would not be cause for discipline, the arbiter concluded that it was reasonable to infer that the parties contemplated that any disciplinary action would be taken only for cause. (R L C & Son Trucking Inc., 70 LA 600)

Rights Surrendered by Negotiating

By asking the union's advice on a certain matter, management may lose its right to assert exclusive control over the subject, according to many arbiters. In making awards, they attempt to find the intent of the parties at the time of the discussion. A company may intend only to obtain the union's views on a subject, but if it has actually become a matter of collective bargaining and an agreement is made, arbiters insist that the employer live up to such agreement.

EXAMPLE: One employer association could not reduce the number of electricians on a ship to five after having agreed with the union that eight would be employed, even though there was no specific contract provision for this. The arbiter said that an employer could not submit a managerial function to collective bargaining, reach an agreement on it, and then repudiate the agreement. (Pacific American Shipowners Assn., 10 LA 736)

Furthermore, if a company brings up a matter in negotiations and fails to reach agreement with the union on it, management may lose the right to take action on the matter, even though it would otherwise be able to do so under the management rights clause.

EXAMPLE: During contract negotiations a company demanded a clause making overtime work compulsory, but the union refused to agree to one. The company signed the contract without it. Later, when some workers were suspended for refusing to work Saturdays, the company claimed it had a right to require overtime work because the agreement was silent on the point. But the arbiter decided that since the matter had been brought up in negotiations and no agreement was reached, the company had lost its absolute right to require employees to work overtime. (Sylvania Electric Products Inc., 24 LA 199)

TECHNOLOGICAL CHANGE

Introduction of New Machines

Employers generally claim the absolute right to install new and improved machinery. When it seems likely that it would result in rate changes or a cut in the number in the work force, the union may challenge management's right to make the change. But usually arbiters have held that a union cannot block technological improvement unless there are specific contract restrictions on the matter.

EXAMPLE: Where one contract specifically allowed a company to install new machines, an arbiter ordered the workers to run them to their full capacity in good faith, even though it meant the piece rates would have to be lowered.

The arbiter stated that there was sound economic justification for upholding management's right to introduce technical improvements. To rule for the union, he said, would lead toward economic stagnation. (Associated Shoe Industries of Southeastern Mass. Inc., 10 LA 535; see also 84 LA 788, 83 LA 39)

Transfer of Work Because of Mechanization

When work is mechanized, does management have the right to assign it to employees outside the bargaining unit? Awards suggest that it depends on how much change takes place in the way the work is performed. If a union can show that the workers in the unit are capable of continuing the work after the new machines are installed, then its gripe against transferring the work is likely to be upheld.

EXAMPLE: Employees in the bottling department of a brewing company had performed a manual testing operation on beer cans for seven or eight years; then the firm purchased a machine that could prepare the cans for testing more efficiently. It proposed turning the operation over to its machinists, who were in another bargaining unit.

The arbiter found that installing the machine would not really change the nature of the testing operation but would simply allow it to be done faster. Accordingly, he concluded that the proposed transfer would violate two sections of the union contract—the recognition clause, which gave the union jurisdiction over the customary work of the bargaining unit; and the job security clause, which reserved jobs in the bottling department for employees on the seniority list there.

All the signs were that the bottlers would be able to operate the machine satisfactorily, the arbiter noted. If they could not after a fair trial, he added, the company could then give the work to the machinists. (Hamm Brewing Co., 28 LA 46)

On the other hand, if a company can show that the nature of the work has changed so that the workers who were assigned to it can no longer handle it efficiently, an arbiter will no doubt uphold a decision to transfer it.

EXAMPLE: Timekeepers claimed that their seniority rights were violated when the company installed automatic data processing equipment that eliminated some of the duties formerly performed by them. In rejecting the timekeepers' claim, an arbiter said that the company had the right to mechanize its work procedures by utilizing data processing equipment. Moreover, he noted, the eliminated duties were not performed by any workers within or outside the bargaining unit, but by a machine. (Bethlehem Steel Co., 35 LA 72; see also Van Norman Machine Co., 28 LA 791)

Similarly, a union's recognition clause did not guarantee that bargaining unit work would continue unchanged indefinitely, according to the arbiter; hence he did not bar transfer of unit work to another department. When a publisher installed a computer in the subscription department, there was no longer any need for an addresso-graph operator. The arbiter held that the recognition clause extended to departments, not to types of work. Thus the union could not claim jurisdiction over a new system introduced into another department. (McCall Corp., 44 LA 201)

On a related matter: An employer had the right to assign technicians, instead of unit personnel, to develop a procedure for producing fuel rod simulators under a test program, an arbiter decided, since the contract gave the employer the right to use management personnel for "experimental purposes." Rejecting the union's argument that since unit personnel used the same tools, instruments and procedures used by the technicians, it followed that the work performed by the technicians was bargaining unit work, the arbiter stressed that this contention overlooked the needs and purpose of the employer's experimental and research work. The assignment of such work was specifically granted to management under the contract, and retained under the recognition clause the arbiter notes, concluding that to hold for the union would be in essence to find that management could not engage in essential experimental and developmental work. (Union Carbide Corp., 72 LA 1318, see also 93 LA 227, 91 LA 329, 85 LA 681, 84 LA 875, 83 LA 838, 82 LA 680, 72 LA 927)

ASSIGNING WORK

Right to Control Plant Operations

In general, arbiters have recognized broad authority in management, absent clear limitations in a contract, to determine and control the methods of its operations. (95 LA 840, 93 LA 48, 92 L A225, 88 LA 963, 88 LA 580, 88 LA 251, 87 LA 853, 85 LA 1079, 84 LA 1260, 84 LA 1020, 84 LA 273, 84 LA 175, 84 LA 15, 82 LA 910, 74 LA 1261, 73 LA 751, 71 LA 396, 65 LA 1309, 64 LA 1283, 64 LA 894, 61 LA 697, 60 LA 1106, 59 LA 1026)

EXAMPLE: One arbiter, ruled that a publisher had the right to use its presses to train management personnel, notwithstanding the union's contention that the bargaining agreement established the union's contention that the bargaining agreement established the union's jurisdiction over operation of the presses. The arbiter pointed out that if the union desired to prevent the publisher from using the presses in this manner, it should have included specific language to that effect in the contract. (Sacramento Newspaper Publishers Assn., 62 LA 1112)

Likewise, arbiters have upheld management's right to schedule work hours and to require overtime. (67 LA 257, 66 LA 1326, 66 LA 1338, 66 LA 577, 63 LA 1, 61 LA 16, 60 LA 905)

Work Not Covered by Job Descriptions

According to one arbiter, management's freedom to assign work is not restricted by job descriptions unless the contract expressly says so. The purpose of job descriptions, he said, is to describe duties for classification purposes; they seldom list all job requirements. Unless the contract says otherwise, he added, management is free to change duties and assignments; workers must perform assigned tasks, saving their protests for the regular grievance channels. (Pittsburgh Steel Co., 34 LA 598; see also 53 LA 1130, 61 LA 808)

Similarly, when a new contract dropped the status quo provisions that had prevented unilateral changes in work assignments, management was no longer bound by a past practice of only assigning one job at a time to mold makers, according to another arbiter. His ruling was that past practice under a prior contract is not binding unless the language giving rise to that practice is continued in the current contract. Therefore, he concluded, dual work assignments could be made unilaterally by management. (Overmyer Co., 43 LA 1006)

Likewise, another arbiter ruled that a publisher had the right to assign the work of filling, transporting and cleaning new portable ink tank equipment to paperhandlers, instead of to pressmen. Since there was a lack of evidence clearly establishing that the work in question was within the traditional scope of pressmen's work, the arbiter decided that the assignment constituted a reasonable management decision. (Detroit News, 62 LA 313)

Eliminating Job

Does a contract clause giving management the right to assign work forces permit the company unilaterally to eliminate a job? A number of arbiters have held that management can eliminate or combine jobs in the interest of efficiency or economy, so long as its action is not arbitrary and is not prohibited by the contract.

EXAMPLE: An employer had the right to assign to "unrepresented" personnel duties that its receptionists had performed prior to the elimination of their jobs as a economy measure, an arbiter ruled. Pointing out that the effect on the bargaining unit was minor, since the work had not been performed exclusively by unit employees, the arbiter emphasized that the job elimination was for good business reasons. Noting that there was no contract language expressly prohibiting the employer from assigning work to non-unit employees when the assignment has been made in good faith and for good reasons, the arbiter upheld management's right to transfer the work. (Lake City Elks Lodge, 72 LA 643; see also 96 LA 844, 91 LA 329, 29 LA 324, 23 LA 561, 15 LA 783)

However, a contract may have other clauses that restrict a company's decision to do away with a job under the management-rights clause.

EXAMPLE: Where a contract gave the company the right to assign work forces, but also prohibited changes in job classifications except where a new job was created or changes made in the production process, one arbiter would not permit the company to wipe out a mouldman-leader's job which had not changed in content. (Bethlehem Steel Co., 17 LA 295).

Eliminating Classification

If there is no longer any work required in a job classification, can an employer do away with it? Awards apparently depend upon the wording in individual contracts.

EXAMPLE: One arbiter held that a company was prohibited from divvying up the duties of the welder-inspector classification and abolishing it without getting the union's approval because its contract specifically said that job descriptions and classifications would remain unchanged unless both parties agreed to change them. (Lone Star Steel Co., 26 LA 160)

EXAMPLE: Even where there was no specific restriction but where the contract established rates of pay for several classifications, an arbiter ruled that the company could not eliminate a classification by itself. He said that the combining and elimination of classifications was a subject for negotiation between the parties. (Kansas Grain Co., 29 LA 242)

EXAMPLE: Although a "bargaining unit work" clause did not freeze work, a company was not allowed to abolish a unit job only to reassign its duties as a non-unit job. The company contended that, since the jobs were clerical, they should not be considered part of the unit. However, the arbiter found no evidence in the contract that the parties had intended to limit the bargaining unit to actual production work. (Gisholt Machine Co., 44 LA 840; see also 84 LA 788)

On the other hand, several arbiters believe that in the absence of contract restrictions, management has the right to eliminate a classification by transferring its duties to others.

EXAMPLE: One arbiter decided that a company did not violate the seniority provisions of the contract by laying off men in one classification and assigning their duties to workers with less seniority. Seniority rights do not guarantee that a job will remain in existence or that its content will not be changed, he reasoned. (Axelson Mfg. Co., 30 LA 444; see also 90 LA 758, 90 LA 67, 89 LA 118, 71 LA 396, 54 LA 365)

Combining Jobs

If the work on a certain job is reduced through technological changes, can the workers be required to take on duties belonging to another classification? In one case an arbiter found nothing in the agreement to prevent combining jobs in this way. But, he warned, such combinations could not be used to fill vacancies.

EXAMPLE: Because of technological changes, a time clerk and a die setter did not have enough work to occupy them full time. To keep them busy, the company had them spend part of their time on work in other classifications. The union argued that this violated the seniority provisions of the contract; if more people were needed in these other classifications, it said, the regular procedure for filling vacancies should have been followed.

An arbiter found nothing in the contract forbidding out-of-classification assignments. On the other hand, he said, the company could not use this device to fill vacancies. To determine whether vacancy existed, the arbiter applied this rule: If either the time clerk or the die setter spent more than 50 percent of his time on work in some other classification, he filled a vacancy in that classification. Since neither employee did so, the company acted within its rights. (Fletcher-Enamel Co., 27 LA 466; see also, 53 LA 33)

EXAMPLE: Another arbiter found nothing wrong with the action of an employer who combined the duties of three jobs into one classification and offered to negotiate with the union over a wage rate for the new job. He said that the job-protection clause primarily was aimed at maintaining the pay scale, not at preventing all changes in classifications. (Sewanee Slica Co., 47 LA 282)

Moving Jobs Between Shifts

Where there was no specific contract ban on it, at least one arbiter ruled that a company could move a vacant job from one shift to another in the interest of efficiency.

EXAMPLE: When a day-shift cleaning job opened up at one company, management posted it as a night-shift job. It figured the cleaning work could be done better when regular employees were out of the way. It assured the union that it was not going to transfer any of the day-shift cleaners but would simply move jobs to the night shift as vacancies occurred. The union nevertheless contended that the job should have been posted as a day-shift vacancy.

An arbiter noted that the posting provision of the contract was of the ordinary type, requiring the posting of new jobs and vacancies. In his view, nothing in the clause limited the company's choice of the shift to which a particular job was assigned. The union's claim that upholding the company's action would pave the way for a wholesale transfer of jobs to the night shift did not impress the arbiter; the existence of night-shift premiums was an effective deterrent, he remarked. (White Motor Co., 29 LA 153)

Determining and Filling Job Vacancies

Arbiters have upheld management's contractual right to determine whether a job vacancy exists and whether it should be filled.

EXAMPLE: Under the management rights clause of a contract, an employer had the right not to fill three computer jobs that it previously posted, an arbiter decided, since contrary to the union's contention, the contract did not limit management's authority to determine whether job vacancies existed in the plant. (Computing & Software Inc., 61 LA 261)

EXAMPLE: An employer had the right to temporarily fill vacant job of production utility during the period that the job was being posted, an arbiter ruled, since the contract gave management this right. (Right Away Food Corp., 60 LA 230; see also 94 LA 1183, 90 LA 577, 86 LA 1102, 86 LA 173, 84 LA 390, 84 LA 36, 83 LA 801, 83 LA 445, 82 LA 708)

However, where duties associated with the vacancy are reassigned and continue to be performed by employees in other jobs, arbiters will examine whether the employer intentionally has avoided contractually required procedures for filling jobs. (Homestake Mining Co., 88 LA 614, see also 85 LA 449, 85 LA 290, 84 LA 390)

WORK BY SUPERVISORS

Absence of Contract Ban on Work by Supervisors

Does management have the right to assign production work to supervisors if the contract does not specifically say they cannot do the work usually performed by members of the bargaining unit? Under these circumstances arbi-

MANAGEMENT RIGHTS

ters permit employers to assign production work to supervisors only so long as the rights of bargaining-unit employees are not violated.

EXAMPLE: One arbiter said that although a company had the right to assign certain work to supervisors, it could not exercise this right if it would deprive employees in the unit of their right to work when sufficient work was available. (Bethlehem Steel Co., 14 LA 159; see also 39 LA 530)

EXAMPLE: Under a contract where the job of gang-boss was made a part of the promotion sequence, a company was not allowed to assign this job to supervisors outside the unit because it violated the seniority provisions. (West Virginia Pulp & Paper Co., 12 LA 1074)

EXAMPLE: Another arbiter held that a company could not assign duties of shopping checker to a foreman without the union's consent because the transfer meant changing the job's content, which had been set by the agreement. (Kraft Foods Corp., 10 LA 254)

However, one arbiter said that under its contract management was allowed to transfer supervisors to bargaining-unit jobs during slack seasons. The contract said that the company could retain as many as 30 employees regardless of their seniority if in the sole judgment of the company, their special training, experience, or ability was needed. Although the union argued that this clause applied to technical workers only, the arbiter said it extended to supervisors. Since the company was "sole judge" of who needed to be retained, it has the right to make 30 transfers of non-unit workers to bargaining-unit jobs, he decided. The only limit on management, he added, was that it could not act in bad faith in selecting the men for transfer or use the clause to subvert the union. (Jefferson City Cabinet Co., 35 LA 117)

Work by Supervisors During Emergency

Contract bans on supervisors' performance of bargaining-unit work often contain an exception permitting such work in an "emergency." Arbitrators generally take a narrow reading of such exceptions and require firm evidence of a true emergency.

EXAMPLE: Sending a supervisor to an airport to pick up a cylinder was held not to be an "emergency." (Masonite Corp., 53 LA 965) Nor were "emergencies" found in the use of supervisors to make withdrawals and requisitions for employees (Masonite Corp., 53 LA 965), or in the performance by supervisors of Sunday washroom work caused by a temporary breakdown at another plant. (F.W. Means & Co., LA 54 874)

However, an employer had the right to assign supervisors to replace a sprinkler valve that had blown off and caused water to spill into an oil room, an arbiter decided. Despite the fact that the work customarily was done by pipefitters, the arbiter upheld management's action since the work was of an emergency nature. (Diamond National Corp. and Paperworkers, 61 LA 567)

Similarly, a brewery did not violate a contract's provision barring supervisory personnel from performing unit work, an arbiter ruled, when, during the course of repair of a malfunctioning crowning machine by a machinist who was not wearing a safety shield, a supervisor pushed away bottles on a conveyor that was moving toward the machine. The danger of an explosion arising from the flow of the bottles constituted an "emergency," the arbiter reasoned. (Anheuser Busch Inc., Jacksonville Plant and Teamsters, 62 LA 1130; see also 74 LA 1175, 71 LA 454)

Application of "De Minimis" Principle

arbiters may decide to overlook a technical violation of a ban on supervisors performing bargaining unit work, where the violation was so minor as to warrant application of the "de minimis principle," which calls for ignoring inconsequential violations.

EXAMPLE: No substantive violation was found in a supervisor's distribution of hand tools to pipefitters while the counterman was off duty (Stauffer Chemical Co., 53 LA 706), or in a supervisor's dusting and sweeping an office where there was no indication that an employee was adversely affected. (Ideal Cement Co., 52 LA 9)

Likewise, a mine operator did not violate a contract when a foreman loaded roof bolting supplies found in a unitrack that he used to transport himself to a certain section of the mine, an arbiter held. Even assuming that the operation of the unitrack with bolting supplies in it was "classified work," the operation, which lasted for 25 minutes, would be covered under the de minimis rule, the arbiter concluded. (Consolidation Coal Co., 65 LA 892; see also 75 LA 569)

Effect of Other Clauses

Even under contracts which do not clearly forbid supervisors to do bargaining-unit work, some arbiters have found the parties' intent in other clauses.

EXAMPLE: In one such situation a working foreman was advanced to assistant superintendent but kept doing production work. The union complained that this violated a clause limiting the number of supervisors to three. But an arbiter held that this must have been meant to limit only the number of working supervisors because a company's right to employ any number of nonworking supervisors is not ordinarily restricted. The company had not exceeded this limit, so the arbiter ruled that the superintendent could continue doing production work. (Mt. Carmel Public Utility Co., 16 LA 59)

EXAMPLE: Under another contract lacking a definite ban on production work by supervisors, an arbiter found help from a clause stating that no employee would be temporarily transferred to a job in another department where the worker regularly handling the job was on layoff. This, the arbiter said, prevented the company from letting a foreman do a job ordinarily done by a bargaining-unit man who was laid off. (Sayles Biltmore Bleacheries Inc., 26 LA 585)

Effect of Past Practice

When faced with ambiguous contracts some arbiters have answered questions of work by supervisors by looking at the company's past practice.

EXAMPLE: One arbiter, noting that a contract definition of bargaining-unit work was ambiguous focused on the way in which the definition had been applied. Over a period of three years, he noted, management had on every occasion withdrawn supervisors from assignments which the union claimed were bargaining-unit work. Since management itself had given this consistent interpretation to the contract terminology, the arbiter found it binding, despite the fact that the union had tried unsuccessfully to negotiate a specific ban on supervisors' doing production work. (Los Angeles Drug Co., 29 LA 38; see also 88 LA 406, 84 LA 549, 83 LA 792, 82 LA 534, 75 LA 963, 74 LA 13, 73 LA 529)

However, one arbiter would not let a company continue assigning supervisors to bargaining-unit work merely because it had done so for several years without the union's forcing arbitration of the issue. (Great Lakes Pipe Line Co., 27 LA 748; see also 75 LA 450)

Monitoring of Automated Machinery

Can management, after installing automatic equipment to operate its machines, assign supervisors to monitor the equipment and eliminate the job of machine operator? Even where the contract contained a prohibition on the performance by supervisors of "work normally performed" by bargaining-unit workers, an arbiter ruled that this was permissible. The machine operator's duties had been taken over by mechanical devices rather than by supervision, he reasoned. Control-room monitoring, he stated, is closer to the normal duties of supervisors than to the work done by bargaining-unit workers.

At the same time, the arbiter held that it would be improper for supervisors to operate the machines manually or to do physical work in cleaning, repairing, or adjusting them. (Goodyear Tire & Rubber Co., 35 LA 917)

Work by Supervisors to Test Standards

Under a contract containing a general ban on the performance of production work by supervisors, one arbiter ruled that management violated the agreement when it assigned supervisors to such work, outside regular hours, to prove that production standards were fair. However, in view of a clause stating that supervisors could do production work for the purpose of instructing workers, he said the assignment in question would have been proper if the workers who regularly performed the work had been called in to observe the demonstration. (National Lead Co., of Ohio, 34 LA 235)

Effect of Strike

A ban on assigning supervisors to bargaining-unit work does not apply during a strike, in the opinion of one arbiter. Such a ban is designed to protect the job rights of union members on duty or available for work, he said. It has no application when the members refuse to work, he reasoned, since in such a case they are not displaced by supervisors. (Texas Gas Corp., 36 LA 1141; see also 75 LA 1302)

Ban Applied to Other Non-Unit Workers

At least one arbiter has decided that a contract clause forbidding supervisors to do bargaining unit work applied to other workers outside the unit as well.

EXAMPLE: At one company, requisitions for materials on night and weekend shifts were too infrequent to justify having a stock clerk on duty. Plant guards, who were not in the bargaining unit, handled the occasional requisitions on those shifts. The union protested. It would have been okay to have some other bargaining unit member take over stock-clerk duties, the union said, but it was wrong for plant guards to do the work.

The arbiter agreed. Although having plant guards handle bargaining-unit work was not specifically forbidden by the contract, the arbiter thought the effect of using them was the same as that of using supervisors; it deprived members of the bargaining unit of work that should have been theirs. Unit members have a vested right in bargaining-unit work, the arbiter stated, and no worker outside the unit has the right to horn in on it. (Reynolds Metals Co., 26 LA 756)

PRODUCTION STANDARDS

Right to Establish Production Standards

If the contract does not provide yardsticks for measuring employee efficiency, can management adopt its own standards? Most arbiters hold that an employer can, so long as whatever standards it sets are fair and reasonable. (90 LA 570, 85 LA 254, 70 LA 1152, 65 LA 405, 65 LA 380, 65 LA 270, 64 LA 885, 60 LA 491, 33 LA 725)

EXAMPLE: One company gave an employee a warning stating that he was producing only 42 percent of the average of other employees doing comparable work. The union squawked, pointing out that the contract made no reference to production or efficiency standards. Neither side meant for such standards to be used in evaluating performance, it claimed. The company, though, figured its action came within the scope of the management rights clause, under which it retained the right to manage the plant, direct the work force, and suspend and discharge employees for just cause.

An arbiter upheld the company's position. The right to manage the plant and direct the work force would be almost meaningless, in his opinion, if the company could not judge efficiency and require a reasonable level to be maintained. If some benchmark was to be used to measure performance, he added, management had to discipline all those individuals whose records compared least favorably with the standard. Failure to apply the standard in an even-handed manner would violate the "just cause" requirement, he commented. (Menasco Mfg. Co., 30 LA 264)

Similarly, another arbiter said management could establish production standards where workers previously had set their own standards. Nothing indicated that the parties intended old practices to be continued indefinitely, he noted, and the union had been notified that the establishment was being contemplated. There was no evidence that the new standards were unreasonable, he said, and the company's failure to exercise a right did not waive that right. Further, the contract allowed management to "establish production and work standards" and to eliminate practices which were inefficient or unreasonable. (Mead Corp., 41 LA 1038)

However, an employer did not have the right to establish a productivity improvement program which imposed predetermined discipline on employees for failing to meet production standards, an arbiter ruled. Rejecting the employer's contention that establishing the program was an exercise of its exclusive and unilateral right to manage the plant, the arbiter decided that the arbitrary application of discipline changed the conditions of employment for the employees. Such a change requires mutual agreement by the parties, the arbiter noted, pointing out that the evidence established that there were no negotiations or mutual agreement with respect to the program, or any implied waiver by the union of such negotiations.

However, the employer would have been entitled to establish the program had it not included the disciplinary features, the arbiter concluded. (Union Carbide Corp., 70 LA 201; see also 86 LA 6)

Right to Change Size of Work Crew

If the contract mentions the number of employees to be used in the work crew on a particular job, can the company adjust the size of the crew because of changes in the volume of business or other factors?

Under a contract which stated that "no less than three men shall be employed in a crew ...." an arbiter ruled that, regardless of workload, the company could not cut the size of the crew for the duration of the contract. (Weston Biscuit Co. Inc., 21 LA 653)

Similarly, in another case, where the contract banned reduction in existing crew size but permitted negotiations on size in certain situations, an arbiter held that management could not negotiate for a smaller crew. Although the contract did not expressly confine negotiations to increasing, rather than decreasing crew sizes, the arbiter thought it was the parties' intent to maintain the state minimum manning, at least for the contract term. Nothing barred them from resolving the issue when the new contract negotiations occurred, he added. (Sinclair Oil Corp., 41 LA 878)

Likewise, when a salt company installed new conveyor equipment, it did not have the right to eliminate workers engaged in sacking the salt, an arbiter decided. The contract's wage schedule specified that the crews consist of 11 workers, and, for this reason, the employer was not allowed to reduce the size of the sacking crews, despite the fact that only nine men were needed. (Barton Salt Co. 46 LA 503; see also 92 LA 453, 86 LA 357)

However, another arbiter upheld a company's action in reducing the size of a work crew after the work had been mechanized and thus required fewer workers. The contract required a certain crew size "under present conditions." The "present conditions" mentioned in the contract no longer existed, the arbiter said. (Theo. Hamm Brewing Co., 35 LA 243)

MANAGEMENT RIGHTS

Similarly, in the absence of a contract requiring an employer to employ a specified number of electricians to operate mechanical devices used at its racing tracks, the employer had the right to employ two, instead of three electricians to perform the work, an arbiter decided. (West Flagler Assoc., LTD, 61 LA 1253)

Likewise, an employer that purchased a folding carton plant of another company properly required pressmen to operate the cutting press machine without help, an arbiter ruled, since the employer made technological modifications on the equipment that rendered a reduction in crew size feasible. (Container Corp. of America, 65 LA 517; see also 92 LA 553, 76 LA 1099, 76 LA 903, 74 LA 820, 71 LA 185)

PLANT TRANSFER

Relocation of Operations

What effect does a contract between a company and a union have on management's right to move the entire plant or relocate some of the operations to locations outside the union's jurisdiction?

The U.S. Supreme Court has ruled that a company that moves a plant to a new location may be required to arbitrate the question of employment rights at the new plant even though (1) the new plant is a considerable distance away and (2) the contract has expired. (Carpenters v. Kimball Co., US SupCt, 1965, 57 LRRM 2628)

EXAMPLE: In one case, an arbiter said management had a right to shut down, buy out a competitor, and transfer operations during contract term. As to its duty to bargain, this meant consulting with the union on its decision to move, he held, not yielding to union opposition to the move. In this case, management refused to give workers any transfer rights, which the union contended violated seniority provisions. However, the arbiter decided the workers had no seniority at the other plants, since these were under contracts with other locals. (Sivyer Steel Casting Co., 39 LA 449)

EXAMPLE: An employer had the right to transfer its bar soap operation from its plant at which employees were represented by a union to its out-of-state plant at which employees were represented by another union, an arbiter held, since the contract prohibited interference with the right of the employer to "permanently eliminate jobs." (Lever Bros. Co., 65 LA 1299; see also 91 LA 849, 74 LA 407, 71 LA 873, 71 LA 120)

Remedy for Improper Relocation

Depending on the circumstances and the wording of the contract, arbiters have fashioned remedies for the workers affected by plant closing and relocation ranging from severance pay to an order directing the company to reestablish the original plant.

EXAMPLE: A contract between a union and a clothing manufacturer specifically prohibited removal of the plant or the manufacture of garments in any other factory without the consent of the union. After a shutdown that the union was told was temporary, the manufacturer moved his operations to a new plant in another state. The move was accomplished at night and over weekends without the union's knowledge.

Finding that the move violated the contract, an arbiter directed the manufacturer to discontinue operations in the new plant, reestablish the factory in the state from which he had moved, and pay the union damages of over $200,000 covering wage, vacation, and welfare-fund payments for 300 workers. (Jack Meilman, 34 LA 771; see also 36 LA 1364)

EXAMPLE: When one company announced that it was going to move its finishing operations from Danbury, Conn., to Philadelphia, the union charged that this would be a lockout in violation of its contract.

An arbiter found that the shift was being made for business reasons. This being so, he said, only an express contract provision could stop the move, since a company's freedom to move is not limited by the mere existence of a contract. Nevertheless he ruled that management should have discussed the move in advance with the union. Moreover, he said, available jobs should have been offered to those employees willing to go to Philadelphia, and their moving expenses paid. Those who did not make the move, he decided, were entitled to severance pay plus a share of the pension fund.

The company voluntarily offered to pay supplemental unemployment benefits totalling about $45,000 to employees staying in Connecticut, but the arbiter figured this was not enough. He was not sure that he had authority to order payment of severance benefits; but to the extent that he did, he ordered the company to set aside $100,000 for severance pay and moving expenses. (John B. Stetson Co., 28 LA 514)

EXAMPLE: An employer was obligated to compensate employees for their loss of pay caused by the relocation of its distribution facility to its main plant in another locality, an arbiter decided, since the management rights clause did not entitle the employer to close the distribution facility for economic reasons. (Sealtest Dairy and Teamsters, 65 LA 858)

EXAMPLE: An employer that phased out its roller bearing operations at its plants in one area was obligated, according to contractual language, to give eligible senior employees hiring preference at its existing plant in another location to which production of some of its rolling bearing operation had been transferred, an arbiter ruled. (Federal-Mogul Corp., 61 LA 745)

MISCELLANEOUS PROBLEMS

Right to Promulgate Reasonable Plant Rules

It is well established that management has the right unilaterally to promulgate reasonable rules—not inconsistent with law or the collective bargaining agreement—and to enforce such rules through disciplinary action. (96 LA 499, 95 LA 729, 92 LA 497, 92 LA 390, 92 LA 181, 92 LA 68, 91 LA 1251, 91 LA 969, 91 LA 375, 90 LA 729, 89 LA 1069, 89 LA 1065, 87 LA 529, 84 LA 688, 77 LA 705, 77 LA 320, 77 LA 249, 76 LA 935, 76 LA 827, 76 LA 249, 74 LA 58, 72 LA 250, 71 LA 306, 63 LA 896, 63 LA 467, 60 LA 924, 60 LA 778)

EXAMPLE: In one case, the arbiter emphasized that the employer clearly has the right, and in fact, the responsibility, to impose the ultimate penalty of discharge where plant rules definitely have been violated. (Walker Manufacturing Co., 60 LA 645)

However, while management generally has the right to promulgate reasonable plant rules, arbiters may restrict that right where the rules are deemed unreasonable, vague, ineffective, or arbitrary. (77 LA 807, 75 LA 975, 74 LA 770, 74 LA 252, 73 LA 443, 73 LA 684, 72 LA 588)

Regulation of Coffee Breaks

Can management, during the term of a contract, unilaterally establish definite rules regarding coffee breaks to replace a practice of allowing individual workers to select their own coffee-break times? According to one arbiter, such an action is a legitimate exercise of management's rulemaking powers.

EXAMPLE: For years employees at one company had been permitted to take breaks for coffee and other refreshments according to their individual wishes. In time this arrangement reached the point where it was seriously hindering production—an employee might take a break that would stop a production line and when he returned another might knock off, and so on down the line. To remedy this situation, the company made a rule limiting breaks to set periods in the morning and afternoon. The union immediately protested that this amounted to a change in working conditions in violation of its contract.

An arbiter pointed out that the firm's action did not end the practice of allowing breaks but actually gave it official recognition and status. This was not a change in working conditions, he concluded. (Dover Corp., 33 LA 860; see also 74 LA 312, 39 LA 1265)

On the other hand, an employer could not unilaterally reduce the number of rest periods which had remained the same for five years. According to the arbiter, such a seasoned practice took on the status of an obligation binding on both parties. It was a working condition set by past practice, and, as such was not subject to unilateral action. (Formica Corp., 44 LA 467)

Similarly, an employer that had a past practice of giving three paid coffee breaks' to its transfer drivers improperly discontinued the third break following the effective date of a new collective bargaining contract, an arbiter decided, since the practice was of long standing and the parties specifically agreed during contract negotiations that the practice would continue under the new contract. (Pacific Clay Products, 62 LA 706)

Likewise, an employer was not entitled to make a unilateral change in coffee breaks from the "honor system," under which employees could take breaks when they wished, an arbiter held, since the honor system was a practice of long standing and the change to a seven-minute break was an unreasonable alternative in view of management's failure to establish that the break period was of sufficient duration. (Ohmstede Machine Works Inc., 62 LA 45; see also 72 LA 470)

Installation of Time Clocks

Does management have the right to install the clocks without first getting the union's go-ahead? Time clocks are a condition of employment over which a company is obligated to bargain, one arbiter has said. But if the subject of installing them is raised in contract negotiations and the union registers no objection, management may be able to put in time clocks without discussing the matter further with the union.

EXAMPLE: Shortly after signing a union contract, a company started requiring office employees to punch time clocks. The union claimed this step violated a contract clause requiring the company to negotiate with the union on conditions of employment. The company maintained that it merely had exercised a management right. Even if the issue were bargainable, the company argued, the union had waived its right to bargain about installation of time clocks by failing to negotiate on the point when management representatives brought it up in negotiations.

An arbiter decided that the company did have an obligation to bargain over the time clocks, but he agreed with management that the union had lost out by failing to pursue the matter in negotiations. The union might have ground for complaint, he added, if the time clocks were used in an unfair way. (Motor Wheel Corp., 26 LA 931)

EXAMPLE: The exact procedures for clocking in and out were within the exclusive authority of management, an arbiter decided. While manual time clocks had been used in the past, the arbiter found nothing wrong with the company's introduction of IBM units for clocking in and out. He said that the installation of new equipment was not a condition of employment, and therefore, not a subject for union involvement. (Babcock & Wilcox Co., 45 LA 897)

EXAMPLE: An employer had the right to install a special time clock outside the restroom and to require employees to punch their time cards on entering and leaving, under guidelines that were instituted to prevent the abuse of emergency use of the restroom, an arbiter ruled. Rejecting the contention that the use of the time clock by female employees was "humiliating and undignified," the arbiter concluded that it was inconceivable that female employees under a female supervisor would experience any embarrassment among practically all female workers. (Cagle's poultry and Egg Co., 73 LA 34)

On the other hand, an employer did not have the right to institute a rule requiring employees to keep a time clock record of all their visits to the toilet in an effort to solve the problem of too much loss of worktime loitering in the washrooms, an arbiter decided. Even though the rule may have resulted in an increase in production, the arbiter rejected its implementation, since it also resulted in a loss of dignity and embarrassment to employees. Although no one can blame the employer for wanting to curb wasteful practices of a small number of loiterers, other methods can be found to reduce the incidence of loitering without imposing onerous and humiliating timekeeping procedures on all employees, the arbiter concluded. (Schmidt Cabinet Co. Inc., 75 LA 397)

Change in Pay Periods

Does management have the right to change the frequency of pay periods during the term of a contract without getting the union's consent? It probably does, arbiters' rulings suggest, if the contract does not say when employees are to be paid.

EXAMPLE: When a company decided to pay employees on a bi-weekly basis instead of weekly, the union argued this was a change in past practice that violated its contract. The arbiter disagreed. In the first place, he said, the dispute was not even arbitrable since the contract said nothing about pay periods and specifically stated that only grievances arising out of the operation or interpretation of the agreement could be arbitrated.

Despite what the agreement said, the arbiter noted that he might have ruled on the merits of the case if the parties had had an informal understanding about pay periods. But although the company had had a weekly pay system for years, the union never said anything about it; such "mute acquiescence" did not establish a binding past practice, the arbiter concluded. (Cone Mills Corp., 30 LA 100)

EXAMPLE: An employer did not improperly eliminate a local working condition when it began to distribute paychecks to bricklayers by mid-afternoon on Tuesdays, instead of at the end of their rotating shift at 8 a.m. on Tuesday, an arbiter ruled, notwithstanding the union's contention that the basis of the local working condition was to save employees the inconvenience of having to return to the plant on their Wednesday or Thursday day off to pick up their paychecks. There was sufficient reason for eliminating the local working condition, the arbiter concluded, because the employer changed its payroll operations so that all employee paychecks were distributed on Tuesday. (Bethlehem Steel Corp., 66 LA 227)

Compulsory Retirement

IN BRIEF

During the later 1940's and early 1950's there could not be any dispute as to the right of an employer to unilaterally set a mandatory retirement age in the absence of specific contractual restriction, according to one arbiter. However, in the middle 1950's, a different theory began to emerge under which if the union did not acquiesce, but instead objected to the institution of a compulsory retirement plan, forcible retirement of an otherwise physically able employee would be held to violate the job security provision of a contract. (Cummins Power Inc., 51 LA 909)

Since then there has been a split of authority on the employer's right unilaterally to set a mandatory retirement age in the absence of a specific contract restriction.

For example, one arbiter ruled that retirement is a very important condition of employment, and a union has the right to bargain for a condition of employment. (Consolidated Packaging Corp., 51 LA 47)

Still, another arbiter decided that discharge, as used in collective bargaining, is not synonymous with termination by retirement, and it is "a well-established principle in arbitration" that in the absence of any contract restriction, the employer has the unilateral right to establish and administer a compulsory retirement policy. (Brown Line Co., 50 LA 597)

Another arbiter ruled that the forced retirement of a physically able and competent employee is a violation of his security and seniority rights, especially where the retirement policy and plan is unilaterally announced and is not spelled out in a jointly-established agreement. (Armour Agricultural Chemical Co., 47 LA 513)

Additionally, the prohibitions against compulsory retirement incorporated in the 1978 amendments to the Age Discrimination in Employment Act, and in some state fair-employment-practice laws, have caused more split decisions in this area. The ADEA amendments removed the 70-year age limitation applicable to employees who are protected under the ADEA; therefore, with limited exceptions — e.g., for persons in a "bona fide executive or a high policy-making position" — compulsory retirement of employees 65 or older is prohibited. (87 LA 985, 87 LA 137, 74 LA 1121, 74 LA 278, 70 LA 245)

GUIDELINES

▶ Since no consistent pattern has emerged in arbiter's rulings on whether a company may require workers to retire at a fixed age, all the circumstances of the particular case must be examined including what the basic contract says, what the company's past practice has been, what has happened in past negotiations, and the like.

▶ Generally a long-standing policy of retiring workers at a certain age may be continued by a company, despite the existence of a bargaining agreement.

▶ If the union has had an opportunity to bargain on the subject of retirement and has passed it up, the employer may be within its rights in putting a policy into effect during the contract term.

▶ It has usually, though not always, been held that a forced retirement does not violate a just-cause discharge provision.

▶ A compulsory retirement policy, to be valid and enforceable during the term of a contract, must have been announced in clear terms to workers and applied consistently.

Long-Standing Policy

If the company has had a compulsory retirement policy in effect for several years before it ever signs a contract with a union, does it retain the right to follow this policy after the contract goes into effect? Many arbiters have held that management does retain the right.

EXAMPLE: An employer properly ordered an employee to retire upon reaching the age 65 pursuant to a retirement plan that it uniformly and consistently administered for almost seven years, an arbiter decided. Although the contract on its face was silent on the subject of mandatory retirement, the arbiter noted that the employer and the union had acknowledged, at a special meeting during contract negotiations, that pre-existing and uniformly applied mandatory retirement plans would be allowed to continue. While the employer's failure to communicate the mandatory retirement plan to employees was inexcusable, the arbiter concluded that this failure by itself did not destory the vitality of the plan. (Illinois-California Express Inc., 63 LA 805)

On the other hand, a school board that had a practice of retiring teachers at age 70 improperly established a new policy compelling them to retire at age 65, an arbiter held, since the contract barred the employer from changing past policy or practice affecting employee wages, hours, or working conditions, without mutual agreement between the employer and the union. An employee's expectation as to the duration of his employment permeates his job performance, his attitude toward his employer, and his job morale in a manner that makes the expectation an "employee working condition," the arbiter concluded. (Jefferson County Bd. of Education, 69 LA 890)

Moreover, even though an employer's mandatory retirement policy predated the bargaining contract and was uniformly imposed upon employees in other parts of the country, an arbiter ruled that the company improperly forced an employee to retire upon reaching the age of 65, since neither the union nor the employees had actual knowledge of the policy's existence (Simpson Building Supply Co., 73 LA 59)

Effect of Negotiations

According to many arbiters, management's right to force workers to retire is strengthened if the union: (1) has had an opportunity to negotiate but failed to do so, or (2) brings to the matter in negotiations but fails to get agreement and signs a contract with no mention of the policy.

EXAMPLE: A person plan providing for automatic retirement at age 65, adopted unilaterally, had been in effect for five years before the union brought a grievance over an employee's forced retirement. An arbitration board said the company could continue to follow its established practice until such time as the policy was restricted through collective bargaining. The board noted that the union had tried unsuccessfully to do this in the most recent bargaining sessions. Generally, the board concluded, employees are entitled only to the rights they have won in the contract. If the right to work beyond age 65 is not specified in the contract, the arbiters said, it does not exist. (Hercules Powder Co., 23 LA 214)

On the other hand, arbiters believe that if a union consistently objects to a compulsory retirement policy, or if the policy contravenes the contract, the company may have no business forcing workers to retire against their wishes.

EXAMPLE: In one case, an arbiter found that the union not only demanded bargaining when a compulsory retirement plan was set up—a request that was refused—but had protested every time the company threatened to enforce it. The arbiter noted that the agreement set forth circumstances under which seniority was lost but did not mention forced retirement. Thus, he ruled, the company had introduced a new reason for loss of seniority without giving prior notice to the union and bargaining as required by law. (TransWorld Airlines Inc., 31 LA 45)

EXAMPLE: An arbiter ruled that an employer did not have the right to require employees, aged 68 and 72 respectively, to accept compulsory retirement due to their having passed age 65. Noting that in the past the retirement of employees at age 65 had not been enforced, the arbiter pointed out that a new pension plan, which the employer accepted during contract negotiations and which in effect became part of the collective bargaining agreement, did not require retirement at age 65. The arbiter concluded that compulsory retirement clearly was in violation of a contractor's provision prohibiting discrimination against employees on the basis of age. (Waterbury Hospital, 62 LA 113)

EXAMPLE: An employer improperly compelled employees to retire at age 65, an arbiter decided, following management's failure to agree to a union proposal that the parties' new contract contain an express provision regarding mandatory retirement. Noting that mandatory retirement was proscribed by the contract's provision barring discrimination against employees "on account of age," the arbiter rejected the employer's contention that the obvious intent of the provision referred to applicable statutory provisions, both federal and state, which do not protect workers 65 or older. (MaGee-Women's Hospital, 62 LA 987)

EXAMPLE: An employer violated the contract when it terminated employees upon their reaching age 65, an arbiter ruled, since there was no compulsory retirement age in the contract's annuity plan. Emphasizing that the evidence did not establish that any employee previously had been involuntarily retired, the arbiter concluded that requiring employees to accept mandatory retirement at age 65 was an attempt by management to impose a new condition of employment that was not negotiated by the parties. (Chicago Zoological Society, 61 LA 387)

Contract Specifying "National Retirement Age"

Where either the contract or a pension plan agreed to by the union and the company expressly provides for compulsory retirement, arbiters find little difficulty in upholding the company's right to compel a worker to retire. But where the contract is silent on the subject and there is no long-standing policy acquiesced in they the union, arbiters generally hold that management does not have the right to compel a worker to retire. In such a case, language specifying a "normal retirement age" and the manner in which the parties have interpreted the language may be important.

EXAMPLE: A contract stated that "age 65 is considered the normal retirement age." The company retired an employee against his wishes when he reached 65, and the union filed a grievance. In upholding the company's right to retire the employee, an arbiter noted that "normal retirement date" was defined in an earlier pension agreement between the parties as the date beyond which a worker could not continue working unless specifically requested to do so by the company. The only logical interpretation of the present language, the arbiter said, was that the parties intended to carry over the same concept of compulsory retirement that had existed under the pension plan. (National Airlines, 35 LA 67)

However, under a pension plan which stated that an "employee may be permitted to remain" at work after the normal retirement age of 65 until he reached age 70 provided he was physically able to do the job and performed his duties satisfactorily, and permitted continued work after age 70 "only upon the request of the company," an arbiter said management could not force retirement of a 65-year-old worker who met the standards. The pension plan was not originally negotiated, but was written by the company, the arbiter noted. Thus, if the company had wanted to make the 65-to-70 privilege exclusively within its control, it could have stated so in concise language, just as it did the provision for workers over age 70, he reasoned. Since this was not done the arbiter concluded that the worker must be allowed to remain at work if he fulfilled the qualifications. (Central Soya Co. 41 LA 370)

Discriminatory Retirement Policy

Some retirement plans allow employers to retire workers at different ages depending on the ability of the individual. Generally arbiters have okayed the use of such flexible retirement policies only as long as they are administered consistently and fairly.

EXAMPLE: A policy that allowed old-age employees to continue working only as long as they continued in the same job was held to be discriminatory and a violation of the contract. (Barrett-Cravens Co., 12 LA 522)

EXAMPLE: Another arbiter ruled that there must be substantial proof that an employee's work is unsatisfactory before he can be forced to retire under a contract giving the company discretion in retiring employees 65 or over. (Ford Motor Co., 20 LA 13)

Similarly, an employer did not have the right to require three employees who reached age 65 to retire, an arbiter decided, where the workers performed their duties satisfactorily, accepted required overtime, had exemplary attendance records and did not have disciplinary records. Noting that the document containing management's unilateral policy requiring compulsory overtime was not placed in the employee's work area, the arbiter pointed out that the policy was not posted until after two of the employees had been notified that they had been retired. Emphasizing that the collective bargaining agreement denied the employer the right to unilaterally terminate seniority because of age, the arbiter observed that the contract also incorporated an express declaration that prohibited discrimination because of age. (Air California, 67 LA 1115)

However, where a retirement policy permitted employees who reached the age of 65 to continue their employment if their continued service was recommended by the department head, cleared by the employee health service, and approved by the administration, an arbiter decided that an employer had the right to force retirement of a 69 year old employee who was unable to adapt to certain operational changes that required expanded duties and responsibilities. While management's policy did not establish a fixed date of retirement and this fact created an impression of inconsistency, the arbiter said that the employer's action was in effect a benefit to some employees who desired to work longer. The fact that the employee was not fully apprised of the mandatory retirement programs was insufficient to render his retirement ineffective, the arbiter concluded. (City of Hope National Medical Center, 67 LA 518)

Physical Condition Warrants Retirement

Arbitrators also have upheld management's decision to compel an employee to retire where the worker's physical condition warrants retirement. (66 LA 1207, 66 LA 849)

EXAMPLE: An employer properly refused to defer retirement of a 66-year-old employee who failed to pass a required physical examination due to liver and other physical problems, an arbiter ruled. Emphasizing that the physical health of employees who are 65 years old or older is an important factor affecting job performance, the arbiter concluded that there was no evidence that the company doctor who recommended the employee's retirement was biased. (Kendall Co., 66 LA 1285)

However, an employer did not have the right to retire involuntarily a 57-year-old employee who was certified by his doctor as disabled, but was considered capable of returning to work by the employer under an employee pension plan giving a benefit committee discretion to retire employees who had worked at the company 30 years or more, an arbiter ruled. Pointing out that involuntary retirement amounted to dismissal under the contract, and therefore was subject to arbitration, the arbiter observed that there was nothing in either the plan or the contract allowing the employer to force retirement of an employee as a means of discipline. Emphasizing that the purpose of the plan was to allow retirement of persons who no longer desire to work or unable to do so, the arbiter concluded that imposing discipline upon employees was not part of the plan. (Pacific Telephone & Telegraph Co., 70 LA 1279)

Subcontracting

IN BRIEF

The right of management to subcontract, in the absence of specific contract restrictions, has been the subject of numerous grievances. Where the bargaining agreement is silent on subcontracting, one important factor considered by arbitrators is the effect of the subcontracting on the bargaining unit or bargaining unit employees. Also relevant is the employer's justification for the subcontracting — e.g., business reasons. (92 LA 271, 91 LA 245, 88 LA 185, 82 LA 805)

Furthermore, in earlier cases pertaining to subcontracting issues, arbitrators generally held that management had the right, if exercised in good faith, to subcontract work to independent contractors. Later cases, however, have held that management's right to subcontract is not unrestricted; but must be judged against the recognition, seniority, wage, and other such clauses of the bargaining agreement. Standards of reasonableness and good faith are applied in determining whether these clauses were violated.

One arbitrator, for example, observed that management is prohibited from subcontracting: (1) unless it acts in good faith; (2) unless it acts in conformity with past practices; (3) unless it acts reasonably; (4) unless the act deprives only a few employees of employment; (5) unless the act was dictated by business requirements; (6) if the act is barred by the recognition clause; (7) if the act is barred by seniority provisions; or (8) if the act violates the spirit of the agreement. (American Sugar Refining Co., 37 LA 334)

GUIDELINES

Arbitrators, generally, apply the following standards in deciding subcontracting cases:

1. *Past practices.* Whether the company has subcontracted work in the past. (97 LA 650, 75 LA 742, 75 LA 665, 73 LA 29, 72 LA 1115, 64 LA 101, 63 LA 1143, 61 LA 526)

2. *Justification.* Whether subcontracting is done for reasons such as economy, maintenance of secondary sources for production, plant security, etc. (62 LA 421, 61 LA 530)

3. *Effect on union.* Whether subcontracting is being used as a method of discriminating against the union and substantially prejudicing the status and integrity of the bargaining unit. (64 LA 602)

4. *Effect on unit employees.* Whether members of the union are discriminated against, displaced, laid off, or deprived of jobs previously available to them, or to lose regular or overtime earnings, by reason of the subcontract.

(63 LA 798, 62 LA 1000, 62 LA 895, 61 LA 333) Where subcontracting has little or no effect on the unit or its members, it is likely to be upheld by arbitrators (97 LA 64, 95 LA 1139, 95 LA 89, 93 LA 101, 92 LA 933, 92 LA 250, 88 LA 995, 88 LA 185, 82 LA 805). However, where subcontracting is used either to replace current employees or in lieu of recalling employees on layoff, it is less likely to be upheld (92 LA 841, 89 LA 1112, 87 LA 40)

5. *Type of work involved.* Whether it is work that is normally done by unit employees, or work that is frequently the subject of subcontracting in the particular industry, or work that is of a "marginal" or "incidental" nature. (97 LA 1216, 97 LA 782, 97 LA 650, 97 LA 614, 97 LA 214, 96 LA 816, 74 LA 1128, 71 LA 155, 62 LA 474)

6. *Availability of properly qualified employees.* Whether the skills possessed by available members of the bargaining unit are sufficient to perform the work. (97 LA 614, 74 LA 616, 74 LA 269, 71 LA 1024, 65 LA 598, 65 LA 431, 63 LA 883)

7. *Availability of equipment and facilities.* Whether necessary equipment and facilities are presently available or can be economically purchased. (64 LA 1244, 63 LA 82, 62 LA 505)

8. *Regularity of subcontracting.* Whether the particular work is frequently or only intermittently subcontracted.

9. *Duration of subcontracted work.* Whether the work is subcontracted for a temporary or limited period, or for a permanent or indefinite period. (92 LA 703)

10. *Unusual circumstances involved.* Whether an emergency, "special" job, strike, or other unusual situation exists necessitating the action.

11. *History of negotiations.* Whether management's right to subcontract has been the subject of contract negotiations. (How Arbitration Works; Elkouri and Elkouri; BNA Books, 1985)

Notification Requirement/ Duty to Bargain

A bargaining contract may require management to notify the union of its intent to subcontract. (54 LA 1207, 53 LA 993, 46 LA 724) In such cases, the notification requirement may be strictly construed.

Where a contract was silent as to subcontracting, an arbitrator emphasized that prior notification generally should be given. (Pittsburgh Brewing Co., 53 LA 470) On the other hand, another arbitrator, in a similar situation, decided that no notice was required. (Haveg Industries, 52 LA 1146)

EXAMPLE: A hospital violated a contract allowing subcontracting of unit work only after 30-day advance notice to the union when it did not give the required notice before subcontracting work involving transcription of medical reports dictated on tapes by doctors, an arbitrator ruled. In effect, the notice requirement was a definite restriction on the employer's right to subcontract the work, the arbitrator reasoned. Unless this condition precedent was fulfilled, there was no contractual right to subcontract the work, the arbitrator continued. If the required 30-day notice was given, then the criteria and standards generally applicable to the various aspects of subcontracting become applicable to any work subcontracted by the employer, the arbitrator concluded. (Kaiser Foundation Hospitals, 61 LA 1008; see also 98 LA 13, 93 LA 666, 75 LA 485, 73 LA 1036)

However, another arbitrator decided that an employer properly contracted out construction and/or installation of manufacturing equipment, following the maintenance manager's meeting with union officers during which the manager gave the officers forms containing a brief description of the project, the contractor to whom the job would be awarded, and other details. (J.T. Baker Chemical Co., 76 LA 1147; see also 95 LA 668, 75 LA 810, 74 LA 1128)

Also, an arbiter ruled that even though a collective bargaining agreement requires a notice of intent to subcontract, the contractual notice requirement is not violated if the employer lacks the necessary equipment and qualified employees and if the subcontracting of work is not expected to become routine. (M.A. Hannah Co., 88 LA 185)

Duty to Bargain

The current NLRB approach for determining whether an employer's decision to subcontract work is a mandatory subject of bargaining is reflected in *Otis Elevator Co.*, (269 NLRB No. 162, 1984, 115 LRRM 1281), where NLRB ruled that a duty to bargain arises when the decision turns on labor costs, rather than on a fundamental change in the direction or nature of the enterprise.

Further, one arbiter has ruled that a union has the right to bargain over the *impact* of subcontracting on the bargaining unit, even where it is clear that the employer has the right unilaterally to contract out the work in question. (Witco Chem. Co., 89 LA 349)

Significance of Recognition Clause

Generally, reliance on recognition, seniority and other such clauses is not persuasive to arbitrators where there is a weak subcontracting clause in the agreement. In all probability, the arbitrator will go with an implied-obligation-residual-rights balancing test to determine the issue. For example, in one case, an arbitrator indicated that the subcontracting clause required "good-faith" efforts by the company not to subcontract work that was normally performed by regular employees. The arbitrator did not specifically repudiate the contract's recognition clause, but chose to treat the issue as if the contract were "silent" on the subcontracting question, thus basing his decision on an implied obligation-residual-rights concept. (Sealtest Foods, 48 LA 797)

Subcontracting Where Work Is Customarily Performed by Unit Employees

Usually, arbitrators confronted with a clause restricting management from subcontracting for work involving the production of parts and equipment normally made by unit employees will hold for the union if there is a significant detriment to the unit.

EXAMPLE: An employer did not have the right unilaterally to contract out unit work of fabricating rollers during the time that maintenance mechanics were on layoff, an arbitrator ruled, even though the magnitude of the job, in addition to the rush nature of the work, justified contracting out a portion of production. Pointing out that the subcontracting deprived unit employees of work customarily performed by them, the arbitrator emphasized that the injuries done to the workers and the potential damage to the union were paramount. Rejecting the employer's contention that the contracting out was not done to undermine the union, the arbitrator concluded that the adverse effect that the subcontracting caused the unit was the same as if there had been an overt intent to undermine the union. (Consolidated Aluminum Co., 66 LA 1170; see also 97 LA 983)

However, another arbitrator ruled that an employer did not commit a subcontracting violation when it purchased stock parts from a supplier. Despite the fact that the contract prohibited subcontracting where employees were on layoff and the work subcontracted was work that they normally performed, the arbitrator reasoned that the purchases were not subcontracting, since they were ready-made stock parts in a catalogue, and thus there was no deprivation of work. (Iowa Manufacturing Co., 68 LA 599)

Subcontracting Where the Company Lacks the Equipment and Facilities

Management's right to subcontract out work may be restricted even where the company lacks the equipment or facilities to do the job.

EXAMPLE: An employer was obligated to pay lost overtime to employees for subcontracting unit work, an arbitrator ruled, despite the fact that the employer did not have the equipment the subcontractor used and the employees did not have training to operate the equipment. The employer was prohibited from subcontracting even if it were required to rent part of the equipment and to train the affected employees in the operation of such equipment, the arbitrator concluded. (Ashland Chemical Co., 64 LA 1244)

On the other hand, an arbitrator ruled that if there was a gross uneconomic effect on the company, an employer could subcontract work, notwithstanding a clause limiting subcontracting, unless there was a lack of equipment and facilities. The arbitrator allowed the employer to subcontract the dismantling and removal of equipment it sold to the subcontractor because, in his judgment, this was not a serious detriment to the unit. In this case, no employees were laid-off as a result of the subcontracting, past practice supported management's action, and the economic savings were substantial, the arbitrator concluded. (Weyerhaeuser Co., 68 LA 7; see also 95 LA 89, 93 LA 465, 74 LA 616, 74 LA 196, 72 LA 1115)

Part 11

Union Rights

Union Rights

IN BRIEF

Although a union's prerogatives usually are specified in the collective bargaining agreement, problems involving the right of a union to conduct business, handle grievances, receive information, or visit an employer's premises to discuss employees' gripes do arise in the arbitral setting. More frequently, however, arbitrators must resolve labor-management disputes centering on the manner in which unions exercise their rights or on the reasonableness of limitations placed on such rights by management. Trouble also may occur with clauses dealing with the use of union bulletin boards. Arbitrators usually have interpreted such provisions broadly, holding that any intended restrictions should be written into the contract.

In this area perhaps more than any other, what the contract says is only part of the story. The union also has important grievance-handling and information rights under the Taft Act.

According to one arbitrator, "the law of labor relations is relatively clear that an employer has no right to interfere with an employee's performance of his valid union activities and his obligations to his union, the same as the union and employee have no right to interfere with the employer's right to manage and operate the plant." (Greif Bros. Corp., 67 LA 1001)

GUIDELINES

Union's Right to Information

Most arbitrators agree that the union should have any information necessary for the processing of grievances and for making sure that the contract isn't being violated with respect to the company's wage administration practices. As one arbitrator pointed out, "The object and purpose of arbitration is to arrive at a fair and just decision, and to this end parties should be assisted in obtaining competent and material evidence where such may reasonably be had." (Chesapeake & Potomac Telephone Co. of West Va., 21 LA 367)

EXAMPLE: One company whose contract specified that it would furnish complete data and figures on the operation of its merit review system refused to disclose the names and department numbers of employees who had received increases. But the arbitrator ruled that the agreement required the employer to give the union such information. (Sperry Gyroscope Co., 18 LA 916)

EXAMPLE: Where a contract required the company to furnish the union with detailed information pertaining to changes in work assignments, another arbitrator ruled that this meant it had to supply all the basic time-study data, not just summaries. (Celanese Corp. of America, 27 LA 845)

EXAMPLE: Still another contract didn't spell out the employer's obligation to furnish the union with specific information, but an arbitrator said the company must give the union a list of pay rates so that it could bargain effectively on merit increases. (I. Lewis Cigar Mfg. Co., 12 LA 661)

EXAMPLE: Since a union was entitled to bargain over an employer's proposed amendments to the retirement plan, an arbitrator held, the employer was required to produce for inspection by the union the text of all proposed and existing amendments and all actuarial data concerning all participants. The actuarial data was considered absolutely necessary in order to evaluate the presence or absence of benefits resulting from employees' contributions, the arbitrator concluded. (Anti-Defamation League B'Nai B'Rith, 53 LA 1332)

EXAMPLE: Another arbitrator decided that an employer who discharged an employee for exceeding his allotted amount of sick leave was obligated to provide the union with the names, addresses, initial employment dates, and seniority dates of other workers who had been allowed to return to work after being absent in excess of their authorized sick leave. The desired information was of sufficient relevance to warrant a requirement that the employer disclose it, the arbitrator reasoned. (Mobil Oil Corp., 63 LA 263)

EXAMPLE: Under a SUB plan providing that the company "will comply with reasonable requests by the union for other statistical information on the operation of the plan," an arbitrator held that the union was entitled to monthly lists of names of recipients and amounts paid. The company's contention that the lists were not "statistical information" placed an unduly narrow restriction on the term, the arbitrator said. The union had a legitimate reason for wanting the information, he said; it wanted to check for possible errors, since the funding obligation of the company was determined by the average weekly amount paid during the preceding year. (Mack Trucks, Inc., 36 LA 1114)

However, under a contract that said nothing about seniority lists, one arbitrator agreed that the union had a right to seniority information only when it specifically asked for it. (Bethlehem Steel Co., 24 LA 699)

Similarly, another union was held to have bargained away its right to be furnished seniority lists where its contract required a grievant to go first to his immediate supervisor, not to the union, and also made seniority disputes subject to the procedure. (Spartan Mills, 27 LA 256)

Likewise, contract provisions making payroll data available upon request didn't require a company to furnish such records for uncovering claims during a dispute over seniority in layoffs, an arbitrator held. The records were to be used only for testing the validity of specific claims, he said. (Santa Clara & Central Calif. Meat Processors' Assn., 36 LA 42; see also 77 LA 1008, 74 LA 96, 72 LA 57)

Right to Represent Employees at Investigative Interviews (Weingarten Rights)

The U.S. Supreme Courts' *Weingarten* decision (1975, 88 LRRM 2689) held that individual employees have the right under the Taft Act to refuse to submit without union representation to an employer investigatory interview which the employee reasonably believes may result in disciplinary action. (see Chevron Chemical Co., 60 LA 1066)

Weingarten and other union-representation cases have gained general acceptance among arbiters, who have generally focused their decisions on the presence or absence of Weingarten principles, according to Elkouri & Elkouri (How Arbitration Works; BNA Books, 1991) (Maui Pineapple Co, 86 LA 907; see also 98 LA 201, 97 LA 271, 96 LA 255, 95 LA 148, 93 LA 203, 92 LA 544, 92 LA 144, 92 LA 127, 90 LA 1133, 90 LA 209, 89 LA 1265, 89 LA 799, 89 LA 393, 88 LA 791, 88 LA 741, 88 LA 651, 88 LA 44, 87 LA 534, 86 LA 907, 84 LA 1112, 83 LA 1248, 83 LA 833, 82 LA 1209, 82 LA 198, 82 LA 1, 81 LA 1024, 81 LA 740, 81 LA 368)

For example, where an employee fails to request or waives union representation, arbiters generally have found employer denial of representation not to be a violation of either the bargaining agreement or *Weingarten.* (86 LA 350, 83 LA 1248) However, arbiters considered the extent to which certain employees would be aware of *Weingarten* rights, in upholding the discipline of a union president, while mitigating discipline for an employee with limited knowledge of English. (86 LA 907, 82 LA 1)

In setting the limits to which *Weingarten* applies to employer investigations, some arbiters have limited the right of union representation to investigatory interviews only. Consequently, there is arbitral authority to prevent union representation during employer searches for physical evidence in employee cars (84 LA 562), and in meetings informing employees to submit to drug screening during a physical examination. (84 LA 1272) Further, an arbiter denied an employee union representation during a performance evaluation, holding that the union had no right to accompany an employee to a supervisor's evaluation before there was a grievance or a grievable event. (84 LA 516; see also 97 LA 728, 97 LA 303)

Also, arbiters have held that where the purpose of a meeting was to administer discipline and not to conduct an investigatory interview, employer denial of union representation did not violate *Weingarten.* (87 LA 572, 87 LA 568, 83 LA 1248; however, compare with 95 LA 82, 94 LA 1229)

Similarly, an arbiter upheld the discipline of an employee, even though she was deprived on union representation during an investigatory interview, where she responded to a supervisor's initial, direct inquiry and failed immediately to request a union representative. (Grand Blanc Community Schools, 97 LA 162)

In addition, an arbiter upheld a sexual-harassment discharge even though an employer improperly limited a union's role at a second investigatory interview, since a union representative fully participated in the first interview, and any prejudice through procedural defect was overcome by clear and convincing evidence that the grievant engaged in the harassment of several workers. (Shell Pipe Line Corp., 97 LA 957; see also 97 LA 343, 96 LA 1020)

Decertified Union's Right to Process Grievance

A decertified union still has the right to prosecute a grievance, one arbitrator held. Thus, where a union had processed a grievance but was decertified before the case reached arbitration, the arbitrator said it had a right to settle the dispute. A distinction exists between the collective bargaining function and the processing of a grievance, he noted. Though a decertified union may not bargain for the workers, he said, federal law does not bar it from representing them in arbitration. (Trumbull Asphalt Co., 38 LA 1093)

Right to Post Union Notices

Usually a union is free to put up any notice dealing with union business, and the company cannot withhold approval unless the material is slanderous or derogatory to the company. Types of union notices against which companies have protested, but which arbitrators have upheld, include: a notice urging members' support for striking members of another union (Wisconsin Tissue Mills, Inc. and Paperworkers, Local 1279, 73 LA 271); a letter from a union international representative which attempted to avoid an imminent wildcat strike and assure members that the union would fight their grievances through legal means (Freuhauf Corp., 54 LA 1096); a notice stating that the purpose of a forthcoming union meeting was to consider strike action against the company (Fairchild Engine & Airplane Corp., 16 LA 678); a seniority list drawn up by the union after the parties had failed to agree on a seniority list (Lennox Furnace Co., 20 LA 788); and a notice urging union members to register for voting (Warren City Mfg. Co., 7 LA 202).

On the other hand, one arbitrator has held that a clause permitting the posting of union "announcements" couldn't be stretched to include organizational material. (General Electric Co., 31 LA 924)

Similarly, when the union posted a listing of nonmembers under the title, "Scabs," it was acting improperly, according to an arbitrator. The lists smacked of coercion and embarrassment and created an atmosphere of intimidation to join the union, the arbitrator pointed out. The underlying purpose was to blacklist employees; an illegitimate recruitment tactic and misuse of information, the arbitrator concluded. (Union Carbide Corp., 44 LA 554)

Likewise, the discharge of an employee for posting unauthorized inflammatory notices pertaining to the employer was upheld by an arbitrator, where the employee had been given repeated warnings concerning other notices he had posted and had been ordered not to post the notice that led to his discharge. (Beaver Precision Products Inc., 51 LA 853)

Furthermore, some arbitrators have interpreted posting clauses calling for company approval of union notices to mean that the employer may refuse to approve a submitted notice for any reason whatsoever. On this theory, arbitrators have okayed management's action in turning thumbs down on a notice consisting of a comparison of wages paid at another of the company's plants and at plants of a competitor (Reynolds Metals Co., 13 LA 278); and an announcement that a strike at another company with which the union had a contract had ended, together with a summary of the provisions of the new agreement at that company. (Danly Specialties Inc., 13 LA 499)

Right to Investigate Grievances

Frequently, union and management disagree on whether the union has the right to represent employees at the early stages of a grievance. Management generally holds the view that the aggrieved employee should go to his supervisor alone before going to his steward and that the union should not enter the picture until after the first step of the grievance procedure. On the other hand, unions often take the position that the steward should handle grievances from the start. Arbitrators, in turn, generally agree that unions should be given considerable latitude in representing employees and investigating grievances, and therefore recognize a right to union representation at least commencing with the first step of the contractual grievance procedure. (75 LA 994, 73 LA 972, 71 LA 452, 69 LA 29, 67 LA 352, 67 LA 349, 66 LA 758, 66 LA 582)

However, in cases where an employee does not request that a union representative be present during a disciplinary interview, or effectively waives the right of representation by his conduct, arbitrators may hold that management has the right to deny the worker representation. (76 LA 719, 76 LA 379, 73 LA 1092)

Restrictions on Right to Represent Employees

Most contracts place restrictions on the union's methods of handling grievances by requiring, for example, that union representatives and employees obtain proper authorization from their superiors before they absent themselves from their work stations in order to discuss a grievance. (67 LA 887, 67 LA 1123)

EXAMPLE: In one case, an arbitrator held that an employer properly determined that a chief steward was on unauthorized leave instead of administrative leave when he left his work station to give employees advice concerning various problems they were experiencing on the job. Although it had been the employer's custom to grant administrative leave to elected union officials for the purpose of investigating grievances, the arbitrator ruled that the steward violated the contract by failing to identify either the specific bargaining unit in which he planned to make the investigation or the particular supervisor who had been contacted.

(National Institutes of Health, 67 LA 788)

In addition to restricting the time and place in which union representatives are authorized to discuss grievances, contract provisions also may specify the union's role at each step of the grievance procedure.

EXAMPLE: Where a contract provided that an employee filing a grievance could be represented at the first step of the grievance process "by an appropriate steward," an arbitrator ruled that a worker was not entitled to have the union's "business" representative represent him at the first-step meeting. Agreeing with the employer's contention that the presence of the union business agent, rather than a steward, at the first step created "an atmosphere of undue sophistication," the arbitrator decided that the parties had intended to try to settle disputes initially through the efforts of the lowest levels of employer and union representatives. (Navy Commissary Store Complex, 62 LA 576)

Right to Investigate Departments Not in Unit

Do union representatives have the right to investigate in departments not covered by the contract? One arbiter ruled that a company had no business refusing to allow a union representative to investigate a possible grievance involving a department specifically excluded from the bargaining unit but also involving a charge that the department was doing bargaining unit work.

EXAMPLE: By decision of NLRB, engineering department employees were excluded from the bargaining unit at one company. So, when the union got wind of a report that people in the department were doing bargaining unit work, the chief steward sought to enter the department to find out whether the report was true. The company blocked his attempt, saying he should tell what he knew to the personnel manager. The latter would then make an investigation and report on his findings, the company said. One reason given by the company for its stand was that some of the work in the engineering department was classified, and the union representative didn't have security clearance. It is also argued that it didn't have to let union representatives roam around on "fishing expeditions."

An arbitrator found no merit in these contentions. The contracts, he pointed out, permitted the union to file grievances on its own motion; the union was not limited to processing grievances that came to it from employees. So if it got word that the contract wasn't being kept, it had a right to make an investigation, regardless of the source of its information. And the arbitrator said the company could not require such an investigation to be made through the personnel manager.

As for the company's fears about security, the arbitrator saw no problem. The firm, he said, could assign a "conductor" to accompany the union investigator and make sure no violation of security regulations occurred. The company's action, the arbitrator concluded, amounted to a violation of the recognition clause of the contract. (Librascope Inc., 30 LA 358)

However, another arbitrator has held that where a union can't initiate grievances, it cannot go all over the plant looking for contract violations.

EXAMPLE: A union suspected that unit work was being done in a department where none of the workers belonged to the unit. To investigate the situation, it requested access to the site; the company turned it down. Under the contract, management noted union officers could leave their work for "the proper handling of grievances." But that did not mean the union could go where there were no unit members and look for trouble, it said.

The arbitrator agreed that the union had the right to police the contract, but in his opinion the right was limited to cases of already-existing disputes. By the terms of the contract, he noted, only the company and the workers could be parties to grievances. Since the union couldn't bring up beefs on its own hook, it couldn't roam the plant looking for them, the arbitrator concluded. (Bendix Aviation Corp., 39 LA 393)

Right of Access to Plant

Many bargaining agreements provide for nonemployee union representatives to come into the plant to investigate grievances or for other purposes. Further, some arbiters suggest that such plant access is inherent in agreements whether explicitly guaranteed or not. (36 LA 815, 32 LA 1004, 30 LA 358) It is essential that union representatives be given the opportunity, as management is, to investigate all circumstances surrounding a grievance. (20 LA 211; see also 53 LA 1061)

While arbiters have upheld union access to a workplace for grievance-related investigations, they have held other non-grievance-related activities under greater scrutiny.

EXAMPLE: An arbiter held that an agreement, which required union representatives to make arrangements with an employer prior to entering the plant to "discuss matters of contract administration," did not allow solicitation of membership by a nonemployee union representative. (Montgomery Ward & Co., 85 LA 913)

However, where an employer repeatedly denied union representative access to a plant to investigate violations of a union-security clause and on one occasion had the union representative arrested for trespassing, an arbiter ruled that the employer interfered with the union's contractual right to visit the premises. Recognizing the union's obligation to refrain form unreasonably interrupting employees during a peak business period, the arbiter held the employer responsible for creating a confrontational situation where the circumstances called for "a spirit of cooperation and consideration." (Piper's Restaurant, 86 LA 809)

Employer rules governing access to a plant must be based on reasonableness.

EXAMPLE: An arbiter found that, where an agreement permitted union safety officials access to an employer's premises, the employer's requirement that union officials sign a waiver releasing the employer from all liability was on its face unreasonable. However, the arbiter said, since the union officials were covered by workers' compensation and since without the waiver, union officials would be given greater rights than employee members, the employer's requirement of waiver of liability for specific visits by union officials was reasonable. (Utah Power & Light, 88 LA 310) Arbitrators have held that when union representatives do not behave in a civilized manner while exercising visitation rights, they may be denied access to the plant. (Associated Hospitals of San Francisco, 67 LA 323)

EXAMPLE: A union representative visited the company president in his office to discuss an alleged contract violation by management. During a heated argument the representative suddenly got out of his chair, stepped behind the president's desk, and began to twist his arm and poke him in the chest. He then invited the president outside to settle the matter. Thereafter the company refused to allow the representative to enter the plant.

Although the contract said that the union agents would have access to the plant during working hours to take up complaints and determine whether the contract was being complied with, an arbitrator ruled that the denial of access was justified. The representative's conduct had no place in labor relations, he said. (Glendale Mfg. Co., 32 LA 223)

EXAMPLE: One arbitrator used the following guidelines in determining the propriety of a union representative's visit to the worksite.

• Visitation rights must be exercised at reasonable times and in a reasonable manner;

• The employer cannot legitimately interfere with the representative's business so long as the visitation rights are exercised reasonably;

• In judging the reasonableness of a visitation's timing, not only the particular hours of visitation but also the number of visitations must be considered;

• The employer cannot place a restriction on visitation rights that is contrary to contractual terms and past practice;

• The employer may establish reasonable rules governing access to the premises as long as they do not unreasonably interfere with the legitimate purpose of the visit. (Roy Demanes & Assoc. Inc., 60 LA 1039)

On the other hand, an arbiter ruled that an employer improperly denied a union's request for use of a former conference room for an after-hours meeting of a union's executive board. The denial, originally based on security, and later on the ground that employer facilities could only be used by employer bargaining-unit employees, was improper the arbiter said, since the bargaining agreement provided that the employer to grant meeting space to whatever subdivision of "the union" requests it "where feasible," regardless of whether the individuals are employees. Further, the refusal was improper since the employer could have provided space without undue cost or inconvenience, the arbiter said. (Ohio Dept. of Health, 97 LA 310)

Also, in a case where management denied the chief steward access to the plant except during his own shift, an arbitrator held that the steward had the privilege of entering the plant at all reasonable times. If he were limited to his own shift, the arbitrator said, he would be no different from a departmental steward, and his plant-wide constituency would be ignored. However, the arbitrator cautioned that the chief steward must not abuse his privileges. (Buddy-L Corp., 41, LA 185)

Similarly, an arbitrator said the union had a right to send in its own international staff man to make a time study of new production standards which the union had challenged. The contract permitted the union to bring in "any representative of the union not an employee of the company" for the purpose of investigating grievances and said the company "recognizes that some grievances by their very nature may require investigation on the job," the arbitrator noted. The union's time-study man wouldn't interfere with work any more than managements' own man had, he added, and there was no basis for the company's fear that its secrets would be divulged to its competitors. (Armstrong Cork Co., 41 LA 1053; see also 72 LA 129)

Right to File Grievance

The grievance-settlement machinery is one of the most vital elements in the union-management relationship. As such it has been the subject of numerous arbitral decisions.

EXAMPLE: A union president had the right to present a grievance, even though the grievance-arbitration clause mentioned only disputes between "an employee and the company" and the subject of the complaint did not affect the union head as an "employee." The protest was on behalf of a union member and was allowed because, according to the arbitrator, "it would be inappropriate to impose a legalistic restriction on the right of the parties to settle their disputes by use of the grievance machinery." (Ohio Power Co., 45 LA 1039)

Similarly, an arbitrator decided that a union could file a grievance even if the workers involved wanted no part of it. If the union could not file on its own, there would be no procedure under which controversies as to interpretation or claims of violation could go to arbitration unless some worker actually affected brought up the matter. (Atlantic Seaboard Corp., 42 LA 865)

Right to Repudiate Changes in Grievance Procedure

When a company and a union orally agreed to certain changes in the grievance procedure, it made no difference that the membership did not formally approve the changes, an arbitrator ruled. An attempt was made to repudiate the changes when the union elected new officers. However, the arbitrator decided that if the union were free to invalidate agreements made by its previous officers, the company would be able to invalidate all agreements by merely replacing its representatives. (Gertman Co., 45 LA 30)

Part 12

Strikes & Lockouts

No-Strike Pledges

IN BRIEF

Prohibitions against strike activity during the life of a bargaining contract are included in nearly all labor-management agreements. Generally, arbiters take the position that any union-inspired activity that interferes with production, whether or not called a strike, is in fact a strike. (98 LA 41, 97 LA 297, 71 LA 1151, 69 LA 1201, 69 LA 93, 67 LA 805, 67 LA 934) However, in some instances, where production suddenly falls off, or where several workers call in sick simultaneously, the situation may not be so clear cut.

GUIDELINES

Union Meetings on Company Time as a Strike

Union meetings called during working hours usually result from some company action which employees do not like, or are intended to allow employees to reach a decision on some matter, which the union thinks requires fast action. Most arbiters have held that such meetings amount to strikes.

EXAMPLE: One arbiter declared that a planned mass departure from the workplace that halts productive work and disrupts the company's production schedule is a work stoppage and violates a contract's no-strike clause. (Nathan Mfg. Co., 7 LA 3)

Similarly, an arbitration board threw out one union's argument that a stoppage has to be for an indefinite period of time to be a strike. The board reasoned that a union meeting during working hours is a strike just as certainly as the company's action would be a lockout if it stopped production to hold a directors' meeting. (Atlantic Foundry Co., 8 LA 807)

Employee Gathering as Strike

Situations may arise where workers feel they have an urgent request or question that must be taken care of before they start working. They may then gather together and say they will not work until management listens to them. Most arbiters take management's side in this situation and consider that when employees gather together informally instead of working they are in effect striking.

EXAMPLE: Employees were engaged in an illegal work stoppage, an arbiter ruled, when, after meeting with their supervisor with respect to an incentive dispute, they refused to go back to work until after a private half-hour session with the union grievance chairman. Both supervisor and higher management officials who came into the meeting later made it clear to the employees that they were to return to work, the arbiter noted. Group pressure of this type to resolve grievances is completely unsanctioned by the contract, the arbiter emphasized, concluding that the agreement provided an orderly method for settling such disputes. (Kaiser Steel Corp., 51 LA 1041; see also Republic Steel Corp., 6 LA 85)

On the other hand, at least one arbiter believes that a gathering of employees does not amount to a strike where they are not making any demands but rather are seeking information concerning a change in their working arrangements.

EXAMPLE: A company decided to change the departmental organization of its crane operators. Under the old arrangement, crane operators were all together in one department and were assigned by supervision in that department to particular cranes in the various departments. Under the new plan, management intended to place the crane operators permanently in the various departments instead of assigning them each day to a department. At the beginning of their shift instead of their time cards crane operators found cards telling them to go to other locations to punch in. There was considerable confusion and the operators were about an hour late in starting work. Management maintained that the delay in starting constituted a strike violation of the contract.

The arbiter held, however, that management itself caused the delay by its failure to tell the employees before-hand about their transfer. This was not a strike but rather a delay resulting from a failure of information, comparable to a delay resulting from a power failure, the arbiter concluded. (Ford Motor Co., 10 LA 148)

Simultaneous Absences as Strike

Unless a union can show evidence that simultaneous absences by employees are a coincidence and that each absent worker's excuse is legitimate, an arbiter will probably consider this to be a strike.

EXAMPLE: Shortly after a union meeting, a group of 20 employees in two departments failed to return to work. Each phoned the company to report that he was sick. The company charged that the mass absences were a strike in violation of the contract and discharged the employees.

An arbiter, asked to decide whether the absences were a strike, ruled that they were. Although testimony was presented to show that several of the employees actually were ill, the excuses of most were not backed up by evidence. It was this lack of proof that led the arbiter to conclude that the mass absence was more than a coincidence and constituted a strike. (American Cyanamid Co., 15 LA 563; see also 87 LA 424, 54 LA 569)

However, a school board did not have the right to add one day to the school schedule to make up for a day it closed the school because one-half of the work force called in sick, an arbiter decided, where the school waited for six weeks and made ratification of the contract contingent upon the teacher's making up the lost workday. Finding that the purpose of the additional workday was to discipline employees for the alleged one-day work stoppage, the arbiter ruled that the attempt was untimely and, therefore not based upon just cause. Although management may view the decision as rewarding illegally striking employees, the arbiter concluded it was too late to determine whether there was a concerted and illegal work stoppage because the employer did not see fit to discipline culpable employees in a timely fashion. (White Cloud Public Schools, 72 LA 179)

Refusal to Work Because of Health & Safety Hazards

Employees who refuse to work under dangerous health or safety conditions may not be considered on strike by arbiters.

EXAMPLE: An employer was not justified in discharging employees who walked off their jobs following management's failure to install fire extinguishers that an OSHA inspector had ordered installed, an arbiter ruled, notwithstanding the employer's contention that the employees should have filed a grievance, instead of engaging in a strike in violation of the contract. As a general rule, no employee is required to render services in a place that may be a hazard to his health and safety, the arbiter emphasized, concluding that conditions existing at the plant were such that the health and safety of the employees were in jeopardy. (RI-JA Machining Co. Inc., 66 LA 474; see also 89 LA 1227)

On the other hand, another arbiter did not feel that good-faith belief that working conditions were a health hazard was enough reason to justify a walkout. According to his interpretation of the issue, it must be demonstrated that a hazard actually does exist. Thus, he denied the request for holiday pay or sick leave passes for the workers who left work prior to quitting time because they felt the poor ventilation coupled with prevailing high temperatures presented a health hazard. (Wilcolator Co., 44 LA 847; see also 52 LA 259)

Similarly, where it was found that workers had refused to work until management agreed never to operate under alleged dangerous conditions in the future, one arbiter held that they were clearly engaging in an illegitimate strike. He said that this was more than just a mere refusal to incur an undue health hazard. (Ford Motor Co., 6 LA 799)

Likewise, employees were not entitled to pay for the time that they did not report for work because the employer would not provide a nurse in the first aid room in its main building, an arbiter ruled, since the employees' action constituted an unlawful strike under the no-strike clause of their contract. While the employees were privileged to refuse work assignments on the ground that working conditions were unsafe, the arbiter concluded that the absence of a nurse on duty did constitute such a condition. (Quaker Oats Co., 69 LA 727)

Slowdown as No-Strike Violation

In some cases, a slowdown in production by employees may constitute an illegal strike in violation of the contract. According to one arbiter, any union action, including a pause at work, that interferes with the employees' duty to do their jobs amounts to a contract violation, particularly where there is a no-strike pledge covering any slowdown, work stoppage, strike, picketing, boycott or other job action. (Restaurant-Hotel Employer's Council of Southern California, 24 LA 429; see also 55 LA 372, 50 LA 1157, 48 LA 1224, 41 LA 1253, 41 LA 607, 38 LA 644, 37 LA 401, 18 LA 449, 18 LA 370, 7 LA 438)

EXAMPLE: Employees were held responsible for a work stoppage that resulted in a stay-in in violation of a contract, an arbiter decided, notwithstanding the union's contention that it was management that decided to close the plant and shut-down operations. Finding that the employer shut down the plant only after it had unsuccessfully tried to stop the stay-in through the use of plant guards and local policemen, the arbiter upheld the employees' discharges since they had been apprised by both the union and the employer that the stay-in violated the contract. (Chrysler Corp., 63 LA 677)

However, not every slowdown in the rate of production need constitute a strike.

EXAMPLE: In deciding that the slowdown of several crews was not a "slowdown" in violation of the contract, an arbiter noted that there was no labor dispute involved. In its normal usage a slowdown implies a dispute in which workers intend to get some advantage from their action. While it was true that the crews were not producing as much as they had previously shown they could, they still were performing at a rate that was considered satisfactory for other workers. He concluded that the only fair way to judge effort and production was by the job, not by the individual. (Kelly-Springfield Tire Co., 42 LA 1162; see also 49 LA 1236, 41 LA 1339, 38 LA 896, 37 LA 593, 32 LA 701, 29 LA 512, 21 LA 428)

Observance of Picket Line

Where there is no contract provision permitting employees to refuse to cross a picket line, arbiters generally agree that a no-strike clause is binding upon the employees concerned. Such employees, governed by a broad no-strike, no work stoppage clause, must cross a peaceful picket line, or face disciplinary action or discharge by the employer, according to the arbiters.

EXAMPLE: An electrical union violated a contract provision barring authorization or sanction of "any" strike an arbiter ruled, when the union's president addressed a letter to a clerks union that was picketing the employer, stating that the electrical union members would "support" any sanctioned strike within the jurisdiction of the clerks union. Pointing out that during the course of the picketing, the electrical workers left the plant with their tools, did not report the following day, and returned to work only after the strike ended, the arbiter said he could not accept the unified action of some 30 to 40 employees statewide as individual judgments, and thus must rule that it was taken in "concert." Noting that the contract contained a broad no-strike clause, the arbiter concluded that the agreement did not allow the union either to render assistance, or engage in a sympathy strike." (American Totalisator Company Inc., 74 LA 377)

Similarly, a carpenters' union violated a no-strike pledge when its members refused to cross a picket line set up by striking members of another union that had a contract with the employer, an arbiter decided, notwithstanding the union's contention that the refusal to cross the picket line resulted from the personal conviction of each striking member. Pointing out that the union admitted to doing nothing to convince its members that they should honor the no-strike clause, the arbiter emphasized that the union was responsible for the employees' action since it did not make a good faith effort to get members to honor their contract. Absent a provision permitting employees to refuse to cross a picket line, the no-strike clause was binding upon the employees, the arbiter concluded. (National Homes Mfg. Co., 72 LA 1127; see also 75 LA 36, 68 LA 401, 54 LA 140)

On the other hand, where two or more unions bargained with a company for different groups of employees, members of one union were entitled to honor the picket line of the other union, since the picket line was set up as the result of a genuine labor dispute, even though the contract had a no-strike clause.

EXAMPLE: Clerical employees of a waterfront terminal company went on strike to enforce their demands. Longshoremen employed by the company refused to cross the picket line set up by the other union.

The company claimed that their contract with the longshoremen required them to cross the picket line, since they had agreed to settle all disputes through final arbitration, without a strike or lockout.

Asked to rule whether the longshoremen were required to cross the picket line, one arbiter ruled that this was the type of legitimate picket line which union members could refuse to cross. The contract contained no promise from the union to pass through another union's picket line, he pointed out.

And in view of a union's basic teaching that it cannot be used to break the strike of another union, the company should have known that the longshoremen would not cross such a line. The clerk's picket line was a legitimate one which grew out of a common and typical labor dispute and could be observed by employees belonging to another union or another unit of the same union. (Waterfront Employers' Association of the Pacific Coast, 8 LA 273)

Similarly, where employees of neutral employers refused to cross picket lines set up by another union against another employer working at the same job site, an arbiter held that the employees did not violate contractual no-strike provisions, in face of valid picket line clauses.

EXAMPLE: When unions representing employees of a general contractor and a mechanical contractor at a construction site honored the picket signs of another union, that were directed at another electrical contractor on the same project, they did not violate the no-strike clauses in their contracts, an arbiter decided. Even though the other union had restricted its picketing to a separate gate of the electrical contractor, the arbiter found no violation since the decision of the employees of the neutral general contractor and the mechanical contractor to consider the picketing as being at their own employers' gates was protected under the picket line clauses of the unions' contracts. Finding that the striking union's picketing was protected primary activity, the arbiter concluded that the picket line clauses may be used to protect the individual decision of neutral employees to honor such activity. (Associated General Contractors of Minnesota, 63 LA 32)

Handling Struck Work

If there is a clear provision in a contract permitting employees to handle work going to or coming from a struck plant, then there may be no problem, when they refuse to handle "struck work". But in the absence of a hot-goods clause, arbiters have held that employees cannot refuse to handle struck work.

EXAMPLE: Communications workers at a cable company refused to forward messages through a company which was on strike during a period when an emergency condition made it impossible to transmit the messages over their own company's facilities. They were suspended for refusing to handle the so-called "hot traffic."

The arbiter held that neither the contract nor past practice gave employees the right to refuse to handle the messages bound for a struck company. He noted that the work in question was not part of the ordinary work flow, but was caused only by a cable break. Allowing employees to refuse to handle the work would amount to adding something to the contract which was not put there by the parties, according to the arbiter . Finally, it was noted that the union should have followed the contractual grievance procedure rather than taking matters in its own hands. The suspensions were upheld. (Commercial Pacific Cable Co., 11 LA 219)

Similarly, an international and local unions violated a no-strike clause when the international threatened to pull the union label on rotogravure work that a customer for a primary employer had placed with the secondary employer following another union's strike against the primary employer, an arbiter decided. Finding that the international improperly determined that the work was "struck work" under the contract, and then ordered the local to refuse to process any of the customer's requirements on the secondary employer's presses, the arbiter ruled that the dispute should have been submitted to arbitration. Pointing out that the local was the agent of the international with respect to the union label, and that the use of the label was indispensable to the secondary employer's uninterrupted production, the arbiter concluded that liability should be apportioned 99.8 percent upon the international and .2 percent upon the local. (Sterling Regal Inc., 69 LA 513)

Union Liability for No-Strike Violation

A union may be liable when its members violate a no-strike clause, if there is evidence that the union, actively or passively, was involved in the illegal action.

EXAMPLE: A union was liable for damages that an employer sustained when a union steward encouraged picketing against the employer in protest against a subcontractor's employees performing bargaining unit work, an arbiter ruled, even though the steward's interpretation of the contract may have been knowingly wrong. Finding that the steward was acting within the scope of his authority when he rendered the interpretation, and the union was responsible for his actions as its agent, the arbitrator concluded that this responsibility continued until the union's business agent took action to overrule the incorrect interpretation, and carried out reasonable means for getting members back to work. (Rust Engineering Co., 77 LA 488)

Similarly, a union that represented mechanics and drivers under separate agreements was liable to an employer for damages for not directing employees to return to work after the mechanics refused to cross picket lines set up by the drivers when their contract expired, an arbiter ruled. The no-strike clause and the provision expressing the union's commitment to see that its members obey all reasonable rules contemplated that the union would order its members to ignore picket lines and take all reasonable steps to end strikes, the arbiter concluded. (Westinghouse Transport Leasing Corp., 69 LA 1210; see also, 66 LA 82, 66 LA 388)

Strike Penalties

IN BRIEF

Violation of a no-strike clause can lead to disciplinary action, including discharge. In most cases, arbiters uphold management's decision to discipline workers who engage in illegal strike activity, unless the union can prove that the penalty was based on anti-union bias or discrimination. Other factors which arbiters consider in determining the propriety of strike penalties include: (1) the predominance of union members or leaders among the discharged and those offered reinstatement; (2) the degree of union activity by the individual worker; and (3) the position of the employer with regard to union membership.

Penalties against union officials who participate in, or fail to try to prevent an illegal strike, frequently, are harsher than those meted out against rank-and-file violators, because a higher degree of responsibility is imposed on union representatives. According to one arbiter, a union steward's responsibility in a wildcat situation is as follows:

"Indeed, a shop steward's duty in the face of an unauthorized work stoppage is well settled. Not only should he make a determined effort to prevent the stoppage before it begins, but upon its development must actively and unequivocally attempt to bring an end of the stoppage at the earliest possible moment. Moreover, he must set an example by either reporting to work himself or by clearly indicating a willingness to work if his employer wishes him to do so. And obviously if he is either requested or directed to work, he must do so. Only in this way can the steward comply with his responsibility to uphold the integrity of the contract and its orderly processes for dispute settlement." (United Parcel Service Inc., 47 LA 1100)

GUIDELINES

Discipline of Union Leaders

Union officials are supposed to set good examples for the rank and file to follow. Holding this view, most arbiters have ruled that, if union officers do not carry out their responsibility of seeing to it that workers live up to a contract's no-strike clause, they can be disciplined. (69 LA 459, 55 LA 31, 36 LA 214)

Indeed, many arbiters have upheld the discharge of union leaders who incited, led, or refused to try to prevent an illegal strike. (88 LA 1230, 84 LA 1315, 69 LA 93, 66 LA 682, 64 LA 428, 63 LA 765, 63 LA 633, 53 LA 154, 7 LA 735, 4 LA 403)

The following cases are examples of instances in which arbiters have sustained disciplinary actions against union officers:

• Discharge of a union steward for violating a work rule and a settlement agreement by leading a work stoppage over an assignment of work which was allegedly contrary to past practice. The settlement agreement ordered his discharge if any further work stoppages occurred at his "direction or participation." (San Francisco Newspaper Agency, 87 LA 537)

• Discharge of a union steward for violating a no-strike clause by attempting to impede the work of probationary employees. (Vernitron Piezoelectric Div., 84 LA 1315)

• Discharge of a union president for failure to take affirmative action to prevent a wildcat strike and to put an end to it as soon as it occurred. (Ford Motor Co., 41 LA 609)

• Discharge of union officers who actively participated in picketing, refusal to work, and other activities. (General American Transportation Corp., 42 LA 142)

• Discharge of shop steward for making no convincing effort either to prevent the walkout or to secure a return to work after it occurred. (Gold Bond Stamp Co. of Georgia, 49 LA 27)

• Discharge of union president for instigating a one-day walkout, even though he subsequently tried to secure a return to work. (McGraw-Edison Co., 39 LA 76)

• Discharge of union committeemen who probably were the instigators of a walkout but who, in any event, were derelict in their duty as union officers to try to get employees back to work. (Bell Bakeries, 43 LA 608)

• Discharge of union officers for participating in an unauthorized work stoppage; the arbiter holding that union officers cannot discharge their responsibility by a passive attitude that would allow them to merely be swept along by the tide of rank-and-file action. (Drake Mfg. Co., 41 LA 732)

• Discharge of shop steward for role as leader in strike during impasse in collective bargaining negotiations. (St. Francois County, 69 LA 102)

• Discharge of union president for instigating and leading illegal work stoppage during the time he was on leave of absence as full time union official receiving pay from the union. (Dravo Corp., 68 LA 618)

• Discharge of union executive board members who were in the forefront of an illegal work stoppage following an employer's refusal to accede to a union's demand for reinstatement of an employee who was discharged for theft of company property. (Clinton Corn Processing Co. and Grain Millers, 71 LA 555)

• Suspensions of union president and recording secretary who recommended through their actions that unit employees not show up for scheduled inventory overtime that they previously had volunteered to perform. (Zellerbach Paper Co. and Paperworkers, 73 LA 1140)

On the other hand, arbiters have rejected or reduced penalties imposed on union officials where:

(1) There were mitigating circumstances;

(2) The company could not show that union leaders were more to blame than other strikers; and,

(3) Union officers *did* carry out their responsibilities by urging employees not to strike, even though their efforts failed and the strike proceeded. (65 LA 1245, 64 LA 1210, 64 LA 425, 55 LA 1159, 33 LA 807, 29 LA 644, 8 LA 758, 7 LA 183)

The following cases are examples of instances in which arbiters have set aside or reduced strike penalties against union officials:

• A steward had his suspension set aside, since the suspension had been based on uncorroborated statements that the steward had encouraged an employee to slow down her production rate and had threatened reprisals if she failed to do so. The evidence of conduct was tenuous and insufficient to overcome the greater latitude accorded a steward in the performance of his or her office duties. (Associated Wholesale Grocers Inc., 89 LA 227)

• Disciplinary suspension, rather than discharge, was the appropriate penalty for a steward who urged a work slowdown in violation of a contract, but where there was no evidence of an actual slowdown. (88 LA 1230)

• Similarly, disciplinary suspension, rather than discharge, was the appropriate penalty for a steward whose expression of dissatisfaction at the way the employer and the union committee had handled a grievance led to an illegal work stoppage. (Quanex, Mac Steel Div. and Steelworkers, 73 LA 9)

• Penalty for one-week suspension was too severe for a union steward for telling a co-worker to relax the rate of production for assembly job under time study that grievant determined could not be met if co-worker were following procedures established by the time study. (Gehl Co. and Industrial Workers, 73 LA 158)

• Penalty of discharge was too severe for a union officer who directed employee not to fill in on lamination department maintenance job that had been removed from unit. (Twain, Mark, Marine Industries Inc., 73 LA 551)

• Participation by a union official in a wildcat strike was not ground for discharge, where he later tried to halt it. The company failed to prove that he promoted the strike; however, his participation was ground for a one-year probation. (Cyclops Corp., 45 LA 560)

• When a union president failed to get his men back to work within five minutes, the company placed him on 60-day suspension. The arbiter set this aside because it was not clear whether the president caused the wildcat strike or was simply caught up in it. (Weatherhead Co., 43 LA 422)

Discipline of Rank and File

As a general rule, arbiters hold that an employer who is confronted with an illegal wildcat strike is not required to deprive itself of the services of all employees participating in the strike. The employer may select those for punishment whom it deems fit, provided the employer's selection is not capricious.

The employer has the right to assign varying penalties, up to and including discharge, on the basis of its evaluation of the degree of seriousness of the conduct of participants in an illegal strike — again, subject to the general principle that the evaluation not be arbitrary or capricious. The employer also should exercise its right of discipline within a reasonable time limit. (98 LA 41, 97 LA 297, 93 LA 1097, 90 LA 24, 89 LA 1296, 86 LA 622, 85 LA 1017, 85 LA 692, 83 LA 608, 82 LA 226, 81 LA 179, 66 LA 626, 63 LA 677, 61 LA 896, 53 LA 75, 53 LA 45, 55 LA 1159, 47 LA 129, 41 LA 609, 46 LA 982, 40 LA 1209, 35 LA 590)

EXAMPLE: An arbiter upheld the discharge of the following employees for their participation in a strike in violation of a no-strike clause, there being evidence that the strikers rejected pleadings of union and company officials to cease and desist: (1) Employee who, upon being asked whether it was he who had club in his hand, replies "It could possibly be;" (2) employee who admitted being included in group of union officers who were asked to talk to employer, the contract stating that union officials agree immediately to instruct membership to cease work stoppage; (3) employee who engaged in obstructing and/or blocking traffic during strike; (4) employee who testified that there were couple of days that he went to plant during strike, there being no need for additional testimony to establish that he was an active participant in strike; (5) employee who was not near plant facilities during second week of strike but who was observed throwing bottles onto parking lot during strike; (6) employee who was at plant every day of strike, thereby confirming charge that he was an active participant; (7) employee who established his motive for supporting strike by being at plant during period of his disciplinary layoff; (8) employee who was at plant for three separate days in first week of strike and on each day of following week; (9) employee who had been officer in union and was acting as their negotiator and spokesman and who admitted being at plant for several days during strike.

However, the arbiter reduced the discharge penalty to disciplinary suspension for an employee who appeared at the plant on two separate days during a strike to get an explanation of a restraining order he had received in the mail, and also for another employee who attempted to prevent the wildcat strike, who worked the first five days of a strike and missed the last three days due to threats received by him and his wife. (Grumman Flxible, 72 LA 326)

EXAMPLE: An arbiter ruled that an employer improperly placed a letter in an employee's file threatening discipline for alleged violation of a no-strike clause by his refusal to cross a sister local's picket line. The no-strike clause — which said that a union and its members will not "authorize, instigate, aid, condone, or engage in work stoppages, slowdowns, refusals to work, or strikes," the arbiter pointed out, did not cover sympathy strikes. Further, he said, the established practice had been that bargaining-unit members would not cross legal picket lines and the employer would provide them with alternate work. Also, the arbiter noted that no employer had ever received such a letter in 16 years that the clause had been in effect. (GTE North Inc., 94 LA 1033)

EXAMPLE: An employer had just cause to discharge an employee whom it determined to have participated in a wildcat strike to a greater degree than other strikers, an arbiter decided, rejecting the union's contention that the employer must establish the employee's participation by a preponderance of credible evidence. It is not incumbent upon management to prove that the employee participated to a greater degree than other strikers before it can impose discipline, the arbiter emphasized, concluding that the employer need only establish that it acted fairly and in good faith. (Price Bros. Co. and Laborers, 74 LA 748)

However, the employer must be able to show some basis for selecting out individual strikers for discipline. (93 LA 1097, 89 LA 1257, 68 LA 805, 67 LA 1250)

EXAMPLE: One arbiter set aside suspensions imposed on five employees accused of being the first to walk out of the plant gate during a wildcat strike, where their identification was based on a supervisor's observation from a window located about 50 yards from the gate from which employees exited in a state of confusion. (W. S. Hodge Foundry Inc., 55 LA 548)

EXAMPLE: Another arbiter held that a two-week suspension was too stiff a penalty for some wildcat strikers, even though they probably were guilty of inciting the strike. The arbiter reasoned that the workers probably did not need much encouragement to strike anyhow and found no evidence that the strike would not have occurred even if the instigators had done nothing. (International Minerals & Chemical Corp., 28 LA 121)

Discipline of Strikers Heeding Back-to-Work Order

According to one arbiter, employees who strike in violation of a contract can be disciplined even though they return to work at the union's request.

EXAMPLE: In a contract the parties agreed that: (1) the company had the right to discipline employees for just and proper cause, (2) the union would not engage in any unauthorized work stoppage, and (3) the company would not hold the union liable for damage resulting from an unauthorized work stoppage provided the union immediately instructed its members to return to work. The last clause further provided that the company could take any disciplinary action it considered appropriate in the event employees ignored a back-to-work order.

Employees who walked off the job on one occasion returned to work at the start of their next shift. When the company slapped them with five-day disciplinary layoffs, the union filed a grievance. In its view, the contract permitted the company to discipline strikers only if the union failed to tell them to go back to work and they continued their walkout. In this case, the union pointed out, it had issued the required instructions, and the men had in fact returned to work.

An arbiter would not buy the union's argument. He figured the union was saying that, because the company had the right under the contract to act in one set of circumstances, it necessarily had forfeited the right to act in other circumstances. The arbiter did not think this was so. Since the contract did not specifically cover the case at hand, he decided it came under the provision affirming the company's general right to impose discipline. Accordingly he upheld the suspensions. (Bell Aircraft Corp., 30 LA 153)

Damage Awards as Penalty

Arbitrators have assessed damages against a union that violates a no-strike pledge. (77 LA 488, 75 LA 189, 67 LA 805, 66 LA 388, 66 LA 82, 63 LA 633)

EXAMPLE: While finding that full compensatory damages were not required due to the limited nature of the union's violation and the employer's share of blame for the underlying dispute, an arbiter allowed damages for breach of the no-strike clause that included: (1) out-of-pocket expenses and lost profit on a specific transaction that the employer was unable to complete due to the violation, and (2) a reasonable portion of overhead expenses and general loss of profits arising from the shutdown. The arbiter refused, however, to allow recovery of attorney's fees sustained in an effort to get an injunction to end the strike. (Mercer, Fraser Co., 54 LA 1125)

EXAMPLE: An arbitration board determined damages allowable to an employer for a breach-of-contract strike amounted to $20,334 for fixed and standby expenses and for demurrage. The board declined to include an award for loss of profits, primarily because of a failure to establish definitely the loss, if any, that had occurred. (Vulcan Mold and Iron Co., 53 LA 875)

EXAMPLE: As a remedy for a strike against a construction company on a highway project, an arbiter allowed damages including labor costs, rental value of its own equipment, rental value of rented equipment, and the prorated costs of traffic protection. (Foster Grading Co., 52 LA 197)

EXAMPLE: An arbitration board decided it had power to award damages for a union's breach-of-contract strike, even though the contract made no mention of this remedy. It declined, however, to award damages for loss of good will, since this was too speculative. (Oregonian Publishing Co., 33 LA 575)

Arbiters' Injunction vs. Strikes

In some instances, and particularly where the parties have a permanent arbitrator, the employer may be able to get a back-to-work order from an arbiter similar to a court injunction.

EXAMPLE: A department store was held entitled to an injunction against sympathetic picketing by its sales employees during lunch hours and before and after work in support of a strike by its warehouse employees. (Macy's New York, 40 LA 954)

EXAMPLE: After finding that the union's work stoppage violated the no-strike clause in its contract, an arbitrator ordered the employees to return to work and the union to secure compliance with the no-strike provisions. The order was issued on an ex parte basis in the absence of the union, since the union had received proper notice and an invitation to appear and had not objected to the employer's taking the dispute to arbitration on an ex parte basis. (Pacific Maritime Assn., 52 LA 1189)

Cancellation of Seniority as Penalty

Even though workers who strike in violation of a contract can be disciplined, at least one arbiter thought that cancellation of seniority was an improper penalty for such conduct.

EXAMPLE: When employees at one company staged a wildcat strike, the company notified all 2,500 strikers that they were suspended for five days and would be terminated if they failed to return to work by a certain deadline. It later informed the strikers that those who failed to report before the deadline would be taken back as new employees.

An arbiter held that the company had the right to fire the strike leaders but ordered it to reinstate the others with the seniority they had prior to the walkout. He did not think the company really intended to discharge all the strikers; it had no reason to think it could find enough replacements. The contract mentioned suspension and discharge as disciplinary measures, the arbiter noted, but said nothing about loss of seniority. Such a penalty was inappropriate, he thought, because seniority is in the nature of a vested right and affects the relative standing of all employees. Upholding the penalty, he commented, would lead to continuing dissension between employees who stayed on the job or returned before the deadline and the "new hires."

The award called for gradual reinstatement of the strikers, in order of their seniority, over a nine-month period. None of the strikers received any compensation for lost wages, however. (Lone Star Steel Co., 30 LA 519, see also 64 LA 955, 63 LA 736)

Docking for Lost Time During Stoppage

Awards suggest that arbiters will allow a company to dock the pay of employees for time lost during a work stoppage if certain conditions are met. These are (1) that there is sure proof that *all* employees took part in the work stoppage and (2) that there was work that could have been done during the stoppage and none of the workers did it.

EXAMPLE: A work stoppage occurred in one department of a trailer company, and management docked every employee who participated for the time lost. The union contended that only those actually responsible for the stoppage should have had pay deductions. The union went on to say that since management could not determine exactly which employees caused the stoppage, the deducted pay should be restored to all employees.

The arbiter held that, if innocent employees had been forced to stop working because of others' activities, they should not have been penalized. Here, however, there was work that could have been done, so "it is quite manifest that each employee who stopped did so upon his own responsibility and should suffer any resultant consequences of such action." He concluded, therefore, that the pay deductions were warranted. (Fruehauf Trailer Co., 1 LA 155)

On the other hand, where an arbiter found it impossible on the basis of the evidence to conclude that all the workers in one shop participated in a stoppage, he decided that none of them could be docked. (S. Co. Inc., 10 LA 924)

Similarly, although production had been halted by a strike, the company broadcast over the radio the message that it would be operating. As a result, some workers showed up for work, but were later told to go home. Others never showed up, as they had been told not to do so by their supervisors. The arbiter held that both of these groups of workers were entitled to pay, even though the contract specified no payment for time lost to strikes. He reasoned that their lost time was primarily attributable to the employer's instructions. (U.S. Steel Corp., 45 LA 509)

Partial Strikes

According to one arbiter, workers can be penalized for engaging in an intermittent work stoppage lasting for part or all of a shift even though the contract does not contain a no-strike clause.

EXAMPLE: When a company refused to arbitrate grievances over the pay of skilled trades — as it had a right to do under its contract — the union proceeded to hold meetings lasting two hours on each of three shifts. The third time this happened, the company warned that further meetings would lead to disciplinary action. The next day, another series of meetings was held, and the participants were given a one-day suspension. Claiming that the discipline was a contract violation, the skilled tradesmen staged a one-day strike, and management told the union that one-day suspensions would again be imposed unless the union promised there would not be any repeat performances. The union did not give any such assurance, and the company followed through with the suspensions.

An arbiter upheld the company's actions. Although the contract gave employees the right to engage in a "whole strike," that was not the same as a "partial strike," he said. An employee must either work or strike; and he cannot set his own working conditions, the arbiter held. The union's attitude suggested that more stoppages might occur; under these circumstances, the arbiter decided the penalties were justified. (General Electric Co., 31 LA 28; see also 39 LA 629)

Discipline for Slowdown

Arbitrators are likely to hold that discharge is too severe a penalty for workers who take part in a slowdown.

EXAMPLE: In one case a group of workers was fired because they had collectively decided not to increase their output when production standards were raised as a result of job changes. But an arbiter reduced their penalty to a month's layoff in view of their long seniority and the fact that they did not acutally decrease their output. (Armour & Co., 8 LA 1)

Similarly, even though another arbiter was convinced that a worker had deliberately pulled a slowdown, he changed his penalty from discharge to a four-week layoff because he had a long record of satisfactory performance. (Reed Roller Bit Co., 29 LA 604)

Likewise, an employer was not justified in discharging a member of a union shop committee for telling employees to slowdown production, an arbiter decided, notwithstanding the employer's contention that the employee violated a contractual provision barring the union from causing or sanctioning work stoppages, strikes, or slowdowns. Emphasizing that the employer failed to apply progressive discipline, the arbiter concluded that the employee was not adequately warned about his discharge. (Stevens Air Systems, 64 LA 425)

Moreover in some cases, arbiters even have held that disciplinary suspensions were too severe for employees who participated in a slowdown. (96 LA 294, 64 LA 56, 62 LA 1289, 61 LA 246)

Discipline of "Silent Partners" in a Slowdown

If a slowdown occurs on an incentive operation, can employees be disciplined who are down the line from the bottleneck and therefore do not have primary responsibility for the drop in production? If such employees do not call management's attention to the fact that they're not getting as much material to process, they must be regarded as "silent partners" in the slowdown, one arbitrator has decided; and they're just as much at fault as those who take the initiative in restricting production. (John Deere Harvester Works, 27 LA 744)

Similarly, disciplinary suspensions were in order for shop committeemen who took part in a slowdown, thus giving it their silent if not active okay, one arbitrator has ruled. He agreed with the company that although the committeemen did not initiate the slowdown, they did avoid their responsibility under the contract's no-strike pledge in not trying to stop it. The company tried to identify the leaders but could not, he noted. The next best approach, the arbiter reasoned, was to make an example of those who had shirked their responsibility to lead. (Philco Corp., 38 LA 889)

Pay Cut for Slowdown

One arbiter decided that if incentive employees engage in a slowdown, they can be denied pay guarantees under an incentive plan and paid only for actual output. (American Steel & Wire Co., 6 LA 392)

On the other hand, another arbiter said that cutting pay below guaranteed levels was a contract violation and therefore an improper penalty for slowdown. (Jacobs Mfg. Co., 29 LA 512)

Discipline for Strike Misconduct

Employees can be disciplined for misconduct during strike activities. Violence is the principal charge leveled against strikers for which management feels it may issue discharge or suspension slips. The violence may cover such varied activities as tossing stink bombs around, attacking supervisors or nonstrikers, throwing stones, and issuing threats from the picket line.

Arbitrators generally will consider the evidence in each case closely. If the accusation is of the more serious type (such as attacking a supervisor) and the evidence supports the charge, the discipline may be allowed to stand. (69 LA 351, 68 LA 706, 66 LA 1020)

On the other hand, where the charge of strike misconduct is not substantiated by the evidence, the arbiter may disallow the disciplinary action taken. (77 LA 483, 75 LA 929, 74 LA 726)

In considering cases involving dismissals for misconduct on a picket line and during a strike, respectively, Arbitrators Clark Kerr and James J. Healy have outlined general criteria which they thought were important. These two sets of guiding principles follow:

Kerr —

"(a) How satisfactory is the evidence? Not all evidence is of equal value. Some is more convincing, some less, and some not at all.

"(b) What is the extent of participation? In any mob situation the degree of involvement of the individual in any action taken is important.

"(c) What was the nature of the violence? This has both quantitative and qualitative aspects. Participation in several incidents is more serious than in only one. Some actions are more reprehensible than others. Shouting insults and shoving are of a different order from striking a person.

"(d) Was the violence provoked? To the extent the violence is retaliatory and defensive it is less culpable than if undertaken as an act of aggression.

"(e) Was the violence premeditated or undertaken on the spur of the moment? Premeditated violence is the more inexcusable.

"(f) What will be the impact of the punishment? Discharge is more of a penalty for an old man, than a young one; for a long service employee than a short service employee.

"(g) Was the disciplinary action discriminatory? A company is under some obligation to treat persons similarly situated in a comparable, although not necessarily identical manner. Violence can hardly be said to be the real basis for discharge if other unjustifiable factors enter in.

"(h) What is the general context of the situation?" (Cudahy Packing Co., 11 LA 1138)

Healy —

"(a) Was the alleged misconduct of the aggrieved proved to the complete satisfaction of the arbiter?

"(b) If the misconduct is proved satisfactorily, was it of such a nature as to warrant discharge?

"(c) If the misconduct is proved, was it the result of certain provocation which mitigates the guilt of the aggrieved?

"(d) Is there evidence that discrimination was a factor in the discharge?

"(e) Was the misconduct of such a nature as to affect employer-employee relationship or was it more appropriately the concern of civil authorities?" (Swift & Co., 12 LA 108)

Amnesty Pledges

The following cases illustrate how arbitrators view management's offer of amnesty to striking employees.

EXAMPLE: When several workers engaged in a wildcat strike, the superintendent promised amnesty to those who began work "without further delay." Of those on strike, 17 did not return until an hour later. They were given one-day suspensions, which they claimed was a violation of the amnesty pledge. The arbitrator disagreed, saying that the pledge was not a continuing offer to be accepted whenever the workers felt like returning. (Bethlehem Steel Corp., 47 LA 524)

Likewise, although an employer's amnesty pledge following a wildcat strike barred discipline for "passive nonviolent participation," it did not bar the discharge of two men who tried to promote a secondary boycott. According to the arbiter, the evidence established that they were guilty of concerted misconduct above and beyond actions protected by the amnesty agreement. (Falls Stamping & Welding Co., 48 LA 107)

On the other hand, an employer's blanket offer of reinstatement "without recrimination" after an illegal strike extended to all workers, including the steward who instigated the strike. The arbitrator, however, directed the company to deny back pay as a penalty for her part in the illegal strike. (Strombeck Manufacturing Co., 45 LA 37)

Part 13

Union Security

Union Security

IN BRIEF

Most collective bargaining agreements contain union-security provisions which require employees to become union members and maintain their membership in good standing as a condition of continued employment. In addition, contracts often include a checkoff clause, providing for the employer to deduct union dues from employees' wages. (88 LA 413)

A union may be entitled to demand the discharge of an employee who fails to join the union and pay dues. However, the Taft Act sharply limits the conditions under which a union may take this action. Even though an arbiter may uphold the discharge of an employee for failing to maintain union membership, NLRB may order reinstatement with back pay if it finds that the worker's rights under the law have been violated.

Under union-shop agreements, the obligation of workers to join the union is clear. However, the lesser forms of union security, such as modified-union-shop and maintenance-of-membership, often give rise to special problems — which workers must join, what constitutes union membership, when workers may resign from the union, etc.

GUIDELINES

Types of Union Security

There are several types of union-security clauses. Following are the principal ones:

- The *closed-shop* agreement, which requires union membership as a condition of employment, is illegal under the Taft Act.
- The *union-shop* contract requires nonunion new hires to become members of a union within a prescribed period after initial employment, and for nonunion employees to become members within a prescribed period after the union-shop contract becomes effective. Under the Taft Act, the union-shop contract may not require the employer to hire only union members.
- The *modified-union-shop* contract limits the membership obligation to new hires, while permitting currently employed workers to continue their nonunion status.
- The *agency shop* also conditions employment on the payment of regular union dues and initiation fees, but, unlike a union shop, it does not require actual union membership. Employees who chose to remain nonunion must pay the union a union-service fee, which usually is equivalent to union dues and initiation fees, since the union must act as a bargaining representative for all employees within a bargaining unit. (94 LA 1272, 93 LA 732, 90 LA 973, 89 LA 1181) Agency-shop provisions are limited by state right-to-work laws (currently in 21 states) which regulate union-security agreements more rigorously than federal law and by religious objections. Also, nonmembers, under *Communications Workers v. Beck* (US SupCt, 1988, 128 LRRM 2729), as reiterated in Executive Order 12800, may object to a union's use of agency fees for nonrepresentational activities — i.e., not related to collective

bargaining, contract administration, or grievance adjustment. Further, nonmembers are protected by First-Amendment free-speech provisions.

• *Maintenance-of-membership contracts* require employees who are union members on the effective date of the agreement to retain that membership for the duration of the agreement.

• *Hiring arrangements* require the use of union hiring halls as employment agencies. A union may charge nonmembers a fee to help pay the expenses of a hiring hall, but the fee cannot be equal to the dues paid by union members.

UNION MEMBERSHIP

Application for Membership

Can an employee be considered a union member if he has never signed an application card? Often when a union and a company sign a contract with a maintenance - of - membership, union shop, or other union security provision, the problem comes up of determining which employees were union members at the time the contract was signed.

One arbiter has laid down the following standards for determining what constitutes union membership:

1. The individual must have signed an official application card showing his intention of joining the union and his desire to have the union act as his representative for collective bargaining.
2. The employee must have paid his first month's union dues.
3. The union must have issued him an official receipt for the first month's dues payment.
4. The union must have furnished him with an official membership card showing that the employee has been accepted for membership.

Only if all these conditions are fulfilled according to the arbiter, can an employee be considered as having joined the union. *At the same time:* Payment of an *initiation fee* is not necessarily a condition of union membership. The arbiter observed that unions frequently waive payment of an initiation fee, particularly during an organizing drive. (Bendix Aviation Corp., Pacific Division, 15 LRRM 2650)

Employees Behind in Dues When Contract Is Signed

Granted that a worker was a union member at one time, the question frequently arises whether he was still a member of the union at the time a maintenance - of - membership contract went into effect. If not, he is not bound to keep up his membership in the union unless he rejoins it of his own accord later on.

Most arbiters who have ruled on this question have based their decisions on the provisions of the constitution or bylaws of the union holding the contract. Ordinarily, the union constitution will provide for automatic suspension of members behind in their dues a certain number of months.

When the record of an employee's dues payments shows that he was so far behind at the time the contract went into effect that he was under automatic suspension from the union, the arbiter will usually hold that he is not bound by the maintenance-of-membership requirement. (Bendix Aviation Corp., Pacific Division, 15 LRRM 2650).

Members in Arrears Carried in Good Standing

Can a union by its action in carrying a delinquent member as a "member in good standing," bar escape of the member from the union at a time when such escape is possible?

This situation usually arises when a membership-maintenance clause is enforceable only against "members in good standing" at a certain date. Arbiters have actually held that the employees must be "members in good standing" and not merely carried as such by the union. (Electrical Workers, 4 LA 443)

EXAMPLE: One arbiter stated that a union could waive the delinquency of its members when no third party interests were affected. It is proper, he said, for a union to continue to carry members even if they are in arrears in their dues because of illness or financial difficulties, if the members do not object. But when he found that carrying a delinquent member as one in good standing meant depriving him of his right to withdraw from the union under the escape clause, he ruled that the worker did not have to be discharged for not maintaining membership. (Monsanto Chemical Co., 12 LA 1175)

Signing Membership Application But Not Paying Dues

Are employees "in good standing" with the union if they have signed a membership application card, but have not remitted dues since the signing of the application?

This situation is frequently presented when unions are successful in organizational drives and obtain many membership applications. Some months later when the unions are successful in securing a contract, they find that many of the employees who have signed the applications have failed to keep up their dues.

EXAMPLE: An employee who signed an application form to become a union member at the request of a friend and in the belief that its only purpose was to get the union certified was improperly discharged for failing to pay union dues, an arbiter ruled. Finding that the employee demanded that his application card be returned to him and that he did not intend to belong to the union in advance of the effective date of the contract, the arbiter concluded that the worker was induced to sign the card under mistake of fact. (Rexnord Inc., 77 LA 1166)

Employer's Obligation to Discharge Delinquent

An employer may be obligated to accede to a union's demand to discharge an employee who is delinquent in paying dues, according to arbiters.

EXAMPLE: An arbiter ordered an employer that refused to discharge employees to whom it had served timely notice of nonpayment of union dues or agency fees to discharge all such employees who, within 10 days from date of award, fail to resolve their financial problems with their union. The union's failure to inform the employees of their agency-fee option could not be used as a defense against the grievance, the arbiter said, since unfair-labor-practice claims are not cognizable in arbitration. (Great Western Carpet Cushion Co., 95 LA 1057; see also 95 LA 1175)

EXAMPLE: An employer was obligated to terminate employees after the union notified management that the employees, who were expelled from the union for non-payment of dues, had not tendered the required dues, an arbiter ruled. Pointing out that the demand that the workers be discharged for not paying dues was in full compliance with the Landrum-Griffin Act, the arbiter concluded that the union was not treating the employees arbitrarily or unfairly by requiring them to pay an initiation fee in order to be reinstated. (Times Journal Publishing Co., 72 LA 971)

Likewise, an arbiter ruled that an employer was obligated, under a union-security agreement, to accede to the demand of unions to terminate employees who refused to pay union dues and fees of varying amounts charged by the jointly-certified unions, despite the contention that the charging of different fees and dues by three unions, that must be operated as a "single union," was not compatible with the concept of joint representative in a single unit. (Frazer & Johnston Co., 66 LA 251, see also 77 LA 424, 76 LA 71, 68 LA 261, 42 LA 989)

However, an arbiter ruled that a union did not have the right to seek the termination of a newly-promoted supervisor because of his failure to pay union dues during a 60-day period in which he continued to accumulate seniority and could decide to return to a bargaining unit. The supervisor, was not a member of the bargaining unit during the 60-day period and has no responsibility to remain a union member in good standing, the arbiter held. (Electric Energy Inc., 92 LA 351)

Duel Union Membership

Can a union withhold membership from workers who belong to a rival union, even though lack of membership is cause for dismissal under a union-shop agreement? One arbiter said no.

EXAMPLE: Three workers were not members of the union that held bargaining rights at the company where they worked. They arranged with a competing union, of which they were members, to pay their dues to the incumbent. The latter union denied them membership until they disaffiliated with its rival and signed a checkoff agreement with it. The men refused, and the union demanded their discharge under the union-security clause because they would not sign the checkoff form and were tardy in paying their dues.

There is no prohibition against a worker's belonging to two or more unions, the arbiter noted. Although the dues were delinquent, he found that they were paid before the deadline. Since their dues were in order, the arbiter ruled that the workers were entitled to membership in the incumbent union and the company had no reason to dismiss them. (Hawaiian Brewing Corp., 35 LA 420)

Refusing to Join Union Because of Religious Belief

Can employees be fired for refusing to join a union and to pay dues on the ground that it is against their religion? One arbiter has held yes.

EXAMPLE: Under a contract requiring an employer on written request of the union to discharge employees who fail to become members of the union in good financial standing, an arbiter ruled that an employer was obligated to discharge an employee who refused to pay the required dues because it was against her religion to join associations such as unions. Despite the contention that requiring the employee to pay dues when her religion forbids her to join unions violated her constitutional guaranteed of freedom of religion, the arbiter found no provision in the contract that exempted bargaining unit employees from the obligation to pay dues. Emphasizing that the requirement to pay dues applied to all unit members, and therefore was not discriminatory, the arbiter concluded that the dues amount required was not onerous. (Benson Shoe Co., 62 LA 1020)

Part-Time Employees

Can a union require part-time employees to pay union dues and fees under a contract that requires full-time employees to join the organization? One arbitrator has ruled no.

EXAMPLE: Under a contract that recognized the union as exclusive bargaining representative of "full-time" employees and which permitted part-time employees to be used to augment regular staff on an on-call basis, an arbiter decided that a union was not entitled to require a part-time employee, who was performing fill in duties, to pay union dues and fees. Finding that the part-time employee was not subject to the terms and conditions of the contract, particularly the agency shop provisions, the arbiter ruled that the worker was not included in the bargaining unit since he received no benefits under the contract. (Saginaw County Juvenile Home, 67 LA 446)

ESCAPE PERIODS

Premature Resignation Letters

Employees who submit their letters of resignation from union membership prior to the escape period nevertheless may be held to have effectively resigned, particularly where the letters were sent close to the escape period.

EXAMPLE: A maintenance-of-membership agreement provided a 15-day escape period immediately following the anniversary date of the agreement. This was variously interpreted as meaning a 15-day period beginning November 7 or November 8. Prior to this first anniversary date, 19 employees submitted letters of resignation in the period October 17 through November 5. On November 22, the union informed these employees that their attempted resignations were not effective, since the 15-day escape period ran from November 7 through November 22.

Holding the resignations effective, an arbiter noted that the employees obviously intended their resignations to become effective on the first possible date. He added that the union was guilty of bad faith in waiting until the last day of the escape period to inform the employees that their resignation letters were invalid. (Carson Mfg. Co., 52 LA 1057)

Similarly, under a contract providing that any employee may withdraw from the union during the seven days prior to April 1 of each year, an arbiter decided that an employee gave timely notice of resignation from the union where he spoke to union officials about resigning and handed a letter to the payroll department requesting his withdrawal from the union "as of April, 1972." Notwithstanding the union's contention that the letter was untimely, in that it carried a date which was before the beginning of the escape period, the arbiter concluded that, the crucial date in the letter was the effective date of the withdrawal. (Continental Oil, 61 LA 610)

Absence of Escape Clause

In the absence of an escape clause in renewed membership - maintenance agreements, can a worker resign from the union on the date an old contract expires and a new one becomes effective?

Most arbiters hold that the union-security relationship between parties to the contract is a continuing one which may be interrupted only by formal action of the parties and not by an individual who has benefited by the contract. If the parties do not provide an "escape" period, then none can be implied.

EXAMPLE: One arbiter with this view said that when the parties to a labor contract resort to every known technique to continue their relationship, that continuing character should be recognized and given effect in proceedings such as arbitration. In this case, he said, since it was a collective agreement, no single worker had any power to create an escape period not provided for by the contract. (Monsanto Chemical Co., 12 LA 1175)

Effect of Renewed Contract on Escape Period

In the absence of specific reference to it, is the escape period in an old contract carried forward to the new contract by the terms of a renewal agreement?

Renewal agreements usually provide that all the provisions of the old contract shall be carried forward in the new contract except those specifically modified by the renewal agreement. An arbiter has held that it is not necessary to provide specifically for the renewal of the escape period as it is renewed with all other provisions. (Fulton Sylphon Co., 7 LA 286)

RESIGNATION FROM UNION

Meaning of Resignation

Under a contract providing for maintenance of membership for union members until they properly resign, what is the meaning of "properly resign" when it is not defined in the contract? In this situation arbiters often will look at the union's constitution for the proper procedure for resigning from the union.

EXAMPLE: Where one union's constitution provided for a 10-day period for resignations an arbiter ruled that workers who had not resigned within this period were still members and so they were subject to the maintenance-of-membership clause of the contract. (Bridgeport Rolling Mills Co., 18 LA 233; see also 66 LA 875)

However, where a union's constitution does not provide for resignation but the labor contract it signs with a firm does have an escape clause, arbiters are likely to hold that members can withdraw during the escape period. The agreement a union makes with an employer comes first, they say, regardless of what its constitution provides. (Shell Oil Co., 14 LA 153; see also 70 LA 230, 61 LA 610)

Verbal Resignation

Can a union member resign from the union just by giving word-of-mouth notice to his department steward? In addition to a strict scrutiny of the constitution and by-laws of the union, the arbiters look to past practice and custom before making their determination

EXAMPLE: An employee, during a 15-day escape period, verbally informed the chief union steward of his desire to resign from the union. He then refused to pay any further dues. The union requested his discharge for violation of the membership-maintenance clause of the contract.

The arbiter found that under the constitution and by-laws of the union, it was clear that the steward was a designated contact person between the union and its members. Therefore, the employee had a right to tender his resignation to the departmental steward. The arbiter further found that neither the constitution and by-laws nor custom and usage in the union required that a resignation be submitted in writing. (Onsrud Machine works Inc., 9 LA 375)

EXAMPLE: Another arbiter has held that "proof of knowledge held by responsible union officers, no matter how received, that a member wishes to drop out of the union" determines whether or not the employee has resigned. He also held that the union's efforts to get the employee to sign a union membership card upon his rehire as a new employee constituted proof of the worker's claim that he had resigned from the union when he left the company. (Chicago Metal Mfg. Co., 9 LA 429)

TRANSFER INTO BARGAINING UNIT

Status of Transferred Workers Under Modified Union Shop

Under a modified union shop, employees who are not members of the union when the contract goes into effect are not required to join, but new employees, hired after the effective date of the contract, must become union members after a specified period of time. Under this arrangement, are old employees transferred into the bargaining unit required to join?

Some arbiters have ruled that employees transferred into the bargaining unit must be treated like new hires and required to join the union. (Chrysler Corp., 18 LA 664; see also 19 LA 85, 35 LA 274)

However, another arbiter held that an employer was justified in refusing to discharge a salaried employee for refusing to join the union on her return to the bargaining unit, since she could not be considered as a "new hire" under the modified union-shop agreement. The employee had been with the company for nearly 28 years and had not been a union member before she was transferred to the salaried supervisory job. (Lord Mfg. Co., 55 LA 1005)

Extension of Modified Union Shop Contract To New Unit

If a master contract containing a modified union shop is extended to cover a new unit, are all employees in the new unit required to join the union on the theory that they were hired after the effective date of the master contract? In this situation, one arbiter has held, the union-security provision cannot be considered retroactive.

EXAMPLE: The union-security clause in the master agreement between a company and a union became effective April 19, 1951. It provided that employees who were not union members on the effective date did not have to join, but that all employees hired after that date had to become members within 30 days.

On November 13, 1952, a new unit was brought under the master agreement and the union claimed that all of the workers in it had to join because they were hired after April 19, 1951.

The arbiter disagreed. For purposes of the new unit, he said, the agreement became effective on November 13, 1952. Hence, employees in the unit at that time who were not union members were not required to join, the arbiter concluded. (Chrysler Corp., 21 LA 45)

Part 14

Checkoff

Checkoff

IN BRIEF

Checkoff is the means of dues collection under union security contracts. By law, checkoff must be authorized voluntarily by each individual employee, and authorizations cannot be irrevocable for more than one year, or the duration of the contract, whichever is the shorter period.

Within this legal framework, various problems may arise. For example, what happens to a checkoff authorization when a worker is discharged or transferred out of the bargaining unit? When the union raises its dues and fees, must the employer check off the higher amounts? These are the kinds of issues considered in this chapter.

GUIDELINES

Effect of Discharge

Where an employee has signed a checkoff authorization which is automatically renewed each year if he fails to revoke it, does the authorization remain effective if his employment is terminated, and then he later returns to work for the company as a new employee? Or will a new authorization be necessary?

EXAMPLE: One arbitrator ruled that a worker's discharge ended his checkoff authorization, even though the contract did not specifically cover the matter. Any other conclusion, he commented, would lead to the "preposterous" result of having a checkoff authorization hanging in a state of suspended animation for a period of several years if a discharged employee did not think to revoke it. (Link Belt Co., 16 LA 242)

Similarly, An arbitrator held that an employer properly refused to honor an old dues checkoff authorization that had been signed by two employees prior to their termination and subsequent re-employment. (Samsonite Corp. and Rubber Workers, Local 724, 53 LA 1125)

Effect of Promotion

What is the status of a checkoff authorization after the employee leaves the bargaining unit to become a supervisor? The status of a checkoff authorization by an employee promoted out of the unit may be unlike that of a discharged employee.

EXAMPLE: One arbitrator decided that, instead of being cancelled, the authorization merely remained in a suspended state.

He noted that the authorization cards contained the phrase "future employment" and ruled that this applied to *any* future employment in the unit. To support his decision, he reminded the company that it had a policy of automatically renewing authorizations for other employees who left the unit because of layoff or who returned to the unit within the life of a single contract. (Temco Aircraft Corp., 23 LA 93)

Similarly, five employees who were promoted to supervisors were obligated to pay their union dues until they completed one year of work outside the bargaining unit, or until they sent written notice revoking their dues checkoff authorization, an arbitrator decided, where the contract stated any employee who transferred from the unit after January 1, 1972 shall pay union dues during that first year in exchange for the right to accumulate seniority. Notwithstanding the employer's contention that the supervisors were no longer members of the union and had the option of paying dues or of forfeiting their accumulated seniority, the arbitrator concluded that the obligation to pay dues was mandatory in face of the supervisors' existing and valid dues checkoff authorization. (Minnesota Mining & Mfg. Co., 62 LA 1013)

Likewise, an employer that erroneously collected union dues from a union member after his promotion to supervisor, and remitted the sum to the union, improperly withheld the amount of dues from moneys owing to the union, in order to repay the worker, an arbitrator decided, since the employee never informed the union of his changed status. Emphasizing that the member equitably was estopped from receiving a windfall return of his dues, the arbitrator concluded that upon receiving the authorization to deduct union dues for the employee, the employer's payroll department held the collected dues in trust for the union which was the soul and rightful owner. (Ogden Air Logistics Center, 75 LA 936)

On the other hand, an employer that stopped checking off union dues for union members on their promotion to supervisory positions was justified in not resuming checkoff upon the supervisors' return to the unit due to a reduction in work force, an arbitrator ruled, despite the union's contention that the supervisors had not revoked their dues authorization cards. Finding that the supervisors ceased being "employees" within the meaning of the contract upon their promotions, the arbitrator concluded that the workers had returned to the unit as new employees who may or may not elect to execute new dues deduction authorization forms. (Armstrong Cork Co., 65 LA 907; see also 65 LA 1035)

Effect of Revocation

Employers, may be obligated to continue to deduct union dues from an employee's wages where the worker's revocation of checkoff authorization is ineffective, arbitrators have ruled.

EXAMPLE: An employer was required to deduct union dues from the wages of an employee who gave notice to the employer that he was withdrawing from union membership, an arbitrator decided, where the checkoff agreement was renewed automatically, unless "specific" notice of revocation was communicated. According to the arbitrator, the employee's communication to both the employer and the union was to the effect that he was withdrawing his union membership, not that he was revoking his dues authorization. Distinguishing withdrawal of membership from revocation of authorization, the arbitrator pointed out that an employee could for personal or other reasons wish to terminate his union membership, but still wish to contribute to the cost of contract administration and thereby, be able to claim assistance from the union, in the event of difficulty. Consequently, it does not automatically follow that communication of an intent to withdraw from the union implies inevitably an intent to no longer pay dues to support the administration of the contract, the arbitrator adds.

Emphasizing that cancellation or revocation of the wage authorization required a notice sufficient to apprise the parties "unequivocably" of that purpose, the arbitrator concluded that at best the employee's notice indicated that he may have, or probably intended, to try to revoke or cancel his dues checkoff. (Asarco, Inc., 71 LA 730; see also 72 LA 937, 71 LA 228, 70 LA 58, 41 LA 1073, 36 LA 933)

Similarly, a struck employer violated a contract's maintenance-of-membership clause, an arbitrator ruled, when it failed to deduct union dues from wages of employees who sought either to revoke their dues checkoff authorizations or to resign from the union after the old contract had expired. Notwithstanding the employer's contentions that since there was no collective bargaining contract containing a union-security clause in effect during the period the employees were free to resign from the union and were not obligated to pay dues to the union after resigning, the arbitrator held that the dues checkoff authorizations remained in effect despite the contract hiatus.

The employees failed to revoke their authorizations in a timely fashion because they acted after the contract had expired, and when the escape periods of their anniversary dates either had passed or were too distant, the arbitrator reasoned. Even assuming that the employees had resigned effectively, the resignations were not revocations, the arbitrator concluded, adding that even if they were, they should have been lodged in a timely fashion in accordance with the irrevocability provisions of the authorizations. (Washington Post Co, 66 LA 553; see also 90 LA 946, 88 LA 497, 66 LA 875, 55 LA 770, 40 LA 398, 38 LA 290, 36 LA 867)

On the other hand, an arbitrator ruled that once an employee effectively resigned from a union, he was no longer member. Thus, management would violate the law if it continued to make dues deductions from his wages, the arbitrator concluded. (C.H. Guenther & Son Inc., 34 LA 800; see also, 82 LA 856, 44 LA 965)

Effect of Decertification

After a union has been decertified, must a company continue paying checked-off contributions to it until the collective bargaining agreement expires? Arbitrators have ruled that companies are not required to continue to check off the dues.

EXAMPLE: One union claimed that the decertification cancelled only those provisions concerning recognition and representation, while the rest of the contract remained in effect until the normal expiration date. However, the arbitrator disagreed. A contract is a bilateral agreement, he pointed out; when the union no longer is able to comply with its contractual obligations as representative of the workers, the company no longer is bound by the contract. (Ferris Sales & Service Inc., 36 LA 848)

EXAMPLE: A similar decision was reached when a union that lost a deauthorization election claimed that the voiding of the union-security provision did not affect the separate checkoff clause. The arbitrator based his decision on contract law and said that the commitment to pay dues was made in the light of an assumed right of the union to compel membership. Since that assumption turned out to be erroneous, the checkoff authorizations became voidable at the option of the workers. (North Hills Electronics Inc., 46 LA 789)

Dues Increase v. Assessment

Suppose a union has a checkoff arrangement calling for the deduction of union dues but not assessments, and then it imposes a levy in addition to regular dues for an indefinite period of time. Can the company refuse to check off the additional amount on the ground that it is an assessment? According to one arbitrator, a company could not refuse to do this.

He found, first of all, that the dues hike was voted by the membership in the form of an amendment to the bylaws, in accordance with the union constitution. Assessments, on the other hand, could be levied by the local executive board without a vote of the membership. Secondly, the additional money was to be used to carry on the regular business of the local, whose treasury had been depleted by a number of strikes, but it was not earmarked specifically as a strike fund, nor was the levy for any set length of time. Finally, the arbitrator noted that when the union had put similar (but smaller) dues increases into effect in the past, the company had not refused to check off the additional amounts. So it could not refuse to do so in the present situation, the arbitrator concluded. (Bates Mfg. Co., 24 LA 643; see also 41 LA 65)

Similarly, an employer's refusal to deduct two hours' pay that a union had certified as monthly dues and fair share assessments for members in the unit was improper, an arbitrator decided, since the union's discretion to decide the amount of dues and assessments which effect each employee in the "same form, manner, and degree" satisfied the contract's uniformity requirement. (Rock County and State, County & Municipal Employees, 64 LA 887)

However, where a contract required the checkoff of "regular union dues," an arbitrator held that a company was not required to honor payroll deductions for the amount of union dues, plus an additional $2.00 per month deduction for coverage under the union's insurance plan, which coverage was optional with the employees and subject to change or cancellation at any time. (South-western Bell Telephone Co., 38 LA 693)

Increase in Fees Subject to Checkoff

If fees are subject to checkoff, can a union increase the amount of the initiation fee, once the checkoff agreement has gone into effect? Unless the contract puts a definite limit on the amount of fees to be checked off, the company can do nothing to stop the union from raising it, according to one arbitrator.

EXAMPLE: When a union upped its initiation fee from $5 to $25, the company protested that the fee was "unreasonable and excessive." When it agreed to the union shop and checkoff provisions in the contract, the company argued, it did so with the understanding that the initiation fee was $5; it had never dreamed that the union would hike the fee to $25. Requiring new employees to pay this amount, it said, might hinder its recruiting efforts.

The arbitrator, however, found nothing in the contract to prevent the union from raising the fee; neither the agreement nor the checkoff form, he noted, said what the fee should be. Noting that NLRB had already ruled that the increased fee was not "excessive or discriminatory," the arbitrator concluded that the company had no voice in setting the amount of the fee, and that the union was under no obligation not to change it. (Engineering & Research Corp., 23 LA 410)

Part 15

Wages and Hours

Incentive-Pay Plans

IN BRIEF

The Department of Labor's Bureau of Labor Statistics has defined incentive pay or wage plans as "a method by which workers receive extra pay for extra production." BLS elaborates that in established incentive pay plans, consideration must be given to: (1) the base rate for a job; (2) the amount of work required to earn the base rate; and, (3) the relationship between extra work above the base and extra pay for extra performance. Further, BLS divides incentive pay plans into "piecework" plans or a form of a "standard-hour" plan.

Most collective bargaining agreements that mention incentive operations do not elaborate on the details of the system. Almost all contract clauses dealing with incentive pay place some limitation on the employer's right to revise standards. (86 LA 6, 85 LA 1183, 82 LA 1145, 82 LA 738, 62 LA 756, 61 LA 132, 61 LA 171)

Arbiters, generally, have interpreted such provisions to mean that workers' earnings opportunities must be protected when standards are revised (Elkhart Brass Mfg. Co., 67 LA 184), and that where a change in the workload is negligible, the employer is not required to negotiate a change in the incentive rates (Jack T. Baillie Co., 84 LA 285).

GUIDELINES

These are some basic guidelines for establishing incentive pay rates:

▶ "The essential standard should be that the workers affected should have free access to the relevant information so that any injustices in the final result may be corrected through the regular grievance procedure.

▶ Workers should be informed as to the results of time studies, the basis for any company estimates of efficiency of the workers are timed, and the company allowances for such factors as fatigue and personal needs.

▶ Pieceworkers affected by any new rate are entitled to a clear and prompt statement of exactly what the new rate is.

▶ An elementary standard of piecework administration requires that a piece rate, once established, should not be changed unless the relevant conditions of work are subsequently changed or unless an error or oversight was made on establishing the original rate." (International Harvester Inc., 1 LA 512)

Time Limit On Revision of Incentive Rate

Most contracts dealing with incentive systems provide that management (sometimes with the advice or consent of the union) can revise existing incentive standards or rates, or set up new rates, when there are changes in the content of the job involved. If there is no time limit on the period during which the rate can be changed, is management free to set a new rate at any time after there have been changes in the job?

According to most arbiters, management has an obligation to revise incentive standards or rates within a "reasonable" time after changes are made in job content.

EXAMPLE: One arbiter, decided that two years was far more than a reasonable time limit for changing an incentive rate. (International Harvester Co., 14 LA 1010; see also 34 LA 497)

Likewise, overnight notification of a speed-up in the rate of output of a potato-chip bagging machine did not meet the contract's requirements of "reasonable prior notice," according to an arbiter. A change in rates could occur only if the union was notified sufficiently in advance to permit meaningful discussion, the arbiter concluded. (Daniel W. Mikesell Inc., 47 LA 986)

However, a delay of 13 months after changes were made before establishing a new rate for the job was okayed in another instance, because the arbiter found that this period of time was necessary to allow a complete restudy of the operation. (Mosaic Tile Co., 16 LA 922)

Basis for Rate Changes

Where the workload of incentive employees changes, arbiters in reviewing the incentive rates, may apply the standard of maintenance of prior earnings on the theory that incentive employees should be able to earn as much under the new standard as under the old. (28 LA 259, 26 LA 812, 17 LA 472) However, the maintenance of prior earnings standard may not be applied where the contract expressly recognizes that the employer, at its discretion, may find it necessary or desirable from time to time to establish new incentive rates or adjust existing incentive rates because of certain conditions. (Timken Co., 85 LA 377; see also 90 LA 1279)

A more nebulous standard requires the maintenance of the same ratio of earnings to effect expended. Use of this standard means that employees receive increased earnings for that part of the increased production that is due to their effort, and management receives the benefit for that part of the production increase that is due to technological improvement. (22 LA 450, 28 LA 129, 10 LA 20)

EXAMPLE: In one case a union objected to an increase in the number of units required and a decrease in the percentage standards on the ground that workers could not earn as much as under the old rates. But an arbiter found that the new method of calculation would permit workers to earn as much as before. (Timken Roller Bearing Co., 28 LA 259)

Similarly, where another arbiter found that greater productivity was the result of machine and engineering changes, he allowed the company to revise the incentive rates. He noted that the stated aim of the incentive agreement was to give workers more money for extra effort above normal. If the rates had remained the same, he reasoned, earnings would have gone up in direct ratio to the increased productivity, even without any extra effort from the workers. He concluded that the rate change did not violate the contract's ban on revisions which lessen the earnings potential of workers. (Libbey-Owens-Ford Glass Fibres Co., 31 LA 662; see also 65 LA 643)

Reduction of Rates

Reduction of incentive rates has been allowed where the introduction of new machinery has resulted in increased production without requiring an increase in effort. (63 LA 384, 11 LA 432, 3 LA 677)

EXAMPLE: An arbiter ruled that an employer did not violate a contract when it reduced incentive time standard for cut, splice, and wind-up element on cutting machine, since an upgrading of the machine to provide automatic feed without excessive jam-ups justified a review of the operation, and the change in standard was commensurate with the degree of change in job content. (Armstrong Tire Co., 95 LA 1050)

Moreover, reduction of incentive rates has been ordered where employees controlled production on new machines at a very low level. (10 LA 534)

Changing Job Standards During Strike

An employer violated its contract by revising incentive standards during a strike following the expiration of the previous contract and then putting them into effect after the strike had ended and the new agreement had been signed, an arbiter ruled.

EXAMPLE: The strike-settling contract, like the pre-strike agreement, said there were to be no changes in incentive standards unless changes were made in the methods of operation. While the stoppage was in progress the firm kept production going after a fashion, but all workers were paid on an hourly basis. Meanwhile, the company's job standards people were told to do some tinkering with certain standards that were considered loose. The tighter standards were made effective when incentive work was resumed a week after the new contract had been signed. The union was told nothing of all this; it became aware of the situation only when workers began complaining about the speed-up.

The arbiter conceded that the company could do as it pleased while the union was on strike. But if it meant to make new standards effective during the term of the new agreement, he said, it had to inform the union of its intention during the negotiations over the new contract, so that the parties could negotiate on the basis of full information. By failing to do this, the arbiter concluded, the firm violated the agreement. (M.H. Rhodes Inc., 25 LA 243)

Allowances

Following is a general statement of a standard for allowances to be paid pieceworkers and examples of its application:

"In all cases where allowances are deemed necessary, the pieceworker should be paid his occupational earned rate or his average piecework earning rate, depending on the degree of effort expected and the responsibility placed upon him under the particular conditions which gave rise to the grievance.

"By way of example, it seems obvious to us that, where a worker encounters hard stock, faulty material, or is given erroneous instructions, and is required to continue with the job after calling the situation to the attention of his supervisor, he has every reason to expect to be guaranteed his average piecework earning rate.

"Similarly, where, because of his special skill and aptitude, he is called upon to leave his regular job to perform experimental or other work not a regular part of his assigned duties and which he performs for the convenience of management, he should also receive his average piecework earning rate.

"However, it seems equally obvious that, where a temporary breakdown occurs and he is called upon to perform some other work to occupy his time, which work does not call for anything more than dayrate effort or efficiency, industrial practice generally does not call for the payment of the average piecework earning rate." (International Harvester Inc., 1 LA 512)

Machine Breakdown

At what rate should incentive workers be paid for periods during which their machines are down for repairs? One arbiter, ruling on the equities of the situation, agreed with a union that incentive workers should be paid average hourly earnings rather than base rates during periods of machine breakdown. (Pantasote Co., 3 LA 545)

However, another arbiter, ruled the other way in interpreting a contract which stated that waiting time caused by machine breakdowns would be paid at the "regular earning rate." The arbiter said that the employer need pay only on the basis of the hourly rate and not on the basis of average earnings, as the union contended. (Kensington Steel Co., 13 LA 545)

On a related matter, a machine operator who worked on an incentive basis and whose machine broke down was entitled to refuse assigned work on a new machine that had the potential of diluting his earnings, an arbiter ruled. The contract, the arbiter noted, provided that if an employee reported for work, and his work was not available, the employer would assign him any available work, and that if any work was refused, the employee would be paid only for elapsed time registered on his time card. Rejecting the employer's contention that the employee only had the right to refuse work at the start of his shift, the arbiter concluded that there was no doubt as to the meaning of the contract giving the employee the right to refuse assigned work. (Mueller Company, 76 LA 965)

Temporary Rate for Materials Shortage

Under a contract calling for payment of a specified hourly rate when a shortage of materials "substantially" reduces an employee's output, how far must the employee's production drop before he is entitled to receive that rate?

A union argued that such a provision meant that an employee should get the specified hourly rate whenever a materials shortage caused his production to drop below the point in the incentive range which is on a level with the hourly rate. But an arbiter ruled that the hourly rate should be paid only when his production drops below the incentive base rate. (Maytag Co., 20 LA 43)

Spoiled Work

If a crew of employees working under a group incentive system have to stop work while one or two members of the crew rework parts which they spoiled, should all the members of the group be paid hourly rates or average earnings?

EXAMPLE: In one arbiter's opinion, the rest of the crew should not be penalized for work spoiled by one or two members of the group. The employees responsible for the spoiled work should be paid their hourly rate, the arbiter said, but the others should get average earnings for the time they waited while the parts were being reworked. (International Harvester Co., 23 LA 184)

However, one arbiter ruled that under a group incentive plan management was justified in apportioning among all workers in its production line the cost of reprocessing work damaged by two men. The union protested that penalizing all the workers for the mistakes of two was unjust. The arbiter, however, held that the earnings deduction was not really a penalty, but the result of an accurate count of acceptable products. Had the men at fault been made to correct the error, they would have earned less than base wages, a contract violation. Furthermore, he said, the assembly line would have been stopped and the other workers paid only base wages. He pointed out that by continuing to operate, the line made up the reprocessing cost and still earned incentive pay. (Westclox, 34 LA 777)

Built-in Delay Allowances

If allowances for delays are built into the rates under an incentive plan, should workers still be paid their hourly rates for down time? Awards differ on this problem depending upon the circumstances in each case.

EXAMPLE: In one instance where a crew of incentive workers were held up for an hour and a half because their supervisor had not got certain equipment ready for them to use, an arbiter ruled that they were entitled to straight-time pay for the down time. He agreed with the union that such long periods of lost time that were the fault of management were not the kind of delays allowed for the incentive rates. (Bethlehem Steel Co., 29 LA 360)

However, another arbiter turned down a union's claim that incentive workers deserved standard hourly rates for a delay that began in the preceding shift and continued into theirs. The union argued that the incentive plan was not in effect until a crew actually started work. But the arbiter disagreed, saying that, in the absence of contract language to the contrary, an incentive plan with built-in delay allowances must be considered as covering all delays no matter when they start. (Kaiser Steel Corp., 31 LA 447)

Hourly Workers Assigned to Piecework

If some employees fill in as utility men on piecework operations in addition to their regular jobs at hourly rates, should they be paid their hourly rate or at piece rates for their piecework assignments?

The common complaint of employees who are assigned piecework on a casual or part-time basis is that they are unfamiliar with the work or the machines and, as a result, may not be able to make as much as they would on their regular jobs at their hourly rate. Taking this fact into consideration, one arbiter ruled that employees in a "hybrid classification" who do piecework in addition to their hourly-paid work must be paid at least the rate of their hourly scale. He noted that, under the contract, regular pieceworkers were customarily paid at a straight hourly rate or at their piece rate, whichever was greater. In the absence of a contract provisions covering hourly workers assigned to piecework, the arbiter reasoned, casual pieceworkers should receive the same treatment. The arbiter further pointed out that standard practice elsewhere called for hourly rates in such a situation. (John Deere & Co., 21 LA 449)

On the other hand, an arbiter decided that electricians who were not on an incentive wage rate, but who were assigned to work with electricians who were on incentive, were not entitled to be paid incentive pay, in the absence of a past practice by which workers who are not on incentive pay are paid such rate when working with incentive pay employees. Despite the union's requests for the arbiter to study "very carefully" the entire contract provisions, that included a joint incentive committee, continuation of wage rates, or new wage rates for new jobs, the arbiter concluded there was nothing in the agreement that supported the union's position. (Jessop Steel Co., 76 LA 641)

Job Evaluation

IN BRIEF

In the absence of an express contractual provision, it is generally recognized that management has the right to establish new jobs or job classifications and change existing jobs and classifications without first bargaining with the union. (93 LA 623, 91 LA 1003)

However, where an agreement contains rigid job classifications, an employer may not be permitted unilaterally to establish new classifications. (84 LA 989) Arbiters have often rejected the contention that job classifications in an agreement automatically preclude elimination or modification of jobs or classifications. (91 LA 329)

Even where management has the right to alter its classification system, the union normally may question changes through the grievance procedure.

GUIDELINES

Arbiters generally agree that an employer has the right to eliminate jobs — and allocate any remaining jobs — (93 LA 227, 86 LA 880, 84 LA 788, 83 LA 792, 82 LA 534, 82 LA 225, 46 LA 43, 30 LA 444, 25 LA 188, 16 LA 955) — or classifications (91 LA 329, 84 LA 875) when justified by improved technology or production efficiencies, and if not expressly prohibited by an agreement. Further, arbiters have held that an employer may combine jobs or job classifications in determining methods of operation. (85 LA 1026, 83 LA 214, 30 LA 81, 19 LA 797)

Changes in methods of operation, unless restricted by the agreement, have been held to be within the prerogatives of management. (39 LA 939, 46 LA 43, 17 LA 268, 6 LA 681) (19 LA 797, 30 LA 81), or a change in the product (46 LA 43)

On the other hand, an employer's act of recognizing a union has been held to carry with it the obligation to refrain from making major changes in employment conditions and circumstances without consulting with the union (25 LA 611). Such obligation may be found to exist under the Taft Act, as a well as under the contract. (71 LA 244)

Management's Right to Change Job Descriptions & Classifications

Does a company have to get the union's permission to change the make-up of a job or classification before putting the change into effect?

Even though job classifications, job descriptions, and job evaluation procedure have been agreed on in the past and have become part of the contractual relationship with the union, the company may still have the right to introduce new jobs or take apart existing jobs. As long as the company pays the established rates and accepts union complaints through the grievance procedure, jobs can be put into effect, described, and evaluated by the company, according to most arbiters.

EXAMPLE: An employer had the right to establish new job classifications and rates for positions, following the advent of a new production process that demanded new skills, an arbiter ruled. Since the contract expressly gave management the power to add to negotiated classifications and rates, the arbiter concluded that the employer's action was taken pursuant to its authority to establish new classifications; which it exercised properly according to the evidence. (T.N.S. Inc., 76 LA 278; see also 76 LA 1220)

Similarly, another arbiter decided that a company's contract did not obligate it to freeze job titles and duties pending the union's consent to a change. Such a requirement, he said, would place the company in an intolerable position. (Dow Chemical Co., 22 LA 336; see also 31 LA 744, 14 LA 510)

Arbiters, however, also agree that even where the contract specifically gives management the right to establish new or revised job descriptions, the union still retains the right to challenge management's evaluation through the grievance and arbitration machinery. (Emhart Mfg. Co., 23 LA 61; see also 23 LA 206)

On the other hand, many arbiters believe that management does not have the right to change the job classifications which are agreed to in a contract, without the union's consent.

EXAMPLE: An employer violated a contract obligating it to notify the union of proposed changes affecting rates of pay, hours of work and other conditions of employment, an arbiter decided, when it unilaterally created a new work group during a reorganization of its operations. (United Telephone Co. of the Carolinas, 71 LA 244)

Similarly, another arbiter ruled that a company could not make a major transfer of job duties from one category to another without the union's consent because it would upset the bargain the parties made when they incorporated the rates and classifications into the contract. (James Vernor Co., 26 LA 415; see also 24 LA 713)

Likewise, an employer did not have the right, under the management-rights clause of the contract, unilaterally to subdivide a job classification into three classifications. Although the change was made in good faith to eliminate a production bottleneck, management was restricted in its freedom to make such changes by other sections of the contract, according to the arbiter. Contrary past practices could not justify the action, since the specific contract language governed the situation. (Barcalo Mfg. Co., 31 LA 269)

Changes Warranting Job Reclassification

Some contracts require reclassification of jobs in which there have been substantial changes since they were classified and the rates set. Arbiters must often determine whether changes in job content are substantial enough to warrant a reclassification. (95 LA 1081, 95 LA 412, 69 LA 198, 54 LA 918, 22 LA 721, 20 LA 463, 11 LA 490)

EXAMPLE: An arbiter decided that an employer improperly reclassified students in its training program as "trainees," rather than as "helper apprentices" belonging to the bargaining unit, following a change in the work duties of the employees. The students' training for production jobs in the shipyard was sufficient to make them "production" employees under the contract the arbiter reasoned, concluding that the fact that none of the employees' training actually was used in the shipyard did not preclude their classification as "production" employees. (Ingalls Shipbuilding Division, 69 LA 294)

On the other hand, an employer had the right to require molding operators to train new employees on pick off or hydraulic presses, an arbiter ruled, rejecting a union's contention that the action constituted a "significant change in job content" requiring a new evaluation for the molding operators. Pointing out that the parties agreed that the molding operators were responsible for training other operators on small presses before the job evaluations became part of the collective bargaining agreement, the arbiter noted that if there were any changes, they were not either as large, or expansive as claimed by the union. The complete record failed to show that there had been a significant change in job content of the operators, the arbiter concluded. (Powder Metal Products Inc. 77 LA 499)

Reclassification After Technological Changes

Where an employer introduced a new machine substantially different from machines in an existing wage rate classifications, it was required to negotiate with the union over rates to be paid the operators of the new machine, and not merely insert the job in an existing classification, an arbiter decided. (Lockheed-Georgia Co., 48 LA 518)

However, a publisher-employer had the right to change job classifications following conversion from a hot metal process to a cold metal process that resulted in a substantial change in equipment and procedures of its composing room, an arbiter ruled, since management had the right to make changes in job duties, to create new job classifications, to eliminate jobs and to combine jobs by unilateral action, absent a provision in the contract imposing a limitation on such action. (Leavenworth Times, 71 LA 396; see also (93 LA 227, 91 LA 329, 86 LA 880, 84 LA 875, 84 LA 788, 85 LA 1026, 83 LA 792, 83 LA 214, 82 LA 534, 82 LA 225, 46 LA 43, 33 LA 1, 30 LA 444, 30 LA 214, 30 LA 81, 25 LA 188, 19 LA 797, 16 LA 955)

Factors in Establishing New Rates

When a new job is set up which does not fit into the existing classification scheme, various factors should be taken into account in establishing the rate for the job.

EXAMPLE: According to one arbiter, the following factors should be considered in setting up the rate range for a new job: (1) nature of the duties and responsibilities of the job as compared to other jobs at the plant; (2) existing wage rate structure; and (3) existing method of in-grade rate progression. (Dumont Electric Corp., 13 LA 763; see also, 62 LA 511, 62 LA 574)

EXAMPLE: Another arbiter determined the job rate for a new classification in light of: (1) the company's past practice, (2) prevailing practice in comparable plants, and (3) the effect on intra-plant wage relationships. (Wetter Numbering Machine Co., 13 LA 177)

Moreover, when two jobs are combined into one, the new job should be evaluated as though it were a completely new job and the rate set accordingly, another arbiter ruled. (Republic Steel Corp., 20 LA 370)

Upgrading under Classification System

Generally, the test that arbiters use for determining if an employee is entitled to be upgraded to the next higher classification is whether the worker is actually performing or is capable of performing the higher classification. (67 LA 1094, 67 LA 23)

EXAMPLE: Employees classified as specialists third class claimed they should be reclassified to specialists first class because they were qualified to do higher-rated work and they were performing the same job duties as employees with the first-class rating. The arbiter turned down their arguments because he found that: (1) their job duties had not changed since they got their third-class ratings, (2) there was no practice of upgrading employees merely on the basis of added skill without the addition of more difficult job duties, and (3) the only reason they were performing the same job duties as employees with a first-class rating was that more difficult work, which would have been assigned to the first-class specialists, was not available at the time. (Bethlehem Steel Co., 19 LA 521)

Similarly, an arbiter held that an employer was not obligated to classify "production layout artists" as "creative artists," even if they had the ability to do the work of the higher classification, since they were not required actually to do this work. An employer is not required to pay for talent he does not use, the arbiter held. (Gill Studies Inc., 52 LA 506; see also 75 LA 531)

Likewise, an employee who held the job of loader crater B for about two months properly was denied upward reclassification to the position of loader crater A held by another employee on leave of absence, an arbiter decided, since the employer had reason to believe that the employee was not capable of performing a significant portion of the loader crater A job duties. (FMC Corp., 61 LA 1240; see also 69 LA 1239, 63 LA 907)

However, a federal agency employer improperly refused to upgrade a research specialist to a higher classification, an arbiter ruled, where the employer had knowledge that the specialist was continually performing the duties of the higher classification. (Economic Opportunity, Office of and Government Employees, 62 LA 496)

Similarly, a federal government employee who held a GS-13 classification when detailed to perform duties of a higher-rated job of GS-14 was entitled to be promoted to the higher-rated job, an arbiter ruled, where the employee continued to perform the higher-rated job duties for a period of two years. (Economic Opportunity, Office of and Government Employees, 64 LA 164; see also 75 LA 1298)

Downgrading under Classification System

Arbiters are likely to approve management's action in downgrading an employee if there is a clear showing that the worker is performing lower-rated duties.

EXAMPLE: A federal agency employer did not improperly reclassify an employee when it changed his job description from "Supervisory Occupational Analyst" to "Occupational Analyst" during the course of a job survey in the division, an arbiter held, it appearing that there was a civil service rule requiring employees holding supervisory title to supervise at least three professionals, which the employee did not. (U.S. Department of Labor, 64 LA 357)

EXAMPLE: One company moved an employee to the next higher classification as part of a negotiated plan to eliminate wage inequities. Six years later it discovered that the employee had been performing the duties of his old classification all along, so he was downgraded to his original classification. The union argued that once the employee's classification had been agreed on jointly, it could not be changed. The arbiter decided, however, that the job descriptions were clear enough to show that the employee's duties fitted his old classification and ruled that the company was free to reclassify him. (Erie Forge & Steel Corp., 22 LA 551)

However, in another case, an arbiter decided that six years was too long a period to wait before correcting a classification error. He pointed out that the wrong classification had continued for several years as a direct result of the failure of management representatives to discover and correct the error earlier. The arbiter agreed that the company had the right to correct its mistakes, but said that management had more than reasonable opportunities in the past to make adjustments. He also noted that the employees had a legitimate right to expect that the rates and classifications were the prevailing and correct ones when they went unchanged for six years. (National Tube Co., 7 LA 575)

Moreover, an employer arbitrarily downgraded three employees on the basis of gradual changes in their duties, an arbitrator ruled. This action would have been okay under the contract, the arbiter said, except that the employer left six or seven other employees doing similar work in the higher classification. (John Deere Harvester Works, 20 LA 665)

Where Job Overlaps Two Classifications

If the contract states that employees performing the duties of two classifications should be paid the rate of the higher classification, they must be paid the higher rate even if they spend only a small part of their time on the higher-rated job duties or do not have the skills originally required for the higher job, an arbiter ruled. (Hotpoint Co., 23 LA 562)

In situations where this point was not covered in the contract, however, arbiters have relied on various factors in determining which job rate should apply.

EXAMPLE: One arbiter said employees should get the lower rate because they performed only a few of the duties of the higher job, even though these duties made their jobs as a whole more difficult than those of other employees in the lower classification. (Douglas Aircraft Co. Inc., 18 LA 387)

EXAMPLE: Another arbiter decided that the proper rate for an employee performing the duties of two jobs was not the one for the job at which he spent most of his time, but the rate for the job for which he had been trained and was responsible — the higher of the two. (Soule Steel Co., 21 LA 88)

EXAMPLE: Still another arbiter ruled that workers were not entitled to the pay for a higher classification than their own just because they were voluntarily performing some of the duties of the higher-rated job. (Phelps Dodge Copper Products Corp., 25 LA 64)

Elimination of Classifications

When it comes to eliminating existing job classifications, management may have less freedom than it does in setting up new or revised classifications. Arbiters sometimes have ruled that where job classifications are included in the contract, the company has no right to abolish any of them without the union's consent as long as the job functions of the classification continue to exist. (Flintkote Co., 41 LA 120)

However, following what he saw as a modern trend among arbiters to give management more leeway in changing and abolishing jobs, one arbiter upheld management's right to abolish job classifications and assign the work to higher-rated jobs. The fact that the classifications were listed in the contract did not mean they were frozen, he said; they were not contracted for, but were bases for rates of pay. Hence, the company could not have given the duties to lower-rated workers. (Georgia-Pacific Corp., 40 LA 769)

Similarly, another arbiter decided that where a larger part of a job's duties had been eliminated, management could abolish the job, even though the contract required it to maintain local working conditions. (Pittsburgh Steel Co., 40 LA 70)

Likewise, job elimination has also been upheld where duties were reduced or eliminated by extensive changes or automation. (Pittsburgh Steel Co., 40 LA 67; see also 40 LA 65)

Furthermore, if all the duties of a job classification are eliminated by technological or other changes, what the company can do, one arbiter suggested, is merely to refrain from assigning any workers to that classification. While it cannot formally abolish the classification without union consent, there's nothing to require the company to keep on assigning workers to the job. This action would have the effect of leaving the classification in a dormant state, he pointed out, which might be useful if the job duties of the classification were ever resumed. (Lone Star Steel Co., 23 LA 164)

Eliminating Red-Circle Rates

Most arbiters agree than an employer cannot get rid of red-circle rates by withholding negotiated general increases. The time and place to do this, they say, is at the bargaining table.

EXAMPLE: Where one company tried to withhold an increase 10 months after discovering that some workers were being overpaid, an arbiter said that it had waited too long to correct the error. (Celluplastic Corp., 28 LA 659; see also 27 LA 858, 72 LA 1178)

However, an employer properly discontinued paying red-circle rate to employee following the execution of a new contract that did not carry over the old contract's clause recognizing existence of red-circle rates, an arbiter ruled, despite the employee's contention that his red-circle rate was provided for in a separate contract which negotiators had no authority to alter. (Everlock Charlotte Inc., 62 LA 1018)

Further, under a contract granting wage increases according to the employees' classifications, former painters who had been reclassified as laborers and permitted to keep their higher painters' wage scales as "red-circle" rates within the laborers classification were not entitled to increases negotiated for the painters' classification. The former painters were classified as laborers when the contact was executed and, therefore, were entitled only to increase applicable to laborers. (Bethlehem Steel Co., 31 LA 104; see also 72 LA 87)

Effect of Transfer & Promotion on Red-Circle Rate

Where a red-circle rate exists for an employee on a particular job, it is not likely that he can carry the top-plus rate with him in the event that he's transferred, even if he stays within the same classification.

EXAMPLE: One arbiter ruled that a red-circle rate applied only to the job involved and was not the property of the employee to take with him wherever he went.

This same arbiter held that a worker who is promoted from a red-circle rate and later demoted back to the same classification has no right to the red-circle padding after demotion. In other words, the promotion has the effect of cancelling the extra red-circle amount. (International Harvester Co., 22 LA 674; see also 53 LA 694)

However, another arbiter ruled that incentive workers were entitled to retain their red-circle rates following their transfer from nickel-line to zinc-line jobs as the result of senior employees bumping into their old jobs. (H.P. Snyder Mfg. Co., 64 LA 801)

Similarly, an arbiter held that an employer that had agreed to a 15-cent red-circle add-on for certain employees improperly discontinued an employee's red-circle rate when he elected to bump in to a lower-rated job. The red-circle advantage had been significantly restricted through grievance settlements and contract negotiations, the arbiter pointed out, but a bumping provision remained silent as to red-circle rates. Further, there was no indication that the union had agreed to give up the red-circle add-on in connection with bumping rights, the arbiter found. (Schauer Manufacturing Corp., 94 LA 1116)

Overtime Work & Pay

IN BRIEF

Grievances concerning overtime work generally fall into one of three categories — (1) challenges of the employer's right to require workers to put in overtime, (2) complaints that overtime work has not been distributed properly, and (3) complaints that work has not been paid for at the proper rate.

While there have been rulings both ways, arbiters have held more often than not that management can require employees to work overtime if the contract does not expressly limit the length of the workday or workweek. The right must, however, be exercised reasonably.

Arbiters disagree on management's right to provide make-up overtime in lieu of pay, where an employer has breached its overtime obligation. (93 LA 4, 89 LA 781)

In general, the Fair Labor Standards Act requires employers to pay employees overtime compensation "at a rate of not less than one and one-half times" the employee's regular rate. It does not, however, prohibit an employer paying an overtime rate of over 150 percent of his or her regular rate.

GUIDELINES

Management Right to Require Overtime

For the most part, an employee's right to have his or her overtime pay computed in accordance with methods approved by the FLSA and its implementing regulations is a right that cannot be waived and that the employee cannot be estopped from asserting. (However, an arbiter ruled FLSA to be irrelevant where contract expressly states method for computing overtime, and an advisory opinion on law was not requested, see Potlatch Corp., 95 LA 737)

Many cases have come to arbitration over the issue of whether management has the right to compel an employee to work overtime and discipline an employee who refuses overtime. If the issue is not expressly settled in the collective bargaining agreement, arbiters have generally ruled that management does have that right.

In general, one arbiter has stated that the burden is not on the employer to find a contractual provision expressly authorizing it to require overtime work; rather, burden is upon the union to point out the contractual prohibition against such mandatory assignment. (Seilon Inc., 51 LA 261)

Another arbiter explained that the underlying theory is that management has retained its inherent right to assign work and overtime. He added, however, that management must be reasonable and fair when demanding overtime. (Van Dorn Co., 48 LA 925)

Still, another arbiter stated that the "vast majority of arbitral awards" supports the position that "overtime is compulsory in the absence of a specific prohibition in the collective bargaining agreement." (Douglas Aircraft Co., 55 LA 1155)

Other arbitral methods of confirming management's overtime powers involve finding implied support of the right in existing contractual provisions, such as clauses recognizing management's authority to control or direct the work force or setting pay rates for hours worked beyond a certain number in a week. (55 LA 31, 52 LA 493, 13 LA 211)

Furthermore, it has been found that specifications in the contract of a "normal" workday or "normal" workweek implies that there will occasionally be "abnormal" workdays or workweeks. Such provisions may serve to affirm management's right to require overtime. (Jones & Laughlin Steel Corp., 29 LA 708)

EXAMPLE: In a case where the contract stipulated that changes in the work schedule must be mutually agreeable to both the company and the union, the union held that a worker should not have been disciplined for refusing to work overtime since such overtime constituted a change in the work schedule. The arbiter found, however, that the overtime was for a limited, specified duration and, hence, not a change which would require union approval. Therefore, management was permitted to require an unwilling employee to work overtime. (McConway & Torley Corp., 55 LA 31)

EXAMPLE: In another instance, an arbiter ruled that a statement in the contract that it was the policy of the company (as opposed to a requirement for the company) to assign overtime to employees willing to accept it did not deny management its right to compel an employee to work overtime — provided management had exhausted all possibilities of locating willing workers. (General Telephone Co., 53 LA 246)

EXAMPLE: A provision of an agreement giving the employer sole discretion in scheduling production has been determined to be legitimate basis for management to require overtime. Past practice, even of many years' duration, of relying exclusively on volunteers to work overtime does not constitute a waiver of this right of management. (Colt Firearms Div., 52 LA 493)

EXAMPLE: An employer that previously assigned overtime to its employees on a voluntary basis was justified in making assignments mandatory, an arbiter decided, since there was nothing in the contract that specifically limited, the right of employer to require overtime. Emphasizing that it is a settled rule that employers retain all power to manage the plant, make rules, and set working hours, the arbiter concluded that the employer's reasonable assignment of overtime did not violate the contract. (Powermatic/Houdaille Inc., 63 LA 1)

EXAMPLE: An employer with a heavy workload properly assigned clerical employees to two hours of mandatory overtime following completion of their eight hour shift on a one-night-a-week basis, an arbiter ruled, where the contract clearly stated that "a fifteen (15) minute relief period shall be assigned as service requirements permit for each full two (2) hours an employee is required to work immediately preceding or following their regular scheduled tour." (General Telephone Co., 63 LA 182; see also 77 LA 698, 75 LA 170, 73 LA 1140, 73 LA 1048, 72 LA 759, 72 LA 668, 72 LA 622, 72 LA 591)

On the other hand, arbiters may rule that management acted unreasonably in compelling employees to work overtime where the employer has not considered the legitimate excuses of employees who refuse to work, does not attempt to find substitute employees who are willing and able to perform the work, or gives insufficient notice that overtime work is required. (76 LA 205, 75 LA 849, 74 LA 1020, 74 LA 967, 71 LA 721, 71 LA 222)

Equal Distribution of Overtime

Contracts frequently provide for the equal sharing of overtime, with equalization generally limited to employees in the same job classification, in the same department, or on the same shift. (65 LA 553, 65 LA 520, 63 LA 441) Ordinarily, when two or more employees have accumulated the same amount of overtime, the one with the greatest seniority is given the option of the overtime assignment.

EXAMPLE: In a case where the contract called for equalization of overtime with consideration given to seniority, management scheduled a specific overtime assignment for all first-shift employees and promised to even-up the overtime of second-shift workers within the allotted time period for equalization. When management subsequently failed to do so, second-shift employees with greater seniority than some of the first-shift men filed a grievance which later came to arbitration. The arbiter upheld the grievance, stating that under the contract it was required to cross shift lines if necessary to equalize overtime with consideration to seniority. (Eaton, Yale & Town Inc., 54 LA 1121; see also 75 LA 608, 75 LA 275, 75 LA 99, 74 LA 699)

EXAMPLE: A collective bargaining agreement required equal distribution of overtime. Management assigned overtime to the employee who had been working on the job in question during regular hours. Another worker who was qualified to do the job and had fewer hours of overtime than the assigned employee filed a grievance. His complaint was upheld. (Vendorlator Manufacturing Co., 53 LA 494)

EXAMPLE: In another ruling, the arbiter found that failure of an employee to show up for prior overtime assignments does not justify passing over that employee for a new overtime assignment when the contract specifies that extra-hours work is to be distributed equally. (Grief Bros. Corp., 55 LA 384)

EXAMPLE: Under a contract providing that overtime in each department shall be divided equally and among employees to the extent that it is practical to do so, an employer improperly awarded overtime during a holiday weekend shutdown to one member of a labor pool, an arbiter ruled, instead of to another member who had fewer overtime hours. (Logan-Long Co., 61 LA 963)

EXAMPLE: An employer violated a contractual provision requiring equalization of overtime by continually by-passing a tooling machinist with low overtime in favor of another machinists who had higher overtime accumulation, an arbiter held, absent any significant functional differences in the work performed by the two machinists that might cause each to be regarded as a "single overtime group." (Norris Industries, 62 LA 632)

EXAMPLE: An employer violated a contract provision requiring equalization of overtime an arbiter decided when stockroom clerks who belonged to finished goods department that had only day shift were allowed to work overtime, instead of night shift stockroom clerks who belonged to parts-in-process department that had both day and night shifts. (Akron Brass Co., 67 LA 267)

EXAMPLE: An employer who failed to contact vacationing employees to determine their availability for scheduled overtime on the date they would have returned to work violated a contract requiring equalization of overtime, an arbiter held, notwithstanding the employer's contention that the employees were ineligible for overtime because they failed to sign the overtime sheet. (General Mills Chemicals Inc., 66 LA 1012; see also 73 LA 1087, 76 LA 1159)

On the other hand, an employer did not violate a contract provision requiring the scheduling of overtime as equally as possible among employees, an arbiter decided, despite over 100 hours' difference between high and low employees within the same classification. (Portec, Inc., Rail Car Operations Paragon Div., 73 LA 56; see also 75 LA 1070, 75 LA 633, 73 LA 827, 73 LA 673, 72 LA 996, 71 LA 412)

Period in Which Overtime Must Be Equalized

Recognizing that it is not always possible to equalize overtime exactly, many contracts specify a permissible spread in the number of overtime hours worked by different employees.

EXAMPLE: One such contract contained a provision that "the Company will distribute available overtime work as equally as possible (within a thirty-six (36) hour limitation)," and further stated that "the employee with the least amount of department overtime will be scheduled first."

An arbiter interpreted these two provisions to mean that the employer should assign scheduled overtime to the employee with the least amount of departmental overtime credit, but may properly give overtime to an employee whose overtime credit does not exceed that of another worker by 36 hours. He further ruled that when an employee is properly assigned extra-hours work, but his overtime credit increases between the assignment and performance of that overtime, management need not reschedule that overtime for another employee. (National Lead Co., 53 LA 687)

In the absence of a contractual time limit, what is a reasonable length of time in which to equalize overtime assignments? One arbiter held that four months was not an excessive period of equalization.

EXAMPLE: One employee complained that a company violated a clause requiring equal distribution of overtime by failing to give him any overtime work during a two-month period when other employees worked as much as 24 hours overtime. In the following two months, his overtime was brought up to that of the other employees. The union claimed he was entitled to pay for overtime missed during the first two months. The arbiter, however, ruled that four months was a reasonable period in which to equalize overtime, since the contract did not set any time limit. (North American Aviation Inc., 17 LA 320)

Avoiding Double-Time Pay

Arbitrators have consistently ruled that management may not assign overtime in such a manner as to avoid paying double-time when such an assignment violates the scheduling of overtime stipulated in the collective bargaining agreement.

EXAMPLE: A contract called for equal distribution of overtime, and provided for double-time pay for hours worked in excess of 12 in any one day. The employer scheduled a group of workers for overtime and then dismissed them after they had worked a total of 12 hours during the day. Another group of employees, who had accumulated more overtime but were not eligible for double-time pay, were assigned to complete the overtime work. The arbiter ruled that the employer was not entitled to avoid paying double-time by assigning overtime to workers with more accumulated extra-hours work, even though the contract failed to specify within what time period overtime must be equalized. (Continental Can Co., 52 LA 118)

Likewise, in two similar situations, the contracts provided for double-time pay for the seventh consecutive day worked and equalization of overtime. Failure to assign extra-hours work to employees with the least amount of accumulated overtime in order to avoid paying double-time constituted a violation of the contract, it was held in both cases. (American Enka Corp., 52 LA 882; U.S. Borax & Chemical Corp., 54 LA 387)

Transferred Employees

In two cases, arbiters found that, when overtime is to be shared equally throughout a department or work group, employees temporarily transferred to another area are entitled to overtime assignments scheduled in their regular group. As one arbiter pointed out, to rule otherwise would mean that management could avoid giving overtime to a particular individual merely by temporarily transferring him prior to assigning overtime. (Massey-Ferguson, Inc., 53 LA 616; see also 54 LA 252)

Qualifications to Perform Overtime Tasks

Certain overtime tasks may require more skill and time than others. This may result in a lack of uniformity in the distribution of overtime, due to some employees' inability to perform frequent-overtime tasks.

Arbitrators have reached differing conclusions regarding management's discretion in assigning overtime when a certain group of workers are able to perform the overtime task, but are not the most proficient group for that task.

EXAMPLE: In one instance, the contract called for equal distribution of overtime departmentally. However, it had been company practice to assign maintenance overtime on the basis of special proficiencies of the maintenance workers. The arbiter ruled that this practice violated the contract, except in cases where the employee having the least overtime was totally unqualified to perform the overtime task. (National Lead Co., 53 LA 687)

EXAMPLE: It was the policy of another company not to require female employees to lift more than 50 pounds. Yet, it was frequently necessary for women workers to do so during regular hours. When an overtime assignment occurred which necessitated lifting of more than 50 pounds, the female workers (who were in line for overtime) were by-passed; and they initiated a grievance. The arbiter ruled that management violated the contract, since the women had demonstrated during regular hours that they were able to perform the work. (Standard Brands Inc., 54 LA 732; see also 75 LA 275, 74 LA 217, 73 LA 1087)

On the other hand, another arbiter held that it was legitimate to assign overtime for purposes of taking inventory on the basis of ability, despite contractual provision for overtime assignments to be made on a seniority basis. The arbiter reasoned that special skills are needed for taking inventory, and inventory is totally unrelated to production activities. (Myers Drum Co., 55 LA 1048)

Similarly, an employer properly assigned a qualified junior tool and die maker, instead of a senior employee, to Saturday overtime to repair a bearing in a paint bake oven, an arbiter ruled, where the employer determined that the junior employee was the only employee "qualified" to handle the job. (Proto Tool Co., 65 LA 588; see also 77 LA 128, 71 LA 412)

Overtime by Job Classification

A contract called for overtime work to be performed by the classification of employees who normally perform that type of work. Given such a provision, an arbiter ruled that it was a violation of the contract for overtime to be assigned to another classification of employees even though the job was to be performed in their work area and they had on occasion performed the particular task. (American Shipbuilding Co., 54 LA 1216; see also 74 LA 699)

Overtime by Seniority

Arbitrators have upheld contracts that provide for overtime to be distributed on the basis of seniority.

EXAMPLE: One such contract contained a clause "Overtime shall be allocated in accordance with departmental seniority unless production would be substantially impaired by strict adherence to this rule." In one instance under this agreement, management gave an overtime job to an employee from another department who was on hand performing other overtime activities and made no attempt to contact the senior employee in the affected department. The arbiter held that management had violated the contract. (Harris Brothers Co., 53 LA 293)

Similarly, an employer violated a contract requiring overtime to be assigned according to department seniority when it assigned group leader in maratex department rather than assistant group leader in jute department to assist maintenance personnel in overtime work involving installation of a sprinkler system in the jute department, an arbiter held, since the assistant group leader had prior claim to overtime work in his own department. (Amtel Inc., 63 LA 357)

Likewise, an electrician who was fifth in seniority standing in his department was entitled to eight hours of overtime pay because he was by-passed for the overtime in favor of another electrician who was sixteenth in seniority standing, an arbiter held, notwithstanding the employer's contention that the employee's grievance was invalid because the four other more senior employees did not elect to file grievances. (Celotex Corp., 63 LA 521)

However, where a contract specified that overtime must be distributed according to seniority, an arbiter ruled that an employer did not violate the contract when it offered overtime to a junior employee after finding that the senior employee who might have been offered the overtime had already left the plant. (Kellogg Co., 62 LA 1217; see also 77 LA 217)

Moreover, management was under no obligation to assign overtime work on the basis of seniority, an arbiter decided, where the collective bargaining agreement did not specifically state that seniority rights shall apply to overtime distribution.

EXAMPLE: A union objected to a company's practice of assigning overtime in a random manner and demanded that senior employees be paid for extra-hours work given junior men. The contract said nothing about overtime distribution, but it did contain a clause stating that "seniority rights for employees shall prevail subject to the terms of this agreement." The union contended this meant that seniority would apply in all situations except as limited by the agreement. The company, on the other hand, argued that the clause meant seniority rights would operate only in the manner spelled out in detail in other parts of the contract.

The arbiter agreed with the company. In the absence of a provision making seniority applicable to overtime work, the union did not have cause for complaint. (Crowe-Guide Cements Co., 30 LA 177)

Probationary and Temporary Employees

When the contract fails to specify whether probationary employees are to be given overtime, the facts in the individual case may determine the arbiter's ruling.

EXAMPLE: A collective bargaining agreement stipulated that overtime was to be distributed equally among employees in a department. When necessary to get additional help from outside the department, overtime was to be given to the senior employee with the least overtime. The contract defined probationary workers as employees.

In a grievance arising under this agreement, the arbiter ruled that the company acted properly when it assigned a probationary employee in the department to overtime work rather than going outside the department. (Hess & Eisenhardt Co., 53 LA 95)

Likewise, under a contract provision stating that an employer was not required to offer overtime to employees who were not qualified to perform work, an employer had the right to assign overtime involving filling of large orders in the warehouse department to experienced temporary employees, an arbiter ruled, instead of to two office employees. Noting that the employer was not obligated to train office employees before using outside help, the arbiter concluded that the employer had the right to assign the overtime to the temporary employees absent a clear showing of discriminatory or arbitrary treatment of the office workers. (Nissan Motor Corp., 66 LA 132; see also 77 LA 393, 72 LA 996)

However, an employer improperly assigned overtime on its valentine candy line only to temporary employees instead of to regular employees in the unit, even though the entire line was staffed by temporary employees, an arbiter ruled, since there existed a past practice under which regular employees were given the first consideration for available overtime whenever there was a mixture of regular and temporary employees on a particular line. (Zachery Confections, Inc., 77 LA 464; see also 55 LA 189)

Notifying Employees of Overtime Work Available

To what extent is management obligated to attempt to reach an employee at home whose turn it is to work overtime? Each case must be judged individually.

EXAMPLE: A contract called for equalization of overtime. The employer called the man with the least overtime at his home to come in for an overtime assignment, but the employee failed to answer the phone. The assignment was properly given to someone else.

Twenty minutes later, however, another overtime assignment became known. The employer assumed that the previously-called employee with the least overtime was still unavailable and failed to try to contact him for the new assignment. The arbiter ruled that the employer could not assume that the employee had not returned home during the twenty-minute interval and, therefore, violated the contract. (Goodyear Aerospace Corp., 52 LA 1098; see also 76 LA 1159, 76 LA 1024, 74 LA 110)

On the other hand, in another case, the contract provided for overtime to be given to the most senior employee classified to do the work. Overtime was necessary for Labor Day, and it was scheduled late in the afternoon of the last working day before the holiday. The most senior employee had been on vacation (his honeymoon), and was not due back until the day after Labor Day. The foreman made no attempt to contact the senior employee and instead assigned the overtime to someone else.

The company argued that it would be unreasonable to have to try to contact the senior employee throughout the holiday weekend. Furthermore should he prove to be unavailable for the overtime assignment on Labor Day, it would be very difficult to get a substitute worker at the last minute. The arbiter upheld the company's contention and agreed that the overtime was properly assigned to someone else. (Carey Salt Co., 51 LA 1170)

Responsibility for an Error in Assigning Overtime

Arbiters generally hold that any mistakes an employer makes when assigning overtime, even if they are perfectly honest and understandable errors, are management's responsibility.

EXAMPLE: Due to a computer error, overtime was improperly assigned to an employee. The arbiter concluded that the aggrieved worker must be compensated — despite the fact that he should have been aware of the error and should have called it to management's attention before the scheduled overtime was performed. (Goodyear Aerospace Corp., 54 LA 579)

Remedy for Overtime Missed

The usual remedy awarded when management makes an erroneous overtime assignment is make-up overtime or payment of money the employee would have earned were the overtime properly assigned. Arbitrators are frequently called upon to determine which of the two remedies is appropriate. (48 LA 923, 48 LA 47)

EXAMPLE: Under a contract providing for equal distribution of overtime within the appropriate overtime group in a classification, the employer improperly gave an overtime assignment to an employee from a different classification. The arbiter ruled for a monetary award — rather than make-up overtime — for the employee who should have been given the assignment. The arbiter explained that to give the grievant make-up overtime would adversely affect the contractual overtime rights of the other employees in his classification. (Trane Co., 52 LA 144)

Similary, in another instance, an employee was mistakenly bypassed for an overtime assignment under a contract stipulating equal distribution of overtime. The assignment was given to another employee in the same overtime group, however. The contract failed to specify any remedy for improper overtime assignments, so the arbiter imposed an award of makeup overtime for the grievant. He felt that the remedy was appropriate since the bypass occurred within the same overtime equalization roster and no inequities would result from make-up overtime. Furthermore, the bypass was unintentional, and the employee would suffer no loss of earnings as long as he received the make-up assignment within a reasonable period. (Kaiser Aluminum & Chemical Corp., 54 LA 613)

Likewise, an employer that committed an honest mistake in its by-pass of an employee to perform emergency overtime work was directed to remedy its violation of the contract by: (1) providing make-up overtime of eight hours for the employee at a time convenient for him and at a time when he otherwise would not be working; (2) insuring that the overtime given does not take away from the employee's other overtime opportunities; and (3) providing eight hours of overtime pay to the employee without his working any make-up over time if he ceases to become an employee or if he is unable to work the make-up overtime within a reasonable period of time. (Kimberly-Clark Corp., 61 LA 1094; see also 76 LA 10)

When the award granted is monetary, arbiters generally will award pay for missed overtime at the overtime rate rather than at straight time.

EXAMPLE: A series of grievances came before an arbiter in which he found that certain employees had been denied their proper opportunity for overtime work. The union argued that the employees should be paid the appropriate premium rates for the hours of work they were denied. The company, however, maintained that they should be paid straight-time rates, saying that the contract specified straight-time as the appropriate rate of pay for any hours not worked. The company also pointed out that it had been established practice at the plant to pay only straight-time in such cases.

Despite the company's past practice, the arbiter ruled for the union. He said that the most important consideraton was that the employees would have been paid at overtime rates if they had worked the hours in question, so he awarded them the "amount of compensation they were denied the opportunity to earn." (John Deere Ottumwa Works, 20 LA 737)

Similarly, an employer who improperly denied employees the opportunity to work holiday overtime which was compensated at double time was ordered to pay employees equivalent to half-time for the hours that they missed, in addition to giving the workers make-up overtime, an arbiter decided. (General Mills Chemicals Inc., 66 LA 1012)

Definition of "Day" for Overtime Purposes

Where overtime pay is required for all work beyond a designated number of hours a day, the manner in which a day is measured becomes crucial.

Some companies use a calendar day, others a 24-hour period following a specified time, and still others recognize the 24-hour period following the start of the particular employee's regular shift.

EXAMPLE: In one case, several employees who normally worked from 3 p.m. to 11 p.m. were ordered to work from 7 p.m. to 7 a.m. on Monday and Tuesday, resuming their normal work schedule on Wednesday. The contract defined the workday for purposes of computing overtime as "24 consecutive hours commencing with the starting time on an employee's regularly assigned shift."

The union contended that the employees were entitled to overtime pay for the hours worked between 3 p.m. and 7 p.m.

on Wednesday. The union argued that the 24-hour period began for these workers at 7 p.m.; hence, 3 p.m. to 7 p.m. Wednesday was the same workday that began Tuesday at 7 p.m. The company countered that the workday began at 3 p.m., the starting time of these employees' regularly assigned shift; and all work performed on Wednesday was to be paid at the straight-time rate. The arbitrator ruled for the company. (Chicago Pneumatic Tool Co., 42 LA 1240)

EXAMPLE: In another case, a problem arose with the initiation of Daylight Saving Time. The contract required overtime pay for all time worked in excess of eight hours in any one day and defined a day as "24 hours beginning at the time an employee starts work on his regular or assigned schedule." The arbiter held that the employees who worked the 7 p.m. to 3 p.m. shift and the 3 p.m. to 11 p.m. shift on the Saturday before Daylight Saving Time went into effect were entitled to overtime pay for the first hour worked on those same shifts the following Sunday. He commented that the contract was very specific in defining a day as 24-hours long, and only 23 hours had elapsed between the start of the Saturday shifts and the start of the Sunday shifts. (Neches Butane Products, 49 LA 1195)

Overtime on Holidays

Under a contract that failed to specify the manner of computing compensation for hours worked in excess of eight on premium-pay days such as holidays, an arbiter found that employees are entitled to one and one-half times the applicable premium hourly rate for such hours. The contract called for time and one-half for overtime work and triple-time for holiday work. The arbiter upheld the union contention that the triple-time holiday pay was the proper base rate to be used for computing overtime on a holiday; hence, overtime on a holiday was to be compensated at four and one-half times the straight-time rate. (Fry's Food Stores, 44 LA 431)

However, an employer properly paid time and one-half rate rather than double time pay to employees who were scheduled to work on a contractual holiday, on a Tuesday, an arbiter decided, notwithstanding the union's contention that the payment of time and one-half was not in keeping with the intent of the contract. The employer, the arbiter reasoned, was entitled to compute the employees' pay by not considering the exception to the contract's no-pyramiding clause, which applied only to work performed on Sunday. (Inland Container Corp., 63 LA 1294)

Holiday As Time Worked for Overtime Purposes

When contracts are silent on the subject of whether or not an unworked holiday is to be counted as hours worked for purposes of calculating weekly overtime, arbiters may rule either way.

EXAMPLE: One company's contract stated that time and one-half would be paid for all work beyond 40 hours in a week and specified a Monday through Friday workweek. When employees worked a Saturday during a week which included an unworked holiday, the union and the company disagreed over whether the employees were entitled to overtime pay for the Saturday work. The company claimed that, since the contract did not specifically say so, holidays need not be counted as time worked.

The arbiter ruled, however, that holidays should be counted as time worked. Otherwise, workers would lose pay (the overtime premium) for the sixth day worked because of a holiday. Concluding that the parties meant for workers to enjoy holidays without losing any money, the arbiter said the company must count holidays as time worked. (Martin Aircraft Tool Co., 25 LA 181)

However, another arbiter, declared that if the contract is silent on the matter, management need not count an unworked holiday as time worked in figuring when overtime pay starts. The contract stipulated time and one-half pay for work after 40 hours a week. It stated that "hours lost by employees from their regular scheduled shift at the request of the company shall count as time worked for the purpose of computing weekly overtime."

In one week, employees put in a total of 40 hours of actual work, apart from time off on a holiday. The union insisted that the time off on the holiday should be counted as time worked — for a total of 48 hours' work in the week, eight of them compensated at the overtime premium.

The arbiter decided otherwise. It was not time lost at the request of the company, he said. He considered the unworked holiday comparable to an unworked Sunday, and it should not be viewed as time worked for overtime purposes. (Goodyear Clearwater Mills, 6 LA 117)

Pyramiding of Daily and Weekly Overtime Pay

Collective bargaining agreements generally provide for overtime or premium pay for work in excess of some specified number of hours per day or in excess of some specified number of hours in a week. It is common for these agreements to also contain a clause prohibiting pyramiding of overtime premiums — hours of daily overtime worked and compensated for cannot be counted again as time worked toward weekly overtime. Problems can arise however, in determining whether certain hours worked, paid for at some premium rate, are in fact overtime hours and consequently cannot be counted toward weekly overtime. (74 LA 345, 71 LA 1055, 71 LA 582)

EXAMPLE: In one such case, the grievant worked 12 hours on his birthday. The contract recognized employees' birthdays as holidays, and provided for time and one-half payment for work done on a holiday. The contract also prohibited pyramiding of overtime premiums.

The grievant was paid time and one-half holiday pay for the first eight hours worked on his birthday, and time and one-half overtime pay for the remaining four hours. The union contended that the first eight hours, the grievant worked should be counted in computing the weekly overtime, since these hours were compensated as holiday work, not overtime work. The arbiter agreed, rejecting the company's argument that such action would amount to pyramiding. (Hooker Chemical Corp., 50 LA 1091)

EXAMPLE: In another case an employee had been paid time and one-half for the hours she worked on her scheduled day off. The arbiter ruled she was also entitled to receive overtime pay for the hours worked in excess of 40 during the week, despite the fact that the contract prohibited payment of both daily and weekly overtime for the same hours. The premium pay which the grievant received for her off-day work is analogous to "penalty pay" for Sunday and holiday work, the arbiter reasoned, rather than to daily overtime. (Safeway Stores Inc., 45 LA 244)

EXAMPLE: Another contract provided for double-time for Sunday work and time and one-half for hours in excess of 40 in a workweek. The contract further prohibited pyramiding of overtime and/or premium pay. Under this agreement, an employee worked Sunday and the following five days. The company paid the worker double-time for the Sunday work, but refused to pay time and one-half for the sixth day, claiming that to do so would be pyramiding of overtime and premium pay. The arbiter, however, concluded that the double-time pay for Sunday was in fact a penalty against the employer, not premium pay. Consequently, he found that the employee was entitled to time and one-half for the sixth day, and that this would not constitute pyramiding. (Safeway Stores Inc., 45 LA 1163)

EXAMPLE: An employee who worked from 3:00 a.m. through 3:00 p.m. on Monday was entitled to: (1) double time pay for working from 3:00 a.m. to 7:00 a.m. Monday, which was considered part of Sunday under the contract, (2) regular pay for working from 7:00 a.m. to 11:00 a.m. and (3) time and one-half for working from 11:00 a.m. to 3:00 p.m., an arbiter ruled, despite the employer's claim that the payment constituted pyramiding. In his decision the arbiter noted that pyramiding meant "piling on" by paying two different rates for the same hours of work. (King-Seely Thermos Co., 61 LA 544)

Premium Pay for Weekend Work

IN BRIEF

Arbitration awards involving premium pay for weekend work provide few general guidelines for application to everyday problems.

Settlement of disputes over premium pay generally depends on a close reading of complex contract language and its application in the context of the particular bargaining situation. (97 LA 45, 94 LA 271, 94 LA 52, 92 LA 23, 91 LA 1043, 90 LA 225, 74 LA 1195, 65 LA 975, 65 LA 636, 62 LA 1008)

GUIDELINES

Sunday Premium

Frequently, contracts call for premium pay for work performed on Sundays. For purposes of such provisions, many contracts limit Sunday worktime eligible for premium pay to work begun after some specified hour on Sunday in order to avoid premium payments for work that is part of a Saturday night shift. Without such a limitation, arbiters will generally hold employers liable for premium pay for all work performed on "Sunday" as defined by the calendar day.

EXAMPLE: One contract defined the "workday" as beginning at 7 a.m. and provided for double-time pay "for all hours worked on Sunday." Third-shift employees regularly scheduled to work from 11 p.m. Saturday until 7 a.m. Sunday claimed that they were entitled to double-time for all work performed after midnight Saturday night until the end of their shift. The company denied their contention, insisting that the Saturday workday began at 7 a.m. and continued for 24 hours until 7 a.m. Sunday. Hence, all work performed by the third shift employees fell on Saturday, the company claimed.

The arbiter, however, found that the contract made no such definition of Sunday. Absent any contractual provision specifically defining the day for overtime or premium pay purposes in some other manner, a day is generally held to mean the calendar day, the arbiter explained. He concluded that in this contract "Sunday" meant from midnight Saturday to midnight Sunday and, therefore, awarded third shift employees double-time pay for all work performed after midnight Saturday. (Trent Engineering Co., 55 LA 1232)

Similarly, employees who worked on Sunday from 7 a.m. through 2:15 p.m. were entitled to eight hours' pay at double-time rate rather than the seven hours' pay they received, an arbiter decided. Despite the contract's ambiguity, the arbiter held that the union's interpretation that once an employee works more than four hours in workday he is entitled to eight hours' pay, was confirmed by past practice. (Construction Industry Committee, 69 LA 14; see also 86 LA 827, 77 LA 1030, 74 LA 1214, 66 LA 1096)

On the other hand, engineers were not entitled to double-time pay for work performed on Sundays after the employer began opening its stores to the public as a regular business day because the Sunday Blue Laws were struck down as unconstitutional, an arbiter ruled, notwithstanding the union's contention that the contract stating that "employees who work on Sunday shall receive double the straight-time hourly rate for worked" meant what it said. (Alexander's Personnel Providers Inc., 68 LA 249)

Similarly, under a contract stating that "double time shall be paid for all work performed on Sunday, excepting shift that overlaps into Sunday," an arbiter ruled that a publisher was not obligated to pay double time pay to an employee who worked portion of Sunday comprising new shift that started at 10 p.m. Sunday and ended 6 a.m. on Monday. (Baltimore News American, 68 LA 1054; see also 90 LA 663, 74 LA 1042)

Seventh-Day Premium

Rather than specify Sunday as a premium day, some contracts generalize and call for premiums on the seventh day worked. Similar problems can arise in determining when the "seventh day" actually begins.

EXAMPLE: An employee at one company regularly worked Monday through Friday, beginning at 7:30 a.m. After working his regular week, he was called in at 11:00 p.m. Saturday, and worked until 8:36 a.m. Sunday, with an hour break for a meal.

The contract provided for time and one half for the sixth day worked and doubletime for work on the seventh day. The workday was defined as eight hours. The employer consequently paid the employee time and one half for the sixth day and double-time for only a few minutes on Sunday morning, claiming that the seventh day did not begin until eight hours had been worked on the sixth day.

The arbiter ruled, however, that the seventh day began at 7:30 Sunday morning since the employee's regular starting time was 7:30 a.m. He ordered that the employee be paid at double-time rates for all work done after 7:30 a.m. Sunday. (City of Lansing, 53 LA 855; see also 87 LA 1269, 83 LA 480)

However, under a contract provision requiring payment of double-time rate to all employees for all work performed on Sunday when it is sixth or seventh day worked in the workweek, an arbiter ruled that an employer was not required to pay employees at double-time rate for work performed before the start of the workweek commencing at 7:00 a.m. Monday, even though the workday was considered a 24-hour period extending from 7:00 a.m. to 7:00 a.m. The pre-shift hours, being continuous with Monday, could not be considered an extension of Sunday, the arbiter held, since there was no reason to conclude that "Sunday" as used in the contract meant anything other than the normal calendar day. Moreover, past practice supported the employer's contention that employees performing pre-shift work in question were paid time and one half, rather than the double-time rate, the arbiter concluded. (Certain-Teed Products Corp., 61 LA 689; see also 86 LA 992, 76 LA 1037)

Pyramiding Premiums

A contract called for time and one half pay for an employee working his first scheduled day off or the sixth day in the workweek, and double-time for working his second scheduled day off or the seventh day in the workweek. The contract also contained the following clause: "The Company shall not be required to pay overtime twice for the same overtime hours worked."

An employee was scheduled to have Tuesday and Wednesday off. However, he was called in to work Wednesday, his second scheduled day off. He also worked Monday and Thursday through Sunday of that week. He was paid for Wednesday and straight time the remainder of the week.

The union claimed the employee was entitled to time and one half for Sunday since it was the sixth day worked in the week. The company argued that such payment would be pyramiding, which was prohibited in the contract clause quoted above, as the employee already received a premium for the Wednesday worked and that time could not be counted again.

The arbiter rejected the company's argument, however. He pointed out that there were two different days involved, and these were not, therefore, "the same overtime hours." He explained that the clause did *not* state that overtime hours worked and compensated for under one provision could not be counted as hours worked for overtime purposes under any other provision. But rather, he said, the clause was intended to prevent paying a double premium in such situations as an employee working the sixth day in the workweek, that same day also happening to be his first scheduled day off. (Dow Chemical Col., 49 LA 480; see also 97 LA 45, 91 LA 1043, 87 LA 130)

On the other hand, an employer properly paid straight time rate, rather than overtime to employees for work performed on Friday in a workweek consisting of Sunday, Monday, Tuesday, Wednesday, Thursday and Friday, an arbiter ruled. Contending that the contract provided for overtime for all work over 40 hours in a payroll week and on a Sunday to Friday schedule, the union argued that overtime should be paid for Friday work because Friday was an overtime day, while Sunday was a premium pay day.

Rejecting the union's contention, however, the arbiter pointed out that if premium pay and overtime pay are the same, as he viewed it, payment for Friday work in a Sunday to Friday schedule would be pyramiding overtime, which was prohibited by the contract. The denial of the employee's grievance was consistent with the generally accepted concept in today's industrial world providing one overtime day in a six-day workweek, the arbiter concluded. (Utah International Inc., 75 LA 212; see also 94 LA 271, 94 LA 52, 92 LA 23, 90 LA 225)

Unworked Days Affecting Premiums

Holidays and other time not worked but paid for may or may not influence the rate of pay on what are normally premium days. Specific contract language is crucial. (68 LA 1006, 63 LA 1294, 62 LA 1008)

EXAMPLE: A contract called for time and one half for all work performed on Saturday. Another provision of the contract provided for "bereavement pay" —pay for up to three days of missed work when an employee attended the funeral of an immediate family member. The contract stipulated that the employee was to be paid bereavement pay for the time he "would have had the opportunity to work" at his "standard hourly wage rate."

An employee under this contract was scheduled to work on Saturday. However, due to a death in his family, he was excused from work that day. The company subsequently paid him eight hours' bereavement pay at the straight-time rate.

The company contended that the "standard hourly wage rate" meant the "straight-time" rate. The union argued that the employee was entitled to eight hours' pay at time and one half, the "standard hourly wage rate" for Saturday. The arbiter agreed with the union's view and awarded for the grievant. (Marlin-Rockwell Co., 54 LA 99)

On the other hand, a contract provided that all work performed on the seventh consecutive day of the employee's workweek was to be paid at double-time. The contract further stipulated that employees were not to lose pay for worktime lost while serving on jury duty.

An employee was absent from work Monday and Wednesday one week while serving on jury duty, for which he was paid by the company for eight hours each day. He worked Tuesday, Thursday, Friday, Saturday, and Sunday of that week. The company paid the employee at the straight-time rate for Sunday.

The union argued that time spent on jury duty and compensated for by the company was to be counted as time worked. Thus Sunday was the seventh consecutive day worked in that employee's workweek, and should have been paid at double-time, the union insisted. But the arbiter found no provision in the contract stating that time spent on jury duty and compensated for by the company was to be counted as time worked. Absent any such provision, the arbiter could not sustain the grievance; and he ruled that the employee had been properly paid. (Cabot Corp., 52 LA 575)

Similarly, another arbiter also concluded that without specific contractual provision to that effect, pay for jury duty was not to be counted as hours worked when computing overtime. (Coleman Company Inc., 52 LA 357)

Premium Pay for Shift Work

IN BRIEF

Clauses providing for payment of a wage differential to employees who work on afternoon or night shifts ordinarily do not give rise to many disputes. Almost all employers requiring night work pay a shift bonus. The rate of payment invariably is specified in the contract, and workers assigned to the particular shift automatically are paid it.

Occasionally, however, there may be questions relating to the payment of shift differentials to night watchmen and similar groups, or to workers who divide their time between shifts. Legally and in the opinion of most arbiters, shift differentials must be included in figuring an employee's overtime rate.

GUIDELINES

When Regular Work Schedule Extends Into Another Shift

If portions of employees' regular work schedule fall into two different shifts, are they entitled to a shift premium for any of the hours? One arbiter held they were not.

EXAMPLE: Workers who normally worked the evening shift (3 p.m. to 11 p.m.) received a 15-cent premium shift differential. When management unilaterally changed the work schedule for this shift to 11 a.m. to 7 p.m., the employees claimed they were entitled to shift differential for the hours of 3 p.m. to 7 p.m. The arbiter rejected their contention, stating that the shift differential was only applicable to the eight-hour evening shift, and not to a few hours worked during that time span. (Diamond Shamrock Corp., 55 LA 827; see also 73 LA 677)

However, an employer that changed the starting time of the shift worked by poster orderlies from 6:30 a.m.-3 p.m. to 7:30 p.m.-4 a.m. on certain workdays was required to pay the employees contractual premium pay for the split shift, an arbiter decided, since the employees were now required to work portions of two shifts. (Miami Inspiration Hospital, 68 LA 898)

Similarly, an employee whose shift began on Friday and extended into Saturday was entitled to straight time pay for work hours that extended into Saturday and an employee whose shift began on Saturday and extended into Sunday was entitled to time and one-half the rate for the hours worked on Sunday, an arbiter ruled, under a contract that stated that time and one-half the employee's regular hourly wage would be paid for all work performed on Saturday and double time the employee's hourly rate would be paid for all work performed on Sunday.

In adopting the words "all work performed on Saturday" the parties meant "Saturday" to consist of shifts beginning on Saturday, and in using the words "all work performed on Sunday," they meant to cover the shifts which began on Sunday the arbiter emphasized, concluding that this interpretation was supported by the parties past practice. (Vlasic Foods Inc., 74 LA 1214)

If a company agrees to pay employees the premium rate required for a shift in which the *majority* of their working hours fall, what rate should be paid an employee who works *exactly* half his time on the day shift and half on the second shift? In one such situation, the arbiter rejected the employee's claim for a shift premium.

EXAMPLE: The employee worked regularly from 12:30 to 9 p.m., with a half-hour for lunch between 4:30 and 5. The regular second shift hours began at 4:30 p.m. Therefore, excluding his lunch period, this employee worked exactly half his hours on the day shift and half his hours on the second shift. The arbiter pointed out that since the lunch period could not be counted as hours worked, the employee could not show that a *majority* of his work time was put in on the second shift and denied his claim for the second shift premium. (Canfield Oil Co., 7 LA 322)

Night Premium for Non-Production Workers

Rulings have gone both ways on whether non-production workers on premium-pay shifts are entitled to shift differentials. Arbitrators, frequently, base their decisions on the employer's past practice or the language of the contract.

EXAMPLE: Under a contract that provided a shift differential for night work, an arbiter ruled that the employer violated the contract by denying the shift differential to janitors who worked on the night shift. Although janitors had not received the differential prior to this contract and the subject was not mentioned during negotiations, the contract language neglected to specifically exclude janitors from receiving the premium. (Journal-Tribune Publishing Co., 51 LA 606; see also 98 LA 312, 95 LA 479, 89 LA 581, 83 LA 17, 81 LA 1118, 81 LA 903, 77 LA 1220, 73 LA 1305)

On the other hand, it was held in another case that night shift premiums did not apply to watchmen, even though the contract did not specifically exclude them. The award was based on a past practice of several years of not paying such workers the premium. (John Lucas & Co., 19 LA 344)

Similarly, in another case, an employer was again not required to pay shift premiums for work at night to charwomen, because they had not received such pay in the six years that they had been covered by the contract. This past practice overrode the fact that the contract made no exceptions to the payment of premium pay for those hours, according to the arbiter. (Morgan Engineering Co., 33 LA 46)

Likewise, a housekeeper was not entitled to premium pay for working a four-hour afternoon schedule from 12:30 p.m.-4:30 p.m., an arbiter decided, notwithstanding the union's contention that the contract provision requiring payment of $.07 per hour night premium for all regularly scheduled "night employees"' obligated the employer to pay premium pay to the employee because "night employees,' and "second shift employees" working the 11:00 a.m. to 7:00 p.m. shift were one in the same. Finding that the term "shift employees" referred only to employees working a work period of eight hours' duration, the arbiter held that that interpretation was in harmony with the commonly accepted definition of "shift." (Huron Valley Public Schools, 63 LA 49; see also 97 LA 447, 74 LA 884)

Inclusion of Shift Premium in Figuring Overtime Pay

If a worker is entitled to a shift premium, his overtime pay must be based on his regular rate plus the shift premium, according to the Wage-Hour Law and arbiters.

EXAMPLE: A company agreed in its union contract that a bonus of five cents an hour would be paid men working on the second and third shifts. When a employee on a late shift performed overtime work, the company contended that he was entitled only to one and one-half times the day rate, while the union argued that he was entitled to one and one-half times the day rate plus five cents.

The arbiter, in upholding the union view, pointed out that the differential for late-shift work becomes an integral part of the employee's wage. Therefore, he ruled that an employee who worked overtime was entitled to receive compensation for those hours at the rate of one and one-half times his full hourly wage, including the shift premium. (Public Service Electric & Gas Co., 2 LA 2)

Overtime Extending Into a Premium-Pay Shift

Arbitrators generally rule that an employee working a day shift who occasionally is assigned overtime which extends into a premium-pay shift is *not* entitled to have the shift differential included in his overtime pay. However, if the overtime occurs on a regular basis or the contract language suggests that the differential is to be paid, the arbiter may award the shift premium.

EXAMPLE: One arbiter found that employees on the first shift were not entitled to a shift differential for the hour worked after the shift's normal quitting time. He ruled that the shift differential was intended only as additional compensation for second-shift employees who had to give up their socializing time of day. Occasional overtime work performed by the first shift did not alter their status as first-shift employees, and the contract specified that the second shift, not the first, was to receive the differential, the arbiter concluded. (Idal Corrugated Box Co., 46 LA 129)

Similarly, in another instance, a case came to arbitration over a company's practice of paying employees who work overtime on their day off on the basis of the shift differential applicable to the shift actually worked rather than on the basis of the shift to which they were regularly assigned. Employees who regularly worked a premium-pay shift were called in on their day off to work the day shift. The company did not include their usual shift differential when computing the overtime pay for the day shift worked.

The arbiter upheld this procedure since the practice had been in effect for several years, and the union had not challenged it before. (Bonanza Air Lines, Inc., 44 LA 698)

However, under a different contract providing a shift differential for second-shift work, another arbiter held that an employee who *regularly* worked a ten-hour day was entitled to the shift differential for the two hours worked daily on the second shift, in addition to the overtime premium for those two hours. The arbiter explained that payment of overtime alone is sufficient for first-shift employees who only *occasionally* work overtime into the second shift. But the additional shift differential must be paid to employees who work overtime into the second shift on a regularly-scheduled basis. (Brighton Electric Steel Casting, 47 LA 518)

Furthermore, where a contract called for shift bonuses for second-and third-shifts for "all work on these shifts," the employer had to include bonuses in the base rate for purposes of computing overtime worked on those shifts by employees regularly assigned to preceding shifts. (Stauffer Chemical Co., 35 LA 529)

Reporting & Call-In Pay

IN BRIEF

Generally, a reporting-pay clause can not be stretched to cover call-ins for emergency work, since there is a clear-cut distinction between reporting pay and call-in pay.

Where an employer is relieved of its reporting-pay obligation when it tells a worker not to report, a properly addressed telegram is usually considered proper notice — even if the worker does not receive it. However, this may not be true if the contract stipulates that workers must "receive" notice not to report.

If work is unavailable through no fault of the employer's, an employer, nevertheless, must notify workers not to report if this is feasible. A failure to give such notice may make the employer liable for reporting pay.

GUIDELINES

Overtime or Call-in

Problems may arise over whether specific time worked outside the normal work schedule is to be compensated as overtime or as a call-in.

EXAMPLE: One arbiter has made the following distinction between overtime and a call-in. Overtime is time worked continuous to the regular work schedule — whether it precedes or follows that shift. Call-in pay, however, is intended to compensate an employee for making a special trip to work; therefore, it is necessary for the employee to be released to leave the workplace immediately after completing an assignment in order for that assignment to qualify as a call-in. (Owens-Illinois Inc., 55 LA 1121; see also 73 LA 478, 69 LA 908)

Also, an arbiter held that an employee who normally had Saturday and Sunday off, that was called on Saturday to work at a garlic mill on Sunday, and returned to the mill on Monday was entitled to contractual double-time call-in pay for Sunday, since the employee was not given the required notice before the end of the last regular shift. (Basic Vegetable Products Inc., 90 LA 666; see also 92 LA 766, 92 LA 361, 88 LA 1307, 85 LA 500, 83 LA 491, 82 LA 1104, 82 LA 48)

Reporting Pay or Call-in

A collective bargaining agreement contained a provision guaranteeing employees a minimum of four hours' work or four hours' pay if called in at some time other than their regular shift or a continuous extension thereof. The contract further provided for a minimum of four hours' work or pay to any employee reporting for work at the start of his normal shift — with certain exceptions, such as when no work is available due to a power failure.

The second shift employees were instructed on Friday afternoon to report for work the following afternoon. Saturday was not a normal workday, but Saturday overtime occurred frequently. A power failure occurred Saturday morning. When employees reported for work as instructed, the company told them to go home.

The employees filed a grievance claiming four hours' call-in pay. The company contended that the situation came under the provisions governing reporting pay, and it was therefore not liable for payment to employees because of the power failure exception. The arbitrator upheld the company's view, stating that the reporting pay provisions applied given the established practice of an extended workweek schedule. (General Dynamics Corp., 54 LA 405; see also 84 LA 675)

EXCEPTIONS TO REPORTING-PAY REQUIREMENTS

Reporting pay provisions generally list certain situations in which the employer is not required to make reporting payments to employees. These exceptions may be situations where work is unavailable for reasons beyond the company's control or where the employer has given workers prior notice not to report. Arbiters are frequently called upon to determine if a given situation is truly beyond the company's control or if the company has given employees proper notice not to report.

Some of these situations are discussed below:

Civil Disturbances

A contract guaranteed four hours' reporting or call-in pay, except where employees are denied work for reasons beyond the control of the company. During the civil disturbances following the assassination of Dr. Martin Luther King, the company cancelled their regular evening shift because of a curfew imposed by the governor. Management made reasonable attempts to notify employees through radio announcements, although such notification was not required under the terms of the contract.

The arbiter denied reporting pay to employees who came to work, holding that the situation was "a classical illustration of 'other causes beyond the control of the Company.'" (Koppers Co. Inc., 54 LA 408)

Similarly, civil disorders in another city prompted a city-wide curfew starting at 3 p.m. Several second-shift employees reported for work at 3 p.m., but were sent home. They subsequently claimed four hours' pay under a reporting pay clause requiring such pay for employees sent home for lack of work. The arbiter interpreted "lack of work" to mean absence of the need for the product with adjustments in the work schedule to reduce output. Since this situation did not exist, the arbiter rejected the employees' claim for reporting pay. (Lockheed-Georgia, 51 LA 720)

Bomb Threats

A company received a bomb threat. Two previous threats had proved to be hoaxes. Believing this to be another hoax, the company gave employees the option of going home and being paid only for the time actually spent on plant premises, or staying and working the entire shift and getting full pay for the time worked. The company said it would not give four hours' reporting pay to employees who elected to go home, under a contractual provision exempting the employer from such reporting pay in case of explosion.

The union later claimed reporting pay, arguing that no explosion actually occurred. The arbiter denied their grievance, however. He felt that if an actual explosion would exempt the company from reporting pay, the same should hold true for the mere threat of an explosion. Otherwise, "any mischief maker ... could drive the corporation out of business with threats of one sort and another." (General Cable Corp., 54 LA 696; see also 73 LA 1252, 62 LA 463)

However, an employer was obligated to pay reporting pay to employees who claimed loss of pay during two separate bomb scares, an arbiter decided. The contract's provision exempting the employer from paying reporting pay if inability to provide work is due to "labor disputes, riots, fire, flood, tornado, lightening, power failure or act of God," was not applicable notwithstanding the employer's contention that its failure to provide work was due to "circumstances beyond its control," the arbiter held, since that reason was not one of those specified. (Miller Printing Machinery Co., 64 LA 141; see also 73 LA 280, 72 LA 1232, 69 LA 511)

Equipment Breakdowns and Power Failures

Arbitrators will look very closely to determine if equipment breakdowns and power failure are, in fact, within the company's control. (63 LA 261, 61 LA 274)

EXAMPLE: A contract provided for reporting pay for employees who report for work but find none available, except "if the plant delay results from causes beyond the control of the company." A flue collapsed, necessitating the shutting down of a furnace used in production operations. The union argued that since the flue had not been inspected for three years and proper inspection could have prevented the collapse, the situation was legitimately within the company's control. The arbiter agreed and awarded the grievants reporting pay. (Bunker Hill Co., 51 LA 873)

Similarly, Under another contract requiring reporting pay unless the unavailability of work is due to a major power interruption or equipment breakdown over which the company has no control, the arbiter awarded reporting pay when a leak in a boiler made work unavailable. The leak occurred following a shutdown and repairs on the boiler, and such leaks were common after boiler shutdowns. Although the leak was beyond the control of the company, the arbiter said that the company should have foreseen the possibility of the leak and made every effort to discover it in time to notify employees not to report to work. (Rubatex Corp., 52 LA 1270; see also 74 LA 1037, 74 LA 513, 54 LA 1218)

However, an arbiter ruled in another instance that employees who were sent home after a power failure in the main electric feeder line were not entitled to four hours' reporting pay under a contract providing for such payment except where the employer "is not able to operate the plant because of reasons beyond its control." The union contended that since the burn-out which precipitated the power failure occurred within the plant, its occurrence was management's responsibility and, therefore, was within its control. The arbiter accepted the argument that the main feeder line was management's responsibility; but since the power failure could not have been anticipated, it was beyond the company's control. The employees' grievance was denied. (Erie Artisan Corp., 51 LA 850)

Similarly, a power failure due to a malfunction in new equipment was judged to be beyond management's control, exempting that company from payment of four-hours' reporting pay. (E.W. Bliss Co., 55 LA 522; see also 73 LA 1117)

Lack of Heat

When employees reported to work Monday morning, the plant was cold. The oil tank had run out of oil over the weekend. The company had been aware of the oil shortage on Friday, but felt there would be enough to last until Monday. An unexpected, though not uncommon, drop in temperature caused the oil to run out earlier than anticipated. A stand-by gas heater was inoperative.

Employees refused to work due to the lack of heat. A short time after the start of the shift, the company president told employees that the oil shipment was on its way, there would soon be heat, and to either get to work or leave. They all went home.

The company did not pay the employees at all that day. The union demanded four hours' reporting pay or at least compensation for the time spent at the plant that morning. The arbiter awarded payment for time spent in the plant, since the situation was within management's control, but denied four hours' reporting pay on the grounds that there were some equities on the company's side. (Dietz Machine Works Inc., 52 LA 1023)

Health Hazard

While first-shift employees were at work, a mechanical detector sounded an alarm indicating the presence of unsafe levels of carbon monoxide in the workplace. The employees evacuated the area. Twenty minutes later the company informed the employees that the alarm was a result of a malfunction in the detector, and instructed employees to return to work. Seventeen of them refused to do so, believing conditions were genuinely unsafe; they requested other work for the one hour remaining in their shift. The company said it could not make substitute work available on such short notice.

The 17 employees subsequently filed a grievance requesting the pay they had been denied for the last hour of their shift. Their claim was based on a contract provision stating that employees who report for their normal shift without prior notification not to report will be given eight hours of work.

The arbiter found that the employees were justified in refusing to return to work under the circumstances. He further found that the contract failed to limit the company's liability to pay the workers in this situation, and thus awarded each one hour's pay. (Miller Printing Machinery Co., 54 LA 69)

However, In another case, when several employees were suddenly taken ill at work, the company tried to ascertain the cause, but was unable to do so. Upon the advise of the state health department, the company closed the plant two hours after the start of the workday, and paid the employees for the two hours worked.

An arbiter denied a grievance for four hours' reporting pay, explaining that the company had made every effort to locate and control the cause. Since its efforts failed, the situation was obviously beyond the company's control, and it was therefore not liable for reporting pay under the provisions of the contract. (Lasko Metal Products Inc., 51 LA 1119)

Inclement Weather

In two cases, employers decided to close down production because they felt that there would be substantial absenteeism due to a snowstorm, making operations inefficient. In both instances, the arbiters awarded reporting pay to those employees who showed up for work. The decision to shut down because of anticipated absenteeism was within the managements' control, they held. (Westinghouse Electric Corp., 51 LA 298; Muskegon Piston Ring Co., 55 LA 685; see also 73 LA 627)

On the other hand, an employer was not obligated to pay reporting pay to employees who were prevented from working by closing of the plant due to icy roads caused by freezing rain, an arbitrator ruled, since freezing rain is an "Act of God" exempting the employer from reporting pay liability. The fact that the employees travelled on the icy roads without difficulty on their way to the plant and had not seen any accidents was not controlling, the arbiter held. (Bangor Products Corp., 63 LA 213; see also 74 LA 191, 73 LA 962, 72 LA 845, 71 LA 1015, 71 LA 716)

Daylight Saving Time

Under a contract guaranteeing a full day's pay if more than half the shift is worked except when employees are sent home early for reasons beyond management's control, the employees demanded a full eight hours' pay even though they only worked seven hours on the evening that Daylight Saving Time went into effect. Management claimed it was not liable to pay for the last, unworked hour because the institution of Daylight Saving Time was beyond its control.

The arbiter upheld the union, however. Management could have scheduled the workers for eight hours, even though it would have created confusion at the start of the next shift; and the situation, the arbiter held, therefore was not beyond management's control. (Magma Copper Co., 51 LA 9)

Proper Notification

The facts of the individual situation may dictate whether management's attempts to notify employees not to report to work were sufficient to exempt the company from reporting pay. (67 LA 1029, 67 LA 792)

EXAMPLE: Following the assassination of Dr. Martin Luther King, severe riots broke out in the city where this plant was located. Concerned for the safety of its employees, the management announced on radio the cancellation of the second shift.

The contract provided for four hours' reporting pay when employees are sent home for lack of work, unless they were notified the night before not to report. Several second shift employees who did not hear the radio announcement reported for work. Along with employees sent home early from the first shift, they requested to be paid four hours' reporting pay. The arbiter denied their request on the grounds that attempts to notify second-shift employees were reasonable under the extreme circumstances, and there was no "lack of work." Furthermore, the arbiter held, the company should not have any present or future deterrent placed in its way when confronted with a decision whether to shutdown for the safety of its employees. (Electronic Communications Inc., 51 LA 692)

However, in a different case, a severe snowstorm caused management to close the plant. Announcements of the closing were broadcast on four major radio stations. One hundred twelve employees did not hear the announcements, however, and reported for work as usual. They were sent home.

Under a contract provision allowing for at least four hours' straight-time pay to be given any employee who reports for his regular shift without having been instructed to the contrary, the 112 employees claimed four hours' reporting pay. The arbiter awarded them their grievance since, despite company efforts to notify the employees, they had not been instructed to remain at home. (Niagara Machine & Tool Works, 55 LA 396)

Similarly, employees who were not given advance notification that the plant would close due to heavy snowfall were entitled to reporting pay, an arbiter decided, since the snowfall did not render operation of the plant impossible. Finding that there were already four or five employees at the plant when the employer decided to close it and that 13 of the regular work force lived within a radius of one mile, the arbiter ordered the employer to compensate the employees for a full shift at the applicable rate of pay. (Hamilton Press Inc., 65 LA 274; see also 71 LA 1106, 71 LA 551, 70 LA 150)

Disciplinary Action

Arbitrators have ruled that an employee is not entitled to reporting pay if he is sent home early for disciplinary reasons, or if he is disciplined, but reports for work anyway. (64 LA 609, 63 LA 483)

EXAMPLE: A little more than an hour after starting work, two employees were sent home for threatening a supervisor, a violation of a company rule. The two employees maintained that they were entitled to four hours' reporting pay under the provisions of the contract. The arbiter disagreed. Although the contract was not particularly clear on this issue, he felt certain that it was not the intention of the parties, in negotiating the agreement, to protect or reward employees who brought about such a situation. (Unarco Industries Inc., 55 LA 421)

EXAMPLE: In another instance, an employee who had a poor attendance record failed to show up for work one day and did not call in his absence. When he reported to work the next day, his foreman stopped him immediately after the employee punched in and asked him why he had been absent. He said he was sick. The foreman did not believe him and suspended him for three days, sending the worker home right away.

The employee filed a grievance requesting four hours' reporting pay for the day he was sent home (but not challenging the suspension). The arbiter denied the grievance explaining that the foreman could not know of the suspension prior to the employee's reporting to work since he did not know if the worker's absence was legitimate. Consequently, he could not have given the worker prior notification not to report. Furthermore, the conditions precipitating the foreman's sending the employee home were beyond management's control. (Barber-Greene Co., 53 LA 1244)

However, employees were entitled to pay for work time that they lost on the day after they had been absent when the employer refused to allow them to work because of their failure to comply with a modified attendance rule. The modified rule required absent employees to notify the employer of their absence at least one-half hour before the start of their shift, or within two hours after the start of the shift if the absence was due to an emergency. Although the arbiter found that the employer had administered the modified rule in a fair manner, he concluded that the employer's implementation of the rule without giving the union an opportunity to negotiate on the subject was sufficient reason to allow the pay. (National Can Corp., 63 LA 766)

Likewise, an employer was obligated to pay call-out pay to employees for the time that they were required to spend at a company disciplinary investigation during their off-duty hours, an arbitrator ruled, despite the employer's contention that the phrase "called back to work" applied only to cases when employees were brought back to perform production activities. If there is to be an exception to the call out provision for disciplinary meetings, it should be stated in the labor agreement, the arbiter concluded. (Mobil Oil Corp., 76 LA 3)

Application of Premium Rates

Under a contract providing that double-time rates are to apply for all work in excess of 12 hours in one day, and further providing for a minimum of four hours' pay at time and one-half for call-in, an employee who had already worked 12 hours was called in for another hour and one-half. The company paid him double-time for the one and one-half hours actually worked, but only time and one-half hours for the remaining two and one-half hours of the four-hour call-in guarantee.

The grievant maintained that he was entitled to double-time pay for the entire four-hour period. But the arbiter held that there was no expressed or implied requirements in the contract that an employee is entitled to the high premium rates for the entire four hours of call-in pay unless he actually works the entire period. The grievance was denied. (General Portland Cement Co., 53 LA 653)

Hours Schedules

IN BRIEF

Generally, arbiters agree that management may set or change working hours if the change is not arbitrary, capricious, or discriminatory, and is not restricted by the collective bargaining agreement. Management is more likely to be given the prerogative to schedule hours of work than to be able to change established schedules. A certain small percentage of collective bargaining agreements permit a change in schedules only by mutual management-union agreement, or require management either to discuss or notify a union of schedule changes.

GUIDELINES

Scheduling Shifts

As long as the contract does not limit management's right to schedule shifts, most arbiters hold that the union's consent is not required to change the schedule. (98 LA 1099, 92 LA 418, 92 LA 48, 90 LA 922, 90 LA 559, 88 LA 969, 88 LA 599, 86 LA 357, 85 LA 1174, 85 LA 815, 85 LA 780, 85 LA 311, 85 LA 18, 84 LA 190, 82 LA 842, 81 LA 903, 81 LA 483, 68 LA 898, 67 LA 782, 65 LA 1089, 65 LA 439, 65 LA 323, 63 LA 431, 27 LA 123, 1 LA 430)

Even where a contract expressly prohibits an employer from making schedule changes without the union's consent, some arbiters have upheld management's unilateral action in doing so.

EXAMPLE: An employer did not violate a contract provision barring a change of present tours of duty without consulting with the union when it changed the tour of duty for file clerks in its radiology service so as to require them to work weekends and holidays, an arbiter ruled. Noting that the employer did not fail to notify the union concerning the proposed change and did not refuse to negotiate with the union concerning the impact of the change, the arbiter pointed out that meetings with union representatives failed to produce a concurrence on the matter. The employer, the arbiter concluded, was not required to wait until the union agreed to the change before implementing it. (Veterans Administration Medical Center, 72 LA 374)

Similarly, under a contract obligating an employer to notify a union of any change in the start of a shift, an employer had the right, without notice to the union, to require a new employee to commence work no later than the normal shift time, an arbiter decided, since the employee in effect was not working the shift but was working a period of time on his first day of work with the company. (Carnation Co., 73 LA 827)

Likewise, an employer did not violate a contract permitting a change in shift hours or the lunch hour only after an agreement had been arranged with the union when it unilaterally changed the time for the "return" of employees to its maintenance shop; but retained the start and end of shift hours and the usual time period for lunch an arbiter ruled, since only a change in shift hours or in the time of the lunch period required negotiation and agreement with the union. (Englehard Minerals & Chemicals Cor., 77 LA 1282; see also 75 LA 1049)

Additionally, arbiters have ruled that management may alter employees' work schedules if it has a legitimate business reason. (74 LA 1254, 73 LA 621, 73 LA 418)

On the other hand, an employer did not have the right to unilaterally assign a trash truck loader to the 6:30 a.m.–2:30 p.m. work shift in an effort to facilitate earlier trash pickup, where the contract set the regular starting time for the second shift as 7 a.m. to 8 a.m., an arbiter ruled, since the management rights clause could not be construed to deprive the union of the right it clearly had under the contract's hours of work clause. (Cyprus Wire & Cable Co., 71 LA 925)

Similarly, an employer did not have the right to assign mine inspectors to a "mantrip-to-mantrip" work schedule that required inspectors to go inside the mine in the morning with the mine crew, to stay with the mine crew and to come back out with crew at the end of the shift, without giving notice to the union which was required by the contract whenever there were changes made in policies, practices, or matters affecting working conditions, an arbiter decided. Notwithstanding the employer's contention that it had an inherent right to direct its work force, the arbiter concluded that the change in the schedule was not merely direction of work, but involved revision of an established working condition. (Mine Health and Safety Administration, 75 LA 369; see also 95 LA 221, 91 LA 1121, 87 LA 9, 85 LA 1144, 84 LA 679, 84 LA 131, 83 LA 1194, 81 LA 973, 35 LA 800)

Contracts Specifying "Normal Week"

Arbiters have differed on whether a specified "normal week" bars management from changing shift schedules.

EXAMPLE: In one case, an arbiter okayed the setting up of a seven-day, continuous-shift operation, even though the contract specified an eight-hour day, five-day week, Monday through Friday. Absent language to the contrary, he held, the "normal week" clause should not be interpreted to bar continuous operations; otherwise management would be prevented from introducing new products requiring such methods. (Stanley Works, 39 LA 374; see also 95 LA 210, 88 LA 129, 86 LA 992)

However, another arbiter ruled that such a clause was not ambiguous in spelling out a fixed workweek, so management had no right to schedule continuous operations. (Traylor Engineering & Mfg. Div., 36 LA 687)

Hours Schedules for Weekend Work

Arbiters have decided that a company does not have to pay any attention to the Monday-through-Friday shift hours in assigning overtime work on a weekend.

EXAMPLE: One company called in a first-shift worker to handle a rush job on Sunday. Because of production difficulties, the worker did not chock out until nearly midnight. The union complained that the first-shift man should not have been allowed to work the second-shift hours.

Rejecting the union's argument, the arbiter said it would lead to undesirable rigidity in scheduling overtime if the company had to follow the standard shift hours for weekend work. Such an interpretation would defeat the purpose of overtime work, which is to get the job done quickly, the arbiter said. (Menasco Mfg. Co., 26 LA 312)

Likewise, an employer was not obligated to pay overtime to employees for work performed on Saturday after changing the workweek schedule from Monday through Friday to Tuesday through Saturday due to economic recession, an arbiter decided. Notwithstanding the union's contention that five day schedules have always run from Monday through Friday and that Saturday was considered a day off that is paid at premium pay if worked, the arbiter held that the employer did not violate a contractual provision which stated that "40 hours per workweek shall constitute a normal week's work." The arbiter noted further that there was no provision in the contract limiting the "normal workweek" to Monday through Friday. (Stephan Chemical Co., 65 LA 630; see also 89 LA 364, 86 LA 992, 77 LA 23, 76 LA 154)

Changing the Workweek

Whether or not the company can change the workweek schedule without getting union approval depends upon the wording of the contract.

EXAMPLE: One arbiter found that a clause setting a regular workweek from Monday through Friday limited the company's right to change its work schedule form Monday through Friday and alternate Saturdays to Tuesday through Saturday and alternate Mondays. Although a different production schedule was needed, the arbiter said, the company had to reach agreement with the union first. (Seamless Rubber Co., 26 LA 758)

Similarly, where a contract established Monday through Friday as the basic workweek wherever "possible," an employer did not have the right to institute unilaterally a workweek of Tuesday through Saturday, an arbiter held. (Norfolk Naval Shipyard, 54 LA 588; see also 92 LA 430, 89 LA 1313, 73 LA 810, 72 LA 411)

However, the fact that a contract said the parties may negotiate" necessary schedules differing from the standard Monday through Friday workweek did not mean the union's consent was required before changes could be made, another arbiter ruled. (Menasco Mfg. Co., 30 LA 465)

Furthermore, where the management-rights clause of an agreement gave the company the right to schedule work, and where 40 percent of the work force had been on a seven-day workweek for a number of years, the employer was allowed to put the rest of the employees on the same schedule. The arbiter held that the company did not have to get the union's approval to do this. (Celanese Corp. of America, 30 LA 797; see also 87 LA 1290)

Change in Schedule to Avoid Premium Pay

Even though a company may have the right under its contract to change work schedules, it may be violating the agreement if it makes such changes to get out of paying premium pay.

EXAMPLE: A contract gave a company the right to revise operations in any way within its discretion. Using this right, the company changed a Monday-to-Friday schedule to a Tuesday-to-Saturday one for one week in which Monday was a holiday. In this way, employees had to work on Saturday at straight time, instead of at the time-and-one-half rate that would have been in effect had the Monday-to-Friday workweek not been changed. The union protested.

The protest was upheld by an arbiter. It was clear, he said, that the company had the right to change schedules, but "it is also clear that it was not the intent of the parties that the company should be allowed to abuse this right by changing shifts in order to avoid the payment of legitimate overtime." (Kennecott Copper Corp., Nevada Mines Div., 6 LA 820; see also 65 LA 1133, 35 LA 893, 30 LA 465)

Change in Schedule to Avoid Contract Benefits

After negotiating a contract granting benefits to part-time employees working 25 hours or more a week, can management limit the working hours of those employees to less than 25 per week? Since the practice of assigning part-time workers to 25 hours or more a week had been in effect for some time, an arbiter ruled against the reduction. Management pointed out that the contract did not guarantee 25 hours to part-time workers or prohibit reducing the hours of work of such employees. However, the arbiter decided that the contract was negotiated on the assumption that the past practice would continue, so the company was bound by that to continue scheduling hours as before. (Kroger Co., 36 LA 129)

Shutdown Before, During, or After Holiday

If a company thinks that very little work would be done on the day before or after a holiday, can it shut down over the union's objection? One arbiter held that a contract permitting shutdowns for lack of work or "other legitimate reasons" allowed a company to do this.

EXAMPLE: One company scheduled no work on Christmas and New Year's Eves because it was afraid employees would start their holiday celebrations on company time. The union demanded pay for the time lost, relying on a clause stating that the company would maintain an eight-hour day and a 40-hour week.

An arbiter pointed out that the contract itself said that the hours-of-work clause was not to be construed as a guarantee of any fixed amount of work. Moreover, he said, the agreement had features, such as a reporting-pay clause, that were inconsistent with the idea of a work guarantee. Noting that there was no showing of bad faith on the part of the company, the arbiter decided the shutdown did not violate the contract. (Pittsburgh Screw & Bolt Co., 29 LA 615; see also 85 LA 398, 83 LA 314, 64 LA 287, 62 LA 1191, 29 LA 795)

However, an arbiter ruled that held that an employer violated contractual seniority, workweek, and maintenance-of-standards provisions of a contract by instituting continuous layoff plans under which certain employees were laid off for four Fridays and recalled on the following Mondays. The result, the arbiter found, was a systematic, perpetual reduction of the workweek from 40 to 32 hours for a portion of the workforce. (Ace Hardware Corp., 88 LA 594)

Scheduling Lunch Periods & Rest Periods

If a contract provides lunch and rest periods but does not say when they are to be taken, does the union have a say in when they should be scheduled? In one case where the contract did not schedule the lunch periods, an arbiter upheld the union's objection to the company's changing them.

EXAMPLE: The practice at one company had been for employees to eat in four half-hour shifts from 11 a.m. to 1 p.m. Then management decided that five lunch periods would work out better than four, so it changed the lunch schedule to run from 10:45 to 1:15 p.m. When the union claimed this was an unreasonable break with past practice, the company pointed out that the contract, while it provided a half-hour lunch period, said nothing about when it should be taken.

The arbiter though, agreed with the union. The obligation to provide a lunch period implied scheduling at a reasonable time, he said; by custom this meant near the middle of the work shift. In this case, the arbiter decided, past practice had been so consistent that 11 a.m. and 1 p.m. must be regarded as the outside limits for lunch periods. (Bakelite Co., 29 LA 555)

Similarly, under a contract that did not limit management's right to schedule rest periods, one arbiter looked at the company's past practice. He found that the employees had always been given a rest period after three hours' work and decided that this was how the parties must have meant to schedule them. (Rath Packing Co., 21 LA 20, see also 62 LA 45)

On the other hand, an arbiter upheld management's right to stagger rest periods after instituting a continuous operation. Under the contract, times for rest periods were determined by foremen, stewards, and workers in each department. This right, the arbiter said, was dependent on the shifts and hours set by the company. When it decided to go on continuous operations, it necessarily followed that rest periods had to be staggered; hence the workers had no cause to complain, he said. (Philco Corp., 40 LA 490; see also 88 LA 599, 75 LA 16, 62 LA 374)

Working During Paid Lunch Period

If a contract provides for a paid lunch period, can employees be required to work during that time? If some employees are not required to look after any job duties during their meal time, but others are, an arbiter is likely to rule that this is an unfair practice.

EXAMPLE: A contract provided for a 20-minute lunch period as part of the normal workday paid for by the company. Employees were relieved from all duties during this paid meal period, except for boiler firemen, who were asked to keep watch over their boilers while they ate.

The union asked that relief men be furnished the boiler firemen so that they could eat without disturbance. The company claimed that there was ample time for them to eat and still keep an eye on the boilers.

The arbiter ruled that the firemen were entitled to relief. Since no exception was made for these employees in the contract, and since they did not receive any extra payment for the additional time spent on the job during their eating time, the arbiter reasoned that they had to be treated like other employees. (Ford Roofing Products Co., 5 LA 182)

Similarly, an employer violated a contract provision requiring lunch periods to be arranged by mutual agreement between parties, an arbiter decided when it compelled employees to operate their looms during scheduled lunch periods. Notwithstanding the employer's contention that continuous operation of the looms was dictated by the need to maintain its competitive position, the arbiter ruled that the clear provision of the contract must be enforced in the absence of a subsequent agreement modifying its terms. (Atlanta Wire Works Inc., 62 LA 945; see also 71 LA 1128)

However, an arbiter held that a company was not required to pay employees for their lunch period when they were asked to perform minor tasks of short duration during their lunch period. The contract called for the company to pay for the lunch break if a worker "works straight through without stopping to eat" and called for "up to thirty minutes" for meals which suggested to the arbiter that uninterrupted meal periods were not intended. (Chevron Oil Co., 52 LA 928)

Coffee Break as Rest Period

Should a coffee break be viewed in the same light as ordinary rest periods? At least one arbiter has ruled that there is no basis for distinguishing between coffee breaks and ordinary rest periods. Therefore, under a contract specifying that the company would continue its past practices with respect to rest periods, it did not have the right to eliminate the practice of allowing certain women employees to take a 10-minute coffee break in the morning in addition to their regular two 15-minute rest periods during the day. (International Harvester Co., 21 LA 194; see also 76 LA 1203, 73 LA 34)

Paid Wash-Up Time

Where a contract is silent on the subject, can management discontinue paid wash-up periods on its own? In one case, an arbiter ruled no, pointing out that for many years, workers had been allowed to clean up during working hours. Arbitrators usually find unwritten practices involving specific benefits for workers to be binding for the duration of the contract, the arbiter concluded; thus, the practice could not be discontinued unilaterally. (Harnischfeger Corp., 40 LA 1329)

However, another arbiter held that a company could reduce, unilaterally, two 15-minute wash-up periods per day to two 5-minute periods. (Ruralist Press Inc., 51 LA 549; see also 68 LA 94, 62 LA 179, 61 LA 891)

Payment for Unrecorded Work

An employee was not entitled to pay for "off-the-clock" work which he could not prove he had performed, an arbiter ruled. He made no claim to the pay until after he resigned from the supermarket at which he was employed the arbiter noted, concluding that there was no "clear and convincing evidence" that the work actually was performed. (Wrigley Stores, 43 LA 225)

Wage Guarantee & SUB Plans

IN BRIEF

Guaranteed pay provisions and supplementary unemployment compensation benefits trusts (SUBs) are likely to be fertile sources of grievances. One reason for this is that management usually tries to interpret such guarantees as narrowly as possible, since it receives no work in return for payments made in fulfillment of a guarantee. (95 LA 1187)

Generally, arbiters have not interpreted a statement of normal working hours as constituting a guarantee of work or pay. Similarly, a listing of weekly salaries for workers probably does not mean the employer cannot pay pro-rata salaries when a reduced workweek is in effect.

GUIDELINES

Regular Workweek Not a Guarantee

If a contract establishes a regular workweek of so many hours, is this a wage or work guarantee? Most arbiters agree that such a contract does not guarantee wages or work.

EXAMPLE: A union, arguing for a guarantee, relied on two articles of the contract. One provided that the regular workday should be eight hours and the regular workweek 44 hours in six days, Monday through Saturday. The other required the company to maintain standards at least at the levels prevailing when the contract was signed. Putting these two clauses together, the union claimed the company violated the contract when it decided to eliminate Saturday work.

The arbiter okayed the company's action on the basis of this reasoning: (1) there was no discussion in negotiations of whether the company was guaranteeing 44 hours' work; had there been any such intention, it would have been stated in explicit contract language, (2) the workweek clause, it appears, was intended merely to set forth hours of work for purposes of computing overtime, and (3) a clause providing four hours' reporting pay implied that there were occasions when a full schedule of work would not be provided; this was inconsistent with the concept of a guarantee (Consumers Service Co., 29 LA 447; see also 97 LA 39, 95 LA 482, 83 LA 314, 81 LA 14, 10 LA 312)

EXAMPLE: An employer was not obligated to pay a full day's pay to employees for each day on which management decided to close the plant and send employees home during a power failure, an arbiter ruled, since neither the contract nor past practice provided a guarantee of hours of work. Emphasizing that the contract provision establishing an eight hour workday and five day workweek was construed to provide only a usual or "standard" workday or workweek, and the word "standard" was not synonymous with either "minimum," "maximum," or a "guarantee," the arbiter concluded that the emergency nature of the event causing plant closure rendered the payment of full pay unconscionable. (Caribe Circuit Breaker Co., 63 LA 261)

Similarly, an arbiter decided that an employer had the right to shut down the plant on the Monday preceding Christmas Eve and the Christmas holidays after the union rejected an offer to work the preceding Saturday at straight-time rate, since the separate contract provision stating that "five days, Monday through Friday, shall constitute a week's work" does not imply a guarantee of 40 hours as standard workweek. (T M Fab Inc., 64 LA 287)

However, another arbiter has held that a contract providing that regular working hours for regular employees shall be a "a full week of forty hours per week" comprised a guaranteed workweek. (Hampden Sales Assn. Inc., 12 LA 62)

Similarly, an arbiter held that employees were not required to do outside work to make up for hours lost when their employer failed to assign them 40 hours of work per week, as guaranteed in the contract. (Market Wholesale Grocery, 86 LA 147; see also 97 LA 724, 91 LA 1118, 82 LA 1026)

Statement of Weekly Salary

The fact that a contract lists weekly salaries for clerical workers does not mean the company cannot pay them pro rata salaries if a reduced workweek is in effect, an arbiter ruled.

EXAMPLE: Protesting a cut in salaries of clerical workers in a steel mill during a period when the workweek was 32 hours instead of 40 hours, a union pointed to a table in the contract listing the "guaranteed salary" of various clerical grades. The union said the company had to pay the "guaranteed salary" whether the workweek was one day or five.

The arbiter, though, thought the union was confusing a guaranteed rate with guaranteed earnings. The "guaranteed salary" is a promise that a salaried worker will be paid at a certain rate, the arbiter said, and the contract also made it clear that the rates shown are based on a 40-hour week. The company could cut these rates according to the actual workweek, he said, since the contract did not specifically say it could not. (Bethlehem Steel Co., 26 LA 784)

When Employees Refuse Assigned Work

Can workers be deprived of a weekly guarantee of work or wages if they refuse to do available work which is different from their usual job? Most arbiters have upheld employers' right to transfer workers to jobs where they are needed in order to make use of them for the guaranteed time.

EXAMPLE: Where a contract gave a 36-hour guarantee for all except those workers who refused to be transferred to available jobs, one arbiter ruled some employees were not eligible for the guaranteed pay because they refused to do some painting which they were assigned to fill in their time. An argument that no "transfer" was involved was rejected. (Bosto Sausage & Provision Co., 5 LA 627)

Similarly, even where a contract did not specifically deny the guarantee to employees refusing transfer to available work, an arbiter ruled that the guarantee did not apply when employees refused such work. He reasoned that it was clear that the company's guarantee of hours involved a corresponding responsibility on the part of employees to perform the work offered. (Kroger Co., 5 LA 154)

However, where a prior arbitration award (42 LA 228) interpreted a Supplemental Unemployment Benefit plan's provisions relating to "lack of work" in terms of plant practice of allowing employees for whom there is no work to decline alternate work, senior employees who declined alternate work when there was not enough alternate work for all of the employees were awarded benefits by an arbiter. Junior workers were also entitled to short-week benefits where the employer failed to exercise his power to "compel acceptance of another job offer," that is, notify an employee of alternate work, order him to accept it, and advise him that refusal to accept such work would result in the loss of benefits. (Pittsburgh Steel Co., 46 LA 774)

Effect of Strike on Guarantee

If one group of employees have a guarantee of hours or wages in their contract and cannot work because of a strike by another group, are they entitled to the guarantee? A lot depends on the wording of the guarantee provision. Some arbiters have said that a clause that just guarantees minimum weekly earnings is not the same guarantee.

EXAMPLE: One arbiter ruled that a clause like this didn't require a baking company to pay drivers their weekly wages during a time they could not work when the bakers were on strike. The arbiter said that the pay guarantee applied only when the drivers could do work. (Junge Bread Co., et al., 1 LA 569; see also 74 LA 987, 53 LA 550)

Likewise, even where a contract contains a specific guarantee of work, on arbiter has held, the guarantee is suspended when employees cannot work because of a walkout by members of the same union under a different contract. He reasoned that all union members must accept responsibility for the actions of any portion of the membership. (Kroger Co., 5 LA 154)

However, in one case an arbiter ordered the company to pay the guarantee where (1) the contract clearly guaranteed 40 hours of work in a week, (2) employees had already worked the first day of the week, and (3) they had no work for three days during the week because members of another union were on strike, (Wheatality Baking Corp., 11 LA 526; see also 74 LA 867)

Effect of Strike on SUB Eligibility

The extent of a worker's involvement in a strike situation may have some influence on whether he is eligible for supplemental unemployment compensation benefits trust (SUB) payments.

EXAMPLE: Workers who were suspended for engaging in a wildcat strike were not entitled to supplemental unemployment benefits, even though they received state unemployment compensation benefits, one arbiter ruled.

The union argued that, under the SUB agreement, a worker was entitled to benefits, even though laid off by reason of a strike, if he was awarded UC benefits for the same week of layoff. However, the arbiter reasoned that the workers were not laid off because of a work stoppage, but for disciplinary action connected with a work stoppage. The contract language clearly treated layoffs for disciplinary reasons separately from those resulting from strikes, he added. (Lehigh Portland Cement Co., 37 LA 996).

But, another arbiter decided that workers on layoff who were eligible for SUB before a strike did not become ineligible when the stoppage began.

EXAMPLE: Following the expiration of the SUB agreement and the beginning of the strike, the company stopped paying SUB to workers who—prior to the strike—had been laid off from the bargaining units which went on strike. It continued the plan in effect for certain workers outside these units. Under the SUB plan's termination provision, the union argued, as long as the plan continued to exist, it had to apply to workers "to whom it had been made applicable."

The arbiter agreed. Although the company was free to terminate the entire plan upon the expiration of the agreement, it could not terminate coverage in these units only. Since none of the workers had originally been laid off because of the strike, he reasoned, the continuance of their lay off could not have been a consequence of the strike. The benefit eligibility rule could not be applied as an additional "strike situation" eligibility rule, he concluded. (Allegheny Ludlum Steel Corp., 37 LA 689)

Guarantee Applied to Partial Workweek After Strike

If workers are called back to work after a strike in the middle of the workweek, are they entitled to a full week's pay under a weekly work guarantee? According to one arbiter the answer is yes. Otherwise a company could get around the contract simply by withholding work on the first day of a regularly scheduled workweek, the arbiter concluded. (Wilson & Co. Inc., 5 LA 454)

On the other hand, an arbiter ruled that employees were not entitled to short-week benefits under their SUB plan that contained a strike disqualification clause for full weekly benefits. He held that if unemployment resulting from strike disqualified the employees from benefits while "wholly unemployed," it surely disqualified them from benefits while "partially unemployed." (E. J. Lavino & Co., 43 LA 213)

Similarly, employees were not entitled to short week benefits under a SUB plan for having worked less than their 32 hours scheduled during a week of contract negotiations, an arbiter ruled, where the employer slowed and later shut down the plant. Although the union contended that the reason the employees did not work was the lack of available work, the arbiter held that the evidence established that the shutdown, in addition to lost time resulting from preparations upon contract agreement, was reasonably related to the union's threat to strike unless an agreement on the new contract was reached. (Bethlehem Steel Corp., 62 LA 54) Effect of Layoff on Guarantee

Does a worker lose a weekly hours' guarantee if he is laid off before the end of a workweek?

One arbiter decided that unless the contract says otherwise, a worker coming under the guarantee probably does not lose the amount guaranteed if removed from the payroll by the company during a workweek. Once the employee starts to work he is entitled to a full week's pay, the arbiter concluded. (Keeshin Motor Express Co. Inc. 2 LA 57)

Similarly, employees who were laid off as a result of a permanent plant shutdown were entitled to supplemental unemployment benefits, an arbiter ruled, despite the employer's contention that the employees were terminated upon receiving severance pay. (Ajax Forging and Casting Co., 64 LA 1309)

However, another arbiter made a distinction between employees who were laid off temporarily and those who were permanently terminated. He said that a weekly guarantee provision did apply to employees who were laid off during the week with the expectation that they would return when more work was available, but did not apply to those whose employment was ended permanently before the end of the workweek. (Walsh, Perini, Groves, & Slattery Cos.,

Effect of Lockout on Guarantee

If an employer locks out employees during an impasse in negotiations for a new contract are the workers entitled to a full week's pay under the guarantee provision of the expired contract? One arbiter has ruled yes.

EXAMPLE: Where the expired contract guaranteed employees 40 straight-time hours of work or a full equivalent of pay for a regular workweek, the arbiter decided that employees who worked the first part of the workweek in which the expiration date of the old contract fell were entitled to be paid for the remainder of the workweek when the employer locked the workers out due to an impasse in negotiations for a new contract. Finding that the guarantee of a week's work or equivalent pay was "triggered" by employees' being "put to work" the first part "of the regular workweek," the arbiter held that the right of the employer to lock out employees did not necessarily excuse it from obligations that attach to other contractual provisions. (Edward Don & Co., 65 LA 1307)

Exclusions from Guarantee

Most wage guarantees contain language relieving the employer of the obligation to pay the guarantee if work is lost due to certain circumstances. This exclusion may be stated generally in terms of conditions "beyond the employer's control," in which case disputes are almost certain to arise concerning whether in a given situation the loss of work was "beyond the employer's control." Or the exclusion may list specific circumstances under which the guarantee would not be applicable. In such case, arbiters tend to restrict the exclusion narrowly to the listed circumstances.

EXAMPLE: An exemption from a weekly wage guarantee for time lost due to causes beyond company control did not apply where a meat packing company laid off the work force because of disruptive absenteeism. The contract specified exemptions for layoffs due to "flood, fire, power failure, breakdown of plant equipment, or other causes beyond reasonable control of employer," The arbiter stated that the company was freed from the guarantee only where a layoff was due to "physical" causes such as those listed. The layoff for absenteeism did not fall in this category, so the employer was not relieved of his obligation under the guarantee. (Ohio Natural Casing & Supply Co., 43 LA 888; see also 71 LA 817, 71 LA 283, 63 LA 257, 68 LA 986)

Effect of Snowstorm on Guarantee

When a severe snowstorm prevented a large part of the work force from reporting to work, an arbiter ruled that the workers were entitled to an Automatic Short Week Benefit as provided in the contract. He said that in the past the company had declared workers on layoff in similar situations and should have done so in this instance. He went on to state that the mere fact of a snowstorm did not entitle employees to SUB payments; each storm would have to be appraised on its own "with the test of reasonableness being the decisive criterion." (Kelsey-Hayes Co., 49 LA 666)

On the other hand, where the contract exempted the employer from SUB liability for time not worked due to an "act of God" workers were not entitled to benefits when a severe snowstorm caused a high degree of absenteeism and forced the suspension of production, resulting in several workers being sent home. As the absenteeism resulted from an "act of God" the employees were not considered on layoff for purposes of SUB payments. (International Harvester Co., 49 LA 892; see also 74 LA 55, 53 LA 9)

Effect of Holiday on Guarantee

Should a holiday be considered a scheduled workday for determining wages under a clause guaranteeing 40 hours' pay for those reporting a certain number of days per week? One arbiter has concluded that it should.

EXAMPLE: A contract guaranteed 40 hours pay to each man who reported for work, upon request, either five or six days in any week, depending on the department's schedule. Several men reported for four scheduled workdays one week, but each worked less than 32 hours. They were paid for their time on the job plus one unworked holiday. The company maintained that an unworked holiday could not be considered a fifth day of work for purposes of the pay guarantee.

The intent of the parties in establishing the 40-hour pay guarantee was to stabilize wages, the arbiter decided. To accomplish this, the company was to schedule production so workers would qualify for the guarantee, the arbiter said. Therefore, he ruled that the occurrence of a holiday did not remove the obligation to do so. The men could count the holiday as a day on which they reported for work, he concluded. (Colonial Baking Co., 35 LA 686)

Likewise, under an SUB plan providing benefits in an amount equal to 65 percent of after-tax pay when added to state benefit and other "wages" or remuneration, an arbiter ruled that employees laid off for a holiday week were entitled to benefits, even though state benefits plus holiday pay paid by the employer came to more than 65 percent of normal take-home pay. The state unemployment compensation agency defined "wages" for a holiday week as not including holiday pay, and the parties had agreed to apply the agency's definitions so the employer's contribution did not count, reducing the pay below the 65 percent level. (Pittsburgh Steel Co., 42 LA 228)

However, another arbiter stated that the closing of a plant on Fridays, following Thursday holidays, did not constitute a layoff under the meaning of the SUB plan, and that the employees were not entitled to benefits. (Western Tool Inc., 42 LA 1064)

Overtime Included in Guarantee

When the contract does not specify whether or not a weekly wage guarantee includes overtime pay, should overtime pay be added to employees' regular earnings before applying the minimum guarantee?

At least one arbiter has ruled that overtime pay should be added to employees' regular wages in calculating gross weekly earnings to which the wage guarantee applies. Since the contract clause did not specify whether or not the guarantee included overtime, the arbiter's decision was based on the fact the overtime rate was computed from the daily base rate rather than from the weekly guaranteed rate. If the parties had intended to exclude overtime, the arbiter said, they would have figured the overtime rate on the basis of the weekly guarantee. (Boller Beverage Co., 19 LA 860)

Eligibility for SUB While Receiving Social Security

If a supplemental unemployment benefits plan disqualifies employees who receive a retirement pension financed wholly or partially by the company, is a worker who is drawing federal social security benefits entitled to payments under the plan?

Interpreting the basic steel SUB plan, one arbiter ruled that an individual cannot be considered to be disqualified just because he receives old-age insurance benefits. Even if social security were considered a pension, he added, it could not be said to be financed either partially or wholly by the company since it is financed by federal taxes. (Various Steel Companies, 32 LA 529; see 88 LA 232, 82 LA 1261)

Disability Retirement

Where a contract provided for an income extension arrangement for use in the event of layoff, a grievant who retired on a disability pension because of a permanent physical disability was not entitled to benefits under the plan. Although income extension aid may be a form of severance pay for employees who are separated through no fault of their own, it is not available to all separated employees, the arbiter noted, but only to those laid off for lack of work or plant closing. (General Electric Co., 49 LA 62)